# Revenue Statistics in Latin America and the Caribbean 2022

# Estadísticas tributarias en América Latina y el Caribe 2022

1990-2020

This work is published under the responsibility of the Secretary-General of the OECD. The opinions expressed and arguments employed herein do not necessarily reflect the official views of the OECD Member countries, the members of its Development Centre or of the United Nations, the Inter-American Center of Tax Administrations (CIAT) or the Inter-American Development Bank (IDB), its Board of Directors, or the countries they represent.

*El presente trabajo se publica bajo la responsabilidad del Secretario General de la OCDE. Las opiniones expresadas y los argumentos utilizados en el mismo no reflejan necesariamente el punto de vista oficial de los Países miembros de la OCDE, ni del Centro de Desarrollo de la OCDE, ni de las Naciones Unidas, ni del Centro Interamericano de Administraciones Tributarias (CIAT), ni del Banco Interamericano de Desarrollo, de su Directorio Ejecutivo ni de los países que representa.*

The names of countries and territories and maps used in this joint publication follow the practice of the OECD.

This document, as well as any data and map included herein, are without prejudice to the status of or sovereignty over any territory, to the delimitation of international frontiers and boundaries and to the name of any territory, city or area.

*Los nombres de los países y territorios y los mapas utilizados en esta publicación conjunta siguen la práctica de la OCDE.*

*Tanto este documento, así como cualquier dato y cualquier mapa que se incluya en él, se entenderán sin perjuicio respecto al estatus o la soberanía de cualquier territorio, a la delimitación de fronteras y límites internacionales, ni al nombre de cualquier territorio, ciudad o área.*

**Please cite this publication as:**
OECD et al. (2022), *Revenue Statistics in Latin America and the Caribbean 2022*, OECD Publishing, Paris, https://doi.org/10.1787/58a2dc35-en-es.

***Por favor, cite esta publicación de la siguiente manera:***
OCDE et al. (2022), *Estadísticas tributarias en América Latina y el Caribe 2022*, OECD Publishing, Paris, https://doi.org/10.1787/58a2dc35-en-es.

ISBN 978-92-64-93914-1 (print/impresa)
ISBN 978-92-64-63044-4 (pdf)

Revenue Statistics in Latin America and the Caribbean/*Estadísticas tributarias en América Latina y el Caribe*
ISSN 2410-4728 (print/impresa)
ISSN 2410-4736 (online/en línea)

*La OCDE no garantiza la exacta precisión de esta traducción y no se hace de ninguna manera responsable de cualquier consecuencia por su uso o interpretación.*

**Photo credits/Imágenes:** Cover/Portada © some of the graphic elements in the main cover illustration were adapted from Freepik.com.

Corrigenda to publications may be found on line at: www.oecd.org/about/publishing/corrigenda.htm.
*Las erratas de las publicaciones se encuentran en línea en: www.oecd.org/about/publishing/corrigenda.htm.*

# Foreword

Revenue Statistics in Latin America and the Caribbean 2022 *is a joint publication by the Organisation for Economic Co-operation and Development (OECD) Centre for Tax Policy and Administration, the OECD Development Centre, the United Nations Economic Commission for Latin America and the Caribbean (UN-ECLAC), the Inter-American Center of Tax Administrations (CIAT) and the Inter-American Development Bank (IDB), with the support of the European Union Regional Facility for Development in Transition for Latin America and the Caribbean. It presents detailed, internationally comparable data on tax revenues for 27 Latin American and Caribbean (LAC) economies, four of which are OECD members.*

Revenue Statistics in Latin America and the Caribbean 2022 *is based on the well-established methodology of the OECD* Revenue Statistics *database, which is an essential reference source for OECD member countries. Comparisons are also made with the average tax indicators for OECD economies. In this publication, the term "taxes" is confined to compulsory, unrequited payments to general government. As outlined in the Interpretative Guide to Revenue Statistics, taxes are "unrequited" in the sense that benefits provided by government to taxpayers are not normally in proportion to their payments. The OECD methodology classifies a tax according to its base: income, profits and capital gains (classified under heading 1000); payroll (heading 3000); property (heading 4000); goods and services (heading 5000); and other taxes (heading 6000). Compulsory social security contributions paid to general government are treated as taxes and classified under heading 2000. Much greater detail on the tax concept, the classification of taxes and the accrual basis of reporting is set out in the Interpretative Guide in Annex A.*

*Extending the OECD methodology to Latin American and Caribbean countries enables comparisons of tax systems on a consistent basis both across this region and with OECD countries. In a few cases, this methodology differs from the approach used by ECLAC, CIAT and IDB; these differences are noted in the text and in the tables.*

*The report provides an overview of the main taxation trends in Latin America and the Caribbean. It examines changes in both the level and the composition of taxation plus the attribution of tax collection by sub-level of government between 1990 and 2020. The report includes two special features: the first one examines fiscal revenues from non-renewable natural resources in the LAC region in 2020 and provides preliminary data on revenues in 2021; the second presents key findings from monthly revenue data during the COVID-19 crisis until the end of August 2021.*

# Presentación

*La publicación* Estadísticas tributarias en América Latina y el Caribe 2022 *ha sido elaborada conjuntamente por el Centro de Política y Administración Tributaria de la Organización para la Cooperación y el Desarrollo Económicos (OCDE), el Centro de Desarrollo de la OCDE, la Comisión Económica para América Latina y el Caribe de las Naciones Unidas (CEPAL-NU), el Centro Interamericano de Administraciones Tributarias (CIAT) y el Banco Interamericano de Desarrollo (BID). Esta publicación presenta datos detallados y comparables a nivel internacional sobre los ingresos tributarios de 27 economías de América Latina y del Caribe (ALC), cuatro de las cuales son miembros de la OCDE.*

*La publicación* Estadísticas tributarias en América Latina y el Caribe 2022 *se basa en la metodología bien establecida de la base de datos* Estadísticas tributarias *de la OCDE, que se ha convertido en una referencia esencial para los países miembros de la OCDE. Se presentan también comparaciones con los promedios de indicadores tributarios para las economías de la OCDE. En la presente publicación, el término "impuestos" se limita exclusivamente a los pagos obligatorios sin contraprestación efectuados al gobierno general. Tal y como lo indica la Guía de Interpretación de* Revenue Statistics, *los impuestos carecen de contraprestación en el sentido en que, normalmente, las prestaciones proporcionadas por el gobierno a los contribuyentes no guardan relación directa con los pagos realizados por estos. La metodología de la OCDE clasifica un impuesto de acuerdo con su base: renta, utilidades y ganancias del capital (categoría 1000); nómina (categoría 3000); propiedad (categoría 4000); bienes y servicios (categoría 5000); y otros impuestos (categoría 6000). Las contribuciones obligatorias a la seguridad social pagadas al gobierno general se tratan aquí como impuestos y se clasifican en la categoría 2000. Para mayor detalle sobre el concepto de impuesto, su clasificación y su registro según el criterio de devengo, véase la Guía de Interpretación que figura en el Anexo A.*

*Aplicar la metodología de la OCDE a América Latina y el Caribe posibilita la comparación de sistemas tributarios a partir de una base coherente en la región, entre los países de ALC, y con los países miembros de la OCDE. Sin embargo, en algunas ocasiones, esta metodología difiere de la empleada por la CEPAL, el CIAT y el BID; en esos casos, las diferencias se han indicado en el texto y los cuadros.*

*El informe ofrece un panorama general de las principales tendencias en materia tributaria en América Latina y en el Caribe. Examina los cambios registrados entre 1990 y 2020 en el nivel y la composición de la tributación, así como en la atribución de la recaudación tributaria a los diversos subsectores de gobierno. El informe incluye dos capitulos especiales: el primero identifica las tendencias de los ingresos fiscales procedentes de los recursos naturales no renovables en la región de ALC en 2020 y proporciona datos preliminares para 2021; el segundo presenta los hallazgos clave de las estadísticas tributarias mensuales durante la crisis del COVID-19 hasta finales de agosto de 2021.*

# Acknowledgements

*Revenue Statistics in Latin America and the Caribbean 2022* was jointly produced by the Organisation for Economic Co-operation and Development (OECD) Centre for Tax Policy and Administration, the OECD Development Centre, the United Nations Economic Commission for Latin America and the Caribbean (UN-ECLAC), the Inter-American Center of Tax Administrations (CIAT) and the Inter-American Development Bank (IDB), with the support of the European Union Regional Facility for Development in Transition for Latin America and the Caribbean.

The staff from these organisations with responsibility for producing the publication were: Emmanuelle Modica of the OECD Centre for Tax Policy and Administration, under the supervision of the Director, Pascal Saint-Amans, the Deputy Director, Grace Perez-Navarro, the Head of the Tax Policy and Tax Statistics Division, David Bradbury, and the Head of the Tax Data and Statistical Analysis Unit, Michelle Harding; Jingjing Xia in collaboration with René Orozco of the OECD Development Centre, under the supervision of the Director, Ragnheiður Elín Árnadóttir, the Deputy Director, Federico Bonaglia, the Head of the Latin America and the Caribbean Unit, Sebastian Nieto Parra, and the Co-ordinator of *Revenue Statistics* for the Development Centre, Alexander Pick; Michael Hanni of the Economic Development Division of UN-ECLAC, under the supervision of Director Daniel Titelman and the Chief of the Fiscal Affairs Unit, Noel Pérez Benítez; Julio Alberto López from the CIAT Tax Studies and Research Directorate, under the supervision of Director Santiago Díaz de Sarralde; and Alberto Barreix, Principal Technical Leader in Fiscal Economics at the IDB, under the supervision of Ubaldo González de Frutos, Sector Lead Specialist in Tax Administration. Michael Hanni of UN-ECLAC authored the Special Feature on fiscal revenues from non-renewable natural resources in the LAC region (Chapter 2); Santiago Díaz de Sarralde of CIAT authored the Special Feature on monthly revenue data during the COVID-19 crisis (Chapter 3).

The authors would like to thank other staff at the OECD Development Centre and the Centre for Tax Policy and Administration for their invaluable support in completing and improving the 2022 edition of this publication. Delphine Grandrieux and Elizabeth Nash from the OECD Development Centre's Communications and Publications team, and statistical editors from the OECD Publications and Communications Directorate, ensured the production of the publication, in both paper and electronic form. Michael Sharratt from the OECD Centre for Tax Policy and Administration provided invaluable assistance with the databases, website and other dissemination tools. Laura Gutiérrez and Juan Nicolás Velandia from the OECD Development Centre provided precious help in the Spanish version of this publication.

Finally, the OECD Centre for Tax Policy and Administration and the OECD Development Centre would like to thank our colleagues working in national entities, with whom we have consulted regularly. In particular, we are grateful to Rosario López Palazzo and Marcelo Adrián Calissano from the Ministry of Finance of Argentina; Fidelia Raulina Pérez Castillo from the

Dominican Republic's Finance Ministry; Diana Vanessa Sánchez Nacevilla and Salomé Velasco Struve from the Ministry of Economy and Finance of Ecuador; Luis Antonio Campos and Sara Guadalupe García de Reyes from the Ministry of Finance of El Salvador; David Fernando Pineda Pinto from the Revenue Administration Service and Kervin Andre Sánchez Valle and Neffy Noel Velásquez Sagastume from the Secretary of Finances in Honduras; Andrea Gregory from Jamaica's Tax Administration and Customs agencies; Emma Isaza from Panama's Finance Ministry; Diego Dominguez from Paraguay's Finance Ministry; and Óscar Núñez Del Arco Mendoza and Jorge Rivera Calderón from Peru's Ministry of Economy and Finance. Additionally, ECLAC would like to acknowledge the valuable contributions of Yannick Gordon from the Ministry of Finance & Corporate Governance of Antigua and Barbuda.

This document was produced with the financial assistance of the European Commission. The opinions expressed and arguments employed herein do not necessarily reflect the official views of OECD member countries or the European Union.

# Agradecimientos

La publicación *Estadísticas tributarias en América Latina y el Caribe 2022* ha sido elaborada conjuntamente por el Centro de Política y Administración Tributaria de la Organización para la Cooperación y el Desarrollo Económicos (OCDE), el Centro de Desarrollo de la OCDE, la Comisión Económica para América Latina y el Caribe de las Naciones Unidas (CEPAL-NU), el Centro Interamericano de Administraciones Tributarias (CIAT) y el Banco Interamericano de Desarrollo (BID), con el apoyo del Fondo Regional para el Desarrollo en Transición para América Latina y el Caribe de la Unión Europea.

Las personas de estas organizaciones responsables de redactar la presente publicación han sido: Emmanuelle Modica del Centro de Política y Administración Tributaria de la OCDE, bajo la supervisión del Director, Pascal Saint-Amans, de la Sub-directora, Grace Perez-Navarro, del Jefe de la División de Políticas y Estadísticas Tributarias, David Bradbury, y de la Jefe de la Unidad de Análisis de Datos Tributarios y Estadísticas, Michelle Harding; Jingjing Xia en colaboración con René Orozco del Centro de Desarrollo de la OCDE, bajo la supervisión de la Directora, Ragnheiður Elín Árnadóttir, del Director adjunto, Federico Bonaglia, del Jefe de la Unidad de América Latina y el Caribe, Sebastián Nieto Parra, y del Coordinador de estadísticas tributarias para el Centro de Desarrollo, Alexander Pick; Michael Hanni de la División de Desarrollo Económico de la CEPAL, bajo la supervisión del Director, Daniel Titelman, y del Jefe de la Unidad de Asuntos Fiscales, Noel Pérez Benítez; Julio Alberto López de la Dirección de Estudios e Investigaciones Tributarias del CIAT, bajo la supervisión del Director, Santiago Díaz de Sarralde; y Alberto Barreix, Líder Técnico Principal en Economía Fiscal del BID bajo la supervisión del Especialista Líder de Sector en Administración Fiscal, Ubaldo González de Frutos. Michael Hanni de la CEPAL-NU es el autor del capítulo especial sobre los ingresos fiscales de recursos naturales no renovables en América Latina y el Caribe (Capítulo 2). Santiago Díaz de Sarralde del CIAT escribió el capítulo especial sobre las estadísticas tributarias mensuales durante la crisis del COVID-19 (Capítulo 3).

Los autores desean agradecer a otras personas del Centro de Desarrollo y del Centro de Política y Administración Tributaria de la OCDE por su invaluable contribución a la mejora y finalización de la edición 2022 de esta publicación. Delphine Grandrieux y Elizabeth Nash, del equipo de Comunicaciones y Publicaciones del Centro de Desarrollo de la OCDE, y editores estadísticos del equipo de Publicaciones y Comunicaciones de la OCDE, aseguraron la producción de la publicación, tanto física como en formato electrónico. Michael Sharratt, del Centro de Política y Administración Tributaria de la OCDE, brindó una valiosa ayuda con las bases de datos, el sitio web y otras herramientas de difusión. Laura Gutiérrez y Juan Nicolás Velandia del Centro de Desarrollo de la OCDE proporcionaron una ayuda preciosa en la versión en español de esta publicación.

Por último, el Centro de Política y Administración Tributaria y el Centro de Desarrollo de la OCDE quisieran agradecer a nuestros colegas de entidades nacionales, a los que hemos consultado con frecuencia. En particular, damos gracias a Rosario López Palazzo y Marcelo

Adrián Calissano, del Ministerio de Hacienda de Argentina; Jorge Richard Muñoz Nuñez, del Ministerio de Hacienda de Costa Rica; Fidelia Raulina Pérez Castillo, del Ministerio de Hacienda de la República Dominicana; Ruben Nehemías Ordoñez Gutiérrez, Diana Vanessa Sánchez Nacevilla y Salomé Velasco Struve del Ministerio de Economía y Finanzas de Ecuador; Luis Antonio Campos y Sara Guadalupe García de Reyes del Ministerio de Hacienda de El Salvador; David Fernando Pineda Pinto, del Servicio de Administración de Rentas, y Kervin Andre Sánchez Valle y Neffy Noel Velásquez Sagastume, de la Secretaría de Finanzas de Honduras; Andrea Gregory, de la Administración de Impuestos y Aduanas de Jamaica; Emma Isaza, del Ministerio de Hacienda de Panamá; Diego Domínguez, del Ministerio de Hacienda de Paraguay; y Óscar Núñez Del Arco Mendoza y Jorge Rivera Calderón, del Ministerio de Economía y Finanzas de Perú. Asimismo, ECLAC quisiera agradecer las valiosas contribuciones realizadas por Yannick Gordom del Ministerio de Finanzas y Governanza Corporativa de Antigua y Barbuda.

Este documento fue producido con el apoyo financiero de la Comisión Europea. Las opiniones expresadas y los argumentos aquí empleados no reflejan necesariamente las opiniones oficiales de los países miembros de la OCDE o de la Unión Europea.

# Table of contents

# *Índice*

## LIST OF TABLES/LISTA DE CUADROS

### Chapter 1/Capítulo 1
### Tax revenue trends, 1990-2020/Tendencias tributarias, 1990-2020



### Chapter 2/Capítulo 2
### Special feature/Sección especial



### Chapter 3/Capítulo 3
### Special feature/Sección especial

Chapter 4/Capítulo 4

**Tax levels and tax structures, 1990-2020/**
**Niveles impositivos y estructuras tributarias, 1990-2020**

## LIST OF FIGURES/LISTA DE GRÁFICOS

### Chapter 1/Capítulo 1
### Tax revenue trends, 1990-2020/Tendencias tributarias, 1990-2020

Chapter 2/Capítulo 2

**Special feature/Sección especial**



Chapter 3/Capítulo 3

**Special feature/Sección especial**

## Follow OECD Publications on:

*http://twitter.com/OECD_Pubs*

*http://www.facebook.com/OECDPublications*

*http://www.linkedin.com/groups/OECD-Publications-4645871*

*http://www.youtube.com/oecdilibrary*

*http://www.oecd.org/oecddirect/*

## This book has...

StatLinks
A service that delivers Excel® files from the printed page!

Look for the *StatLinks* at the bottom of the tables or graphs in this book. To download the matching Excel® spreadsheet, just type the link into your Internet browser, starting with the *http://dx.doi.org* prefix, or click on the link from the e-book edition.

## Siga las publicaciones de la OCDE en:

*http://twitter.com/OECD_Pubs*

*http://www.facebook.com/OECDPublications*

*http://www.linkedin.com/groups/OECD-Publications-4645871*

*http://www.youtube.com/oecdilibrary*

*http://www.oecd.org/oecddirect/*

## Este libro contiene...

StatLinks
¡Un servicio que transfiere ficheros Excel® utilizados en los cuadros y gráficos!

Busque el logotipo *StatLinks* en la parte inferior de los cuadros y gráficos de esta publicación. Para descargar la correspondiente hoja de cálculo Excel®, sólo tiene que introducir el enlace en la barra de direcciones de su navegador incluyendo primero el prefijo *http://dx.doi.org* o bien haga clic en el enlace de la versión electrónica.

# Executive summary

*Revenue Statistics in Latin America and the Caribbean 2022* provides internationally comparable data on tax levels and tax structures for 27 Latin American and Caribbean (LAC) countries: Antigua and Barbuda, Argentina, the Bahamas, Barbados, Belize, Bolivia, Brazil, Chile, Colombia, Costa Rica, Cuba, the Dominican Republic, Ecuador, El Salvador, Guatemala, Guyana, Honduras, Jamaica, Mexico, Nicaragua, Panama, Paraguay, Peru, Saint Lucia, Trinidad and Tobago, Uruguay and Venezuela.

In this publication, "taxes" are defined as compulsory, unrequited payments to general government. Compulsory social security contributions (SSCs) paid to general government are classified as taxes. More information on the tax classification is set out in the Interpretative Guide in Annex A.

## Tax-to-GDP ratios in the LAC region in 2020

In 2020, against the backdrop of the COVID-19 crisis, the average tax-to-GDP ratio in the LAC region was 21.9%, a decrease of 0.8 percentage points (p.p.) relative to 2019. The LAC average represents the unweighted average of 26 countries included in this publication, but excludes Venezuela due to data availability issues.

Tax-to-GDP ratios varied widely across the region in 2020, ranging from 12.4% in Guatemala to 37.5% in Cuba. Between 2019 and 2020, they decreased in 20 countries, largely due to the impact of COVID-19 in the region. In most LAC countries, a decline in nominal tax revenues was accompanied by a decline in nominal GDP; taxes decreased by more than GDP in a majority of cases, causing widespread declines in tax-to-GDP ratios. In contrast, the average tax-to-GDP ratio across the OECD increased by 0.1 p.p. in 2020, with the tax-to-GDP ratio increasing in 20 out of the 38 OECD countries.

Taxes on goods and services across the LAC region were the most strongly impacted by the COVID-19 crisis, decreasing by 0.7% of GDP on average between 2019 and 2020, almost four times the decline in income taxes. Value-added taxes (VAT) recorded a decrease of 0.2 p.p., excises declined by 0.1 p.p. and other consumption taxes (OCT), such as import and export duties and non-VAT general taxes, declined by 0.4 p.p. over this period. Revenues from income taxes decreased by 0.2 p.p. on average between 2019 and 2020, driven entirely by a fall in revenues from corporate income taxes (CIT). Revenues from personal income taxes (PIT) remained unchanged as a percentage of GDP while SSCs increased by 0.1 p.p. between 2019 and 2020. However, in nominal terms, revenues from all main tax categories decreased on average across the region between 2019 and 2020.

The impact of COVID-19 on different tax types varied significantly between the LAC region and the OECD. VAT and other consumption taxes as a percentage of GDP declined strongly in the LAC region whereas no change was observed in these revenues for the OECD average. Excises declined by 0.1 p.p. in both regions. CIT revenues in LAC countries on average experienced a smaller decline (half that of the OECD average of 0.4 p.p.). PIT and SSCs were relatively stable in the LAC region, whereas the OECD average for PIT and SSCs increased as a share of GDP by 0.3 p.p. for both.

Across the LAC sub-regions, average tax-to-GDP ratios in the Caribbean, in Central America and Mexico, and in South America stood at 23.8%, 20.4% and 21.8% respectively in 2020. In all three sub-regions, tax-to-GDP ratios decreased by 0.8 p.p. between 2019 and 2020, and revenues from taxes from goods and services were more affected than revenues from income taxes. The decrease in consumption tax revenues (VAT, excises and OCT) was largest in the Caribbean. In Central America and Mexico and in South America, CIT revenues also declined over the period (by 0.4 p.p. and 0.3 p.p. respectively).

## Evolution of tax-to-GDP ratios in the LAC region since 1990

The average tax-to-GDP ratio for the LAC region rose by more than 6 p.p. between 1990 and 2020 (from 15.6% to 21.9%), due largely to increases in revenues from VAT and taxes on income and profits (of 3.5 p.p. and 2.7 p.p., respectively). The gap between the LAC and OECD average tax-to-GDP ratios narrowed considerably over this period, although the difference widened from 10.7 p.p. in 2019 to 11.6 p.p. in 2020 due to the impact of the COVID-19 pandemic on the LAC region.

On average, South America's tax revenues recorded the strongest growth among the sub-regions between 1990 and 2020, increasing by 8.2% of GDP. South America's average tax-to-GDP ratio was higher than the LAC average between 2004 and 2018 but has declined steadily since 2015, falling below the LAC average from 2019. The Caribbean's average tax-to-GDP ratio was consistently higher than the LAC average between 1990 and 2020, while the average tax-to-GDP ratio of Central America and Mexico increased gradually over this period but remained below the LAC average.

## Tax structures in the LAC region

In 2020, the average tax mix of the LAC region was heavily reliant on revenues from taxes on goods and services, which made up about half of total tax revenues (48.4%), compared with a third in the OECD (32.6% in 2019, the latest year available). VAT revenues were the principal source of these revenues in the LAC region in 2020, on average accounting for 27.5% of total tax revenues and 5.7% of GDP. In comparison, VAT revenues amounted to 20.3% of total tax revenues and 6.7% of GDP in 2019 in the OECD.

The LAC region received 26.9% of tax revenues from taxes on income and profits in 2020 (5.9% of GDP). In 2020, CIT and PIT revenues accounted for 15.6% and 9.8% of total tax revenues on average, compared with 9.6% and 23.5% in the OECD (2019 figures). Similarly, the average share of SSCs in total tax revenues was 18.4% in the LAC region in 2020, well below the OECD average of 25.9% (2019 figure). The remainder of tax revenues in the LAC region was derived from property taxes, unallocable income tax revenues and other taxes, which amounted to 7.9% of total tax revenues in 2020.

## Special feature: Trends in fiscal revenues from non-renewable natural resources

Amidst turmoil in global oil markets due to the COVID-19 crisis, hydrocarbon-related revenues in the LAC region declined from 3.1% of GDP on average in 2019 to 2.1% in 2020, driven by external price shocks and decreases in production. Meanwhile, revenues from mining as a proportion of GDP fell to 0.3% on average in 2020 from 0.4% in 2019. This decline was driven by weak international prices for most minerals and metals as well as lower production partly attributable to measures to limit the spread of the COVID-19 virus. Estimates for 2021 point to a rebound in revenues from non-renewable natural resources (3.0% of GDP for oil and gas revenues and 0.6% of GDP for mining revenues), supported by growing global demand, favourable prices and higher production.

## Special feature: Key findings from monthly revenue data during the COVID crisis

This special feature examines monthly trends in tax revenues during the COVID crisis in 18 LAC countries, with a particular focus on income taxes, VAT and excises. It demonstrates that revenues from these tax types experienced sharp declines in real terms during the second quarter of 2020. The different tax types recovered at varying speeds across the different sub-regions during the second half of 2020, but in cumulative terms remained significantly below revenues in 2019 until the end of 2020. During the first eight months of 2021, tax revenues recovered across the LAC region: on a cumulative basis, the selected tax types for the 18 LAC countries were up 21.3% compared with the same period in 2020 and were 4.6% higher than in the first eight months of 2019. The chapter also examines the evolution of tax revenues with different mobility indicators, especially in the first half of 2020.

# Resumen ejecutivo

*Estadísticas tributarias en América Latina y el Caribe 2022* proporciona datos comparables a nivel internacional sobre los niveles y las estructuras tributarias de 27 países de América Latina y el Caribe (ALC): Antigua y Barbuda, Argentina, Bahamas, Barbados, Belice, Bolivia, Brasil, Chile, Colombia, Costa Rica, Cuba, República Dominicana, Ecuador, El Salvador, Guatemala, Guyana, Honduras, Jamaica, México, Nicaragua, Panamá, Paraguay, Perú, Santa Lucía, Trinidad y Tobago, Uruguay y Venezuela.

En la presente publicación, los «impuestos» se definen como pagos obligatorios y sin contraprestación a las administraciones públicas. En esta clasificación, también se incluyen las contribuciones a la seguridad social (CSS) obligatorias que se pagan a las administraciones públicas. En la Guía interpretativa del Anexo A se ofrece más información sobre la clasificación de los impuestos.

## La recaudación tributaria como proporción del PIB en la región de ALC en 2020

En 2020, con la crisis de COVID-19, el promedio de recaudación tributaria como proporción del PIB de la región de ALC fue del 21.9%, una reducción de 0.8 puntos porcentuales (p.p.) respecto a 2019. El promedio de ALC representa el promedio no ponderado de 26 países de la región incluidos en esta publicación, sin contar con Venezuela, debido a problemas de disponibilidad de datos.

En 2020, el promedio de recaudación tributaria como proporción del PIB presentó variaciones considerables en toda la región, desde el 12.4%, de Guatemala, al 37.5%, de Cuba. Entre 2019 y 2020, este indicador se redujo en 20 países, en gran medida, como consecuencia del impacto del COVID-19. En la mayoría de los países de ALC, la reducción de los ingresos tributarios nominales estuvo acompañada de un descenso del PIB nominal y, en casi todos los casos, los impuestos se redujeron más que el PIB, por lo que se produjeron descensos generalizados en los respectivos coeficientes tributarios. En comparación, en 2020, el promedio de recaudación tributaria como proporción del PIB en los países miembros de la OCDE aumentó 0.1 p.p. Este indicador aumentó en 20 de los 38 países miembros.

Entre 2019 y 2020, los impuestos sobre bienes y servicios de toda la región de ALC fueron los más afectados por la crisis de COVID-19, con una reducción media del PIB del 0.7%, casi cuatro veces la caída que sufrieron los impuestos sobre la renta. Además, los impuestos sobre el valor añadido (IVA) registraron una reducción de 0.2 p.p., los impuestos especiales experimentaron una disminución de 0.1 p.p. y otros impuestos sobre el consumo (OIC), como derechos de importación y exportación y los impuestos generales distintos del IVA, se contrajeron 0.4 p.p. Durante el 2020, la recaudación de los impuestos sobre la renta se redujo un promedio de 0.2 p.p., debido en su totalidad a la disminución de los ingresos procedentes de los impuestos sobre sociedades (IS). Asimismo, la recaudación de los impuestos sobre la renta de las personas físicas (IRPF) como proporción del PIB no sufrió variaciones, mientras que la de las CSS aumentó 0.1 p.p. Sin embargo, en términos nominales, entre 2019 y 2020, los ingresos procedentes de las principales categorías de impuestos se redujeron, en promedio, en toda la región.

El impacto del COVID-19 en los diferentes tipos de impuestos varió enormemente entre la región de ALC y la OCDE. El promedio de los ingresos procedentes del IVA y otros impuestos sobre el consumo como porcentaje del PIB sufrió un fuerte descenso en la región de ALC y permaneció igual en la OCDE. Los impuestos especiales disminuyeron 0.1 p.p. en ambas regiones. La recaudación media del IS en los países de ALC experimentó una pequeña reducción (la mitad que el promedio de la OCDE, que fue de 0.4 p.p.). El IRPF y las CSS se mantuvieron relativamente estables en la región de ALC, mientras que el promedio del coeficiente tributario de la OCDE relativo a estos dos impuestos aumentó 0.3 p.p., en ambos casos.

En 2020, para las subregiones de ALC, el promedio de recaudación tributaria como proporción del PIB correspondiente al Caribe, América Central y México y América del Sur se mantuvo en el 23.8%, el 20.4% y el 21.8%, respectivamente. Entre 2019 y 2020, en las tres subregiones, los coeficientes tributarios se redujeron 0.8 p.p. y los ingresos procedentes de los impuestos sobre bienes y servicios se vieron más afectados que los de los impuestos sobre la renta. La mayor caída de la recaudación de los impuestos sobre el consumo (IVA, impuestos especiales y OIC) se produjo en el Caribe. Los ingresos por el IS en América Central y México y en América del Sur también sufrieron un descenso (0.4 p.p. y 0.3 p.p., respectivamente), en este periodo.

## Evolución de la recaudación tributaria como proporción del PIB en la región de ALC desde 1990

Entre 1990 y 2020, el promedio de recaudación tributaria como proporción del PIB de la región de ALC aumentó más de 6 p.p. (del 15.6% al 21.9%), en buena medida, gracias al aumento de la recaudación del IVA y de los impuestos sobre la renta y los beneficios (de 3.5 p.p. y 2.7 p.p., respectivamente). La diferencia entre estos coeficientes en ALC y la OCDE se acortó considerablemente a lo largo de este periodo, aunque aumentó de 10.7 p.p., en 2019, a 11.6 p.p., en 2020, como consecuencia del impacto de COVID-19.

En promedio, de entre las subregiones de ALC, América del Sur registró el mayor crecimiento entre 1990 y 2020, con un aumento del 8.2% del PIB. Entre 2004 y 2018, el promedio de recaudación tributaria como proporción del PIB de América del Sur fue superior al de ALC, aunque, a partir de 2015, fue reduciéndose progresivamente, hasta situarse por debajo en 2019. Entre 1990 y 2020, el promedio de recaudación tributaria como proporción del PIB del Caribe fue sistemáticamente superior al de ALC y el de América Central y México aumentó gradualmente, aunque se mantuvo por debajo del promedio de ALC.

## Estructuras tributarias en la región de ALC

En 2020, la estructura tributaria promedio de la región de ALC dependía enormemente de los ingresos procedentes de impuestos sobre bienes y servicios, que constituían cerca de la mitad de la recaudación impositiva total (48.4%), frente a un tercio en la OCDE (32.6%, en 2019, el último año del que se dispone de datos). En 2020, en la región ALC, la recaudación del IVA fue la principal fuente de estos ingresos y representaba, en promedio, el 27.5% de los ingresos tributarios totales y el 5.7% del PIB. En comparación la recaudación del IVA en la OCDE alcanzó el 20.3% de los ingresos tributarios totales y el 6.7% del PIB en 2019.

El 26.9% de los ingresos tributarios de la región de ALC de 2020 procedía de impuestos sobre la renta y los beneficios (5.9% del PIB). El mismo año, el IS y el IRPF representaron el 15.6% y el 9.8% de los ingresos tributarios totales, en promedio, frente al 9.6% y el 23.5% de la OCDE (cifras de 2019). Del mismo modo, en 2020, la participación media de las CSS en los ingresos tributarios totales fue del 18.4%, en la región de ALC, muy inferior al promedio de la OCDE, que se situó en el 25.9% (cifras de 2019). Los restantes ingresos tributarios de 2020, en la región de ALC, provenían de impuestos sobre la propiedad, de ingresos del impuesto sobre la renta no clasificables y otros impuestos, que representaron el 7.9% de los ingresos tributarios totales.

## Sección especial: Tendencias de los ingresos tributarios provenientes de recursos naturales no renovables

En medio de la conmoción de los mercados mundiales de petróleo como consecuencia de la crisis generada por el COVID-19, los ingresos relacionados con los hidrocarburos se redujeron, en la región de ALC, en promedio, del 3.1% del PIB, en 2019, al 2.1%, en 2020, por la evolución de los precios externos y la reducción de la producción. Al mismo tiempo, la recaudación procedente de la minería como proporción del PIB cayó, en promedio, desde el 0.4%, en 2019, al 0.3%, en 2020. Esta reducción se debió a la debilidad de los precios internacionales de la mayoría de los minerales y metales, así como a la menor producción, como consecuencia, en parte, de las medidas adoptadas para impedir la propagación del virus causante del COVID-19. Las previsiones para 2021 señalan la recuperación de los ingresos provenientes de los recursos naturales no renovables (3.0% del PIB para los ingresos derivados del gas y el petróleo y el 0.6% del PIB para los ingresos procedentes de la minería), gracias al aumento de la demanda mundial, a unos precios favorables y una mayor producción.

## Sección especial: Principales conclusiones extraídas de los datos de ingresos mensuales durante la crisis de COVID-19

Esta sección especial analiza las tendencias mensuales de los ingresos tributarios, durante la crisis de COVID-19, en 18 países de ALC, con especial atención a los impuestos sobre la renta, el IVA y los impuestos especiales. Se pone de manifiesto que los ingresos procedentes de estos tipos de impuestos sufrieron fuertes caídas, en términos reales, durante el segundo trimestre de 2020. En cada una de las subregiones, los diferentes tipos de impuestos se recuperaron a distintas velocidades, durante la segunda mitad de 2020, pero, en términos acumulativos, se mantuvieron significativamente por debajo de los ingresos de 2019 hasta finales de 2020. En los primeros ocho meses de 2021, los ingresos tributarios se recuperaron en toda la región de ALC: de forma acumulativa, la recaudación de los tipos de impuestos seleccionados para los 18 países de ALC aumentó un 21.3%, en comparación con el mismo periodo de 2020, y fue un 4.6% superior a la de los ocho primeros meses de 2019. A lo largo del capítulo también se analiza la evolución de los ingresos tributarios con diferentes indicadores de movilidad, especialmente, en la primera mitad de 2020.

*Chapter 1*

# Tax revenue trends, 1990-2020

*Capítulo 1*

# Tendencias tributarias, 1990-2020

*Chapter 1*

# Tax revenue trends, 1990-2020

Financing the development agenda of Latin America and the Caribbean (LAC) and the achievement of the Sustainable Development Goals in the LAC region requires a step change in domestic resource mobilisation. The current COVID-19 crisis has deepened the need for LAC countries to strengthen tax revenues to address structural weaknesses in their fiscal, social protection and health systems. The region was already challenged by social unrest and subdued growth when the COVID-19 crisis began. While countries were quick to implement health and fiscal measures in response to the crisis to support the most vulnerable households and firms, these efforts were hindered by high levels of informality, underdeveloped social protection systems and limited fiscal space (OECD et al., 2021[1]; OECD et al., 2021[2]). Once the region has emerged from the pandemic, tax systems will need to be reformed and strengthened to support an inclusive economic recovery and to ensure a sustainable and fair fiscal position in the medium-to-long term.

Fiscal policy has an important role to play in catalysing inclusive economic growth in the region once the COVID-19 crisis has passed. In the long term, higher levels of revenue generation will be crucial to address demands from citizens across the region to improve equity via the provision of public goods, mitigating high levels of vulnerability, particularly in the labour market, and implementing comprehensive social protection systems. Improving the structure of the taxation system is important to promote entrepreneurship and enhance redistribution. Taxes can also incentivise a transition to cleaner forms of energy in the context of the climate crisis.

*Revenue Statistics in Latin America and the Caribbean* provides internationally comparable data on tax revenues in 27 countries in the region both as a basis for in-depth policy analysis and as a common starting point for knowledge-sharing and capacity development. This edition of the report shows the impact of COVID-19 on tax revenues in 2020, the first year of the pandemic. The first chapter discusses the evolution of several key tax indicators between 1990 and 2020, including the tax-to-GDP ratio, the tax mix and the share of tax revenue generated by different levels of government. It also analyses revenues from environmental taxes. Chapters 5 and 6 provide a detailed country-by-country breakdown of tax revenues.

## Tax-to-GDP ratios

### *Tax-to-GDP ratios in 2020*

The tax-to-GDP ratio measures tax revenues (including social security contributions paid to the general government) as a proportion of gross domestic product (GDP). The LAC average represents the unweighted average of 26 of the countries included in this publication and excludes Venezuela due to lack of data.

The average tax-to-GDP ratio in the LAC region was 21.9% in 2020 (Figure 1.1). Levels varied widely across the region, ranging from 12.4% in Guatemala to 37.5% in Cuba. With the exceptions of Barbados and Cuba, all LAC countries recorded a tax-to-GDP ratio below the OECD average[1] of 33.5%.

The highest tax-to-GDP ratios in the LAC region were registered by Cuba (37.5%), Barbados (35.2%) and Brazil (31.6%). The countries with the lowest tax-to-GDP ratios were Guatemala (12.4%), the Dominican Republic (12.6%) and Paraguay (13.4%).

Figure 1.1. **Tax-to-GDP ratios in the LAC region, 2020**

Total tax revenues as percentage of GDP

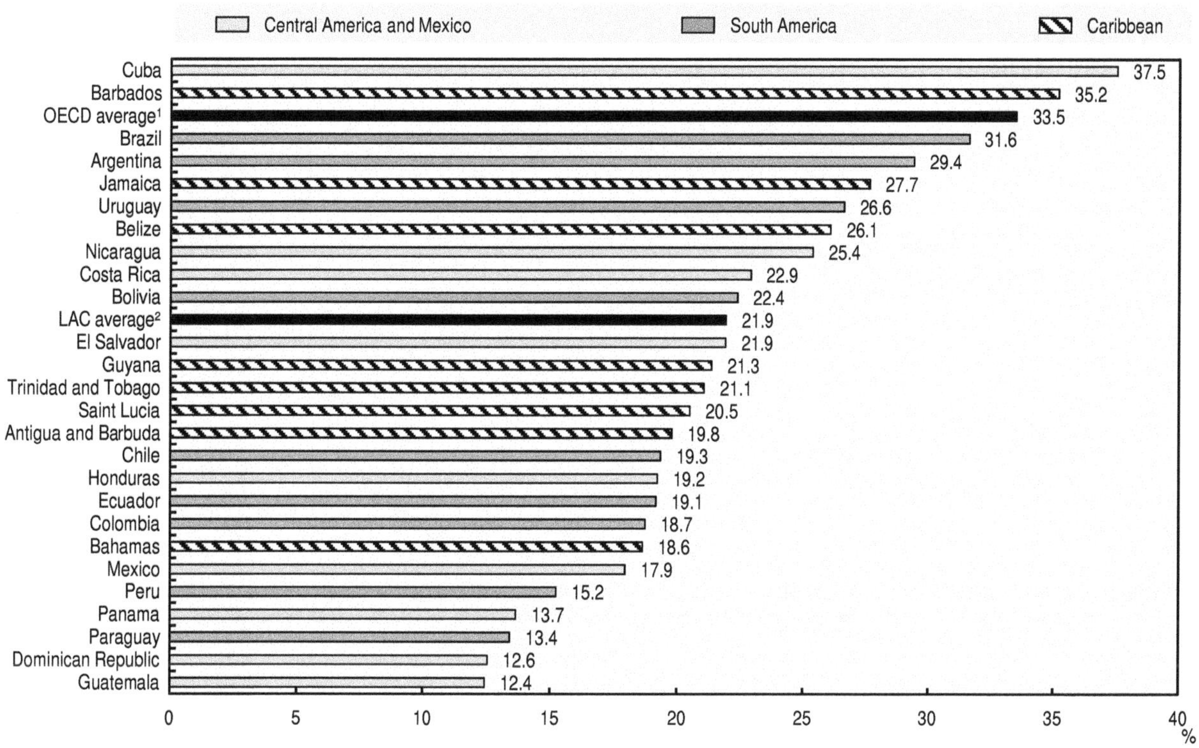


*Note:* The classification of countries into different sub-regions follows ECLAC's classification and is based on the spoken language of countries. The "Caribbean" includes the English-speaking countries and Guyana, while "Central America and Mexico" covers Spanish-speaking countries including Dominican Republic and Cuba.

The figures exclude local government revenues for Antigua and Barbuda, Argentina (but include provincial revenues), the Bahamas, Barbados, Cuba (except for 2002-12), the Dominican Republic, Saint Lucia, Trinidad and Tobago, and Venezuela as the data are not available.

1. Represents the unweighted average of the 38 OECD member countries. Chile, Colombia, Costa Rica and Mexico are also part of the OECD (38).
2. Represents the group of 26 Latin American and Caribbean countries included in this publication and excludes Venezuela due to data availability issues.

*Source:* OECD et al. (2022[3]), Table 4.1.

StatLink https://doi.org/10.1787/888934307478

In 2020, the average LAC tax-to-GDP was 0.8 percentage points (p.p.) lower than in 2019. Changes in tax-to-GDP ratios between 2019 and 2020 varied greatly across the region (Figure 1.2). Twenty countries recorded decreases in their tax-to-GDP ratio over this period while increases were seen in six. In comparison, the average OECD tax-to-GDP ratio increased by 0.1 p.p. in 2020 relative to 2019, and 20 out of 38 OECD countries recorded increases in their tax-to-GDP ratios.

The decreases in the tax-to-GDP ratio exceeded 1 p.p. in ten LAC countries between 2019 and 2020. Over the same period, tax-to-GDP ratios in five LAC countries increased by more than 1 p.p. However, the decreases in the tax-to-GDP ratios were typically more significant than the increases. The largest decreases in the LAC region between 2019 and 2020 were observed in Cuba (4.6 p.p.), Trinidad and Tobago (3.3 p.p.) and Belize (3.0 p.p.). By contrast, Antigua and Barbuda and Mexico recorded the largest increases in their tax-to-GDP ratios, of 1.7 p.p. and 1.6 p.p. respectively.

Figure 1.2. **Change in tax-to-GDP ratios in the LAC region in 2019 and 2020**

Percentage points of GDP

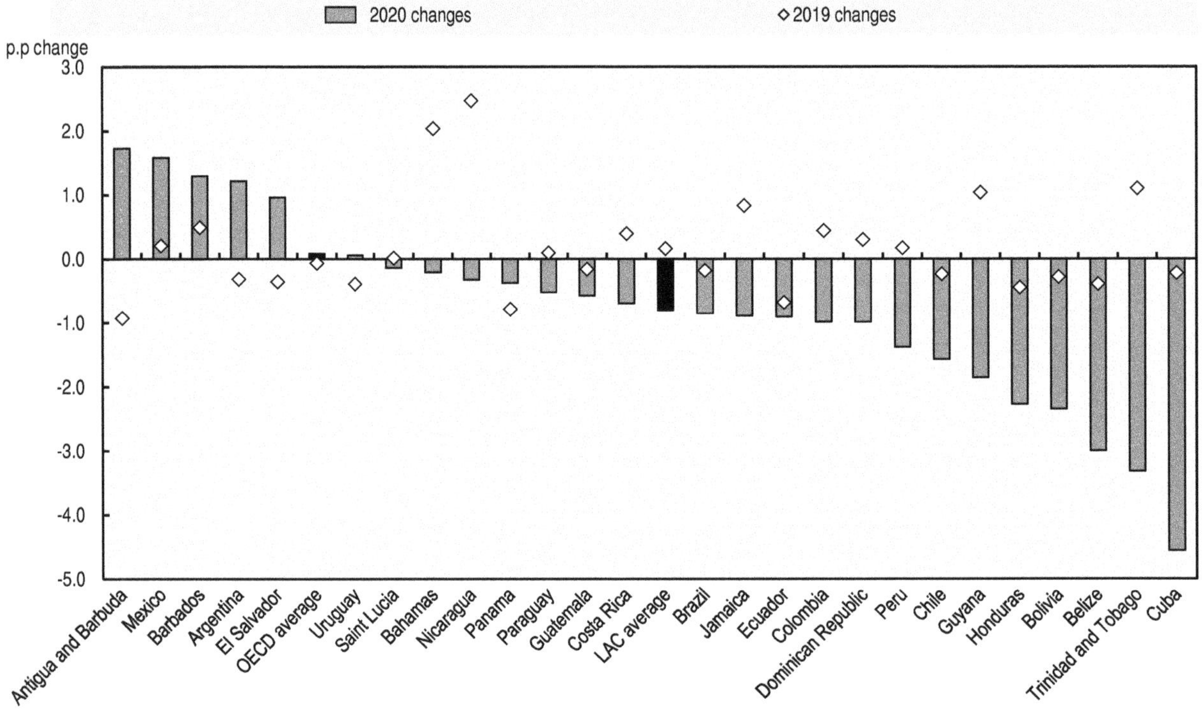


*Note:* The LAC average represents the unweighted average of 26 LAC countries included in this publication and excludes Venezuela due to data availability issues. The OECD average represents the unweighted average of the 38 OECD member countries. Chile, Colombia, Costa Rica and Mexico are also part of the OECD (38).

*Source:* Authors' calculations based on OECD et al. (2022[3]), Table 4.1.

StatLink https://doi.org/10.1787/888934307497

## *Impact of COVID-19 on tax revenues: Changes in 2020 relative to 2019*

### *Overview of changes in tax revenues and in GDP*

To provide further insights into the impact of the COVID-19 crisis, this section analyses changes in nominal tax revenues and nominal GDP between 2019 and 2020. The value of the tax-to-GDP ratio depends on two components; its numerator (tax revenue) and its denominator (GDP) (see Box 1.1). This means that the changes in tax-to-GDP ratios between 2019 and 2020 reflect changes in nominal tax revenues as well as changes in nominal GDP over the same period.

The COVID-19 pandemic resulted in historic falls in nominal tax revenues and nominal GDP. Twenty-two out of 26 countries covered by this report recorded falls in nominal tax revenues between 2019 and 2020, and nominal tax revenues fell by 8.0% on average over the period (unweighted figure). Seventeen LAC countries recorded decreases in nominal GDP between 2019 and 2020, and nominal GDP fell on average by 4.9% (unweighted figure). In contrast, nominal tax revenues fell by 1.2% and nominal GDP increased by 1.8% on average between 2008 and 2009 as a result of the Global Financial Crisis (GFC).

Figure 1.3 shows the relative falls in nominal tax revenues and nominal GDP between 2019 and 2020 for all LAC and OECD countries. In 16 LAC countries, a decline in nominal tax revenues accompanied a decline in nominal GDP and for 13 of these countries nominal tax revenues fell by more than nominal GDP, leading to a decline in the tax-to-GDP ratios. For three countries (Antigua and Barbuda, Barbados and El Salvador), nominal tax revenues fell by less than nominal GDP between 2019 and 2020, leading to an increase in their tax-to-GDP ratio. Another six LAC countries reported decreases in nominal tax revenues while their nominal GDP increased, also decreasing their tax-to-GDP ratios.

### Box 1.1. **The tax-to-GDP ratio methodology**

The tax ratios shown in this publication express aggregate tax revenues as a percentage of GDP. The value of this ratio depends on its denominator (GDP) and its numerator (tax revenues). Both the numerator and the denominator may be subject to historical revision.

In 22 LAC countries, the reporting year coincides with the calendar year. The remaining five countries report on a fiscal year basis:

- The fiscal year in Barbados, Belize and Saint Lucia runs from April to March. This means that reporting year 2020 is Q2/2020–Q1/2021.
- The fiscal year in Trinidad and Tobago covers October to September. The reporting year 2020 spans Q4/2019–Q3/2020.
- The fiscal year for the Bahamas ends on 30th June. The reporting year 2020 includes Q2/2019–Q2/2020.

**The numerator (tax revenues)**

This publication uses tax revenue figures that are submitted by focal points or published annually by national Ministries of Finance, tax administrations or statistics offices. Historical tax revenue data are subject to revisions each year, with more important revisions in later years. Past figures may also change from one edition to the next when new data are obtained.

**The denominator (GDP)**

The GDP figures used in this publication are mainly sourced from national sources (such as National Statistical Institutes or Central Banks) and the *World Economic Outlook* (WEO) published by the IMF. GDP figures are also revised and updated to reflect better data sources and improved estimation procedures, or to move towards new internationally agreed guidelines for measuring the value of GDP. The most recent available figures from WEO were published in October 2021 (IMF, 2021[5]) and include GDP revisions made by some countries to align with the most recent System of National Accounts (SNA 2008).

The GDP figures for the four LAC countries that are also members of the OECD – Chile, Colombia, Costa Rica and Mexico – are based on the OECD Annual National Accounts (SNA, 2009[6])

Panama and Saint Lucia recorded the largest decreases in 2020 relative to 2019 (over 20%) in nominal GDP as well as in nominal tax revenues. Although these falls were significant, the declines in tax revenues as percentage of GDP between 2019 and 2020 were relatively modest (0.1 p.p. for Saint Lucia and 0.4 p.p. for Panama) due to the similar magnitude of the falls in nominal tax revenues and nominal GDP.

Only four LAC countries (Argentina, Mexico, Nicaragua and Uruguay) recorded increases in their nominal tax revenues between 2019 and 2020, of which three also had increases in nominal GDP. Mexico is the only country whose tax-to-GDP ratio rose because nominal tax revenues rose while nominal GDP declined.

The COVID-19 crisis impacted the tax revenues and GDP of countries around the world. Across OECD countries, the impact was typically smaller than in LAC countries. The OECD average tax-to-GDP ratio increased by 0.1 p.p. between 2019 and 2020 and 18 countries reported higher tax-to-GDP ratios over the period. However, these increases occurred against a backdrop of falling nominal tax revenues in 31 OECD countries between 2019 and 2020. The average drop in nominal tax revenues and nominal GDP between 2019 and 2020 in OECD countries amounted to 2.1% for both (OECD, 2021[4]). Between 2019 and 2020, 25 OECD countries recorded declines both in nominal GDP and in nominal tax revenues. However, in 14 of these countries, nominal tax revenues fell by less than nominal GDP, resulting in higher tax-to-GDP ratios in 2020.

Figure 1.3. **Changes in nominal tax and nominal GDP, 2019-20**

Year-on-year % change

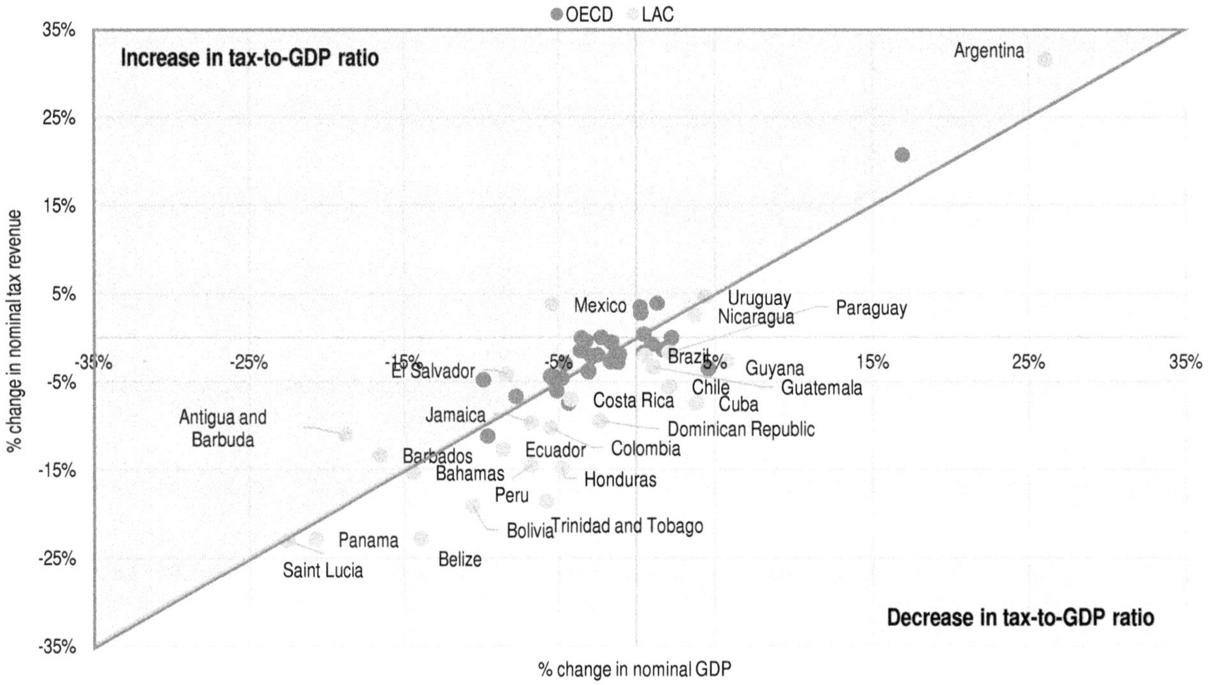


*Note:* OECD data for 2020, reflected by the blue dots, are preliminary and should be interpreted with caution. The diagonal line across the graph represents the point at which the change in tax revenues and in GDP were of the same magnitude and therefore the point at which the tax-to-GDP ratio remained unchanged. Countries above the diagonal line had increases in their tax to GDP ratios; countries below it, had falls.

*Source:* OECD figures are sourced from (OECD, 2021[4]). LAC figures are authors' calculations based on OECD et al. (2022[3])

StatLink https://doi.org/10.1787/888934307516

## *Major changes in tax-to-GDP ratios in LAC countries in 2020*

This section examines in greater detail the largest changes in tax-to-GDP ratios in LAC countries in 2020 relative to 2019 and provides possible contributing factors. In general, countries most affected by the pandemic in 2020 were those reliant on tourism (due to the impact of travel restrictions on tourist arrivals) and resource-rich countries (as commodity prices plummeted in the second quarter of 2020 – see Chapter 2). The three countries that registered the largest decreases in their tax-to-GDP ratio between 2019 and 2020 rely on tourism (Cuba and Belize) or on oil and gas activities (Trinidad and Tobago).

The largest decline in tax revenues as a percentage of GDP between 2019 and 2020 occurred in Cuba, at 4.6 p.p. This was mainly driven by decreases in non-VAT taxes on goods and services (of 2.9 p.p.; Cuba does not have a VAT) and revenues from income taxes (1.2 p.p.) (Figure 1.4). Cuba's economy relies greatly on tourism (revenue from international tourism represented 22% of total exports in 2019); by the end of December 2020, Cuba had experienced a 74.6% drop in international visitors relative to 2019 (Havana Times, 2021[7]). In addition, Cuba implemented one of the tightest lockdowns in the world for six months to prevent the spread of the coronavirus (CNN, 2020[8]).

Figure 1.4. **Changes in tax-to-GDP ratios in LAC countries by main tax heading between 2019 and 2020**

Percentage points of GDP

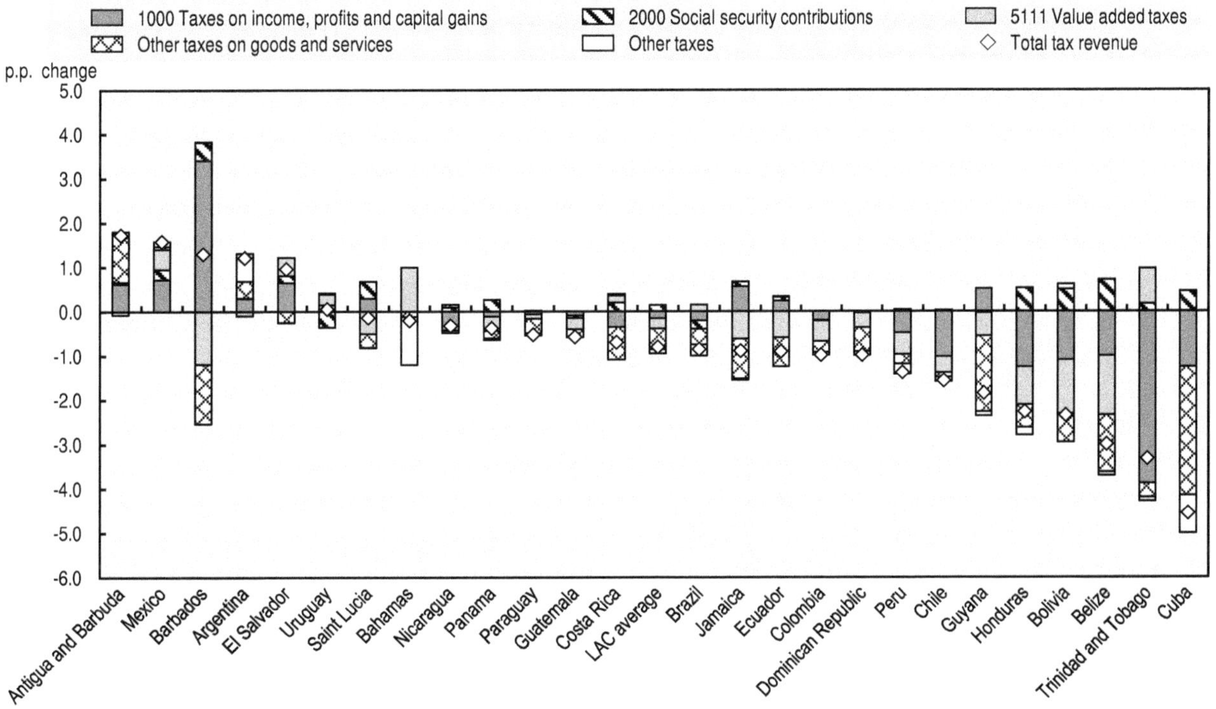


*Note:* The LAC average represents the unweighted average of 26 LAC countries included in this publication and excludes Venezuela due to data availability issues.

*Source:* Authors' calculations based on OECD et al. (2022[3]), Chapter 4.

StatLink https://doi.org/10.1787/888934307535

Trinidad and Tobago recorded the second-largest decline in tax revenues as a percentage of GDP across the LAC region between 2019 and 2020. The drop, of 3.3 p.p., was driven by a decline of 3.9 p.p.in revenues from taxes on income and profits, which accounted for more than half of total tax revenues in 2019. Trinidad and Tobago's tax revenues were affected by the dramatic drop in oil and gas prices and the slump in global demand for crude oil in 2020 (Hon. Colm Imbert, 2020[9]), (ECLAC, 2021[10]). Although oil prices started to recover after April 2020, they did not reach pre-crisis levels in 2020. In addition, revenues from energy production in Trinidad and Tobago declined in 2020 due to unanticipated maintenance activity in some energy facilities and the closure of several petrochemical plants (IMF, 2021[11]).

The decline in the tax-to-GDP ratio of Belize, of 3.0 p.p., was the third-largest in the region. Declines were observed across the main tax categories, including a 1.0 p.p. fall in revenues from taxes on income and profits and a 1.3 p.p. drop in revenues from both VAT and other taxes on goods and services. (ECLAC, 2021[10]) estimates that service sector activity fell by 18.2% in 2020 due to a 71.1% contraction in the tourism sector. In response to the crisis, Belize announced fiscal stimulus amounting to 1% of GDP in 2020 to provide short-term relief to employees affected by the crisis, especially in the tourism sector (IMF, 2021[12]) (ECLAC, 2021[13]).

Six LAC countries experienced an increase in their tax-to-GDP ratio between 2019 and 2020. For three of these countries, the increases were a result of nominal tax revenues falling by less than nominal GDP (Antigua and Barbuda, Barbados and El Salvador) whereas for Mexico the increase was as a result of nominal tax revenues increasing with a falling nominal GDP. Reforms to tax policy or administration in some of these countries may have limited the declines in tax revenues or contributed to their increase.

- In Antigua and Barbuda, revenue from corporate income taxes (CIT) increased by 0.6 p.p. between 2019 and 2020, contributing to the overall increase in tax-to-GDP ratio over the period (1.7 p.p.). Antigua and Barbuda introduced legislation in December 2018 deleting the corporate tax exemption for international business corporations now taxed at the general tax rate of 25% (Council of European Union, 2019[14]). Taxes owed by these companies for the year 2019 were paid at the start of 2020, which led to a significant increase in CIT revenues that year.
- Mexico's tax administration implemented several measures, including tax controls targeting evasion and avoidance, which contributed to the increase of 1.6 p.p. in the overall tax-to-GDP ratio in 2020 relative to 2019 (ECLAC, 2021[13]).
- CIT revenues in El Salvador increased by 0.4 p.p. between 2019 and 2020 as a result of a tax amnesty implemented that year (ECLAC, 2021[13]). This contributed to an overall increase in the tax-to GDP-ratio of 1.0 p.p. over the period.
- With respect to Barbados, the 1.3% increase in tax revenues as a percentage of GDP was due to one-off receipts from CIT in 2020, which were due to higher rates on foreign exchange companies and the higher profitability of these companies (Central Bank of Barbados, 2020 and 2021[15]). Estimated taxes reported by a number of these entities were underpaid during the prepayment periods in 2019 (IMF, 2021[16]) and the shortfalls were paid in the first quarter of 2020, leading to an increase in corporate tax receipts of 4.2% of GDP between 2019 and 2020. This more than offset a decrease equivalent to 2.5% of GDP in revenues from taxes on goods and services over the same period.

#### Impact of the pandemic on different tax types

Between 2019 and 2020, taxes on goods and services were the most strongly impacted by the COVID-19 crisis, decreasing on average by 0.7% of GDP across the region. This decline was almost four times larger than that of revenues from income taxes.

Within taxes on goods and services, VAT showed a decrease of 0.2 p.p. while excises recorded a decrease of 0.1 p.p. Other consumption taxes (OCT), which include customs and imports duties, non-VAT general taxes (such as sales taxes), taxes on the use of goods (such motor vehicles taxes) and taxes to perform activities (such as professional business licences), declined by 0.4 p.p. between 2019 and 2020. Within the OCT category, customs and imports duties recorded the most important decrease at 0.1 p.p.

Revenues from income taxes decreased by 0.2 p.p. on average across the LAC region between 2019 and 2020, driven entirely by a fall in CIT revenues over the same period. Revenues from personal income tax (PIT) as a percentage of GDP remained unchanged while social security contributions (SSCs) increased by 0.1 p.p. between 2019 and 2020.

In nominal terms, revenues from all main tax categories decreased on average across the region between 2019 and 2020. PIT and SSCs declined by 3.0% and 0.7% respectively over this period, a smaller decline than the 4.9% drop in nominal GDP (Table 1.1.). In nominal terms, revenues from the other main tax categories – CIT, VAT and excises – declined respectively by 5.6%, 8.1% and 8.9% over the period.

Table 1.1. **Changes in tax revenues by main tax categories in the LAC region (p.p. and as a percentage)**

| | p.p. | % |
|---|---|---|
| PIT | 0.0 | -3.0 |
| CIT | -0.2 | -5.6 |
| SSCs | 0.1 | -0.7 |
| Prop. | -0.1 | -14.2 |
| VAT | -0.2 | -8.1 |
| Exc. | -0.1 | -8.9 |
| OCT | -0.4 | -15.7 |
| Res. | 0.0 | -12.1 |
| **Total tax** | **-0.8** | **-8.0** |

*Note:* The LAC average excludes Venezuela due to data availability issues. The PIT and CIT averages exclude Ecuador due to data quality issues. The OCT average includes Cuban excises as it is not possible to separate them from other OCT revenues.

*Source:* Authors' calculations based on OECD et al. (2022[3])

StatLink https://doi.org/10.1787/888934308200

The two largest decreases in nominal terms in 2020 relative to 2019 were observed for other consumption taxes (15.7%) and property taxes (14.2%). However, as property taxes represented less than 4% of total taxation on average in the LAC region in 2019, the impact on the tax-to-GDP ratio was smaller than that of declines in other main categories such as VAT or excises, which accounted for a higher share of total tax revenues.

Figure 1.5 presents the overall distribution of changes in tax types as a percentage of GDP between 2019 and 2020. Sixteen LAC countries saw decreases in CIT revenues as a share of GDP and in six LAC countries the decreases in CIT revenues exceeded 0.6 p.p. of GDP. CIT revenues show the widest dispersion across all the tax categories: the changes between 2019 and 2020 ranged from -3.3 p.p. (Trinidad and Tobago) to 4.2 p.p. (Barbados).

Wide variation can also be observed in changes to OCT revenues (i.e. non-VAT & excises consumption taxes). Twenty-two LAC countries saw decreases in OCT revenues as a share of GDP between 2019 and 2020. Cuba registered the largest decrease (2.9 p.p.), mainly driven by a 2.6 p.p. decline in sales tax revenues as a consequence of the COVID-19 crisis.

Seventeen LAC countries saw decreases in VAT revenues as a share of GDP and for half of the LAC countries, the decreases exceeded 0.3 p.p. The largest decrease in VAT revenues amounted to 1.3 p.p. in Belize and the largest increase in VAT was observed in the Bahamas (1.0 p.p.). The increase in VAT revenues in the Bahamas was due to the shift from stamp tax to VAT on real estate following a tax reform. This led to a 1.1 p.p. decrease in property taxes in the Bahamas in 2020 (The Government of the Bahamas, 2020[17]).

Sixteen LAC countries recorded decreases in excise revenues as a share of GDP. Guyana posted the largest decrease, of 1.1 p.p.

Figure 1.5. **Changes in tax revenues by category as a share of GDP in the LAC region, 2019-20**

Percentage points of GDP

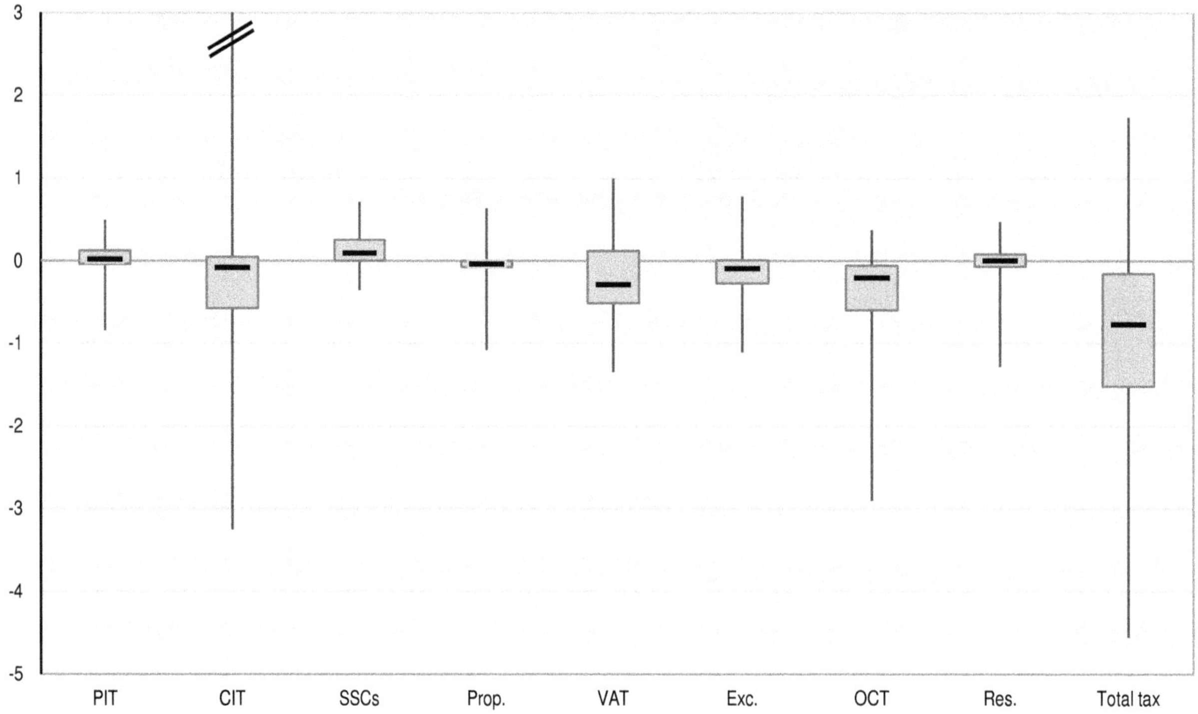


*Note:* The LAC average excludes Venezuela due to data availability issues. The PIT and CIT averages exclude Ecuador due to data quality issues. The OCT average includes Cuban excises as it is not possible to separate them from other OCT revenues. In the figure, the lowest point represents the minimum country change for the tax type between 2019 and 2020; the box represents the changes for countries between the lower and upper quartiles (i.e. 50% of countries had changes within the range shown by each box); and the upper point for each tax type represents the maximum country change. The line in each box represents the median country change (i.e. half of countries were above this line and half were below).

*Source:* Authors' calculations based on OECD et al. (2022[3]).

StatLink https://doi.org/10.1787/888934307554

As a share of GDP, revenues from PIT and SSCs showed smaller changes than other categories, demonstrating the relatively limited impact of COVID-19 on these two categories compared to the others. Revenues of these two taxes were more stable compared to taxes such as VAT and CIT, which have more volatile tax bases. As a percentage of GDP, PIT revenues increased in 14 countries and SSCs increased in 21 countries over the period.

Figure 1.6 presents the overall distribution of relative 2019-20 changes in nominal tax revenues by main categories. In nominal terms, changes are more widespread and the negative impact of COVID-19 is clearly visible for all tax categories. For all of them, the median is negative, meaning that more than half of the countries showed declines in nominal tax revenues between 2019 and 2020.

With respect to taxes on goods and services, the number of countries showing declines in VAT, excises and OCT revenues were 19, 18 and 23 respectively. Within the income tax category, 15 and 16 countries recorded decreases in nominal tax revenues between 2019 and 2020 for PIT and CIT respectively. Meanwhile, SSCs declined in 15 countries in nominal terms and 23 out 26 countries recorded declines in nominal property tax revenues.

Figure 1.6. **Relative changes in nominal tax revenues by category in the LAC region, 2019-20**

Year-on-year % change

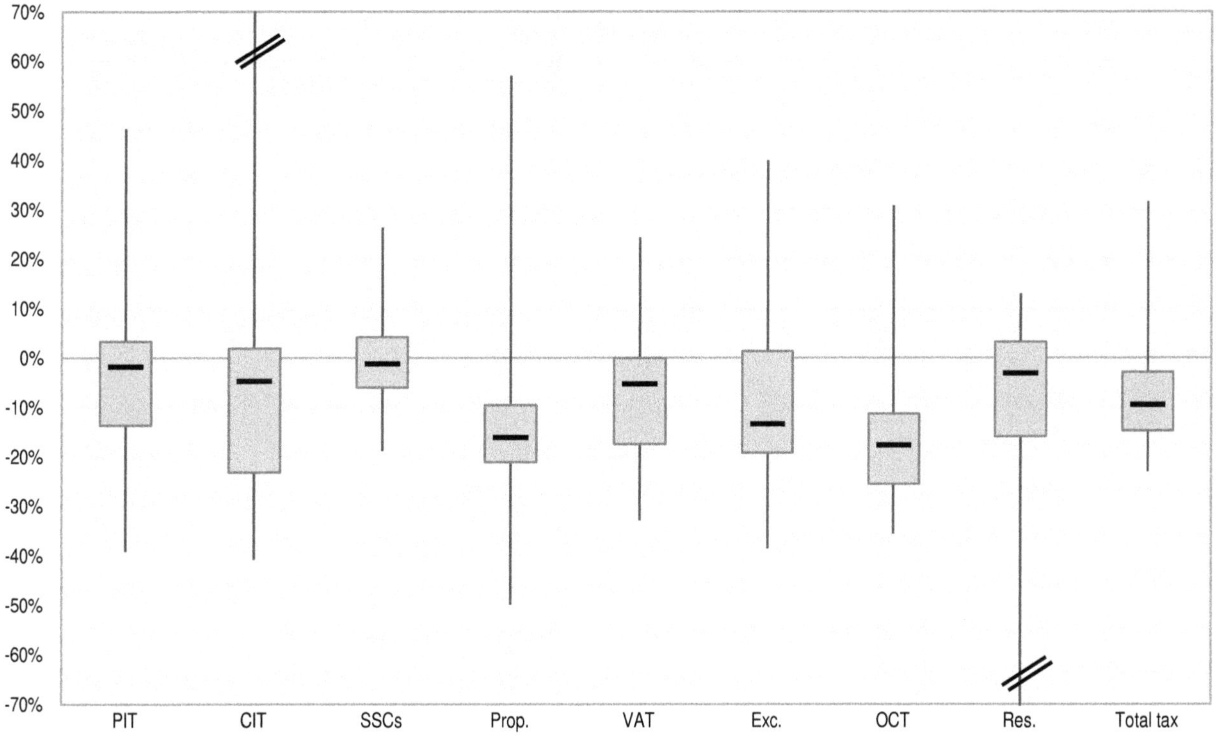


*Note:* The LAC average excludes Venezuela due to data availability issues. The PIT and CIT averages exclude Ecuador due to data quality issues. The OCT average includes Cuban excises as it is not possible to separate them from other OCT revenues. In the figure, the lowest point represents the minimum country change for the tax type between 2019-2020; the box represents the changes for countries between the lower and upper quartiles (i.e. 50% of countries had changes within the range shown by each box); and the upper point for each tax type represents the maximum country change. The line in each box represents the median country change (i.e. half of countries were both above this line and half below).

*Source:* Authors' calculations based on OECD et al. (2022[3]).

StatLink https://doi.org/10.1787/888934307573

In 2020, the impact of COVID-19 on different tax types in the LAC region varied significantly from its impact in the OECD (Figure 1.7):

- In the OECD, PIT and SSCs increased as a share of GDP (0.3 p.p. for both on average) (OECD, 2021[4]). Revenues from both tax categories rose in 2020 in the majority of OECD countries as a share of GDP (28 and 29 countries respectively, representing nearly three-quarters of the OECD countries). For both, half of the OECD countries had increases above 0.2 p.p. In comparison, only six out of 26 LAC countries had increases in PIT revenues that exceeded 0.2 p.p. and eight LAC countries had increases in SSCs above that level.
- In the OECD, CIT revenues experienced a significant decline (OECD, 2021[4]). The average fall of CIT revenues in the OECD average was 0.4 p.p., double that of the LAC average for CIT (0.2 p.p.). CIT revenues fell in 26 OECD countries, more than two-thirds of the total countries. Half of the OECD countries had decreases over 0.3 p.p. whereas in the LAC region eight out of 26 countries (less than a third) had decreases above that level.
- No change was seen in VAT or the other consumption taxes as a percentage of GDP for the OECD average (OECD, 2021[4]) whereas VAT and other consumption taxes declined strongly (by 0.2 p.p. and 0.4 p.p. respectively) in the LAC region. Figure 1.7 illustrates the

greater magnitude of decreases in VAT and OCT revenues as a percentage of GDP across LAC countries compared to the OECD. Half of the LAC countries had decreases in VAT revenues above 0.3 p.p. whereas only seven OECD countries had decreases above that level.

- A decrease of 0.1 p.p. was seen for excise revenues in both regions. Revenues from excise taxes in the OECD on average saw the most widespread declines in revenues of all tax types, with falls in 28 countries (OECD, 2021[4]). Excise revenues fell in 16 out of 25 LAC countries for which data is available.
- Property tax revenues remained unchanged in the OECD whereas they declined by 0.1 p.p.in LAC countries on average.

Figure 1.7. **Changes in tax revenues by category as a share of GDP, OECD and LAC, 2019-20**

Percentage points of GDP

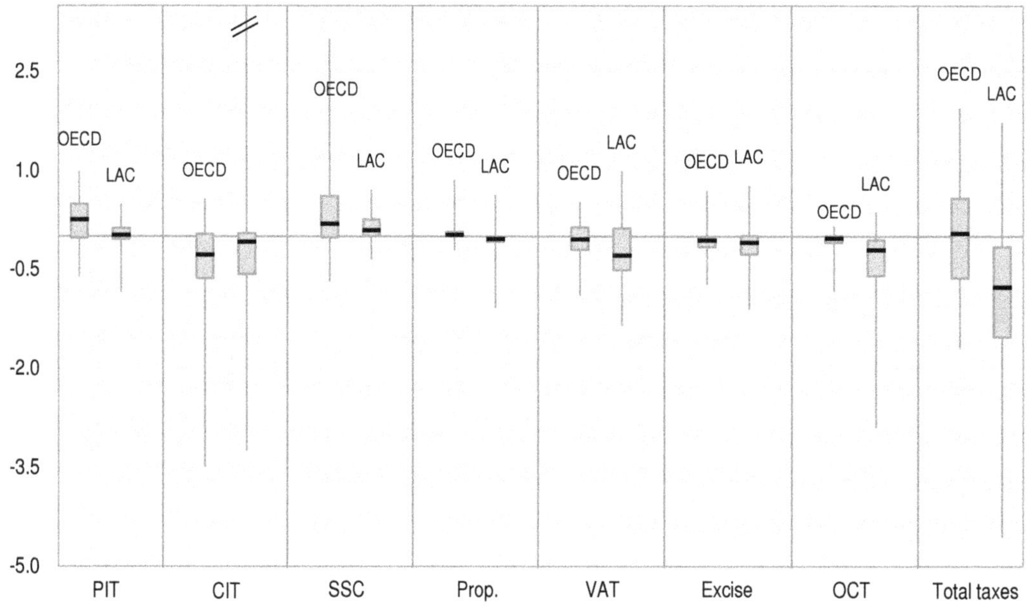


*Note:* The LAC average excludes Venezuela due to data availability issues. The PIT and CIT LAC averages exclude Ecuador due to data quality issues. The OCT LAC average includes Cuban excises as it is not possible to separate them from other OCT revenues. In the figure, the lowest point represents the minimum country change for the tax type between 2019-2020; the box represents the changes for countries between the lower and upper quartiles (i.e. 50% of countries had changes within the range shown by each box); and the upper point for each tax type represents the maximum country change. The line in each box represents the median country change (i.e. half of countries were both above this line and half below). OECD data for 2020 are preliminary and should be interpreted with caution.

*Source:* OECD figures are sourced from (OECD, 2021[4]). LAC figures are authors' calculations based on OECD et al. (2022[3]).

StatLink https://doi.org/10.1787/888934307592

It is important to note that most tax revenues in OECD countries are reported on an accruals basis (when the tax liability is determined, rather than at the time of payment), whereas tax revenues in all LAC countries are reported on a cash basis. Tax revenues in some OECD countries may include liability amounts – notably for VAT – that will not be remitted by businesses to tax authorities in the short term or at all in the future due to tax measures adopted in some OECD countries in response to the COVID-19 crisis, such as deferrals of VAT payments or write-offs for the output-VAT for unpaid invoices. This means that tax revenues in some OECD countries may be overestimated in 2020, in particular for VAT. On the other hand, reporting on a cash basis in the LAC region may mean that changes in the crisis are more pronounced due to the impact of deferrals on the payment of tax liabilities as part of countries' COVID-19 response.

**Impact on different sub-regions**

The three LAC sub-regions have been affected by the COVID-19 crisis in different ways, reflecting their own economic characteristics. The Caribbean was hit hard by COVID-19 in 2020 due to the collapse in tourism. The South American sub-region, which is a net exporter, in particular of non-renewable natural resources, suffered from sharp declines in commodity prices during 2020.

Average tax-to-GDP ratios in the Caribbean, Central America and Mexico and South America stood at 23.8%, 20.4% and 21.8% respectively in 2020. Although the tax-to-GDP ratios decreased by 0.8 p.p. in all three sub-regions between 2019 and 2020, the pandemic's impact on different tax categories varied for each of them.

For all three sub-regions, revenues from taxes from goods and services were more affected than revenues from income taxes. Revenue from taxes from goods and services decreased on average by 0.9 p.p., 0.7 p.p. and 0.6 p.p. respectively in the Caribbean, Central America and Mexico, and South America. In contrast, revenue from taxes from income and profits decreased on average in Central America and Mexico (by 0.2 p.p.) and in South America (by 0.3 p.p.) whereas they increased by 0.1 p.p. in the Caribbean. The 2019-20 increase in income tax revenues in the Caribbean was mainly due to the exceptional increase of these revenues between 2019 and 2020 in Barbados explained earlier. Excluding Barbados, revenue from taxes from income and profits fell by 0.4 p.p. over the period

Table 1.2 presents changes in tax revenues in 2020 relative to 2019 for the Caribbean, Central America and Mexico, and South America by main tax types.

- In the Caribbean, the largest decreases in revenues as a share of GDP in 2020 were recorded in VAT and OCT (0.3 p.p. and 0.4 p.p. respectively). Within OCT, customs and import duties and taxes to perform activities were most affected, with falls of 0.2 p.p. for both. Property taxes recorded a decrease of 0.2 p.p. between 2019 and 2020 due to the tax reform in the Bahamas that shifted taxation on real estate transactions from stamp duties to VAT as explained earlier. Excluding the Bahamas, the decrease in property tax revenues in the Caribbean between 2019 and 2020 amounted to 0.1 p.p. whereas the decrease in VAT revenues over the period was 0.5 p.p. The Caribbean also recorded the largest fall in excise revenues (0.2 p.p.) compared to the other two sub-regions, which both saw a decrease of 0.1 p.p.
- In Central America and Mexico, the largest decreases in revenues as a share of GDP in 2020 were recorded in CIT and OCT (both down 0.4 p.p.). With respect to CIT, Costa Rica, Cuba and Honduras registered the largest decreases, all down more than 0.9 p.p. from 2019. Within the OCT category, sales tax revenues were most affected, recording a decline of 0.3 p.p., mainly due by the fall in these revenues in Cuba. Central America showed the lowest decrease in VAT revenues, at 0.1 p.p. over the period, compared to the Caribbean and South America, which both recorded declines of 0.3 p.p.
- In South America, the largest decreases in revenues as a share of GDP in 2020 were recorded in CIT and VAT (both down 0.3 p.p.). OCT revenues were less affected, declining by 0.2 p.p. between 2019 and 2020. Within this category, import duties experienced the largest decrease (of 0.1 p.p.). Bolivia and Peru recorded the largest falls in CIT revenues (1.1 p.p. and 0.6 p.p. respectively) between 2019 and 2020. Bolivia also recorded the largest

fall in VAT revenues (of 1.2 p.p.). The sharp declines in Bolivia were partly due to weaker revenues from hydrocarbon activities (ECLAC, 2021[18]). In addition, Bolivia implemented a VAT refund targeted at low-income groups in November 2020, which further contributed to the fall of VAT revenues in 2020 (ECLAC, 2021[18]).

Table 1.2. **Changes in tax revenues by category as a share of GDP, LAC and sub-regions, 2019-20**

Percentage points of GDP

| | LAC | Caribbean | Central America + Mexico | South America |
|---|---|---|---|---|
| PIT | 0.0 | -0.1 | 0.1 | 0.0 |
| CIT | -0.2 | 0.1 | -0.4 | -0.3 |
| SSCs | 0.1 | 0.2 | 0.2 | 0.0 |
| Prop. | -0.1 | -0.2 | 0.0 | 0.0 |
| VAT | -0.2 | -0.3 | -0.1 | -0.3 |
| Exc. | -0.1 | -0.2 | -0.1 | 0.0 |
| OCT | -0.4 | -0.4 | -0.4 | -0.2 |
| Res. | 0.0 | 0.0 | 0.0 | -0.1 |
| **Total tax** | **-0.8** | **-0.8** | **-0.8** | **-0.8** |

*Note:* The LAC average excludes Venezuela due to data availability issues. The PIT and CIT averages for LAC and the South American sub-region exclude Ecuador due to data quality issues. The OCT average includes Cuban excises as it is not possible to separate them from other OCT revenues for the LAC and Central America + Mexico averages.
*Source:* Authors' calculations based on OECD et al. (2022[3]).

StatLink https://doi.org/10.1787/888934308219

### *The economic context*

Latin America and the Caribbean has been negatively impacted by the COVID-19 pandemic both economically and socially (OECD et al., 2021[2]). Regional GDP experienced the largest contraction of the past 100 years in 2020, contracting by 6.8% in real terms, while GDP per capita fell by 7.7% on average (ECLAC, 2021[18]). This contraction was among the largest registered by developing regions. Despite the general decline, performance varied between different economic sectors. For example, the agricultural sector has shown strong resilience against the COVID shock, with production expanding in many regional economies in 2020, while manufacturing-related sectors suffered initial downturns but recovered swiftly. The digital economy has received the greatest boost due to lockdown and quarantine measures. Many firms migrated their businesses online to mitigate the lack of physical presence during the pandemic.

In contrast, foreign trade, tourism, passenger air transport and other service sectors were devastated by the pandemic (ECLAC, 2021[19]), In 2020, international goods exports decreased by 9.6% in value and by 4.9% in volume, while international goods imports fell by 15.5% in value and by 11.2% in volume in Latin America (ECLAC, 2021[18]). Net foreign direct investment in the LAC region dropped to USD 90.1 billion in 2020, its lowest level since the GFC, while the region's total external debt climbed to 48% of GDP, the highest level since 1990 (ECLAC, 2022[20]). The region faces a complex context in 2022 amid continued uncertainty regarding the pandemic's evolution, supply disruptions, slowdowns in key trade partners, constrained fiscal policy and tighter monetary and financing conditions. After a relatively strong recovery of 6.2% in 2021, growth is projected to slow to 2.1% in 2022 (ECLAC, 2022[21]).

The COVID-19 pandemic has led to considerable job losses, unprecedented increases in unemployment and widespread bankruptcies, particularly among micro, small and medium-sized enterprises (MSMEs), which represent the majority of businesses in the

LAC region and generate more than half of local jobs. Lockdown measures and restrictions on activities have played a significant role (OECD, 2020[22]). More than 2.7 million formal businesses, 19% of the total, had closed by the end of 2020, among which about 2.6 million were microenterprises (ECLAC, 2020[23]). The largest share of these businesses were in the wholesale and retail trade sector, followed by tourism (ECLAC, 2020[23]).

The COVID-19 crisis had a much bigger negative impact on jobs than previous crises, leading to a historic 9% decline in the number of employed persons and a 4.9 p.p. drop in the labour participation rate (ECLAC, 2021[18]). Even for those who were employed, underemployment was a problem: the number of hours worked declined considerably across the LAC region according to estimates by the International Labour Organisation. Working hours declined by 16.2% from 2019 to 2020, compared with a global loss of 8.8%, making it the worst-hit region in the world (ILO, 2021[24]).

Poverty and inequality have increased throughout the LAC region due to the COVID-19 crisis, which has exacerbated other structural problems that existed before the pandemic (ECLAC, 2021[19]; OECD et al., 2021[2]). The crisis had a disproportionate impact on informal workers and women, as they represent a larger share of the workers in some of the hardest-hit economic sectors (ECLAC, 2021[25]; OECD et al., 2021[2]). Compared with formal workers, especially those in high-income sectors, workers in the informal sector often found it more difficult to carry out their jobs during lockdowns and did not have access to social protection mechanisms such as unemployment insurance. A bigger contraction was thus observed for informal jobs than formal jobs in the region (ECLAC, 2021[18]; OECD et al., 2021[2]). Meanwhile, women typically account for a major share of labour force in the domestic and care sector, which was particularly affected by lockdowns and social distancing.

### *Support measures implemented*

Countries across the region were quick to adopt ambitious fiscal measures to support public healthcare systems, vulnerable households and affected businesses, and to protect productive capacity to facilitate the post-pandemic economic recovery (ECLAC, 2020[26]) (OECD, 2020[22]). While public expenditure served as the central pillar of the fiscal response, tax policy was also used across LAC as an instrument to mitigate the impact of the COVID-19 crisis on families and firms. Compared with programmes that required budgetary reallocations and additional spending, tax policies could often be implemented relatively quickly (OECD et al., 2021[1]).

The unprecedented scale of the health crisis has put significant pressure on healthcare systems in the region, which in many cases were under-developed. Most countries quickly adopted measures to reduce the cost of key medical goods, mainly in the form of temporary exemptions or zero-ratings of medical supplies from import duties. Some countries, such as Colombia, exempted medical goods from VAT, while others provided temporary reductions for PIT and CIT to encourage donations to healthcare systems (OECD et al., 2021[1]).

Tax-relief measures were implemented to compensate households and workers for loss of wages and to support consumption. The most common tax measures for this purpose have included tax deferrals, suspensions of advance payments and the creation of favourable tax payment facilities for VAT and PIT, such as instalment plans with no interest or penalties. Many countries have implemented additional tax policies to further support families and workers (OECD et al., 2021[1]).

Tax relief for firms consisted principally of temporary measures to boost cash flow through tax deferrals and suspension of advance payments of VAT and CIT, in some cases targeting small businesses or sectors most affected by the crisis, such as construction, tourism and personal services. VAT relief played an important role in the region, especially for MSMEs. In addition to CIT and VAT relief, countries also provided support to companies through modifications to social security contributions (OECD et al., 2021[1]).

Despite the rapid rollout of tax-relief measures, the effectiveness of tax policies was hampered by the region's large informal sector and the limited participation of individuals and small businesses in tax and social security systems (OECD et al., 2021[1]; OECD et al., 2021[2]).

### Evolution of tax-to-GDP ratios

#### Evolution of tax-to-GDP ratios since 1990

Notwithstanding the pandemic-induced decline in 2020, the average tax-to-GDP ratio for the LAC region has risen since 1990 (Figure 1.8). It rose by more than 7 p.p. between 1990 and 2019 (from 15.6% to 22.7%) before dropping by 0.8 p.p. in 2020. This trend contrasts with that of OECD countries, where the average tax-to-GDP ratio has been relatively stable since 1990 (although at a higher level than the LAC average); the OECD tax-to-GDP ratio reached 33.5% in 2020, 2.7 p.p. above its level in 1990. The difference between the LAC and OECD average tax-to-GDP ratio has thus reduced considerably over time and in 2019 it reached one of its lowest points at 10.7 p.p. However, the difference between the LAC and OECD average tax-to-GDP ratio widened to 11.6 p.p. in 2020 due to COVID-19's more significant impact on tax revenues in the LAC region.

#### Factors influencing tax-to-GDP ratios

Tax-to-GDP ratios are influenced by a range of economic and structural factors, including GDP per capita (see Box 1.2). Differences between the LAC and OECD average tax-to-GDP ratios are consistent with the tendency for countries at higher income levels to have higher tax-to-GDP ratios. The data implies a positive correlation between GDP per capita (a measure of the level of income of a country) and tax-to-GDP ratios (Figure 1.9). In general, OECD countries have higher average incomes than LAC countries and collect higher tax revenues as a proportion of GDP. Argentina, Barbados, Brazil, and Uruguay show similar tax-to-GDP ratios and levels of income to some OECD countries. Empirical analysis suggests that stronger tax collection, accompanied by better institutions, education and skills, and economic diversification allowed many OECD countries to evade the middle income trap, in contrast to LAC (Melguizo et al., 2017[27]).

Box 1.2. **Factors influencing tax-to-GDP ratios**

The economic and structural factors that influence tax-to-GDP ratios include GDP per capita, openness to trade, the extent of the informal economy, natural resource endowments and the importance of agriculture in the economy. The power of tax administrations, levels of corruption and tax morale (the willingness of people to pay taxes) are also strongly linked to the level of tax revenues (OECD, 2014[28]; OECD, 2019[29]).

The tax-to-GDP ratio also reflects political choices regarding the role of the government and its size. For example, the extent of state participation in financing social security is an important factor behind disparate tax ratios in the LAC region. From the 1980s onwards, many LAC countries, such as Chile, El Salvador and

### Box 1.2. **Factors influencing tax-to-GDP ratios** *(cont.)*

Mexico, privatised healthcare and pensions to greater or lesser degrees: these contributions to private institutions are not considered SSC revenues. In Colombia and Peru, private and public programmes compete and employees opt between them (OECD et al., 2015[30]; OECD/IDB/The World Bank, 2014[31]). On the other hand, Argentina, Brazil and Uruguay follow a model where public and private systems are complementary. In these countries, substantial reforms were undertaken to extend coverage of social security systems to those previously excluded. This has also been instrumental in the increase of tax revenues (ECLAC, 2014[32]).

Informality is another factor that constrains tax collection in LAC by significantly reducing the taxable base. Informal employment accounts for close to 60% of workers in Latin America and the Caribbean (OECD, 2020[22]).

The region loses significant amounts of tax revenues to tax evasion and aggressive tax planning. Foregone revenues due to tax non-compliance in LAC was estimated at 6.1% of GDP in 2018, mainly in income tax (3.8% of GDP) and VAT (2.3% of GDP) (ECLAC, 2020[26]).

In addition, geographic location and historical factors can influence tax-to-GDP ratios: for example, landlocked countries are less able to impose taxes on goods and services at a port of entry than coastal countries. Socio-demographic determinants are also important, such as the level of education or female participation in the labour force. Finally, international factors, including the tax policies of other countries, can impact tax-to-GDP ratios.

Figure 1.8. **Tax-to-GDP ratios, LAC and OECD averages, 1990-2020**

Percentage of GDP

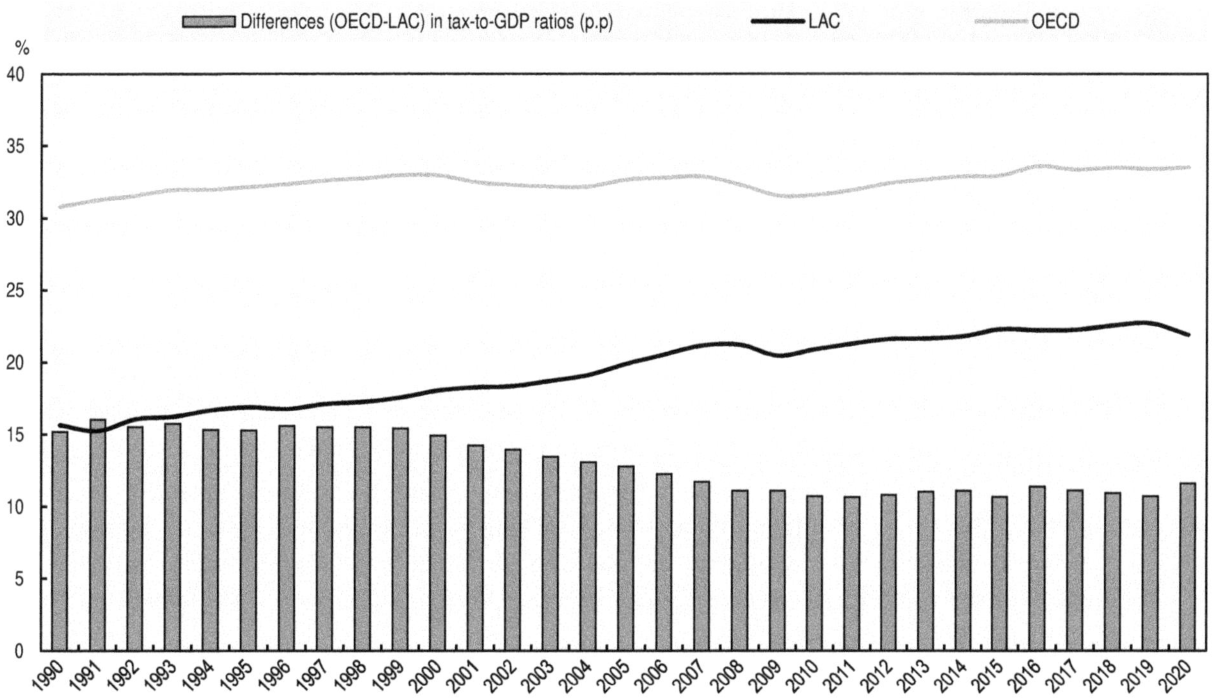


*Note:* The LAC average represents the unweighted average of 26 LAC countries included in this publication and excludes Venezuela due to data availability issues. The OECD average represents the unweighted average of the 38 OECD member countries. Chile, Colombia, Costa Rica and Mexico are also part of the OECD (38).

*Source:* Authors' calculations based on OECD et al. (2022[3]), "Revenue Statistics in Latin America: Comparative tables", *OECD Tax Statistics* (database), *http://dx.doi.org/10.1787/data-00641-en.*

StatLink *https://doi.org/10.1787/888934307611*

Figure 1.9. **GDP per capita in PPP (USD) and tax-to-GDP ratios for countries in the LAC region, the OECD, and a group of African, Asian and Pacific economies, 2019**

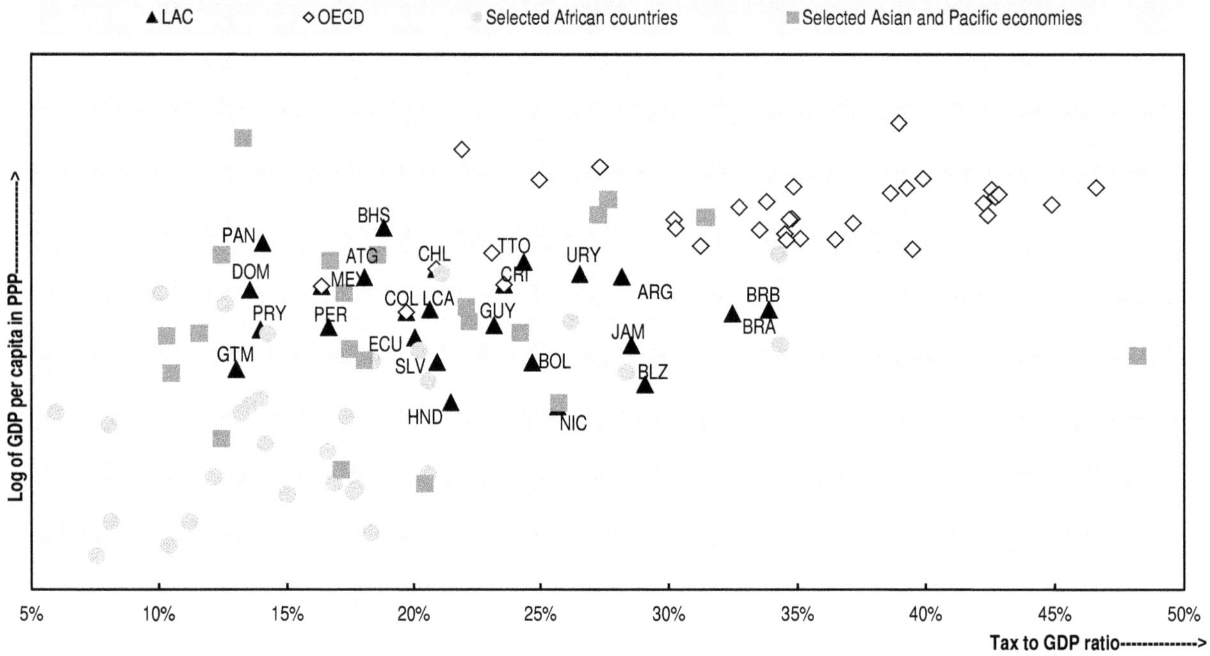


*Note:* The year of comparison is 2019 as 2020 data for the tax-to-GDP ratios are not available for the selected African, Asian and Pacific economies. Cuba and Venezuela are not included in this figure due to data availability issues. The purchasing-power-parity (PPP) between two countries is the rate at which the currency of one country needs to be converted into that of a second country to ensure that a given amount of the first country's currency will purchase the same volume of goods and services in the second country as it does in the first. The implied PPP conversion rate is expressed as national currency per current international dollar. An international dollar has the same purchasing power as the U.S. dollar has in the United States. An international dollar is a hypothetical currency that is used as a means of translating and comparing costs from one country to the other using a common reference point, the US dollar (USD).

*Source:* (IMF, 2021[5]) for figures of GDP per capita. Tax-to-GDP ratios are sourced from the *Global Revenue Statistics Database (http://www.oecd.org/tax/tax-policy/global-revenue-statistics-database.htm).*

StatLink https://doi.org/10.1787/888934307630

### *Evolution of tax-to-GDP ratios in the Caribbean, Central America and Mexico and South America since 1990*

Figure 1.10 shows the evolution of the average tax-to-GDP ratio for the three LAC sub-regions since 1990. While tax levels in all three sub-regions have shown an upward trend during the last three decades, their trajectory shows notable differences:

- On average, South America recorded the strongest growth between 1990 and 2020, of 8.2 p.p. South America recorded a strong increase in its tax-to-GDP ratio during the 1990s and exceeded the LAC average in 2004. Since 2015, however, South America's tax-to-GDP ratio has declined towards the LAC average, and in 2019 and 2020 it was lower than the LAC average.
- The increase in the average tax-to-GDP ratio for Central America and Mexico over the period has been more gradual. Between 1990 and 2020, the average tax-to-GDP ratio of this sub-region remained below the average for the LAC region.

- The Caribbean average tax-to-GDP ratio increased by 4.6 p.p. between 1990 and 2020, and it has been consistently higher than the LAC average. The difference has widened between 2017 and 2019 due to the relatively sharp increase in the tax-to-GDP ratio of the Caribbean in these two years.

Figure 1.10. **Average tax-to-GDP ratios, LAC and sub-regions, 1990-2020**

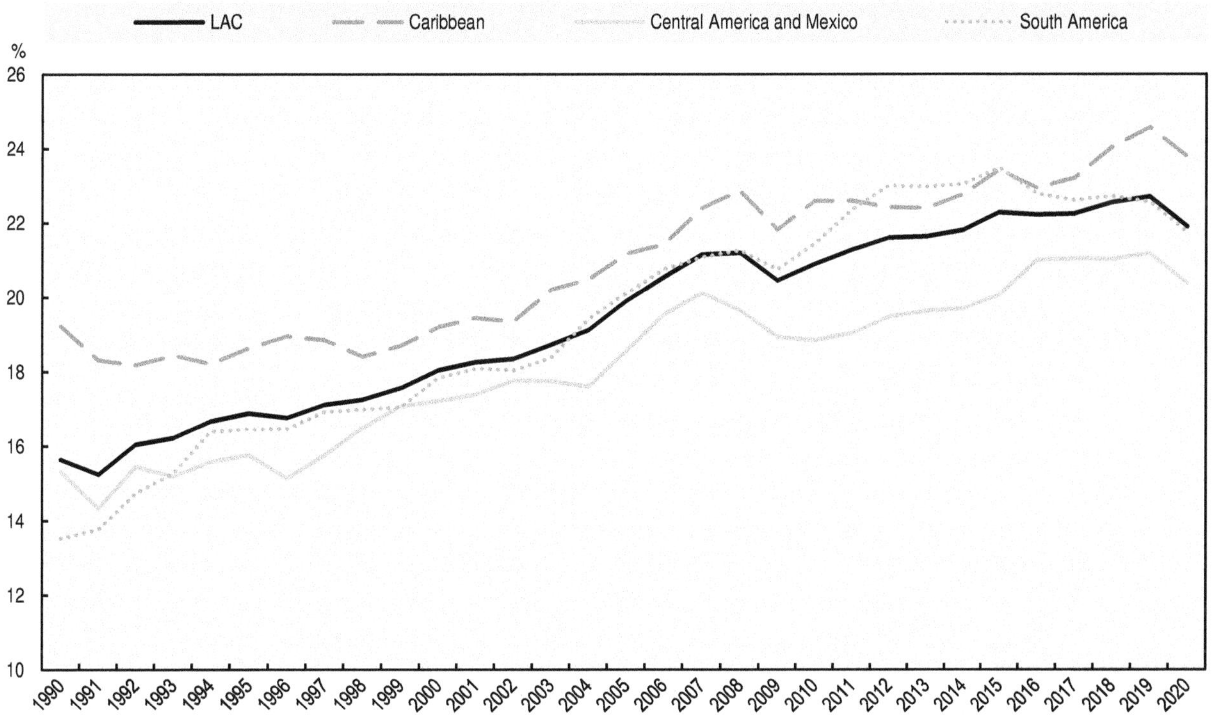


*Note:* The LAC average represents the unweighted average of LAC countries included in this publication and excludes Venezuela due to data availability issues. The Caribbean includes eight countries (Antigua and Barbuda, Bahamas, Barbados, Belize, Guyana, Jamaica, Saint Lucia and Trinidad and Tobago), Central America and Mexico nine countries (Costa Rica, Cuba, Dominican Republic, El Salvador, Guatemala, Honduras, Mexico, Nicaragua and Panama) and South America nine countries (Argentina, Bolivia, Brazil, Chile, Colombia, Ecuador, Paraguay, Peru and Uruguay). The classification of countries into the different sub-regions follows ECLAC's classification and is based on the spoken language of countries. The Caribbean includes the English-speaking countries and Guyana while Central America and Mexico covers Spanish-speaking countries including Dominican Republic and Cuba.

*Source:* Authors' calculations based on OECD et al. (2022[3]), "Revenue Statistics in Latin America: Comparative tables", *OECD Tax Statistics* (database), *http://dx.doi.org/10.1787/data-00641-en*.

StatLink https://doi.org/10.1787/888934307649

### *Evolution of tax revenues by tax types since 1990*

Tax-to-GDP ratios in LAC countries increased in the early 1990s after a decade of macroeconomic instability. During the 1980s, many countries ran large fiscal imbalances and some resorted to alternative ways of financing expenditure (borrowing or printing money). This caused rapid inflation across the region, which eroded the real value of tax revenues. Reforms in the 1990s focused on price stability, trade liberalisation and fiscal discipline. Most LAC governments reduced spending and implemented policies aimed at increasing tax revenues; budget management and fiscal balances improved considerably. Policy makers implemented reforms to tax policy and administration to reinforce tax systems against inflationary episodes by shortening collection lags and indexing tax liabilities (ECLAC, 2018[33]).

The introduction of VAT has been the most significant tax reform in LAC of the past three decades. By the early 1990s, almost all countries were implementing a VAT system and reforms aimed to increase its rate, to widen the tax base and to improve collections. Several countries have moved towards single-rate VAT schemes (ECLAC, 2018[33]).

LAC countries have undertaken significant efforts to modernise tax administration over the last two decades. New information technology systems have been implemented, tax collection systems became more efficient and staff have gained expertise (IDB, 2013[34]). Tax reforms included the introduction or development of simplified regimes for small taxpayers, the taxation of property based on presumed incomes and the expansion of taxation to labour and capital income, including dividends. Reforms have also included the establishment of minimum taxes, taxes on financial transactions and gradual reductions in the real income level taxed at the top marginal rate (ECLAC, 2013[35]; ECLAC, 2018[33]).

The increase in the average tax-to-GDP ratio in the LAC region since 1990 has largely been driven by increases in revenues from income tax and VAT, which increased by 2.9 and 3.7 p.p. respectively between 1990 and 2019 before both declined by 0.2 p.p. in 2020. In 2020, revenues from VAT amounted to 5.7% of GDP while revenues from taxes on income and profits were equivalent to 5.9% of GDP (Figure 1.11).

Between 1990 and 2020, revenues from non-VAT consumption taxes in LAC decreased as a percentage of GDP. Besides a decrease of 0.5 p.p. in 2020 due to the COVID-19 pandemic, there has been longer-term decline associated with trade liberalisation, as a result of which LAC countries changed the way they tax imported and exported goods as well as specific goods and services. These changes included a reduction of import tariffs, narrowing the base of products and services subject to excises, and the elimination of taxes on exports. One important exception is Argentina, where taxes on exports were re-established in 2002, partly abolished in 2015, and reintroduced in September 2018.

Five distinct phases in the evolution of tax revenues can be distinguished:

- Between 1990 and 2002, VAT contributed more to the increase in tax revenues than taxes on income and profits (1.9% of GDP versus 1.0%). Over that period, five countries introduced a VAT (Barbados, Belize, El Salvador, Jamaica and Paraguay). Several other countries increased their standard VAT rates as well as undertaking reforms to widen the tax base and improve revenue collection.
- Between 2002 and 2008, the opposite is observed: revenue from taxes on income and profits contributed more than VAT revenues to the increase in the average tax-to-GDP ratio (the increases amounted to 1.7% and 1.3% of GDP respectively). The increase in income taxes was partly explained by the commodity price boom after 2003, which drove up CIT revenue from the natural resources sector (ECLAC, 2014[32]; Barreix, Benítez and Pecho, 2017[36]). In several countries, it was also a result of policies that reduced tax incentives in free-trade zones, the introduction of minimum taxes for corporations, reforms in international taxation and agreements between countries to fight tax evasion.
- VAT and revenues from income taxes declined strongly during the GFC. During the subsequent recovery, VAT revenues grew quickly to reach 5.9% of GDP in 2016, a similar level to income tax revenues. During this period, two more Caribbean countries introduced VAT (Saint Lucia in 2012 and Bahamas in 2015). Commodity prices declined steadily and then sharply in 2015.

- Between 2016 and the start of the COVID-19 crisis, commodity prices recovered and income tax revenues rebounded. Between 2017 and 2018, revenues from income taxes recorded their largest increase since 2011, at 0.3 p.p. on average, due to strong profits in the mining and oil and gas extraction sectors. In 2019, the increase in income tax revenues (driven by CIT revenue) was more modest, at 0.1 p.p.
- In 2020, all main tax categories except for PIT and SSCs declined as a consequence of the COVID-19 pandemic, as explained in the previous section.

Figure 1.11. **Revenue from selected taxes in the LAC region, 1990-2020**

Percentage of GDP

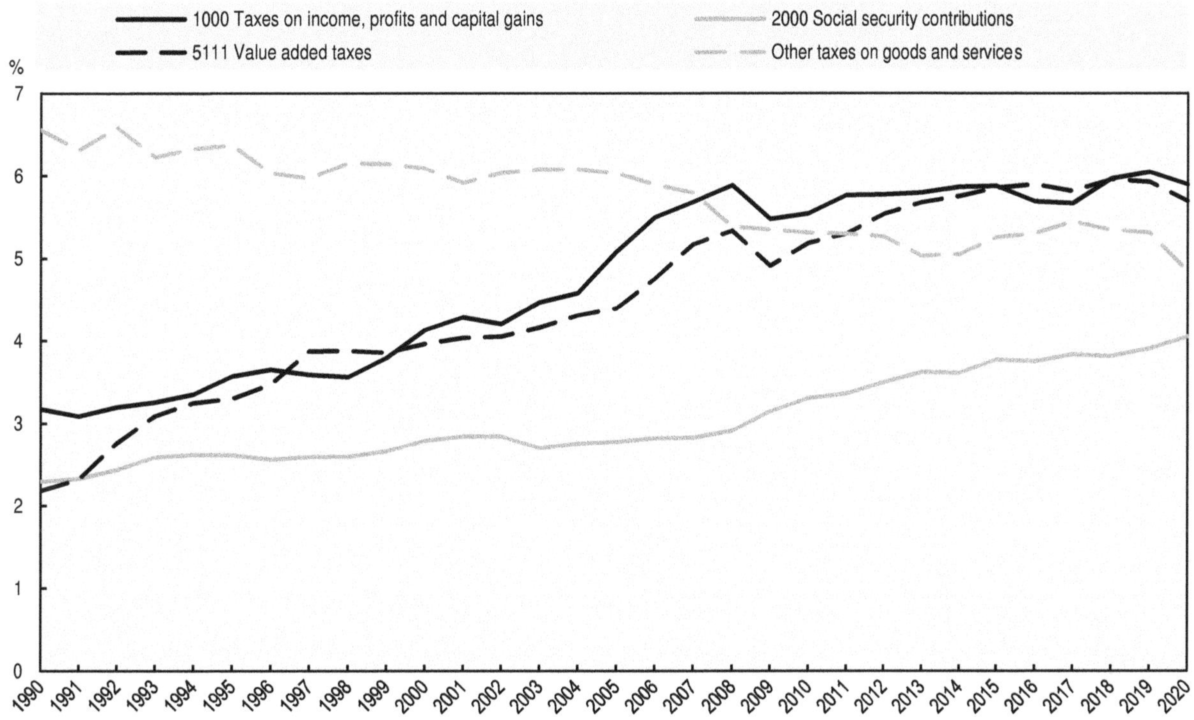


*Note:* The LAC average represents the unweighted average of 26 LAC countries included in this publication and excludes Venezuela due to data availability issues.

*Source:* Authors' calculations based on OECD et al. (2022[3]), "Revenue Statistics in Latin America: Comparative tables", *OECD Tax Statistics* (database), *http://dx.doi.org/10.1787/data-00641-en.*

StatLink https://doi.org/10.1787/888934307668

Figure 1.12 shows the evolution of CIT and PIT since 2005. In 2020, the LAC averages for CIT and PIT revenues stood at 3.4% and 2.2% of GDP respectively. Over this period, CIT revenues as a percentage of GDP have been more volatile than revenues from PIT, which have steadily increased on average across the region and were more resilient than CIT revenues during the GFC and the COVID-19 crisis.

There are notable differences between the three LAC sub-regions in the evolution of the main tax categories in the last three decades:

- In the Caribbean, VAT revenues as a percentage of GDP on average increased greatly in the last three decades as seven of the eight Caribbean countries implemented[2] a VAT system over the period, later than most countries in Central America and Mexico and in South America. VAT revenues were the main driver in the overall tax-to-GDP ratio increase of the Caribbean over the period.

- In Central America and Mexico and in South America, taxes on income and profits contributed most to the increase in the overall tax-to-GDP ratio followed by VAT revenues. Revenues from taxes on income and profits (and indirectly from VAT) were influenced by increases in mineral and oil prices between 2003 and 2010.

Figure 1.12. **Revenue from taxes on income and profits, CIT and PIT in the LAC region, 2005-20**

Percentage of GDP

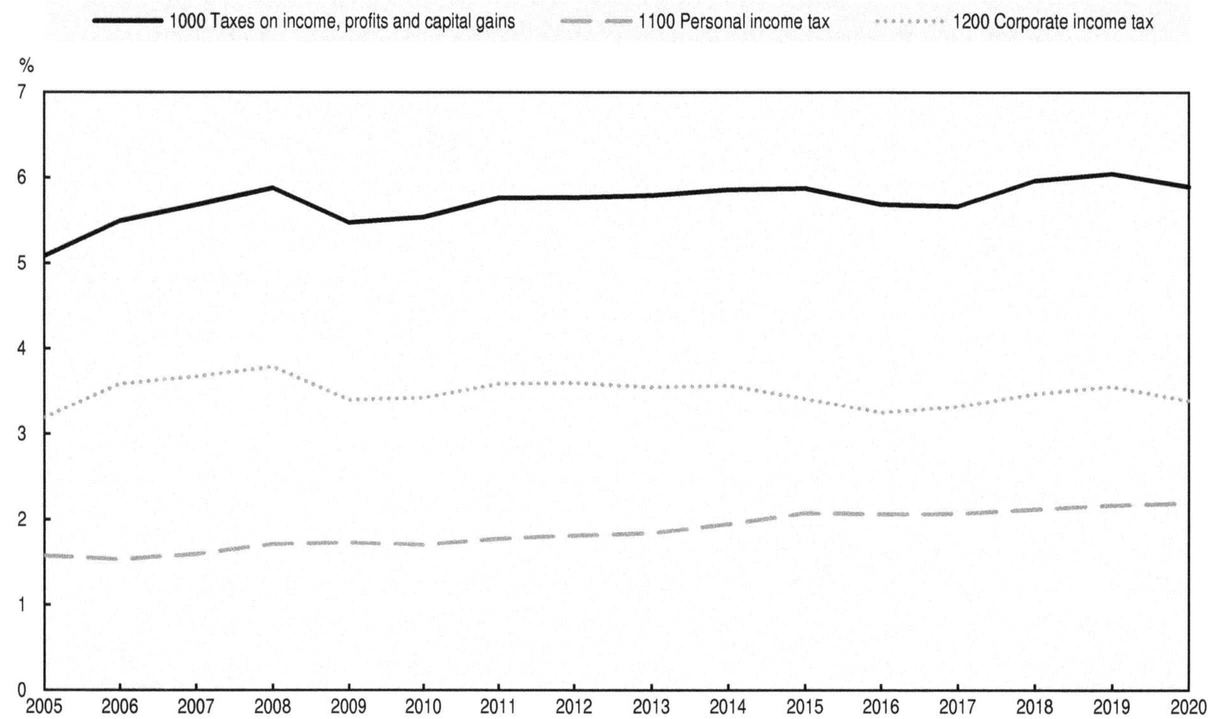


*Note:* The LAC average excludes Venezuela due to data availability issues. Average CIT and PIT as a percentage of GDP should be interpreted with caution as Ecuador is excluded from the calculation. Ecuador is excluded from the LAC average for CIT and PIT revenues as a percentage of GDP as more than a third of its revenue from taxes on income and profits cannot be allocated to either CIT revenue (1200) or PIT revenue (1100).

*Source:* OECD et al. (2022[3]), "Revenue Statistics in Latin America and the Caribbean: Comparative tables", *OECD Tax Statistics* (database), *http://dx.doi.org/10.1787/data-00641-en*.

StatLink *https://doi.org/10.1787/888934307687*

## Tax structures

The tax structure (defined as the share of major tax types in total tax revenue) depicts the composition of tax revenues by different tax types. It is an important indicator for understanding the economic and social effects of tax systems in the LAC region.

### *Evolution of tax structures*

Taxes on goods and services provided the largest share of total tax revenues in the LAC region in 2020, representing nearly half of total taxation on average. During the last three decades, the average LAC mix shifted towards VAT, taxes on income and profits and social security contributions and away from other taxes on goods and services.

- The share of VAT revenues in total tax revenues reached 27.5% in 2020, corresponding to an increase of 12.0 p.p. since 1990. The revenue share of other taxes on goods and services (including excises, customs and import duties) declined by 21.3 p.p. over the same period (Figure 1.13).

- The share of revenues from taxes on incomes and profits grew by 7.4 p.p. (from 19.5% to 26.9% of total tax revenues) between 1990 and 2020.
- The share of social security contributions in total tax revenues increased by 4.5 p.p. from 1990 to 18.4% in 2020. Two major (and opposing) factors have influenced the trajectory of social security contributions in the region. While rising personal incomes have led to higher collections, this was counter-balanced by the full or partial privatisation of social security that occurred in many countries principally between the mid-1990s and 2010 (OECD et al., 2015[30]).

Figure 1.13. **Average tax structure in the LAC region, 1990-2020**

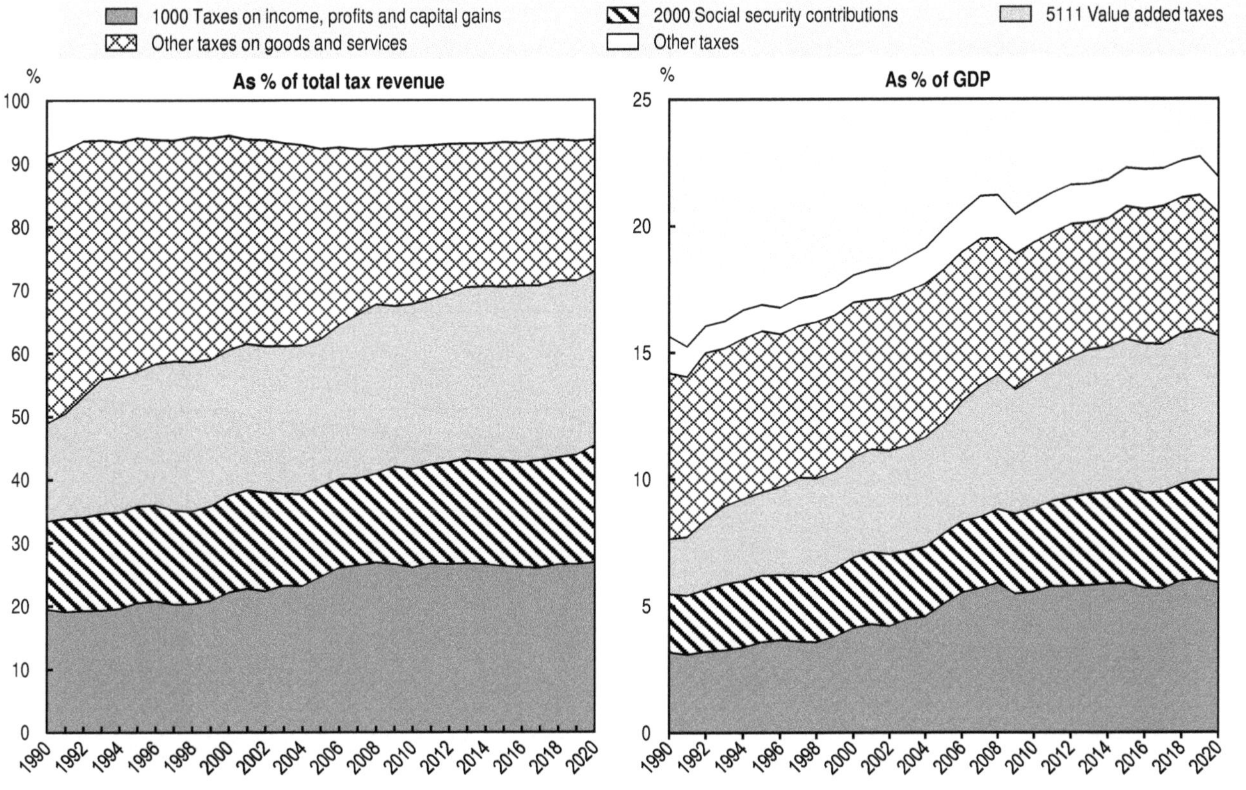


*Note:* The LAC average represents the unweighted average of 26 LAC countries included in this publication and excludes Venezuela due to data availability issues.

*Source:* Authors' calculations based on OECD et al. (2022[3]), Chapter 4.

StatLink https://doi.org/10.1787/888934307706

The share of PIT revenues grew from 7.7% of total tax revenues in 2005 to 9.8% in 2020, in part due to increases in personal incomes across the region in the last two decades before COVID-19. However, the average share of PIT revenue remains low in LAC countries despite some countries implementing reforms to expand their tax base. After the GFC, several countries established flat rates on capital income that had previously been exempt and implemented progressive rates on labour income (ECLAC, 2014[32]). More recently, Ecuador has introduced a new tax reform that came into force at the beginning of 2022 affecting PIT and taxation on wealth, profits and foreign assets. In addition to increasing revenues, this tax reform is expected to increase the progressivity of Ecuador's tax system.

In the LAC region, there are relatively few personal income taxpayers, given the concentration of income earners at low-income levels: in 2013, only 10% of the population in Latin America were registered taxpayers (IDB, 2013[34]).

Several other factors continue to limit PIT revenues, including a small tax base that is comprised primarily of wages (since tax privileges are often granted to returns on capital) and high levels of evasion (Barreix, Benítez and Pecho, 2017[36]; ECLAC, 2014[32]). (ECLAC, 2020[26]) finds that the evasion rates for PIT are high in selected LAC countries that conducted tax evasion studies, ranging from 18.7% in Mexico (2016 figure, equivalent to tax revenue losses of 0.8% of GDP) to 69.9% in Guatemala (2006 figure equivalent to tax revenue losses of 0.5% of GDP). Evasion is more common among the self-employed than employees. A study for Mexico that disaggregated the evasion rate for different groups concluded that the tax revenue losses as a percentage of GDP are nearly five times higher for individuals with business activities than for wage earners (ECLAC, 2020[26]).

Figure 1.14. **Average tax structure in the LAC region, 2005-20**

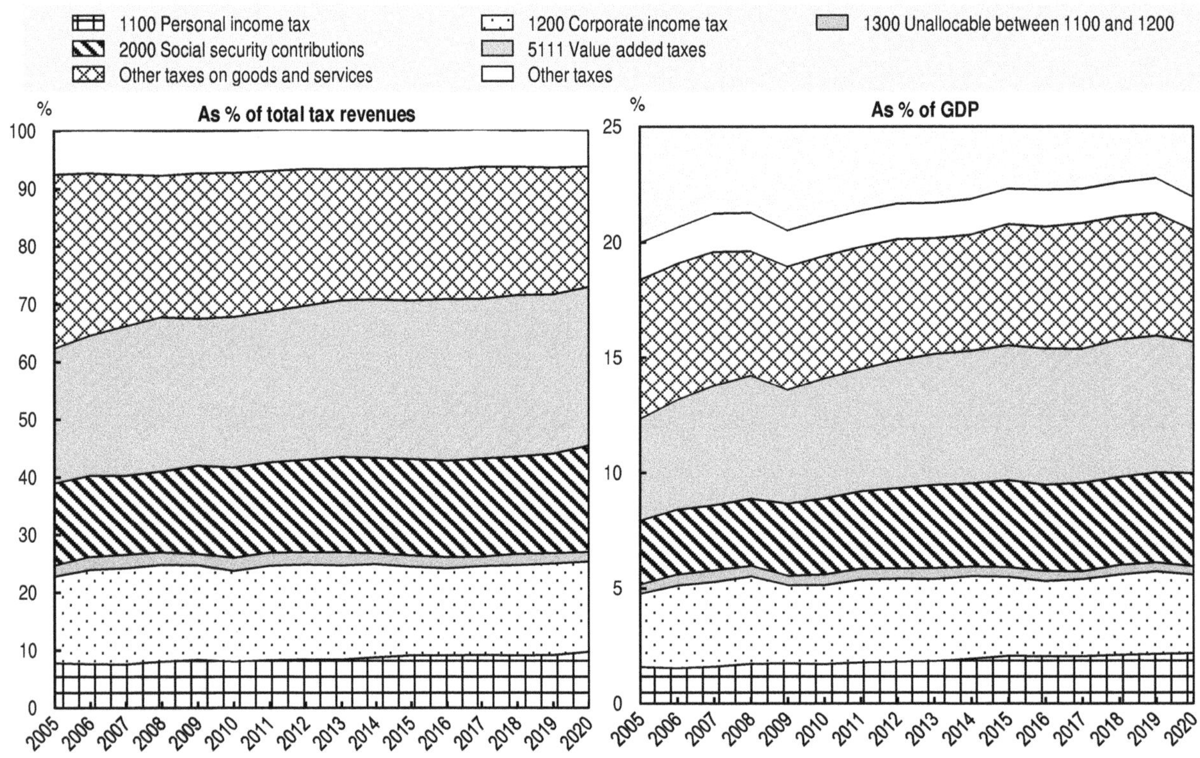


*Note*: The LAC average excludes Venezuela due to data availability issues. Average CIT and PIT as a percentage of GDP should be interpreted with caution as Ecuador is excluded from the calculation. Ecuador is excluded from the LAC average for CIT and PIT revenues as a percentage of GDP as more than a third of its revenue from taxes on income and profits cannot be allocated to either CIT revenue (1200) or PIT revenue (1100).

*Source*: Authors' calculations based on OECD et al. (2022[3]), "Revenue Statistics in Latin America: Comparative tables", *OECD Tax Statistics* (database), *http://dx.doi.org/10.1787/data-00641-en*.

StatLink *https://doi.org/10.1787/888934307725*

The share of CIT revenues in total tax revenues increased by 0.5 p.p. between 2005 and 2020, reaching 15.6% in the latter year. CIT evasion is also a significant issue in the LAC region, with higher evasion rates than for PIT. ECLAC (2020[26]) states that "evasion rates for corporate income tax range from 19.9% in Mexico to almost 80% in Guatemala". Because of high evasion rates, tax revenue losses are estimated to exceed 4% of GDP in the Dominican Republic, Guatemala, Peru and Panama.

In 2020, there were notable differences in average tax structures across the sub-regions. The largest share of revenue in the Caribbean was derived from taxes on goods and services other than VAT, which on average represented 27.9% of total tax revenues. In contrast, South America had the highest share of VAT revenue in 2020 at 30.3% on average, compared with 27.5% in the Caribbean and 24.7% in Central America and Mexico. Social security contributions were lowest in the Caribbean in 2020, at 12.9% of total tax revenues on average. This was slightly less than half of the average for the other sub-regions (20.9% in both Central America and Mexico, and in South America). All three sub-regions generated higher revenues from CIT than from PIT.

### *Average tax structure in LAC and the OECD*

The average tax mix in the LAC region exhibits low revenues from PIT and social security contributions relative to the OECD average (Figure 1.15). On the other hand, LAC countries rely more on taxes on goods and services, which make up just under half of tax revenues on average, compared with around one-third in OECD economies on average. As a percentage of GDP, revenues from taxes on goods and services in the LAC and OECD regions were similar in 2019, at 11.2% and 10.8% respectively.[3]

By contrast, the combined share of taxes on income and profits and social security contributions was much lower in the LAC region than in the OECD (44.1% versus 60.0% in 2019, on average). As a percentage of GDP, these two categories amounted to 10.0% in the LAC region, less than half the average OECD level (20.2%). The tendency towards private provision of social security in many LAC countries explains some of this difference.

On average, CIT generated 15.8% of total tax revenues in the LAC region, compared with 9.6% in the OECD (respectively 3.6% and 3.0% of GDP) (Figure 1.15). The most striking difference relates to revenues from PIT, which contributed 23.5% of total tax revenues in the OECD on average in 2019, and 9.2% of total tax revenues in the LAC region. PIT revenues were 2.2% of GDP in the LAC region on average, compared with 8.0% for the OECD.

Taxes on immovable property and payroll (contained within the category "other taxes") are a less important source of revenue for the LAC region on average than in the OECD, although there are challenges with data availability for property taxes.

### *Tax structures in LAC countries*

Taxes on goods and services are the main source of revenue for all LAC countries except Mexico, Panama, and Trinidad and Tobago. For Mexico and Trinidad and Tobago, revenue from taxes on income and profits accounted for the largest share, whereas revenue from SSCs was the most important source of tax revenue for Panama (Figure 1.16).

Figure 1.15. **Average tax structure in the LAC and OECD regions, 2019**

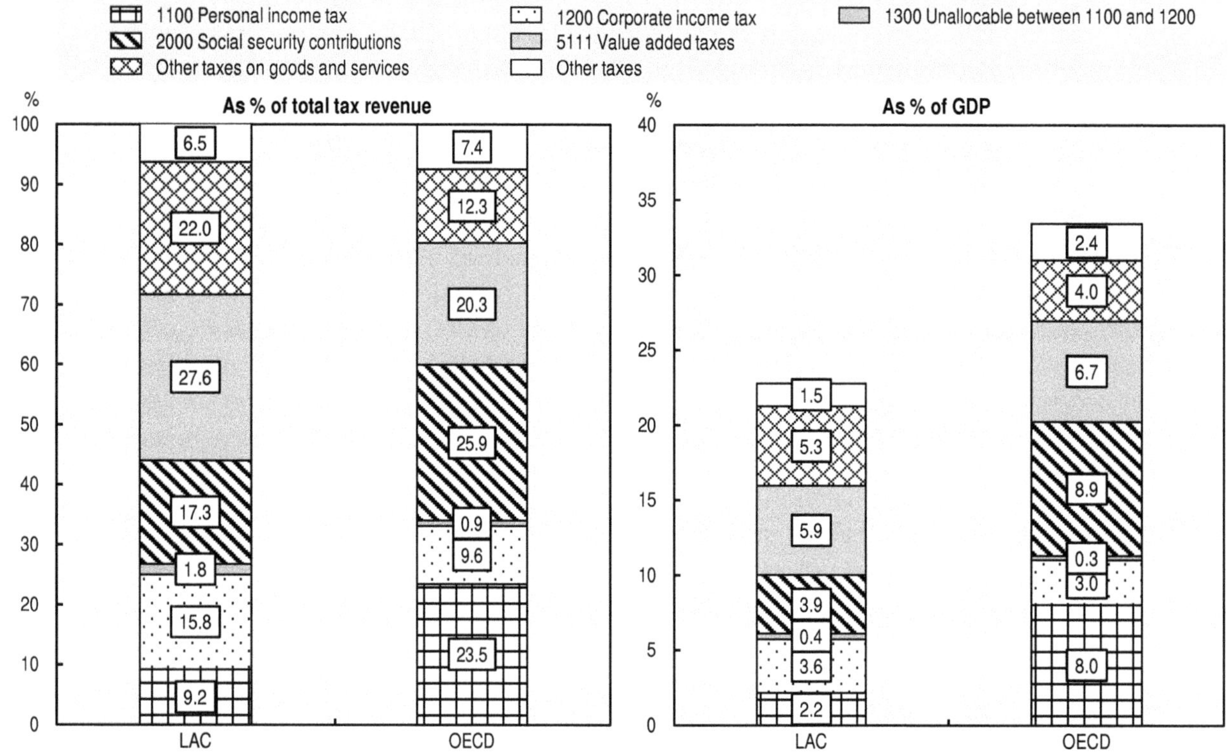


*Note:* The LAC average excludes Venezuela due to data availability issues. The year of comparison is 2019 as the 2020 tax structure data for the OECD average are not available. The average CIT and PIT as a percentage of GDP for LAC should be interpreted with caution as Ecuador is excluded from the calculation. Ecuador is excluded from the LAC average for CIT and PIT revenues as a percentage of GDP as more than a third of its revenue from taxes on income and profits cannot be allocated to CIT (1200) or PIT (1100). The OECD average represents the unweighted average of the 38 OECD member countries. Chile, Colombia, Costa Rica and Mexico are also part of the OECD (38).

*Source:* Authors' calculations based on OECD et al. (2022[3]), "Revenue Statistics in Latin America: Comparative tables", *OECD Tax Statistics* (database), *http://dx.doi.org/10.1787/data-00641-en*.

StatLink *https://doi.org/10.1787/888934307744*

In most of the countries where taxes on goods and services are the main source of revenues, VAT contributed a larger share than non-VAT taxes on goods and services such as excises and import duties. Of these countries, 18 recorded higher tax revenues from VAT, ranging from 26.3% of total tax revenues in Uruguay to 41.8% in the Bahamas. In contrast, five countries (including four in the Caribbean) received a larger share of revenue from taxes on goods and services other than VAT. This group includes Argentina, which sourced 27.5% of total tax revenues from taxes on goods and services other than VAT: export taxes represented just under a quarter of this category and were equivalent to 1.4% of GDP, compared with less than 0.1% of GDP on average in the region.

In 2020, social security contributions ranged from 0.5% of total tax revenues in the Dominican Republic to 44.6% in Panama. The level of these revenues reflects choices about how to finance social security (see Box 1.2): in countries with public or mixed social security schemes (including Brazil, Costa Rica, Panama, Paraguay and Uruguay), social security contributions accounted for over 20% of total tax revenues.

Figure 1.16. **Tax structures in LAC countries, 2020**

**Percentage of total tax revenue**

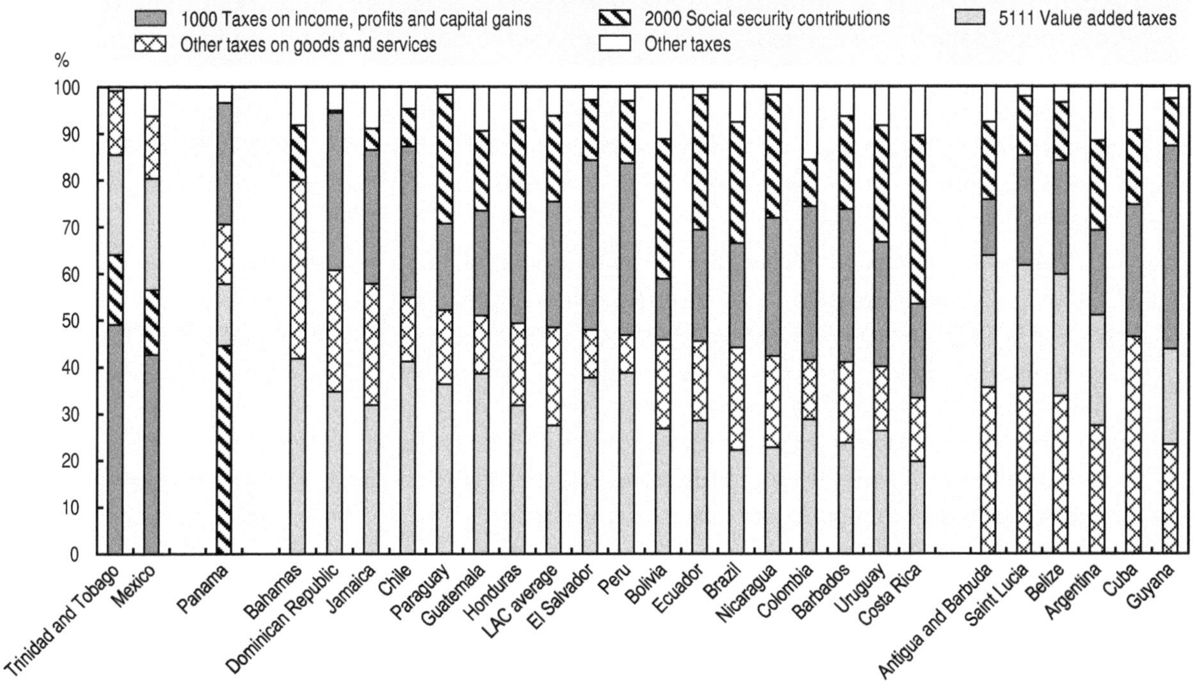


*Note:* Countries are grouped by the main share of tax revenues among 1000 taxes on income and profits, 2000 social security contributions, 5111 value added taxes and other taxes on goods and services. The Bahamas does not tax income. There is no VAT system in Cuba. The LAC average represents the unweighted average of 26 LAC countries included in this publication and excludes Venezuela due to data availability issues.

*Source:* Authors' calculations based on OECD et al. (2022[3]), Chapter 4.

StatLink https://doi.org/10.1787/888934307763

## Environmental tax revenues

Through the Paris Agreement of 2016, countries have committed to decarbonise their economies by mid-century, implying a shift away from fossil fuels as a source of energy. Environmentally related taxes, and price-based policy instruments more generally, play an increasingly significant role in many countries. By incorporating a price signal into consumer decisions, these taxes give effect to the polluter-pays principle and encourage businesses and households to consider the environmental costs of their behaviour.

An environmentally related tax is a tax whose base is a physical unit (or a proxy of a physical unit) of something that has a proven, specific harmful impact on the environment regardless of whether the tax is intended to change behaviours or is levied for another purpose (OECD, 2005[37]).

A detailed examination of country-specific taxes[4] for 24 LAC countries in this report demonstrates that, on average, environmentally related tax revenues (ERTR) amounted to 1.0%[5] of GDP in 2020, a lower level than the OECD average of 2.0% of GDP (estimated 2020 figure) (OECD, 2021[38]).

In 2020, revenues from energy taxes (most commonly excises from diesel and petrol) generated the highest share of total ERTR in the LAC region. Revenues from energy products amounted to 0.7% of GDP on average in 2020 and represented around 65.6% of ERTR. Revenues from motor vehicle and transport services amounted to 0.3% of GDP and represented most of the remainder (32.5%) of ERTR. Revenues from taxes levied on other environmentally related bases were negligible. ERTR for the OECD were higher than the LAC region across the different bases, notably for energy and transport-related taxes (OECD, 2021[38]). The OECD averages for energy and transport-related tax revenues in 2020 amounted to 1.4% and 0.5% of GDP respectively.

There were notable differences in the composition of ERTR across the LAC sub-regions in 2020, on average (Figure 1.17). While energy-related tax revenues represented the highest share of ERTR in Central America and Mexico and South America in 2020, in the Caribbean the largest share was derived from transport-related taxes. Transport-related taxes in Central America and Mexico and in South America were at 0.2% and 0.3% of GDP respectively whereas in the Caribbean they amounted to 0.5% of GDP. Transport-related tax revenues for most Caribbean countries were mainly sourced from travel or departure taxes, an important source of revenues for countries reliant on tourism.

Figure 1.17. **Environmentally related tax revenue for the OECD, LAC and sub-region averages by main tax base, 2020**

Percentage of GDP

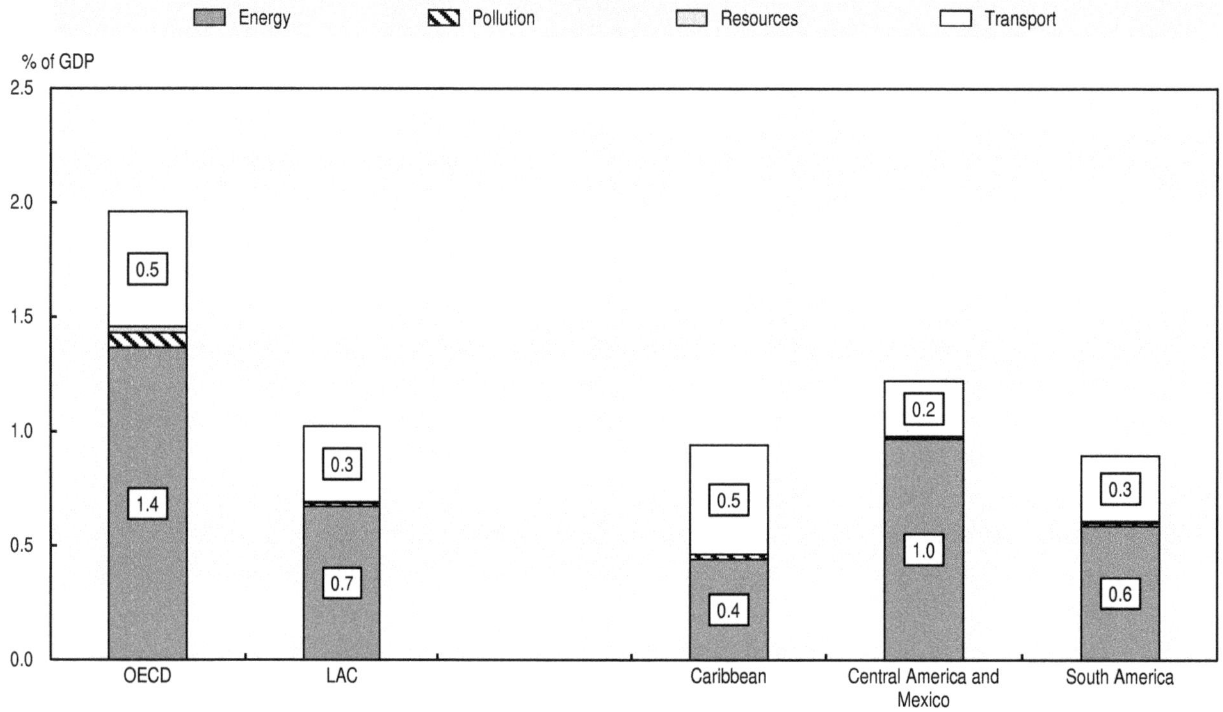


*Note:* The LAC average represents the unweighted average of 24 LAC countries included in this publication and excludes Cuba,Costa Rica and Venezuela due to data availability issues. Chile, Colombia and Mexico are also part of the OECD.

*Source: PINE* database for Chile, Colombia and Mexico, and authors' calculations for other countries based on OECD et al. (2022[3]), Chapter 5.

StatLink https://doi.org/10.1787/888934307782

Between 2019 and 2020, ERTR in the LAC region declined by 0.1% of GDP, a similar decrease to that experienced by OECD countries on average over the same period. In the LAC region, this decline was equally driven by the decreases in energy tax revenues and transport-related tax revenues. Most decreases in energy taxes were partly caused by falls in fuel excises due to pandemic-related mobility restrictions, lockdowns and teleworking.

These factors also had an impact on revenues from transport-related taxes. In particular they contributed to declines in tourist arrivals that have affected revenues from travel and departure taxes, mainly in the Caribbean. Between 2019 and 2020, the Caribbean recorded the strongest decrease in ERTR on average (0.3 p.p. compared to a decrease of 0.1 p.p. in Central America and Mexico and no change in South America). The strongest decreases between 2019 and 2020 occurred in revenues from energy- and transport-related taxes in the Caribbean and from energy taxes in Central America and Mexico, all of them down by 0.1 p.p.

ERTR in 2020 ranged from 0.1% of GDP in Belize to 2.8% in Guyana (Figure 1.18). In Guyana, the tax on the import of petroleum products represented 1.7% of GDP in 2020. Between 2019 and 2020, 14 out of the 24 LAC countries for which data are available recorded decreases in ERTR. Guyana recorded the largest decrease of 1.2 p.p. over the period. Decreases in the other LAC countries that saw a fall in ERTR between 2019 and 2020 were more modest, ranging from 0.1 p.p. in Antigua and Barbuda to 0.6 p.p. in Jamaica. The decrease in Jamaica was due to falls in travel tax revenues over the period.

Figure 1.18. **Environmentally related tax revenue in LAC countries by main tax base, 2020**

Percentage of GDP

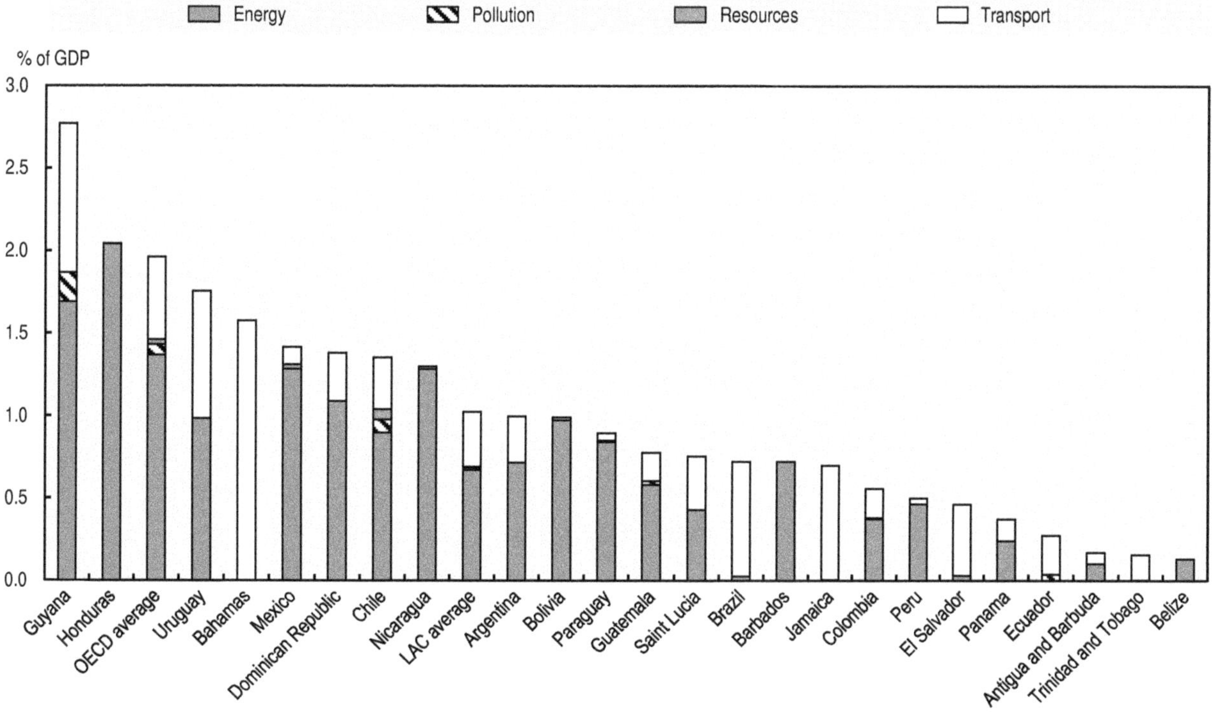


*Note:* The LAC average represents the unweighted average of 24 LAC countries included in this publication and excludes Cuba,Costa Rica and Venezuela due to data availability issues. The figure does not include Jamaica's revenues from the special consumption tax on petroleum products (estimated to be more than 2.0% of GDP in 2018) (OECD, 2021[39]) as the data are not available. Chile, Colombia and Mexico are also part of the OECD;

*Source: PINE* database for Chile, Colombia and Mexico, and author's calculations for other countries based on OECD et al. (2022[3]), Chapter 5.

StatLink https://doi.org/10.1787/888934307801

LAC countries have been slow to implement ERTR. Although they have introduced fuel taxes (mainly for revenue collection rather than environmental purposes), many countries also provide subsidies for energy products (Lorenzo, 2016[40]) in order to mitigate the impact of high and volatile petroleum prices, control inflation, boost competitiveness and protect the poorest sections of the population. Energy subsidies can put a strain on national budgets. However, energy tax revenues were greater than the cost of subsidies for five of the six LAC countries included in a recent OECD report (OECD, 2021[39]) (Costa Rica, Dominican Republic, Guatemala, Jamaica and Uruguay, with the exception being Ecuador), representing on average a net positive impact on public finances in these six countries (roughly 0.6% of GDP in 2018 on average).

Beyond taxes on fuel and the registration or use of vehicles, environmental taxes are still underdeveloped across the LAC region. However, a few LAC countries have introduced significant green tax reforms, including Chile, Mexico and Colombia.

## Taxes by level of government

In LAC countries, tax revenues are collected predominantly by central or federal entities. Sub-national public spending is financed through transfers from upper to lower levels of government to a greater extent than in OECD countries. Where sub-national data for LAC countries is available, it indicates that tax revenues collected by central government accounted for more than two-thirds of the total collections, whereas the corresponding figure for OECD countries was about 60% (2019 figure). Brazil is a notable exception: central government tax revenue amounted to 42.4% of tax collected in 2020[6] (Table 1.3).

There are two statistical issues to consider when comparing the attribution of revenues for LAC countries with that of OECD members. First, revenues of both groups have been attributed to different levels of government according to guidelines set out in the 2008 System of National Accounts (SNA).[7] The second issue is that some LAC countries lack tax revenue statistics at sub-national level.

For the 18 LAC countries in this report for which sub-national data is available, the share of sub-national tax revenues in total tax revenue was below 9.0% in 2020 except in Argentina, Brazil and Colombia. In Brazil, states and municipalities collect about 31.6% of total tax revenues, indicating a significant degree of decentralisation of tax collection. A large part of the VAT (ICMS – *imposto sobre operações relativas à circulação de mercadorias e prestação de serviços de transporte interestadual e intermunicipal e de comunicação*) is collected at the state level. Sub-national tax revenue in Argentina and Colombia account for more than 16% of total tax revenue. Argentina has a significant collection at state level, which is explained in part by the provincial sales tax (*impuesto sobre los ingresos brutos*).

These figures reflect the fact that sub-national governments in LAC countries tend to have a relatively narrow range of taxes under their jurisdiction. The taxes most frequently assigned to sub-national entities are property taxes, motor-vehicle licenses, taxes on specific services and municipal fees. The revenue-generation potential of these instruments is limited relative to the tax bases under central jurisdiction, such as VAT and income taxes. The Covid-19 crisis has highlighted the need for structural reforms to improve the collection of revenues at the sub-national level. These include improvements in information and statistics regarding revenues from these taxes, the administrative capacity to collect at the local level, effective co-ordination with national authorities, and the need to promote sustainable and stable sources of tax revenues at the sub-national level (Nieto-Parra and Orozco, 2020[41]).

## Table 1.3. **Attribution of tax revenue to sub-sectors of general government in LAC countries**[1]

Percentage of total tax revenue

| | Central government | | | State or regional government | | | Local government | | | Social security funds | | |
|---|---|---|---|---|---|---|---|---|---|---|---|---|
| | 1995 | 2000 | 2020 | 1995 | 2000 | 2020 | 1995 | 2000 | 2020 | 1995 | 2000 | 2020 |
| **Federal countries** | | | | | | | | | | | | |
| Argentina | 59.0 | 66.4 | 64.1 | 17.5 | 17.8 | 16.8 | .. | .. | .. | 23.4 | 15.8 | 19.2 |
| Brazil | 44.8 | 47.9 | 42.4 | 26.5 | 25.0 | 25.6 | 3.7 | 3.4 | 6.1 | 25.0 | 23.7 | 26.0 |
| Mexico[3] | 73.9 | 78.3 | 80.7 | 2.8 | 2.7 | 3.9 | 1.5 | 1.0 | 1.5 | 21.8 | 18.0 | 13.9 |
| Venezuela[4] | 94.6 | 94.6 | .. | .. | .. | .. | .. | .. | .. | 5.4 | 5.4 | .. |
| **Regional countries** | | | | | | | | | | | | |
| Colombia[5] | 63.2 | 68.7 | 71.9 | 5.5 | 5.6 | 4.8 | 8.6 | 9.4 | 13.3 | 22.7 | 16.3 | 9.9 |
| **Unitary countries** | | | | | | | | | | | | |
| Antigua and Barbuda[2] | 100.0 | 100.0 | 83.3 | | | | .. | .. | .. | 0.0 | 0.0 | 16.7 |
| Bahamas[2] | 89.1 | 88.1 | 88.3 | | | | .. | .. | .. | 10.9 | 11.9 | 11.7 |
| Barbados | 85.6 | 84.4 | 80.1 | | | | .. | .. | .. | 14.4 | 15.6 | 19.9 |
| Belize | 93.2 | 93.5 | 86.9 | | | | 0.5 | 0.7 | 0.7 | 6.3 | 5.8 | 12.4 |
| Bolivia | 94.3 | 86.4 | 65.3 | | | | 5.7 | 6.3 | 4.8 | .. | 7.3 | 29.9 |
| Chile | 89.9 | 87.8 | 84.7 | | | | 6.5 | 7.9 | 8.6 | 3.6 | 4.4 | 6.7 |
| Costa Rica | 65.5 | 63.3 | 55.2 | | | | 1.6 | 1.9 | 3.1 | 33.0 | 34.8 | 41.6 |
| Cuba[6] | .. | .. | .. | | | | .. | .. | .. | 11.3 | 10.4 | 16.0 |
| Dominican Republic | 99.3 | 99.0 | 99.5 | | | | .. | .. | .. | 0.7 | 1.0 | 0.5 |
| Ecuador | 70.5 | 87.7 | 68.4 | | | | 4.0 | 1.6 | 2.8 | 25.5 | 10.7 | 28.8 |
| El Salvador | 80.9 | 80.5 | 85.0 | | | | .. | .. | 2.0 | 19.1 | 19.5 | 13.0 |
| Guatemala | 83.3 | 83.6 | 82.0 | | | | 0.7 | 0.9 | 1.0 | 16.1 | 15.5 | 17.1 |
| Guyana | 92.6 | 88.6 | 89.8 | | | | .. | .. | .. | 7.4 | 11.4 | 10.1 |
| Honduras | 86.1 | 85.3 | 75.6 | | | | 4.4 | 5.2 | 3.8 | 9.5 | 9.4 | 20.6 |
| Jamaica | 100.0 | 99.3 | 93.9 | | | | .. | 0.7 | 1.5 | 0.0 | 0.0 | 4.6 |
| Nicaragua[2] | 78.0 | 72.5 | 67.6 | | | | 5.1 | 9.5 | 6.1 | 16.8 | 18.0 | 26.4 |
| Panama | 67.2 | 59.6 | 53.8 | | | | .. | 2.2 | 1.6 | 32.8 | 38.2 | 44.6 |
| Paraguay | 92.0 | 74.4 | 69.8 | | | | .. | .. | 2.6 | 8.0 | 25.6 | 27.6 |
| Peru | 88.7 | 86.5 | 84.2 | | | | .. | 1.6 | 2.3 | 11.3 | 11.9 | 13.4 |
| Saint Lucia | 100.0 | 90.0 | 87.3 | | | | .. | .. | .. | 0.0 | 10.0 | 12.7 |
| Trinidad and Tobago | 96.8 | 93.6 | 85.0 | | | | .. | .. | .. | 3.2 | 6.4 | 15.0 |
| Uruguay[2] | 61.7 | 63.6 | 69.3 | | | | 8.8 | 8.9 | 5.6 | 29.5 | 27.5 | 25.0 |

1. The figures exclude local government revenues for Antigua and Barbuda, Argentina (but include provincial revenues), the Bahamas, Barbados, Cuba, the Dominican Republic, Saint Lucia, Trinidad and Tobago and Venezuela as the data are not available. Local government revenue data have been available since 1991 for Nicaragua, since 1994 for Bolivia, since 1995 for Guatemala, since 1998 for Jamaica, since 1999 for Panama, since 2000 for Peru, since 2002 for El Salvador and Guyana, since 2006 for Paraguay and since 1990 for all other countries.
2. The data include the following estimations: Antigua and Barbuda (social security contributions for 2019 and 2020), Bahamas (social security contributions for 2019 and 2020), Nicaragua (local tax revenues for 2020) and Uruguay (local tax revenues for 2020). See the corresponding country tables for more information.
3. Preliminary data for 2020 are used for Mexico's state and local tax revenues.
4. Some tax revenue data between 2014 and 2017 and all data since 2018 have not been available. The breakdown by sub-sectors of general government is not available for those years.
5. Colombia is constitutionally a unitary country with high autonomy of its territorial entities.
6. Data for sub-sectors of general government in Cuba are only available between 2002 and 2012.

*Source:* OECD et al. ($2022_{[3]}$), Table 4.11.

StatLink https://doi.org/10.1787/888934308238

In 2020, all subnational tax revenue in Belize, Guatemala and Jamaica, and more than 50% of tax revenue collected at the sub-national level in Peru, Uruguay and Ecuador were sourced from property taxes (Figure 1.19). All other countries in the region rely principally on revenues from taxes on goods and services. Mexico is the only country that also collected revenue from different tax bases. In 2020, 47% of sub-national tax revenue in Mexico came from payroll taxes. In OECD countries, sub-national entities tend to have much broader potential tax bases. A substantial proportion of revenue collection by sub-national governments in OECD countries comes through income taxes and profits (representing more than a third of the total collected at sub-national level on average).

Figure 1.19. **Tax mix of sub-national tax revenue in LAC countries, 2020**

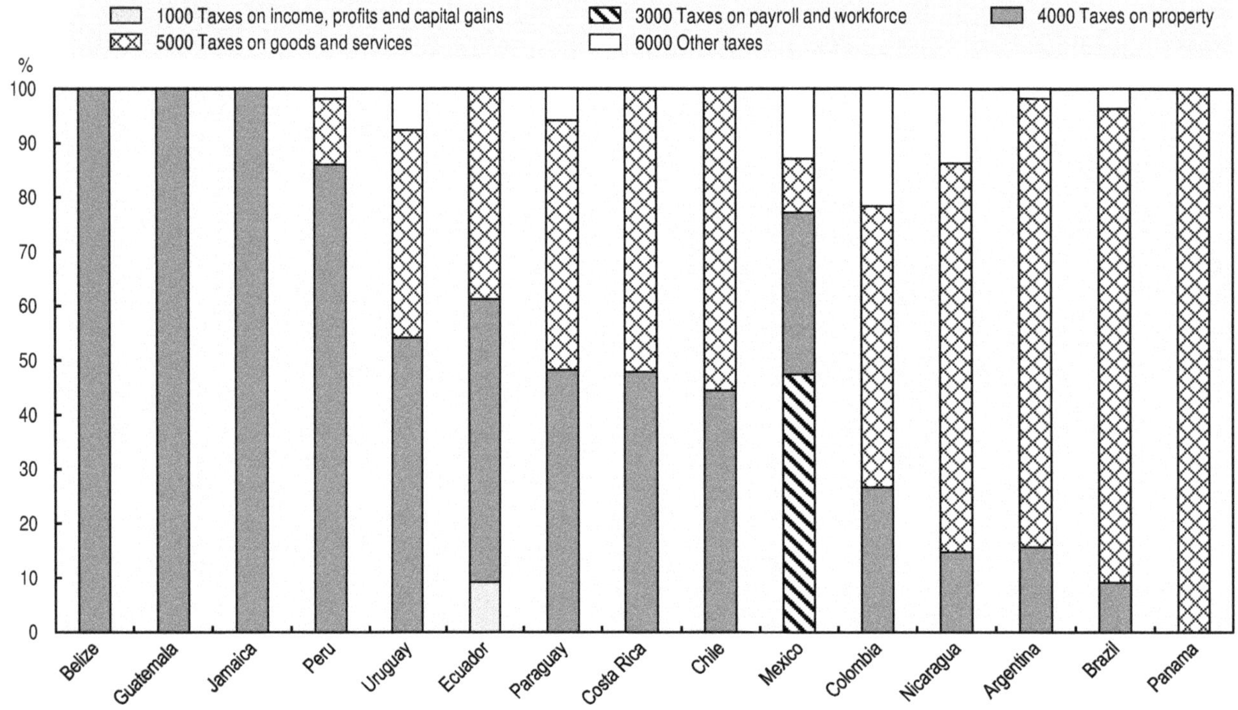


*Note:* Figures for Antigua and Barbuda, Bahamas, Barbados, Bolivia, Cuba, Dominican Republic, El Salvador, Guyana, Honduras, Saint Lucia, Trinidad and Tobago and Venezuela are excluded as either the sub-national tax revenue data or the breakdown of sub-national tax revenue data by the main type of tax category is not available. Figures exclude local government revenues for Argentina but include provincial revenues.

*Source:* Authors' calculations based on OECD et al. (2022[3]), Chapter 6.

StatLink https://doi.org/10.1787/888934307820

Low tax revenues at the sub-national level in LAC countries may result from a lack of administrative and technical capacity. Property taxes require sophisticated systems and information, and collecting this revenue is expensive. Appropriate property registers are lacking in many countries; where they exist, they are rarely updated (Canavire-Bacarreza, Martínez-Vázquez and Sepúlveda, 2012[42]; OECD et al., 2019[43]). As a result, tax authorities lack access to accurate valuations of lands and buildings and real estate registries are often reluctant to share this information. Property tax also suffers from a high level of informality: buildings are constructed without permits, properties are not registered and reported prices of some real estate transactions are falsified. As property tax is one of the most controversial taxes with citizens and has high political costs, local politicians are often unwilling to invest the appropriate resources to levy this revenue.

## Notes

1. The figure is provisional and is based on preliminary data provided for the year 2020. The data need to be interpreted with caution as they are subject to revisions in future years that can affect the magnitude, and less commonly, the direction, of change between the last two years of data.

2. VAT was introduced in 1991 for Jamaica, 1997 for Barbados, 2006 for Belize (the General Sales Tax), 2007 for Guyana and Antigua and Barbuda, 2012 for Saint Lucia and 2014 for the Bahamas.
3. The year of comparison is 2019 as the average tax structure for OECD countries in 2020 is not available.
4. Although environmentally related tax revenues are not separately identified in the standard OECD classification of tax revenues, they can be identified through the detailed list of specific taxes included for most countries within this overarching classification. It is on this basis that they are included in the OECD Policy Instruments for the Environment (PINE) database (OECD, 2021[38]). In 2020, the OECD started the collection of Environmentally Related Tax Revenue accounts in line with the System of Environmental and Economic Accounting and ERTR accounts are disaggregated by industries and households (OECD, 2021[44]).
5. Unweighted average of 38 OECD countries.
6. Preliminary data for 2020 are used for Mexico's state and local tax revenues.
7. This means that revenues are generally attributed to the level of government that exercises the authority to impose the tax or has the final discretion to set and vary the tax rate. This has implications for situations where one level of government collects tax revenues and transfers them in whole or in part to other levels. Regional examples of this type of mechanism are the Co-participation Law in Argentina, federal participations in Mexico (mandated in the Fiscal Co-ordination Law) and participation funds in Brazil (defined in Article 159 of the Constitution).

## *References*


Barreix, A., J. Benítez and M. Pecho (2017), "Revisiting personal income tax in Latin America: Evolution and impact", *OECD Development Centre Working Papers*, No. 338, OECD Publishing, Paris, *https://dx.doi.org/10.1787/16d42b4a-en.* [36]

Canavire-Bacarreza, G., J. Martínez-Vázquez and C. Sepúlveda (2012), *Sub-national Revenue Mobilization in Peru, IDB Working Paper Series No. 299*, Inter-American Development Bank, *https://publications.iadb.org/en/sub-national-revenue-mobilization-peru.* [42]

Central Bank of Barbados (2020 and 2021), *Quarterly Press Conferences*, *http://www.centralbank.org.bb/media/press-conferences/quarterly-press-conferences.* [15]

CNN (2020), *'There's no one': Cuba is suffering from tourism's standstill*, *https://edition.cnn.com/travel/article/cuba-coronavirus-lockdown-tourism/index.html.* [8]

Council of European Union (2019), "Antigua and Barbuda's International Business Corporations regime", *https://data.consilium.europa.eu/doc/document/ST-7461-2019-INIT/en/pdf#:~:text=The%20general%20tax%20rate%20for,from%20the%20date%20of%20incorporation.* [14]

ECLAC (2022), *CEPALSTAT (database)*, Economic Commission for Latin America and the Caribbean, Santiago, *https://statistics.cepal.org/portal/cepalstat/dashboard.html?theme=2&lang=en.* [20]

ECLAC (2022), *Preliminary Overview of the Economies of Latin America and the Caribbean 2021*, Economic Commission for Latin America and the Caribbean, Santiago, *https://www.cepal.org/en/pressreleases/latin-america-and-caribbeans-growth-will-slow-21-2022-amid-significant-asymmetries.* [21]

ECLAC (2021), *Economic Survey of Latin America and the Caribbean 2021*, Economic Commission for Latin America and the Caribbean, Santiago, *http://www.repositorio.cepal.org/bitstream/handle/11362/47193/10/S2100607_en.pdf.* [18]

ECLAC (2021), *Fiscal Panorama of Latin America and the Caribbean: Fiscal policy challenges for transformative recovery post-COVID-19*, Economic Commission for Latin America and the Caribbean, Santiago, *https://repositorio.cepal.org/bitstream/handle/11362/46809/1/S2100169_en.pdf.* [13]

ECLAC (2021), *Preliminary Overview of the Economies of Latin America and the Caribbean 2020*, Economic Commission for Latin America and the Caribbean, Santiago, *https://www.cepal.org/en/publications/46504-preliminary-overview-economies-latin-america-and-caribbean-2020.* [10]

ECLAC (2021), *Social Panorama of Latin America, 2020*, Economic Commission for Latin America and the Caribbean, Santiago, *https://www.cepal.org/en/publications/46688-social-panorama-latin-america-2020.* [25]

ECLAC (2021), *The recovery paradox in Latin America and the Caribbean, Special Report COVID-19*, Economic Commission for Latin America and the Caribbean, Santiago, *https://www.cepal.org/sites/default/files/presentation/files/covid-19_special_report_no_11_launch_ppt_final-visto_jl.pdf.* [19]

ECLAC (2020), *Fiscal Panorama of Latin America and the Caribbean 2020: Fiscal policy amid the crisis arising from the coronavirus disease (COVID-19) pandemic*, Economic Commission for Latin America and the Caribbean, *https://www.cepal.org/en/publications/45731-fiscalpanorama-latin-america-and-caribbean-2020-fiscal-policy-amid-crisis.* [26]

ECLAC (2020), *Sectors and businesses facing COVID-19: emergency and reactivation*", Economic Commission for Latin America and the Caribbean, Santiago, *https://www.cepal.org/sites/default/files/presentation/files/ppt_specialreport_sectorsandbusinesses_en.pdf.* [23]

ECLAC (2018), *The Fiscal Panorama of Latin America and the Caribbean*, United Nations, *https://www.cepal.org/en/publications/43406-fiscal-panorama-latin-america-and-caribbean-2018-public-policy-challenges.* [33]

ECLAC (2014), *Tax policy in Latin America: Assessment and guidelines for a second generation of reforms*, United Nations, *https://repositorio.cepal.org/handle/11362/36806.* [32]

ECLAC (2013), *Fiscal Panorama of Latin America and the Caribbean: Tax reform and renewal of the fiscal covenant*, United Nations, *https://www.cepal.org/en/publications/3101-fiscal-panorama-latin-america-and-caribbean-2013-tax-reform-and-renewal-fiscal.* [35]

Havana Times (2021), *The Impact of COVID-19 on Tourism in Cuba*, *https://havanatimes.org/features/the-impact-of-covid-19-on-tourism-in-cuba/.* [7]

Hon. Colm Imbert, M. (2020), *Statement by the Hon. Colm Imbert, Minister of Finance, to the House of Representatives on the Economic Effect and Financial Response to the Covid-19 Pandemic*, *https://www.finance.gov.tt/2020/04/27/statement-by-the-hon-colm-imbert-minister-of-finance-to-the-house-of-representatives-on-the-economic-effect-and-financial-response-to-the-covid-19-pandemic/.* [9]

IDB (2013), *More than revenues, Taxation as a development tool*, Inter-American Development Bank, *https://publications.iadb.org/en/publication/more-revenue-taxation-development-tool-executive-summary.* [34]

ILO (2021), *Employment and informality in Latin America and the Caribbean: An insufficient and unequal recovery*, International Labour Organisation, Geneva. [24]

IMF (2021), Policy responses to COVID-19, Policy tracker, *https://www.imf.org/en/Topics/imf-and-covid19/Policy-Responses-to-COVID-19#F.* [12]

IMF (2021), "Barbados: Fifth Review Under the Extended Arrangement, Request for Waiver of Nonobservance of Performance Criterion, and Modification of Performance Criteria-Press Release; Staff Report; and Statement by the Executive Director for Barbados", *https://www.elibrary.imf.org/view/journals/002/2021/128/article-A001-en.xml#A001fn02.* [16]

IMF (2021), *Trinidad and Tobago: Staff Concluding Statement of the 2021 Article IV Mission*, *https://www.imf.org/en/News/Articles/2021/11/19/trinidad-and-tobago-staff-concluding-statement-of-the-2021-article-iv-mission.* [11]

IMF (2021), *World Economic Outlook Database, October 2021*, *https://www.imf.org/en/Publications/WEO/weo-database/2021/October* (accessed on 20 September 2021). [5]

Lorenzo, F. (2016), *Inventario de instrumentos fiscales verdes en América Latina*, CEPAL, *https://agua.org.mx/biblioteca/inventario-instrumentos-fiscales-verdes-en-america-latina-experiencias-efectos-alcances/.* [40]

Melguizo, A. et al. (2017), "No sympathy for the devil! Policy priorities to overcome the middle-income trap in Latin America", *OECD Development Centre Working Papers*, No. 340, OECD, *http://dx.doi.org/10.1787/26b78724-en.* [27]

Nieto-Parra, S. and R. Orozco (2020), *Potencializar los impuestos subnacionales en América Latina y el Caribe en tiempos del Covid-19 in Los desafíos de las finanzas intergubernamentales ante el Covid-19*, AIFIL - Asociación Iberoamericana de Financiación, *https://www.aifil-jifl.org/wp-content/uploads/2020/11/AIFIL-2.11.pdf.* [41]

OECD (2021), *Environmental policy: Environmentally related tax revenue accounts, OECD Environment Statistics (database)*, *https://stats.oecd.org/Index.aspx?DataSetCode=ERTR_ACC.* [44]

OECD (2021), *OECD Revenue Statistics 2021: The Initial Impact of COVID-19 on OECD Tax Revenues*, OECD Publishing, Paris, *https://doi.org/10.1787/6e87f932-en.* [4]

OECD (2021), *PINE database*, OECD Publishing, Paris, *http://www.oecd.org/environment/tools-evaluation/environmentaltaxation.htm.* [38]

OECD (2021), *Taxing Energy Use for Sustainable Development*, OECD Publishing, Paris, *https://www.oecd.org/tax/tax-policy/taxing-energy-use-for-sustainable-development.htm.* [39]

OECD (2020), *COVID-19 in Latin America and the Caribbean: Regional socio-economic implications and policy priorities*, OECD Publishing, Paris, *http://www.oecd.org/coronavirus/policy-responses/covid-19-in-latinamerica-and-the-caribbean-regional-socio-economic-implications-and-policy-priorities-93a64fde/*. [22]

OECD (2019), *Tax Morale: What Drives People and Businesses to Pay Tax?*, OECD Publishing, Paris, *https://doi.org/10.1787/f3d8ea10-en*. [29]

OECD (2014), *Development Co-operation Report 2014: Mobilising Resources for Sustainable Development*, OECD Publishing, Paris, *https://dx.doi.org/10.1787/dcr-2014-en*. [28]

OECD (2005), *Glossary of statistical terms*, *https://stats.oecd.org/glossary/detail.asp?ID=6437*. [37]

OECD et al. (2022), *Revenue Statistics in Latin America and the Caribbean 2022*, OECD Publishing, Paris, *http://dx.doi.org/TBC*. [3]

OECD et al. (2021), *Latin American Economic Outlook 2021: Working Together for a Better Recovery*, OECD Publishing, Paris, *https://doi.org/10.1787/5fedabe5-en*. [2]

OECD et al. (2021), *Revenue Statistics in Latin America and the Caribbean 2021*, *https://doi.org/10.1787/96ce5287-en-es*. [1]

OECD et al. (2019), *Revenue Statistics in Latin America and the Caribbean 2019*, OECD Publishing, Paris, *https://doi.org/10.1787/25666b8d-en-es*. [43]

OECD et al. (2015), *Revenue Statistics in Latin America and the Caribbean 2015*, OECD Publishing, Paris, *https://dx.doi.org/10.1787/rev_lat-2015-en-fr*. [30]

OECD/IDB/The World Bank (2014), *Pensions at a Glance: Latin America and the Caribbean*, OECD Publishing, Paris, *https://dx.doi.org/10.1787/pension_glance-2014-en*. [31]

SNA (2009), *System of National Accounts 2008*, *https://unstats.un.org/unsd/nationalaccount/docs/SNA2008.pdf*. [6]

The Government of the Bahamas (2020), "Combined nine month fiscal snapshot and report on budgetary performance", *https://www.bahamas.gov.bs/wps/wcm/connect/b65ccbe4-64ee-4b94-b692-7a19cd509ba2/Combined+9-Month+Fiscal+Snapshot+%26+Report_Final+April+30%2C+2020+-+Compressed.pdf?MOD=AJPERES*. [17]

*Capítulo 1*

# Tendencias tributarias, 1990-2020

La financiación de la agenda de desarrollo de América Latina y el Caribe (ALC) y el logro de los Objetivos de Desarrollo Sostenible (ODS) exigen cambios significativos en la movilización de los recursos internos. La actual crisis de COVID-19 ha intensificado aún más la necesidad de los países de ALC de incrementar la recaudación tributaria para hacer frente a las debilidades estructurales de sus sistemas tributarios, de protección social y de salud. Cuando surgió esta crisis, la región ya se enfrentaba a un amplio malestar social y un débil crecimiento. A pesar de que los países dieron una rápida respuesta a la crisis adoptando medidas sanitarias y fiscales para apoyar a los hogares y las empresas más vulnerables, sus esfuerzos se vieron obstaculizados por unos altos niveles de informalidad, unos sistemas de protección social poco desarrollados y un espacio tributario limitado (OCDE et al., 2021[1]; OCDE et al., 2021[2]). Cuando la región salga de la pandemia de COVID-19, será necesario reformar y fortalecer los regímenes tributarios para apoyar una recuperación económica inclusiva y garantizar una posición fiscal sostenible y justa a medio y largo plazo.

Una vez que la crisis de COVID-19 quede en el pasado, la política presupuestaria deberá desempeñar un papel importante como catalizador de un crecimiento económico inclusivo en la región. A largo plazo, lograr unos niveles más altos de ingresos será crucial para hacer frente a las necesidades de los ciudadanos en toda la región y mejorar la equidad a través de la prestación de servicios públicos, a fin de reducir los altos niveles de vulnerabilidad, en particular, en el mercado laboral, y desarrollar unos sistemas de protección social amplios. Mejorar la estructura de los sistemas impositivos es importante para fomentar el espíritu empresarial e impulsar la redistribución. Los impuestos también pueden incentivar la transición a formas más limpias de energía en el contexto del cambio climático.

El informe *Estadísticas tributarias en América Latina y el Caribe* proporciona datos comparables internacionalmente sobre los ingresos tributarios de 27 países de la región, datos que pueden servir de base para emprender análisis detallados de las políticas y ser el punto de partida para el intercambio de conocimiento y el desarrollo de capacidades. Esta edición del informe refleja el impacto que el COVID-19 ha tenido en los ingresos tributarios de 2020, primer año de la pandemia. En el primer capítulo se aborda la evolución de varios indicadores tributarios desde 1990 hasta 2020, entre ellos, la recaudación tributaria como proporción del PIB, la estructura tributaria y la proporción de ingresos tributarios que generan los diferentes niveles gubernamentales. También se analizan los ingresos procedentes de los impuestos ambientales. Los capítulos 5 y 6 contienen un desglose minucioso por países de los ingresos tributarios.

## La recaudación tributaria como proporción del PIB

### *La recaudación tributaria como proporción del PIB en 2020*

La recaudación tributaria como proporción del PIB mide los ingresos tributarios (incluidas las contribuciones a la seguridad social que reciben las administraciones públicas) como porcentaje del producto interior bruto (PIB). El promedio de los países de ALC refleja el promedio no ponderado de 26 de los países incluidos en esta publicación, pues se excluye a Venezuela debido a la falta de datos.

En 2020, el promedio de recaudación tributaria como proporción del PIB para la región de ALC se situó en el 21.9% (Gráfico 1.1). La región presentó variaciones considerables, que van desde el 12.4%, de Guatemala, al 37.5%, de Cuba. Salvo en Barbados y Cuba, la recaudación tributaria como proporción del PIB para todos los países de ALC fue inferior al promedio de la OCDE[1], que se situó en el 33.5%.

Los porcentajes más altos de este indicador se registraron en Cuba (37.5% como proporción del PIB), Barbados (35.2%) y Brasil (31.6%). Los más bajos fueron los de Guatemala (12.4%), República Dominicana (12.6%) y Paraguay (13.4%).

Gráfico 1.1. **Recaudación tributaria como proporción del PIB en la región de ALC, 2020**

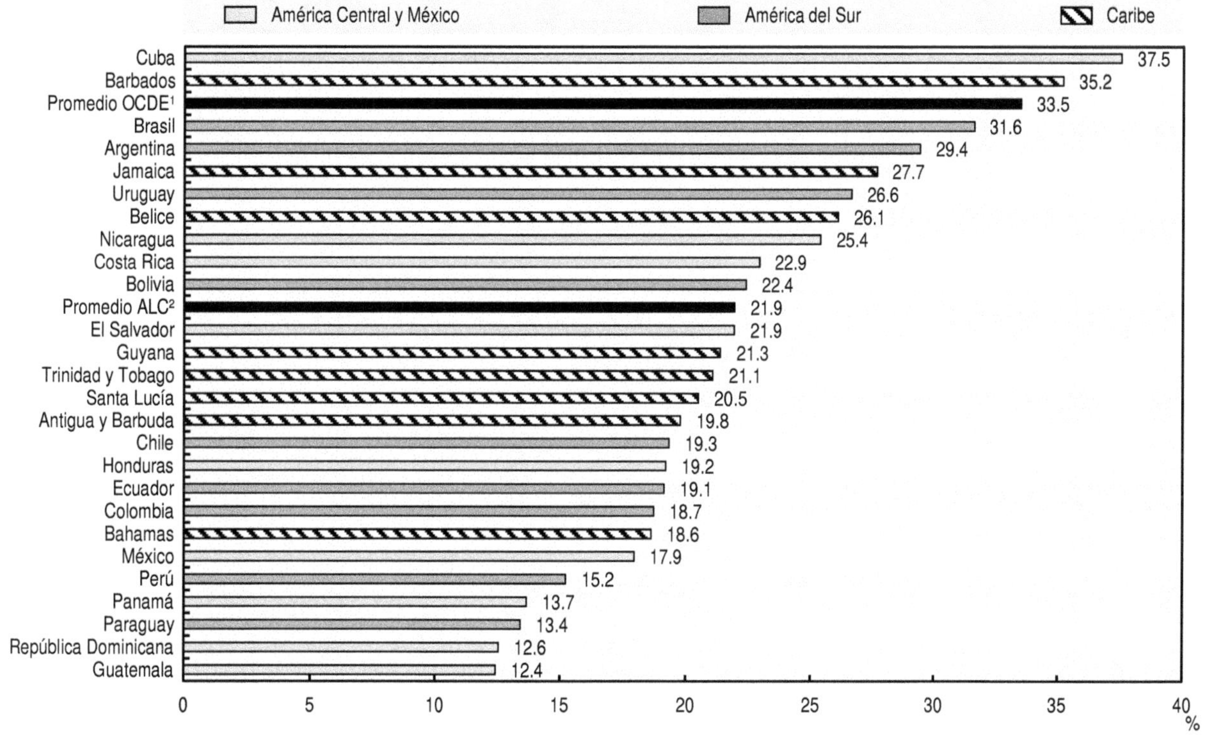


*Nota:* La clasificación de los países en diferentes subregiones respeta la clasificación de la CEPAL y se basa en el idioma de cada uno de ellos. En el «Caribe» se incluyen los países de habla inglesa y Guyana, mientras que «América Central y México» abarca países hispanohablantes e incluye a la República Dominicana y Cuba.

Las cifras no incluyen los ingresos de la administración local de Antigua y Barbuda, Argentina (aunque sí los ingresos de las provincias), las Bahamas, Barbados, Cuba (salvo para el periodo comprendido entre 2002 y 2012), la República Dominicana, Santa Lucía, Trinidad y Tobago y Venezuela por la falta de datos disponibles.

1. Representa el promedio no ponderado de los 38 países miembros de la OCDE. Chile, Colombia, Costa Rica y México también forman parte de la OCDE (38).
2. Representa el grupo de 26 países de ALC incluidos en esta publicación y excluye a Venezuela, por la falta de datos disponibles.

*Fuente:* (OCDE et al., 2022[3]), Cuadro 4.1.

StatLink https://doi.org/10.1787/888934307839

En 2020, el promedio de recaudación tributaria como proporción del PIB para ALC fue 0.8 puntos porcentuales (p.p.) más bajo que en 2019. Los cambios de este indicador, entre 2019 y 2020, variaron mucho en toda la región (Gráfico 1.2). Durante este periodo, la recaudación tributaria como proporción del PIB se redujo en 20 países y aumentó en seis. En comparación, en 2020, el promedio de este indicador para los países miembros de la OCDE aumentó 0.1 p.p. con relación a 2019 y 20 de los 38 países de la OCDE registraron un aumento.

Gráfico 1.2. **Variación de la recaudación tributaria como proporción del PIB para la región de ALC en 2019 y 2020**

Puntos porcentuales del PIB

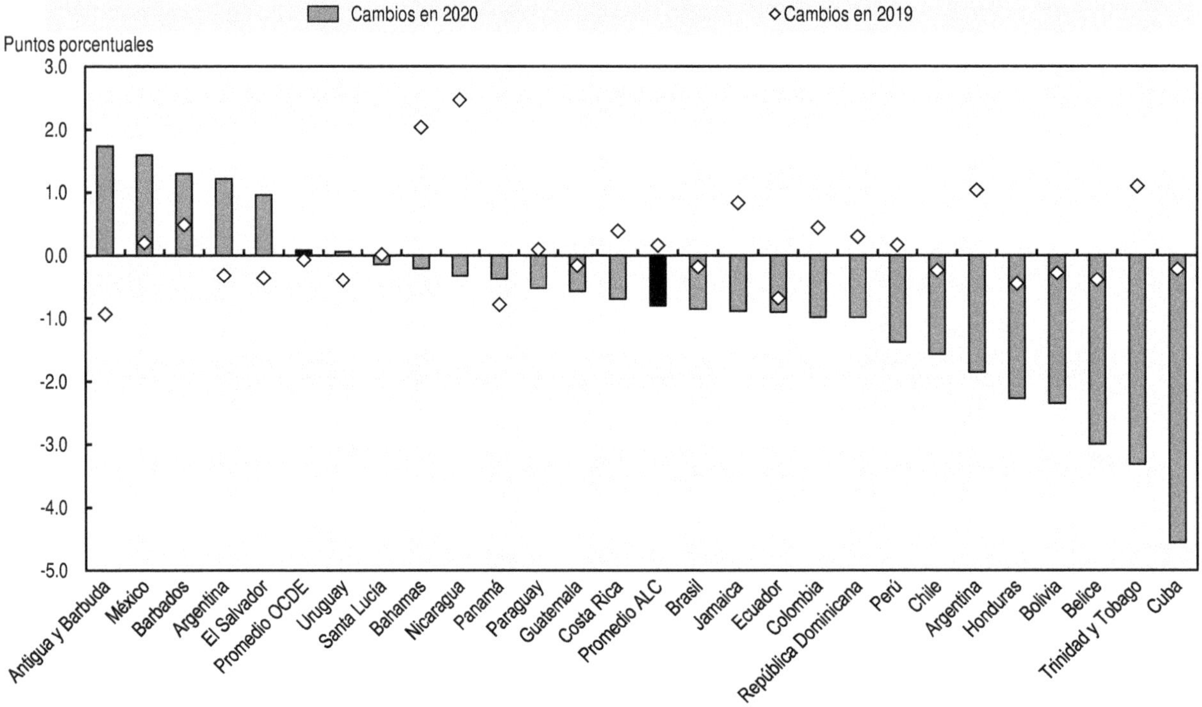


*Nota:* El promedio de ALC representa el promedio no ponderado de 26 países de la región incluidos en esta publicación, sin contar con Venezuela, debido a los problemas de disponibilidad de datos. El promedio de la OCDE representa el promedio no ponderado de los 38 países miembros de la OCDE. Chile, Colombia, Costa Rica y México forman parte de la OCDE (38).

*Fuente:* Cálculos propios basados en (OCDE et al., 2022[3]), Cuadro 4.1.

StatLink https://doi.org/10.1787/888934307858

Entre 2019 y 2020, la recaudación tributaria como proporción del PIB se redujo en más de 1 p.p. en diez países de ALC. Durante el mismo periodo, los coeficientes tributarios de cinco países de la región aumentaron más de 1 p.p. Sin embargo, las reducciones fueron, en general, más acentuadas que los aumentos. Las mayores reducciones en la región de ALC durante este periodo se observaron en Cuba (4.6 p.p.), Trinidad y Tobago (3.3 p.p.) y Belice (3.0 p.p.). En cambio, Antigua y Barbuda y México registraron los mayores aumentos en sus coeficientes, 1.7 p.p. y 1.6 p.p., respectivamente.

## *El impacto de la pandemia de COVID-19 sobre los ingresos tributarios: variaciones de 2020 respecto a 2019*

### *Perspectiva general de las variaciones en los ingresos tributarios y el PIB*

A fin de lograr una mejor compresión del impacto de la crisis de COVID-19, en este apartado se analizan las variaciones que han experimentado los ingresos tributarios nominales y el PIB nominal entre 2019 y 2020.

El valor del cociente entre la recaudación tributaria y el PIB depende de dos elementos: su numerador (recaudación tributaria) y su denominador (PIB) (véase Recuadro 1.1). Esto significa que las variaciones del coeficiente entre 2019 y 2020 reflejan la variación de los ingresos tributarios nominales y la variación del PIB nominal durante el mismo periodo. En épocas de crisis, las variaciones en términos nominales (normalmente, reducciones) pueden ser más significativas que en otros momentos.

### Recuadro 1.1. **Metodología de cálculo de la recaudación tributaria como proporción del PIB**

Los coeficientes tributarios que se reflejan en esta publicación expresan la recaudación tributaria total como porcentaje del PIB. El valor de este cociente depende de su denominador (PIB) y su numerador (recaudación tributaria). Ambos, numerador y denominador, pueden experimentar una corrección histórica.

En 22 países de ALC, el año de referencia para el informe coincide con el año natural. Los cinco países restantes ofrecen datos relativos al ejercicio presupuestario:

- El ejercicio presupuestario en Barbados, Belice y Santa Lucía va de abril a marzo. Esto significa que el año de referencia del informe 2020 se corresponde con el periodo comprendido entre el segundo trimestre de 2020 al primer trimestre de 2021.
- El ejercicio presupuestario en Trinidad y Tobago abarca de octubre a septiembre, de modo que el año de referencia del informe 2020 comprende desde el cuarto trimestre de 2019 al tercer trimestre de 2020.
- El ejercicio presupuestario de las Bahamas termina el 30 de junio. El año de referencia del informe 2020 abarca desde el segundo trimestre de 2019 al segundo trimestre de 2020.

**El numerador (recaudación tributaria)**

Esta publicación utiliza las cifras relativas a los ingresos tributarios que presentan los centros de referencia o que publican anualmente los ministerios de Hacienda, las administraciones tributarias o las oficinas de estadística nacionales. Los datos históricos de ingresos tributarios están supeditados a correcciones anuales, que han sido más importantes durante los últimos años. Las cifras anteriores también pueden variar de una edición a otra cuando se obtienen nuevos datos.

**El denominador (PIB)**

Las cifras relativas al PIB utilizadas en la presente publicación proceden, en su mayoría, de fuentes nacionales (como los Institutos Nacionales de Estadística o los Bancos Centrales) y del informe *Perspectivas de la economía mundial* (informe WEO, por sus siglas en inglés) que publica el FMI. Los datos relativos al PIB también se revisan y actualizan para reflejar unas mejores fuentes de datos y procedimientos de cálculo más precisos o para acercarse a nuevas directrices internacionales para calcular el valor del PIB. Las últimas cifras disponibles del informe WEO se publicaron en octubre de 2021 (FMI, 2021[5]) e incluyen las correcciones efectuadas en el PIB de algunos países para adaptarse al último Sistema de Cuentas Nacionales (SCN, 2016[6]).

Las cifras relativas al PIB para los cuatro países de ALC que también son miembros de la OCDE (Chile, Colombia, Costa Rica y México) se basan en las Cuentas Nacionales anuales de la OCDE.

La pandemia de COVID-19 se tradujo en caídas históricas de los ingresos tributarios nominales y del PIB nominal. Entre 2019 y 2020, veintidós de los 26 países a que se refiere este informe sufrieron caídas en sus ingresos tributarios nominales, que se redujeron un 8.0% en promedio (cifra no ponderada). Durante el mismo periodo, diecisiete países de ALC registraron caídas en sus respectivos PIB nominales, que se redujeron un 4.9% en promedio (cifra no ponderada). En cambio, los ingresos tributarios nominales cayeron un 1.2% y el PIB nominal aumentó un 1.8% de media entre 2008 y 2009 como consecuencia de la crisis financiera mundial.

El Gráfico 1.3 muestra la caída de los ingresos tributarios nominales y el PIB nominal, entre 2019 y 2020, en todos los países de ALC y la OCDE. En 16 países de ALC, la reducción de los ingresos tributarios nominales fue aparejada de una reducción del PIB nominal y en 13 de estos países la caída de los ingresos tributarios nominales fue mayor que la del PIB nominal, lo que provocó una disminución de la recaudación tributaria como proporción del

PIB. En tres países (Antigua y Barbuda, Barbados y El Salvador), entre 2019 y 2020, los ingresos tributarios nominales cayeron menos que el PIB nominal, lo que se tradujo en un aumento de los coeficientes tributarios. Otros seis países de ALC registraron una reducción de sus ingresos tributarios nominales y un aumento de su PIB nominal, lo que también provocó que se redujeran sus respectivos coeficientes tributarios.

Gráfico 1.3. **Variaciones de los ingresos tributarios nominales y el PIB nominal, 2019-20**

Variación porcentual interanual

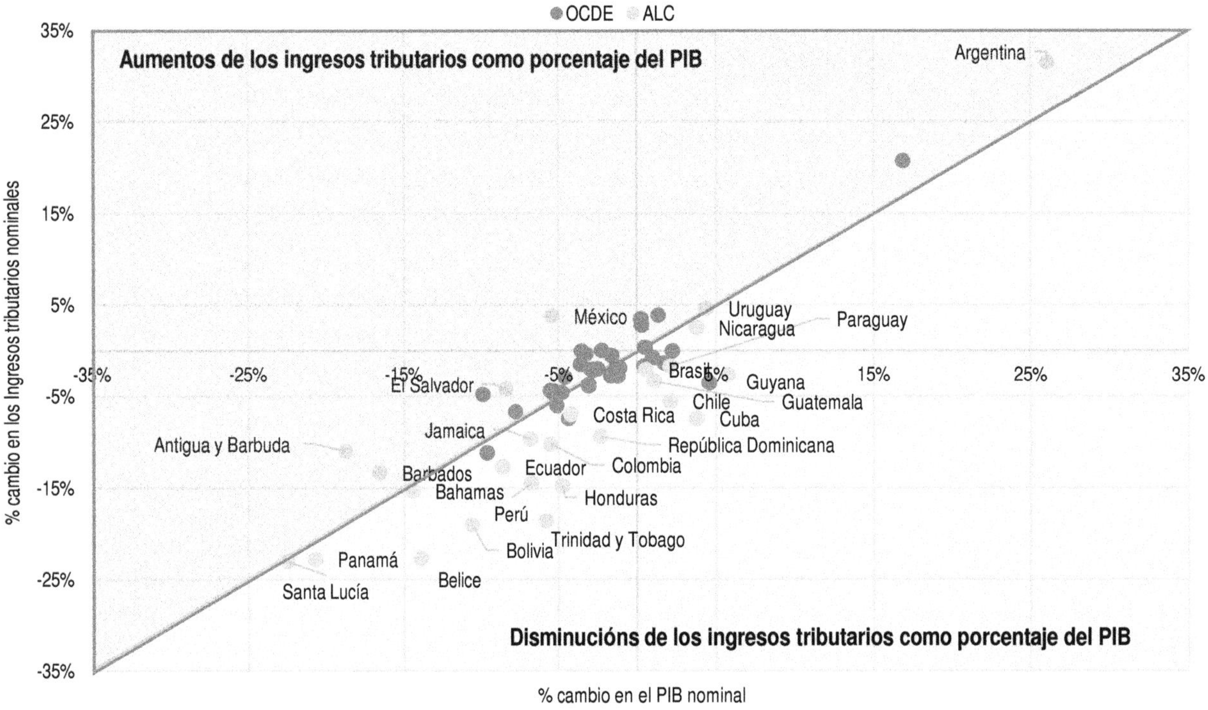


*Nota:* Los datos de la OCDE para 2020, que se representan mediante puntos azules, son preliminares y deben interpretarse con prudencia. La línea diagonal que atraviesa el gráfico representa el punto en el que la variación en los ingresos tributarios y el PIB fueron de la misma magnitud y, por tanto, el punto en el que la recaudación tributaria como proporción del PIB se mantuvo inalterada. En los países situados por encima de la diagonal aumentó la presión fiscal y en los países que están por debajo, se redujo.

*Fuente:* Las cifras relativas a la OCDE proceden de (OCDE, 2021[4]). Los datos relativos a ALC son cálculos propios basados en (OCDE et al., 2022[3]).

StatLink https://doi.org/10.1787/888934307877

Panamá y Santa Lucía registraron la mayor reducción en 2020 con relación a 2019 (más del 20%) tanto del PIB nominal como de los ingresos tributarios nominales. Pese a que estas caídas fueron significativas, la disminución de la recaudación tributaria como porcentaje del PIB de estos países, entre 2019 y 2020, fue relativamente modesta (0.1 p.p., en Santa Lucía, y 0.4 p.p., en Panamá), pues la magnitud de la caída de ambos de parámetros fue semejante.

Solo en cuatro países de ALC (Argentina, México, Nicaragua y Uruguay) aumentaron los ingresos tributarios nominales entre 2019 y 2020 y, en tres de ellos, también aumentó el PIB nominal. México es el único país cuyo coeficiente tributario aumentó debido a que los ingresos tributarios nominales se incrementaron mientras que el PIB nominal se redujo.

La crisis generada por la pandemia de COVID-19 ha afectado a los ingresos tributarios y al PIB de todos los países del mundo. Entre los países de la OCDE, el impacto ha sido, en general, menos intenso que en los países de ALC. Entre 2019 y 2020, la presión fiscal media en la OCDE aumentó un 0.1 p.p. y 18 países experimentaron un aumento de la recaudación tributaria como proporción del PIB durante este periodo. Sin embargo, estos incrementos se produjeron en un contexto de disminución de los ingresos tributarios nominales en 31 países de la OCDE, entre 2019 y 2020. La reducción media de los ingresos tributarios nominales y el PIB nominal, en este periodo, en los países de la OCDE, se situó en el 2.1% en ambos casos (OCDE, 2021[4]). Entre 2019 y 2020, 25 países de la OCDE registraron disminuciones en el PIB nominal y en los ingresos tributarios nominales. Sin embargo, en 14 de esos países, los ingresos tributarios nominales cayeron menos que el PIB nominal, lo que se tradujo en una mayor presión fiscal en 2020.

### *Las mayores variaciones en la recaudación tributaria como proporción del PIB, en los países de ALC, en 2020*

En este apartado se analizan de manera pormenorizada las variaciones más llamativas de la recaudación tributaria como proporción del PIB en los países de ALC, producidas en 2020 con relación a 2019, y se señalan los posibles factores contribuyentes.

En general, los países más afectados por la pandemia son aquellos que dependen del turismo (puesto que las restricciones a los viajes produjeron una drástica reducción de la llegada de turistas) y los países ricos en recursos (dado que los precios de los productos básicos se desplomaron en el segundo trimestre de 2020 – véase el capítulo 2). Los tres países que experimentaron las mayores reducciones de la recaudación tributaria como proporción del PIB, entre 2019 y 2020, dependen del turismo (Cuba y Belice) o de actividades relacionadas con el petróleo y el gas (Trinidad y Tobago).

La mayor reducción de la recaudación tributaria como proporción del PIB, entre 2019 y 2020, se produjo en Cuba, con 4.6 p.p. Esto se debió sobre todo al descenso de los impuestos sobre bienes y servicios distintos del IVA (de 2.9 p.p.; Cuba no tiene de IVA) y de los ingresos procedentes de los impuestos sobre la renta (1.2 p.p.) (Gráfico 1.4). La economía de Cuba depende enormemente del turismo (los ingresos procedentes del turismo internacional representaron el 22% de las exportaciones totales de Cuba, en 2019); a finales de diciembre de 2020, Cuba había sufrido una reducción del 74.6% en el número de visitantes internacionales respecto a 2019 (Havana Times, 2021[7]). Además, Cuba impuso uno de los confinamientos más estrictos del mundo durante seis meses para evitar la propagación del coronavirus (CNN, 2020[8]).

Trinidad y Tobago experimentó la segunda mayor reducción de la recaudación tributaria como proporción del PIB de toda la región de ALC, entre 2019 y 2020. La caída, de 3.3 p.p., se debió a una reducción de 3.9 p.p. en los ingresos de los impuestos sobre la renta y los beneficios, que representaban más de la mitad de la recaudación tributaria total de 2019 (Gráfico 1.4). Los ingresos tributarios de Trinidad y Tobago se vieron afectados por la fuerte caída de los precios del petróleo y el gas y el desplome de la demanda mundial de crudo en 2020 (Hon. Colm Imbert, 2020[9]). (CEPAL, 2021[10]). Aunque los precios del petróleo empezaron a recuperarse en abril de 2020, no alcanzaron los niveles anteriores a la crisis en 2020. Además, en 2020, los ingresos procedentes de la producción de energía también se redujeron en Trinidad y Tobago como consecuencia de la actividad de mantenimiento imprevista en algunas instalaciones energéticas y el cierre de varias plantas petroquímicas (FMI, 2021[11]).

La reducción de la recaudación tributaria como proporción del PIB de Belice, de 3.0 p.p., fue la tercera más acentuada de la región de ALC. La recaudación de todas las grandes categorías tributarias se contrajo, como por ejemplo los ingresos procedentes de impuestos sobre la renta y los beneficios, que experimentaron una caída de 1.0 p.p., y la recaudación del IVA y otros impuestos sobre bienes y servicios, que se redujo 1.3 p.p. (CEPAL, 2021[10]) calculó que la actividad del sector servicios se redujo un 18.2% en 2020 como consecuencia de la contracción del 71.1% que sufrió el sector del turismo. En respuesta a la crisis, en 2020, Belice anunció estímulos fiscales que ascendían al 1% del PIB para proporcionar un alivio a corto plazo a los trabajadores afectados por la crisis, sobre todo, del sector turístico (FMI, 2021[12]) (CEPAL, 2021[13]).

Gráfico 1.4. **Variaciones en la recaudación tributaria como proporción del PIB de los países ALC, según las principales partidas tributarias, entre 2019 y 2020**

Puntos porcentuales del PIB

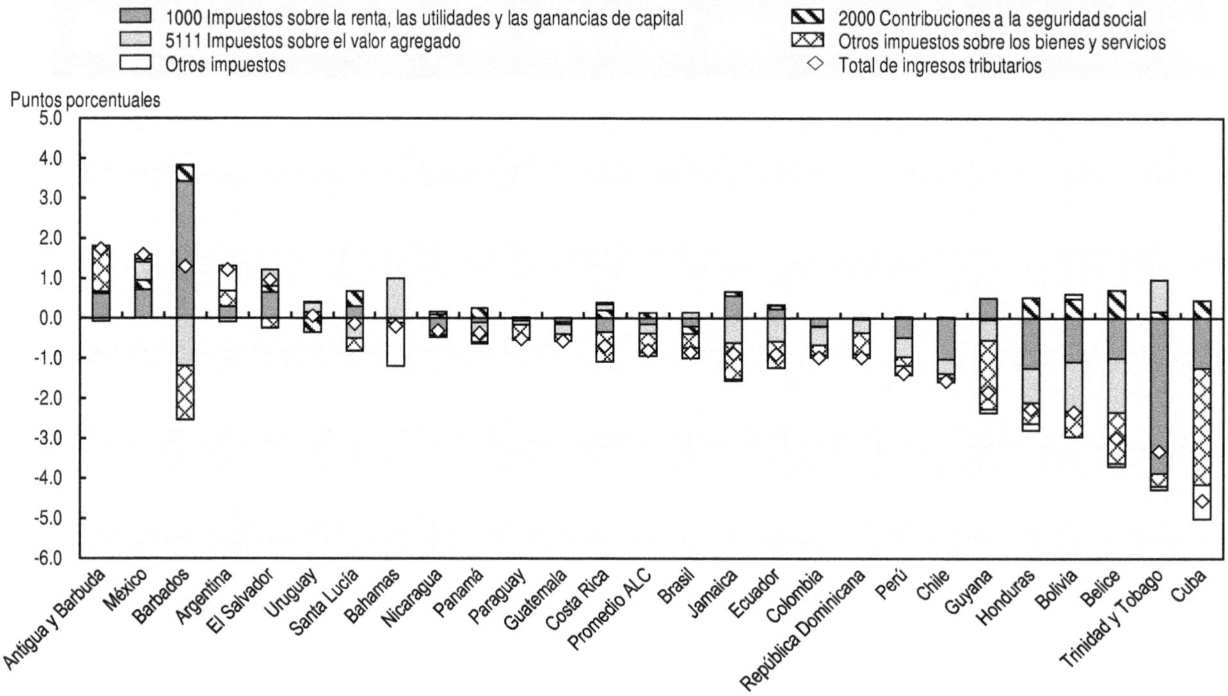


*Nota:* El promedio de ALC representa el promedio no ponderado de los 26 países de la región incluidos en esta publicación, sin contar a Venezuela debido a los problemas de disponibilidad de datos.

*Fuente:* Cálculos propios basados en (OCDE et al., 2022[3]), Capítulo 4.

StatLink https://doi.org/10.1787/888934307896

Entre 2019 y 2020, seis países de ALC experimentaron un aumento de la recaudación tributaria como proporción del PIB. En tres de ellos, los incrementos se debieron a que la reducción de los ingresos tributarios nominales fue menor que la del PIB nominal (Antigua y Barbuda, Barbados y El Salvador), mientras que, en México, el aumento se debió al incremento de ingresos tributarios nominales acompañado de una caída del PIB nominal. Las reformas administrativas o políticas en materia tributaria llevadas a cabo en algunos de estos países pueden haber limitado el derrumbe de la recaudación tributaria o haber contribuido a su aumento.

- En Antigua y Barbuda, los ingresos procedentes del impuesto sobre la renta de sociedades (IS) aumentaron 0.6 p.p. entre 2019 y 2020, lo que contribuyó al aumento general de la recaudación tributaria como proporción del PIB durante este periodo (1.7 p.p.). En diciembre de 2018, Antigua y Barbuda suprimió la exención del impuesto sobre sociedades de la cual disfrutaban las corporaciones mercantiles internacionales, que ahora tributan al tipo impositivo general del 25% (Consejo de la Unión Europea, 2019[14]). Los impuestos adeudados por estas sociedades correspondientes a 2019 se pagaron a principios de 2020, lo que supuso un importante aumento de la recaudación por IS en ese año.

- La Administración tributaria de México adoptó varias medidas que incluían inspecciones tributarias centradas en la evasión y la elusión, lo que contribuyó a aumentar en 1.6 p.p. la recaudación tributaria como proporción del PIB en 2020 con respecto a 2019 (CEPAL, 2021[13]).
- Los ingresos procedentes del IS en El Salvador, entre 2019 y 2020, aumentaron 0.4 p.p., gracias a la amnistía fiscal de ese año (CEPAL, 2021[13]). Esto contribuyó a un aumento general de la recaudación tributaria como proporción del PIB de 1.0 p.p. durante este periodo.
- Con relación a Barbados, el aumento del 1.3% en la recaudación tributaria como porcentaje del PIB se debió a los ingresos únicos de 2020 por IS, como consecuencia de los tipos más elevados impuestos a las empresas de cambio de divisas y a la mayor rentabilidad de estas empresas (Banco Central de Barbados, 2020 y 2021[15]). En 2019, un cierto número de estas empresas no efectuaron el pago a cuenta íntegro dentro del plazo correspondiente para efectuar los pagos anticipados de los impuestos (FMI, 2021[16]) cuyas diferencias ingresaron en el primer trimestre de 2020, lo que provocó un aumento de los ingresos procedentes del impuesto sobre sociedades de 4.2% del PIB, entre 2019 y 2020. Esto compensó con creces una reducción equivalente al 2.5% del PIB en la recaudación por los impuestos sobre bienes y servicios, durante el mismo periodo.

### Impacto de la pandemia sobre los diferentes tipos de impuestos

Entre 2019 y 2020, los impuestos sobre bienes y servicios fueron los más afectados por la crisis de COVID-19 con una reducción media del 0.7% del PIB en toda la región. Este descenso fue más de cuatro veces superior al sufrido por los ingresos procedentes de impuestos sobre la renta.

Entre los impuestos sobre bienes y servicios, el IVA fue el que experimentó la mayor reducción, de 0.2 p.p., mientras que los impuestos especiales sufrieron una caída de 0.1 p.p. Otros impuestos sobre el consumo (OIC), entre los que se incluyen los derechos de aduana y de importación, los impuestos generales distintos del IVA (como los impuestos sobre las ventas), los impuestos por el uso de determinados bienes (como los impuestos de circulación) y los impuestos para desarrollar ciertas actividades (como las licencias de actividades comerciales y profesionales), se redujeron 0.4 p.p. entre 2019 y 2020. Dentro de la categoría OIC, los derechos de aduana y de importación registraron el mayor descenso de todos, de 0.11 p.p.

Entre 2019 y 2020, los ingresos procedentes de los impuestos sobre la renta se redujeron, en promedio, 0.2 p.p., en toda la región de ALC, impulsados por una reducción equivalente de los ingresos por el IS. La recaudación del impuesto sobre la renta de las personas físicas (IRPF) como porcentaje del PIB permaneció sin cambios, mientras que las contribuciones a la seguridad social (CSS) aumentaron 0.1 p.p. en este periodo.

En términos nominales, entre 2019 y 2020, el promedio de la recaudación de todas las categorías tributarias principales se redujo en toda la región. El IRPF y las CSS disminuyeron un 3.0% y un 0.7%, respectivamente, durante este periodo, un descenso más pequeño que la caída del 4.9% en el PIB nominal (Cuadro 1.1). En términos nominales, la recaudación de las demás categorías tributarias principales (IS, IVA e impuestos especiales) se redujo, respectivamente, un 5.6%, un 8.1% y un 8.9%, durante este periodo.

Cuadro 1.1. **Variaciones de los ingresos tributarios de las principales categorías de impuestos en ALC (en puntos porcentuales y como porcentaje)**

| | p. p. | % |
|---|---|---|
| IRPF | 0.0 | -3.0 |
| IS | -0.2 | -5.6 |
| CSS | 0.1 | -0.7 |
| Prop. | -0.1 | -14.2 |
| IVA | -0.2 | -8.1 |
| I. esp. | -0.1 | -8.9 |
| OIC | -0.4 | -15.7 |
| Res. | 0.0 | -12.1 |
| **Total impuestos** | **-0.8** | **-8.0** |

*Nota:* El promedio de ALC excluye a Venezuela debido a los problemas de disponibilidad de datos. Los promedios del IRPF y el IS no tienen en cuenta a Ecuador por problemas relacionados con la calidad de los datos. El promedio de los OIC (otros impuestos sobre el consumo) incluye los impuestos especiales Cubanos, ya que no es posible separarlos de otros ingresos de OIC.
*Fuente:* Cálculos propios basados en (OCDE et al., 2022[3]).

StatLink https://doi.org/10.1787/888934308257

Los dos mayores descensos en términos nominales, en 2020 respecto a 2019, se observaron en otros impuestos sobre el consumo (15.7%) y los impuestos sobre la propiedad (14.2%). Sin embargo, como en 2019 los impuestos sobre la propiedad representaban menos del 4% de la imposición total media en la región ALC, el impacto en la recaudación tributaria como proporción del PIB fue más reducida que las reducciones sufridas por otras de las principales categorías tributarias, tales como el IVA o los impuestos especiales, que representaban una mayor participación en los ingresos tributarios totales.

El Gráfico 1.5 presenta la distribución general de las variaciones experimentadas por la recaudación de los principales tipos de impuestos como porcentaje del PIB entre 2019 y 2020. Dieciséis países de ALC vieron reducirse su recaudación por el IS como proporción del PIB: en seis países, la reducción de los ingresos por IS fue superior a 0.6 p.p. del PIB. La recaudación por IS presenta la dispersión más amplia de todas las categorías tributarias: las variaciones entre 2019 y 2020 oscilaron entre -3.3 p.p. (Trinidad y Tobago) y 4.2 p.p. (Barbados).

Esta amplia variación también puede observarse en las diferencias habidas en la recaudación de otros impuestos sobre el consumo (esto es, los impuestos sobre el consumo distintos del IVA). Veintidós países de la región de ALC vieron como, entre 2019 y 2020, se reducía su recaudación por otros impuestos sobre el consumo como proporción del PIB. Cuba registró la mayor reducción (2.9 p.p.), impulsada principalmente por una disminución de 2.6 p.p. en la recaudación de los impuestos sobre las ventas como consecuencia de la crisis de COVID-19.

En diecisiete países de ALC, se redujo la recaudación del IVA como proporción del PIB; para la mitad de los países de la región, esta se redujo más de 0.3 p.p. La mayor caída de los ingresos por IVA fue de 1.3 p.p., en Belice, y el mayor aumento se observó en las Bahamas (1.0 p.p.). El aumento de la recaudación del IVA en las Bahamas se debe al cambio del impuesto sobre el timbre por el IVA sobre los bienes inmuebles, como consecuencia de la reforma tributaria. Esto condujo a una reducción de 1.1 p.p. en los impuestos sobre la propiedad, en las Bahamas, en 2020 (Gobierno de las Bahamas, 2020[17]).

Gráfico 1.5. **Variaciones de los ingresos tributarios por categoría como proporción del PIB para la región de ALC, 2019-20**

Puntos porcentuales del PIB

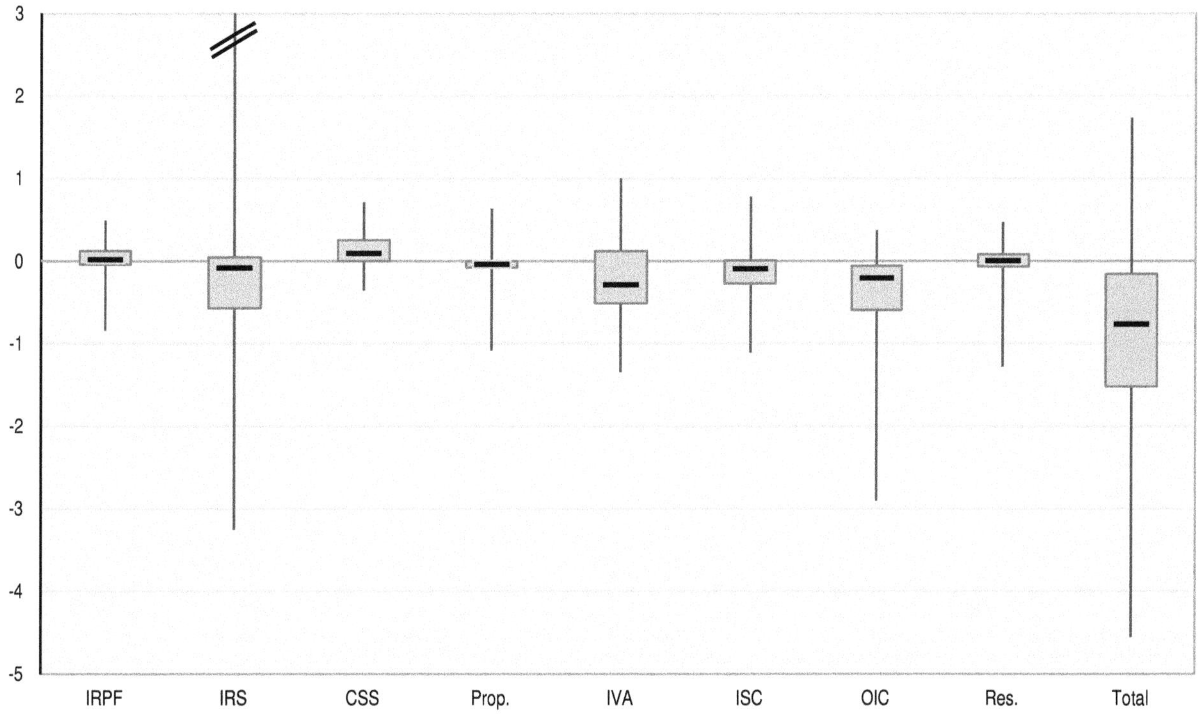


*Nota:* El promedio de ALC excluye a Venezuela debido a los problemas de disponibilidad de datos. Los promedios del IRPF y el IS no tienen en cuenta a Ecuador por problemas relacionados con la calidad de los datos. El promedio de los OIC (otros impuestos sobre el consumo) incluye los impuestos especiales Cubanos, ya que no es posible separarlos de otros ingresos de OIC. En el gráfico, el punto más bajo representa la variación nacional de menor envergadura para el tipo de impuesto entre 2019 y 2020; el recuadro representa las variaciones para los países entre el cuartil inferior y el superior (es decir, el 50% de los países experimentó variaciones dentro del intervalo mostrado en cada recuadro); y el punto superior de cada tipo de impuesto representa la variación nacional máxima. La línea en cada recuadro representa la variación nacional media (es decir, la mitad de los países estaban por encima de esta línea y la otra mitad por debajo).

*Fuente:* Cálculos propios basados en (OCDE et al., 2022[3]).

StatLink https://doi.org/10.1787/888934307915

Dieciséis países de ALC registraron un descenso en la recaudación de los impuestos especiales como proporción del PIB. Guyana experimentó el mayor de todos ellos, de 1.1 p.p.

Como proporción del PIB, la variación en la recaudación del IRPF y las contribuciones a la seguridad social fueron de menor entidad que en otras categorías, lo que demuestra el impacto relativamente limitado del COVID-19 sobre estas dos categorías frente a las demás. La recaudación de estos dos impuestos fue más estable que la de otros impuestos, como el IVA y el IS, cuyas bases imponibles son más volátiles. Durante este periodo, la recaudación del IRPF aumentó en 14 países y la de las contribuciones a la seguridad social, en 21 países.

El Gráfico 1.6 refleja la distribución general de las variaciones relativas a 2019-20 en los ingresos tributarios nominales, por categorías principales. En términos nominales, las variaciones están más generalizadas y el impacto negativo del COVID-19 se siente claramente en todas las categorías tributarias. En todas ellas, la mediana es negativa, lo que significa que, entre 2019 y 2020, en más de la mitad de los países, se redujeron sus ingresos tributarios nominales.

Gráfico 1.6. **Variación relativa en los ingresos tributarios nominales por categoría para la región de ALC, 2019-20**

Variación porcentual interanual

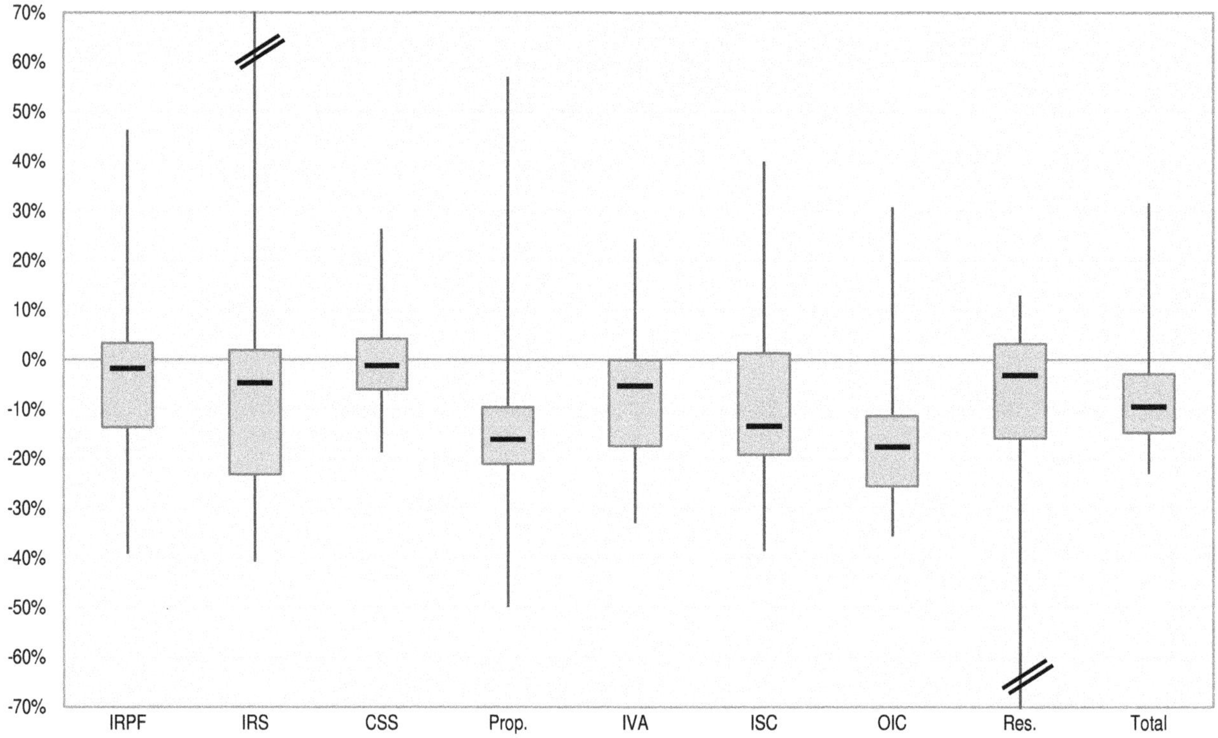


*Nota:* El promedio de ALC excluye a Venezuela debido a los problemas de disponibilidad de datos. Los promedios del IRPF y el IS no tienen en cuenta a Ecuador por problemas relacionados con la calidad de los datos. El promedio de los OIC (otros impuestos sobre el consumo) incluye los impuestos especiales Cubanos, ya que no es posible separarlos de otros ingresos de OIC. En el gráfico, el punto más bajo representa la variación nacional de menor envergadura para el tipo de impuesto entre 2019-2020; el recuadro representa las variaciones para los países entre el cuartil inferior y el superior (es decir, el 50% de los países experimentó variaciones dentro del intervalo mostrado en cada recuadro); y el punto superior de cada tipo de impuesto representa la variación nacional máxima. La línea en cada recuadro representa la variación nacional media (es decir, la mitad de los países estaban por encima de esta línea y la otra mitad por debajola).

*Fuente:* Cálculos propios basados en (OCDE et al., 2022[3]).

StatLink https://doi.org/10.1787/888934307934

Con relación a los impuestos sobre bienes y servicios, el número de países que presentaron una reducción de las recaudaciones del IVA, los impuestos especiales y de otros impuestos sobre el consumo fueron 19, 18 y 23, respectivamente. Dentro de la categoría de impuestos sobre la renta, 15 y 16 países registraron reducciones en los ingresos tributarios nominales por IRPF e IS, entre 2019 y 2020, respectivamente. Por su parte, la recaudación procedente de las contribuciones a la seguridad social, en términos nominales, se redujo en 15 países y, en 23 de 26 países, disminuyeron los ingresos tributarios nominales del impuesto sobre la propiedad.

En comparación con la OCDE, en 2020, el impacto del COVID-19 sobre los diferentes tipos de impuestos en la región de ALC varió significativamente (Gráfico 1.7):

- En la OCDE, el IRPF y las contribuciones a la seguridad social aumentaron como proporción del PIB (0.3 p.p. en promedio, en ambos casos (OCDE, 2021[4])). En 2020, la recaudación de ambas categorías de impuestos como proporción del PIB aumentó en la mayoría de los países de la OCDE (28 y 29 países, respectivamente, que representan casi tres cuartas partes de los países de la OCDE). En ambas categorías tributarias, la mitad de los países de la OCDE experimentó un aumento de más de 0.2 p.p. En cambio, en solo seis de 26 países de ALC aumentó la recaudación del IRPF más de 0.2 p.p. y, en ocho países de ALC, el aumento en la recaudación de las contribuciones a la seguridad social rebasó ese nivel.

- En la OCDE, la recaudación del IS experimentó una disminución significativa (OCDE, 2021[4]). La caída media de la recaudación del IS en el promedio de la OCDE fue de 0.4 p.p., el doble que el promedio de ALC relativo al IS (0.2 p.p.). La recaudación del IS se redujo en 26 países de la OCDE, lo que supone más de dos tercios de todos los países. En la mitad de los países de la OCDE, los descensos fueron superiores a 0.3 p.p., mientras que, en la región de ALC, en ocho de 26 países (menos de un tercio), el descenso rebasó ese nivel.
- En el promedio de la OCDE, no hubo variación en el IVA u otros impuestos sobre el consumo como porcentaje del PIB (OCDE, 2021[4]), mientras que, en la región de ALC, estos impuestos sufrieron un fuerte descenso, de 0.2 y 0.4 p.p., respectivamente. El Gráfico 1.7 refleja la mayor de las magnitudes del descenso de la recaudación del IVA y otros impuestos sobre el consumo como porcentaje del PIB en los países de ALC frente a los países de la OCDE. En la mitad de los países de ALC se redujo la recaudación del IVA por encima de 0.3 p.p., mientras que solo siete países de la OCDE rebasaron ese nivel.
- En ambas regiones, se observó una reducción de 0.1 p.p. en la recaudación de los impuestos especiales. En la OCDE, los ingresos procedentes de estos impuestos experimentaron, en promedio, la reducción más generalizada de todos los tipos de impuestos, al caer en 28 países (OCDE, 2021[4]). La recaudación de los impuestos especiales cayó en 16 de los 25 países de ALC para los que se dispone de datos.
- La recaudación de los impuestos sobre la propiedad no experimentó ninguna variación en la OCDE mientras que se redujo 0.1 p.p., en promedio, en los países de ALC.

Gráfico 1.7. **Variaciones en los ingresos tributarios por categoría como proporción del PIB, OCDE y ALC, 2019-20**

Puntos porcentuales del PIB

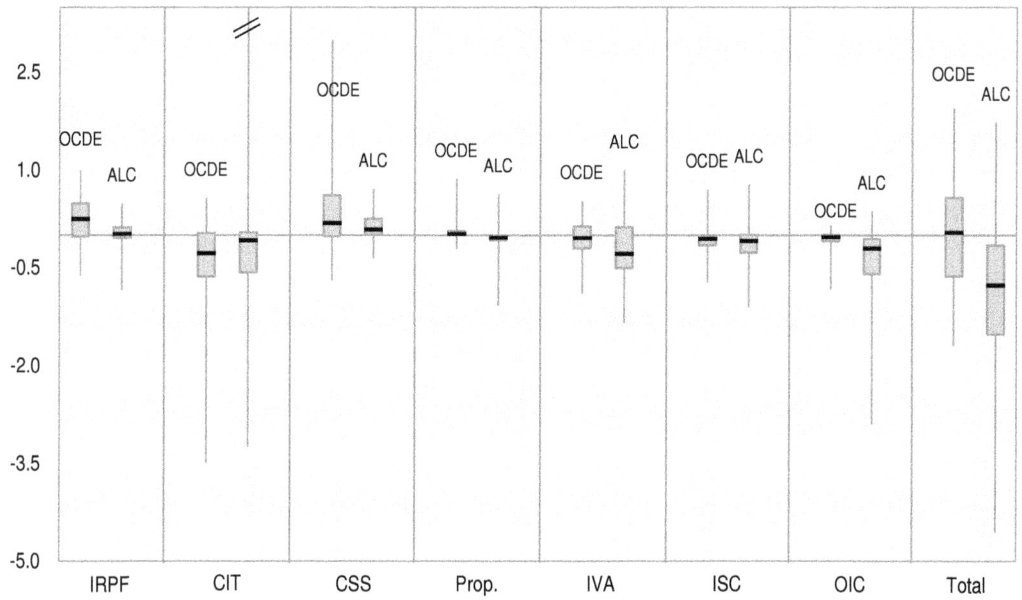


*Nota:* El promedio de ALC excluye a Venezuela debido a los problemas de disponibilidad de datos. Los promedios del IRPF y el IS para ALC no tienen en cuenta a Ecuador por problemas relacionados con la calidad de los datos. El promedio de ALC de los OIC (otros impuestos sobre el consumo) incluye los impuestos especiales Cubanos, ya que no es posible separarlos de otros ingresos de OIC. En el gráfico, el punto más bajo representa la variación nacional de menor envergadura para el tipo de impuesto entre 2019 y2020; el recuadro representa las variaciones para los países entre el cuartil inferior y el superior (es decir, el 50% de los países experimentó variaciones dentro del intervalo mostrado en cada recuadro); y el punto superior de cada tipo de impuesto representa la variación nacional máxima. La línea en cada recuadro representa la variación nacional media (es decir, la mitad de los países estaban por encima de esta línea y la otra mitad por debajo). Los datos de la OCDE para 2020 son provisionales y deben interpretarse con prudencia.

*Fuente:* Los datos relativos a la OCDE provienen de (OCDE, 2021[4]). Las cifras relativas a ALC son cálculos propios basados en (OCDE et al., 2022[3]).

StatLink https://doi.org/10.1787/888934307953

Valga señalar que la mayoría de los ingresos tributarios de los países de la OCDE se registran conforme al principio de devengo (cuando nace la obligación tributaria, aunque el pago aún no sea exigible), mientras que en todos los países de ALC los ingresos tributarios se registran según el criterio de caja. Los ingresos tributarios en algunos países de la OCDE pueden incluir pasivo acumulado —en particular, para el IVA— que las empresas no remitirán a las haciendas públicas en un corto plazo o nunca gracias a las medidas fiscales adoptadas en algunos países de la OCDE como respuesta al COVID-19, tales como aplazamientos del IVA o la condonación del IVA repercutido en facturas no cobradas. Esto implica que, en 2020, en algunos países de la OCDE, es posible que se haya sobrevalorado la recaudación tributaria, en particular, del IVA. Por otro lado, el registro según el criterio de caja en la región de ALC puede suponer que las variaciones durante la crisis sean más acentuadas por el impacto de los aplazamientos del pago de las deudas tributarias que los países adoptaron como respuesta al COVID-19.

**Impacto en las diferentes subregiones**

La crisis de COVID-19 ha afectado a cada una de las tres subregiones de ALC de manera distinta, como consecuencia de sus propias características económicas. En 2020, el COVID-19 ha afectado gravemente al Caribe por el colapso del turismo. La subregión América del Sur, que es exportadora neta, sobre todo de recursos naturales no renovables, también sufrió las fuertes caídas de los precios de los productos básicos durante ese año.

En 2020, el promedio de recaudación tributaria como proporción del PIB en el Caribe, América Central y México y América del Sur se situó en el 23.8%, el 20.4% y el 21.8%, respectivamente. Aunque los coeficientes se redujeron 0.8 p.p. en las tres subregiones entre 2019 y 2020, el impacto de la pandemia en las diferentes categorías tributarias varía en función de cada una de ellas.

En las tres subregiones, la recaudación de los impuestos sobre bienes y servicios sufrió un mayor impacto que la correspondiente a los impuestos sobre la renta. La recaudación de los impuestos sobre bienes y servicios se redujo, en promedio, 0.9, 0.7 y 0.6 p.p., en el Caribe, América Central y México y América del Sur, respectivamente. En contraste, en este periodo, los ingresos procedentes de impuestos sobre la renta y los beneficios se redujeron, en promedio, en América Central y México (0.2 p.p.) y en América del Sur (0.3 p.p.) y aumentaron en el Caribe (0.1 p.p.). Este último incremento se debe íntegramente al excepcional aumento de estos ingresos, durante este periodo, en Barbados, al que ya nos hemos referido en este capítulo. Sin contar Barbados, la recaudación de los impuestos sobre la renta y los beneficios cayó, durante el periodo, 0.4 p.p.

El Cuadro 1.2 refleja las variaciones en los ingresos tributarios en 2020 respecto a 2019, para el Caribe, América Central y México y América del Sur, respecto a los principales tipos de impuestos.

- En el Caribe, el mayor descenso en la recaudación tributaria como proporción del PIB, en 2020, se registró en el IVA y otros impuestos sobre el consumo (0.3 y 0.4 p.p., respectivamente). Dentro de los otros impuestos sobre el consumo (OIC), los derechos de aduana y de importación y los impuestos para desarrollar ciertas actividades fueron los más afectados, con caídas de 0.2 p.p., en ambos casos. Los impuestos sobre la propiedad tuvieron un descenso de 0.2 p.p., entre 2019 y 2020, como consecuencia de la reforma tributaria en las Bahamas que comenzó a gravar las transacciones relativas a bienes inmuebles con el IVA en vez de con el impuesto sobre el timbre, como ya se ha explicado antes en este capítulo. Sin contar con las Bahamas, el descenso de la recaudación del impuesto sobre la propiedad en el Caribe, entre 2019 y 2020, fue de 0.1 p.p., mientras que la reducción de los ingresos del IVA durante este periodo fue de 0.5 p.p. Además, el Caribe registró la mayor caída en la recaudación de impuestos especiales (0.2 p.p.) en comparación con las otras dos subregiones, en las que la reducción fue de 0.1 p.p. en ambas.

- En América Central y México, el mayor descenso de ingresos como proporción del PIB, en 2020, se registró en el IS y otros impuestos sobre el consumo (en ambos de 0.4 p.p.). Con relación al IS, Costa Rica, Cuba y Honduras registraron el mayor descenso de todos, en todos los casos de más de 0.9 p.p., desde 2019. En la categoría de otros impuestos sobre el consumo (OIC), los ingresos por los impuestos sobre las ventas fueron los más afectados, al registrar una disminución de 0.3 p.p., sobre todo, como consecuencia de la reducción que sufrieron en Cuba. América Central presentó el mayor descenso en la recaudación del IVA, 0.1 p.p. durante todo el periodo, en comparación con el Caribe y América del Sur, que sufrieron una disminución de 0.3 p.p. en ambos casos.
- En América del Sur, en 2020, el mayor descenso de los ingresos tributarios como proporción del PIB se registró en el IS y el IVA (con una caída en ambos casos de 0.3 p.p.). Los ingresos de otros impuestos sobre el consumo se vieron menos afectados, con una disminución de 0.2 p.p., entre 2019 y 2020. En esta categoría, los derechos de importación experimentaron el mayor descenso (0.1 p.p.). Bolivia y Perú registraron las mayores caídas en los ingresos del IS (1.1 y 0.6 p.p., respectivamente) entre 2019 y 2020. Bolivia también registró la mayor caída en la recaudación del IVA (1.2 p.p.). El fuerte descenso de los ingresos en Bolivia se debe, en parte, a los ingresos menos sólidos de las actividades de hidrocarburos (CEPAL, 2021[18]). Además, en noviembre de 2020, Bolivia aplicó una devolución del IVA a grupos con bajos ingresos, que contribuyó aún más a la caída de la recaudación del impuesto, en 2020 (CEPAL, 2021[18]).

Cuadro 1.2. **Variaciones en los ingresos tributarios por categoría como proporción del PIB, ALC y subregiones, 2019-20**

Puntos porcentuales del PIB

| | ALC | Caribe | América Central + México | América del Sur |
|---|---|---|---|---|
| IRPF | 0.0 | -0.1 | 0.1 | 0.0 |
| IS | -0.2 | 0.1 | -0.4 | -0.3 |
| CSS | 0.1 | 0.2 | 0.2 | 0.0 |
| Prop. | -0.1 | -0.2 | 0.0 | 0.0 |
| IVA | -0.2 | -0.3 | -0.1 | -0.3 |
| I. esp. | -0.1 | -0.2 | -0.1 | 0.0 |
| OIC | -0.4 | -0.4 | -0.4 | -0.2 |
| Res. | 0.0 | 0.0 | 0.0 | -0.1 |
| **Total impuestos** | **-0.8** | **-0.8** | **-0.8** | **-0.8** |

*Nota:* El promedio de ALC excluye a Venezuela debido a los problemas de disponibilidad de datos. Los promedios del IRPF y el IS para ALC y América del Sur no tienen en cuenta a Ecuador por problemas relacionados con la calidad de los datos. El promedio de los OIC (otros impuestos sobre el consumo) incluye los impuestos especiales cubanos en los promedios de ALC y América Central y México, ya que no es posible separarlos de otros ingresos de OIC.

*Fuente:* Cálculos propios basados en (OCDE et al., 2022[3]).

StatLink https://doi.org/10.1787/888934308276

## *El contexto económico*

La pandemia de COVID-19 ha afectado negativamente a la región de ALC tanto desde un punto de vista económico como social (OCDE et al., 2021[2]). En 2020, el producto interior bruto sufrió la mayor recesión de los últimos 100 años y se contrajo un 6.8% en términos reales, mientras que el PIB per cápita caía un 7.7%, en promedio (CEPAL, 2021[18]). Esta ha sido una de las mayores recesiones de las regiones en desarrollo, en 2020. Pese al declive general, los resultados han variado entre los diferentes sectores económicos. Por ejemplo, el sector agrícola ha presentado una mayor resistencia frente a la crisis de COVID-19 y, en 2020, llegó a aumentar la producción en muchas economías regionales, mientras que los sectores industriales sufrieron una desaceleración inicial para recuperarse después rápidamente. La economía digital ha recibido el mayor impulso como consecuencia de los confinamientos y las cuarentenas. Muchas empresas también se vieron obligadas a migrar sus negocios a internet para mitigar la falta de presencia física, durante la pandemia.

En cambio, la pandemia devastó los sectores del comercio exterior, el turismo, el transporte aéreo de pasajeros y otros servicios (CEPAL, 2021[19]). En 2020, en América Latina, el valor de las exportaciones internacionales de mercancías se contrajo un 9.6% y su volumen, un 4.9%, mientras que el valor de las importaciones internacionales de mercancías cayó un 15.5% y su volumen, un 11.2% (CEPAL, 2021[18]). En 2020, la inversión extranjera directa neta en la región de ALC cayó hasta los 90.100 millones de dólares estadounidenses, su nivel más bajo desde la crisis financiera global de 2008-2009, mientras que la deuda externa total de la región se elevó hasta el 48% del PIB, su nivel más alto desde 1990 (CEPAL, 2022[20]). En 2022, la región va a enfrentar un contexto complejo, pues la incertidumbre acerca de la evolución de la pandemia aún se mantiene. Asimismo, la región seguirá enfrentando interrupciones en los suministros, retrasos de socios comerciales esenciales, políticas presupuestarias limitadas y condiciones monetarias y de financiación más ajustadas. Tras una relativamente fuerte recuperación del 6.2%, en 2021, se espera que, en 2022, se ralentice el crecimiento un 2.1% (CEPAL, 2022[21]).

Desde el punto de vista social, la pandemia de COVID-19 ha provocado la pérdida de numerosos puestos de trabajo y un aumento sin precedentes del desempleo, como consecuencia de las quiebras generalizadas, sobre todo, de micro, pequeñas y medianas empresas (MiPyME), que son la inmensa mayoría en la región de ALC y que generan más de la mitad de los puestos de trabajo locales (OCDE, 2020[22]). Los confinamientos y las restricciones a las actividades también han desempeñado un importante papel (OCDE, 2020). Más de 2.7 millones de empresas formales, que representan el 19% del total, había cerrado a finales de 2020, de las cuales cerca de 2.6 millones eran microempresas (CEPAL, 2020[23]). La mayor parte de estas empresas pertenecían al sector del comercio mayorista y minorista, seguido por el sector turístico (CEPAL, 2020[23]).

La crisis de COVID-19 tuvo un impacto negativo mucho mayor sobre el empleo que la anterior crisis y ha provocado una reducción histórica del 9% del número de personas ocupadas y una caída de 4.9 p.p. en la tasa de actividad (CEPAL, 2021[18]). Incluso para aquellas personas que tenían empleo, el desempleo era un problema: el número de horas trabajadas se redujo considerablemente en toda la región de ALC, según los cálculos de la Organización Internacional del Trabajo (OIT). De 2019 a 2020, las horas de trabajo se redujeron un 16.2%, frente a la pérdida global del 8.8%, con lo que la región fue la más afectada del mundo (OIT, 2021[24]).

La pobreza y la desigualdad aumentaron en toda la región de ALC a raíz de la crisis de COVID-19, que ha agravado otros problemas estructurales que ya existían antes de la pandemia (CEPAL, 2021[19]; OCDE et al., 2021[2]). La crisis ha tenido un impacto desproporcionado en los trabajadores informales y las mujeres, ya que estos representan la mayor proporción de trabajadores en algunos de los sectores económicos más perjudicados (CEPAL, 2021[25]; OCDE et al., 2021[2]). En comparación con los trabajadores formales, sobre todo aquellos de sectores de ingresos elevados, los trabajadores de los sectores informales tenían más dificultades para seguir realizando sus trabajos durante los confinamientos y no tenían acceso a mecanismos de protección social, como los seguros de desempleo. Por consiguiente, en ALC, se observó una mayor contracción en los trabajos informales que en los formales (CEPAL, 2021[18]; OCDE et al., 2021[2]). Por otro lado, en la región, las mujeres suelen representar una parte importante de la mano de obra en los sectores del trabajo doméstico y asistencial, que se vieron especialmente perjudicados por la pandemia como consecuencia de los confinamientos y las medidas de distancia social aplicadas.

### *Medidas de apoyo aplicadas*

Los países de toda la región adoptaron rápidamente medidas presupuestarias ambiciosas para apoyar a los sistemas públicos de salud, los hogares vulnerables y las empresas afectadas, así como para proteger la capacidad productiva a fin de facilitar la recuperación económica después de la pandemia (CEPAL, 2020[26]) (OCDE, 2020[22]). Aunque, en toda la región de ALC, el gasto público fue el eje central de la respuesta fiscal, también se recurrió a la política tributaria como instrumento para mitigar el impacto de la crisis de COVID-19 sobre las familias y las empresas. Frente a los programas que necesitan la reasignación de recursos presupuestarios y gastos adicionales, las políticas tributarias se suelen poder aplicar con relativa rapidez (OCDE et al., 2021[1]).

Las proporciones nunca antes vistas de esta pandemia han ejercido una enorme presión sobre los sistemas sanitarios de la región, que, en muchos casos, estaban poco desarrollados. La mayoría de los países adoptaron rápidamente medidas dirigidas a reducir el coste de productos sanitarios esenciales, principalmente a través de exenciones temporales o de la aplicación de tasas o tipos impositivos del 0% a la importación de material sanitario. Algunos países, como Colombia, también aprobaron exenciones del IVA para los productos sanitarios, mientras que otros ratificaron reducciones temporales de los impuestos IRPF y IS a fin de incentivar las donaciones a los sistemas de salud (OCDE et al., 2021[1]).

Se aplicaron medidas de desgravación fiscal para compensar a los hogares y los trabajadores por la pérdida de salarios, así como para apoyar el consumo. Para ello, las medidas fiscales más comunes fueron el aplazamiento de impuestos, la suspensión de los pagos anticipados y la creación de formas de pago de impuestos favorables para el IVA y el IRPF, como los planes de fraccionamiento del pago sin intereses ni multas. Muchos países han aplicado políticas tributarias complementarias para ofrecer un apoyo adicional a las familias y los trabajadores (OCDE et al., 2021[1]).

La desgravación fiscal para empresas consistió principalmente en medidas temporales para aumentar el flujo de caja mediante el aplazamiento y la suspensión de los pagos anticipados del IVA y el IS, en algunos casos, centradas en las pequeñas empresas o los sectores más afectados por la crisis, como la construcción, el turismo y los servicios a las personas. La reducción del IVA desempeñó un papel importante en la región, sobre todo para las MiPyME. Junto con la reducción del IS y el IVA, los países apoyaron a las empresas mediante modificaciones en las contribuciones a la seguridad social (OCDE et al., 2021[1]).

Pese la rápida aplicación de las medidas de reducción de impuestos, la eficacia de las políticas tributarias tropezó en el amplio sector informal de la región y la escasa participación de las personas y pequeñas empresas en los sistemas impositivos y de seguridad social (OCDE et al., 2021[1]; OCDE et al., 2021[2]).

## Evolución de la recaudación tributaria como proporción del PIB

### Evolución de la recaudación tributaria como proporción del PIB desde 1990

Pese a la reducción causada por la pandemia en 2020, el promedio de recaudación tributaria como proporción del PIB para la región de ALC ha aumentado desde 1990 (Gráfico 1.8). Este indicador aumentó más de 7 p.p. entre 1990 y 2019 (del 15.6% al 22.7%), para caer 0.8 p.p., en 2020. Esta tendencia contrasta con la de los países de la OCDE, donde el promedio de recaudación tributaria como proporción del PIB se ha mantenido relativamente estable desde 1990 (aunque a un nivel más alto que el promedio de ALC).

La recaudación tributaria como proporción del PIB de la OCDE alcanzó el 33.5%, en 2020, 2.7 p.p. por encima de su nivel de 1990. De este modo, la diferencia entre los promedios de este coeficiente tributario para ALC y la OCDE se ha reducido considerablemente a lo largo del tiempo y, en 2019, alcanzó uno de sus niveles más bajos, al situarse en 10.7 p.p. Sin embargo, la diferencia entre el promedio de recaudación tributaria como proporción del PIB para la región de ALC y de la OCDE se ensanchó hasta los 11.6 p.p. en 2020 dado el mayor impacto del COVID-19 en los ingresos tributarios de ALC.

Gráfico 1.8. **Recaudación tributaria como proporción del PIB, promedios para ALC y la OCDE, 1990-2020**

Porcentaje del PIB

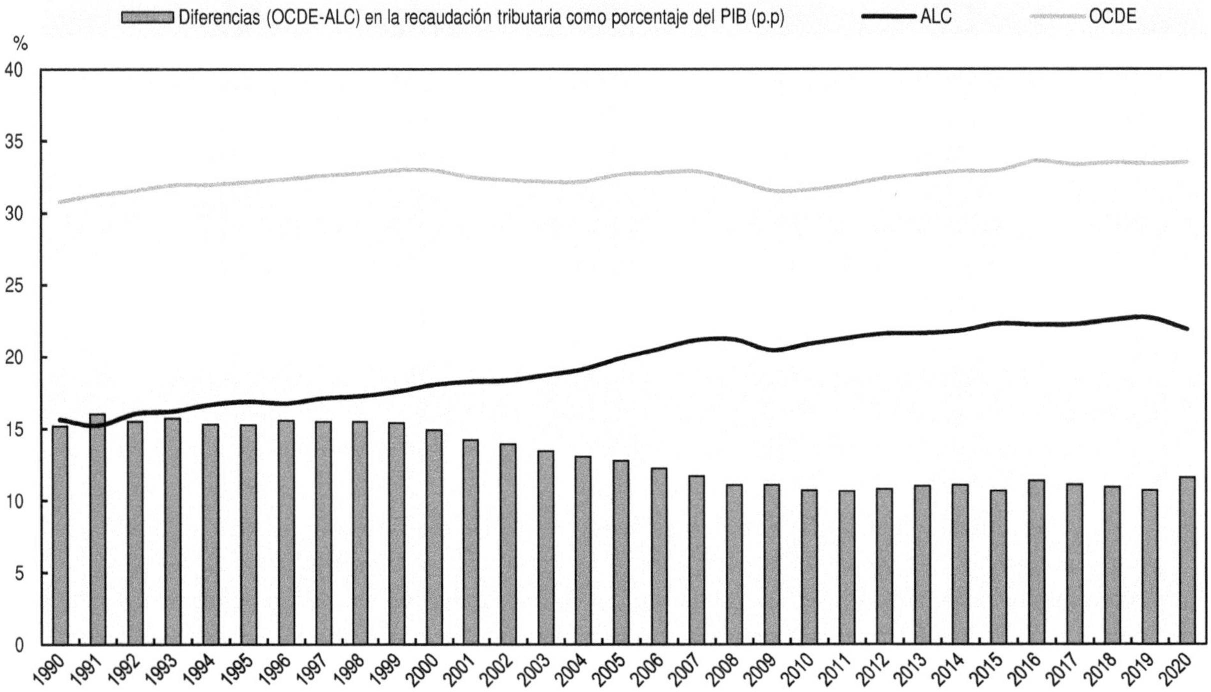


*Nota:* El promedio de ALC representa el promedio no ponderado de 26 países de la región incluidos en esta publicación, sin contar con Venezuela, debido a los problemas de disponibilidad de datos. El promedio de la OCDE representa el promedio no ponderado de los 38 países miembros de la OCDE. Chile, Colombia, Costa Rica y México forman parte de la OCDE (38).

*Fuente: Cálculos propios basados en* (OCDE et al., 2022[3]), «Revenue Statistics in Latin America: Comparative tables», *OECD Tax Statistics* (database), *http://dx.doi.org/10.1787/data-00641-en.*

StatLink https://doi.org/10.1787/888934307972

### *Factores que influyen en la recaudación tributaria como proporción del PIB*

Existe una serie de factores económicos y estructurales, entre los que se incluye el PIB per cápita, que influyen en la recaudación tributaria como proporción del PIB (véase Recuadro 1.2). Las diferencias entre el promedio de recaudación tributaria como proporción del PIB entre ALC y la OCDE son congruentes con la tendencia de los países con niveles de renta más elevados de presentar también mayores coeficientes tributarios. Los datos comportan una correlación positiva entre el PIB per cápita (una medida del nivel de renta de un país) y la recaudación tributaria como proporción del PIB (Gráfico 1.9).

#### Recuadro 1.2. **Factores que influyen en la recaudación tributaria como proporción del PIB**

El PIB per cápita, la apertura comercial, la extensión de la economía informal, las dotaciones de recursos naturales y la importancia de la agricultura en la economía son factores económicos y estructurales que influyen en la recaudación tributaria como proporción del PIB. El poder de las administraciones tributarias, los niveles de corrupción y la moral tributaria (la predisposición de las personas a pagar impuestos) también están íntimamente relacionados con el nivel de ingresos tributarios (OCDE, 2014[28]; OCDE, 2019[29]).

La recaudación tributaria como proporción del PIB también refleja las opciones políticas acerca del papel que desempeña el gobierno y su tamaño. Por ejemplo, el alcance de la participación pública en la financiación de la seguridad social es un factor importante que subyace a los dispares coeficientes tributarios en la región de ALC. Desde la década de 1980, muchos países de ALC, como Chile, El Salvador y México, han privatizado la salud y las pensiones, en mayor o menor medida: estas aportaciones a entidades privadas no se consideran ingresos por contribuciones a la seguridad social. En Colombia y Perú, los sistemas públicos y privados conviven y los trabajadores pueden optar entre ellos (OCDE et al., 2015[30]; OCDE/BID/El Banco Mundial, 2014[31]). Por otro lado, Argentina, Brasil y Uruguay siguen un modelo de complementariedad entre los sistemas público y privado. En estos países, se emprendieron reformas sustanciales para ampliar la cobertura de los sistemas de seguridad social a las personas que estaban excluidas. Esto también ha sido fundamental para el aumento de los ingresos tributarios (CEPAL, 2014[32]).

La informalidad es otro factor que lastra la recaudación de tributos en la región al reducir considerablemente la base imponible. El empleo informal representa cerca del 60% de los trabajadores en ALC (OCDE, 2020[22]).

La región pierde cantidades importantes de ingresos tributarios como consecuencia de la evasión impositiva y la planificación fiscal abusiva. Se calcula que los ingresos no recaudados fruto del incumplimiento tributario en ALC alcanzaron el 6.1% del PIB, en 2018, principalmente del impuesto sobre la renta (3.8% del PIB) y el IVA (2.3% del PIB) (CEPAL, 2020[26]).

Asimismo, la ubicación geográfica y factores históricos también pueden afectar a la recaudación tributaria como proporción del PIB: por ejemplo, los países sin litoral tienen menos capacidad de gravar los bienes y servicios en un puerto de entrada que los costeros. Además, los condicionantes sociodemográficos también son importantes, como el nivel educativo o la participación femenina en el mercado laboral. Por último, factores internacionales, como las políticas tributarias de otros países, pueden tener un efecto sobre la recaudación tributaria como proporción del PIB.

Gráfico 1.9. **PIB per cápita en PPA (USD) y recaudación tributaria como proporción del PIB en la región de ALC, la OCDE y un grupo de economías de África, Asia y el Pacífico, 2019**

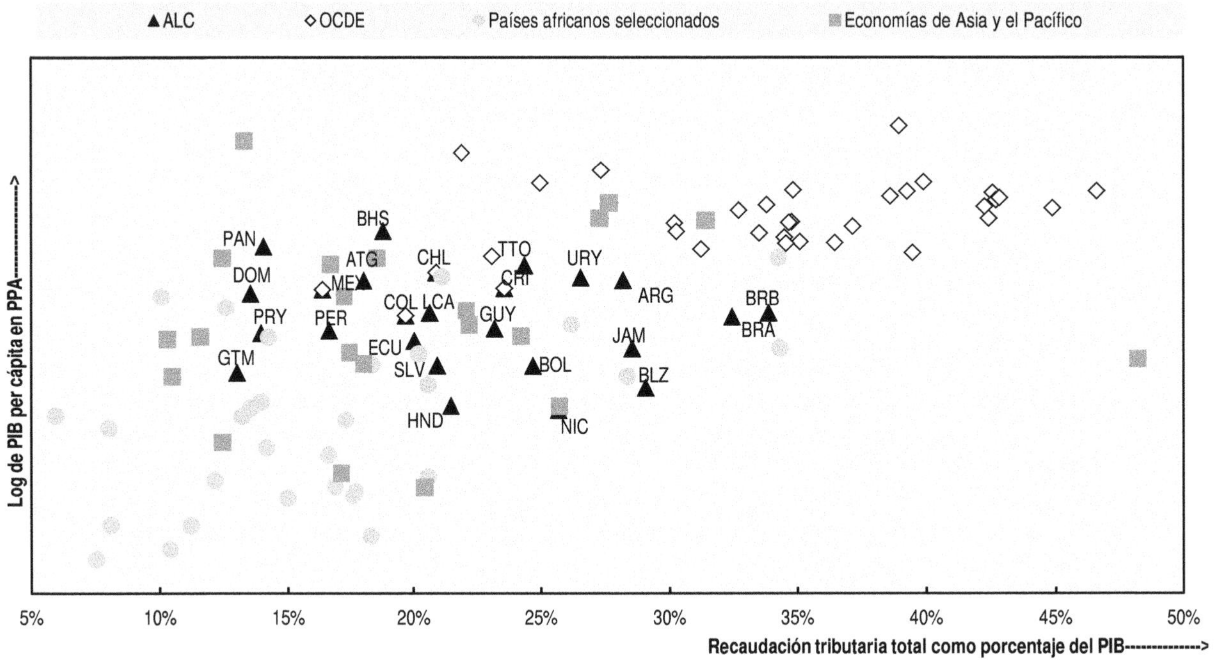


*Nota:* El año de comparación es 2019, dado que los datos relativos a la recaudación tributaria como proporción del PIB para 2020 no están disponibles para las economías seleccionadas de África, Asia y el Pacífico. No se incluyen Cuba y Venezuela debido a los problemas de disponibilidad de datos. La paridad de poder adquisitivo (PPA) entre dos países es el tipo de cambio entre las divisas de dos países para garantizar que una determinada suma en la moneda del primer país sirve para adquirir la misma cantidad de bienes y servicios en el segundo país. El tipo de conversión PPA implícito se expresa como moneda nacional por dólar internacional actual. El dólar internacional tiene el mismo poder adquisitivo que el dólar estadounidense en los Estados Unidos. El dólar internacional es una moneda hipotética que se utiliza como medio para convertir y comparar los costos de un país a otro utilizando un punto de referencia común: el dólar estadounidense (USD).

*Fuente:* (FMI, 2021[5]) para las cifras del PIB per cápita. La fuente de la recaudación tributaria como proporción del PIB es la base de datos de estadísticas tributarias mundiales *Global Revenue Statistics Database* (*http://www.oecd.org/tax/tax-policy/global-revenue-statistics-database.htm*).

StatLink https://doi.org/10.1787/888934307991

En general, los países de la OCDE tienen una renta media más elevada que los países de ALC y una mayor recaudación tributaria como proporción del PIB. Argentina, Barbados, Brasil y Uruguay presentan unos coeficientes tributarios y niveles de renta similares a los de algunos países de la OCDE. Los análisis empíricos sugieren que una recaudación impositiva más sólida, acompañada de unas mejores instituciones, educación y conocimientos y diversificación económica permitió a varios países de la OCDE evitar la trampa de las rentas medias, a diferencia de ALC (Melguizo et al., 2017[27]).

### *Evolución de la recaudación tributaria como proporción del PIB en el Caribe, América Central y México y América del Sur desde 1990*

El Gráfico 1.10 muestra la evolución, desde 1990, del promedio de recaudación tributaria como proporción del PIB de las tres subregiones de ALC. Aunque los niveles tributarios en las tres subregiones han mostrado una tendencia creciente durante las últimas tres décadas, sus trayectorias reflejan importantes diferencias:

- En promedio, América del Sur ha experimentado un fuerte crecimiento entre 1990 y 2020, de 8.2 p.p. América del Sur presentó el mayor aumento de su recaudación tributaria como proporción del PIB durante la década de 1990 y superó el promedio de ALC en 2004. Sin embargo, a partir de 2015, el cociente se fue acercando al promedio de ALC hasta que, en 2019 y 2020, se situó por debajo de él.

- El aumento del promedio de recaudación tributaria como proporción del PIB en América Central y México durante este periodo ha sido más gradual. Entre 1990 y 2020, la presión fiscal media de la subregión se mantuvo por debajo del promedio para la región de ALC.
- Entre 1990 y 2020, el promedio de recaudación tributaria como proporción del PIB del Caribe aumentó 4.6 p.p. y ha se ha mantenido constantemente por encima de la media de ALC. La diferencia se ha ensanchado entre 2017 y 2019, como consecuencia del relativamente pronunciado aumento de este cociente para el Caribe en estos dos años.

Gráfico 1.10. **Promedio de recaudación tributaria como proporción del PIB, ALC y subregiones, 1990-2020**

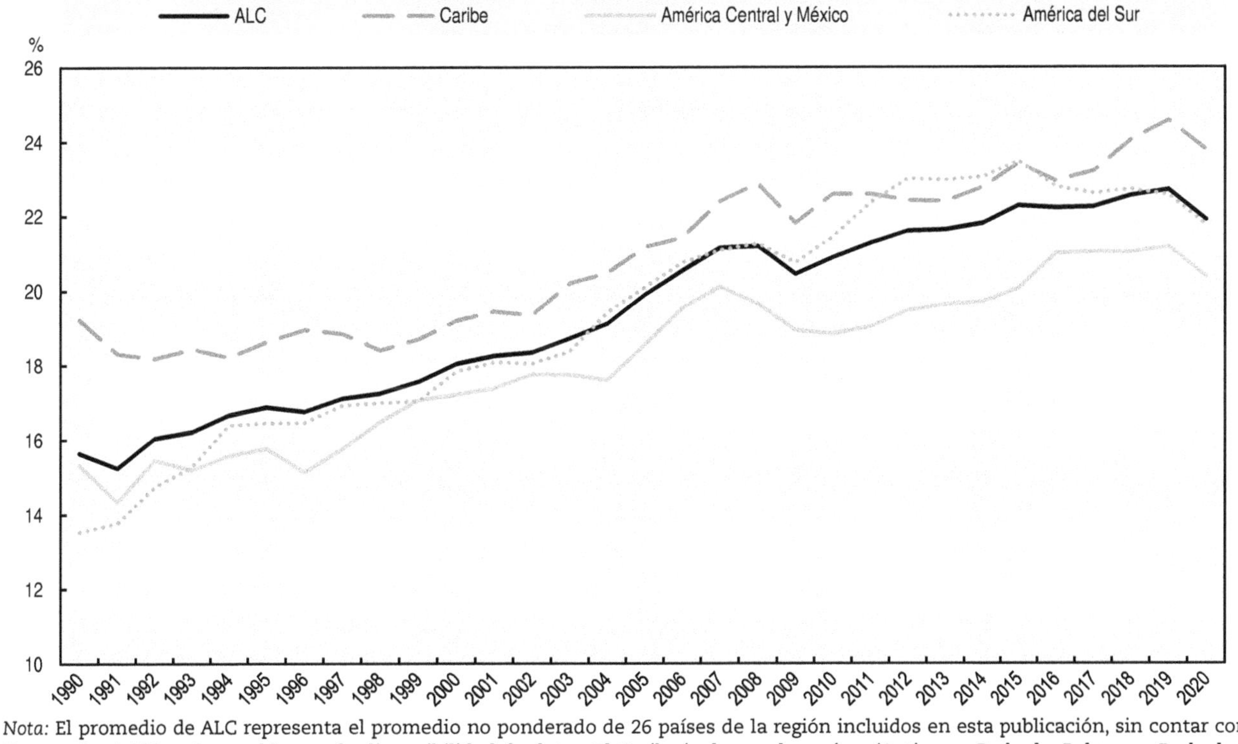


*Nota:* El promedio de ALC representa el promedio no ponderado de 26 países de la región incluidos en esta publicación, sin contar con Venezuela, debido a los problemas de disponibilidad de datos. El Caribe incluye ocho países (Antigua y Barbuda, Bahamas, Barbados, Belice, Guyana, Jamaica, Santa Lucía y Trinidad y Tobago), América Central y México, nueve países (Costa Rica, Cuba, República Dominicana, El Salvador, Guatemala, Honduras, México, Nicaragua y Panamá) y América del Sur, nueve países (Argentina, Bolivia, Brasil, Chile, Colombia, Ecuador, Paraguay, Perú y Uruguay). La clasificación de los países en las diferentes subregiones sigue la clasificación de CEPAL y se basa en el idioma oficial de cada uno de ellos. El Caribe comprende los países de habla inglesa y Guyana, mientras que América Central y México abarca países hispanohablantes e incluye a la República Dominicana y Cuba.

*Fuente:* Cálculos propios basados (OCDE et al., 2022[3]), «Revenue Statistics in Latin America: Comparative tables», *OECD Tax Statistics* (database), *http://dx.doi.org/10.1787/data-00641-en.*

StatLink https://doi.org/10.1787/888934308010

### *Evolución de la recaudación por tipo de impuesto desde 1990*

La recaudación tributaria como proporción del PIB en los países de ALC aumentó a principios de los años 1990, tras una década de inestabilidad macroeconómica. Durante los años ochenta, muchos países sufrieron grandes desequilibrios presupuestarios y algunos recurrieron a formas alternativas de financiación del gasto (préstamos o emisión de moneda), con lo que se originó una rápida inflación en toda la región, que menoscabó el valor real de los ingresos tributarios. Las reformas emprendidas en los años noventa se centraron en la estabilidad de los precios, la liberalización del comercio y la disciplina presupuestaria. La mayoría de los gobiernos de ALC redujeron el gasto y aplicaron políticas dirigidas a aumentar los ingresos tributarios; la gestión presupuestaria y el equilibrio presupuestario mejoraron de forma significativa. Los responsables políticos pusieron en marcha reformas en la política impositiva y la administración encaminadas a reforzar los regímenes tributarios frente a los episodios inflacionistas, reduciendo los desfases recaudatorios e indexando las deudas tributarias (CEPAL, 2018[33]).

La introducción del IVA ha sido la reforma tributaria más importante de ALC, en las últimas tres décadas. A principios de la década de 1990, casi todos los países estaban implantando el régimen del IVA y realizando reformas dirigidas a aumentar su tipo o tasa impositiva, a fin de ampliar la base imponible y aumentar la recaudación. Varios países han pasado a regímenes de IVA de tipo único (CEPAL, 2018[33]).

Durante las dos últimas décadas, los países de ALC han realizado grandes esfuerzos para modernizar la administración tributaria. Se han implantado sistemas informáticos nuevos, los sistemas de recaudación se han hecho más eficientes y el personal ha adquirido experiencia (BID, 2013[34]). Las reformas tributarias incluían la introducción o el desarrollo de regímenes simplificados para pequeños contribuyentes, la tributación de la propiedad en regímenes de rentas presuntas y la ampliación de la tributación a los rendimientos del trabajo y del capital, incluidos los dividendos. Las reformas también han incluido la creación de impuestos mínimos, impuestos sobre las operaciones financieras y reducciones graduales en el nivel de ingresos reales gravados al tipo marginal máximo (CEPAL, 2013[35]; CEPAL, 2018[33]).

Desde 1990, el incremento del promedio de recaudación tributaria como proporción del PIB de la región de ALC se ha visto en gran medida impulsado por los aumentos de la recaudación del impuesto sobre la renta y el IVA, que se alzaron 2.9 y 3.7 p.p., respectivamente, entre 1990 y 2019, antes de la caída de 0.2 p.p. que ambos sufrieron en 2020. En este año, la recaudación del IVA equivalía al 5.7% del PIB, mientras que los ingresos procedentes de los impuestos sobre la renta y los beneficios representaban el 5.9% del PIB (Gráfico 1.11).

Entre 1990 y 2020, la recaudación en ALC de otros impuestos sobre el consumo se redujo como porcentaje del PIB. Además de la reducción de 0.5 p.p. sufrida en 2020, como consecuencia de la pandemia de COVID-19, se ha producido una reducción a largo plazo asociada a la liberación del mercado, cuyo resultado fue que los países de ALC cambiaron la forma de gravar los bienes importados y exportados, así como determinados bienes y servicios. Estos cambios incluyeron una reducción de los derechos de importación, la limitación de la base de productos y servicios sujetos a impuestos especiales y la eliminación de los impuestos sobre las exportaciones. Una importante excepción es Argentina, donde los impuestos sobre las exportaciones se restablecieron en 2002, se abolieron parcialmente en 2015 y se reintrodujeron en septiembre de 2018.

Gráfico 1.11. **Recaudación de algunos impuestos en la región de ALC, 1990-2020**

Porcentaje del PIB

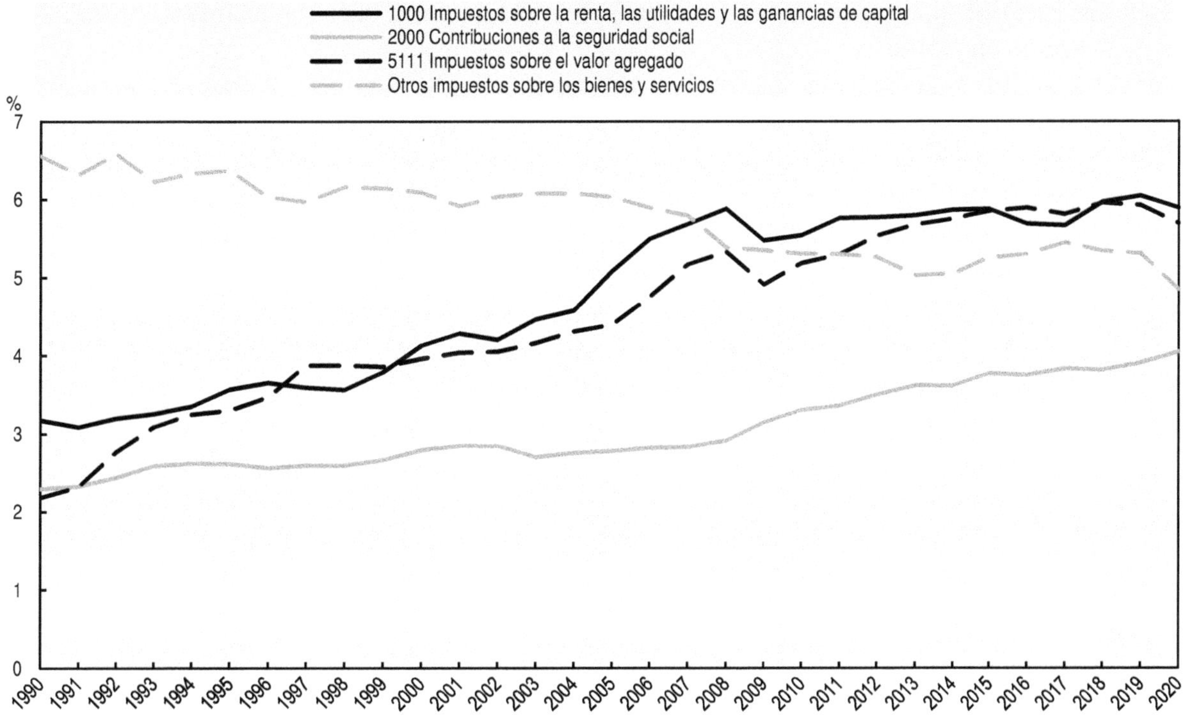


*Nota:* El promedio de ALC representa el promedio no ponderado de 26 países de ALC incluidos en esta publicación, se excluye a Venezuela, dada la falta de datos disponibles.

*Fuente:* Cálculos propios basados en OCDE et al. (OCDE et al., 2022[3]), «Revenue Statistics in Latin America: Comparative tables», *OECD Tax Statistics* (database), *http://dx.doi.org/10.1787/data-00641-en*.

StatLink https://doi.org/10.1787/888934308029

Pueden diferenciarse cinco etapas en la evolución de los ingresos tributarios:

- Entre 1990 and 2002, el IVA contribuyó más al aumento de los ingresos tributarios que los impuestos sobre la renta y los beneficios (el 1.4% del PIB frente al 1.0%). Durante este periodo, cinco países introdujeron el IVA (Barbados, Belice, El Salvador, Jamaica y Paraguay). Otros países aumentaron sus tipos generales de IVA y emprendieron reformas para incrementar la base imponible y la recaudación tributaria.
- Entre 2002 y 2008, se produjo el efecto contrario: los ingresos procedentes de los impuestos sobre la renta y los beneficios contribuyeron más que los del IVA al aumento de la recaudación tributaria como proporción del PIB (los incrementos representaron el 1.7% y el 1.3% del PIB, respectivamente). El incremento de los impuestos sobre la renta se explica, en parte, por la fuerte alza que experimentaron los precios de los productos básicos a partir de 2003, que impulsó los ingresos por el IS del sector de los recursos naturales (CEPAL, 2014[32]; Barreix, Benítez and Pecho, 2017[36]). En varios países, este incremento también se explica por las políticas que redujeron los estímulos fiscales en las zonas de libre comercio, la introducción de impuestos mínimos para las sociedades, las reformas en la tributación internacional y los acuerdos entre países para luchar contra la evasión de impuestos.
- El IVA y los ingresos procedentes de los impuestos sobre la renta sufrieron un fuerte descenso durante la crisis financiera mundial. Durante la recuperación posterior, la recaudación del IVA aumentó rápidamente hasta alcanzar el 5.9% del PIB, en 2016, un

nivel similar al de los ingresos procedentes del impuesto sobre la renta. Durante este periodo, dos nuevos países del Caribe introdujeron el IVA (Santa Lucía, en 2012, y Bahamas, en 2015). Los precios de los productos básicos se redujeron de forma constante y, en 2015, cayeron en picado.

- Entre 2016 y el principio de la crisis de COVID-19, se recuperaron los precios de los productos básicos y repuntaron los ingresos procedentes del impuesto sobre la renta. Entre 2017 y 2018, los ingresos por impuestos sobre la renta experimentaron su mayor aumento desde 2011, de 0.3 p.p. en promedio, gracias a las fuertes ganancias generadas en los sectores de la minería y extracción de gas y petróleo. En 2019, este aumento (impulsado por la recaudación del IS) fue más moderado, de 0.1 p.p.
- En 2020, todas las categorías de impuestos principales, salvo el IRPF y las contribuciones a la seguridad social, sufrieron un descenso como consecuencia de la pandemia de COVID-19, tal y como se ha explicado en el apartado anterior.

El Gráfico 1.12 muestra la evolución del IS y el IRPF desde 2005. En 2020, los promedios de los ingresos por estos dos impuestos en ALC se situaron en el 3.4% y el 2.2% del PIB, respectivamente. En este periodo, la recaudación del IS como ha sido más volátil que la del IRPF, que ha ido aumentando de forma constante en toda la región y resistió mejor la crisis financiera mundial y la del COVID-19.

Gráfico 1.12. **Recaudación de los impuestos sobre la renta y los beneficios, IS e IRPF en la región de ALC, 2005-20**

Porcentaje del PIB

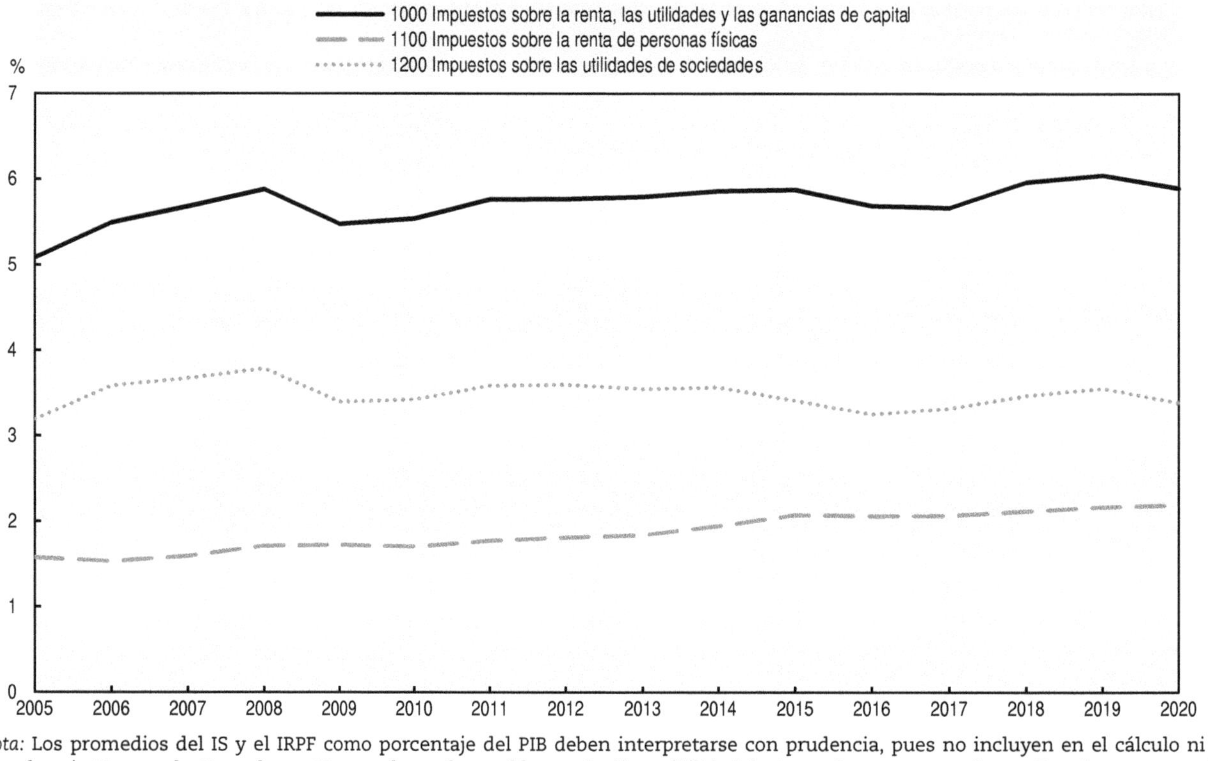


*Nota:* Los promedios del IS y el IRPF como porcentaje del PIB deben interpretarse con prudencia, pues no incluyen en el cálculo ni a Ecuador ni a Venezuela. Se excluye a Venezuela por los problemas de disponibilidad de datos. A su vez, se excluye a Ecuador porque más de un tercio de los ingresos procedentes de los impuestos sobre la renta y los beneficios no pueden atribuirse a los ingresos por el IS (1200) ni el IRPF (1100).

*Fuente:* (OCDE et al., 2022[3]), «Revenue Statistics in Latin America and the Caribbean: Comparative tables», *OECD Tax Statistics* (database), *http://dx.doi.org/10.1787/data-00641-en.*

StatLink https://doi.org/10.1787/888934308048

En las últimas tres décadas se aprecian importantes diferencias en la evolución de las principales categorías tributarias entre las tres subregiones de ALC:

- En las últimas tres décadas, el Caribe registró un considerable aumento del promedio de ingresos del IVA como porcentaje del PIB. Siete de los ocho países caribeños implantaron[2] el régimen del IVA durante este periodo, más tarde que la mayoría de los países de América Central y México y América del Sur. Los ingresos por IVA fueron el principal impulsor del aumento que experimentó la recaudación tributaria total como proporción del PIB del Caribe durante este periodo.
- En América Central y México y en América del Sur, los impuestos sobre la renta y los beneficios fueron los que más contribuyeron al aumento de la recaudación tributaria total como proporción del PIB, seguida de la recaudación del IVA. El aumento de los precios de los minerales y el petróleo, entre 2003 y 2010, condicionó los ingresos procedentes de los impuestos sobre la renta y los beneficios (e indirectamente del IVA).

## Estructuras tributarias

La estructura tributaria (definida como la participación de los principales tipos de impuestos en la recaudación tributaria total) refleja la composición de los ingresos tributarios según los diferentes tipos de impuestos. Se trata de un importante indicador para entender los efectos económicos y sociales de los regímenes tributarios en la región de ALC.

### *Evolución de las estructuras tributarias*

En 2020, los impuestos sobre bienes y servicios representaron la mayor proporción de los ingresos tributarios totales en la región de ALC, lo que constituye, en promedio, cerca de la mitad de la tributación total. Durante las últimas tres décadas, la estructura tributaria, en promedio, de ALC se ha desplazado hacia el IVA, los impuestos sobre la renta y los beneficios y las contribuciones a la seguridad social y se ha alejado de otros impuestos sobre sobre bienes y servicios.

- En 2020, la participación de la recaudación del IVA en los ingresos tributarios totales alcanzó el 27.5%, que representa un aumento de 12.0 p.p. desde 1990. La participación en la recaudación de otros impuestos sobre bienes y servicios (como los impuestos especiales, y los derechos de aduana y de importación) se redujo 21.3 p.p., durante el mismo periodo (Gráfico 1.13).
- Entre 1990 y 2020, la participación de la recaudación de los impuestos sobre la renta y los beneficios creció 7.4 p.p. (del 19.5% al 26.9% de los ingresos tributarios totales).
- Desde 1990, la participación de las contribuciones a la seguridad social en los ingresos tributarios totales ha aumentado 4.5 p.p. hasta alcanzar el 18.4%, en 2020. Dos factores fundamentales (y opuestos) han influido en la trayectoria de las contribuciones a la seguridad social en la región. Aunque el aumento de la base imponible regular se tradujo en una mayor recaudación, esta se vio contrarrestada por la privatización total o parcial de la seguridad social que se produjo en muchos países, sobre todo entre mediados de los años noventa y 2010 (OCDE et al., 2015[30]).

La participación de la recaudación del IRPF en los ingresos tributarios totales creció del 7.7%, en 2005, al 9.8%, en 2020, en parte, gracias al incremento de las rentas de las personas físicas en toda la región, durante las últimas dos décadas, antes del impacto del COVID-19. No obstante, la participación media de la recaudación del IRPF se mantiene en niveles bajos en los países de ALC, a pesar de que algunos países han introducido reformas para ampliar su base imponible.

Gráfico 1.13. **Estructura tributaria promedio en la región de ALC, 1990-2020**

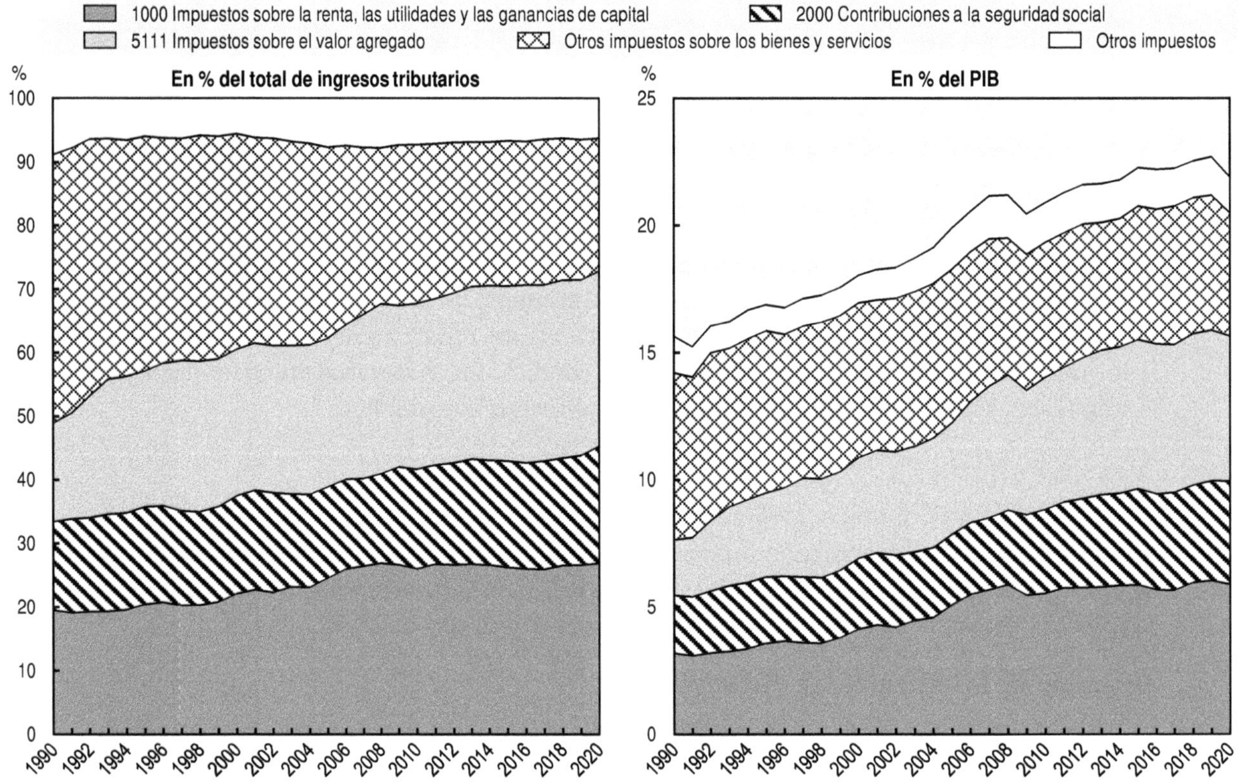


*Nota:* El promedio de ALC representa el promedio no ponderado de 26 países de la región incluidos en esta publicación, sin contar con Venezuela, debido a los problemas de disponibilidad de datos.

*Fuente:* Cálculos propios basados en (OCDE et al., 2022[3]), Capítulo 4.

StatLink https://doi.org/10.1787/888934308067

Tras la crisis financiera mundial, varios países establecieron tipos fijos sobre las rentas del capital que antes estaban exentas y aplicaron tipos progresivos sobre las rentas del trabajo (CEPAL, 2014[32]). Recientemente, Ecuador emprendió una nueva reforma tributaria, que entró en vigor a principios de 2022, que afecta al IRPF y a la tributación de la riqueza, los beneficios y los activos extranjeros. Además de impulsar el aumento de los ingresos impositivos, esta reforma tributaria debería mejorar la progresividad en Ecuador.

En la región de ALC, hay relativamente pocos sujetos pasivos del IRPF, pues la mayor parte de la población se concentra en los niveles de bajos ingresos: en 2013, solo el 10% de la población de América Latina estaba registrado como contribuyentes (BID, 2013[34]).

Existe otra serie de factores que contribuyen a limitar los ingresos del IRPF, como la existencia de una base imponible reducida integrada principalmente por salarios (puesto que los privilegios fiscales se suelen otorgar a los rendimientos del capital) y los elevados niveles de evasión (Barreix, Benítez and Pecho, 2017[36]; CEPAL, 2014[32]). En (CEPAL, 2020[26]), se concluye que existen unas altas tasas de evasión del IRPF en determinados países de ALC, según los datos que arrojan estudios efectuados sobre la evasión de impuestos, que oscilan entre el 18.7%, en México (cifra de 2016, equivalente a unas pérdidas de ingresos tributarios del 0.8% del PIB), y el 69.9%, en Guatemala (cifra de 2016, equivalente a unas pérdidas de ingresos tributarios del 0.5% del PIB). La evasión es más habitual entre los autónomos que entre los trabajadores por cuenta ajena. Un estudio relativo a México que desglosa el porcentaje de evasión en función de diferentes grupos concluyó que las pérdidas de ingresos tributarios como porcentaje del PIB es casi cinco veces superior entre personas que desarrollan actividades profesionales que entre asalariados (CEPAL, 2020[26]).

Gráfico 1.14. **Estructura tributaria promedio en la región de ALC, 2005-20**

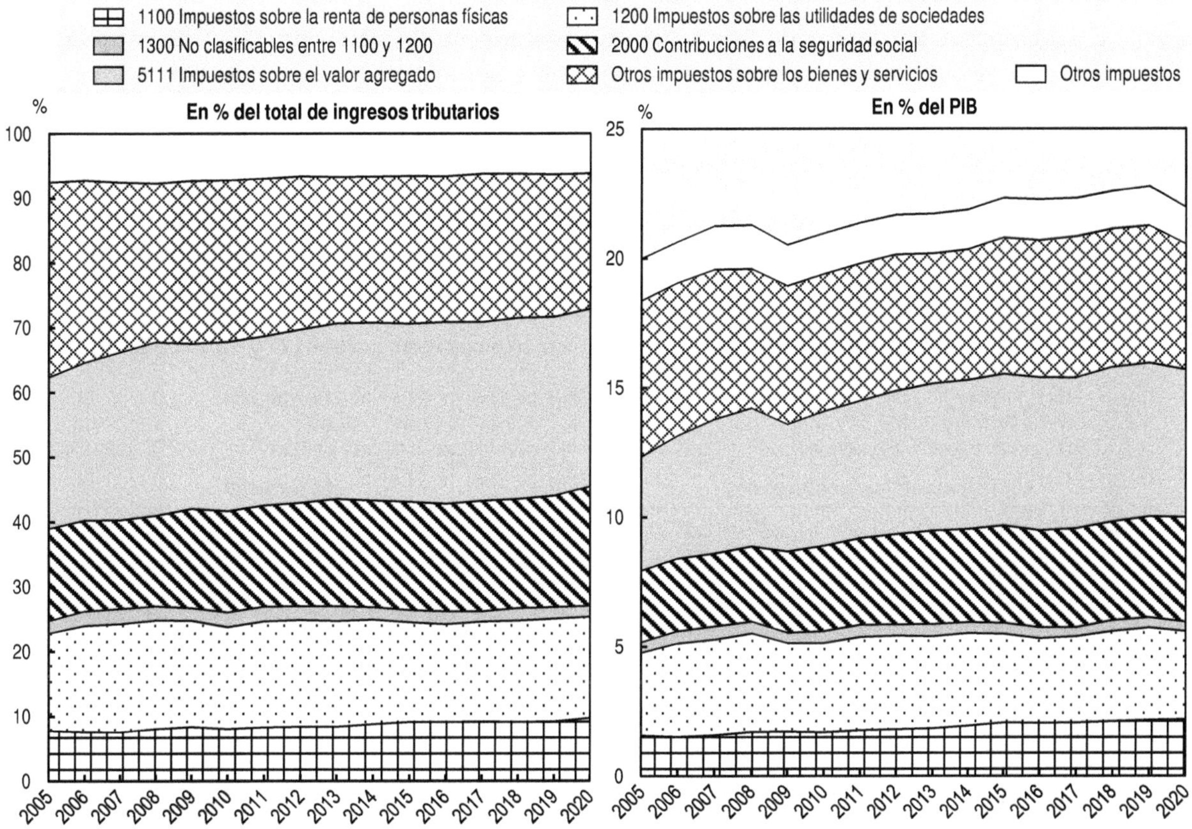


*Nota:* El promedio del IS y el IRPF como porcentaje del PIB debe interpretarse con prudencia puesto que Ecuador y Venezuela no están incluidos en el cálculo. El promedio de ALC excluye a Venezuela por los problemas de disponibilidad de datos. Se excluye a Ecuador del promedio de la recaudación del IS como porcentaje del PIB para ALC porque más de un tercio de los ingresos procedentes de los impuestos sobre la renta y los beneficios no pueden atribuirse a los ingresos por el IS (1200) ni el IRPF (1100).

*Fuente:* Cálculos propios basados en (OCDE et al., 2022[3]), «Revenue Statistics in Latin America: Comparative tables», *OECD Tax Statistics* (database), *http://dx.doi.org/10.1787/data-00641-en*.

StatLink https://doi.org/10.1787/888934308086

La participación del IS en los ingresos tributarios totales aumentó 0.5 p.p. entre 2005 y 2020, alcanzando el 15.6% durante el último año. La evasión del impuesto sobre sociedades también es un importante problema en la región de ALC, con unas elevadas tasas de evasión, superiores a las del IRPF. En (CEPAL, 2020[26]) se afirma que «las tasas de evasión en el impuesto sobre sociedades oscilan entre el 19.9%, de México, a casi el 80%, de Guatemala». Como consecuencia de las elevadas tasas de evasión, se calcula que las pérdidas de recaudación superan el 4% del PIB en la República Dominicana, Guatemala, Perú y Panamá.

En 2020, se produjeron notables diferencias en la estructura tributaria promedio en todas las subregiones. En el Caribe, la mayor participación en los ingresos correspondía a los impuestos sobre bienes y servicios distintos del IVA, que, en promedio, representaba el 27.9% de los ingresos tributarios totales. Por el contrario, en 2020, América del Sur presentó la mayor participación del IVA, con un 30.3% de media, frente al 27.5%, en el Caribe, y el 24.7%, en América Central y México. En 2020, las contribuciones a la seguridad social más bajas fueron las del Caribe, que representaron el 12.9% de los ingresos tributarios totales, en promedio. Esta cifra se sitúa ligeramente por debajo de la media de las otras subregiones (el 20.9%, tanto en América Central y México como en América del Sur). Las tres subregiones generaron más ingresos procedentes del IS que del IRPF.

### *Estructura tributaria promedio en ALC y la OCDE*

La composición media de la estructura tributaria de la región de ALC refleja unos ingresos más bajos procedentes del impuesto sobre la renta de las personas físicas y las contribuciones a la seguridad social que el promedio de la OCDE (Gráfico 1.15). En particular, los países de ALC dependen fuertemente de los impuestos sobre bienes y servicios, que representan, en promedio, algo menos de la mitad de los ingresos tributarios, frente al aproximadamente un tercio de las economías de la OCDE. Sin embargo, como porcentaje del PIB, en 2019, la recaudación procedente de los impuestos sobre bienes y servicios en ALC y la OCDE fueron similares, un 11.2% y un 10.8%, respectivamente[3].

Gráfico 1.15. **Estructura tributaria promedio en las regiones de ALC y la OCDE, 2019**

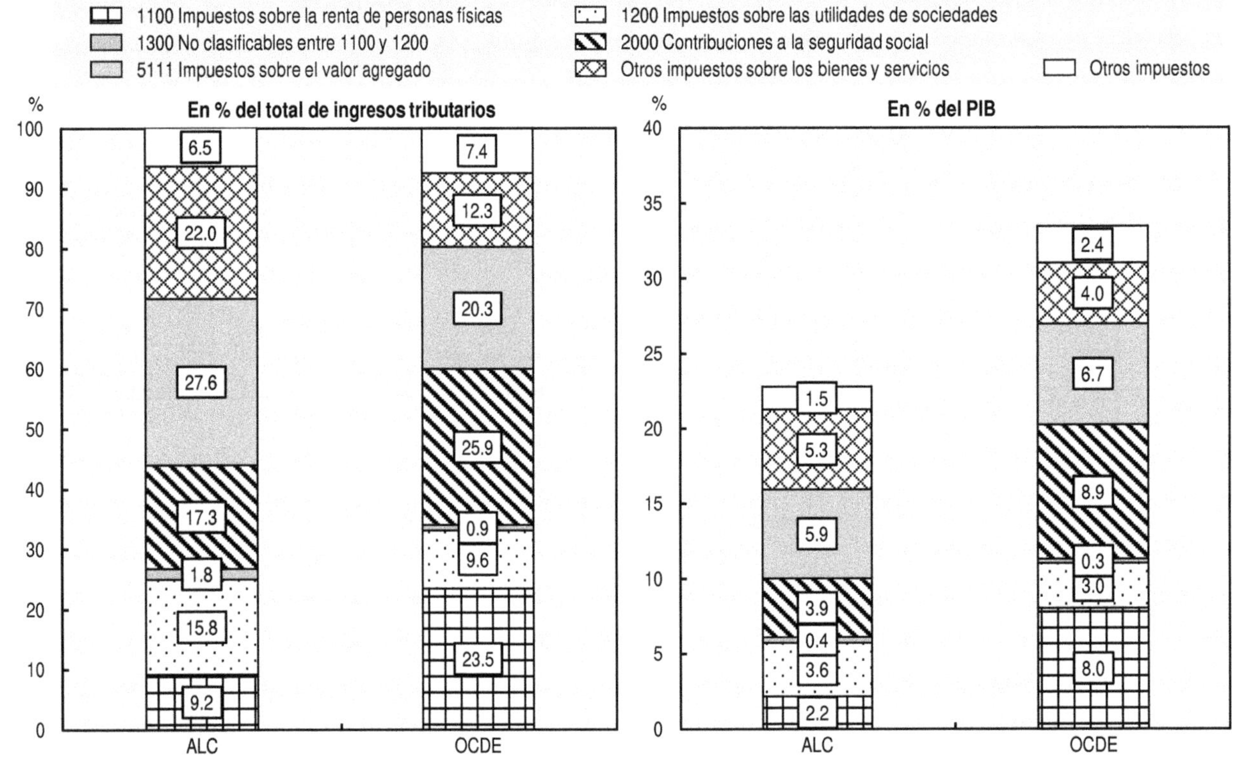


*Nota:* El año de comparación es 2019, puesto que los datos relativos al promedio de la OCDE del año 2020 no están disponibles. Los promedios del IS y el IRPF como porcentaje del PIB para ALC deben interpretarse con prudencia, puesto que en los cálculos no se incluyen ni Ecuador ni Venezuela. Se excluye a Venezuela del promedio de ALC por los problemas de disponibilidad de datos. A su vez, se excluye a Ecuador del promedio de ALC relativo a la recaudación del IS y del IRPF como porcentaje del PIB porque más de un tercio de los ingresos procedentes de los impuestos sobre la renta y los beneficios no pueden atribuirse a los ingresos por el IS (1200) ni el IRPF (1100). El promedio de la OCDE representa el promedio no ponderado de los 38 países miembros de la OCDE. Chile, Colombia, Costa Rica y México también forman parte de la OCDE (38).

*Fuente:* Cálculos propios basados en (OCDE et al., 2022[3]), «Revenue Statistics in Latin America: Comparative tables», *OECD Tax Statistics* (database), *http://dx.doi.org/10.1787/data-00641-en*.

StatLink *https://doi.org/10.1787/888934308105*

Por el contrario, la participación combinada de los impuestos sobre la renta y los beneficios y las contribuciones a la seguridad social fue mucho menor en la región de ALC que en la OCDE (el 44.1% frente al 60.0%, en 2019, como promedio). Como porcentaje del

PIB, estas dos categorías alcanzaron el 10.0% en la región de ALC, menos de la mitad del promedio de la OCDE (que se sitúa en el 20.2%). Esta diferencia se explica por la tendencia a privatizar las prestaciones de la seguridad social en muchos países de ALC.

Como promedio, el IS generó el 15.8% de los ingresos tributarios totales en la región de ALC frente al 9.6% en la zona de la OCDE (el 3.6% y el 3.0% del PIB, respectivamente) (Gráfico 1.15). La diferencia más llamativa entre los promedios de ambas regiones se relaciona con la recaudación del IRPF, que, en 2019, representó el 23.5% de los ingresos tributarios totales en la OCDE y el 9.2% en la región de ALC. Como promedio, la recaudación del IRPF supuso el 2.2% del PIB, en la región de ALC, frente al 8.0% en la OCDE.

En la región de ALC, los impuestos sobre los bienes inmuebles y las nóminas (que se incluyen en la categoría «otros impuestos»), en promedio, son una fuente de ingresos menos relevante que en la OCDE, aunque hay dificultades de disponibilidad de datos relativos a los impuestos sobre la propiedad.

### *Estructura tributaria en los países de ALC*

Los impuestos sobre los bienes y servicios son la principal fuente de ingresos en todos los países de ALC, excepto en México, Panamá y Trinidad y Tobago. En México y Trinidad y Tobago, la recaudación procedente de los impuestos sobre la renta y los beneficios representa la mayor proporción, mientras que, en Panamá, la principal fuente de ingresos son las contribuciones a la seguridad social (Gráfico 1.16).

Gráfico 1.16. **Estructuras tributarias en los países de ALC, 2020**

% de los ingresos tributarios totales

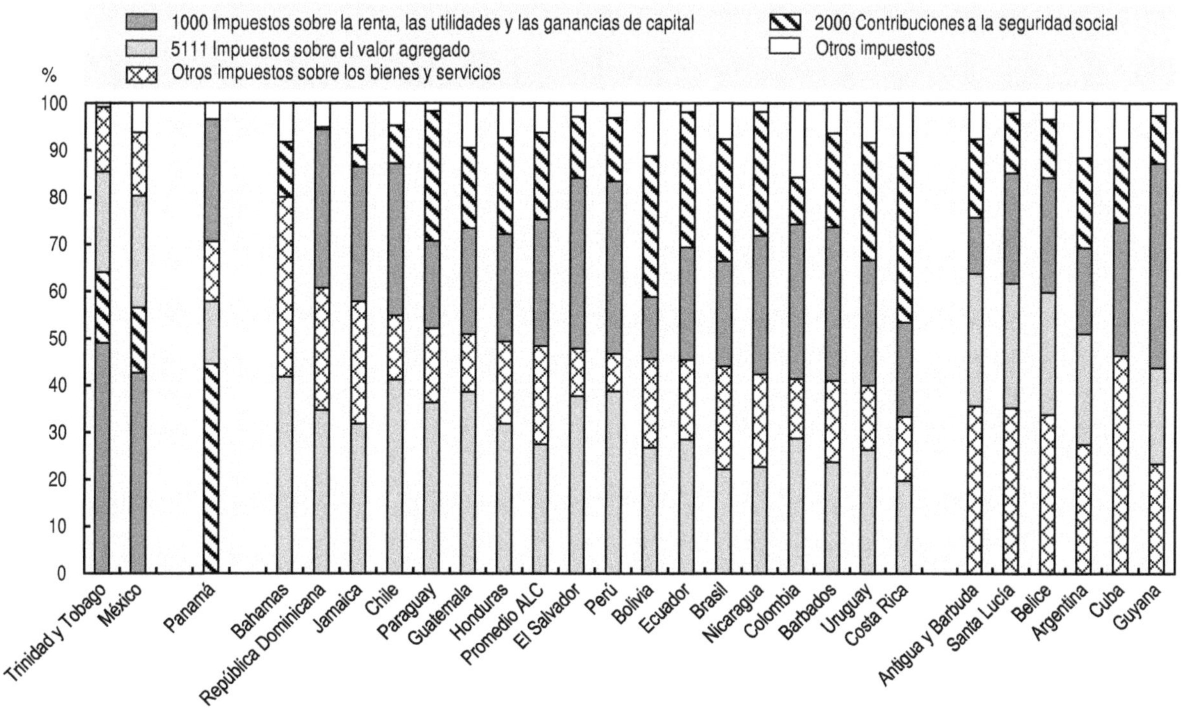


*Nota:* Los países están agrupados en función de la principal proporción de ingresos tributarios entre 1000 Impuestos sobre la renta y los beneficios, 2000 Contribuciones a la seguridad social, 5111 Impuestos sobre el valor añadido y otros impuestos sobre bienes y servicios. Bahamas no grava la renta. En Cuba, no existe el régimen del IVA. El promedio de ALC representa el promedio no ponderado de 26 países de ALC incluidos en esta publicación, sin contar con Venezuela por los problemas de disponibilidad de datos.

*Fuente:* Cálculos propios basados en (OCDE et al., 2022[3]), Capítulo 4.

StatLink https://doi.org/10.1787/888934308124

En la mayoría de los países en los que los impuestos sobre bienes y servicios son la principal fuente de ingresos, la recaudación del IVA supuso una mayor proporción que la de los impuestos sobre bienes y servicios distintos del IVA, tales como los impuestos especiales y los derechos de importación. Dieciocho países presentaron mayores ingresos tributarios procedentes del IVA, que variaban desde el 26.3% de la recaudación total, en Uruguay, al 41.8%, en las Bahamas. Por el contrario, en cinco países (de los cuales, cuatro eran del Caribe), la mayor proporción de la recaudación procedía de los impuestos sobre bienes y servicios distintos del IVA. En este grupo se incluye a Argentina, que obtuvo el 27.6% de sus ingresos tributarios totales de impuestos sobre bienes y servicios distintos del IVA: los impuestos a la exportación representaron casi una cuarta parte de esta categoría y equivalían al 1.9% del PIB, frente al menos del 0.1% del PIB, en promedio, de la región.

En 2020, las contribuciones a la seguridad social oscilaron entre el 0.5% de los ingresos tributarios totales de la República Dominicana y el 44.6%, de Panamá. El nivel de estos ingresos refleja las opciones de financiación de la seguridad social (véase Recuadro 1.2): en países que cuentan con sistemas de seguridad social públicos o mixtos (como Argentina, Brasil, Costa Rica, Panamá, Paraguay y Uruguay), las contribuciones a la seguridad social representaron más del 20% de los ingresos tributarios totales.

## Ingresos tributarios relacionados con el medioambiente

A raíz del Acuerdo de París de 2016, los países se han comprometido a reducir las emisiones de carbono de sus economías para mediados de siglo, lo que implica el abandono de los combustibles fósiles como fuente de energía. En muchos países, los impuestos relacionados con el medioambiente y, en general, los instrumentos políticos basados en los precios desempeñan un papel cada vez más importante. Al introducir una señal de precios en las decisiones del consumidor, estos impuestos aplican el principio de «quien contamina, paga» y fomentan que tanto las empresas como los hogares se planteen los costes ambientales de sus acciones.

Un impuesto relacionado con el medioambiente es un impuesto cuya base es una unidad física (o un equivalente a una unidad física) de algo que tiene un efecto negativo específico y contrastado sobre el medioambiente, con independencia de si el impuesto tiene por objeto cambiar las conductas o si persigue otro propósito (OCDE, 2005[37]).

Un análisis pormenorizado de los impuestos específicos de cada país[4] para los 24 países de ALC incluidos en este informe demuestra que, en promedio, los ingresos por impuestos relacionados con el medioambiente representaron el 1.0%[5] del PIB, en 2020, un nivel inferior que el promedio de la OCDE, que se situó en el 2.0% del PIB (cifra estimada de 2020) (OCDE, 2021[38]).

En 2020, los ingresos por impuestos sobre la energía (normalmente, impuestos especiales sobre el diésel y la gasolina) representaron la mayor proporción de los ingresos por impuestos relacionados con el medioambiente totales en la región de ALC. En 2020, los ingresos procedentes de los productos energéticos ascendieron al 0.7% del PIB, en promedio, y representaron cerca del 65.6% de los ingresos por impuestos medioambientales. Los ingresos procedentes de los impuestos de circulación y sobre los servicios de transporte equivalieron al 0.3% del PIB y representaron la mayor proporción del resto (32.5%) de los ingresos por impuestos relacionados con el medioambiente. Los ingresos procedentes de impuestos que gravan otras bases relacionadas con el medioambiente fueron insignificantes. Los ingresos por impuestos relacionados con el medioambiente en la OCDE fueron más elevados que en la región de ALC para todas las bases imponibles, sobre todo, respecto a los impuestos relacionados con la energía y los transportes (OCDE, 2021[38]). En 2020, los promedios de la OCDE para los ingresos procedentes de impuestos relacionados con la energía y el transporte alcanzaron el 1.4% y el 0.5% del PIB, respectivamente.

En 2020, hubo importantes diferencias en la composición media de los ingresos por impuestos relacionados con el medioambiente entre las subregiones (Gráfico 1.17). Mientras que, en América Central y México y en América del Sur, los ingresos procedentes de impuestos relacionados con la energía representaron la mayor proporción en los ingresos por impuestos relacionados con el medioambiente; en el Caribe, la mayor participación procedía de los impuestos sobre el transporte. Estos últimos, en América Central y México y en América del Sur, fueron del 0.2% y el 0.3% del PIB, respectivamente, mientras que, en el Caribe, ascendieron al 0.5% del PIB. En la mayoría de los países del Caribe, los ingresos procedentes de impuestos relacionados con el transporte procedían principalmente de las tasas de viaje o salida, una importante fuente de ingresos en países que dependen del turismo.

Gráfico 1.17. **Recaudación por impuestos relacionados con el medioambiente en la OCDE, ALC y subregiones, en promedio, por base imponible principal, 2020**

Porcentaje del PIB

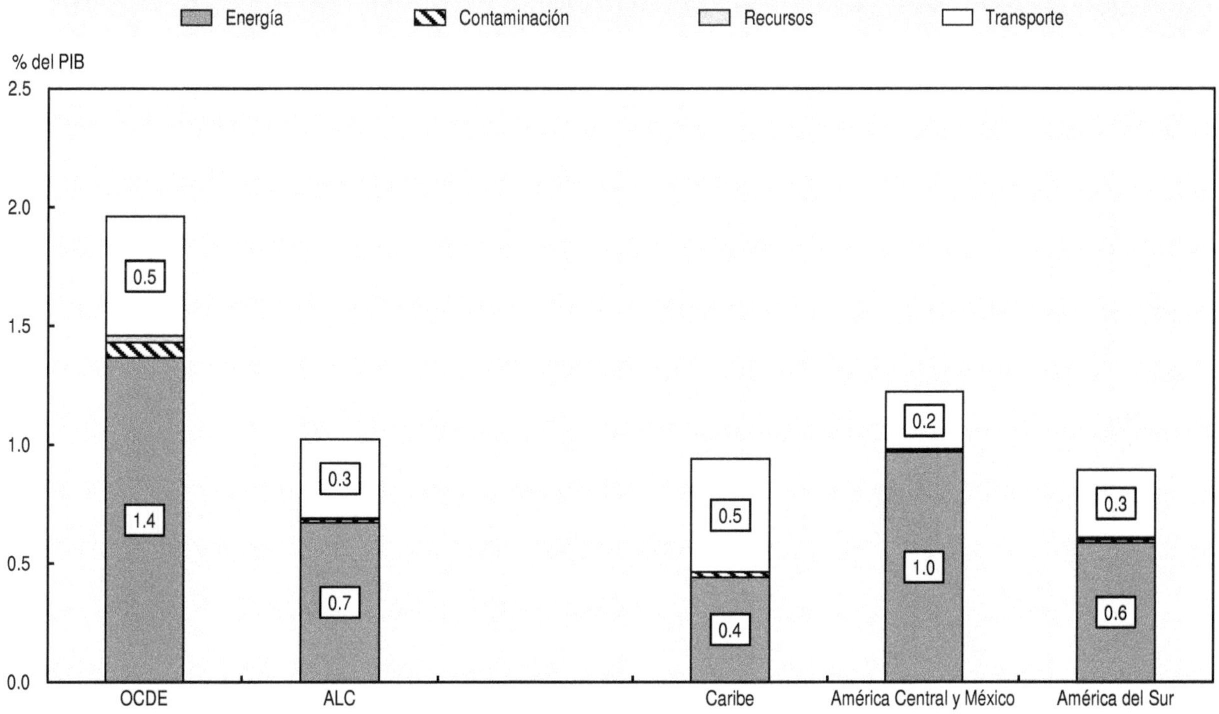


*Nota:* El promedio de ALC representa el promedio no ponderado de 24 países de ALC incluidos en esta publicación, sin contar con Cuba,Costa Rica y Venezuela por los problemas de disponibilidad de datos. El promedio de la OCDE representa el promedio no ponderado de los 38 países miembros de la OCDE. Chile, Colombia y México también forman parte de la OCDE.

*Fuente:* Base de datos *PINE* para Chile, Colombia,y México y cálculos propios para los demás países basados (OCDE et al., 2022[3]), Capítulo 5.

StatLink https://doi.org/10.1787/888934308143

Entre 2019 y 2020, los ingresos por impuestos relacionados con el medioambiente en la región de ALC se redujeron 0.1 p.p., un descenso similar al que experimentaron, en promedio, los países de la OCDE. En la región de ALC, este descenso se debió por igual a la disminución de los ingresos procedentes de los impuestos sobre la energía y sobre el transporte. La mayoría de las reducciones en los impuestos sobre la energía se debieron, en parte, a la caída de los impuestos especiales sobre los combustibles como consecuencia de las restricciones a la movilidad relacionadas con el COVID-19, los confinamientos y el teletrabajo.

Estos factores también tuvieron un importante impacto en los ingresos procedentes de impuestos relacionados con el transporte, en particular, contribuyeron al desplome de las llegadas de turistas que afectaron a los ingresos derivados de las tasas de viaje y salida, sobre todo, en el Caribe. Entre 2019 y 2020, el Caribe registró el mayor descenso en el promedio de ingresos por impuestos medioambientales (0.3 p.p. frente al descenso de 0.1 p.p. en América Central y México, y la misma situación anterior, en América del Sur). Entre 2019 y 2020, las mayores caídas se produjeron en los ingresos procedentes de los impuestos sobre la energía y los impuestos relacionados con el transporte, en el Caribe, y de los impuestos sobre la energía, en América Central y México, en todos casos de 0.1 p.p.

En 2020, los ingresos por impuestos relacionados con el medioambiente oscilaron entre el 0.1% del PIB, en Belice, y el 2.8%, en Guyana (Gráfico 1.18). En Guyana, ese mismo año, el impuesto sobre la importación de productos petrolíferos representó el 1.7% del PIB.

Gráfico 1.18. **Ingresos por impuestos medioambientales en los países de ALC, por base imponible principal, 2020**

Porcentaje del PIB

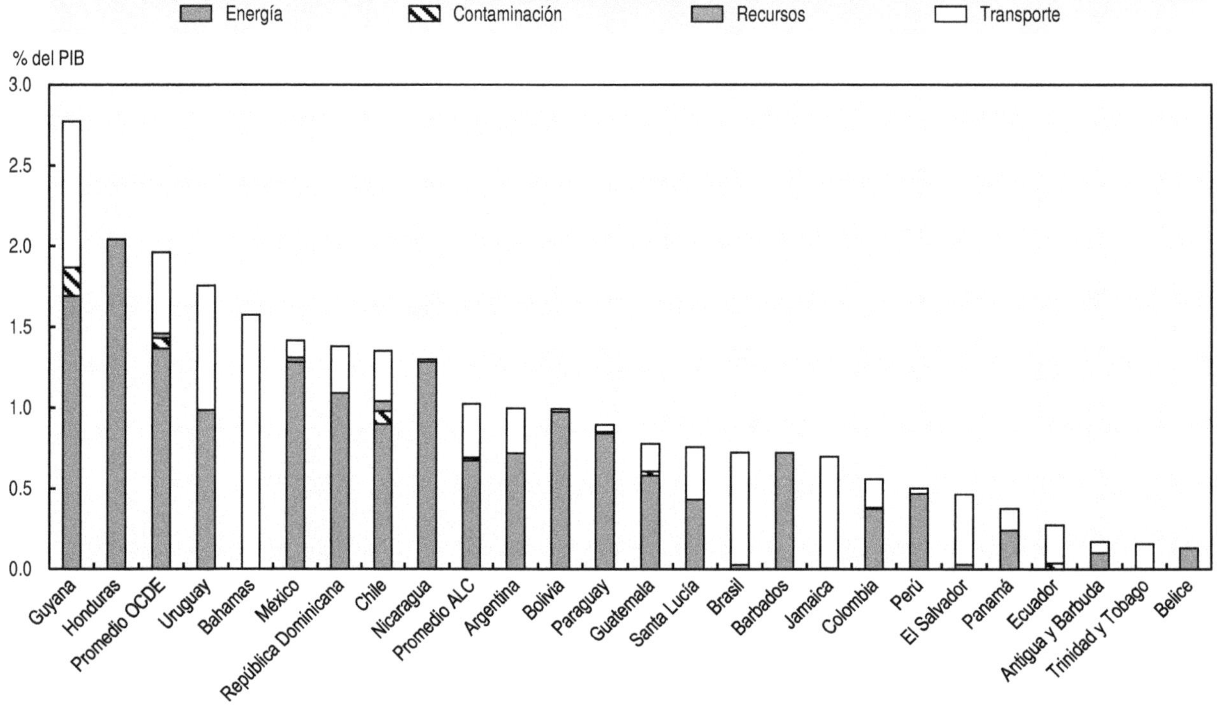


*Nota:* El promedio de ALC representa el promedio no ponderado de 24 países de ALC incluidos en esta publicación, sin contar con Cuba, Costa Rica y Venezuela por los problemas de disponibilidad de datos. El gráfico no incluye los ingresos procedentes de impuestos especiales sobre el consumo de productos petrolíferos de Jamaica (que se calcula que fue superior al 2.0% del PIB, en 2018) (OCDE, 2021[39]), puesto que los datos no están disponibles. Chile, Colombia y México también forman parte de la OCDE.

*Fuente:* Base de datos *PINE* para Chile, Colombia y México y cálculos propios para los demás países basados en (OCDE et al., 2022[3]), Capítulo 5.

StatLink https://doi.org/10.1787/888934308162

Entre 2019 y 2020, 14 de los 24 países de ALC para los que se dispone de datos registraron un descenso de los ingresos por impuestos medioambientales. Guyana sufrió la caída más acusada, de 1.4 p.p., durante este periodo. Los descensos en los demás países de ALC que vieron caer sus ingresos por impuestos medioambientales fueron más modestos y oscilaron entre 0.1 p.p., en Antigua y Barbuda, y 0.6 p.p., en Jamaica. El descenso en Jamaica se debió a la caída que experimentaron los ingresos procedentes de las tasas de viaje durante este periodo.

Los países de ALC han tardado en aplicar los impuestos medioambientales. Aunque se han introducido impuestos sobre los combustibles (más para percibir ingresos que por finalidades medioambientales), muchos países también ofrecen subvenciones a los productos energéticos (Lorenzo, 2016[40]) para mitigar el impacto de unos precios del petróleo elevados y volátiles, controlar la inflación, estimular la competitividad y proteger a las capas más pobres de la población. Las subvenciones energéticas pueden suponer una carga para los presupuestos nacionales. Sin embargo, los ingresos por impuestos energéticos fueron superiores al coste de las subvenciones en cinco de los seis países de ALC incluidos en un reciente informe de la OCDE (OCDE, 2021[39]) (Costa Rica, República Dominicana, Guatemala, Jamaica y Uruguay, con la excepción de Ecuador), que supone un impacto neto positivo, en promedio, sobre las cuentas públicas de estos seis países (aproximadamente el 0.6% del PIB en 2018, en promedio).

Al margen de los impuestos sobre los combustibles y los impuestos de matriculación y circulación de vehículos, los impuestos medioambientales aún están poco desarrollados en la región de ALC. Sin embargo, un número reducido de países de ALC, como Chile, México y Colombia, han introducido importantes reformas en los impuestos ecológicos.

## Impuestos por nivel gubernamental

En los países de ALC, la recaudación de tributos está en manos mayoritariamente de la administración central o federal. El gasto público de las administraciones de ámbito inferior al nacional se financia mediante transferencias de los niveles gubernamentales superiores a los inferiores en mayor grado que en los países de la OCDE. En los casos en los que se disponen de datos a nivel subnacional de los países de ALC, estos arrojan que la recaudación de tributos por parte del gobierno central representaba más de dos tercios de la recaudación total, mientras que la correspondiente cifra en los países de la OCDE se situó cerca del 60% (cifras de 2019). Brasil constituye una notoria excepción: la recaudación tributaria del gobierno central supuso el 42.4% de la recaudación tributaria en 2020[6] (Cuadro 1.3).

Existen dos problemas estadísticos que deben tenerse en cuenta cuando se comparan la asignación de ingresos en los países de ALC y en la OCDE. En primer lugar, los ingresos de ambos grupos han sido asignados a diferentes niveles gubernamentales de acuerdo con las directrices establecidas en el Sistema de Cuentas Nacionales (SCN) de 2008[7]. En segundo lugar, algunos países de ALC no disponen de estadísticas tributarias relativas al nivel subnacional.

Para los 18 países de ALC de este informe para los cuales se dispone de datos relativos al nivel subnacional, en 2020, la proporción de los ingresos tributarios procedentes de este nivel respecto del total de la recaudación se situó por debajo del 9.0%, excepto en Argentina, Brasil y Colombia. En Brasil, los estados y los municipios recaudan aproximadamente el 31.6% del total de los ingresos tributarios, lo que indica un grado significativo de descentralización de la recaudación tributaria. Una buena parte del IVA brasileño (que, en Brasil, es el ICMS – *imposto sobre operações relativas à circulação de mercadorias e prestação de serviços de transporte interestadual e intermunicipal e de comunicação*) lo recaudan los estados. La recaudación de tributos a nivel subnacional en Argentina y Colombia representa más del 16% de los ingresos tributarios totales. La importante recaudación a nivel estatal de Argentina se explica, en parte, por el impuesto sobre los ingresos brutos, de ámbito provincial.

Estas cifras reflejan el hecho de que los gobiernos subnacionales en los países de ALC suelen tener un relativamente pequeño número de impuestos bajo su jurisdicción. Los impuestos que más se suelen ceder a las entidades subnacionales son los impuestos sobre la propiedad, los permisos de circulación, los impuestos sobre determinados servicios y las tasas municipales. La capacidad de generar ingresos de estos instrumentos es relativamente limitada, en comparación con las bases imponibles que están en manos de la administración central, como el IVA y los impuestos sobre la renta. La crisis de Covid-19 ha puesto de manifiesto la necesidad de llevar a cabo reformas estructurales encaminadas a mejorar la recaudación y las fuentes de ingresos en el ámbito subnacional. Esto incluye introducir mejoras en la información y las estadísticas relativas a los ingresos procedentes de estos impuestos, la capacidad recaudatoria de la administración local, la coordinación eficaz con las autoridades nacionales y la necesidad de fomentar fuentes de ingresos impositivos a nivel subnacional que sean sostenibles y estables (Nieto-Parra and Orozco, 2020[41]).

En 2020, todos los ingresos tributarios recaudados a nivel subnacional en Belice, Guatemala y Jamaica y más del 50% de los ingresos tributarios recaudados a nivel subnacional en Perú, Uruguay y Ecuador provenían de impuestos sobre la propiedad (Gráfico 1.19). Todos los demás países de la región dependen principalmente de los impuestos sobre bienes y servicios. México es el único país que también recaudó ingresos de diferentes bases imponibles. En 2020, el 47% de los ingresos tributarios obtenidos a nivel subnacional en México provenían de los impuestos sobre las nóminas. En los países de la OCDE, las entidades subnacionales suelen contar con bases imponibles en potencia mucho más amplias. Una parte importante de la recaudación de impuestos que llevan a cabo las administraciones subnacionales en los países de la OCDE se debe a los impuestos sobre la renta y los beneficios (que representan más de un tercio de la recaudación, en promedio, que se obtiene en el nivel subnacional).

Gráfico 1.19. **Estructura tributaria de los ingresos tributarios a nivel subnacional en los países de ALC, 2020**

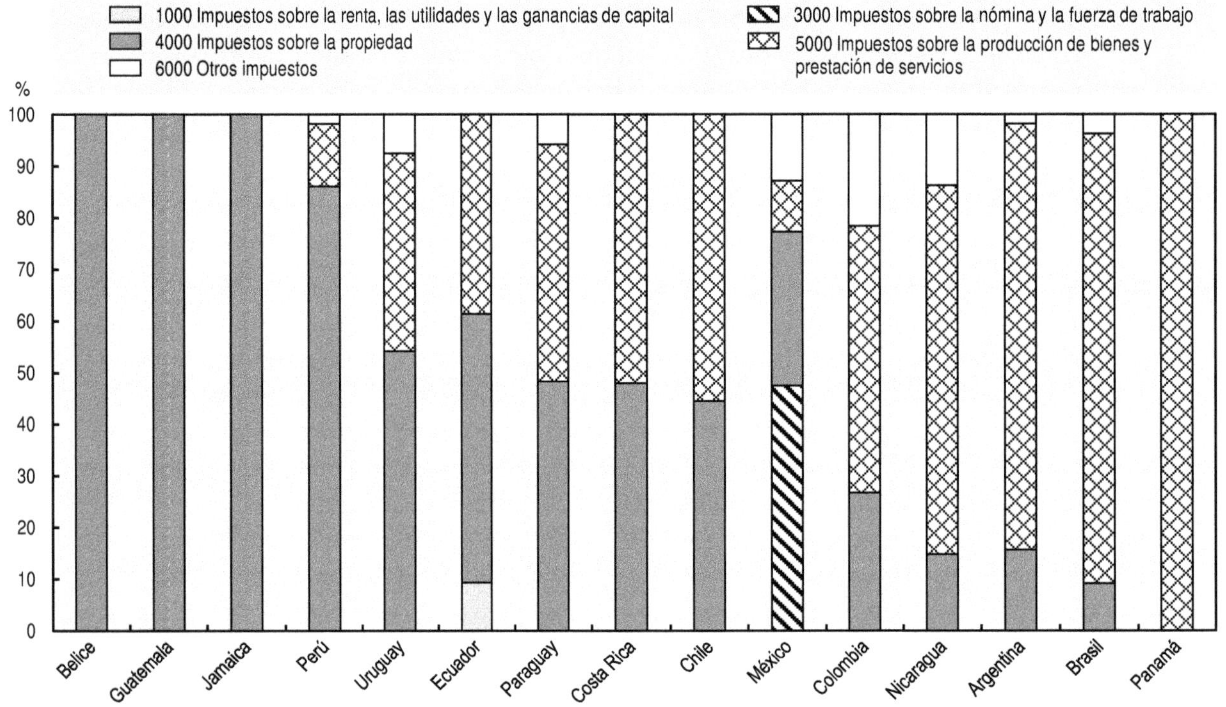


*Nota:* No se incluyen las cifras de Antigua y Barbuda, Bahamas, Barbados, Bolivia, Cuba, República Dominicana, El Salvador, Guyana, Honduras, Santa Lucía, Trinidad y Tobago y Venezuela por la falta de datos relativos a los ingresos tributarios a nivel subnacional o de datos sobre la composición de los ingresos tributarios a nivel subnacional por categoría impositiva principal. Las cifras no incluyen la recaudación local de Argentina pero sí la de ámbito provincial.

*Fuente:* Cálculos propios basados en (OCDE et al., 2022[3]), Capítulo 6.

StatLink https://doi.org/10.1787/888934308181

## Cuadro 1.3. **Asignación de ingresos tributarios a los subsectores de la administración general en los países de ALC[1]**

Porcentaje de los ingresos tributarios totales

| | Gobierno central | | | Gobierno estatal o regional | | | Administraciones locales | | | Fondos de seguridad social | | |
|---|---|---|---|---|---|---|---|---|---|---|---|---|
| | 1995 | 2000 | 2020 | 1995 | 2000 | 2020 | 1995 | 2000 | 2020 | 1995 | 2000 | 2020 |
| **Países federales** | | | | | | | | | | | | |
| Argentina | 59.0 | 66.4 | 64.1 | 17.5 | 17.8 | 16.8 | .. | .. | .. | 23.4 | 15.8 | 19.2 |
| Brasil | 44.8 | 47.9 | 42.4 | 26.5 | 25.0 | 25.6 | 3.7 | 3.4 | 6.1 | 25.0 | 23.7 | 26.0 |
| Mexico[3] | 73.9 | 78.3 | 80.7 | 2.8 | 2.7 | 3.9 | 1.5 | 1.0 | 1.5 | 21.8 | 18.0 | 13.9 |
| Venezuela[4] | 94.6 | 94.6 | .. | .. | .. | .. | .. | .. | .. | 5.4 | 5.4 | .. |
| **Países regionales** | | | | | | | | | | | | |
| Colombia[5] | 63.2 | 68.7 | 71.9 | 5.5 | 5.6 | 4.8 | 8.6 | 9.4 | 13.3 | 22.7 | 16.3 | 9.9 |
| **Países unitarios** | | | | | | | | | | | | |
| Antigua y Barbuda[2] | 100.0 | 100.0 | 83.3 | | | | .. | .. | .. | 0.0 | 0.0 | 16.7 |
| Bahamas[2] | 89.1 | 88.1 | 88.3 | | | | .. | .. | .. | 10.9 | 11.9 | 11.7 |
| Barbados | 85.6 | 84.4 | 80.1 | | | | .. | .. | .. | 14.4 | 15.6 | 19.9 |
| Belice | 93.2 | 93.5 | 86.9 | | | | 0.5 | 0.7 | 0.7 | 6.3 | 5.8 | 12.4 |
| Bolivia | 94.3 | 86.4 | 65.3 | | | | 5.7 | 6.3 | 4.8 | .. | 7.3 | 29.9 |
| Chile | 89.9 | 87.8 | 84.7 | | | | 6.5 | 7.9 | 8.6 | 3.6 | 4.4 | 6.7 |
| Costa Rica | 65.5 | 63.3 | 55.2 | | | | 1.6 | 1.9 | 3.1 | 33.0 | 34.8 | 41.6 |
| Cuba[6] | .. | .. | .. | | | | .. | .. | .. | 11.3 | 10.4 | 16.0 |
| República Dominicana | 99.3 | 99.0 | 99.5 | | | | .. | .. | .. | 0.7 | 1.0 | 0.5 |
| Ecuador | 70.5 | 87.7 | 68.4 | | | | 4.0 | 1.6 | 2.8 | 25.5 | 10.7 | 28.8 |
| El Salvador | 80.9 | 80.5 | 85.0 | | | | .. | .. | 2.0 | 19.1 | 19.5 | 13.0 |
| Guatemala | 83.3 | 83.6 | 82.0 | | | | 0.7 | 0.9 | 1.0 | 16.1 | 15.5 | 17.1 |
| Guyana | 92.6 | 88.6 | 89.8 | | | | .. | .. | .. | 7.4 | 11.4 | 10.1 |
| Honduras | 86.1 | 85.3 | 75.6 | | | | 4.4 | 5.2 | 3.8 | 9.5 | 9.4 | 20.6 |
| Jamaica | 100.0 | 99.3 | 93.9 | | | | .. | 0.7 | 1.5 | 0.0 | 0.0 | 4.6 |
| Nicaragua[2] | 78.0 | 72.5 | 67.6 | | | | 5.1 | 9.5 | 6.1 | 16.8 | 18.0 | 26.4 |
| Panamá | 67.2 | 59.6 | 53.8 | | | | .. | 2.2 | 1.6 | 32.8 | 38.2 | 44.6 |
| Paraguay | 92.0 | 74.4 | 69.8 | | | | .. | .. | 2.6 | 8.0 | 25.6 | 27.6 |
| Perú | 88.7 | 86.5 | 84.2 | | | | .. | 1.6 | 2.3 | 11.3 | 11.9 | 13.4 |
| Santa Lucía | 100.0 | 90.0 | 87.3 | | | | .. | .. | .. | 0.0 | 10.0 | 12.7 |
| Trinidad y Tobago | 96.8 | 93.6 | 85.0 | | | | .. | .. | .. | 3.2 | 6.4 | 15.0 |
| Uruguay[2] | 61.7 | 63.6 | 69.3 | | | | 8.8 | 8.9 | 5.6 | 29.5 | 27.5 | 25.0 |

1. Las cifras no incluyen los ingresos de la administración local de Antigua y Barbuda, Argentina (aunque incluye los ingresos provinciales), las Bahamas, Barbados, Cuba, la República Dominicana, Santa Lucía, Trinidad y Tobago y Venezuela porque no se dispone de dicha información. Los datos sobre la recaudación de la administración local están disponibles desde 1991, para Nicaragua; desde 1994, para Bolivia; desde 1995, para Guatemala; desde 1998, para Jamaica; desde 1999, para Panamá; desde 2000, para Perú; desde 2002, para El Salvador y Guyana; desde 2006, para Paraguay; y desde 1990, para el resto de países.
2. Los datos incluyen las siguientes estimaciones: Antigua y Barbuda (contribuciones a la seguridad social para 2019 y 2020), Bahamas (contribuciones a la seguridad social para 2019 y 2020), Nicaragua (ingresos tributarios locales para 2020) y Uruguay (ingresos tributarios locales para 2020). Para más información, consulte los cuadros relativos a cada país.
3. Se utilizan datos provisionales de 2020 para los ingresos tributarios estatales y locales de México.
4. No están disponibles algunos datos relativos a los ingresos tributarios de 2014 a 2017 y ninguno de los datos relativos a 2018. No está disponible desglose por subsectores de la administración general para estos años.
5. Colombia es constitucionalmente un estado unitario cuyas entidades territoriales gozan de una amplia autonomía.
6. Solo se dispone de datos para los subsectores de la administración general de Cuba para el periodo comprendido entre 2002 y 2012.

*Fuente:* (OCDE et al., $2022_{[3]}$), Cuadro 4.11.

StatLink https://doi.org/10.1787/888934308295

La escasa recaudación tributaria del nivel subnacional en los países de ALC puede deberse a una falta de capacidad administrativa y técnica. Los impuestos sobre la propiedad requieren una información y sistemas sofisticados y recaudarlos es costoso. Muchos países no tienen registros de la propiedad adecuados y cuando existen no suelen estar actualizados (Canavire-Bacarreza, Martínez-Vázquez and Sepúlveda, $2012_{[42]}$; OCDE et al., $2019_{[43]}$). Por consiguiente, las autoridades tributarias no tienen acceso a valoraciones precisas de los terrenos y los edificios y los registros de la propiedad suelen mostrarse reacios a comunicar esta información. Además, los impuestos sobre la propiedad también sufren los altos niveles de informalidad: se construyen edificios sin licencia, no se registran las propiedades y los precios que se comunican relativos a algunas de las operaciones con bienes raíces son falsos. Habida cuenta que el impuesto sobre la propiedad es uno de los impuestos más polémicos entre la ciudadanía, al que se asocia un gran coste político, los políticos locales suelen ser reacios a invertir en recursos adecuados para recaudarlo.

## Notas

1. La cifra es provisional y se basa en datos preliminares relativos a 2020. Los datos deben interpretarse con prudencia, pues están sujetos a futuras revisiones que pueden afectar a la magnitud y, con menos frecuencia, a la dirección del cambio entre los dos últimos años de datos.
2. El IVA se introdujo en Jamaica, en 1991; en Barbados, en 1997; en Belice (el Impuesto General sobre las Ventas), en 2006; en Guyana y Antigua y Barbuda, en 2007; en Santa Lucía, en 2012; y el Bahamas, en 2014.
3. El año de comparación es 2019 al no disponer de la información relativa a la estructura tributaria, en promedio, correspondiente a 2020 para los países de la OCDE.
4. Pese a que en la clasificación normalizada de ingresos tributarios de la OCDE no se pueden identificar los ingresos tributarios relacionados con el medio ambiente, estos sí aparecen identificados en la pormenorizada lista de impuestos específicos incluidos, para la mayoría de los países, en esta clasificación general. En consecuencia, se incluyen en la base de datos de la OCDE de Instrumentos de Política Ambiental (PINE, por sus siglas en inglés) (OCDE, 2021[38]). En 2020, la OCDE empezó la recopilación de las cuentas de los Ingresos Tributarios Medioambientales de conformidad con el Sistema de Contabilidad Ambiental y Económica Integrada y desglosa las cuentas de ingresos por impuestos medioambientales por sectores y hogares (OCDE, 2021[44]).
5. Promedio no ponderado de 38 países miembros de la OCDE.
6. En los ingresos tributarios estatales y locales de México se utilizan datos provisionales de 2020.
7. Esto significa que los ingresos se suelen asignar al nivel gubernamental que ostenta las potestades para imponer el impuesto o que tiene la facultad de decisión última para modificar el tipo impositivo. Esto tiene implicaciones en aquellos casos en los que un nivel gubernamental recauda tributos y los transfiere, total o parcialmente, a otros niveles. Los ejemplos regionales de este tipo de mecanismo los encontramos en la Ley de Coparticipación en Argentina, las participaciones federales en México (establecidas en la Ley de Coordinación Fiscal) y los fondos de participación en Brasil (definidos en el Artículo 159 de la Constitución).

## Referencias

Banco Central de Barbados (2020 y 2021), *Quarterly Press Conferences*, *http://www.centralbank.org.bb/media/press-conferences/quarterly-press-conferences.* [15]

Barreix, A., J. Benítez y M. Pecho (2017), "Revisiting personal income tax in Latin America: Evolution and impact", *OECD Development Centre Working Papers*, No. 338, Publicaciones de la OCDE, París, *https://dx.doi.org/10.1787/16d42b4a-en.* [36]

BID (2013), *More than revenues, Taxation as a development tool*, Banco Interamericano de Desarrollo, Nueva York, *https://publications.iadb.org/en/publication/more-revenue-taxation-development-tool-executive-summary.* [34]

Canavire-Bacarreza, G., J. Martínez-Vázquez y C. Sepúlveda (2012), *Sub-national Revenue Mobilization in Peru, IDB Working Paper Series No. 299*, Banco Interamericano de Desarrollo, Nueva York, *https://publications.iadb.org/en/sub-national-revenue-mobilization-peru.* [42]

CEPAL (2022), *CEPALSTAT (base de datos)*, Comisión Económica para América Latina y el Caribe, Santiago, *https://statistics.cepal.org/portal/cepalstat/dashboard.html?theme=2&lang=en.* [20]

CEPAL (2022), *Preliminary Overview of the Economies of Latin America and the Caribbean 2021*, Comisión Económica para América Latina y el Caribe, Santiago, *https://www.cepal.org/en/pressreleases/latin-america-and-caribbeans-growth-will-slow-21-2022-amid-significant-asymmetries.* [21]

CEPAL (2021), *Economic Survey of Latin America and the Caribbean 2021*, Comisión Económica para América Latina y el Caribe, Santiago, *http://www.repositorio.cepal.org/bitstream/handle/11362/47193/10/S2100607_en.pdf*. [18]

CEPAL (2021), *Fiscal Panorama of Latin America and the Caribbean: Fiscal policy challenges for transformative recovery post-COVID-19*, Comisión Económica para América Latina y el Caribe, Santiago, *https://repositorio.cepal.org/bitstream/handle/11362/46809/1/S2100169_en.pdf*. [13]

CEPAL (2021), *Preliminary Overview of the Economies of Latin America and the Caribbean 2020*, Comisión Económica para América Latina y el Caribe, Santiago, *https://www.cepal.org/en/publications/46504-preliminary-overview-economies-latin-america-and-caribbean-2020*. [10]

CEPAL (2021), *Social Panorama of Latin America, 2020*, Comisión Económica para América Latina y el Caribe, Santiago, *https://www.cepal.org/en/publications/46688-social-panorama-latin-america-2020*. [25]

CEPAL (2021), *The recovery paradox in Latin America and the Caribbean, Special Report COVID-19*, Comisión Económica para América Latina y el Caribe, Santiago, *https://www.cepal.org/sites/default/files/presentation/files/covid-19_special_report_no_11_launch_ppt_final-visto_jl.pdf*. [19]

CEPAL (2020), *Fiscal Panorama of Latin America and the Caribbean 2020: Fiscal policy amid the crisis arising from the coronavirus disease (COVID-19) pandemic*, Comisión Económica para América Latina y el Caribe, *https://www.cepal.org/en/publications/45731-fiscalpanorama-latin-america-and-caribbean-2020-fiscal-policy-amid-crisis*. [26]

CEPAL (2020), *Sectors and businesses facing COVID-19: emergency and reactivation"*, Comisión Económica para América Latina y el Caribe, Santiago, *https://www.cepal.org/sites/default/files/presentation/files/ppt_specialreport_sectorsandbusinesses_en.pdf*. [23]

CEPAL (2018), *The Fiscal Panorama of Latin America and the Caribbean*, Comisión Económica para América Latina y el Caribe, *https://www.cepal.org/en/publications/43406-fiscal-panorama-latin-america-and-caribbean-2018-public-policy-challenges*. [33]

CEPAL (2014), *Tax policy in Latin America: Assessment and guidelines for a second generation of reforms*, Comisión Económica para América Latina y el Caribe, *https://repositorio.cepal.org/handle/11362/36806*. [32]

CEPAL (2013), *Fiscal Panorama of Latin America and the Caribbean: Tax reform and renewal of the fiscal covenant*, Comisión Económica para América Latina y el Caribe, *https://www.cepal.org/en/publications/3101-fiscal-panorama-latin-america-and-caribbean-2013-tax-reform-and-renewal-fiscal*. [35]

CNN (2020), *'There's no one': Cuba is suffering from tourism's standstill*, *https://edition.cnn.com/travel/article/cuba-coronavirus-lockdown-tourism/index.html*. [8]

Consejo de la Unión Europea (2019), "Antigua and Barbuda's International Business Corporations regime", *https://data.consilium.europa.eu/doc/document/ST-7461-2019-INIT/en/pdf#:~:text=The%20general%20tax%20rate%20for,from%20the%20date%20of%20incorporation*. [14]

FMI (2021), Policy responses to COVID-19, Policy tracker, *https://www.imf.org/en/Topics/imf-and-covid19/Policy-Responses-to-COVID-19#F*. [12]

FMI (2021), "Barbados: Fifth Review Under the Extended Arrangement, Request for Waiver of Nonobservance of Performance Criterion, and Modification of Performance Criteria-Press Release; Staff Report; and Statement by the Executive Director for Barbados", *https://www.elibrary.imf.org/view/journals/002/2021/128/article-A001-en.xml#A001fn02*. [16]

FMI (2021), *Trinidad and Tobago: Staff Concluding Statement of the 2021 Article IV Mission*, *https://www.imf.org/en/News/Articles/2021/11/19/trinidad-and-tobago-staff-concluding-statement-of-the-2021-article-iv-mission*. [11]

FMI (2021), *World Economic Outlook Database, October 2021*, *https://www.imf.org/en/Publications/WEO/weo-database/2021/October* (accessed on 20 September 2021). [5]

Gobierno de las Bahamas (2020), "Combined nine month fiscal snapshot and report on budgetary performance", *https://www.bahamas.gov.bs/wps/wcm/connect/b65ccbe4-64ee-4b94-b692-7a19cd509ba2/Combined+9-Month+Fiscal+Snapshot+%26+Report_Final+April+30%2C+2020+-+Compressed.pdf?MOD=AJPERES*. [17]

Havana Times (2021), *The Impact of COVID-19 on Tourism in Cuba*, *https://havanatimes.org/features/the-impact-of-covid-19-on-tourism-in-cuba/*. [7]

Hon. Colm Imbert, M. (2020), *Statement by the Hon. Colm Imbert, Minister of Finance, to the House of Representatives on the Economic Effect and Financial Response to the Covid-19 Pandemic*, *https://www.finance.gov.tt/2020/04/27/statement-by-the-hon-colm-imbert-minister-of-finance-to-the-house-of-representatives-on-the-economic-effect-and-financial-response-to-the-covid-19-pandemic/*. [9]

Lorenzo, F. (2016), *Inventario de instrumentos fiscales verdes en América Latina*, CEPAL, *https://agua.org.mx/biblioteca/inventario-instrumentos-fiscales-verdes-en-america-latina-experiencias-efectos-alcances/*. [40]

Melguizo, A. et al. (2017), *No sympathy for the devil! Policy priorities to overcome the middle-income trap in Latin America*, OECD, *http://dx.doi.org/10.1787/26b78724-en*. [27]

Nieto-Parra, S. y R. Orozco (2020), *Potencializar los impuestos subnacionales en América Latina y el Caribe en tiempos del Covid-19 in Los desafíos de las finanzas intergubernamentales ante el Covid-19*,, AIFIL - Asociación Iberoamericana de Financiación, *https://www.aifil-jifl.org/wp-content/uploads/2020/11/AIFIL-2.11.pdf*. [41]

OCDE (2021), *Environmental policy: Environmentally related tax revenue accounts, OECD Environment Statistics (base de datos)*, *https://stats.oecd.org/Index.aspx?DataSetCode=ERTR_ACC*. [44]

OCDE (2021), *OECD Revenue Statistics 2021: The Initial Impact of COVID-19 on OECD Tax Revenues*, Publicaciones de la OCDE, París, *https://doi.org/10.1787/6e87f932-en*. [4]

OCDE (2021), *PINE database*, Publicaciones de la OCDE, París, *http://www.oecd.org/environment/tools-evaluation/environmentaltaxation.htm*. [38]

OCDE (2021), *Taxing Energy Use for Sustainable Development*, Publicaciones de la OCDE, París, *https://www.oecd.org/tax/tax-policy/taxing-energy-use-for-sustainable-development.htm*. [39]

OCDE (2020), *COVID-19 in Latin America and the Caribbean: Regional socio-economic implications and policy priorities*, Publicaciones de la OCDE, París, *http://www.oecd.org/coronavirus/policy-responses/covid-19-in-latinamerica-and-the-caribbean-regional-socio-economic-implications-and-policy-priorities-93a64fde/*. [22]

OCDE (2019), *Tax Morale: What Drives People and Businesses to Pay Tax?*, Publicaciones de la OCDE, París, *https://doi.org/10.1787/f3d8ea10-en*. [29]

OCDE (2014), *Development Co-operation Report 2014: Mobilising Resources for Sustainable Development*, Publicaciones de la OCDE, París, *https://dx.doi.org/10.1787/dcr-2014-en*. [28]

OCDE (2005), *Glossary of statistical terms*, *https://stats.oecd.org/glossary/detail.asp?ID=6437*. [37]

OCDE et al. (2022), *Estadísticas tributarias en América Latina y el Caribe 2022*, Publicaciones de la OCDE, París, *http://dx.doi.org/TBC*. [3]

OCDE et al. (2021), *Perspectivas económicas de América Latina 2021: Avanzando juntos hacia una mejor recuperación*, Publicaciones de la OCDE, París, *https://doi.org/10.1787/2958a75d-es*. [2]

OCDE et al. (2021), *Estadísticas tributarias en América Latina y el Caribe 2021*, Publicaciones de la OCDE, París, *https://doi.org/10.1787/96ce5287-en-es*. [1]

OCDE et al. (2019), *Estadísticas tributarias en América Latina y el Caribe 2019*, Publicaciones de la OCDE, París, *https://doi.org/10.1787/25666b8d-en-es*. [43]

OCDE/BID/El Banco Mundial (2014), *Pensions at a Glance: Latin America and the Caribbean*, Publicaciones de la OCDE, París, *https://dx.doi.org/10.1787/pension_glance-2014-en*. [31]

OCDE et al. (2015), *Estadísticas tributarias en América Latina y el Caribe 2015*, Publicaciones de la OCDE, París, *https://dx.doi.org/10.1787/rev_lat-2015-en-fr*. [30]

OIT (2021), *Employment and informality in Latin America and the Caribbean: An insufficient and unequal recovery*, Organizacion Internacional del Trabajo, Ginebra. [24]

SCN (2016), *Sistema de Cuentas Nacionales 2008*, *https://unstats.un.org/unsd/nationalaccount/docs/SNA2008Spanish.pdf*. [6]

*Chapter 2*

# SPECIAL FEATURE

# Fiscal revenues from non-renewable natural resources in Latin America and the Caribbean

*Capítulo 2*

# SECCIÓN ESPECIAL

# Ingresos fiscales provenientes de recursos naturales no renovables en América Latina y el Caribe

*Chapter 2*

# SPECIAL FEATURE

# Fiscal revenues from non-renewable natural resources in Latin America and the Caribbean

### Principal findings

**Fiscal accounts in Latin America and the Caribbean were adversely impacted in 2020 by falling fiscal revenues from non-renewable natural resources**

Faced with an unprecedented economic and social crisis, countries in Latin America and the Caribbean (LAC) employed fiscal policy to alleviate the impact of the COVID-19 pandemic on public health systems, households, and the productive structure. Crisis-related fiscal measures, largely based on discretionary public expenditure, combined with falling public revenues created substantial strain on public accounts. For producers of non-renewable natural resources in the region, particularly crude oil exporters, the decline in overall revenues in 2020 was aggravated by external price shocks that severely undercut oil and gas revenues. In some countries, the decline in these revenues accounted for half or more of the overall contraction in general government revenues.

**Hydrocarbon revenues declined sharply in 2020 amidst turmoil in global oil markets**

Fiscal revenues from exploration and production of hydrocarbons in the region fell to 2.1% of GDP in 2020, compared to 3.1% of GDP in 2019. While production levels in the region generally fell, the principal driver of lower hydrocarbon revenues was the price shock originating in international markets. For the year, oil and gas revenues were down by 59.7% in US dollar terms, falling to USD 33.1 billion, a level not seen since 2002.

**Mining revenues gave ground in 2020 as public health measures strongly impacted production**

Mining revenues in the region contracted during 2020, reflecting the combined effect of lower international prices for most minerals and base metals as well as lower production due in part to public health measures adopted to limit the spread of the COVID-19 virus. Tax revenues, particularly corporate income tax (CIT) receipts, plunged as a result. For the year, revenues from mining fell to 0.3% of GDP, from 0.4% of GDP in 2019, or a decline of 15.4% in US dollar terms.

**A recovery in fiscal revenues from non-renewable natural resources is forecast for 2021**

Estimates and preliminary data for selected countries point to a sharp increase in non-renewable natural resource revenues in 2021. Mining revenues are estimated to have been especially buoyant, doubling their 2020 level to reach 0.6% of GDP, supported by growing global demand, favourable prices and expanded domestic production. Oil and gas revenues are also estimated to have recovered in 2021 to reach 3.0% of GDP, just below the level registered in 2019.

## Falling fiscal revenues from non-renewable natural resources had a material impact on LAC's public accounts in 2020

The outbreak of the COVID-19 pandemic had a dramatic and immediate impact on global activity and social welfare. The profound shocks to supply and demand caused by public health measures, including quarantines and limits on movement, rippled through the global economy, causing severe dislocations in global trade, investment and employment. Global economic output contracted by -3.3% in 2020, the lowest rate recorded in the period beginning in 1980, easily surpassing the decline of -0.1% registered in 2009 during the global financial and economic crisis (IMF, 2021[1]).

Commodity markets were likewise buffeted by supply and demand shocks, causing significant moves in international prices. International trade and travel collapsed, which, when coupled with restrictions on mobility, led to a historic decline in demand for liquid hydrocarbon products. Spot prices for crude oil plummeted, turning negative during some days as traders sought to unwind positions for product they could no longer store. Mineral and metal markets were similarly affected, although rapid rebounds in China's industrial activity and fixed capital formation bolstered prices by the end of the first half of the year.

LAC was not spared the consequences of COVID-19's rapid propagation. Economic output contracted by -6.8%, the largest decline since 1900 (ECLAC, 2021[2]). Measures to halt the spread of the pandemic contributed to a significant decline in employment (-9.0%), which could not be made up by greater informal employment – the traditional labour market shock absorber – as quarantines forced workers to remain at home. Against this backdrop, the crisis provoked a serious erosion of socio-economic wellbeing, aggravating existing structural development gaps, while creating an unprecedented rise in poverty.

Countries in the region sought to temporarily fill these gaps by adopting packages of fiscal support measures of broad scope and scale, averaging 4.6% of GDP in Latin America (ECLAC, 2021[3]). Fiscal policy served as a key tool of public policy to strengthen crumbling public health systems, support struggling families and protect the region's productive capacity. However, these efforts were accompanied by a significant erosion in public accounts, with exceptionally large deficits and a substantial increase in public debt.

The region's fiscal situation in 2020 was also complicated by the turmoil in commodity markets, which had a direct impact on fiscal revenues from non-renewable natural resources. While the bulk of the erosion of public balances was due to public spending, total general government revenues fell significantly in some countries. This was especially severe in countries with an elevated dependence on hydrocarbon revenues, such as Bolivia (Plurinational State of), Colombia, Ecuador, Mexico, and Trinidad and Tobago. The contraction of oil and gas revenues in Ecuador (-3.4 percentage points [p.p.] of GDP), Colombia (-1.2 p.p. of GDP) and Trinidad and Tobago (-3.3 p.p. of GDP) accounted for half or more of the overall decline in total revenues (Figure 2.1).

Countries specialising in mining, or where mining makes up the bulk of fiscal revenues from non-renewable natural resources, were in general less impacted. Mining in Chile and Peru, among the principal metal producers in the world, registered a limited decline with a concomitantly small impact on public accounts. This reflected the rapid reactivation of mine output in the second half and favourable international prices but was also a result of the relatively small import of these revenues, which had progressively fallen from a regional average of 0.9% of GDP in 2009 to 0.3% of GDP in 2020.

Estimates for central government operations in 2021 point to a significant rebound in public revenues, bolstered in part by higher fiscal revenues from non-renewable natural resources (ECLAC, 2021[4]). Crude oil prices rose sharply during the year, with the spot price of Brent crude up 67% on the 2020 annual average, and 10% higher than in 2019. Hydrocarbon revenues – heavily weighted toward property rents calculated on the commercial value of production – in the region are therefore set to recover significantly in 2021, with estimates suggesting an increase to 3.0% of GDP from 2.1% of GDP in 2020 (Figure 2.2).

Figure 2.1. **Selected countries: Year-on-year variation of total general government revenues, by component, 2019-20**

Percentage points of GDP

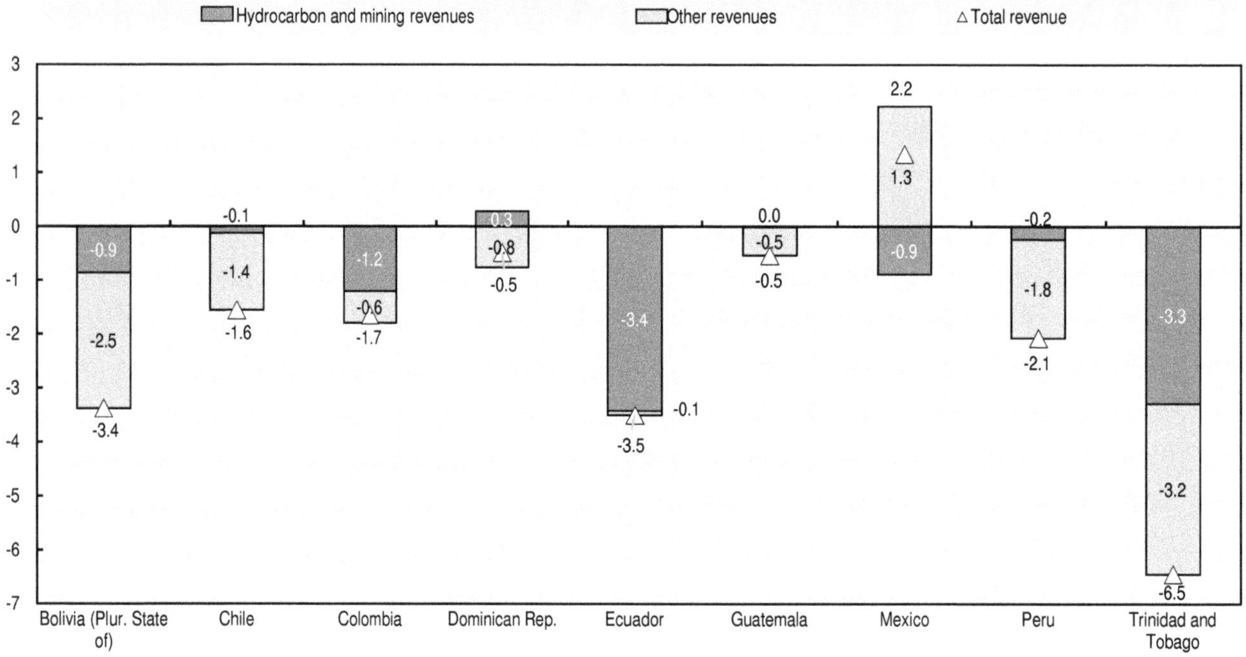


*Note:* Data for Mexico correspond to the federal government, which exclude own revenues of Pemex, the state-owned oil and gas producer. In Ecuador, data correspond to oil revenues derived from exports of the non-financial public sector. Data for the Dominican Republic, Guatemala, and Trinidad and Tobago refer to the central government.

*Source:* Economic Commission for Latin America and the Caribbean (ECLAC), based on data from ECLAC's Fiscal Revenues from Non-Renewable Natural Resources in Latin America and the Caribbean database.

StatLink https://doi.org/10.1787/888934308314

In an analogous way, prices for a wide range of minerals and metals rose during in 2021, including substantial increases for coal (+127%), copper (+51%) and iron ore (+48%). Increases in royalty payments and other property rents derived from mining have been estimated, but the primary driver of higher mining revenues was a surge in corporate income tax (CIT) payments. Higher profitability and the impact of the withdrawal of tax relief measures employed in 2020 resulted in an up-tick in the liquidation of previous year tax liabilities and pre-payments of the current fiscal year. As a result, mining revenues are estimated to double on average in the region, from 0.3% of GDP in 2020 to 0.6% of GDP (Figure 2.2).

Preliminary data on fiscal revenues from non-renewable natural resources are supportive of estimates for annual revenues for the region. Mining revenues rose sharply in 2021 in Chile and Peru, doubling or more levels recorded in 2019 (Figure 2.2). However, part of this increase was due to significant one-off payments. Codelco, Chile's state-owned copper producer, made a pre-payment on 2021 dividends equivalent to 0.4% of GDP to the central government (DIPRES, 2021[5]). In Peru, two mining companies – Compañía Minera Buenaventura and Cerro Verde – settled outstanding tax debts with payments equivalent to 0.4% of GDP.[1]

Oil and gas revenues also showed signs of recovery, especially in Ecuador, where issues with oil infrastructure were progressively resolved and prices surpassed 2019 levels. The recovery of hydrocarbon revenues in Mexico was less pronounced, partly reflecting measures taken to reduce the fiscal burden on Pemex, such as reducing the rate used in the calculation of the payment of the profit-sharing duty (Derecho por la Utilidad Compartida).

Figure 2.2. **General government fiscal revenues from non-renewable natural resources, 2000-21 (forecast), and preliminary data for selected countries, 2019-21 (preliminary)**

Percentage of GDP

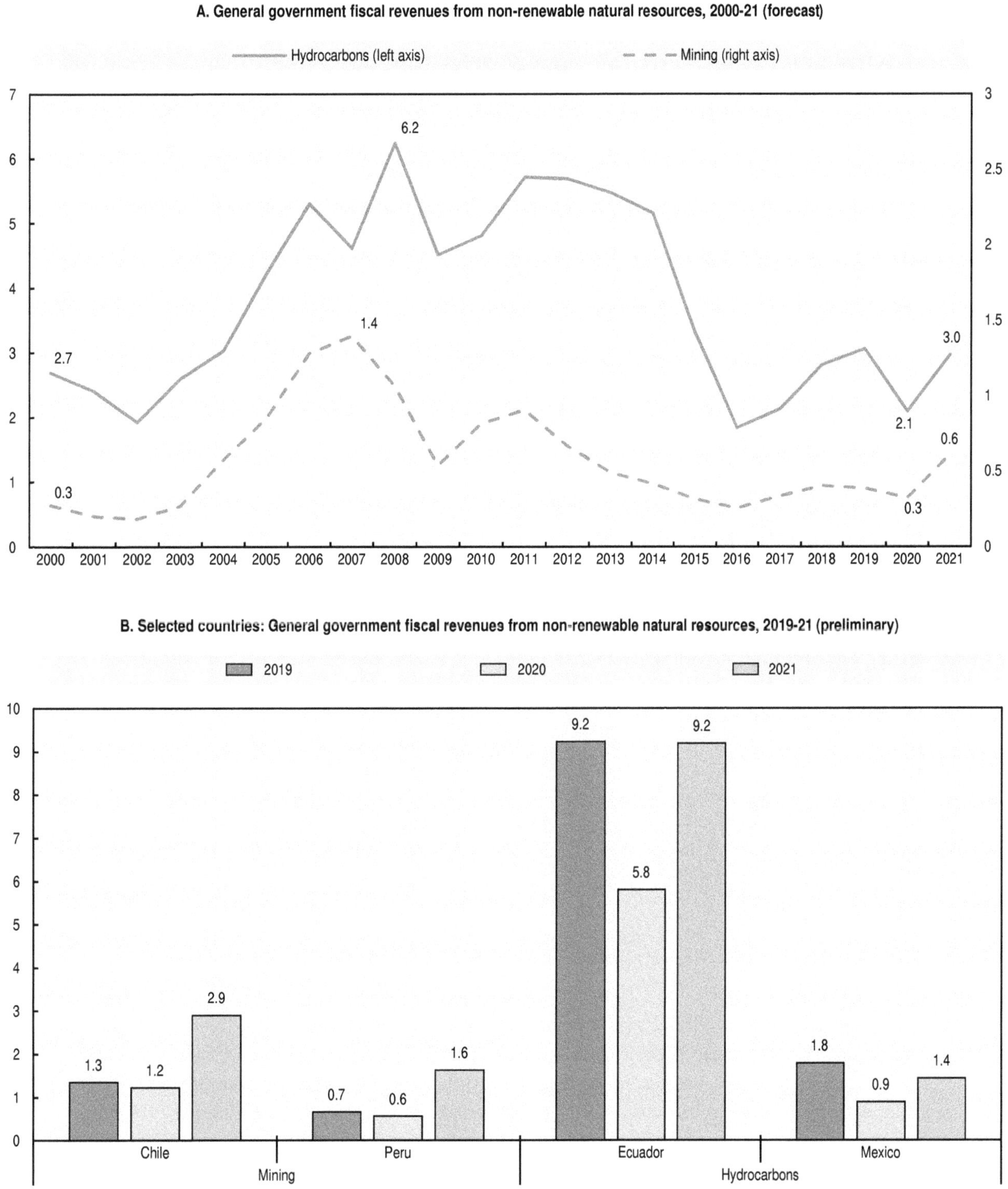


*Note:* Data for Mexico correspond to federal government oil revenue, they exclude own revenues of Pemex, the State-owned oil and gas producer. Data for Ecuador correspond to oil revenues of the non-financial public sector derived from exports of crude oil.

*Source:* Economic Commission for Latin America and the Caribbean (ECLAC), based on data from ECLAC's Fiscal Revenues from Non-Renewable Natural Resources in Latin America and the Caribbean database.

StatLink https://doi.org/10.1787/888934308333

## Turmoil in global hydrocarbon markets during 2020 roiled hydrocarbon revenues in LAC

The outbreak of the COVID-19 pandemic and the associated public health measures, including restrictions on mobility and quarantines, resulted in a near-instantaneous rupture in international oil markets. Global consumption of petroleum and other liquids began to contract sharply at the end of the first quarter of 2020 (Figure 2.3), a slide that accelerated in the second quarter with a staggering 15% year-on-year decline, as the twin supply and demand shocks caused by the crisis engulfed the global economy. For context, before 2020 the largest single quarter declines were registered in the fourth quarter of 2008 (-3.4%) and the first quarter of 2009 (-3.3%), at the height of the global financial and economic crisis.

Figure 2.3. **World liquid fuels production and consumption balance and international spot prices for crude oil, 2019-20**

Million barrels per day and dollars per barrel

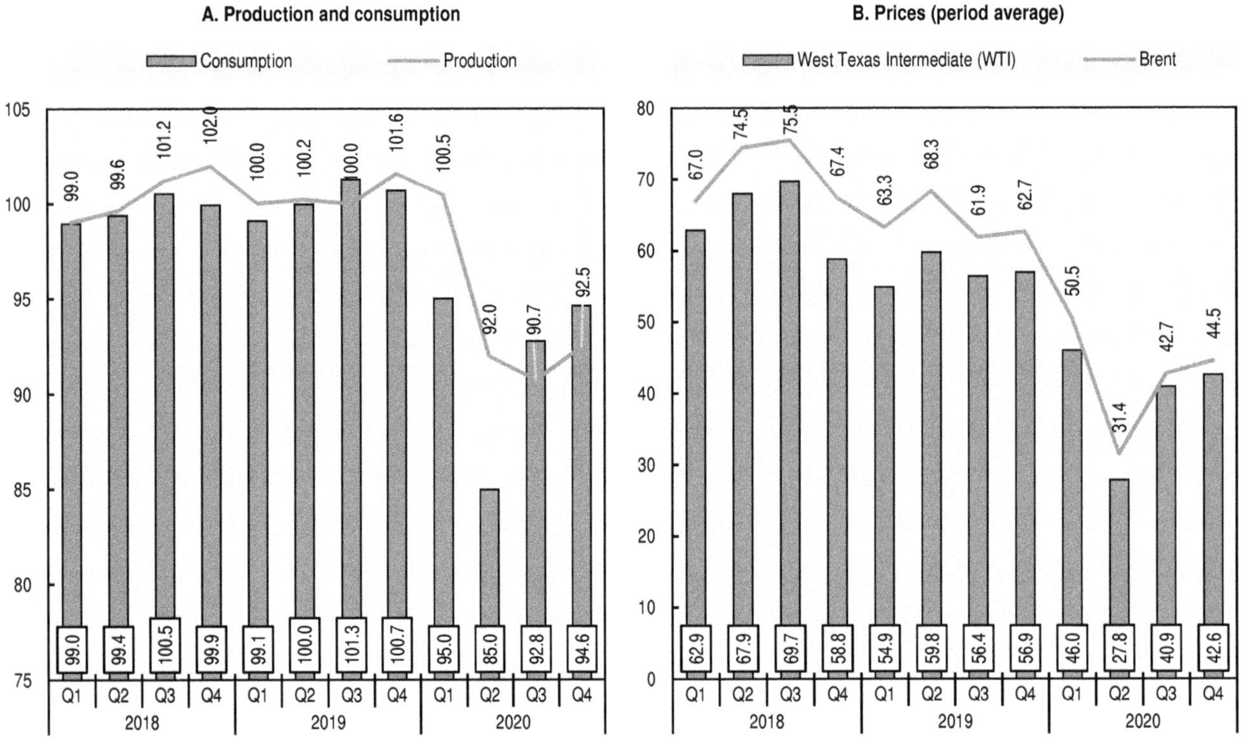


*Source:* Economic Commission for Latin America and the Caribbean (ECLAC), on the basis of Short-Term Energy Outlook Data Browser, U.S. Energy Information Administration (EIA) and World Bank Commodity Price Data (The Pink Sheet), World Bank.

StatLink https://doi.org/10.1787/888934308352

Crude oil prices in global markets tumbled in reaction to this fall in overall demand. Spot prices for Brent and West Texas Intermediate fell precipitously in February 2020. In April 2020, with global economic activity largely paralysed and international trade and transport effectively shut down, the spot price for Brent experienced a historic 74% year-on-year contraction. Price dynamics were also influenced by a significant oversupply of hydrocarbons globally and an acute lack of additional storage space to accommodate growing inventories. On 20 April 2020, the price of West Texas Intermediate fell from USD 17.85 per barrel to a negative USD 37.62 per barrel, the largest one-day decline until that point, as traders sought to sell May contracts for oil volumes of which they could not take delivery for lack of available storage (CRS, 2020[6]).

In response to the unfolding economic crisis and falling crude oil prices, OPEC and allied countries – the so-called OPEC+, which includes the Russian Federation – agreed to a significant cut in oil production in April 2020 to close imbalances in global supply and demand. The agreement established a downward adjustment of 9.7 million barrels per day between May and June, 7.7 million barrels per day between July and December and 5.8 million barrels per day through from January 2021 to April 2022.[2] The agreement was subsequently amended to include additional voluntary production cuts of 0.5 million barrels per day beginning in January 2021.[3]

Turmoil in global oil markets spread rapidly to the LAC region, where hydrocarbon producers are particularly exposed to external shocks. Crude oil exports account for around 70% or more of average daily production in Colombia, Ecuador, Mexico and the Bolivarian Republic of Venezuela. Similarly, the Plurinational State of Bolivia exports roughly 75% of average daily natural gas production, principally to Argentina and Brazil. Nevertheless, the shock to production and exports was not uniformly felt at the country level (Table 2.1). Crude oil output rose in Brazil, Guyana – where full-scale crude oil production began in 2020 – and Mexico. This up-tick in production was accompanied by higher exports from Brazil and Guyana, which offset declines in other countries and led to an increase in exports of crude oil from the region (+2.0%), excluding the Bolivarian Republic of Venezuela.

Table 2.1. **Latin America and the Caribbean and selected country groupings: crude oil and natural gas production and exports, 2019-20**

Thousand barrels daily, billion cubic metres and percentages

| Selected country groupings and countries | Crude oil (thousand barrels daily) | | | | | | Natural gas (billion cubic metres) | | | | | |
|---|---|---|---|---|---|---|---|---|---|---|---|---|
| | Production | | | Exports | | | Production | | | Exports | | |
| | 2019 | 2020 | % | 2019 | 2020 | % | 2019 | 2020 | % | 2019 | 2020 | % |
| ***Latin America and the Caribbean*** | 7519 | 7197 | -4.3 | 4496 | 4204 | -6.5 | 194 | 183 | -5.7 | 36 | 29 | -17.9 |
| *excluding Venezuela* | 6642 | 6670 | 0.4 | 3650 | 3718 | 1.9 | 174 | 165 | -4.9 | .. | .. | .. |
| Argentina | 508 | 480 | -5.4 | .. | .. | .. | 43 | 39 | -9.2 | 1 | 1 | -13.6 |
| Bolivia | 39 | 37 | -5.5 | .. | .. | .. | 17 | 16 | -3.9 | 13 | 12 | -2.0 |
| Brazil | 2788 | 2940 | 5.5 | 1301 | 1401 | 7.7 | 22 | 21 | -7.1 | .. | .. | .. |
| Colombia | 886 | 781 | -11.8 | 612 | 541 | -11.6 | 10 | 10 | -1.7 | .. | .. | .. |
| Ecuador | 531 | 479 | -9.7 | 398 | 362 | -9.1 | 0 | 0 | -3.2 | .. | .. | .. |
| Guatemala | 9 | 8 | -12.2 | .. | .. | .. | .. | .. | .. | .. | .. | .. |
| Guyana | 1 | 74 | 6251.7 | 0 | 73 | n.a. | .. | .. | .. | .. | .. | .. |
| Mexico | 1704 | 1710 | 0.4 | 1200 | 1199 | -0.1 | 32 | 37 | 15.5 | .. | .. | .. |
| Peru | 53 | 40 | -25.1 | .. | .. | .. | 14 | 12 | -10.2 | 5 | 4 | -18.3 |
| Suriname | 15 | 15 | -3.7 | .. | .. | .. | .. | .. | .. | .. | .. | .. |
| Trinidad and Tobago | 59 | 56 | -4.0 | 58 | 56 | -4.9 | 36 | 30 | -16.0 | 17 | 12 | -29.7 |
| Venezuela | 877 | 527 | -39.9 | 847 | 487 | -42.5 | 21 | 18 | - 12 | .. | .. | .. |
| Other LAC | 50 | 49 | -2.0 | 81 | 87 | 7.8 | 1 | 1 | -8.8 | .. | .. | .. |
| **Total World** | 82 340 | 76 101 | -7.6 | 45 222 | 41 988 | -7.2 | 4 086 | 3 962 | -3.0 | 1 332 | 1 244 | -6.6 |
| OPEC | 31 386 | 27 550 | -12.2 | 22 478 | 19 701 | -12.4 | 642 | 637 | -0.8 | 111 | 105 | -5.3 |
| Saudi Arabia | 9 981 | 9 406 | -5.8 | 7 038 | 6 659 | -5.4 | .. | .. | .. | .. | .. | .. |
| Non-OPEC | 50 954 | 48 551 | -4.7 | 22 744 | 22 287 | -2.0 | 3 444 | 3 325 | -3.5 | 1 220 | 1 138 | -6.7 |
| Russian Federation | 10 847 | 9 865 | -9.1 | 5 253 | 4 654 | -11.4 | 693 | 649 | -6.3 | .. | .. | .. |
| United States | 12 248 | 11 308 | -7.7 | 2 982 | 3 175 | 6.5 | 964 | 948 | -1.6 | .. | .. | .. |

*Source:* Economic Commission for Latin America and the Caribbean (ECLAC), on the basis of Short-Term Energy Outlook Data Browser, U.S. Energy Information Administration (EIA) and OPEC Annual Statistical Bulletin 2021, Organization of the Petroleum Exporting Countries (OPEC).

StatLink https://doi.org/10.1787/888934308466

Fiscal revenues from hydrocarbon production and exploration – up-stream activities – experienced a sharp decline in 2020, reflecting the interplay of global and domestic dynamics (Table 2.2). In absolute terms, total oil and gas revenues fell to USD 33.1 billion in 2020, a 59.5% reduction from the level of USD 81.8 billion in 2019. This represented the lowest annual total since 2002, when revenues reached USD 23.5 billion. In relative terms, hydrocarbon revenues fell to an average of 2.1% of GDP in 2020 from 3.1% of GDP in 2019. However, these figures were impacted by shifts in nominal GDP – which fell in most LAC countries (see Chapter 1) – and currency depreciations, which boosted revenues expressed in national currency terms.

### Table 2.2. **Latin America and the Caribbean (10 countries): General government fiscal revenues from oil and gas exploration and production, by type of revenue, 2019-20**

Percentage of GDP, percentage points of GDP and percentages

| Type of revenue | Period | Region / country | | | | | | | | | | |
|---|---|---|---|---|---|---|---|---|---|---|---|---|
| | | LAC | Argentina | Bolivia (Plurinational State of) | Brazil | Colombia | Ecuador | Guatemala | Guyana | Mexico | Peru | Trinidad and Tobago |
| **Total revenues** | 2019 | **3.1** | 0.56 | 3.9 | 1.9 | 2.2 | 9.2 | 0.05 | .. | 1.8 | 0.5 | 7.4 |
| | 2020 | **2.1** | 0.44 | 3.8 | 0.7 | 1.2 | 5.8 | 0.03 | 3.62 | 0.9 | 0.4 | 4.1 |
| | 2020-2019 (p.p. of GDP) | **-1.0** | -0.12 | -0.1 | -1.2 | -1.0 | -3.4 | -0.02 | .. | -0.9 | -0.1 | -3.3 |
| | 2020-2019 (% change in NC) | **n.a.** | -1.1 | -13.7 | -64.2 | -48.0 | -42.5 | -38.4 | .. | -53.1 | -31.6 | -48.4 |
| | 2020-2019 (% change in USD) | **-59.5** | -32.5 | -13.7 | -72.6 | -53.8 | -42.5 | -38.6 | .. | -58.0 | -34.7 | -48.3 |
| **Tax revenues** | 2019 | **0.5** | 0.13 | 0.3 | 0.1 | 0.4 | 0.0 | 0.02 | .. | 0.02 | 0.1 | 3.5 |
| | 2020 | **0.3** | 0.09 | 0.2 | 0.0 | 0.1 | 0.0 | 0.01 | .. | 0.03 | 0.1 | 1.8 |
| | 2020-2019 (p.p. of GDP) | **-0.3** | -0.04 | -0.1 | -0.1 | -0.3 | .. | -0.01 | .. | 0.01 | 0.0 | -1.6 |
| | 2020-2019 (% change in NC) | **n.a.** | -13.5 | -45.7 | -77.8 | -81.9 | .. | -45.1 | .. | 19.5 | -37.8 | -50.8 |
| | 2020-2019 (% change in USD) | **-59.7** | -41.0 | -45.7 | -83.0 | -83.9 | .. | -45.2 | .. | 7.2 | -40.6 | -50.7 |
| **Non-tax revenues** | 2019 | **2.5** | 0.43 | 3.6 | 1.7 | 1.8 | 9.2 | 0.03 | .. | 1.8 | 0.4 | 3.9 |
| | 2020 | **1.9** | 0.35 | 3.6 | 0.6 | 1.1 | 5.8 | 0.02 | 3.62 | 0.9 | 0.3 | 2.3 |
| | 2020-2019 (p.p. of GDP) | **-0.7** | -0.08 | 0.0 | -1.1 | -0.7 | -3.4 | -0.01 | .. | -0.9 | -0.1 | -1.7 |
| | 2020-2019 (% change in NC) | **n.a.** | 2.7 | -10.6 | -63.1 | -40.0 | -42.5 | -34.6 | .. | -54.1 | -29.5 | -46.2 |
| | 2020-2019 (% change in USD) | **-58.9** | -29.9 | -10.6 | -71.8 | -46.7 | -42.5 | -34.8 | .. | -58.8 | -32.7 | -46.2 |
| *of which: royalties and production levies* | 2019 | **2.2** | 0.42 | 3.6 | 0.8 | 0.6 | 9.2 | 0.03 | .. | 1.8 | 0.4 | 2.7 |
| | 2020 | **1.8** | 0.35 | 3.6 | 0.6 | 0.4 | 5.8 | 0.02 | 3.62 | 0.9 | 0.3 | 2.2 |
| | 2020-2019 (p.p. of GDP) | **-0.4** | -0.07 | 0.0 | -0.1 | -0.2 | -3.4 | -0.01 | .. | -0.9 | -0.1 | -0.5 |
| | 2020-2019 (% change in NC) | **n.a.** | 4.0 | -10.6 | -16.5 | -33.1 | -42.5 | -34.6 | .. | -54.1 | -29.5 | -25.5 |
| | 2020-2019 (% change in USD) | **-45.5** | -29.0 | -10.6 | -36.1 | -40.6 | -42.5 | -34.8 | .. | -58.8 | -32.7 | -25.4 |

*Note:* Data for Mexico correspond to federal government oil revenue, they exclude own revenues of Pemex, the State-owned oil and gas producer. Data for Ecuador correspond to oil revenues of the non-financial public sector derived from exports of crude oil. Revenue-to-GDP ratios for Latin America and the Caribbean correspond to a simple average of the countries included in the sample. Figures may not sum due to rounding.

*Source:* Economic Commission for Latin America and the Caribbean (ECLAC), based on data from ECLAC's Fiscal Revenues from Non-Renewable Natural Resources in Latin America and the Caribbean database.

StatLink https://doi.org/10.1787/888934308485

The principal driver of the reduction in hydrocarbon revenues was the contraction in payments of royalties and other participations in production, as the commercial value of production fell in line with prices and production levels. This decrease was offset to some extent by new hydrocarbon revenues in Guyana and currency depreciations in some countries. Tax revenues also dipped as lower prices reduced operating profits and due to the high base of comparison with the previous year in Trinidad and Tobago caused by one-off receipts. These overall regional trends notwithstanding, results at the country level were highly heterogeneous.

Hydrocarbon revenues in **Argentina** during 2020 were influenced by various, in some cases offsetting, factors. While total revenues expressed in US dollars fell in line with the price of oil, they retreated only marginally in national currency terms as the Argentinian peso depreciated significantly (47%). However, oil and gas revenues nonetheless fell in relative terms – from 0.56% of GDP in 2019 to 0.44% of GDP – in an inflationary context characterised by the rapid growth of nominal GDP. Royalty payments rose during the year in part due to the application of Decree 488/2020, which came into force in May.[4] The measure established a price level of USD 45 per barrel for domestic oil deliveries and for the liquidation of royalty payments. The decree was to remain in effect until the end of the year or until the futures price for Brent surpassed a stipulated price level for ten consecutive days, a condition that was met in August. In contrast, tax revenues – principally CIT receipts – collapsed as some companies (such as YPF, the State-controlled oil company) reported large financial losses.

In the **Plurinational State of Bolivia**, oil and gas revenues registered a modest decline in 2020, both in absolute and relative terms (from 3.9% of GDP in 2019 to 3.8% of GDP), supported in part by a recovery in export volumes in the second half of the year. Although natural gas production fell (-3.8%), export volumes for the year rose (+2.1%) as higher exports to Argentina compensated for a decline in sales to Brazil (MEFP, 2021[7]). Nevertheless, exports to Brazil recovered by mid-year, exceeding the lower minimum purchase volumes – 14 million cubic meters per day (MMmcd) of natural gas, down from 24.06 MMmcd under the prior agreement – stipulated as part of the new multi-year supply contract between the country and Petrobras (Brazil), which was signed in March (YPBF, 2021[8]). As a result, non-tax revenues from royalty payments and other property rents – which represent the bulk of hydrocarbon revenues – fell marginally and were flat relative to GDP.

Hydrocarbon revenues in **Brazil** fell sharply in 2020 (from 1.9% of GDP in 2019 to 0.7% of GDP) due in part to the high base effect caused by extraordinary revenues booked in 2019. The Transfer of Rights Surplus bidding round held in November 2019 resulted in a large signing bonus (0.9% of GDP), which pushed non-tax revenues higher. Likewise, the 16th round of oil concessions held in October 2019 and the 6th round of "pre-sal" auctions in November 2019 generated additional signing bonuses equivalent to 0.2% of GDP. Excluding this base effect, royalties and other participations in the value of production also registered declines as the impact of lower prices was only partially offset by higher production and the depreciation of the Brazilian real. Tax revenues fell precipitously in absolute terms, with Petrobras' payments of CIT and the social contribution on net income falling by 89.8% in national currency terms (Petrobras, 2020[9]; Petrobras, 2021[10]).

**Colombia** registered a significant decline in oil and gas revenues in 2020 (falling from 2.2% of GDP in 2019 to 1.2% of GDP) in a context of lower oil production and exports. While the depreciation of the Colombian peso softened the blow of lower crude oil prices, non-tax revenues from royalties and payments of economic rights to the government (derechos económicos) fell sharply. Non-tax revenues were also impacted by lower dividend payments by Ecopetrol to the central government, which declined from 1.1% of GDP in 2019 to 0.7% of GDP (Ecopetrol, 2021[11]). CIT revenues tumbled, reflecting the weak financial condition of companies in the sector and as a result of Law 2010, adopted in December 2019, which established a gradual reduction in the corporate tax rate from 33% in 2019 to 32% in 2020 and 30% in 2022.

Total oil revenues from exports in **Ecuador** fell precipitously in 2020, from 9.2% of GDP in 2019 to 5.8% of GDP[5]. The decline in absolute terms relative to the US dollar – and implicitly in national currency as Ecuador is a dollarised economy – was in line with the reduction in global crude oil prices and the contraction of oil production (-9.7%). Oil output trended lower in line with demand but was also impacted by the rupture of the Trans-Ecuadorian Oil Pipeline System and the Heavy Crude Oil Pipeline as a result of a landslide in April caused by rapid erosion of the banks of the Coca river (CBE, 2021[12]).

Similarly, in **Guatemala**, lower exports and reduced domestic demand undercut hydrocarbon revenues, which fell from 0.05% of GDP in 2019 to 0.03% of GDP. Export volumes – nearly entirely to the United States and which represent slightly more than half of crude oil production – fell by 28.8%. Revenues related to royalties and state participation in the production of hydrocarbons contracted, roughly in line with the commercial value of production. Tax revenues, which account for a higher share of oil revenues than in most countries, also slid as receipts of the CIT and the solidarity tax (impuesto de solidaridad) contracted.

In **Guyana**, crude oil production began in December 2019 and ramped up during 2020, despite mechanical issues that affected production at the Liza Destiny well operated by ExxonMobil (CBG, 2021[13]). Revenues derived from oil production, currently royalties and profit oil, are deposited in the Natural Resource Fund, a sovereign wealth fund that was established to manage the country's natural resource wealth and that can be tapped to support certain public activities, such as national development investments, especially those targeting an inclusive green economy, and to finance natural disaster relief efforts. The 2021 Natural Resource Fund Act, which included several modifications to the original enabling legislation adopted in 2019, stipulates that all petroleum-related revenues – including, but not limited to, royalties, profit oil, income tax and signature bonuses – must be deposited in the fund.[6] By the end of 2020, hydrocarbon revenues deposited in the fund were equivalent to 3.6% of GDP.

General government oil and gas revenues in **Mexico** were driven down by lower prices, production and policy measures adopted in 2020. Total revenues fell from 1.8% of GDP in 2019 to 0.9% of GDP, due largely to lower property rents as the commercial value of production plummeted. Oil output fell as a result of the decline in demand but also as a consequence of production cuts agreed by OPEC+, of which Mexico is a member, in April. Non-tax revenues were also influenced by the adoption of several policy measures to provide fiscal relief to Pemex, the state-owned oil company. In December 2019, the rate by which the profit-sharing duty (Derecho por la Utilidad Compartida), the most important fiscal instrument for the sector, is assessed was reduced from 65% in 2019 to 58% in 2020.[7] Additionally, in April 2020, the government provided Pemex a fiscal credit of MXN 65 million (0.3% of GDP) to be applied to the payments of the profit-sharing duty.[8]

Hydrocarbon revenues in **Peru** were strongly impacted by public health measures taken to limit the spread of COVID-19 and social conflicts. The shuttering of the Norperuano oil pipeline as a result of social conflicts that were aggravated by the outbreak of the pandemic accentuated existing market-related pressures, leading to a decline in production (PeruPetro, 2021[14]). Natural gas production also contracted but began to rebound in the second half of the year. Lower prices and reduced production caused a contraction in non-tax revenues, which represent the majority of hydrocarbon revenues, and a concomitant decline in total revenues from the sector, which fell from 0.5% of GDP in 2019 to 0.4% of GDP.

Oil and gas revenues in **Trinidad and Tobago** registered a sharp contraction in 2020 – falling from 7.4% of GDP in 2019 to 4.1% of GDP – due to oil market dynamics and a strong base effect associated with extraordinary one-off revenues booked in 2019. Unlike the many hydrocarbon producers in the region for which property rents are the principal source of hydrocarbon revenues, in Trinidad and Tobago tax revenues play a significant role as the sector is largely controlled by private-sector operators. During 2020, tax revenues registered a marked contraction, not only due to weakening profits but also due to a base effect caused by one-off receipts (0.5% of GDP) from the sector related to a tax amnesty in 2019. Similarly, the year-on-year change in non-tax revenues was influenced by a payment (1.2% of GDP) in 2019 by a subsidiary of Royal Dutch Shell to resolve outstanding tax issues. These issues notwithstanding, property rents in the form of royalties also declined in line with global market conditions.

## Falling annual prices for a range of minerals and base metals and lower production undercut mining revenues in 2020

As with global oil markets, the outbreak of the COVID-19 pandemic quickly affected mineral and metal markets. Spot prices for many minerals and base metals dipped in the first half of 2020 as global demand contracted and production in some countries was shuttered as a result of public health measures adopted to limit the spread of the pandemic (Figure 2.4).

Figure 2.4. **International spot prices for selected minerals and metals, 2019-20**

Index 100 = January 2020

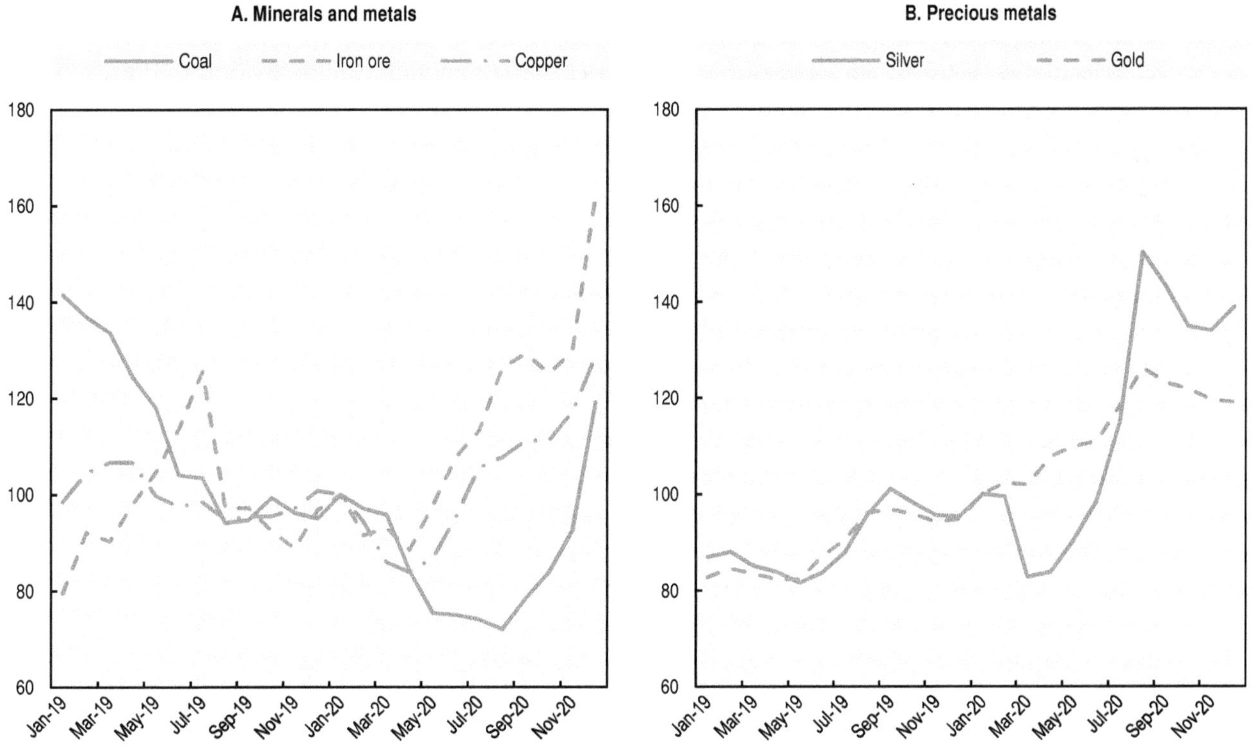


*Source:* Economic Commission for Latin America and the Caribbean (ECLAC), on the basis of World Bank Commodity Price Data (The Pink Sheet), World Bank.

StatLink https://doi.org/10.1787/888934308371

However, market fundamentals for minerals and metals improved markedly in the second half of 2020 as fixed capital formation and industrial activity accelerated in China. Iron ore prices registered a significant increase (rising 16.1% for the year) as steel production in China reached a historic level (+5% year-on-year) (Vale, 2021[15]). Base metals also benefited from increased demand, although annual prices generally fell. Coal prices were particularly impacted, as demand for thermal coal – largely used in power generation – tumbled in May as China adopted a series of import restrictions (Vale, 2021[15]). In contrast, prices for precious metals rose, reflecting their traditional use as a safe-haven asset, a tendency which in the case of silver was heightened by a record inflow of silver-backed financial instruments (World Bank, 2020[16]).

At the regional level, mineral and metals production was significantly impacted by the application of public health measures adopted to limit the spread of the COVID-19 pandemic, especially in Argentina and Peru (Table 2.3). These measures frequently resulted in the shuttering of mines, which were essentially run on a maintenance basis. Output of all major base metals, as well as coal, declined, although with significant variation at the country level. Copper production in Chile – the world's largest producer – fell by less than 1% in 2020, while Peru experienced a 12.4% decline. Coal production in Colombia plummeted (-38.6%), in line with global trends for thermal coal. In contrast, iron ore output rose – principally in Brazil – due to strong Chinese demand. Paradoxically, production of precious metals fell, despite higher prices, as output declined in Argentina, Dominican Republic and Peru.

The interplay of lower average annual prices and reduced production levels resulted in a significant contraction in mining revenues in the region during 2020. Although the decline was modest in relative terms, falling on average from 0.4% of GDP in 2019 to 0.3% of GDP, this was due in part to the dynamics of nominal GDP and currency depreciations, which bolstered revenues from US dollar sources when expressed in national currency (Table 2.4). The decline was more appreciable in absolute terms, with overall mining revenues falling 15.4% in US dollar terms to USD 11.3 billion in 2020.

These trends notwithstanding, there was a pronounced difference in the movements of mining receipts by instrument. Tax revenues at the regional level fell sharply (-20.8% in US dollar terms), largely due to weak profits in 2019 that led, in some cases, to tax refunds in 2020 when advance payments exceeded tax liabilities. Additionally, tax relief measures adopted to offset the impact of the crisis had a strong inter-temporal effect on tax payments, pushing some receipts from 2020 to 2021. Non-tax revenues, in contrast, registered a more modest decline in the region (-2.2%), driven by strong receipts in Chile. At the country level, there was significant heterogeneity, reflecting the varying impact of the pandemic on production, the composition of each country's mining offering and, in some cases, the existence of large one-off transactions in 2019.

Mining revenues contracted in **Argentina** as gold and silver production – the country's principal mining product exports – registered significant declines in 2020. Total mining revenues fell in both relative, from 0.10% of GDP in 2019 to 0.06% of GDP, and absolute (-49.6% in US dollars) terms. Several major producers suspended operations in the first half of the year in response to public health measures, including a mandatory nationwide quarantine in March. Operations at Newmont's Cerro Negro gold mine were restricted to maintenance, with mine production still in the process of ramping up by year-end (Newmont, 2021[17]). Despite the reduction in precious metal production, higher international prices limited the fall in the commercial value of production and in turn in non-tax property rents from royalties.

Table 2.3. **Latin America and the Caribbean (selected countries): International prices and production of metals and minerals, 2019-20**

Percentages, US dollars and thousands of metric tons unless otherwise specified

| Metals and minerales | Year and percent change | Price | Production by country in thousands of metric tons unless otherwise specified | | | | | | | | | | |
|---|---|---|---|---|---|---|---|---|---|---|---|---|---|
| | | | LAC-10 | Argentina | Bolivia | Brazil | Chile | Colombia | Dominican Republic | Ecuador | Jamaica | Mexico | Peru |
| **Copper** | 2019 | 6 010 | 9 324 | | 4 | 584 | 5 787 | | 6 | | | 487 | 2 455 |
| | 2020 | 6 174 | 8 935 | | 3 | 554 | 5 733 | | 2 | | | 492 | 2 150 |
| | % change | 2.7 | -4.2 | | -37.0 | -5.1 | -0.9 | | -63.7 | | | 1.0 | -12.4 |
| **Zinc** | 2019 | 2 550 | 2 484 | 19 | 528 | 196 | 6 | | 6 | | | 325 | 1 404 |
| | 2020 | 2 266 | 2 319 | 11 | 358 | 189 | 29 | | 2 | | | 394 | 1 335 |
| | % change | -11.1 | -6.6 | -41.8 | -32.1 | -3.3 | 410.0 | | -57.3 | | | 21.2 | -5.0 |
| **Lead** | 2019 | 1 997 | 588 | 43 | 88 | | | | | | | 149 | 308 |
| | 2020 | 1 825 | 505 | 23 | 65 | | | | | | | 176 | 242 |
| | % change | -8.6 | -14.1 | -46.4 | -26.6 | | | | | | | 18.2 | -21.6 |
| **Tin** | 2019 | 18 661 | 53 | | 17 | 16 | | | | | | | 20 |
| | 2020 | 17 125 | 52 | | 15 | 17 | | | | | | | 21 |
| | % change | -8.2 | -1.3 | | -14.1 | 6.0 | | | | | | | 4.0 |
| **Nickel** | 2019 | 13 914 | 144 | | | 75 | | 41 | 28 | | | | |
| | 2020 | 13 787 | 175 | | | 117 | | 36 | 22 | | | | |
| | % change | -0.9 | 21.5 | | | 55.8 | | -11.0 | -22.7 | | | | |
| **Iron** | 2019 | 94 | 301 386 | | | 275 031 | 8 427 | 667 | | | | 7 141 | 10 120 |
| | 2020 | 109 | 315 545 | | | 290 114 | 9 891 | 787 | | | | 5 859 | 8 894 |
| | % change | 16.1 | 4.7 | | | 5.5 | 17.4 | 18.0 | | | | -17.9 | -12.1 |
| **Coal** | 2019 | 78 | 91 786 | | | | | 85 169 | | | | 6 617 | |
| | 2020 | 61 | 56 544 | | | | | 52 317 | | | | 4 227 | |
| | % change | -22.0 | -38.4 | | | | | -38.6 | | | | -36.1 | |
| **Bauxite / alumina** | 2019 | 1 794 | 30 671 | | | 19 463 | | 18 | 0 | | 11 190 | | |
| | 2020 | 1 704 | 28 529 | | | 19 337 | | 10 | 9 | | 9 173 | | |
| | % change | -5.0 | -7.0 | | | -0.6 | | -46.8 | n.a. | | -18.0 | | |
| **Gold (metric tons)** | 2019 | 1 392 | 466 | 53 | 5 | 91 | 38 | 38 | 32 | 6 | | 73 | 128 |
| | 2020 | 1 770 | 438 | 35 | 3 | 121 | 34 | 48 | 28 | 9 | | 72 | 88 |
| | % change | 27.1 | -6.1 | -34.2 | -48.6 | 33.0 | -11.9 | 27.5 | -11.5 | 44.4 | | -2.4 | -31.8 |
| **Silver (metric tons)** | 2019 | 16 | 11 068 | 1 071 | 1 153 | 50 | 1 309 | 14 | 109 | 3 | | 3 498 | 3 860 |
| | 2020 | 21 | 9 969 | 767 | 930 | 50 | 1 576 | 20 | 88 | 2 | | 3 809 | 2 727 |
| | % change | 26.6 | -9.9 | -28.4 | -19.4 | 0.4 | 20.4 | 37.7 | -19.1 | -38.0 | | 8.9 | -29.3 |

*Source:* Economic Commission for Latin America and the Caribbean (ECLAC), on the basis of World Bank Commodity Price Data (The Pink Sheet), World Bank; Secretaría de Minería de Argentina, Sistema Federal de Información Minera; Instituto Nacional de Estadísticas del Estado Plurinacional de Bolivia, estadísticas mineras; Agência Nacional de Mineração do Brasil, Anuário Mineral Brasileiro: Principais Substâncias Metálicas; Comisión Chilena de Cobre (Cochilco), Anuario de Estadísticas del Cobre y Otros Minerales 2000-2020; Agencia Nacional de Minería de Colombia, Sistema de Información Minero Colombiano; Oficina Nacional de Estadística de la República Dominicana, estadísticas mineras; Statistical Institute of Jamaica, mineral production statistics; Banco Central del Ecuador, Reporte de Minería; Instituto Nacional de Estadística y Geografía de México, estadísticas mineras; and, Instituto Nacional de Estadística e Informática de Perú, estadísticas mineras.

StatLink https://doi.org/10.1787/888934308504

Public health measures significantly curtailed mining activity in the **Plurinational National State of Bolivia**. Lower international prices, particularly for zinc – which is the principal base metal export by value – put downward pressure on non-tax revenues from royalties. However, rising gold prices bolstered the value of exports of metallic gold, compensating in part for the contractions registered for other mining productions. However, the principal driver of the decline in overall mining revenues, which fell from 1.15% of GDP in 2019 to 0.43% of GDP, was a collapse in tax revenues from the sector (-95.8% in US dollar terms). CIT payments reached an artificially elevated level in 2019 as the San Cristóbal mining company made a large advance payment on its tax liabilities for the fiscal year 2019, which was not repeated in 2020 (MSC, 2021[18]).

Table 2.4. **Latin America and the Caribbean (11 countries): General government fiscal revenues from mining, by type of revenue, 2019-20**

Percentage of GDP, percentage points of GDP and percentages

| Type of revenue | Period | Region / country | | | | | | | | | | | |
|---|---|---|---|---|---|---|---|---|---|---|---|---|---|
| | | LAC | Argentina | Bolivia (Plurinational State of) | Brazil | Chile | Colombia | Dominican Republic | Ecuador | Guatemala | Jamaica | Mexico | Peru |
| **Total revenues** | 2019 | **0.4** | 0.10 | 1.15 | 0.19 | 1.35 | 0.28 | 0.23 | 0.09 | 0.01 | 0.04 | 0.18 | 0.66 |
| | 2020 | **0.3** | 0.06 | 0.43 | 0.24 | 1.23 | 0.20 | 0.50 | 0.09 | 0.02 | 0.03 | 0.19 | 0.56 |
| | 2020-2019 (p.p. of GDP) | **-0.1** | -0.04 | -0.72 | 0.06 | -0.12 | -0.07 | 0.28 | 0.00 | 0.01 | -0.01 | 0.01 | -0.10 |
| | 2020-2019 (% change in NC) | **n.a.** | -26.2 | -66.6 | 32.4 | -7.4 | -29.6 | 117.8 | -11.2 | 55.6 | -26.3 | -2.0 | -20.8 |
| | 2020-2019 (% change in USD) | **-15.4** | -49.6 | -66.6 | 1.3 | -17.9 | -37.5 | 97.6 | -11.2 | 55.1 | -31.0 | -12.2 | -24.4 |
| **Tax revenues** | 2019 | **0.3** | 0.09 | 0.67 | 0.11 | 1.02 | 0.06 | 0.17 | 0.05 | 0.01 | 0.00 | 0.18 | 0.46 |
| | 2020 | **0.2** | 0.04 | 0.03 | 0.15 | 0.73 | 0.06 | 0.37 | 0.05 | 0.01 | 0.00 | 0.19 | 0.39 |
| | 2020-2019 (p.p. of GDP) | **-0.1** | -0.04 | -0.64 | 0.04 | -0.30 | 0.00 | 0.20 | -0.01 | 0.00 | 0.00 | 0.01 | -0.07 |
| | 2020-2019 (% change in NC) | **n.a.** | -38.6 | -95.8 | 34.9 | -27.5 | -12.6 | 111.9 | -20.8 | 67.3 | .. | -2.0 | -21.1 |
| | 2020-2019 (% change in USD) | **-20.8** | -58.1 | -95.8 | 3.2 | -35.8 | -22.4 | 92.3 | -20.8 | 66.8 | .. | -12.2 | -24.6 |
| **Non-tax revenues** | 2019 | **0.1** | 0.02 | 0.48 | 0.07 | 0.33 | 0.22 | 0.05 | 0.04 | 0.00 | 0.04 | 0.00 | 0.20 |
| | 2020 | **0.1** | 0.02 | 0.40 | 0.09 | 0.50 | 0.15 | 0.13 | 0.04 | 0.01 | 0.03 | 0.00 | 0.17 |
| | 2020-2019 (p.p. of GDP) | **0.0** | 0.00 | -0.08 | 0.02 | 0.17 | -0.07 | 0.08 | 0.00 | 0.00 | -0.01 | 0.00 | -0.03 |
| | 2020-2019 (% change in NC) | **n.a.** | 31.7 | -25.4 | 28.5 | 55.2 | -34.3 | 137.1 | 3.7 | 34.7 | -26.3 | .. | -20.1 |
| | 2020-2019 (% change in USD) | **-2.2** | -10.1 | -25.4 | -1.7 | 37.6 | -41.7 | 115.2 | 3.7 | 34.3 | -31.0 | .. | -23.7 |
| *of which: royalties and production levies* | 2019 | **0.1** | 0.02 | 0.48 | 0.07 | 0.33 | 0.22 | 0.05 | 0.03 | 0.00 | 0.04 | 0.00 | 0.20 |
| | 2020 | **0.1** | 0.02 | 0.40 | 0.09 | 0.41 | 0.15 | 0.13 | 0.04 | 0.00 | 0.03 | 0.00 | 0.17 |
| | 2020-2019 (p.p. of GDP) | **0.0** | 0.00 | -0.08 | 0.02 | 0.08 | -0.07 | 0.08 | 0.01 | 0.00 | -0.01 | .. | -0.03 |
| | 2020-2019 (% change in NC) | **n.a.** | 31.7 | -25.4 | 29.1 | 25.9 | -34.3 | 137.1 | 6.2 | 68.2 | -26.3 | .. | -19.3 |
| | 2020-2019 (% change in USD) | **-8.1** | -10.1 | -25.4 | -1.2 | 11.6 | -41.7 | 115.2 | 6.2 | 67.6 | -31.0 | .. | -22.9 |

*Note:* Revenue-to-GDP ratios for Latin America and the Caribbean correspond to a simple average of the countries included in the sample. Figures may not sum due to rounding.

*Source:* Economic Commission for Latin America and the Caribbean (ECLAC), based on data from ECLAC's Fiscal Revenues from Non-Renewable Natural Resources in Latin America and the Caribbean database.

StatLink https://doi.org/10.1787/888934308523

Mining revenues in **Brazil** registered a modest increase in 2020 (+1.3% in US dollar terms, from 0.19% of GDP in 2019 to 0.24% of GDP), despite higher production levels and rising international prices for iron ore, particularly in the latter half of the year. Non-tax revenues from royalties – including the federal CFEM and state-level levies applied in Mato Grosso do Sul, Minas Gerais and Pará – rose in national currency terms largely due to the depreciation of the Brazilian real, as for most of the year they were liquidated at a price comparable to those in 2019. Tax revenues, however, were positively impacted by the annual increase in prices, leading to a boost in CIT payments, which were likewise flattered by the movement of the national currency.

In **Chile**, mining revenues retreated – falling from 1.35% of GDP in 2019 to 1.20% of GDP, or by -17.9% in US dollar terms – as the result of a decline in tax revenues from the sector. CIT receipts fell as estimated tax payments for fiscal year 2020 made in 2019 were greater than final tax liabilities (DIPRES, 2020[19]). However, the fall in tax revenues was partially compensated by an increase in non-tax revenues. Overall, copper output proved resilient, despite temporary production suspensions and labour conflicts, which combined with rising prices in the second year resulted in receipts of the export levy applied to the state-owned producer Codelco. Additionally, Codelco made a substantial pre-payment of 2021 dividends (0.1% of GDP) in December 2020 (DIPRES, 2021[5]).

**Colombia** experienced a significant decline in mining revenues in light of the exceptionally weak global market for coal during 2020. Overall, fiscal revenues from the sector fell from 0.28% of GDP in 2019 to 0.20% of GDP, led by a sharp contraction in non-tax revenues. Property rents from royalties fell 41.7% in US dollar terms, reflecting the combined impact of lower coal prices (-22%) and reduced coal production (-38.6%). Coal output was also impacted by a strike at the Cerrejón mine – the largest open-cast coal mine in the region – between 31 August and 30 November, which concluded with the signing of a new collective employment agreement. Gold production, in contrast, reached a four-year high, resulting in a near-doubling of related royalty receipts[9].

Mining revenues in the **Dominican Republic** nearly doubled in US dollar terms in 2020, with higher prices offsetting a decline in gold and silver production. Total revenues rose from 0.23% of GDP in 2019 to 0.5% of GDP, bolstered by a significant increase in CIT receipts. Likewise, revenues from the mining profits tax (Impuesto sobre las Utilidades Mineras) also rose, reflecting its sliding scale of rates based on market prices. Non-tax revenues more than doubled, as the increase in gold prices easily offset the decline in production. However, another key factor was a one-off advance payment on 2021 royalties – equivalent to 0.06% of GDP – made by Barrick Gold Corporation, the operator of the Pueblo Viejo mine (DIGEPRES, 2021[20]).

In **Ecuador**, mining revenues held steady relative to GDP – at 0.09% of GDP – although they fell in US dollar terms. Gold exports, which represent a significant share of large-scale mining activity in the country, rose 4.4% in volume terms, with a near doubling in value. Nevertheless, non-tax revenues from royalties registered a modest increase. This was largely due to the existence of large royalty pre-payments made in 2019. Excluding these, royalties doubled in value, reflecting the combined impact of increased gold production (+44.4%) and higher gold prices (+27.1%). Tax revenues declined in 2020, due in part to high base of comparison with 2019, when Executive Decree No. 1109 mandated the advance payment of 2020 CIT liabilities.[10]

Strong exports bolstered mining revenues in **Guatemala**, which rose from 0.01% of GDP in 2019 to 0.02% of GDP. Trade of ferro-nickel, particularly with China, increased in terms of both volume and value (+75%).[11] Mining activity in the country has been substantially curtailed by order of the Constitutional Court, which mandated that the Ministry of Energy and Mines conduct consultations with local communities impacted by mining projects within the framework of ILO Convention 169. During 2020, the Constitutional Court further ordered the suspension of mining activities related to the Fenix mine – finding that the process of authorising the original permit violated the right of local communities impacted by the project – until a consultation process was concluded. All consultations are at an incipient stage, with preparatory meetings to be held in early 2021.

The combination of lower bauxite and alumina production and a reduction in the global prices for these goods contributed to the contraction of mining revenues in **Jamaica** during 2020. Fiscal revenues from the sector remain exceptionally low, at 0.03% of GDP in 2020 compared with a recent high of 0.2% of GDP in 2015. Falling non-tax revenues accounted for the decline in overall revenues as tax revenues consistently registered 0.0% of GDP since 2012. Property rents from royalty payments were impacted in part by the temporary closure of the Jiuquan Iron and Steel Company (JISCO) Alumina refinery, which began in September 2019 and continued into 2020, and lower global demand, especially from China. The country maintains several bespoke fiscal agreements with individual producers but information about revenues derived from these contracts is not available.

Revenues from mining in **Mexico** contracted in 2020, although they rose relative to GDP (from 0.18% of GDP in 2019 to 0.19% of GDP), reflecting the interaction of several factors. The commercial value of production rose sharply (+23.3%) as rising mine output either offset price declines or amplified higher prices for some products (SGM, 2021$_{[21]}$). Higher sales values translated into increased profits for some major producers, including for Grupo México's mining division – which also includes some operations in Peru – where operating profits in 2020 rose 21.6% in US dollar terms (Grupo México, 2021$_{[22]}$). Nevertheless, overall tax revenues fell in absolute terms due to lower receipts from the special mining right (derecho especial sobre minería), a 7.5% tax on profits from mining operations. The annual full-year payment of this tax is due in March of the following year, therefore revenues registered in 2020 represent 2019 results, when weak prices and labour conflicts impacted the profitability of several major metal producers.[12]

Mining production in **Peru** was strongly impacted by public health measures taken to curtail the spread of the COVID-19 pandemic. Mines were shuttered in mid-March, limited to activities to maintain facilities ready for the eventual restart of operations (MEMP, 2021$_{[23]}$). Mining operations progressively reopened in May, resulting in a quick recovery in production levels in June and July for some products. Nevertheless, yearly mine output was sharply lower, with copper production declining 12.4% compared to 0.9% in neighboring Chile. Falling production and lower international prices for some products reduced the commercial value of production and operating profits with a concomitant impact on mining revenues, which fell from 0.66% of GDP in 2019 to 0.56 % of GDP (-24.4% in US dollar terms). These dynamics were not, however, uniform throughout the sector. For example, operating profits and CIT payments of Shougang Hierro Peru – the country's principal iron ore producer – rose sharply, in line with the increase in iron ore prices (Shougang Hierro, 2021$_{[24]}$).

### Notes

1. SUNAT (National Superintendency of Customs and Tax Administration), Press release, "SUNAT: Compañía Minera Buenaventura paga deuda por s/ 2,134 millones", Lima, 5 August 2021 [online] *https://www.sunat.gob.pe/salaprensa/2021/agosto/NotaPrensaN0612021.doc*; Press release, "SUNAT: Minera Cerro Verde pagó s/ 1,040 millones de deuda", Lima, 13 August 2021 [online] *https://www.sunat.gob.pe/salaprensa/2021/agosto/NotaPrensaN0642021.doc.*
2. Organization of Petroleum Exporting Countries, Press release, "The 10th (Extraordinary) OPEC and non-OPEC Ministerial Meeting concludes" [online], *https://www.opec.org/opec_web/en/press_room/5891.htm.*
3. Organization of Petroleum Exporting Countries, Press release, "The 12th OPEC and non-OPEC Ministerial Meeting concludes" [online], *https://www.opec.org/opec_web/en/press_room/6257.htm.*
4. Decree 488/2020, 18 May 2020, "Petróleo Crudo en el Mercado Local. Establécese Precio para Facturación de Entregas." [online], *https://www.argentina.gob.ar/normativa/nacional/decreto-488-2020-337678/texto.*

5. Statistics related to oil revenues were significantly modified in 2020, as data from 2012 onwards were recalculated to align with the Manual of Government Finance Statistics 2014 and were disaggregated by revenues from crude oil exports (up-stream) and those from the domestic sale of hydrocarbon derivatives (down-stream).
6. Official Gazette of Guyana, Act No. 19 of 2021, Natural Resource Fund Act 2021 [online], *https://finance.gov.gy/wp-content/uploads/2021/03/NRF-Act.pdf.*
7. Secretaría de Gobernación, Diario Oficial de la Federación, "DECRETO por el que se reforman y adicionan diversas disposiciones de la Ley de Ingresos sobre Hidrocarburos", 9 December 2019 [online], *http://www.diputados.gob.mx/LeyesBiblio/pdf/LIH_110121.pdf.*
8. Secretaría de Gobernación, Diario Oficial de la Federación, "DECRETO por el que se otorgan beneficios fiscales a los contribuyentes que se indican", 21 April 2020 [online], *https://www.dof.gob.mx/nota_detalle.php?codigo=5591969&fecha=21/04/2020*
9. Agencía Nacional de Minería de Colombia, "Colombia logró en 2020 la producción de oro más alta de los últimos cuatro años", Press release, 26 March 2021 [online] *https://www.anm.gov.co/?q=colombia-logro-en-2020-la-produccion-de-oro-mas-alta-de-los-ultimos-cuatro-a%C3%B1os.*
10. Servicio de Rentas Internas, "De enero a septiembre de 2021 la recaudación tributaria creció un 11%", Comunicado de prensa, 11 October 2021 [online], *https://www.sri.gob.ec/detalle-noticias?idnoticia=835&marquesina=1*
11. Banco Central de Guatemala, Estadísticas del Comercio Exterior (Exportaciones/Importaciones) [online], *https://www.banguat.gob.gt/es/page/sector-externo-0.*
12. Preliminary results for 2021 show that revenues from the special mining right increased sharply, reflecting the favourable operating profits generated in 2020.

## *References*


CBE (2021), *Reporte del sector petrolero IV Trimestre de 2020*, Central Bank of Ecuador, *https://contenido.bce.fin.ec/documentos/Estadisticas/Hidrocarburos/ASP202004.pdf.* [12]

CBG (2021), *Annual Report 2020*, Central Bank of Guyana, *https://bankofguyana.org.gy/bog/images/research/Reports/ANNREP2020.pdf.* [13]

CRS (2020), *Crude Oil Futures Prices Turn Negative*, Congressional Research Service, *https://crsreports.congress.gov/product/pdf/IN/IN11354#:~:text=On%20April%2020%2C%202020%2C%20the,at%20negative%20%2437.62%20per%20barrel.* [6]

DIGEPRES (2021), *Ejecución presupuestaria del gobierno central, organismos autónomos y descentralizados no financieros e instituciones públicas de la seguridad social*, Dirección General de Presupuesto, *https://www.digepres.gob.do/wp-content/uploads/2021/04/Informe-de-ejecucion-Enero-Diciembre-2020-vf1.pdf.* [20]

DIPRES (2020), *Informe de Finanzas Públicas: Tercer Trimestre 2020*, Dirección de Presupuestos de Chile, *https://www.dipres.gob.cl/598/articles-210554_Informe_PDF.pdf.* [19]

DIPRES (2021), *Informe de ejecución del gobierno central cuarto trimestre 2020*, Dirección de Presupuestos de Chile, *https://www.dipres.gob.cl/598/articles-201613_doc_pdf_Presentacion_IT.pdf.* [5]

ECLAC (2021), *Economic Survey of Latin America and the Caribbean 2021*, Economic Commission for Latin America and the Caribbean, Santiago, *https://www.cepal.org/es/publicaciones/47192-estudio-economico-america-latina-caribe-2021-dinamica-laboral-politicas-empleo.* [2]

ECLAC (2021), *Fiscal Panorama of Latin America and the Caribbean 2021*, Economic Commission for Latin America and the Caribbean, Santiago, *https://www.cepal.org/es/publicaciones/46808-panorama-fiscal-america-latina-caribe-2021-desafios-la-politica-fiscal-la.* [3]

ECLAC (2021), *Preliminary Overview of the Economies of Latin America and the Caribbean 2021*, Economic Commission for Latin America and the Caribbean, Santiago, *https://www.cepal.org/es/publicaciones/47669-balance-preliminar-economias-america-latina-caribe-2021.* [4]

Ecopetrol (2021), *Form 20-F for Fiscal Year 2020*, *https://www.ecopetrol.com.co/wps/wcm/connect/9da6508e-05b3-422b-8c19-a4b14f53b64e/Reporte+20F+2020.pdf?MOD=AJPERES&attachment=false&id=1617974293673.* [11]

Grupo México (2021), *Annual Report 2020*, *https://www.gmexico.com/GMDocs/ReportesFinancieros/ING/2020/RF_EN_2020_IFN.pdf.* [22]

IMF (2021), *World Economic Outlook: October 2021*, International Monetary Fund, Washington D.C., *https://www.imf.org/en/Publications/WEO/weo-database/2021/October*. [1]

MEFP (2021), *Memoria de la Economía Boliviana 2020*, Ministerio de Economía y Finanzas Públicas, *https://www.economiayfinanzas.gob.bo/memoria-de-la-economia-boliviana-2020.html*. [7]

MEMP (2021), *Boletín Estadístico Minero 2020*, Ministerio de Energía y Minas del Perú, *https://www.gob.pe/institucion/minem/informes-publicaciones/1649957-boletin-estadistico-minero-diciembre-2020*. [23]

MSC (2021), *Reporte de Sostenibilidad 2020*, Minera San Cristóbal, *http://www.minerasancristobal.com/reportedesostenibilidad/wp-content/uploads/2021/08/MSC-Reporte-Sostenibilidad-2020-1.pdf*. [18]

Newmont (2021), *2020 Annual Report and Form 10-K*, *https://s24.q4cdn.com/382246808/files/doc_financials/2020/ar/386219(1)_17_Newmont_AR_WR.pdf*. [17]

PeruPetro (2021), *Memoria Institucional 2020*, *https://www.perupetro.com.pe/wps/wcm/connect/corporativo/93e6b149-8a3b-4796-b274-ca2014457703/MEMORIA+PERUPETRO+2020d.pdf?MOD=AJPERES&Memoria%20Perupetro%202020*. [14]

Petrobras (2020), *Tax Report 2019: Petrobras economic and social contribution*, *https://api.mziq.com/mzfilemanager/v2/d/25fdf098-34f5-4608-b7fa-17d60b2de47d/82d39144-bc84-6df6-a33c-c019b6b4fc3c?origin=1*. [9]

Petrobras (2021), *Tax Report 2020*, *https://api.mziq.com/mzfilemanager/v2/d/25fdf098-34f5-4608-b7fa-17d60b2de47d/3d74be35-c5f0-b698-cf39-effdc0abea98?origin=1*. [10]

SGM (2021), *Anuario estadístico de la minería mexicana 2020*, Servicio Geológico Mexicano, *https://www.sgm.gob.mx/productos/pdf/Anuario_2020_Edicion_2021.pdf*. [21]

Shougang Hierro (2021), *Memoria Anual Año 2020*, *https://www.smv.gob.pe/ConsultasP8/temp/Memoria%20SHP%20-%202020.pdf*. [24]

Vale (2021), *Form 20-F for Fiscal Year 2020*, *https://api.mziq.com/mzfilemanager/v2/d/53207d1c-63b4-48f1-96b7-19869fae19fe/348c0de9-5017-4a98-a9b7-4ba755a91f51?origin=1*. [15]

World Bank (2020), *Commodity Markets Outlook, October 2020*, World Bank, Washington D.C., *https://openknowledge.worldbank.org/handle/10986/34621*. [16]

YPBF (2021), *Rendición pública de cuentas final 2020*, *https://www.ypfb.gob.bo/images/ypfb/Transparencia/RendicionPresidencia2020/RendicionDeCuentas2020.pdf*. [8]

*Capítulo 2*

# SECCIÓN ESPECIAL

# Ingresos fiscales provenientes de recursos naturales no renovables en América Latina y el Caribe

### Mensajes principales

**Las cuentas fiscales de América Latina y el Caribe se vieron afectadas negativamente en 2020 por la caída de los ingresos fiscales provenientes de los recursos naturales no renovables**

Ante una crisis económica y social sin precedentes, los países de América Latina y el Caribe (ALC) recurrieron a la política fiscal para paliar los impactos de la pandemia del COVID-19 en los sistemas públicos de salud, los hogares y la estructura productiva. Las medidas fiscales relacionadas con la crisis, basadas en gran medida en el gasto público discrecional, combinadas con la caída de los ingresos públicos crearon una presión sustancial sobre las cuentas públicas. Para los productores de recursos naturales no renovables de la región, en particular los exportadores de petróleo crudo, la disminución de los ingresos totales en 2020 se vio agravada por las perturbaciones de los precios externos que socavaron gravemente los ingresos del petróleo y el gas. En algunos países, la disminución de estos ingresos representó la mitad o más de la contracción general de los ingresos del gobierno general.

**Los ingresos por hidrocarburos disminuyeron significativamente en 2020, en medio de las perturbaciones en los mercados petroleros mundiales**

Los ingresos fiscales por exploración y producción de hidrocarburos en la región cayeron al 2.1% del PIB en 2020, en comparación con el 3.1% del PIB en 2019. Si bien los niveles de producción en la región en general cayeron, el principal impulsor de la contracción de los ingresos por hidrocarburos fue el shock de precios que se originó en los mercados internacionales. Para el año, los ingresos por petróleo y gas cayeron un 59.7% en términos de dólares estadounidenses, para ubicarse en 33.1 millones de USD, un nivel no visto desde 2002.

**Los ingresos mineros cedieron terreno en 2020 debido a que las medidas de salud pública afectaron fuertemente la producción**

Los ingresos mineros en la región se contrajeron durante 2020, reflejando el efecto combinado de precios internacionales más bajos para la mayoría de los minerales y metales básicos, así como una menor producción debido en parte a las medidas de salud pública adoptadas para limitar la propagación del virus COVID-19. Como resultado, los ingresos tributarios, en particular los ingresos por el impuesto a las utilidades corporativas, se desplomaron. En el año, los ingresos de la minería cayeron al 0.3% del PIB, desde el 0.4% del PIB en 2019, equivalente a una disminución del 15.4% en términos de dólares estadounidenses.

**Para 2021 se pronostica una rápida recuperación de los ingresos fiscales por recursos naturales no renovables**

Las estimaciones y los datos preliminares para países seleccionados apuntan a un fuerte aumento en los ingresos fiscales provenientes de recursos naturales no renovables en 2021. Se estima que los ingresos de la minería han sido especialmente dinámicos, duplicando su nivel de 2020 para alcanzar el 0.6% del PIB, respaldados por una demanda global creciente, precios favorables y un aumento de la producción interna. También se estima que los ingresos por petróleo y gas se recuperaron en 2021 para alcanzar el 3.0% del PIB, justo por debajo del nivel registrado en 2019.

## La caída de los ingresos fiscales provenientes de los recursos naturales no renovables tuvo un impacto significativo en las cuentas públicas de ALC en 2020

El estallido de la pandemia de COVID-19 tuvo un impacto dramático e inmediato en la actividad global y el bienestar social. Los profundos impactos en la oferta y la demanda causados por las medidas de salud pública, incluidas las cuarentenas y las restricciones al movimiento de las personas, se extendieron por la economía mundial y tuvieron graves repercusiones en el comercio, la inversión y el empleo a nivel mundial. La producción económica mundial se contrajo un -3.3% en 2020, la tasa más baja registrada desde 1980, superando fácilmente la caída del -0.1% registrada en 2009 durante la crisis financiera y económica mundial (FMI, 2021[1]).

Los mercados de materias primas también se vieron golpeados por choques de oferta y de demanda, lo que provocó movimientos significativos en los precios internacionales. El comercio internacional y los viajes colapsaron lo que, junto con las restricciones a la movilidad, condujeron a una caída histórica en la demanda de productos de hidrocarburos líquidos. Los precios al contado del petróleo crudo se desplomaron, volviéndose negativos durante algunos días, ya que los comerciantes buscaban deshacerse de posiciones de productos que ya no podían almacenar. Los mercados de minerales y metales se vieron afectados de manera similar, aunque los rápidos repuntes en la actividad industrial de China y la formación de capital fijo impulsaron los precios al final del primer semestre del año.

ALC no se salvó de las consecuencias de la rápida propagación del COVID-19. La producción económica se contrajo -6.8%, equivalente a la mayor caída desde 1900 (CEPAL, 2021[2]). Las medidas para frenar la propagación de la pandemia contribuyeron a una importante caída del empleo (-9.0%), que no pudo ser compensada por una mayor informalidad -el tradicional amortiguador del mercado laboral-, ya que las cuarentenas obligaron a los trabajadores a quedarse en casa. En este contexto, la crisis provocó una grave erosión del bienestar socioeconómico, agravando las brechas de desarrollo estructural existentes, al tiempo que generó un aumento sin precedentes de la pobreza.

Los países de la región buscaron llenar temporalmente estos vacíos mediante la adopción de paquetes de medidas de apoyo fiscal de amplio alcance y escala, con un promedio de 4.6% del PIB para América Latina (CEPAL, 2021[3]). La política fiscal se volvió una herramienta clave de la política pública para fortalecer los colapsados sistemas de salud pública, apoyar a las familias en dificultades y proteger la capacidad productiva de la región. Sin embargo, estos esfuerzos fueron acompañados de una importante erosión de las cuentas públicas, con déficits excepcionalmente elevados y un aumento sustancial de la deuda pública.

La situación fiscal de la región en 2020 también se vio complicada por las turbulencias registradas en los mercados de materias primas, que tuvieron un impacto directo en los ingresos fiscales provenientes de la explotación de los recursos naturales no renovables. Si bien la mayor parte de la erosión de los saldos públicos se debió al gasto público, los ingresos totales del gobierno central cayeron significativamente en algunos países. Esto fue especialmente grave en países con una elevada dependencia de los ingresos por hidrocarburos, como Bolivia (Estado Plurinacional de), Colombia, Ecuador, México y Trinidad y Tobago. La contracción de los ingresos por petróleo y gas en Ecuador (-3.4 puntos porcentuales [pp] del PIB), Colombia (-1.2 pp del PIB) y Trinidad y Tobago (-3.3 pp del PIB) representó la mitad o más de la caída general en ingresos totales (véase el Gráfico 2.1).

Los países especializados en actividades mineras, o dónde la minería constituye la mayor parte de los ingresos fiscales de los recursos naturales no renovables, por lo general se vieron menos afectados. La minería en Chile y Perú – entre los principales productores de metales del mundo – registró una caída limitada con un impacto concomitantemente marginal en las cuentas públicas. Esto reflejó la rápida reactivación de la producción minera en el segundo semestre asociada a precios internacionales favorables. También, fue el resultado de la participación relativamente reducida de estos ingresos, que habían caído progresivamente de un promedio regional de 0.9% del PIB en 2009 a 0.3% del PIB en 2020.

Gráfico 2.1. **Países seleccionados: variación % anual de los ingresos totales del gobierno general por componentes, 2019-20**

Puntos porcentuales del PIB

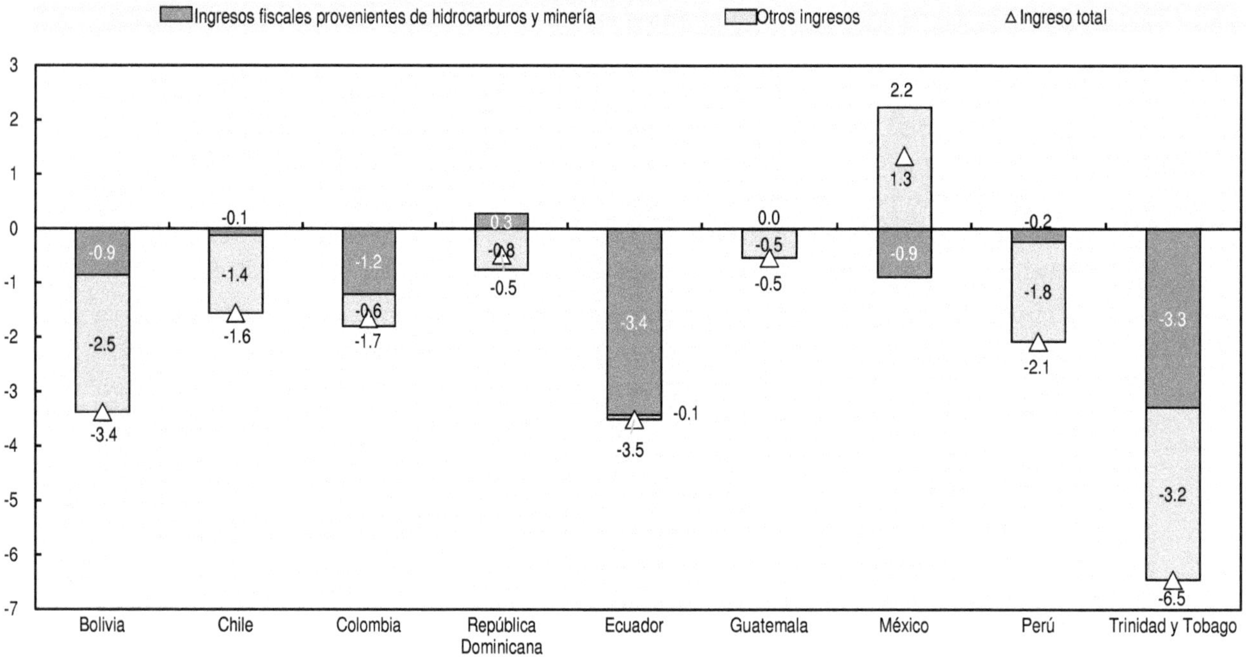


*Nota:* Los datos de México corresponden al gobierno federal que excluyen los ingresos propios de Pemex, la empresa estatal productora de petróleo y gas. En Ecuador, los datos corresponden a los ingresos petroleros derivados de las exportaciones del sector público no financiero. Los datos de República Dominicana, Guatemala y Trinidad y Tobago se refieren al gobierno central.

*Fuente:* Comisión Económica para América Latina y el Caribe (CEPAL) sobre la base información de la base de datos Ingresos Fiscales de los Recursos Naturales No Renovables en América Latina y el Caribe de la CEPAL.

StatLink https://doi.org/10.1787/888934308390

Las cifras preliminares para las operaciones del gobierno central en 2021 indican un repunte significativo de los ingresos públicos, impulsado en parte por mayores ingresos fiscales provenientes de recursos naturales no renovables (CEPAL, 2021[4]). Los precios del petróleo crudo aumentaron considerablemente durante el año, con un aumento del precio spot del crudo Brent del 67% en comparación con el promedio anual de 2020 y del 10% en comparación con 2019. Por lo tanto, los ingresos por hidrocarburos en la región, fuertemente ponderados por las rentas de propiedad calculadas sobre el valor comercial de la producción, se recuperarán significativamente en 2021, con estimaciones que sugieren un aumento al 3.0% del PIB desde el 2.1% del PIB en 2020 (véase el Gráfico 2.2).

De manera similar, los precios de una amplia gama de minerales y metales aumentaron durante 2021, incluidos incrementos sustanciales para el carbón (+127%), el cobre (+51%) y el mineral de hierro (+48%). Se han estimado aumentos en los pagos de regalías y otras rentas de propiedad derivadas de la minería, pero el principal impulsor de los mayores ingresos públicos mineros fue un aumento en los pagos del impuesto a las utilidades corporativas. La mayor rentabilidad y el impacto del retiro de las medidas de alivio fiscal empleadas en 2020 dieron como resultado un repunte en la liquidación de obligaciones tributarias del año anterior y en los pagos anticipados del ejercicio en curso. Como resultado, se estima que los ingresos mineros se duplicarán en promedio en la región, de 0.3% del PIB en 2020 a 0.6% del PIB (véase el Gráfico 2.2).

Gráfico 2.2. **Ingresos fiscales del gobierno general provenientes de recursos naturales no renovables, 2000-21 (proyección) y datos preliminares para países seleccionados, 2019-21 (preliminar)**

Porcentajes del PIB

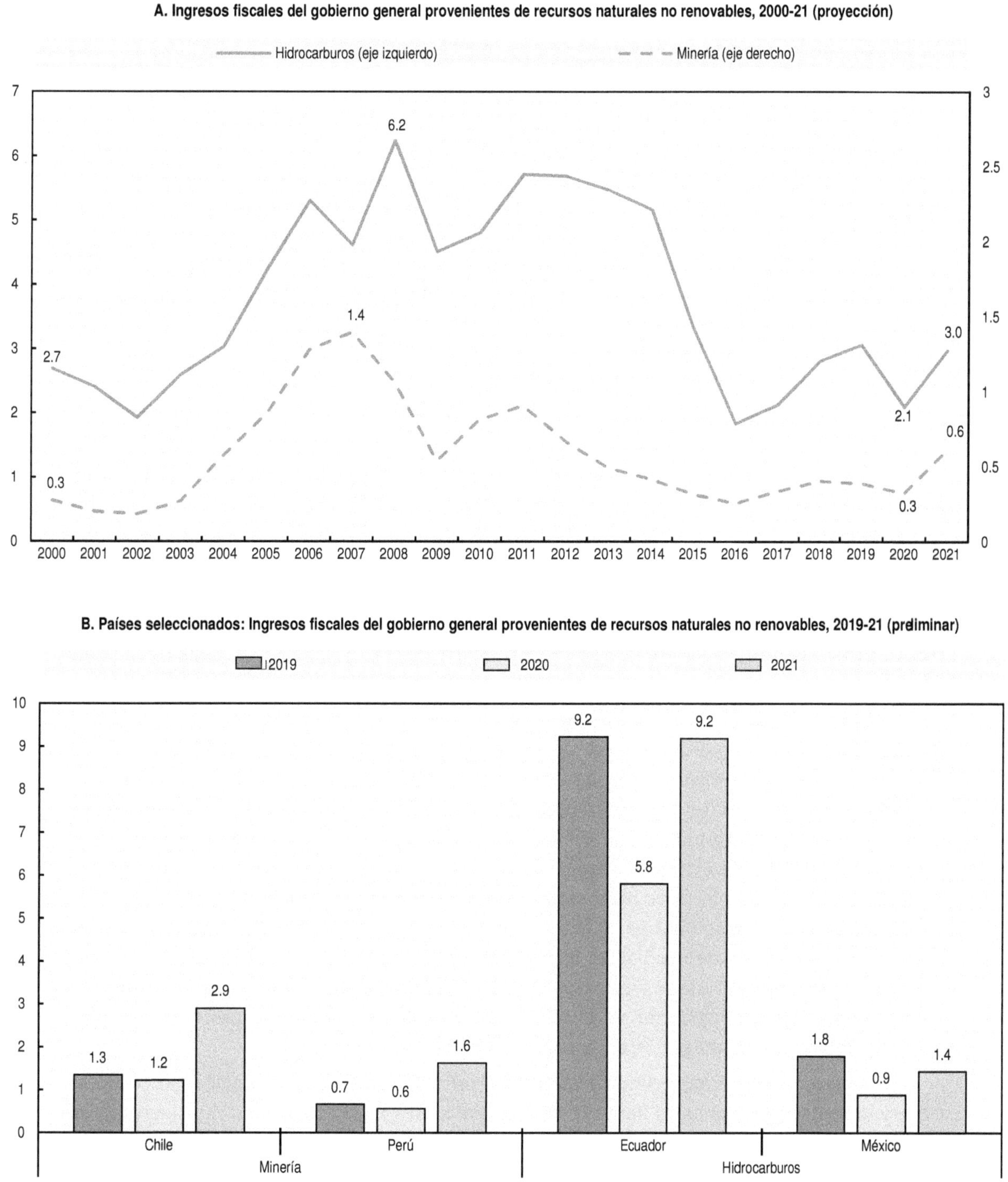


*Nota:* Los datos de México corresponden al gobierno federal que excluyen los ingresos propios de Pemex, la empresa estatal productora de petróleo y gas. En Ecuador, los datos corresponden a los ingresos petroleros derivados de las exportaciones del sector público no financiero.

*Fuente:* Comisión Económica para América Latina y el Caribe (CEPAL) sobre la base información de la base de datos Ingresos Fiscales de los Recursos Naturales No Renovables en América Latina y el Caribe de la CEPAL.

StatLink https://doi.org/10.1787/888934308409

Los datos preliminares sobre los ingresos fiscales provenientes de los recursos naturales no renovables respaldan las estimaciones de ingresos anuales para la región. Los ingresos mineros aumentaron considerablemente en 2021 en Chile y Perú, duplicando o superando los niveles registrados en 2019 (Gráfico 2.2). Sin embargo, parte de este aumento se debió a importantes pagos únicos. Codelco, la productora estatal de cobre de Chile, realizó un prepago de dividendos de 2021 equivalente al 0.4% del PIB al gobierno central (DIPRES, 2021$_{[5]}$). En Perú, dos empresas mineras, Compañía Minera Buenaventura y Cerro Verde, liquidaron deudas tributarias pendientes con pagos equivalentes al 0.4% del PIB[1].

Los ingresos por petróleo y gas también mostraron signos de recuperación, especialmente en Ecuador, donde los problemas con la infraestructura petrolera se resolvieron progresivamente mientras los precios superaron los niveles de 2019. La recuperación de los ingresos por hidrocarburos en México fue menos pronunciada, reflejando en parte las medidas adoptadas para reducir la carga fiscal de Pemex, como la reducción de la tasa utilizada en el cálculo del pago del derecho de participación en las utilidades (Derecho por la Utilidad Compartida).

## Las perturbaciones en los mercados mundiales de hidrocarburos durante 2020 afectaron los ingresos por hidrocarburos en ALC

El estallido de la pandemia de COVID-19 y las medidas de salud pública asociadas, incluidas las restricciones a la movilidad y las cuarentenas, conllevaron una ruptura casi instantánea en los mercados petroleros internacionales. El consumo mundial de petróleo y otros líquidos comenzó a contraerse de forma pronunciada a fines del primer trimestre de 2020 (véase el Gráfico 2.3) mientras la caída se aceleró en el segundo trimestre con una asombrosa contracción interanual del 15%, ya que los choques parejos de la oferta y de la demanda causados por la crisis hundieron la economía global. Estas caídas son históricas ya que antes de 2020, las mayores contracciones en un solo trimestre se registraron en el cuarto trimestre de 2008 (-3.4%) y el primer trimestre de 2009 (-3.3%), en el peak de la crisis financiera global.

Los precios del crudo en los mercados mundiales se desplomaron como reacción a esta caída de la demanda general. Los precios al contado del Brent y del West Texas Intermediate (WTI) cayeron precipitadamente en febrero de 2020. En abril de 2020, con la actividad económica mundial en gran medida paralizada y el cierre efectivo del comercio y del transporte internacionales, el precio al contado del Brent experimentó una contracción interanual histórica del 74%. La dinámica de los precios también se vio influenciada por un importante exceso de oferta de hidrocarburos a nivel mundial y una grave falta de espacio de almacenamiento adicional para acomodar los crecientes inventarios. El 20 de abril de 2020, el precio del WTI cayó de US$ 17.85 por barril a un precio negativo de 37.62 de USD por barril, correspondiendo a la mayor caída en un día hasta ese momento. La razón radica en que los comerciantes intentaron vender los contratos de mayo por volúmenes de petróleo que no podían almacenar por falta de espacio disponible (CRS, 2020$_{[6]}$).

En respuesta a la crisis económica en desarrollo y la caída de los precios del crudo, la OPEP y los países asociados (la llamada OPEP+, que incluye a la Federación Rusa) acordaron un recorte significativo en la producción de petróleo en abril de 2020 para cerrar los desequilibrios en la oferta y la demanda global. El acuerdo estableció un ajuste a la baja de 9.7 millones de barriles diarios entre mayo y junio; 7.7 millones de barriles diarios entre julio y diciembre y 5.8 millones de barriles diarios de enero de 2021 a abril de 2022[2]. Posteriormente, el acuerdo se modificó para incluir recortes de producción voluntarios adicionales de 0.5 millones de barriles por día a partir de enero de 2021[3].

Gráfico 2.3. **Balance mundial de producción y consumo de combustibles líquidos y precios internacionales al contado del petróleo crudo, 2019-20**

Millones de barriles diarios y dólares por barril

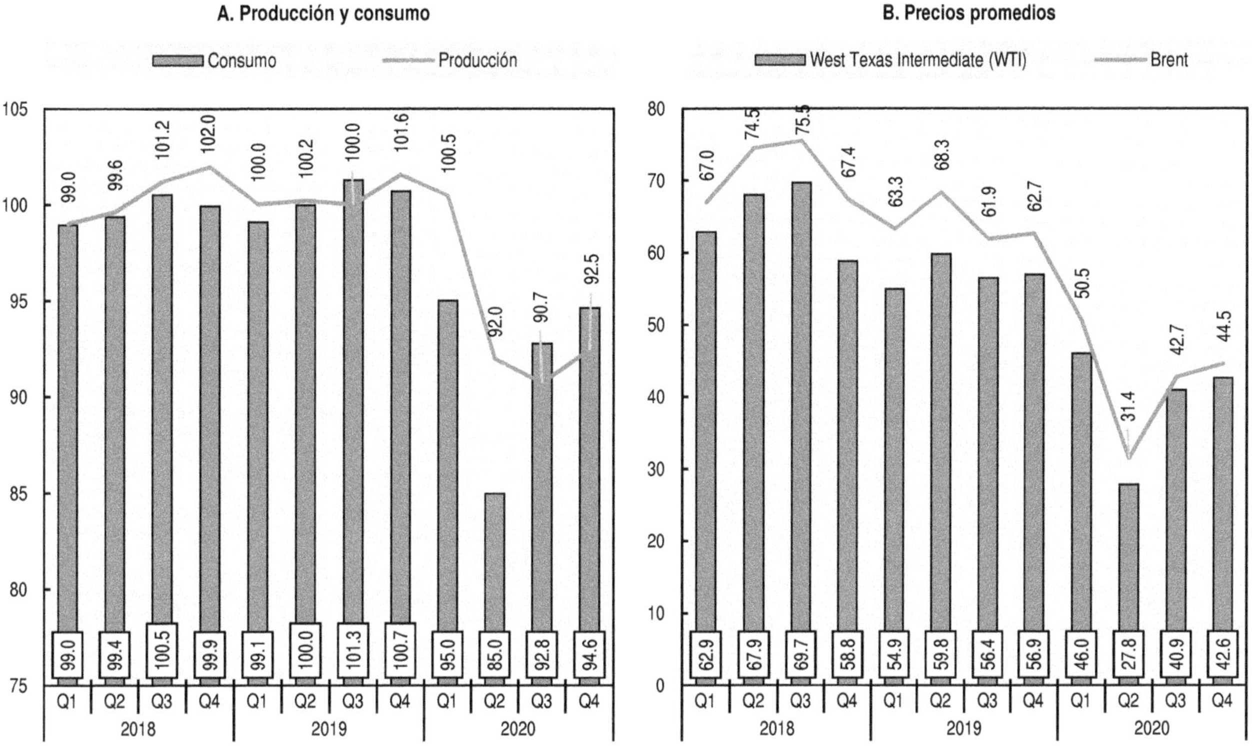


*Fuente:* Comisión Económica para América Latina y el Caribe (CEPAL), sobre la base de Short-Term Energy Outlook Data Browser, U.S. Energy Information Administration (EIA) y de World Bank Commodity Price Data (The Pink Sheet), Banco Mundial.

StatLink https://doi.org/10.1787/888934308428

Las perturbaciones en los mercados petroleros mundiales se extendieron rápidamente a la región de ALC, donde los productores de hidrocarburos están especialmente expuestos a las tendencias externas. Las exportaciones de crudo representan alrededor del 70% o más de la producción diaria promedio en Colombia, Ecuador, México y la República Bolivariana de Venezuela. Asimismo, el Estado Plurinacional de Bolivia exporta aproximadamente el 75% de la producción diaria promedio de gas natural, principalmente hacia Argentina y Brasil. Sin embargo, el impacto en la producción y las exportaciones no se sintió uniformemente a nivel de país (véase el Cuadro 2.1). La producción de petróleo crudo aumentó en Brasil, México y Guyana, donde comenzó la producción de petróleo crudo a gran escala en 2020. Este repunte de la producción estuvo acompañado de mayores exportaciones de Brasil y Guyana, que compensaron las caídas de otros países y dieron lugar a un aumento de las exportaciones de crudo de la región (+2.0%), excluyendo a la República Bolivariana de Venezuela.

Los ingresos fiscales derivados de la producción y exploración de hidrocarburos (actividades upstream) experimentaron una fuerte caída en 2020, lo que refleja la interacción de la dinámica global y nacional (véase el Cuadro 2.2). En términos absolutos, los ingresos fiscales totales por petróleo y gas cayeron a 33.1 millones de USD en 2020 a nivel regional, una reducción del 59.5% con respecto al nivel de 81.8 millones de USD de 2019. Este resultado anual es el más bajo desde 2002, cuando los ingresos alcanzaron los 23.5 millones de USD. En términos relativos, los ingresos por hidrocarburos cayeron a un promedio de 2.1% del

PIB en 2020 desde 3.1% del PIB en 2019. Sin embargo, estas cifras se vieron afectadas por cambios en el PIB nominal, que cayó en la mayoría de los países de ALC (véase el Capítulo 1), y depreciaciones de la moneda, lo que impulsó los ingresos expresados en moneda nacional.

Cuadro 2.1. **América Latina y el Caribe y grupos de países seleccionados: Producción y exportación de petróleo crudo y gas natural, 2019-20**

Miles de barriles diarios, Miles de millones de metros cúbicos y porcentajes

| Grupos de países y países seleccionados | Petróleo crudo (miles de barriles diarios) | | | | | | Gas natural (miles de millones de metros cúbicos) | | | | | |
|---|---|---|---|---|---|---|---|---|---|---|---|---|
| | Producción | | | Exportaciones | | | Producción | | | Exportaciones | | |
| | 2019 | 2020 | % | 2019 | 2020 | % | 2019 | 2020 | % | 2019 | 2020 | % |
| **América Latina y el Caribe** | 7519 | 7197 | -4.3 | 4496 | 4204 | -6.5 | 194 | 183 | -5.7 | 36 | 29 | -17.9 |
| excluyendo Venezuela | 6642 | 6670 | 0.4 | 3650 | 3718 | 1.9 | 174 | 165 | -4.9 | .. | .. | .. |
| Argentina | 508 | 480 | -5.4 | .. | .. | .. | 43 | 39 | -9.2 | 1 | 1 | -13.6 |
| Bolivia | 39 | 37 | -5.5 | .. | .. | .. | 17 | 16 | -3.9 | 13 | 12 | -2.0 |
| Brasil | 2788 | 2940 | 5.5 | 1301 | 1401 | 7.7 | 22 | 21 | -7.1 | .. | .. | .. |
| Colombia | 886 | 781 | -11.8 | 612 | 541 | -11.6 | 10 | 10 | -1.7 | .. | .. | .. |
| Ecuador | 531 | 479 | -9.7 | 398 | 362 | -9.1 | 0 | 0 | -3.2 | .. | .. | .. |
| Guatemala | 9 | 8 | -12.2 | .. | .. | .. | .. | .. | .. | .. | .. | .. |
| Guyana | 1 | 74 | 6251.7 | 0 | 73 | n.a. | .. | .. | .. | .. | .. | .. |
| México | 1704 | 1710 | 0.4 | 1200 | 1199 | -0.1 | 32 | 37 | 15.5 | .. | .. | .. |
| Perú | 53 | 40 | -25.1 | .. | .. | .. | 14 | 12 | -10.2 | 5 | 4 | -18.3 |
| Surinam | 15 | 15 | -3.7 | .. | .. | .. | .. | .. | .. | .. | .. | .. |
| Trinidad y Tobago | 59 | 56 | -4.0 | 58 | 56 | -4.9 | 36 | 30 | -16.0 | 17 | 12 | -29.7 |
| Venezuela | 877 | 527 | -39.9 | 847 | 487 | -42.5 | 21 | 18 | - 12 | .. | .. | .. |
| **Otro ALC** | 50 | 49 | -2.0 | 81 | 87 | 7.8 | 1 | 1 | -8.8 | .. | .. | .. |
| **Total mundial** | 82 340 | 76 101 | -7.6 | 45 222 | 41 988 | -7.2 | 4 086 | 3 962 | -3.0 | 1 332 | 1 244 | -6.6 |
| OPEP | 31 386 | 27 550 | -12.2 | 22 478 | 19 701 | -12.4 | 642 | 637 | -0.8 | 111 | 105 | -5.3 |
| Arabia Saudita | 9 981 | 9 406 | -5.8 | 7 038 | 6 659 | -5.4 | .. | .. | .. | .. | .. | .. |
| No-OPEP | 50 954 | 48 551 | -4.7 | 22 744 | 22 287 | -2.0 | 3 444 | 3 325 | -3.5 | 1 220 | 1 138 | -6.7 |
| Federación Rusa | 10 847 | 9 865 | -9.1 | 5 253 | 4 654 | -11.4 | 693 | 649 | -6.3 | .. | .. | .. |
| Estados Unidos | 12 248 | 11 308 | -7.7 | 2 982 | 3 175 | 6.5 | 964 | 948 | -1.6 | .. | .. | .. |

*Fuente:* Comisión Económica para América Latina y el Caribe (CEPAL) sobre la base de Short-Term Energy Outlook Data Browser, U.S. Energy Information Administration (EIA) y Organización de los Países Exportadores de Pretroleo (OPEP) Annual Statistical Bulletin 2021.

StatLink https://doi.org/10.1787/888934308542

El principal impulsor de la reducción de los ingresos por hidrocarburos fue la contracción en los pagos de regalías y otras participaciones en la producción, ya que el valor comercial de la producción cayó en línea con los precios y los niveles de producción. Esta disminución fue compensada en cierta medida por nuevos ingresos por hidrocarburos en Guyana y depreciaciones de la moneda en algunos países. Los ingresos fiscales también se contrajeron debido a que los precios más bajos redujeron las ganancias operativas y debido a la alta base de comparación con el año anterior en Trinidad y Tobago causada por ingresos extraordinarios. A pesar de estas tendencias regionales generales, los resultados a nivel de país fueron muy heterogéneos.

Los ingresos por hidrocarburos en **Argentina** durante 2020 estuvieron influenciados por diversos factores, en algunos casos compensatorios. Si bien los ingresos totales expresados en dólares estadounidenses cayeron en línea con el precio del petróleo, retrocedieron solo marginalmente en términos de moneda nacional debido a que el peso argentino se depreció significativamente (47%). No obstante, los ingresos por petróleo y gas cayeron en términos relativos –del 0.56% del PIB en 2019 al 0.44% del PIB– en un contexto inflacionario caracterizado por el rápido crecimiento del PIB nominal. Los pagos de regalías aumentaron durante el año en parte por la aplicación del Decreto 488/2020 que entró en vigor en mayo[4]. La medida estableció un nivel de precios de US$ 45 por barril para las entregas nacionales de petróleo y para la liquidación de pagos de regalías. El decreto debía permanecer vigente hasta fin de año o hasta que el precio del futuro del Brent superara un nivel de precio estipulado durante 10 días consecutivos, condición que se cumplió en agosto. Por el contrario, los ingresos tributarios —principalmente los ingresos por concepto de impuesto a sociedades— colapsaron dado que algunas empresas (como YPF, la empresa petrolera controlada por el Estado) registraron grandes pérdidas financieras.

Cuadro 2.2. **América Latina y el Caribe (10 países): Ingresos fiscales del gobierno general provenientes de la exploración y producción de petróleo y gas, por tipo de ingreso, 2019-20**

Porcentajes del PIB, puntos porcentuales del PIB y porcentajes

| Tipos de ingresos | Período | Regional / país | | | | | | | | | | |
|---|---|---|---|---|---|---|---|---|---|---|---|---|
| | | ALC | Argentina | Bolivia (Estado Plurinacional de) | Brasil | Colombia | Ecuador | Guatemala | Guyana | México | Perú | Trinidad y Tabago |
| **Ingresos totales** | 2019 | **3.1** | 0.56 | 3.9 | 1.9 | 2.2 | 9.2 | 0.05 | ... | 1.8 | 0.5 | 7.4 |
| | 2020 | **2.1** | 0.44 | 3.8 | 0.7 | 1.2 | 5.8 | 0.03 | 3.62 | 0.9 | 0.4 | 4.1 |
| | 2020-2019 (pp del PIB) | **-1.0** | -0.12 | -0.1 | -1.2 | -1.0 | -3.4 | -0.02 | ... | -0.9 | -0.1 | -3.3 |
| | 2020-2019 (% variación % en MN) | **n.a.** | -1.1 | -13.7 | -64.2 | -48.0 | -42.5 | -38.4 | ... | -53.1 | -31.6 | -48.4 |
| | 2020-2019 (% variación % en USD) | **-59.5** | -32.5 | -13.7 | -72.6 | -53.8 | -42.5 | -38.6 | ... | -58.0 | -34.7 | -48.3 |
| **Ingresos tributarios** | 2019 | **0.5** | 0.13 | 0.3 | 0.1 | 0.4 | 0.0 | 0.02 | ... | 0.02 | 0.1 | 3.5 |
| | 2020 | **0.3** | 0.09 | 0.2 | 0.0 | 0.1 | 0.0 | 0.01 | ... | 0.03 | 0.1 | 1.8 |
| | 2020-2019 (pp del PIB) | **-0.3** | -0.04 | -0.1 | -0.1 | -0.3 | ... | -0.01 | ... | 0.01 | 0.0 | -1.6 |
| | 2020-2019 (% variación % en MN) | **n.a.** | -13.5 | -45.7 | -77.8 | -81.9 | ... | -45.1 | ... | 19.5 | -37.8 | -50.8 |
| | 2020-2019 (% variación % en USD) | **-59.7** | -41.0 | -45.7 | -83.0 | -83.9 | ... | -45.2 | ... | 7.2 | -40.6 | -50.7 |
| **Ingresos no tributarios** | 2019 | **2.5** | 0.43 | 3.6 | 1.7 | 1.8 | 9.2 | 0.03 | ... | 1.8 | 0.4 | 3.9 |
| | 2020 | **1.9** | 0.35 | 3.6 | 0.6 | 1.1 | 5.8 | 0.02 | 3.62 | 0.9 | 0.3 | 2.3 |
| | 2020-2019 (pp del PIB) | **-0.7** | -0.08 | 0.0 | -1.1 | -0.7 | -3.4 | -0.01 | ... | -0.9 | -0.1 | -1.7 |
| | 2020-2019 (% variación % en MN) | **n.a.** | 2.7 | -10.6 | -63.1 | -40.0 | -42.5 | -34.6 | ... | -54.1 | -29.5 | -46.2 |
| | 2020-2019 (% variación % en USD) | **-58.9** | -29.9 | -10.6 | -71.8 | -46.7 | -42.5 | -34.8 | ... | -58.8 | -32.7 | -46.2 |
| **de los cuales: regalías y gravámenes a la producción** | 2019 | **2.2** | 0.42 | 3.6 | 0.8 | 0.6 | 9.2 | 0.03 | ... | 1.8 | 0.4 | 2.7 |
| | 2020 | **1.8** | 0.35 | 3.6 | 0.6 | 0.4 | 5.8 | 0.02 | 3.62 | 0.9 | 0.3 | 2.2 |
| | 2020-2019 (pp del PIB) | **-0.4** | -0.07 | 0.0 | -0.1 | -0.2 | -3.4 | -0.01 | ... | -0.9 | -0.1 | -0.5 |
| | 2020-2019 (% variación % en MN) | **n.a.** | 4.0 | -10.6 | -16.5 | -33.1 | -42.5 | -34.6 | ... | -54.1 | -29.5 | -25.5 |
| | 2020-2019 (% variación % en USD) | **-45.5** | -29.0 | -10.6 | -36.1 | -40.6 | -42.5 | -34.8 | ... | -58.8 | -32.7 | -25.4 |

*Nota:* Los datos de México corresponden a los ingresos petroleros del gobierno federal, excluyendo a los ingresos propios de Pemex que es el productor estatal de petróleo y gas. Los datos de Ecuador corresponden a los ingresos petroleros del sector público no financiero derivados de las exportaciones de crudo. La relación ingresos/PIB de América Latina y el Caribe corresponde a un promedio simple de los países incluidos en la muestra. Las cifras pueden no sumar debido al redondeo.

*Fuente:* Comisión Económica para América Latina y el Caribe (CEPAL), sobre la base de la base de datos Ingresos Fiscales de los Recursos Naturales No Renovables en América Latina y el Caribe de la CEPAL.

StatLink https://doi.org/10.1787/888934308561

En el **Estado Plurinacional de Bolivia**, los ingresos por petróleo y gas registraron una modesta reducción en 2020, tanto en términos absolutos como relativos (del 3.9% del PIB en 2019 al 3.8% del PIB), apoyados en parte por una recuperación en los volúmenes de exportación en la segunda mitad del año. Aunque la producción de gas natural cayó (-3.8%), los volúmenes exportados en el año aumentaron (+2.1%) por las mayores exportaciones a Argentina que compensaron la caída de las ventas a Brasil (MEFP, 2021[7]). No obstante, las exportaciones a Brasil se recuperaron a mediados de año, superando los menores volúmenes mínimos de compra – 14 millones de metros cúbicos por día (MMmcd) de gas natural, por debajo de los 24.06 MMmcd del acuerdo anterior – estipulados como parte del nuevo suministro plurianual acordado entre el país y Petrobras (Brasil) a través de un acuerdo firmado en marzo (YPBF, 2021[8]). Como resultado, los ingresos no tributarios por pagos de regalías y otras rentas de propiedades, que representan la mayor parte de los ingresos por hidrocarburos, cayeron marginalmente y se mantuvieron estables en relación con el PIB.

Los ingresos por hidrocarburos en **Brasil** cayeron fuertemente en 2020 (del 1.9% del PIB en 2019 al 0.7% del PIB) debido en parte al alto efecto base causado por los ingresos extraordinarios registrados en 2019. La ronda de licitación de Excedentes de Cesión de Derechos celebrada en noviembre de 2019 resultó en un importante bono de firma (0.9% del PIB), lo que impulsó al alza los ingresos no tributarios. Asimismo, la 16° ronda de concesiones petroleras realizada en octubre de 2019 y la 6° ronda de subastas "pre-sal" en noviembre de 2019 generaron bonos de firma adicionales equivalentes al 0.2% del PIB. Excluyendo este efecto base, las regalías y otras participaciones en el valor de la producción registraron disminuciones ya que el impacto de los precios más bajos fue solo parcialmente compensado por una mayor producción y la depreciación del real brasileño. Los ingresos tributarios cayeron abruptamente en términos absolutos, y los pagos de Petrobras del ISR y la contribución social sobre la utilidad neta se redujeron en un 89.8% en términos de moneda nacional (Petrobras, 2020[9]; Petrobras, 2021[10]).

**Colombia** registró una caída significativa en los ingresos por petróleo y gas en 2020 (pasando de 2.2% del PIB en 2019 a 1.2% del PIB en 2020) en un contexto de menor producción y exportación de petróleo. Si bien la depreciación del peso colombiano suavizó el golpe de los precios más bajos del crudo, los ingresos no tributarios por concepto de regalías y pagos de derechos económicos al gobierno cayeron considerablemente. Los ingresos no tributarios también se vieron afectados por el menor pago de dividendos de Ecopetrol al gobierno central, que pasó de 1.1% del PIB en 2019 a 0.7% del PIB (Ecopetrol, 2021[11]). Los ingresos del ISR se desplomaron, reflejando la débil situación financiera de las empresas del sector y el resultado de la Ley 2010, aprobada en diciembre de 2019, que estableció una reducción gradual de la tasa del impuesto a sociedades del 33% en 2019 al 32% en 2020 y al 30% en 2022.

Los ingresos petroleros totales por exportaciones en **Ecuador** cayeron de manera muy importante en 2020, del 9.2% del PIB en 2019 al 5.8% del PIB[5]. La caída en términos absolutos con respecto al dólar estadounidense, e implícitamente en moneda nacional, ya que Ecuador es una economía dolarizada, estuvo en línea con la reducción de los precios mundiales del crudo y la contracción de la producción de petróleo (-9.7%). La producción de petróleo tuvo una tendencia a la baja en línea con la demanda, pero también se vio afectada por la ruptura del Sistema de Oleoducto Transecuatoriano y el Oleoducto de Crudos Pesados como resultado de un deslizamiento de tierra en abril causado por la rápida erosión de las orillas del río Coca (BCE, 2021[12]).

De manera similar, en **Guatemala**, las menores exportaciones y la reducción de la demanda interna socavaron los ingresos por hidrocarburos, que cayeron de 0.05% del PIB en 2019 a 0.03% del PIB. Los volúmenes de exportación – casi en su totalidad dirigidos a los Estados Unidos y que representan algo más de la mitad de la producción de crudo – cayeron un 28.8%. Los ingresos relacionados con regalías y participación estatal en la producción de hidrocarburos contratados se cayeron en línea con el valor comercial de la producción. Los ingresos tributarios, que representan una parte más alta de los ingresos petroleros que en la mayoría de los países, también se contrajeron a medida que se redujeron los ingresos derivados del ISR de las empresas y del impuesto de solidaridad.

En **Guyana**, la producción de crudo comenzó en diciembre de 2019 y aumentó durante 2020, a pesar de problemas mecánicos que afectaron la producción en el pozo Liza Destiny operado por ExxonMobil (BCG, 2021[13]). Los ingresos derivados de la producción de petróleo, actualmente formados por regalías y ganancias del petróleo, se depositan en el Fondo de Recursos Naturales que es un fondo soberano creado para administrar la riqueza generada por la explotación de recursos naturales del país y que se puede aprovechar para apoyar ciertas actividades públicas, como las inversiones de desarrollo nacional – especialmente aquellas que apuntan a una economía verde inclusiva – y para financiar los esfuerzos de alivio en casos de desastres naturales. La Ley del Fondo de Recursos Naturales de 2021, que incluyó varias modificaciones a la legislación original adoptada en 2019, estipula que todos los ingresos relacionados con el petróleo, incluidos, entre otros, regalías, ganancias del petróleo, impuestos sobre la renta y bonos de firma, deben depositarse en el Fondo[6]. Al cierre de 2020, los ingresos de hidrocarburos depositados en el Fondo equivalen a 3.6% del PIB.

Los ingresos por petróleo y gas del gobierno general en **México** se vieron reducidos por los precios más bajos, la producción y las medidas de política adoptadas en 2020. Los ingresos totales cayeron del 1.8% del PIB en 2019 al 0.9% del PIB, debido en gran parte a menores rentas de propiedades ya que el valor comercial de la producción se desplomó. La producción de petróleo cayó como resultado de la caída de la demanda, pero también como consecuencia de los recortes de producción acordados por la OPEP+ en abril, de la cual México es miembro. Los ingresos no tributarios también se vieron influenciados por la adopción de varias medidas de política para proporcionar un alivio fiscal a Pemex, la compañía petrolera estatal. En diciembre de 2019 se redujo del 65% en 2019 al 58% en 2020 la tasa que grava el Derecho por la Utilidad Compartida, el instrumento fiscal más importante del sector[7]. Adicionalmente, en abril de 2020, el Gobierno otorgó a Pemex un crédito fiscal de MXN$ 65 mil millones (0.3% del PIB) para ser utilizado al pago del derecho de participación en las utilidades[8].

Los ingresos por hidrocarburos en **Perú** se vieron fuertemente impactados por las medidas de salud pública tomadas para limitar la propagación del COVID-19 y los conflictos sociales. El cierre del oleoducto Norperuano como resultado de los conflictos sociales que se agravaron con el estallido de la pandemia acentuó las presiones existentes relacionadas con el mercado, lo que provocó una caída en la producción (PeruPetro, 2021[14]). La producción de gas natural también se contrajo durante 2020, pero comenzó a recuperarse en la segunda mitad del año. Los menores precios y la menor producción provocaron una contracción de los ingresos no tributarios, que representan la mayor parte de los ingresos por hidrocarburos, y una disminución concomitante de los ingresos totales del sector, que disminuyeron del 0.5% del PIB en 2019 al 0.4% del PIB en 2020.

Los ingresos por petróleo y gas en **Trinidad y Tobago** registraron una fuerte contracción en 2020, pasando del 7.4% del PIB en 2019 al 4.1% del PIB en 2020, debido a la dinámica del mercado petrolero y un fuerte efecto de base asociado con los ingresos extraordinarios registrados en 2019. A diferencia de muchos productores de hidrocarburos en la región para los cuales las rentas de propiedad son la principal fuente de ingresos por hidrocarburos, en Trinidad y Tobago los ingresos tributarios juegan un papel importante ya que el sector está controlado en gran medida por operadores del sector privado. Durante 2020, los ingresos tributarios registraron una marcada contracción, no solo por el debilitamiento de las utilidades sino también por un efecto base provocado por los ingresos extraordinarios (0.5% del PIB) del sector relacionados con una amnistía tributaria en 2019. Adicionalmente, la variación % interanual de los ingresos no tributarios se vio influida por un pago único equivalente a 1.2% del PIB en 2019 por parte de una filial de Royal Dutch Shell para resolver situaciones tributarias pendientes. En paralelo, las rentas de la propiedad en forma de regalías disminuyeron en línea con las condiciones del mercado global.

## La caída de los precios anuales de una variedad de minerales y metales básicos, así como la menor producción, socavaron los ingresos mineros en 2020

Al igual que con los mercados petroleros mundiales, el brote de la pandemia de COVID-19 afectó rápidamente a los mercados de minerales y metales. Los precios al contado de muchos minerales y metales básicos cayeron en la primera mitad de 2020 debido a que la demanda mundial se contrajo y la producción en algunos países se cerró como resultado de las medidas de salud pública adoptadas para limitar la propagación de la pandemia (véase el Gráfico 2.4).

Sin embargo, los fundamentos del mercado de minerales y metales mejoraron notablemente en la segunda mitad de 2020 a medida que se aceleró la formación de capital fijo y la actividad industrial en China. Los precios del mineral de hierro registraron un aumento significativo (subiendo un 16.1% en el año) ya que la producción de acero en China alcanzó un nivel histórico (+5% interanual) (Vale, 2021[15]). Los metales básicos también se beneficiaron del aumento de la demanda, aunque los precios anuales en general cayeron. Los precios del carbón se vieron particularmente afectados, ya que la demanda de carbón térmico, utilizado en gran medida en la generación de energía, se desplomó en mayo cuando China adoptó una serie de restricciones a la importación (Vale, 2021[15]). Por el contrario, los precios de los metales preciosos aumentaron, reflejando su uso tradicional como activo refugio, una tendencia que en el caso de la plata se vio acentuada por una entrada récord de inversiones en instrumentos financieros respaldados por plata (Banco Mundial, 2020[16]).

A nivel regional, la producción de minerales y metales se vio significativamente afectada por la aplicación de las medidas de salud pública adoptadas para limitar la propagación de la pandemia de COVID-19, especialmente en Argentina y Perú (véase el Cuadro 2.3). Estas medidas con frecuencia resultaron en el cierre de minas, que básicamente funcionaban con fines de mantenimiento. La producción de todos los principales metales básicos, así como del carbón, disminuyó, aunque con una variación % significativa a nivel de país. La producción de cobre en Chile, el mayor productor mundial, cayó menos del 1% en 2020, mientras que Perú experimentó una caída del 12.4%. La producción de carbón en Colombia se desplomó (-38.6%), en línea con la tendencia mundial del carbón térmico. Por el contrario, la producción de mineral de hierro aumentó, principalmente en Brasil, debido a la fuerte demanda china. Paradójicamente, la producción de metales preciosos cayó, a pesar de los precios más altos, ya que la producción disminuyó en Argentina, República Dominicana y Perú.

Gráfico 2.4. **Precios internacionales al contado de minerales y metales seleccionados, 2019-20**

Índice 100 = enero 2020

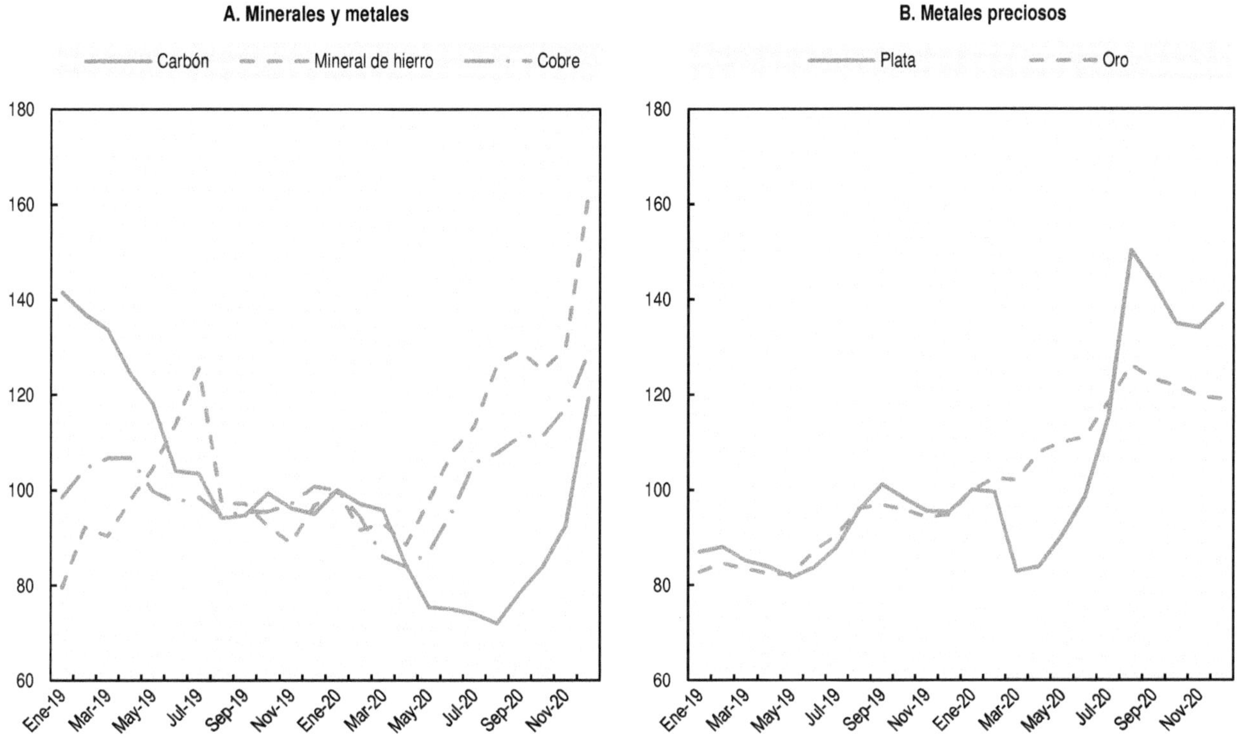


*Fuente:* Comisión Económica para América Latina y el Caribe (CEPAL), sobre la base de World Bank Commodity Price Data (The Pink Sheet), Banco Mundial.

StatLink https://doi.org/10.1787/888934308447

La interacción de precios promedio anuales más bajos y niveles de producción reducidos resultó en una contracción significativa en los ingresos mineros en la región durante 2020. Aunque la disminución fue modesta en términos relativos, cayendo en promedio de 0.4% del PIB en 2019 a 0.3% del PIB, esto se debió en parte a la dinámica del PIB nominal y a las depreciaciones de la moneda que impulsaron los ingresos provenientes de fuentes en dólares estadounidenses cuando se expresaron en moneda nacional (véase el Cuadro 2.4). La disminución fue más apreciable en términos absolutos, con una caída general de los ingresos mineros del 15.4% en términos de dólares estadounidenses para situarse en 11.3 millones de USD en 2020.

A pesar de estas tendencias, hubo una diferencia pronunciada en los movimientos de los ingresos mineros por instrumento. Los ingresos tributarios a nivel regional cayeron fuertemente (-20.8% en términos de dólares estadounidenses), en gran parte debido a las débiles ganancias en 2019 que llevaron, en algunos casos, a devoluciones de impuestos en 2020 cuando los anticipos excedieron las obligaciones tributarias. Además, las medidas de desgravación fiscal adoptadas para compensar el impacto de la crisis tuvieron un fuerte efecto intertemporal en los pagos de impuestos, empujando algunos ingresos de 2020 a 2021. Los ingresos no tributarios, en cambio, registraron una caída más modesta en la región (-2.2%), impulsado por fuertes ingresos en Chile. A nivel de países, hubo una heterogeneidad significativa, reflejando el impacto variable de la pandemia en la producción, la composición de la oferta minera de cada país y, en algunos casos, la existencia de grandes transacciones extraordinarias en 2019.

### Cuadro 2.3. **América Latina y el Caribe (países seleccionados): Precios internacionales y producción de metales y minerales, 2019-20**

Porcentajes, dólares estadunidenses y miles de toneladas métricas a menos que se especifique lo contrario

| Metales y minerales | Año y variación porcentual | Precio | Produccin por pas en miles de toneladas mtricas a menos que se especifique lo contrario | | | | | | | | | |
|---|---|---|---|---|---|---|---|---|---|---|---|---|
| | | | ALC-10 | Argentina | Bolivia | Brasil | Chile | Colombia | Ecuador | Jamaica | México | Perú | República Dominicana |
| **Cobre** | 2019 | 6 010 | 9 324 | | 4 | 584 | 5 787 | | | | 487 | 2 455 | 6 |
| | 2020 | 6 174 | 8 935 | | 3 | 554 | 5 733 | | | | 492 | 2 150 | 2 |
| | variación % | 2.7 | -4.2 | | -37.0 | -5.1 | -0.9 | | | | 1.0 | -12.4 | -63.7 |
| **Zinc** | 2019 | 2 550 | 2 484 | 19 | 528 | 196 | 6 | | | | 325 | 1 404 | 6 |
| | 2020 | 2 266 | 2 319 | 11 | 358 | 189 | 29 | | | | 394 | 1 335 | 2 |
| | variación % | -11.1 | -6.6 | -41.8 | -32.1 | -3.3 | 410.0 | | | | 21.2 | -5.0 | -57.3 |
| **Plomo** | 2019 | 1 997 | 588 | 43 | 88 | | | | | | 149 | 308 | |
| | 2020 | 1 825 | 505 | 23 | 65 | | | | | | 176 | 242 | |
| | variación % | -8.6 | -14.1 | -46.4 | -26.6 | | | | | | 18.2 | -21.6 | |
| **Estao** | 2019 | 18 661 | 53 | | 17 | 16 | | | | | | 20 | |
| | 2020 | 17 125 | 52 | | 15 | 17 | | | | | | 21 | |
| | variación % | -8.2 | -1.3 | | -14.1 | 6.0 | | | | | | 4.0 | |
| **Niquel** | 2019 | 13 914 | 144 | | | 75 | | 41 | | | | | 28 |
| | 2020 | 13 787 | 175 | | | 117 | | 36 | | | | | 22 |
| | variación % | -0.9 | 21.5 | | | 55.8 | | -11.0 | | | | | -22.7 |
| **Mineral de hierro** | 2019 | 94 | 301 386 | | | 275 031 | 8 427 | 667 | | | 7 141 | 10 120 | |
| | 2020 | 109 | 315 545 | | | 290 114 | 9 891 | 787 | | | 5 859 | 8 894 | |
| | variación % | 16.1 | 4.7 | | | 5.5 | 17.4 | 18.0 | | | -17.9 | -12.1 | |
| **Carbón** | 2019 | 78 | 91 786 | | | | | 85 169 | | | 6 617 | | |
| | 2020 | 61 | 56 544 | | | | | 52 317 | | | 4 227 | | |
| | variación % | -22.0 | -38.4 | | | | | -38.6 | | | -36.1 | | |
| **Bauxita / alúmina** | 2019 | 1 794 | 30 671 | | | 19 463 | | 18 | | 11 190 | | | 0 |
| | 2020 | 1 704 | 28 529 | | | 19 337 | | 10 | | 9 173 | | | 9 |
| | variación % | -5.0 | -7.0 | | | -0.6 | | -46.8 | | -18.0 | | | n.a. |
| **Oro (toneladas metricas)** | 2019 | 1 392 | 466 | 53 | 5 | 91 | 38 | 38 | 6 | | 73 | 128 | 32 |
| | 2020 | 1 770 | 438 | 35 | 3 | 121 | 34 | 48 | 9 | | 72 | 88 | 28 |
| | variación % | 27.1 | -6.1 | -34.2 | -48.6 | 33.0 | -11.9 | 27.5 | 44.4 | | -2.4 | -31.8 | -11.5 |
| **Plata (toneladas metricas)** | 2019 | 16 | 11 068 | 1 071 | 1 153 | 50 | 1 309 | 14 | 3 | | 3 498 | 3 860 | 109 |
| | 2020 | 21 | 9 969 | 767 | 930 | 50 | 1 576 | 20 | 2 | | 3 809 | 2 727 | 88 |
| | variación % | 26.6 | -9.9 | -28.4 | -19.4 | 0.4 | 20.4 | 37.7 | -38.0 | | 8.9 | -29.3 | -19.1 |

*Fuente:* Comisión Económica para América Latina y el Caribe (CEPAL), sobre la base de World Bank Commodity Price Data (The Pink Sheet), World Bank; Secretaría de Minería de Argentina, Sistema Federal de Información Minera; Instituto Nacional de Estadísticas del Estado Plurinacional de Bolivia, estadísticas mineras; Agência Nacional de Mineração do Brasil, Anuário Mineral Brasileiro: Principais Substâncias Metálicas; Comisión Chilena de Cobre (Cochilco), Anuario de Estadísticas del Cobre y Otros Minerales 2000-2020; Agencia Nacional de Minería de Colombia, Sistema de Información Minero Colombiano; Oficina Nacional de Estadística de la República Dominicana, estadísticas mineras; Statistical Institute of Jamaica, mineral production statistics; Banco Central del Ecuador, Reporte de Minería; Instituto Nacional de Estadística y Geografía de México, estadísticas mineras; y, Instituto Nacional de Estadística e Informática de Perú, estadísticas mineras.

StatLink https://doi.org/10.1787/888934308580

Los ingresos mineros se contrajeron en **Argentina** por la producción de oro y plata – principales productos mineros de exportación del país – que registró caídas significativas en 2020. Los ingresos mineros totales cayeron tanto en términos relativos (del 0.10% del PIB en 2019 al 0.06% del PIB) como absolutos (-49.6% en dólares estadounidenses). Varios productores importantes suspendieron sus operaciones en la primera mitad del año en respuesta a las medidas de salud pública, incluida una cuarentena nacional obligatoria en marzo. Las operaciones en la mina de oro Cerro Negro de Newmont se restringieron al mantenimiento, mientras la producción de la mina aún estaba en proceso de recuperación para fines de año (Newmont, 2021[17]). A pesar de la reducción en la producción de metales preciosos, los precios internacionales más altos limitaron la caída en el valor comercial de la producción y, a su vez, en las rentas de propiedad no tributaria por regalías.

### Cuadro 2.4. **América Latina y el Caribe (11 países): Ingresos fiscales del gobierno general provenientes de la minería, por tipo de ingreso, 2019-20**

Porcentajes del PIB, puntos porcentuales del PIB y porcentajes

| Tipos de ingresos | Período | Regional / país | | | | | | | | | | | |
|---|---|---|---|---|---|---|---|---|---|---|---|---|---|
| | | ALC | Argentina | Bolivia | Brasil | Chile | Colombia | Ecuador | Guatemala | Jamaica | México | Perú | República Dominicana |
| **Ingresos totales** | 2019 | 0.4 | 0.10 | 1.15 | 0.19 | 1.35 | 0.28 | 0.09 | 0.01 | 0.04 | 0.18 | 0.66 | 0.23 |
| | 2020 | 0.3 | 0.06 | 0.43 | 0.24 | 1.23 | 0.20 | 0.09 | 0.02 | 0.03 | 0.19 | 0.56 | 0.50 |
| | 2020-2019 (pp del PIB) | -0.1 | -0.04 | -0.72 | 0.06 | -0.12 | -0.07 | 0.00 | 0.01 | -0.01 | 0.01 | -0.10 | 0.28 |
| | 2020-2019 (% variación en MN) | n.a. | -26.2 | -66.6 | 32.4 | -7.4 | -29.6 | -11.2 | 55.6 | -26.3 | -2.0 | -20.8 | 117.8 |
| | 2020-2019 (% variación en USD) | -15.4 | -49.6 | -66.6 | 1.3 | -17.9 | -37.5 | -11.2 | 55.1 | -31.0 | -12.2 | -24.4 | 97.6 |
| **Ingresos tributarios** | 2019 | 0.3 | 0.09 | 0.67 | 0.11 | 1.02 | 0.06 | 0.05 | 0.01 | 0.00 | 0.18 | 0.46 | 0.17 |
| | 2020 | 0.2 | 0.04 | 0.03 | 0.15 | 0.73 | 0.06 | 0.05 | 0.01 | 0.00 | 0.19 | 0.39 | 0.37 |
| | 2020-2019 (pp del PIB) | -0.1 | -0.04 | -0.64 | 0.04 | -0.30 | 0.00 | -0.01 | 0.00 | 0.00 | 0.01 | -0.07 | 0.20 |
| | 2020-2019 (% variación en MN) | n.a. | -38.6 | -95.8 | 34.9 | -27.5 | -12.6 | -20.8 | 67.3 | .. | -2.0 | -21.1 | 111.9 |
| | 2020-2019 (% variación en USD) | -20.8 | -58.1 | -95.8 | 3.2 | -35.8 | -22.4 | -20.8 | 66.8 | .. | -12.2 | -24.6 | 92.3 |
| **Ingresos no tributarios** | 2019 | 0.1 | 0.02 | 0.48 | 0.07 | 0.33 | 0.22 | 0.04 | 0.00 | 0.04 | 0.00 | 0.20 | 0.05 |
| | 2020 | 0.1 | 0.02 | 0.40 | 0.09 | 0.50 | 0.15 | 0.04 | 0.01 | 0.03 | 0.00 | 0.17 | 0.13 |
| | 2020-2019 (pp del PIB) | 0.0 | 0.00 | -0.08 | 0.02 | 0.17 | -0.07 | 0.00 | 0.00 | -0.01 | 0.00 | -0.03 | 0.08 |
| | 2020-2019 (% variación en MN) | n.a. | 31.7 | -25.4 | 28.5 | 55.2 | -34.3 | 3.7 | 34.7 | -26.3 | .. | -20.1 | 137.1 |
| | 2020-2019 (% variación en USD) | -2.2 | -10.1 | -25.4 | -1.7 | 37.6 | -41.7 | 3.7 | 34.3 | -31.0 | .. | -23.7 | 115.2 |
| *de los cuales: regalías y gravámenes a la producción* | 2019 | 0.1 | 0.02 | 0.48 | 0.07 | 0.33 | 0.22 | 0.03 | 0.00 | 0.04 | 0.00 | 0.20 | 0.05 |
| | 2020 | 0.1 | 0.02 | 0.40 | 0.09 | 0.41 | 0.15 | 0.04 | 0.00 | 0.03 | 0.00 | 0.17 | 0.13 |
| | 2020-2019 (pp del PIB) | 0.0 | 0.00 | -0.08 | 0.02 | 0.08 | -0.07 | 0.01 | 0.00 | -0.01 | .. | -0.03 | 0.08 |
| | 2020-2019 (% variación en MN) | n.a. | 31.7 | -25.4 | 29.1 | 25.9 | -34.3 | 6.2 | 68.2 | -26.3 | .. | -19.3 | 137.1 |
| | 2020-2019 (% variación en USD) | -8.1 | -10.1 | -25.4 | -1.2 | 11.6 | -41.7 | 6.2 | 67.6 | -31.0 | .. | -22.9 | 115.2 |

*Nota:* La relación ingresos/PIB de América Latina y el Caribe corresponde a un promedio simple de los países incluidos en la muestra. Las cifras pueden no sumar debido al redondeo.

*Fuente:* Comisión Económica para América Latina y el Caribe (CEPAL), sobre la base de la base de datos Ingresos fiscales de los recursos naturales no renovables en América Latina y el Caribe de la CEPAL.

StatLink https://doi.org/10.1787/888934308599

Las medidas de salud pública redujeron significativamente la actividad minera en el **Estado Plurinacional de Bolivia**. Los precios internacionales más bajos, en particular para el zinc, que es el principal metal básico de exportación por valor, ejercen una presión a la baja sobre los ingresos no tributarios por regalías. El aumento de los precios del oro impulsó el valor de las exportaciones de oro metálico, compensando en parte las contracciones registradas por otras producciones mineras. Sin embargo, el principal factor detrás de la disminución de los ingresos totales de la minería, que cayeron del 1.15% del PIB en 2019 al

0.43% del PIB en 2020, fue el colapso de los ingresos tributarios del sector (-95.8% en términos de dólares estadounidenses). Los pagos del ISR alcanzaron un nivel artificialmente elevado en 2019 debido a que la empresa minera San Cristóbal realizó un importante pago anticipado de sus obligaciones tributarias del ejercicio fiscal 2019, que no se repitió en 2020 (MSC, 2021[18]).

Los ingresos mineros en **Brasil** registraron un modesto aumento en 2020 (+1.3% en términos de dólares estadounidenses, pasando de 0.19% del PIB en 2019 a 0.24% del PIB), a pesar de los mayores niveles de producción y del aumento de los precios internacionales del mineral de hierro, particularmente en la segunda mitad del año. Los ingresos no tributarios por regalías, incluidos el Compensação Financeira pela Exploração de Recursos Minerais (CFEM) federal y los gravámenes estatales aplicados en Mato Grosso do Sul, Minas Gerais y Pará, aumentaron en términos de moneda nacional en gran parte debido a la depreciación del real brasileño, ya que durante la mayor parte del año fueron liquidados a un precio comparable al de 2019. Los ingresos tributarios, sin embargo, se vieron impactados positivamente por el aumento anual de los precios, lo que generó un impulso en los pagos del ISR, que también se vieron favorecidos por el movimiento de la moneda nacional.

En **Chile**, los ingresos mineros retrocedieron, pasando del 1.35% del PIB en 2019 al 1.20% del PIB en 2020, lo que equivale a una caída de -17.9% en términos de dólares estadounidenses, como resultado de una disminución de los ingresos tributarios del sector. Los ingresos del ISR cayeron debido a que los pagos de impuestos estimados para el año fiscal 2020 realizados en 2019 fueron mayores que las obligaciones tributarias finales (DIPRES, 2020[19]). Sin embargo, la caída de los ingresos tributarios fue parcialmente compensada por un aumento de los ingresos no tributarios. En general, la producción de cobre demostró ser resistente, a pesar de las suspensiones temporales de la producción y los conflictos laborales lo que, combinado con el aumento de los precios en el segundo año, resultó en mayores ingresos del impuesto a la exportación aplicado al productor estatal Codelco. Adicionalmente, Codelco realizó un prepago sustancial de los dividendos de 2021 (0.1% del PIB) en diciembre de 2020 (DIPRES, 2021[5]).

**Colombia** experimentó una disminución significativa en los ingresos de la minería en línea con el mercado mundial excepcionalmente débil del carbón durante 2020. Los ingresos fiscales del sector cayeron del 0.28% del PIB en 2019 al 0.20% del PIB, liderados por una fuerte contracción en los ingresos tributarios. Las rentas de propiedad por regalías cayeron un 41.7% en términos de dólares estadounidenses a raíz del impacto combinado de los precios más bajos del carbón (-22%) y de la reducción de la producción de carbón (-38.6%). La producción de carbón también se vio afectada por una huelga en la mina Cerrejón – la mina de carbón a cielo abierto más grande de la región – entre el 31 de agosto y el 30 de noviembre, que concluyó con la firma de un nuevo contrato colectivo de trabajo. La producción de oro, por el contrario, alcanzó un máximo de cuatro años, lo que resultó en una casi duplicación de los ingresos por regalías relacionadas[9].

En **Ecuador**, los ingresos mineros se mantuvieron estables en relación con el PIB en un 0.09% del PIB, aunque cayeron en términos de dólares estadounidenses. Las exportaciones de oro, que representan una parte importante de la actividad minera en el país, aumentaron un 4.4% en términos de volumen y casi se duplicaron en valor. No obstante, los ingresos no tributarios por regalías registraron un modesto aumento debido a importantes pagos anticipados de regalías realizados en 2019. Excluyendo este factor, las regalías duplicaron su valor, lo que refleja el impacto combinado de una mayor producción de oro (+44.4%) y mayores precios del oro (+27.1%). Los ingresos tributarios disminuyeron en 2020 dada la alta base de comparación con 2019, cuando el Decreto Ejecutivo No. 1109 ordenó el pago anticipado de las obligaciones del ISR de 2020[10].

Las fuertes exportaciones impulsaron los ingresos mineros en **Guatemala**, que aumentaron del 0.01% del PIB en 2019 al 0.02% del PIB. El comercio de ferroníquel, particularmente con China, aumentó tanto en volumen como en valor (+75%)[11]. La actividad minera en el país se ha reducido sustancialmente por orden de la Corte Constitucional, que ordenó que el Ministerio de Energía y Minas realizara consultas con las comunidades locales afectadas por proyectos mineros en el marco del Convenio 169 de la OIT. Durante 2020, la Corte Constitucional ordenó además la suspensión de las actividades mineras relacionadas con la mina Fénix, encontrando que el proceso de autorización del permiso original violó el derecho de las comunidades locales impactadas por el proyecto, hasta que se concluya un proceso de consulta. Todas las consultas se encuentran en una etapa incipiente, con reuniones preparatorias que se realizarán a principios de 2022.

La combinación de una menor producción de bauxita y aluminio junto con una reducción en los precios globales de estos bienes contribuyó a la contracción de los ingresos mineros en **Jamaica** durante 2020. Los ingresos fiscales del sector siguen siendo excepcionalmente bajos, en 0.03% del PIB en 2020 en comparación con el 0.2% del PIB registrado en 2015. La caída de los ingresos no tributarios explica la disminución de los ingresos totales, ya que los ingresos tributarios registraron constantemente un 0.0% del PIB desde 2012. Las rentas de propiedad por pagos de regalías se vieron afectadas en parte por el cierre temporal de Jiuquan Iron y la refinería de alúmina de Steel Company (JISCO), que comenzó en septiembre de 2019 y continuó hasta 2020. También, fueron impactadas por una menor demanda mundial, especialmente de China. Jamaica mantiene varios acuerdos fiscales a medida con productores individuales, pero no se dispone de información sobre los ingresos derivados de estos contratos.

Los ingresos de la minería en **México** también se contrajeron en 2020, aunque aumentaron levemente en relación con el PIB (de 0.18% del PIB en 2019 a 0.19% del PIB), reflejando la interacción de varios factores. El valor comercial de la producción aumentó considerablemente (+23.3%) ya que el aumento de la producción de la mina compensó las caídas de precios o amplificó el efecto de los precios más altos de algunos productos (SGM, 2021[20]). Los valores de venta más altos se tradujeron en mayores ganancias para algunos de los principales productores, incluida la división minera de Grupo México, que también incluye algunas operaciones en Perú donde las ganancias operativas en 2020 aumentaron 21.6% en términos de dólares estadounidenses (Grupo México, 2021[21]). Sin embargo, los ingresos fiscales totales cayeron en términos absolutos debido a los menores ingresos del derecho especial sobre minería que grava en el 7.5% las ganancias de las operaciones mineras. El pago anual completo de este impuesto vence en marzo del año siguiente, por lo que los ingresos registrados en 2020 representan los resultados de 2019, cuando los precios débiles y los conflictos laborales afectaron la rentabilidad de varios de los principales productores de metales[12].

La producción minera en **Perú** se vio fuertemente afectada por las medidas de salud pública adoptadas para reducir la propagación de la pandemia de COVID-19. Las minas se cerraron a mediados de marzo de 2020, limitándose a actividades para mantener las instalaciones listas para el eventual reinicio de operaciones (MEMP, 2021[22]). Las operaciones mineras reabrieron progresivamente en mayo, lo que resultó en una rápida recuperación de los niveles de producción en junio y julio para algunos productos. Sin embargo, la producción minera anual fue marcadamente menor, con una disminución de la producción de cobre del 12.4% en comparación con la reducción del 0.9% registrada en el vecino Chile. La caída de la producción y los menores precios internacionales de algunos productos redujeron el valor comercial de la producción y las ganancias operativas con un impacto concomitante en los ingresos mineros, que cayeron del 0.66% del PIB en 2019 al 0.56% del PIB (-24.4% en términos de dólares estadounidenses). Sin embargo, esta dinámica no fue uniforme en todo el sector. Por ejemplo, las ganancias operativas y los pagos de ISR de Shougang Hierro Perú, el principal productor de mineral de hierro del país, aumentaron considerablemente, en línea con el aumento de los precios del mineral de hierro (Shougang Hierro, 2021[23]).

Los ingresos mineros en la **República Dominicana** casi se duplicaron en términos de dólares estadounidenses en 2020 con los precios más altos que compensaron una disminución en la producción de oro y plata. Los ingresos totales aumentaron del 0.23% del PIB en 2019 al 0.5% del PIB, impulsados por un aumento significativo en los ingresos de ISR. Asimismo, aumentaron los ingresos por el Impuesto a las Ganancias Mineras (Impuesto sobre las Utilidades Mineras), reflejando su escala móvil de tasas basadas en precios de mercado. Los ingresos no tributarios se duplicaron con creces, ya que el aumento de los precios del oro compensó fácilmente la disminución de la producción. Sin embargo, otro factor clave fue un anticipo único de regalías de 2021, equivalente al 0.06% del PIB, realizado por Barrick Gold Corporation en tanto operador de la mina Pueblo Viejo (DIGEPRES, 2021[24]).

## Notas

1. Superintendencia Nacional de Aduanas y de Administración Tributaria (SUNAT), Comunicado de prensa, "SUNAT: Compañía Minera Buenaventura paga deuda por s/ 2,134 millones", Lima, 5 de agosto de 2021 [en línea] *https://www.sunat.gob.pe/salaprensa/2021/agosto/NotaPrensaN0612021.doc*; Comunicado de prensa, "SUNAT: Minera Cerro Verde pagó s/ 1,040 millones de deuda", Lima, 13 de agosto de 2021 [en línea] *https://www.sunat.gob.pe/salaprensa/2021/agosto/NotaPrensaN0642021.doc*.
2. Organización de Países Exportadores de Petróleo, Comunicado de prensa, "The 10th (Extraordinary) OPEC and non-OPEC Ministerial Meeting concludes" [online] *https://www.opec.org/opec_web/en/press_room/5891.htm*.
3. Organización de Países Exportadores de Petróleo, Comunicado de prensa, "The 12th OPEC and non-OPEC Ministerial Meeting concludes" [online] *https://www.opec.org/opec_web/en/press_room/6257.htm*.
4. Decreto 488/2020, 18 de mayo de 2020, "Petróleo Crudo en el Mercado Local. Establécese Precio para Facturación de Entregas.", [en línea] *https://www.argentina.gob.ar/normativa/nacional/decreto-488-2020-337678/texto*.
5. Las estadísticas relacionadas con los ingresos petroleros se modificaron significativamente en 2020, ya que los datos de 2012 en adelante se recalcularon para alinearse con el Manual de Estadísticas de Finanzas Públicas de 2014 y se desagregaron por ingresos por exportaciones de crudo (upstream) y por venta interna de hidrocarburos derivados (downstream).
6. Official Gazette of Guyana, Act No. 19 de 2021, Natural Resource Fund Act 2021 [en línea] *https://finance.gov.gy/wp-content/uploads/2021/03/NRF-Act.pdf*.
7. Secretaría de Gobernación, Diario Oficial de la Federación, "DECRETO por el que se reforman y adicionan diversas disposiciones de la Ley de Ingresos sobre Hidrocarburos", 9 de diciembre de 2019 [en línea] *http://www.diputados.gob.mx/LeyesBiblio/pdf/LIH_110121.pdf*.
8. Secretaría de Gobernación, Diario Oficial de la Federación, "DECRETO por el que se otorgan beneficios fiscales a los contribuyentes que se indican", 21 de abril de 2020 [en línea] *https://www.dof.gob.mx/nota_detalle.php?codigo=5591969&fecha=21/04/2020*.
9. Agencia Nacional de Minería de Colombia, "Colombia logró en 2020 la producción de oro más alta de los últimos cuatro años", Comunicado de prensa, 26 de marzo de 2021 [en línea] *https://www.anm.gov.co/?q=colombia-logro-en-2020-la-produccion-de-oro-mas-alta-de-los-ultimos-cuatro-a%C3%B1os*.

10. Servicio de Rentas Internas, "De enero a septiembre de 2021 la recaudación tributaria creció un 11%", Comunicado de prensa, 11 de octubre de 2021 [en línea] *https://www.sri.gob.ec/detalle-noticias?idnoticia=835&marquesina=1.*
11. Banco Central de Guatemala, Estadísticas del Comercio Exterior (Exportaciones/Importaciones) [en línea] *https://www.banguat.gob.gt/es/page/sector-externo-0.*
12. Los resultados preliminares de 2021 muestran que los ingresos del derecho especial minero aumentaron considerablemente, reflejando las favorables ganancias operativas generadas en 2020.

## Referencias


Banco Mundial (2020), *Commodity Markets Outlook, October 2020*, Banco Mundial, Washington D.C., *https://openknowledge.worldbank.org/handle/10986/34621.* [16]

BCE (2021), *Reporte del sector petrolero IV Trimestre de 2020*, Banco Central del Ecuador, *https://contenido.bce.fin.ec/documentos/Estadisticas/Hidrocarburos/ASP202004.pdf.* [12]

BCG (2021), *Annual Report 2020*, Banco Central de Guyana, *https://bankofguyana.org.gy/bog/images/research/Reports/ANNREP2020.pdf.* [13]

CEPAL (2021), *Estudio Económico de América Latina y el Caribe*, Comisión Económica para América Latina y el Caribe, Santiago, *https://www.cepal.org/es/publicaciones/47192-estudio-economico-america-latina-caribe-2021-dinamica-laboral-politicas-empleo.* [2]

CEPAL (2021), *Panorama Fiscal de América Latina y el Caribe 2021*, Comisión Económica para América Latina y el Caribe, Santiago, *https://www.cepal.org/es/publicaciones/46808-panorama-fiscal-america-latina-caribe-2021-desafios-la-politica-fiscal-la.* [3]

CEPAL (2021), *Balance Preiliminar de las economías de América Latina y el Caribe 2021*, Comisión Económica para América Latina y el Caribe, Santiago, *https://www.cepal.org/es/publicaciones/47669-balance-preliminar-economias-america-latina-caribe-2021.* [4]

CRS (2020), *Crude Oil Futures Prices Turn Negative*, Congressional Research Service, *https://crsreports.congress.gov/product/pdf/IN/IN11354#:~:text=On%20April%2020%2C%202020%2C%20the,at%20negative%20%2437.62%20per%20barrel.* [6]

DIGEPRES (2021), *Ejecución presupuestaria del gobierno central, organismos autónomos y descentralizados no financieros e instituciones públicas de la seguridad social*, Dirección General de Presupuesto, *https://www.digepres.gob.do/wp-content/uploads/2021/04/Informe-de-ejecucion-Enero-Diciembre-2020-vf1.pdf.* [24]

DIPRES (2020), *Informe de Finanzas Públicas: Tercer Trimestre 2020*, Dirección de Presupuestos de Chile, *https://www.dipres.gob.cl/598/articles-210554_Informe_PDF.pdf.* [19]

DIPRES (2021), *Informe de ejecución del gobierno central cuarto trimestre 2020*, Dirección de Presupuestos de Chile, *https://www.dipres.gob.cl/598/articles-201613_doc_pdf_Presentacion_IT.pdf.* [5]

Ecopetrol (2021), *Form 20-F for Fiscal Year 2020*, *https://www.ecopetrol.com.co/wps/wcm/connect/9da6508e-05b3-422b-8c19-a4b14f53b64e/Reporte+20F+2020.pdf?MOD=AJPERES&attachment=false&id=1617974293673.* [11]

FMI (2021), *World Economic Outlook: October 2021*, Fondo Monetario Internacional, Washington D.C., *https://www.imf.org/en/Publications/WEO/weo-database/2021/October.* [1]

Grupo México (2021), *Annual Report 2020*, *https://www.gmexico.com/GMDocs/ReportesFinancieros/ING/2020/RF_EN_2020_IFN.pdf.* [21]

MEFP (2021), *Memoria de la Economía Boliviana 2020*, Ministerio de Economía y Finanzas Públicas, *https://www.economiayfinanzas.gob.bo/memoria-de-la-economia-boliviana-2020.html.* [7]

MEMP (2021), *Boletín Estadístico Minero 2020*, Ministerio de Energía y Minas del Perú, *https://www.gob.pe/institucion/minem/informes-publicaciones/1649957-boletin-estadistico-minero-diciembre-2020.* [22]

MSC (2021), *Reporte de Sostenibilidad 2020*, Minera San Cristóbal, *http://www.minerasancristobal.com/reportedesostenibilidad/wp-content/uploads/2021/08/MSC-Reporte-Sostenibilidad-2020-1.pdf.* [18]

Newmont (2021), *2020 Annual Report and Form 10-K*, *https://s24.q4cdn.com/382246808/files/doc_financials/2020/ar/386219(1)_17_Newmont_AR_WR.pdf.* [17]

PeruPetro (2021), *Memoria Institucional 2020*, *https://www.perupetro.com.pe/wps/wcm/connect/corporativo/93e6b149-8a3b-4796-b274-ca2014457703/MEMORIA+PERUPETRO+2020d.pdf?MOD=AJPERES&Memoria%20Perupetro%202020.* [14]

Petrobras (2020), *Tax Report 2019: Petrobras economic and social contribution*, *https://api.mziq.com/mzfilemanager/v2/d/25fdf098-34f5-4608-b7fa-17d60b2de47d/82d39144-bc84-6df6-a33c-c019b6b4fc3c?origin=1.* [9]

Petrobras (2021), *Tax Report 2020*, *https://api.mziq.com/mzfilemanager/v2/d/25fdf098-34f5-4608-b7fa-17d60b2de47d/3d74be35-c5f0-b698-cf39-effdc0abea98?origin=1.* [10]

SGM (2021), *Anuario estadístico de la minería mexicana 2020*, Servicio Geológico Mexicano, *https://www.sgm.gob.mx/productos/pdf/Anuario_2020_Edicion_2021.pdf.* [20]

Shougang Hierro (2021), *Memoria Anual Año 2020*, *https://www.smv.gob.pe/ConsultasP8/temp/Memoria%20SHP%20-%202020.pdf.* [23]

Vale (2021), *Form 20-F for Fiscal Year 2020*, *https://api.mziq.com/mzfilemanager/v2/d/53207d1c-63b4-48f1-96b7-19869fae19fe/348c0de9-5017-4a98-a9b7-4ba755a91f51?origin=1.* [15]

YPBF (2021), *Rendición pública de cuentas final 2020*, *https://www.ypfb.gob.bo/images/ypfb/Transparencia/RendicionPresidencia2020/RendicionDeCuentas2020.pdf.* [8]

*Chapter 3*

# SPECIAL FEATURE

# Key findings from monthly revenue data during the COVID crisis

*Capítulo 3*

# SECCIÓN ESPECIAL

# Principales conclusiones de los datos de recaudación mensuales durante la crisis de la COVID

*Chapter 3*

# SPECIAL FEATURE

# Key findings from monthly revenue data during the COVID crisis

This research is based on CIAT Reports elaborated by Santiago Díaz de Sarralde, Dalmiro Morán, Gaspar Maldonado and Julio López.

## Summary


- **Tax collection** in a sample of 18 countries in **Latin America and the Caribbean** declined by 10.9% in real terms in 2020, which was larger than the contraction in GDP. Excise taxes fell by -13.4% from the previous year while income taxes declined by -9.3% and VAT by -7.8%.
- The Central American and Dominican Republic sub-region experienced the largest decline (-14.4%), followed by the Caribbean (-12.0%), Andean countries + Chile (-11.7%), and Mercosur + Mexico (-3.2%).
- There was significant heterogeneity **between countries**, with changes in tax collection ranging from declines of -26.9% in Panama and -22.5% in Honduras to an increase of 0.8% in Mexico.
- In cumulative terms, unweighted average revenues in the 18 countries followed a **downward trend** in 2020, moving from on-year gains during the first quarter of 2020 to negative territory as of April. **The size of the cumulative year-on-year decline grew until June then gradually narrowed during the second half of the year.**
- Econometric analysis shows that the evolution of tax collection was, in general, **correlated with different mobility indicators**, especially in the first half of 2020.
- The latest data from CIAT's *Revenue Reports Covid-19* indicate that revenues recovered during the first eight months of **2021**. Tax revenues in the 18 LAC countries increased by a cumulative 21.3% over this period relative to the same period in 2020, and were up 4.6% compared with the 2019 figure.
- The CIAT website provides additional detailed information on the monthly and cumulative evolution – in constant and current values – of all the tax administrations analysed.


## Regional overview of monthly revenue by groups of selected countries

The COVID-19 crisis created an unprecedented situation that made information more necessary than ever for understanding the problems and designing responses. CIAT's *Revenue Reports COVID-19* offered a statistical database of international scope, which made it possible to monitor and analyse the monthly evolution of tax collection.

This database makes it possible to identify certain general trends, both in terms of tax revenues and indicators of personal mobility (used as a proxy for economic activity). However, as is usually the case, within the averages there is a high degree of heterogeneity.

This chapter groups the countries for which official information is available according to geographic-economic criteria to better analyse these peculiarities, which are also found in Chapter 1. For this chapter, the following country groupings are considered:

- **Mercosur + Mexico**: Argentina, Brazil, Paraguay, Uruguay and Mexico.[1]
- **Andean countries[2] + Chile**: Chile, Ecuador, Colombia and Peru.
- **Caribbean**: Jamaica and Trinidad and Tobago.
- **Central America + Dominican Republic**: Costa Rica, El Salvador, Guatemala, Honduras, Nicaragua, Panama and Dominican Republic.
- **Others**: United States, Spain, Italy and Morocco.
- **Latin America and the Caribbean, henceforth the LAC (18)**: Argentina, Brazil, Chile, Colombia, Costa Rica, Ecuador, El Salvador, Guatemala, Honduras, Jamaica, Mexico, Nicaragua, Panama, Paraguay, Peru, Dominican Republic, Trinidad and Tobago, and Uruguay.

### Box 3.1. **Complementary use of monthly revenue data and harmonised annual revenue statistics**

Data on revenues are critical for governments in formulating tax policies and in assessing the impact of policy and economic changes on the government's fiscal position. The CIAT monthly data and the annual data contained in *Revenue Statistics in Latin America and the Caribbean* are both useful sources of information for this purpose, with differences in their coverage, characteristics and application.

Annual data for nominal taxes, tax-to-GDP ratios and tax structures, which are standardised at the international level (such as those provided by the Revenue Statistics publications), have well-known advantages in terms of comparability and technical soundness. They allow for more robust comparison of data across countries and over time. However, they take more time to compile and to prepare, given the need to collect complete datasets from across government agencies, clean and verify the data then classify it appropriately (see Box 3.2).

While annual data of this kind are invaluable for longer-term analysis and strategic policy changes, they therefore have limitations as a basis for decision-making in times of crisis, such as the impact of the COVID-19 pandemic in 2020 and 2021. At such times, monthly data can complement annual data by offering more timely information and permitting faster policy reactions, as well as facilitating predictions in real time and the short-term evaluation of different events and/or policy measures.

It should be noted that the monthly data in this chapter comes directly from the tax administrations of CIAT member countries and might not give a complete picture of tax revenues in a given country, since different agencies may be responsible for different taxes, such as customs duties or social security contributions. Data will also be affected by different monthly collection and accounting schedules, variation in publication times and formats. Many countries also offered taxpayers deferrals of tax payment or reporting requirements as a measure to improve cashflow during the pandemic, which can affect the month-to-month revenue profile without necessarily reflecting a change in the underlying fiscal picture. In some cases, the data are supplemented with information from other public institutions to reflect, for example, tax revenues at subnational level. Such specificities should be borne in mind when interpreting this data.

Between the start of the pandemic in March 2020 and the end of that year, there were clear differences by country group in terms of **monthly variations in overall tax collection**. The Andean, the Caribbean and, especially, the Central American countries were most affected by the contractionary effects of the pandemic (Table 3.1).

The evolution of revenues in these three groups contrasts with those of the Mercosur countries (including Mexico) and "Others", where average total revenue collection was more resilient in March, showed more vigorous and sustained recoveries from May and June, and shifted to positive year-on-year variations as of August. Towards the end of the year, there was a gradual improvement for all groups, approaching in general to neutral or positive values towards the end of 2020.

In terms of cumulative revenue collections, all country groups remained in negative territory up to and including December 2020. However, there was a stronger recovery in Mercosur, Others and even in the Caribbean, especially from July. The evolution observed in the different groups (except for "Others") is combined in the LAC (18) average, where monthly reductions of more than -20% were observed during the second quarter of 2020. These were partially offset in the following months. On a cumulative basis, tax revenues across the 18 countries ended December 2020 with an average decline of 10.9%.

Table 3.1. **Evolution of total collection by country group (in percentages with respect to the same month of the previous year; constant prices; January to December 2020)**

Monthly percentage change

| Regions or country groups | Jan 20/19 | Feb 20/19 | Mar 20/19 | Apr 20/19 | May 20/19 | Jun 20/19 | Jul 20/19 | Aug 20/19 | Sep 20/19 | Oct 20/19 | Nov 20/19 | Dec 20/19 |
|---|---|---|---|---|---|---|---|---|---|---|---|---|
| Mercosur + Mexico | 2.5 | -1.7 | 2.6 | -25.8 | -23.7 | -10.4 | -6.9 | 2.6 | 5.6 | 2.3 | 6.9 | 15.1 |
| Andeans + Chile | 8.1 | -0.8 | -2.5 | -34.5 | -26.4 | -28.6 | -17.8 | -18.6 | -6.0 | -5.1 | -0.6 | 2.6 |
| Central America + Dom. Rep. | 5.5 | 16.1 | -19.5 | -26.7 | -33.2 | -31.3 | -7.6 | -12.6 | -9.1 | -6.7 | 0.3 | -9.4 |
| The Caribbean | -1.0 | -3.8 | -11.0 | -16.3 | -13.6 | -15.6 | -11.5 | -10.8 | -22.3 | -4.7 | -4.7 | -9.5 |
| Others | 6.4 | 8.6 | 6.3 | -32.0 | -23.9 | -16.2 | 26.3 | 4.9 | 5.1 | -6.6 | 33.1 | -11.1 |
| **LAC (18)** | **4.5** | **5.0** | **-9.2** | **-27.9** | **-27.6** | **-24.0** | **-10.7** | **-10.1** | **-7.0** | **-3.9** | **1.1** | **0.1** |

Cumulative percentage change

| Regions or country groups | Jan 20/19 | Feb 20/19 | Mar 20/19 | Apr 20/19 | May 20/19 | Jun 20/19 | Jul 20/19 | Aug 20/19 | Sep 20/19 | Oct 20/19 | Nov 20/19 | Dec 20/19 |
|---|---|---|---|---|---|---|---|---|---|---|---|---|
| Mercosur + Mexico | 2.5 | 0.6 | 1.2 | -6.4 | -9.9 | -10.0 | -9.5 | -8.2 | -6.6 | -5.7 | -4.5 | -3.2 |
| Andeans + Chile | 8.1 | 4.1 | 1.9 | -10.6 | -13.0 | -15.3 | -15.6 | -16.0 | -15.0 | -14.1 | -12.9 | -11.7 |
| Central America + Dom. Rep. | 5.5 | 10.5 | -2.1 | -9.5 | -13.7 | -17.3 | -16.3 | -15.9 | -15.2 | -14.3 | -13.2 | -14.4 |
| The Caribbean | -1.0 | -2.1 | -6.8 | -8.8 | -9.8 | -10.9 | -10.9 | -11.0 | -13.2 | -12.6 | -12.3 | -12.0 |
| Others | 6.4 | 7.1 | 6.7 | -5.9 | -9.2 | -10.0 | -5.7 | -4.3 | -3.4 | -3.8 | -1.0 | -2.3 |
| **LAC (18)** | **4.5** | **4.8** | **-1.2** | **-9.3** | **-12.6** | **-14.7** | **-14.3** | **-13.8** | **-13.3** | **-12.4** | **-11.3** | **-10.9** |

*Note:* Mercosur includes Argentina, Brazil, Paraguay and Uruguay; Andeans includes Ecuador, Colombia and Peru; Caribbean includes Jamaica and Trinidad and Tobago; Central America includes Costa Rica, El Salvador, Guatemala, Honduras, Nicaragua and Panama; others include United States, Spain, Italy and Morocco; LAC (18) includes Argentina, Brazil, Chile, Colombia, Costa Rica, Ecuador, El Salvador, Guatemala, Honduras, Jamaica, Mexico, Nicaragua, Panama, Paraguay, Peru, Dominican Republic, Trinidad and Tobago, Uruguay.

*Source:* Authors' calculations based on official information from tax administrations.

StatLink https://doi.org/10.1787/888934308884

Figure 3.1. **Evolution of monthly total collection by country group (percentage change year-on-year; constant prices; January-December 2020)**

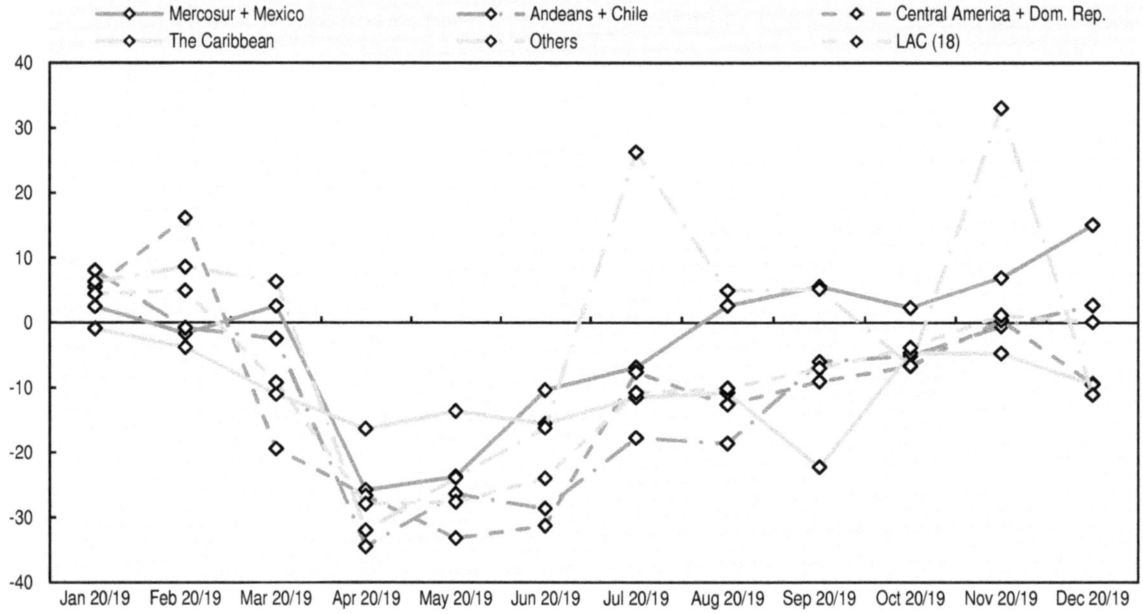


*Note:* Mercosur includes Argentina, Brazil, Paraguay and Uruguay; Andeans includes Ecuador, Colombia and Peru; Caribbean includes Jamaica and Trinidad and Tobago; Central America includes Costa Rica, El Salvador, Guatemala, Honduras, Nicaragua and Panama; others include United States, Spain, Italy and Morocco; LAC (18) includes Argentina, Brazil, Chile, Colombia, Costa Rica, Ecuador, El Salvador, Guatemala, Honduras, Jamaica, Mexico, Nicaragua, Panama, Paraguay, Peru, Dominican Republic, Trinidad and Tobago, Uruguay.

*Source:* Authors' calculations based on official information from tax administrations.

StatLink https://doi.org/10.1787/888934308618

Figure 3.2. **Evolution of cumulative total collection by country group (percentage change year-on-year; constant prices; January-December 2020)**

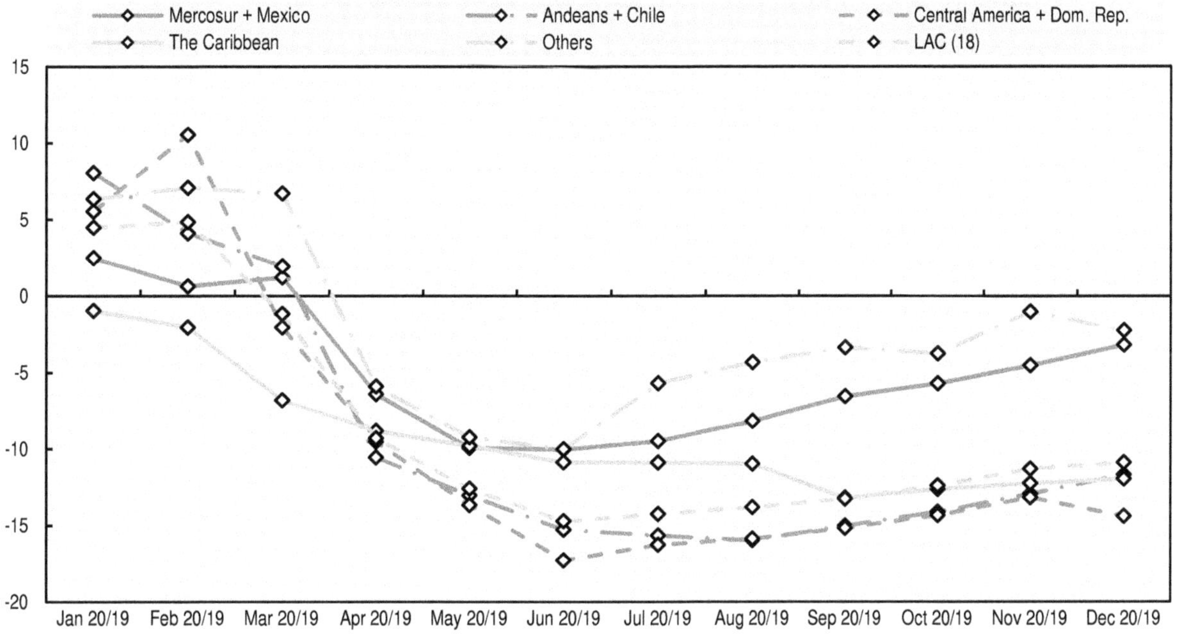


*Note:* Mercosur includes Argentina, Brazil, Paraguay and Uruguay; Andeans includes Ecuador, Colombia and Peru; Caribbean includes Jamaica and Trinidad and Tobago; Central America includes Costa Rica, El Salvador, Guatemala, Honduras, Nicaragua and Panama; others include United States, Spain, Italy and Morocco; LAC (18) includes Argentina, Brazil, Chile, Colombia, Costa Rica, Ecuador, El Salvador, Guatemala, Honduras, Jamaica, Mexico, Nicaragua, Panama, Paraguay, Peru, Dominican Republic, Trinidad and Tobago, Uruguay.

*Source:* Authors' calculations based on official information from tax administrations.

StatLink *https://doi.org/10.1787/888934308637*

Revenues from **income tax** experienced a strong decline in the second quarter of 2020 across all country groups, with a gradual recovery in the third quarter led by the Mercosur countries + Mexico, Central America + Dominican Republic, and Others (notably the United States). The Andean countries, including Chile, only showed a slight recovery in September and more limited variations towards the end of the year, while the Caribbean countries experienced continuous year-on-year falls between March and the end of December (Table 3.2).

### Box 3.2. **Differences in assumptions and terminology between the CIAT monthly data and *Revenue Statistics in Latin America and the Caribbean***

In addition to the different frequency – monthly versus annual data – there are a number of important differences between the data analysed in this chapter vis-à-vis that contained in Chapter 1 of this report. These differences prevent direct comparison of the results in the respective chapters; as explained in Box 3.1, these differences mean that the data fulfil a distinct but complementary purpose.

The principal differences between the data presented in this chapter and in Chapter 1 include:

- Countries included: Chapter 1 analyses annual data on tax revenues for 26 LAC countries. The regional sample in this chapter comprises 18 countries.

Box 3.2. **Differences in assumptions and terminology between the CIAT monthly data and *Revenue Statistics in Latin America and the Caribbean*** *(cont.)*

- Sub-regional configurations: The configuration and composition of the sub-regions analysed in this chapter differ from those examined in Chapter 1, which follows ECLAC's classification of sub-regions according to countries' geographical location and spoken language.
- Timeframe: This chapter focuses on changes to government revenues during the COVID-19 pandemic, analysing tax revenues from the start of 2020 until the end of August 2021. The information in Chapter 1 is provided on an annual basis, typically from 1 January to 31 December, and covers the period from 1990-2020 (see Box 1.1).
- Revenues covered: This chapter focuses on data from three major revenue sources (VAT, income taxes and excises). Its calculations for total revenues in each country are the sum of these three categories. Chapter 1 includes revenues from all tax types for the 26 countries, thereby providing a complete picture of tax revenues.
- Classification: Tax revenues analysed in Chapter 1 are classified and harmonised according to the definition of different tax types set out in the Interpretative Guide (Annex A). This chapter uses countries' definitions of broad tax categories, some components of which might vary from country to country.
- Nominal versus real prices: While this chapter reports tax revenues adjusted for inflation, Chapter 1 uses nominal levels of revenues and GDP.
- Source: The data in this chapter comes from directly from tax administrations, often via monthly or quarterly bulletins, with the specificities noted in Box 3.1. The data in Chapter 1 are gathered from a variety of sources, including publicly available datasets and officials in countries, as detailed in Chapter 5 of the publication.

Table 3.2. **Average changes in income tax collection by country group (in percentages compared to the same month of the previous year; constant prices; January to December 2020)**

Monthly percentage change

| Regions or country groups | Jan 20/19 | Feb 20/19 | Mar 20/19 | Apr 20/19 | May 20/19 | Jun 20/19 | Jul 20/19 | Aug 20/19 | Sep 20/19 | Oct 20/19 | Nov 20/19 | Dec 20/19 |
|---|---|---|---|---|---|---|---|---|---|---|---|---|
| Mercosur + Mexico | -1.7 | 0.9 | 5.0 | -29.8 | -23.4 | -2.8 | -7.8 | 9.8 | 8.1 | 8.4 | 10.2 | 47.6 |
| Andeans + Chile | 11.8 | 4.1 | -5.4 | -37.0 | -2.2 | -28.5 | -9.4 | -15.0 | 8.9 | -5.3 | -3.6 | 5.4 |
| Central America + Dom. Rep. | 12.3 | 34.9 | -27.1 | -15.2 | -15.5 | -33.6 | 10.4 | 3.3 | -6.7 | 2.1 | 28.1 | -18.8 |
| The Caribbean | -0.6 | 1.1 | -14.0 | -5.8 | -3.2 | -16.3 | -10.6 | -12.8 | -23.9 | -0.4 | -5.2 | -15.4 |
| Others | 7.4 | 9.2 | 9.6 | -37.9 | -20.2 | -13.3 | 59.3 | 6.1 | 8.5 | -10.8 | 58.2 | -15.0 |
| **LAC (18)** | **6.8** | **14.9** | **-12.7** | **-23.4** | **-13.6** | **-22.9** | **-2.0** | **-1.4** | **-2.4** | **1.9** | **12.1** | **4.6** |

Cumulative percentage change

| Regions or country groups | Jan 20/19 | Feb 20/19 | Mar 20/19 | Apr 20/19 | May 20/19 | Jun 20/19 | Jul 20/19 | Aug 20/19 | Sep 20/19 | Oct 20/19 | Nov 20/19 | Dec 20/19 |
|---|---|---|---|---|---|---|---|---|---|---|---|---|
| Mercosur + Mexico | -1.7 | -1.0 | 0.7 | -10.2 | -13.7 | -12.2 | -11.3 | -9.9 | -7.5 | -6.2 | -4.7 | -2.6 |
| Andeans + Chile | 11.8 | 8.2 | 3.3 | -16.2 | -14.1 | -16.1 | -15.2 | -15.2 | -13.1 | -12.4 | -11.7 | -10.4 |
| Central America + Dom. Rep. | 12.3 | 22.4 | -3.7 | -10.4 | -11.4 | -17.7 | -15.1 | -13.7 | -13.2 | -12.0 | -10.1 | -10.7 |
| The Caribbean | -0.6 | 0.6 | -8.9 | -8.1 | -7.6 | -9.6 | -9.6 | -9.8 | -13.0 | -12.4 | -12.3 | -12.6 |
| Others | 7.4 | 7.7 | 8.7 | -9.7 | -11.4 | -10.9 | -2.5 | -1.1 | -0.2 | -1.8 | 1.3 | -1.3 |
| **LAC (18)** | **6.8** | **10.4** | **-2.0** | **-11.8** | **-12.6** | **-15.5** | **-14.0** | **-13.1** | **-12.3** | **-11.2** | **-9.9** | **-9.3** |

*Note:* Mercosur includes Argentina, Brazil, Paraguay and Uruguay; Andeans includes Ecuador, Colombia and Peru; Caribbean includes Jamaica and Trinidad and Tobago; Central America includes Costa Rica, El Salvador, Guatemala, Honduras, Nicaragua and Panama; others include United States, Spain, Italy and Morocco; LAC (18) includes Argentina, Brazil, Chile, Colombia, Costa Rica, Ecuador, El Salvador, Guatemala, Honduras, Jamaica, Mexico, Nicaragua, Panama, Paraguay, Peru, Dominican Republic, Trinidad and Tobago, Uruguay.

*Source:* Authors' calculations based on official information from tax administrations.

StatLink https://doi.org/10.1787/888934308903

After recording sharp declines in the second quarter, especially in April (-23.4%) and June (-22.9%), average monthly income tax collections for the LAC region as a whole were approximately neutral in the third quarter of the year due to the contrasting evolutions of the different country groups. A rebound was visible during the final quarter, with three consecutive monthly increases (reaching 4.6% in December).

The average cumulative declines in income tax varied in 2020 for all the groups analysed, within a range of -1.3% for the "Others" group and -12.6% for the Caribbean countries. On average, the cumulative decline for the LAC 18 was -9.3% in the last month of the year.

Amid the sharp generalised declines in tax revenues caused by the pandemic and associated mobility restrictions, monthly data shows that valued-added tax (**VAT**) was initially more resilient than other tax types. However, as the crisis continued, the size of the VAT declines increased from those observed in March-April for all country groups except the Caribbean (Table 3.3).

On average across the LAC region, the largest decline in VAT receipts, of -29.9%, occurred in May 2020. Despite a moderation in the third quarter, annual variations remained in negative territory until November and December, when VAT revenues rose by 2.1% and 8.4% year-on-year respectively.

In cumulative terms, all country groups except the Caribbean, including the LAC region (-7.8% at the end of the year), ended 2020 in negative territory, within a range of -2.6% in Mercosur + Mexico to -11.7% in Central America and -12.2% in Andean countries.

Table 3.3. **Average changes in VAT collection by country group (in percentages compared to the same month of the previous year; constant prices; January-December 2020)**

Monthly percentage change

| Regions or country groups | Jan 20/19 | Feb 20/19 | Mar 20/19 | Apr 20/19 | May 20/19 | Jun 20/19 | Jul 20/19 | Aug 20/19 | Sep 20/19 | Oct 20/19 | Nov 20/19 | Dec 20/19 |
|---|---|---|---|---|---|---|---|---|---|---|---|---|
| Mercosur + Mexico | 7.7 | -0.7 | 1.0 | -15.4 | -20.1 | -12.5 | -7.3 | -0.7 | 0.5 | 0.0 | 8.8 | 10.4 |
| Andeans + Chile | 8.1 | -2.1 | -6.3 | -26.6 | -39.1 | -31.6 | -22.8 | -20.6 | -10.5 | -5.4 | 4.6 | 3.4 |
| Central America + Dom. Rep. | 4.8 | 4.5 | -7.7 | -28.3 | -37.5 | -25.9 | -18.5 | -15.7 | -11.0 | -8.7 | -3.8 | 4.5 |
| The Caribbean | 1.5 | -7.8 | 3.2 | -14.2 | -6.3 | 23.5 | -1.5 | -3.0 | 17.7 | -1.4 | 0.7 | 17.9 |
| Others | 5.6 | 2.7 | 3.8 | -17.2 | -20.4 | -15.5 | -9.9 | -0.2 | 2.6 | 1.1 | -0.5 | 8.1 |
| **LAC (18)** | **6.0** | **-0.2** | **-3.6** | **-23.5** | **-29.9** | **-16.7** | **-14.6** | **-11.4** | **-3.5** | **-4.8** | **2.1** | **8.4** |

Cumulative percentage change

| Regions or country groups | Jan 20/19 | Feb 20/19 | Mar 20/19 | Apr 20/19 | May 20/19 | Jun 20/19 | Jul 20/19 | Aug 20/19 | Sep 20/19 | Oct 20/19 | Nov 20/19 | Dec 20/19 |
|---|---|---|---|---|---|---|---|---|---|---|---|---|
| Mercosur + Mexico | 7.7 | 3.8 | 2.9 | -1.5 | -5.5 | -6.7 | -6.9 | -6.1 | -5.4 | -4.9 | -3.7 | -2.6 |
| Andeans + Chile | 8.1 | 3.3 | 0.3 | -5.8 | -13.0 | -15.6 | -16.9 | -17.2 | -16.6 | -15.4 | -13.6 | -12.2 |
| Central America + Dom. Rep. | 4.8 | 4.6 | 0.7 | -6.4 | -12.6 | -14.7 | -15.3 | -15.4 | -14.9 | -14.3 | -13.3 | -11.7 |
| The Caribbean | 1.5 | -2.8 | -1.2 | -4.4 | -5.0 | -2.1 | -1.9 | -2.1 | -0.1 | -0.2 | -0.1 | 1.1 |
| Others | 5.6 | 4.7 | 3.5 | -1.9 | -5.8 | -7.0 | -7.8 | -6.8 | -6.0 | -5.1 | -4.7 | -3.6 |
| **LAC (18)** | **6.0** | **3.1** | **1.0** | **-4.9** | **-10.1** | **-11.4** | **-11.9** | **-11.8** | **-11.0** | **-10.4** | **-9.2** | **-7.8** |

*Note:* Mercosur includes Argentina, Brazil, Paraguay and Uruguay; Andeans includes Ecuador, Colombia and Peru; Caribbean includes Jamaica and Trinidad and Tobago; Central America includes Costa Rica, El Salvador, Guatemala, Honduras, Nicaragua and Panama; others include United States, Spain, Italy and Morocco; LAC (18) includes Argentina, Brazil, Chile, Colombia, Costa Rica, Ecuador, El Salvador, Guatemala, Honduras, Jamaica, Mexico, Nicaragua, Panama, Paraguay, Peru, Dominican Republic, Trinidad and Tobago, Uruguay.

*Source:* Authors' calculations based on official information from tax administrations.

StatLink https://doi.org/10.1787/888934308922

**Excise taxes** were, on average, the category most damaged by the pandemic in all regions, with sharp declines in revenues during the second quarter of the year and (partial) recoveries only in the "Mercosur + Mexico" and "Others" group during the third quarter (Table 3.4).

Table 3.4. **Average changes in excise taxes collection by country group (in percentages compared to the same month of the previous year; constant prices; January to December 2020)**

Monthly percentage change

| Regions or country groups | Jan 20/19 | Feb 20/19 | Mar 20/19 | Apr 20/19 | May 20/19 | Jun 20/19 | Jul 20/19 | Aug 20/19 | Sep 20/19 | Oct 20/19 | Nov 20/19 | Dec 20/19 |
|---|---|---|---|---|---|---|---|---|---|---|---|---|
| Mercosur + Mexico | 0.3 | -3.4 | -7.6 | -28.9 | -26.5 | -18.8 | 1.6 | 1.7 | 6.0 | -8.0 | 4.9 | 2.9 |
| Andeans + Chile | 1.6 | 2.8 | 13.2 | -34.0 | -49.1 | -31.5 | -30.5 | -27.3 | -30.3 | -7.4 | -7.2 | 15.2 |
| Central America + Dom. Rep. | 1.8 | 9.3 | -2.4 | -36.6 | -42.1 | -34.0 | -17.5 | -22.4 | -12.8 | -13.4 | -3.6 | 2.8 |
| The Caribbean | -2.3 | 0.7 | 5.5 | -30.5 | -21.9 | -17.3 | -8.3 | -10.8 | -24.3 | -7.6 | -12.4 | -0.8 |
| Others | -4.5 | 14.6 | -4.1 | -46.5 | -47.1 | -32.4 | -21.0 | -2.6 | 18.1 | -9.2 | 76.1 | -43.8 |
| **LAC (18)** | **0.8** | **3.4** | **0.8** | **-34.9** | **-38.3** | **-28.3** | **-14.5** | **-16.1** | **-14.1** | **-10.3** | **-3.7** | **5.1** |

Cumulative percentage change

| Regions or country groups | Jan 20/19 | Feb 20/19 | Mar 20/19 | Apr 20/19 | May 20/19 | Jun 20/19 | Jul 20/19 | Aug 20/19 | Sep 20/19 | Oct 20/19 | Nov 20/19 | Dec 20/19 |
|---|---|---|---|---|---|---|---|---|---|---|---|---|
| Mercosur + Mexico | 0.3 | -2.0 | -3.8 | -9.9 | -13.1 | -14.0 | -11.9 | -10.5 | -8.7 | -8.7 | -7.5 | -6.6 |
| Andeans + Chile | 1.6 | 0.9 | 3.0 | -4.5 | -14.2 | -17.0 | -19.5 | -20.9 | -22.2 | -20.9 | -19.7 | -17.5 |
| Central America + Dom. Rep. | 1.8 | 5.0 | 2.4 | -8.0 | -15.1 | -18.1 | -18.1 | -18.7 | -18.1 | -17.6 | -16.4 | -14.7 |
| The Caribbean | -2.3 | -1.2 | 0.8 | -7.4 | -10.5 | -12.2 | -11.7 | -11.8 | -13.4 | -12.9 | -12.8 | -11.8 |
| Others | -4.5 | 3.7 | 0.7 | -12.0 | -19.4 | -21.8 | -21.7 | -19.1 | -12.8 | -12.2 | -4.6 | -8.9 |
| **LAC (18)** | **0.8** | **1.4** | **0.7** | **-8.1** | **-14.4** | **-16.7** | **-16.6** | **-16.8** | **-16.6** | **-16.0** | **-14.9** | **-13.4** |

*Note:* Mercosur includes Argentina, Brazil, Paraguay and Uruguay; Andeans includes Ecuador, Colombia and Peru; Caribbean includes Jamaica and Trinidad and Tobago; Central America includes Costa Rica, El Salvador, Guatemala, Honduras, Nicaragua and Panama; others include United States, Spain, Italy and Morocco; LAC (18) includes Argentina, Brazil, Chile, Colombia, Costa Rica, Ecuador, El Salvador, Guatemala, Honduras, Jamaica, Mexico, Nicaragua, Panama, Paraguay, Peru, Dominican Republic, Trinidad and Tobago, Uruguay.
*Source:* Authors' calculations based on official information from tax administrations.

StatLink https://doi.org/10.1787/888934308941

By the end of the year, a more generalised recovery could be observed, especially for the Andean and Central American countries in December (up 15.2% and 2.8%, respectively), which contributed to the first average year-on-year increase (5.1%) for the LAC (18) since March 2020. At the regional level, in line with the evolution of VAT, cumulative variations stagnated in negative territory during the second half of the year, ending with a decline of -13.4% in December.

## Evolution of mobility as proxy for economic activity and its impact on tax revenue

After the World Health Organization (WHO) classified the COVID-19 situation as a global[3] pandemic, events, consequences and policy responses developed at a frenetic, erratic and uncertain pace in most countries around the world. In general, although with differences in criteria, governments were forced to implement various measures to control and restrict economic activity and mobility, which had a significant negative impact on tax collection. In order to compare and contrast the impact of these measures, CIAT analysed mobility data collected and disseminated by Google, which also allowed us to partially anticipate short-term future trends.

Figure 3.3 shows what happened, on average, to mobility between February 2020 and February 2021 across four different categories[4]. After the deep drop during the months of March and, especially, April 2020 – when journeys to stores and places of leisure, as well to transit stations were most affected – a growth trend was observed, indicating a gradual recovery of economic activity even though mobility was still limited relative to pre-pandemic levels.

Tax collection and mobility indicators (a proxy variable for the level of economic activity), showed a clear correlation (Figure 3.4), which allowed anticipating, to some extent, the evolution of revenue collections in the following months. A simple linear regression model between both variables[5] achieves a high level of fit ($R^2$=0.8662; 87%), with an estimated parameter for variations in mobility (Retail and Recreation) of 0.60 (60% of the variation in mobility would have a direct impact on variations in total revenue).

Figure 3.3. **Variation in the mobility of persons (monthly average by category for all countries analysed, in percentage terms)**

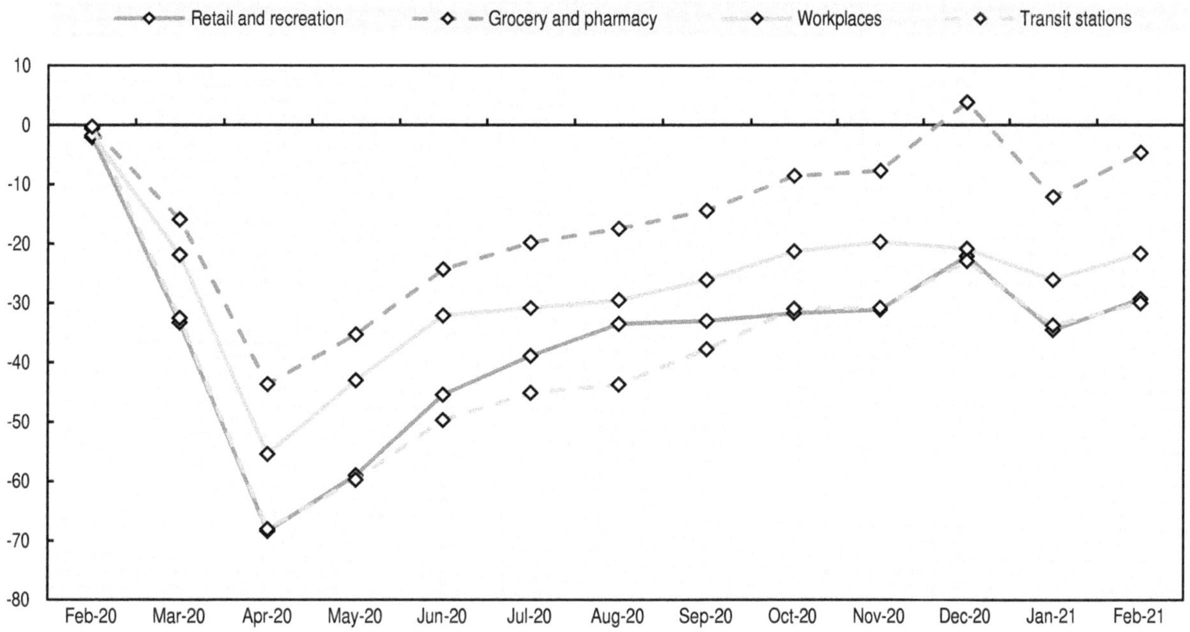


*Source:* Own elaboration based on Google LLC "Google COVID-19 Community Mobility Reports", *https://www.google.com/covid19/mobility/* (Accessed: 1 March 2021).

StatLink https://doi.org/10.1787/888934308656

Figure 3.4. **Average monthly changes in total revenue and people's mobility in retail and recreation (monthly average; in percentages; February to December 2020)**

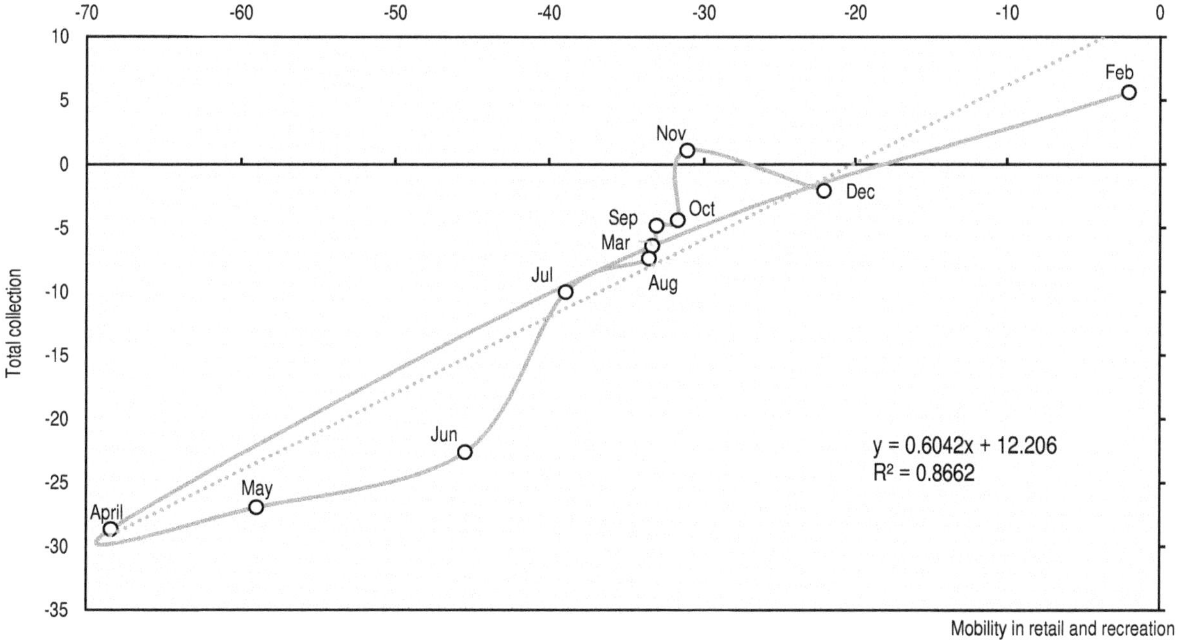


*Source:* Own elaboration based on Google LLC "Google COVID-19 Community Mobility Reports", *https://www.google.com/covid19/mobility/* (Accessed: March 1, 2021) and RRC Database (CIAT).

StatLink https://doi.org/10.1787/888934308675

However, the scatter plot suggests that this relationship was not stable throughout the year. Up to June 2020 (Figure 3.5a), the explanatory capacity of variations in mobility was very high ($R^2$ of 0.94) while from the middle to the end of the year (Figure 3.5b,) the relationship becomes more diffuse ($R^2$ of 0.46 and parameter of the explanatory variable "mobility" of 0.48).

Figure 3.5. **Average monthly changes in total revenue and people's mobility in retail and recreation (monthly average; in percentages; February-June and July-December 2020)**

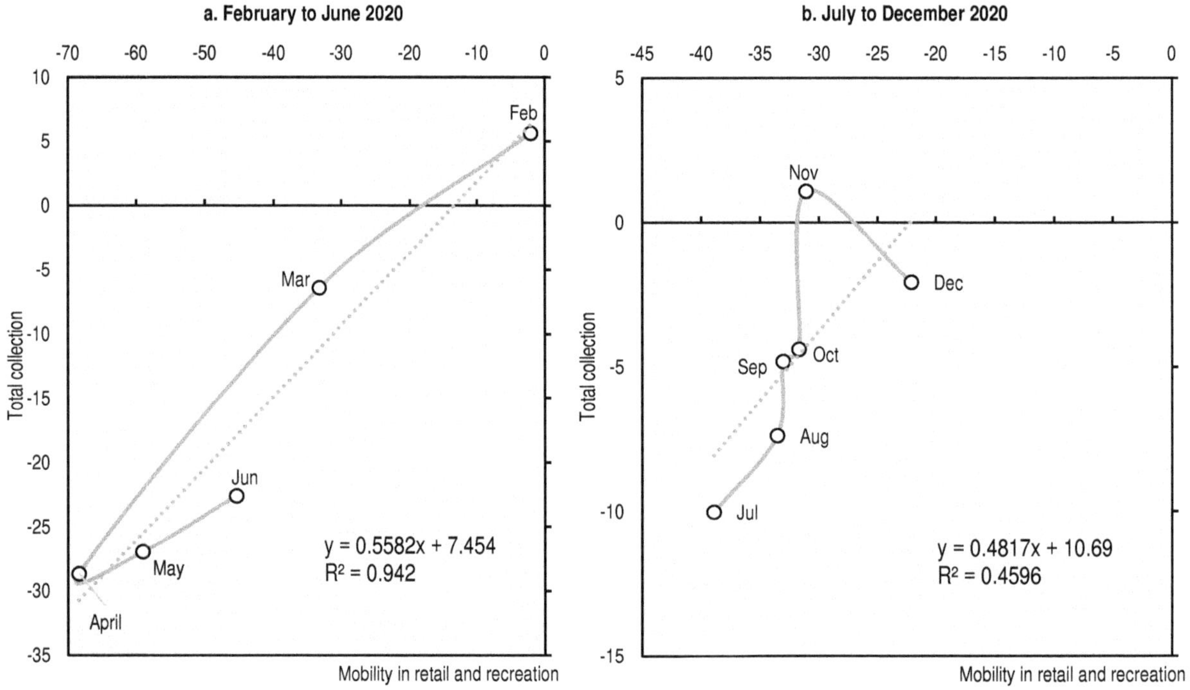


*Source:* Own elaboration based on Google LLC "Google COVID-19 Community Mobility Reports", *https://www.google.com/covid19/mobility/* (Accessed: 1 March 2021) and RRC Database (CIAT).

StatLink *https://doi.org/10.1787/888934308694*

To deepen analysis of this relationship by period and tax category, it is possible to use panel data for a group of 21 countries from February to December 2020 for the revenue and mobility ("Retail&Recreation") variables. Figure 3.6 summarises the results of the estimations for total revenue and each of the revenue categories for the 11 months as a whole, for the first semester (February to June) and for the second semester (July to December).

For the full 11 months, the estimated parameters for the explanatory variable (mobility) are significant in all cases, attaining a value of 0.48 for total tax collection, with a maximum value for Excise Taxes of 0.65, followed by VAT (0.49) and income taxes (0.44). However, with the exception of VAT, the explanatory quality of the model (expressed in the $R^2$) is weak.

When estimations distinguish between the two time periods, the mobility restrictions are correlated with revenue changes in the first half of the year (the $R^2$ coefficients exceed 0.5 in the estimates for Total, VAT and excise taxes). Estimated parameters place the impact at up to 65% for excise taxes and between 40% and 50% in the other cases (with the exception of Other revenues).

Figure 3.6. **Mobility (retail and recreation) and collections panel data estimation results**

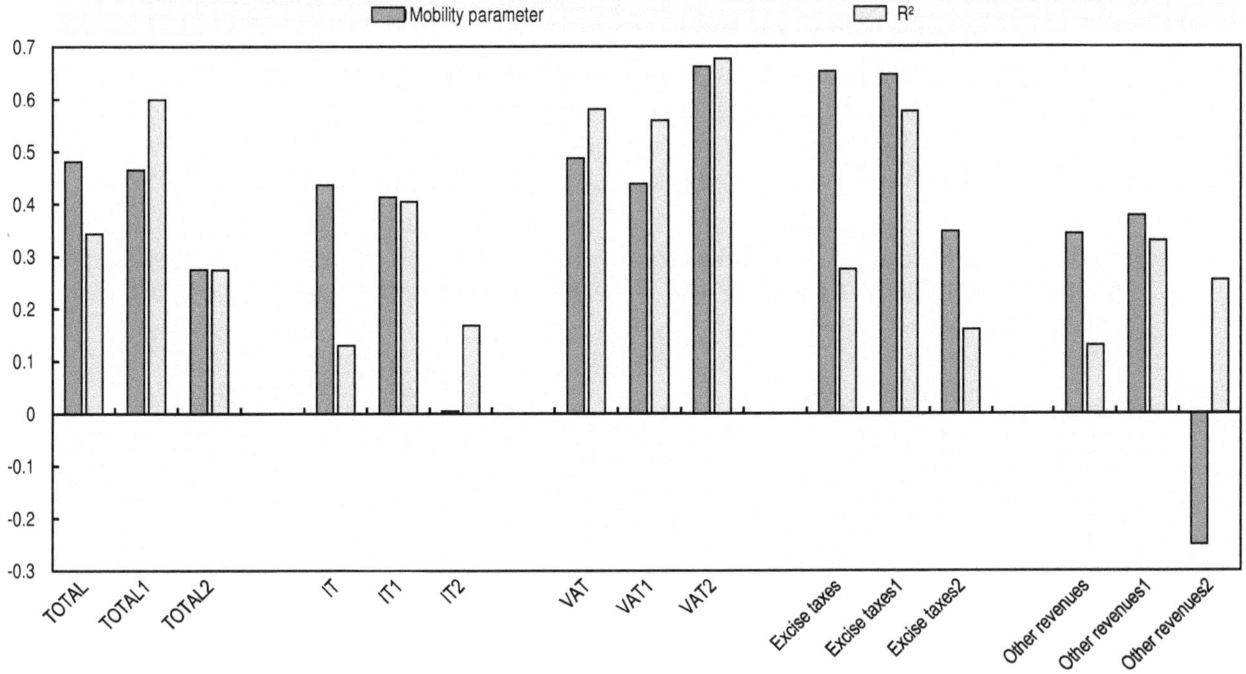


*Note:* Panel data estimation with Gretl (21 countries; 11 months; divided into two periods for partial estimations 1: February-June; 2: July-December); fixed effects and robust estimation of standard errors (with respect to heteroscedasticity and autocorrelation). The estimation is considered conditional on the selection of countries used (not random sample). It considers heterogeneity between countries (different constant or intercept).

*Source:* Own elaboration based on Google LLC "Google COVID-19 Community Mobility Reports", *https://www.google.com/covid19/mobility/* (Accessed: March 1, 2021) and RRC Database (CIAT).

StatLink *https://doi.org/10.1787/888934308713*

A change can be observed in the second period: the relationship between collection and mobility restrictions weakens in income and excise taxes, with estimated parameters not significantly different from zero and reduced levels of adjustment. This is probably due to a combination of factors, including the reversal of tax payment deferrals (especially in the case of income tax), gradual adaptation of consumer and producer behaviour, and growth in digital economic activity.

That said, it should be noted that the relationship remained clear and even strengthened during the second period in the case of VAT: the adjustment was 68% in the second period against 56% in the first, and 66% of the variation in mobility in the second period was transferred to revenue versus 44% in the first period. Given the weight of VAT in the tax structure of most countries, especially in the LAC region, these data facilitate short-term projections for revenue collections based on the trajectory of the pandemic and mobility restrictions associated with its containment.

## Conclusions and early results from 2021

Tracking tax revenues on a monthly basis is a useful tool for monitoring the effects of the Covid-19 crisis on public finances across the LAC region, differentiating between countries, sub-regions and tax categories. The effects of social distancing measures on mobility help explain variations in revenues, which in turn facilitated improvements in short-term revenue forecasts during the pandemic, especially in the first half of 2020. This data could be used to develop further research on the efficiency of the measures adopted during this extraordinary crisis and to learn how to deal with future events.

As long as the crisis continues, monthly tax statistics will remain useful. The latest data from CIAT's *Revenue Reports Covid-19* show that a recovery was underway across the region during the first eight months of 2021. On average, LAC's revenues rose a cumulated 21.3% between January and August 2021 from the same period in 2020 in real terms (Figure 3.7a).

Figure 3.7. **Average evolution of cumulative tax collection by type of tax in 2021 (year-on-year changes – compared to 2020 (a) and 2019 (b); constant prices; in percentages)**

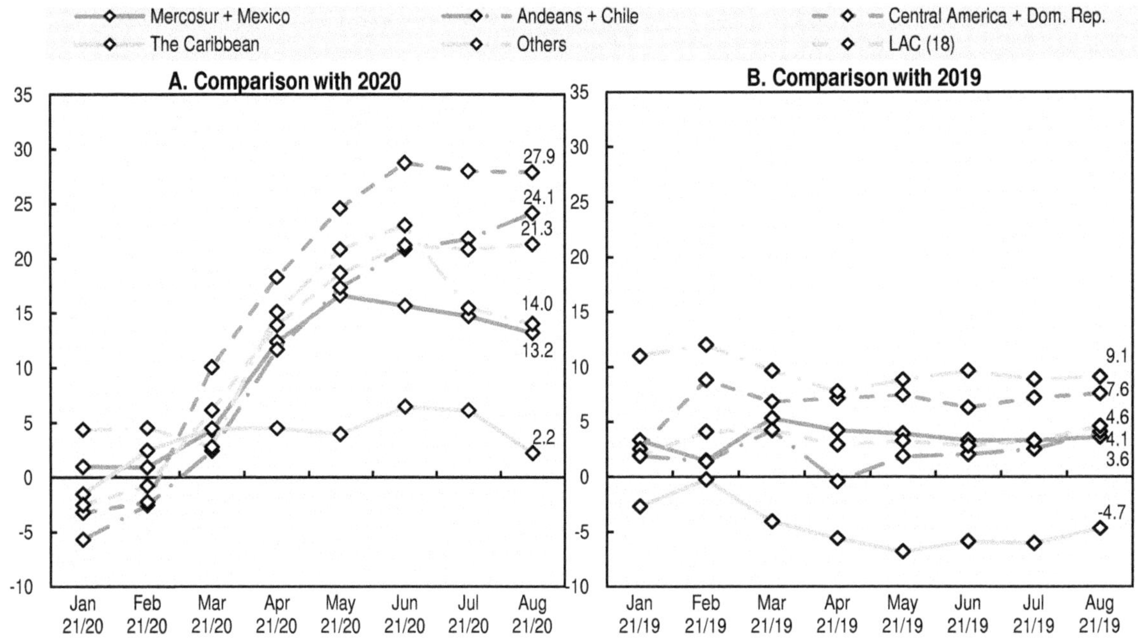


*Note:* Mercosur includes Argentina, Brazil, Paraguay and Uruguay; Andeans includes Ecuador, Colombia and Peru; Caribbean includes Jamaica and Trinidad and Tobago; Central America includes Costa Rica, El Salvador, Guatemala, Honduras, Nicaragua and Panama; others include United States, Spain, Italy and Morocco; LAC (18) includes Argentina, Brazil, Chile, Colombia, Costa Rica, Ecuador, El Salvador, Guatemala, Honduras, Jamaica, Mexico, Nicaragua, Panama, Paraguay, Peru, Dominican Republic, Trinidad and Tobago, Uruguay.
*Source:* Authors' calculations based on official information from tax administrations.

StatLink https://doi.org/10.1787/888934308732

As always – and especially amid one of the biggest economic crises of the recent centuries – it is necessary to be cautious when interpreting these results. First, because the rhythms of the recovery are very different across regions and countries with, for example, the Central America region leading the recovery (with the exception of Panama). Secondly, because the time series has been so disrupted by the extraordinary fall in tax revenues and GDP during 2020.

In this context, comparing the cumulative performance over the first eight months of 2021 with the same period in 2019 is a better guide as to the strength of the recovery. This shows a less dramatic but nonetheless encouraging increase in tax revenues: on a cumulative basis, revenues for the LAC (18) average from January to August were up 4.6% on the equivalent period in 2019 (Figure 3.7b).

## Notes

1. Although Mexico could be grouped with Central American countries due to geographic location, its macroeconomic and tax characteristics make it more comparable to the Mercosur countries, especially Argentina and Brazil.
2. Bolivia would also be included in this group but has been excluded to avoid biases in the average values given the extraordinary variations observed in its collections throughout the period for which official information is available.
3. According to the speech made on 11 March 2020 by the Director of the WHO (Dr. T.A. Ghebreyesus).
4. Data show the rate of change in the number of visitors to the categorised sites (or the time spent there) compared to a "reference day", which represents a normal value on that day of the week and is calculated as the average value for the five-week period from 3 January to 6 February 2020. This paper considers the monthly average of the daily data for each of the countries analysed by CIAT.
5. In the short run, "Retail&Recreation" serves as a better proxy for general economic activity and tax collection than only basic goods (Grocery&Pharmacy) or physical mobility to transit stations or workplaces (taking into account teleworking). However, the evolution of the different indices runs parallel so the basic conclusions of the analysis do not change.

*Capítulo 3*

# SECCIÓN ESPECIAL

# Principales conclusiones de los datos de recaudación mensuales durante la crisis de la COVID

Esta investigación se basa en los Reportes de Recaudación del CIAT elaborados por Santiago Díaz de Sarralde, Dalmiro Morán, Gaspar Maldonado y Julio López.

## Resumen

- **Las recaudaciones de impuestos** en **América Latina y el Caribe** registraron en 2020 un descenso del 10.9% en términos reales, superior a la contracción del PIB. Los impuestos selectivos cayeron un -13.4%, los impuestos sobre la renta un -9.3% y el IVA un -7.8%.
- La región Centroamericana + República Dominicana experimentó el mayor descenso (-14.4%), seguida del Caribe (-12.0%), los países andinos + Chile (-11.7%) y Mercosur + México (-3.2%).
- Hubo una heterogeneidad significativa **entre países**, con cambios en la recaudación de impuestos que van desde caídas de -26.9% en Panamá y -22.5% en Honduras hasta un aumento de 0.8% en México.
- En términos de ingresos acumulados, el promedio simple de los países estudiados siguió una **tendencia a la baja**, pasando de ganancias interanuales durante el primer trimestre de 2020 a territorio negativo a partir de abril. **La magnitud del descenso interanual acumulado creció hasta junio y luego se recuperó gradualmente durante el segundo semestre**.
- El análisis econométrico de las cifras muestra que la evolución de la recaudación tributaria estuvo, en general, **correlacionado con diferentes indicadores de movilidad**, especialmente en el primer semestre de 2020.
- Los últimos datos de los *Reportes de Recaudación COVID-19* del CIAT, indican que los ingresos se recuperaron durante los primeros ocho meses de **2021**. Los ingresos fiscales en la región de América Latina y el Caribe aumentaron en un 21.3% acumulado durante este período en relación con el mismo período de 2020, y aumentaron un 4.6% en comparación con la cifra de 2019.
- El sitio web del CIAT (*Reporte de Recaudación Covid-19* | Centro Interamericano de Administraciones Tributarias (ciat.org)) proporciona información adicional detallada sobre la evolución mensual y acumulada - en valores constantes y corrientes-de todas las administraciones tributarias analizadas.

## Panorama regional de los ingresos mensuales por grupos de países seleccionados

La crisis del COVID-19 creó una situación sin precedentes que hizo que la información fuera más necesaria que nunca para comprender los problemas y diseñar respuestas. Los *Reportes de Recaudación COVID-19* del CIAT (RRC) ofrecieron una base de datos estadísticos de alcance internacional que permitió seguir y analizar la evolución mensual de la recaudación de impuestos.

Esta base de datos facilita la identificación de ciertas tendencias generales, tanto en términos de ingresos tributarios como de indicadores de movilidad personal (utilizados como indicador de la actividad económica). Sin embargo, como suele ocurrir, dentro de los promedios hay un alto grado de heterogeneidad.

En este capítulo se agrupan los países de los que se dispone de información oficial de acuerdo con criterios geográfico-económicos para analizar mejor estas peculiaridades, que también se encuentran en el Capítulo 1. Para este capítulo, se consideran los siguientes grupos de países:

- **Mercosur + México**: Argentina, Brasil, Paraguay, Uruguay y México[1].
- **Países andinos**[2] **+ Chile**: Chile, Ecuador, Colombia y Perú.
- **Caribe**: Jamaica y Trinidad y Tobago.

- **América Central + Rep. Dominicana**: Costa Rica, El Salvador, Guatemala, Honduras, Nicaragua, Panamá y República Dominicana.
- **Otros**: Estados Unidos, España, Italia y Marruecos.
- **América Latina y el Caribe, en adelante ALC (18)**: Argentina, Brasil, Chile, Colombia, Costa Rica, Ecuador, El Salvador, Guatemala, Honduras, Jamaica, México, Nicaragua, Panamá, Paraguay, Perú, República Dominicana, Trinidad y Tobago, y Uruguay.

Entre el comienzo de la pandemia en marzo de 2020 y el final de ese año, hubo claras diferencias por grupo de países en lo que respecta a **variaciones mensuales en la recaudación general de impuestos**. Los países andinos, caribeños y, especialmente, los centroamericanos fueron los más afectados por los efectos contractivos de la pandemia (Cuadro 3.1).

La evolución de los ingresos en estos tres grupos contrasta con la de los países del Mercosur (incluido México) y "Otros", donde la recaudación total promedio de ingresos fue más resistente en marzo, mostró recuperaciones más vigorosas y sostenidas a partir de mayo y junio, y cambió a variaciones positivas interanuales a partir de agosto. Hacia finales de año, hubo una mejora gradual para todos los grupos, acercándose en general a valores neutrales o positivos hacia finales de 2020.

### Recuadro 3.1. **Uso complementario de los datos de recaudación mensuales y de las *Estadísticas Tributarias en América Latina y El Caribe* anuales armonizadas**

Los datos sobre los ingresos son fundamentales para que los gobiernos formulen políticas fiscales y evalúen el impacto de los cambios políticos y económicos en la posición fiscal del gobierno. Tanto los datos mensuales del CIAT como los datos anuales de las *Estadísticas Tributarias en América Latina y El Caribe* son fuentes de información útiles para este fin, con diferencias en su cobertura, características y aplicación.

Los datos anuales de los impuestos nominales, de la relación entre impuestos y PIB y de las estructuras impositivas, que están normalizados a nivel internacional (como los proporcionados por las publicaciones de las Estadísticas Tributarias), tienen ventajas bien conocidas en términos de comparabilidad y solidez técnica. Permiten una comparación más sólida de los datos entre países y a lo largo del tiempo. Sin embargo, su elaboración requiere más tiempo, ya que es necesario recopilar conjuntos de datos completos de todos los organismos públicos, limpiar y verificar los datos y clasificarlos adecuadamente (véase el Recuadro 3.2).

Si bien los datos anuales de este tipo tienen un valor incalculable para el análisis a largo plazo y los cambios políticos estratégicos, tienen limitaciones como base para la toma de decisiones en tiempos de crisis, como el impacto de la pandemia del COVID-19 en 2020 y 2021. En esos momentos, los datos mensuales pueden complementar los datos anuales ofreciendo una información más rápida y permitiendo reacciones políticas más inmediatas, además de facilitar las predicciones en tiempo real y la evaluación a corto plazo de diferentes acontecimientos y/o medidas de política económica.

Hay que tener en cuenta que los datos mensuales de este capítulo proceden directamente de las administraciones tributarias de los países miembros del CIAT, y podrían no dar una imagen completa de los ingresos fiscales en un país determinado, ya que diferentes organismos pueden ser responsables de distintos impuestos, como los derechos de aduana o las contribuciones a la seguridad social. Los datos también se verán afectados por los diferentes calendarios mensuales de recaudación y contabilidad, así como por la variación de los plazos y formatos de publicación. Muchos países también ofrecieron a los contribuyentes aplazamientos en el pago de impuestos o en la presentación de informes como medida para mejorar la liquidez durante la pandemia, lo que puede afectar al perfil de ingresos mes a mes sin reflejar necesariamente un cambio en el panorama fiscal subyacente. En algunos casos, los datos se complementan con información de otras instituciones públicas para reflejar, por ejemplo, los ingresos fiscales a nivel subnacional. Estas especificidades deben tenerse en cuenta a la hora de interpretar estos datos.

## Cuadro 3.1. **Evolución de la recaudación total por grupos de países (en porcentajes con respecto al mismo mes del año anterior; precios constantes; enero a diciembre de 2020)**

Variación Porcentual Mensual

| Regiones o grupos de países | Ene 20/19 | Feb 20/19 | Mar 20/19 | Abr 20/19 | May 20/19 | Jun 20/19 | Jul 20/19 | Ago 20/19 | Sep 20/19 | Oct 20/19 | Nov 20/19 | Dic 20/19 |
|---|---|---|---|---|---|---|---|---|---|---|---|---|
| Mercosur + México | 2.5 | -1.7 | 2.6 | -25.8 | -23.7 | -10.4 | -6.9 | 2.6 | 5.6 | 2.3 | 6.9 | 15.1 |
| Andinos + Chile | 8.1 | -0.8 | -2.5 | -34.5 | -26.4 | -28.6 | -17.8 | -18.6 | -6.0 | -5.1 | -0.6 | 2.6 |
| Centroamerica + Rep. Domin. | 5.5 | 16.1 | -19.5 | -26.7 | -33.2 | -31.3 | -7.6 | -12.6 | -9.1 | -6.7 | 0.3 | -9.4 |
| Caribe | -1.0 | -3.8 | -11.0 | -16.3 | -13.6 | -15.6 | -11.5 | -10.8 | -22.3 | -4.7 | -4.7 | -9.5 |
| Otros | 6.4 | 8.6 | 6.3 | -32.0 | -23.9 | -16.2 | 26.3 | 4.9 | 5.1 | -6.6 | 33.1 | -11.1 |
| **ALC (18)** | **4.5** | **5.0** | **-9.2** | **-27.9** | **-27.6** | **-24.0** | **-10.7** | **-10.1** | **-7.0** | **-3.9** | **1.1** | **0.1** |

Variación Porcentual Acumulada

| Regiones o grupos de países | Ene 20/19 | Feb 20/19 | Mar 20/19 | Abr 20/19 | May 20/19 | Jun 20/19 | Jul 20/19 | Ago 20/19 | Sep 20/19 | Oct 20/19 | Nov 20/19 | Dic 20/19 |
|---|---|---|---|---|---|---|---|---|---|---|---|---|
| Mercosur + México | 2.5 | 0.6 | 1.2 | -6.4 | -9.9 | -10.0 | -9.5 | -8.2 | -6.6 | -5.7 | -4.5 | -3.2 |
| Andinos + Chile | 8.1 | 4.1 | 1.9 | -10.6 | -13.0 | -15.3 | -15.6 | -16.0 | -15.0 | -14.1 | -12.9 | -11.7 |
| Centroamerica + Rep. Domin. | 5.5 | 10.5 | -2.1 | -9.5 | -13.7 | -17.3 | -16.3 | -15.9 | -15.2 | -14.3 | -13.2 | -14.4 |
| Caribe | -1.0 | -2.1 | -6.8 | -8.8 | -9.8 | -10.9 | -10.9 | -11.0 | -13.2 | -12.6 | -12.3 | -12.0 |
| Otros | 6.4 | 7.1 | 6.7 | -5.9 | -9.2 | -10.0 | -5.7 | -4.3 | -3.4 | -3.8 | -1.0 | -2.3 |
| **ALC (18)** | **4.5** | **4.8** | **-1.2** | **-9.3** | **-12.6** | **-14.7** | **-14.3** | **-13.8** | **-13.3** | **-12.4** | **-11.3** | **-10.9** |

*Nota:* Mercosur incluye Argentina, Brasil, Paraguay y Uruguay; Andinos incluye Ecuador, Colombia y Perú; Caribe incluye Jamaica, y Trinidad y Tobago; Centroamerica incluye Costa Rica, El Salvador, Guatemala, Honduras, Nicaragua y Panamá; otros incluyen EEUU, España, Italia y Marruecos; ALC (18) incluye Argentina, Brasil, Chile, Colombia, Costa Rica, Ecuador, El Salvador, Guatemala, Honduras, Jamaica, México, Nicaragua, Panamá, Paraguay, Perú, República Dominicana, Trinidad y Tobago, Uruguay.

*Fuente:* Cálculos de los autores basados en información oficial de las administraciones tributarias.

StatLink https://doi.org/10.1787/888934308960

## Gráfico 3.1. **Evolución de la recaudación mensual total por grupo de países (variación porcentual interanual; precios constantes; enero a diciembre de 2020)**

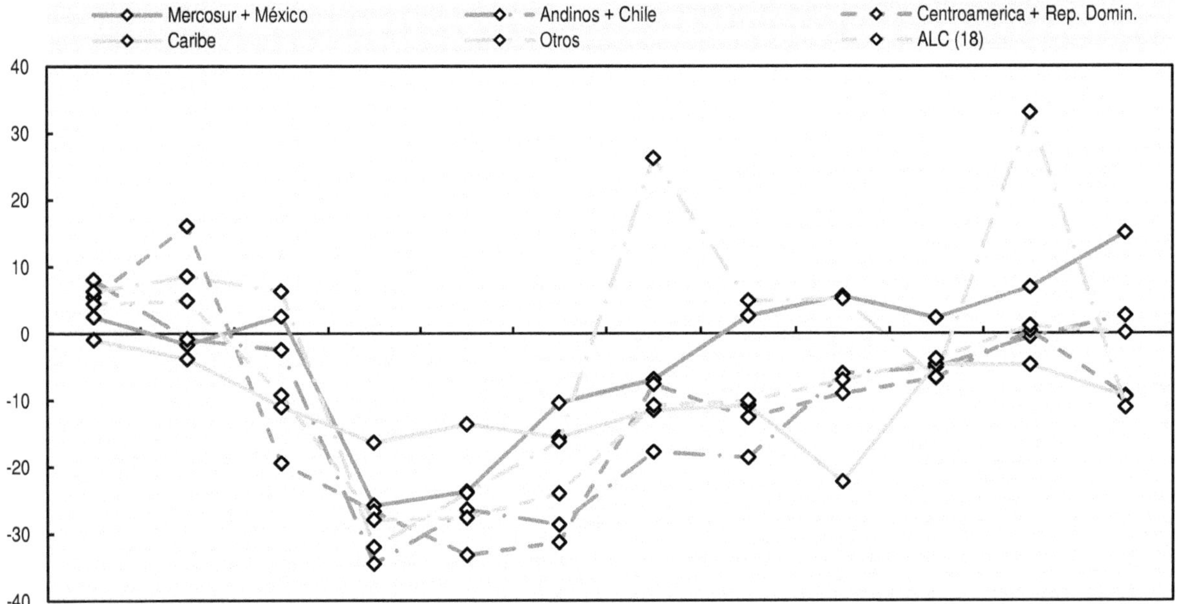


*Nota:* Mercosur incluye Argentina, Brasil, Paraguay y Uruguay; Andinos incluye Ecuador, Colombia y Perú; Caribe incluye Jamaica, y Trinidad y Tobago; Centroamerica incluye Costa Rica, El Salvador, Guatemala, Honduras, Nicaragua y Panamá; otros incluyen EEUU, España, Italia y Marruecos; ALC (18) incluye Argentina, Brasil, Chile, Colombia, Costa Rica, Ecuador, El Salvador, Guatemala, Honduras, Jamaica, México, Nicaragua, Panamá, Paraguay, Perú, República Dominicana, Trinidad y Tobago, Uruguay.

*Fuente:* Cálculos de los autores basados en información oficial de las administraciones tributarias.

StatLink https://doi.org/10.1787/888934308751

En cuanto a las recaudaciones acumuladas, todos los grupos de países permanecieron en territorio negativo hasta diciembre inclusive. Sin embargo, hubo una mayor recuperación en Mercosur, Otros e incluso en el Caribe, especialmente a partir de julio. La evolución observada en los diferentes grupos (a excepción de “Otros”) se combina en el promedio de ALC (18), donde se observaron reducciones mensuales de más del -20% durante el segundo trimestre de 2020. Estas se compensaron parcialmente en los meses siguientes. En términos acumulados, los ingresos fiscales de los 18 países terminaron en diciembre de 2020 con un descenso promedio del 10.9%.

Gráfico 3.2. **Evolución de la recaudación total acumulada por grupos de países (variación porcentual interanual; precios constantes; enero a diciembre de 2020)**

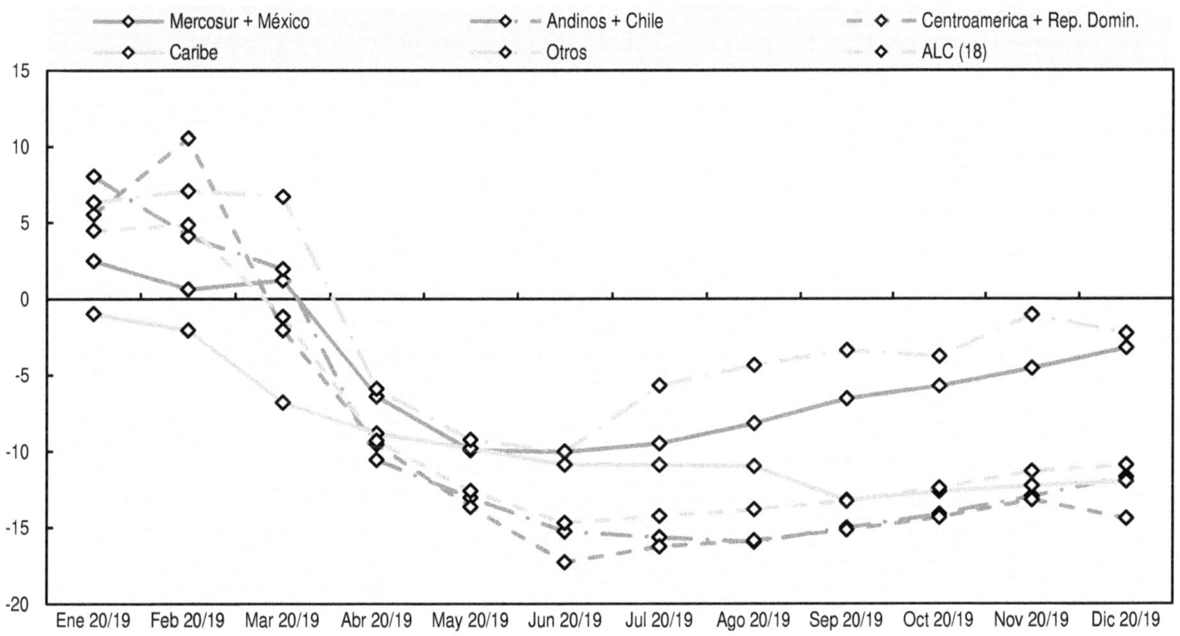


*Nota:* Mercosur incluye Argentina, Brasil, Paraguay y Uruguay; Andinos incluye Ecuador, Colombia y Perú; Caribe incluye Jamaica, y Trinidad y Tobago; Centroamerica incluye Costa Rica, El Salvador, Guatemala, Honduras, Nicaragua y Panamá; otros incluyen EEUU, España, Italia y Marruecos; ALC (18) incluye Argentina, Brasil, Chile, Colombia, Costa Rica, Ecuador, El Salvador, Guatemala, Honduras, Jamaica, México, Nicaragua, Panamá, Paraguay, Perú, República Dominicana, Trinidad y Tobago, Uruguay.

*Fuente:* Cálculos de los autores basados en información oficial de las administraciones tributarias.

StatLink https://doi.org/10.1787/888934308770

Los ingresos procedentes del **Impuesto a la renta** experimentaron un fuerte descenso en el segundo trimestre de 2020 en todos los grupos de países, con una recuperación gradual en el tercer trimestre liderada por los países del Mercosur + México, Centroamérica + República Dominicana y Otros (especialmente Estados Unidos). Los países andinos, incluido Chile, solo mostraron una ligera recuperación en septiembre y variaciones más limitadas hacia fines de año, mientras que los países del Caribe experimentaron caídas continuas interanuales entre marzo y fines de diciembre (Cuadro 3.2).

Después de registrar fuertes descensos en el segundo trimestre, especialmente en abril (-23.4%) y junio (-22.9%), la recaudación mensual promedio de impuestos sobre la renta para la región de América Latina y el Caribe en su conjunto fue aproximadamente neutral en el tercer trimestre del año debido a las evoluciones contrastantes de los diferentes grupos de países. Se observó un repunte durante el último trimestre, con tres incrementos mensuales consecutivos (alcanzando el 4.6% en diciembre).

### Recuadro 3.2. Diferencias en los supuestos y la terminología entre los datos mensuales del CIAT y las *Estadísticas Tributarias en América Latina y El Caribe*

Además de la distinta periodicidad - datos mensuales frente a datos anuales - hay una serie de diferencias importantes entre los datos analizados en este capítulo frente a los contenidos en el capítulo 1 de este informe. Estas diferencias impiden la comparación directa de los resultados en los respectivos capítulos; como se explica en el recuadro 3.1, estas diferencias hacen que los datos cumplan un propósito distinto pero complementario.

Las principales diferencias entre los datos presentados en este capítulo y en el capítulo 1 son:

- Países incluidos: En el capítulo 1 se analizan los datos anuales de los ingresos tributarios de 26 países de ALC. La muestra regional de este capítulo comprende 18 países.
- Configuraciones subregionales: La configuración y composición de las subregiones analizadas en este capítulo difieren de las examinadas en el capítulo 1, que sigue la clasificación de subregiones de la CEPAL según la ubicación geográfica de los países y la lengua hablada
- Marco temporal: Este capítulo se centra en los cambios en los ingresos públicos durante la pandemia de COVID-19, analizando los ingresos tributarios desde el inicio de 2020 hasta el final de agosto de 2021. La información del capítulo 1 se proporciona con carácter anual, normalmente del 1 de enero al 31 de diciembre, y abarca el período comprendido entre 1990 y 2020 (véase el recuadro 1.1).
- Ingresos cubiertos: Este capítulo se centra en los datos de tres fuentes de ingresos principales (IVA, impuestos sobre la renta e impuestos selectivos). Sus cálculos para los ingresos totales de cada país son la suma de estas tres categorías. El capítulo 1 incluye los ingresos de todos los tipos de impuestos de los 26 países, proporcionando así una imagen completa de los ingresos tributarios
- Clasificación: Los ingresos tributarios analizados en el capítulo 1 se clasifican y armonizan según la definición de los distintos tipos de impuestos que figura en la Guía Interpretativa (anexo A). Este capítulo utiliza las definiciones de los países de las categorías tributarias generales, algunos de cuyos componentes pueden variar de un país a otro.
- Precios nominales frente a precios reales: Mientras que en este capítulo se informa de los ingresos tributarios ajustados a la inflación, en el capítulo 1 se utilizan los niveles nominales de los ingresos y del PIB.
- Fuente: Los datos de este capítulo proceden directamente de las administraciones tributarias, a menudo a través de boletines mensuales o trimestrales, con las especificidades señaladas en el Recuadro 3.1. Los datos del capítulo 1 proceden de diversas fuentes, como los conjuntos de datos disponibles públicamente y los funcionarios de los países, como se detalla en el capítulo 5 de la publicación.

Los descensos acumulados promedio en el impuesto sobre la renta variaron en 2020 para todos los grupos analizados dentro de un rango de -1.3% para el grupo "Otros" y -12.6% para los países del Caribe. En promedio, el descenso acumulado para los países de LAC (18) fue de -9.3% en el último mes del año.

Cuadro 3.2. **Cambios medios en la recaudación del impuesto sobre la renta por grupo de países (en porcentajes en comparación con el mismo mes del año anterior; precios constantes; enero a diciembre de 2020)**

Variación porcentual mensual

| Regiones o grupos de países | Ene 20/19 | Feb 20/19 | Mar 20/19 | Abr 20/19 | May 20/19 | Jun 20/19 | Jul 20/19 | Ago 20/19 | Sep 20/19 | Oct 20/19 | Nov 20/19 | Dic 20/19 |
|---|---|---|---|---|---|---|---|---|---|---|---|---|
| Mercosur + México | -1.7 | 0.9 | 5.0 | -29.8 | -23.4 | -2.8 | -7.8 | 9.8 | 8.1 | 8.4 | 10.2 | 47.6 |
| Andinos + Chile | 11.8 | 4.1 | -5.4 | -37.0 | -2.2 | -28.5 | -9.4 | -15.0 | 8.9 | -5.3 | -3.6 | 5.4 |
| Centroamerica + Rep. Domin. | 12.3 | 34.9 | -27.1 | -15.2 | -15.5 | -33.6 | 10.4 | 3.3 | -6.7 | 2.1 | 28.1 | -18.8 |
| Caribe | -0.6 | 1.1 | -14.0 | -5.8 | -3.2 | -16.3 | -10.6 | -12.8 | -23.9 | -0.4 | -5.2 | -15.4 |
| Otros | 7.4 | 9.2 | 9.6 | -37.9 | -20.2 | -13.3 | 59.3 | 6.1 | 8.5 | -10.8 | 58.2 | -15.0 |
| **ALC (18)** | **6.8** | **14.9** | **-12.7** | **-23.4** | **-13.6** | **-22.9** | **-2.0** | **-1.4** | **-2.4** | **1.9** | **12.1** | **4.6** |

Variación porcentual acumulada

| Regiones o grupos de países | Ene 20/19 | Feb 20/19 | Mar 20/19 | Abr 20/19 | May 20/19 | Jun 20/19 | Jul 20/19 | Ago 20/19 | Sep 20/19 | Oct 20/19 | Nov 20/19 | Dic 20/19 |
|---|---|---|---|---|---|---|---|---|---|---|---|---|
| Mercosur + México | -1.7 | -1.0 | 0.7 | -10.2 | -13.7 | -12.2 | -11.3 | -9.9 | -7.5 | -6.2 | -4.7 | -2.6 |
| Andinos + Chile | 11.8 | 8.2 | 3.3 | -16.2 | -14.1 | -16.1 | -15.2 | -15.2 | -13.1 | -12.4 | -11.7 | -10.4 |
| Centroamerica + Rep. Domin. | 12.3 | 22.4 | -3.7 | -10.4 | -11.4 | -17.7 | -15.1 | -13.7 | -13.2 | -12.0 | -10.1 | -10.7 |
| Caribe | -0.6 | 0.6 | -8.9 | -8.1 | -7.6 | -9.6 | -9.6 | -9.8 | -13.0 | -12.4 | -12.3 | -12.6 |
| Otros | 7.4 | 7.7 | 8.7 | -9.7 | -11.4 | -10.9 | -2.5 | -1.1 | -0.2 | -1.8 | 1.3 | -1.3 |
| **ALC (18)** | **6.8** | **10.4** | **-2.0** | **-11.8** | **-12.6** | **-15.5** | **-14.0** | **-13.1** | **-12.3** | **-11.2** | **-9.9** | **-9.3** |

*Nota:* Mercosur incluye Argentina, Brasil, Paraguay y Uruguay; Andinos incluye Ecuador, Colombia y Perú; Caribe incluye Jamaica, y Trinidad y Tobago; Centroamerica incluye Costa Rica, El Salvador, Guatemala, Honduras, Nicaragua y Panamá; otros incluyen EEUU, España, Italia y Marruecos; ALC (18) incluye Argentina, Brasil, Chile, Colombia, Costa Rica, Ecuador, El Salvador, Guatemala, Honduras, Jamaica, México, Nicaragua, Panamá, Paraguay, Perú, República Dominicana, Trinidad y Tobago, Uruguay.

*Fuente:* Cálculos de los autores basados en información oficial de las administraciones tributarias.

StatLink https://doi.org/10.1787/888934308979

En medio de los fuertes descensos generalizados de las recaudaciones fiscales causados por la pandemia y las restricciones de movilidad asociadas, los datos mensuales muestran que el impuesto sobre el valor añadido (**IVA**) fue inicialmente más resistente que otros tipos de impuestos. Sin embargo, a medida que continuó la crisis, la magnitud de las disminuciones del IVA aumentó en comparación con las observadas en marzo y abril para todos los grupos de países, excepto el Caribe (Cuadro 3.3).

En promedio, en toda la región de América Latina y el Caribe, la mayor disminución de los ingresos por IVA, de -29.9%, se produjo en mayo de 2020. A pesar de una moderación en el tercer trimestre, las variaciones anuales se mantuvieron en territorio negativo hasta noviembre y diciembre, cuando los ingresos por IVA aumentaron un 2.1% y un 8.4% interanual, respectivamente.

En términos acumulados, todos los grupos de países, excepto el Caribe, incluida la región de América Latina y el Caribe (-7.8% al final del año), terminaron 2020 en territorio negativo, dentro de un rango de -2.6% en Mercosur + México a -11.7% en América Central y -12.2% en los países andinos.

**Los Impuestos Selectivos** fueron, en promedio, la categoría más afectada por la pandemia en todas las regiones, con fuertes descensos en los ingresos durante el segundo trimestre del año y recuperaciones (parciales) solo en el grupo "Mercosur + México" y "Otros" durante el tercer trimestre (Cuadro 3.4).

## Cuadro 3.3. **Cambios medios en la recaudación del IVA por grupo de países (en porcentajes en comparación con el mismo mes del año anterior; precios constantes; enero a diciembre de 2020)**

Variación porcentual mensual

| Regiones o grupos de países | Ene 20/19 | Feb 20/19 | Mar 20/19 | Abr 20/19 | May 20/19 | Jun 20/19 | Jul 20/19 | Ago 20/19 | Sep 20/19 | Oct 20/19 | Nov 20/19 | Dic 20/19 |
|---|---|---|---|---|---|---|---|---|---|---|---|---|
| Mercosur + México | 7.7 | -0.7 | 1.0 | -15.4 | -20.1 | -12.5 | -7.3 | -0.7 | 0.5 | 0.0 | 8.8 | 10.4 |
| Andinos + Chile | 8.1 | -2.1 | -6.3 | -26.6 | -39.1 | -31.6 | -22.8 | -20.6 | -10.5 | -5.4 | 4.6 | 3.4 |
| Centroamerica + Rep. Domin. | 4.8 | 4.5 | -7.7 | -28.3 | -37.5 | -25.9 | -18.5 | -15.7 | -11.0 | -8.7 | -3.8 | 4.5 |
| Caribe | 1.5 | -7.8 | 3.2 | -14.2 | -6.3 | 23.5 | -1.5 | -3.0 | 17.7 | -1.4 | 0.7 | 17.9 |
| Otros | 5.6 | 2.7 | 3.8 | -17.2 | -20.4 | -15.5 | -9.9 | -0.2 | 2.6 | 1.1 | -0.5 | 8.1 |
| **ALC (18)** | **6.0** | **-0.2** | **-3.6** | **-23.5** | **-29.9** | **-16.7** | **-14.6** | **-11.4** | **-3.5** | **-4.8** | **2.1** | **8.4** |

Variación porcentual acumulada

| Regiones o grupos de países | Ene 20/19 | Feb 20/19 | Mar 20/19 | Abr 20/19 | May 20/19 | Jun 20/19 | Jul 20/19 | Ago 20/19 | Sep 20/19 | Oct 20/19 | Nov 20/19 | Dic 20/19 |
|---|---|---|---|---|---|---|---|---|---|---|---|---|
| Mercosur + México | 7.7 | 3.8 | 2.9 | -1.5 | -5.5 | -6.7 | -6.9 | -6.1 | -5.4 | -4.9 | -3.7 | -2.6 |
| Andinos + Chile | 8.1 | 3.3 | 0.3 | -5.8 | -13.0 | -15.6 | -16.9 | -17.2 | -16.6 | -15.4 | -13.6 | -12.2 |
| Centroamerica + Rep. Domin. | 4.8 | 4.6 | 0.7 | -6.4 | -12.6 | -14.7 | -15.3 | -15.4 | -14.9 | -14.3 | -13.3 | -11.7 |
| Caribe | 1.5 | -2.8 | -1.2 | -4.4 | -5.0 | -2.1 | -1.9 | -2.1 | -0.1 | -0.2 | -0.1 | 1.1 |
| Otros | 5.6 | 4.7 | 3.5 | -1.9 | -5.8 | -7.0 | -7.8 | -6.8 | -6.0 | -5.1 | -4.7 | -3.6 |
| **ALC (18)** | **6.0** | **3.1** | **1.0** | **-4.9** | **-10.1** | **-11.4** | **-11.9** | **-11.8** | **-11.0** | **-10.4** | **-9.2** | **-7.8** |

*Nota:* Mercosur incluye Argentina, Brasil, Paraguay y Uruguay; Andinos incluye Ecuador, Colombia y Perú; Caribe incluye Jamaica, y Trinidad y Tobago; Centroamerica incluye Costa Rica, El Salvador, Guatemala, Honduras, Nicaragua y Panamá; otros incluyen EEUU, España, Italia y Marruecos; ALC (18) incluye Argentina, Brasil, Chile, Colombia, Costa Rica, Ecuador, El Salvador, Guatemala, Honduras, Jamaica, México, Nicaragua, Panamá, Paraguay, Perú, República Dominicana, Trinidad y Tobago, Uruguay.

*Fuente:* Cálculos de los autores basados en información oficial de las administraciones tributarias.

StatLink https://doi.org/10.1787/888934308998

## Cuadro 3.4. **Cambios medios en la recaudación de impuestos selectivos por grupo de países (en porcentajes en comparación con el mismo mes del año anterior; precios constantes; enero a diciembre de 2020)**

Variación porcentual mensual

| Regiones o grupos de países | Ene 20/19 | Feb 20/19 | Mar 20/19 | Abr 20/19 | May 20/19 | Jun 20/19 | Jul 20/19 | Ago 20/19 | Sep 20/19 | Oct 20/19 | Nov 20/19 | Dic 20/19 |
|---|---|---|---|---|---|---|---|---|---|---|---|---|
| Mercosur + México | 0.3 | -3.4 | -7.6 | -28.9 | -26.5 | -18.8 | 1.6 | 1.7 | 6.0 | -8.0 | 4.9 | 2.9 |
| Andinos + Chile | 1.6 | 2.8 | 13.2 | -34.0 | -49.1 | -31.5 | -30.5 | -27.3 | -30.3 | -7.4 | -7.2 | 15.2 |
| Centroamerica + Rep. Domin. | 1.8 | 9.3 | -2.4 | -36.6 | -42.1 | -34.0 | -17.5 | -22.4 | -12.8 | -13.4 | -3.6 | 2.8 |
| Caribe | -2.3 | 0.7 | 5.5 | -30.5 | -21.9 | -17.3 | -8.3 | -10.8 | -24.3 | -7.6 | -12.4 | -0.8 |
| Otros | -4.5 | 14.6 | -4.1 | -46.5 | -47.1 | -32.4 | -21.0 | -2.6 | 18.1 | -9.2 | 76.1 | -43.8 |
| **ALC (18)** | **0.8** | **3.4** | **0.8** | **-34.9** | **-38.3** | **-28.3** | **-14.5** | **-16.1** | **-14.1** | **-10.3** | **-3.7** | **5.1** |

Variación porcentual acumulada

| Regiones o grupos de países | Ene 20/19 | Feb 20/19 | Mar 20/19 | Abr 20/19 | May 20/19 | Jun 20/19 | Jul 20/19 | Ago 20/19 | Sep 20/19 | Oct 20/19 | Nov 20/19 | Dic 20/19 |
|---|---|---|---|---|---|---|---|---|---|---|---|---|
| Mercosur + México | 0.3 | -2.0 | -3.8 | -9.9 | -13.1 | -14.0 | -11.9 | -10.5 | -8.7 | -8.7 | -7.5 | -6.6 |
| Andinos + Chile | 1.6 | 0.9 | 3.0 | -4.5 | -14.2 | -17.0 | -19.5 | -20.9 | -22.2 | -20.9 | -19.7 | -17.5 |
| Centroamerica + Rep. Domin. | 1.8 | 5.0 | 2.4 | -8.0 | -15.1 | -18.1 | -18.1 | -18.7 | -18.1 | -17.6 | -16.4 | -14.7 |
| Caribe | -2.3 | -1.2 | 0.8 | -7.4 | -10.5 | -12.2 | -11.7 | -11.8 | -13.4 | -12.9 | -12.8 | -11.8 |
| Otros | -4.5 | 3.7 | 0.7 | -12.0 | -19.4 | -21.8 | -21.7 | -19.1 | -12.8 | -12.2 | -4.6 | -8.9 |
| **ALC (18)** | **0.8** | **1.4** | **0.7** | **-8.1** | **-14.4** | **-16.7** | **-16.6** | **-16.8** | **-16.6** | **-16.0** | **-14.9** | **-13.4** |

*Nota:* Mercosur incluye Argentina, Brasil, Paraguay y Uruguay; Andinos incluye Ecuador, Colombia y Perú; Caribe incluye Jamaica, y Trinidad y Tobago; Centroamerica incluye Costa Rica, El Salvador, Guatemala, Honduras, Nicaragua y Panamá; otros incluyen EEUU, España, Italia y Marruecos; ALC (18) incluye Argentina, Brasil, Chile, Colombia, Costa Rica, Ecuador, El Salvador, Guatemala, Honduras, Jamaica, México, Nicaragua, Panamá, Paraguay, Perú, República Dominicana, Trinidad y Tobago, Uruguay.

*Fuente:* Cálculos de los autores basados en información oficial de las administraciones tributarias.

StatLink https://doi.org/10.1787/888934309017

A finales de año, se pudo observar una recuperación más generalizada, especialmente para los países andinos y centroamericanos en diciembre (un aumento del 15.2% y el 2.8%, respectivamente), lo que contribuyó al primer aumento promedio interanual (5.1%) para ALC (18) desde marzo de 2020. A nivel regional, en línea con la evolución del IVA, las variaciones acumuladas se estancaron en territorio negativo durante el segundo semestre del año, terminando con un descenso del -13.4% en diciembre.

## Evolución de la movilidad como indicador de la actividad económica y su impacto en los ingresos fiscales

Después de que la Organización Mundial de la Salud (OMS) clasificara la situación del COVID-19 como pandemia global[3], los acontecimientos, las consecuencias y las respuestas políticas se desarrollaron a un ritmo frenético, errático e incierto en la mayoría de los países del mundo. En general, aunque con criterios diferentes, los gobiernos se vieron obligados a aplicar diversas medidas para controlar y restringir la actividad económica y la movilidad, lo que tuvo un efecto muy negativo en la recaudación de impuestos. Para comparar y contrastar el impacto de estas medidas, el CIAT analizó los datos de movilidad recopilados y difundidos por Google, lo que también nos permitió anticipar parcialmente las tendencias futuras a corto plazo.

El Gráfico 3.3 muestra lo que ocurrió, en promedio, con la movilidad entre febrero de 2020 y febrero de 2021 en cuatro categorías diferentes[4]. Después de la profunda caída durante los meses de marzo y, especialmente, abril de 2020 – cuando los viajes a tiendas y lugares de ocio, así como a estaciones de tránsito, se vieron más afectados - se observó una tendencia creciente, que indica una recuperación gradual de la actividad económica a pesar de que la movilidad seguía siendo limitada en relación con los niveles previos a la pandemia.

Gráfico 3.3. **Variación de la movilidad de las personas (promedio mensual por rubro para todos los países analizados, en términos porcentuales)**

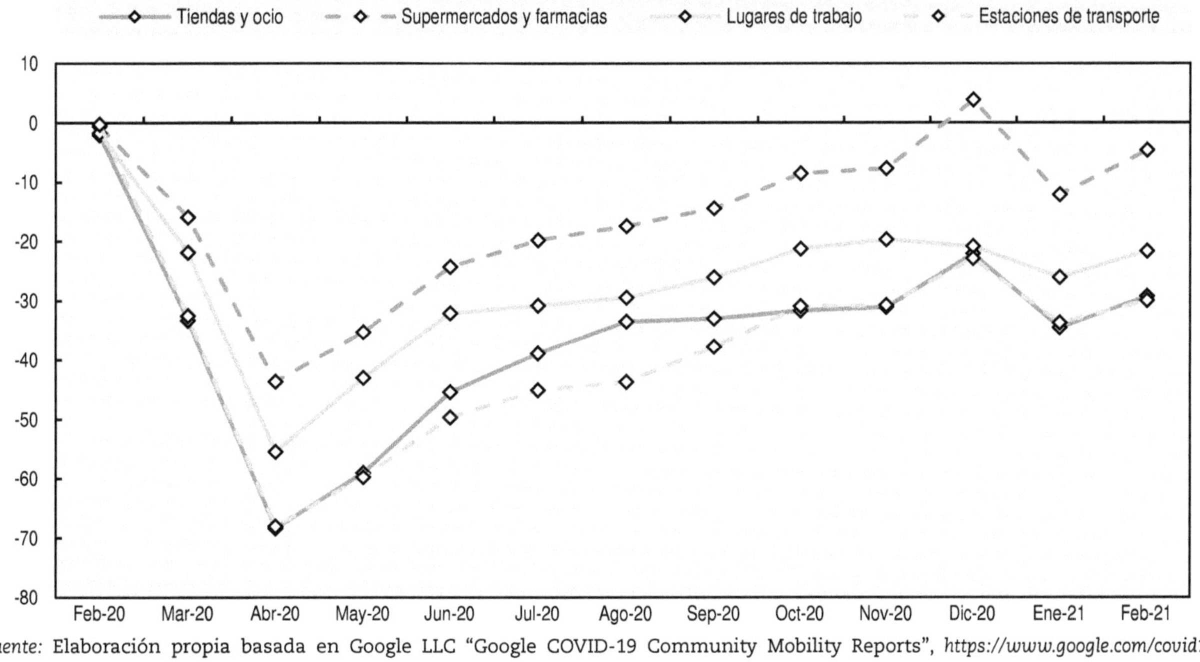


*Fuente:* Elaboración propia basada en Google LLC "Google COVID-19 Community Mobility Reports", *https://www.google.com/covid19/mobility/* (Consultado: 1 de marzo de 2021).

StatLink https://doi.org/10.1787/888934308789

Los indicadores de recaudación de impuestos y movilidad (variable sustitutiva del nivel de actividad económica), mostraron una clara correlación (Gráfico 3.4), que permitió anticipar, en cierta medida, la evolución de la recaudación de ingresos en los meses siguientes. Un modelo de regresión lineal simple entre ambas variables[5] logra un alto nivel de ajuste ($R^2$= 0.8662; 87%), con un parámetro estimado para las variaciones en la movilidad (Tiendas y Ocio) de 0.60 (el 60% de la variación en la movilidad tendría un impacto directo en las variaciones en los ingresos totales).

Gráfico 3.4. **Variaciones mensuales promedio de la recaudación total y la movilidad de las personas en Tiendas y Ocio (promedio mensual; en porcentajes; febrero a diciembre de 2020)**

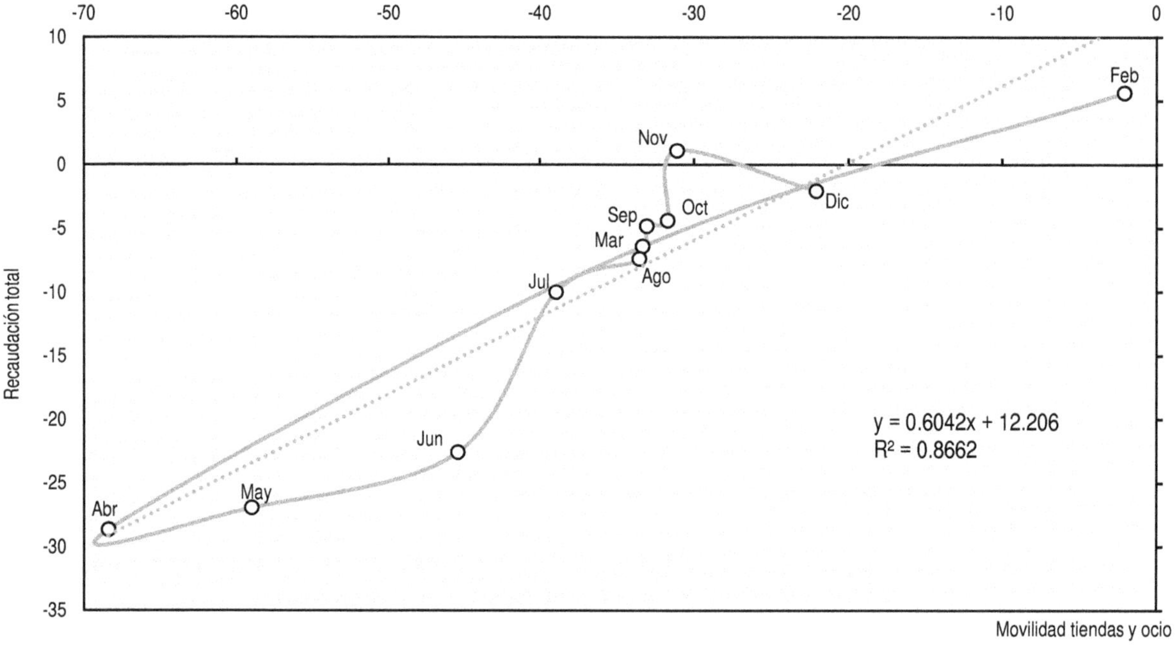


*Fuente:* Elaboración propia basada en Google LLC "Google COVID-19 Community Mobility Reports", *https://www.google.com/covid19/mobility/* (Consultado: 1 de marzo de 2021) y la Base de datos del CRR (CIAT).

StatLink https://doi.org/10.1787/888934308808

Sin embargo, el gráfico de dispersión sugiere que esta relación no fue estable a lo largo del año. Hasta junio de 2020 (Gráfico 3.5a), la capacidad explicativa de las variaciones en la movilidad era extraordinariamente elevada ($R^2$ de 0.94), mientras que de mediados a finales de año (Gráfico 3.5b) la relación se vuelve más difusa ($R^2$ de 0.46 y parámetro de la variable explicativa "movilidad" de 0.48).

Para profundizar en el análisis de esta relación por período y categoría impositiva, es posible utilizar datos de panel para un grupo de 21 países de febrero a diciembre de 2020 para las variables de ingresos y movilidad ("Tiendas y ocio"). El Gráfico 3.6 resume los resultados de las estimaciones de ingresos totales y de cada una de las categorías de ingresos para el conjunto de los 11 meses, para el primer semestre (febrero a junio) y para el segundo semestre (julio a diciembre).

Para los 11 meses completos, los parámetros estimados para la variable explicativa (movilidad) son significativos en todos los casos, alcanzando un valor de 0.48 para la recaudación total de impuestos, con un valor máximo para los impuestos sobre consumos específicos de 0.65, seguido del IVA (0.49) y el impuesto sobre la renta (0.44). Sin embargo, con la excepción del IVA, la calidad explicativa del modelo (expresada en el $R^2$) es débil.

Cuando las estimaciones distinguen entre los dos períodos de tiempo, las restricciones de movilidad se correlacionan con los cambios en los ingresos en el primer semestre del año (Los coeficientes $R^2$ superan 0.5 en las estimaciones de Total, el IVA y los impuestos selectivos). Los parámetros estimados sitúan el impacto en un 65% para los impuestos selectivos y entre el 40% y el 50% en los demás casos (con excepción del Resto de los ingresos).

Gráfico 3.5. **Variaciones mensuales promedio de la recaudación total y la movilidad de las personas en Tiendas y Ocio (promedio mensual; en porcentajes; febrero-junio y julio-diciembre de 2020)**

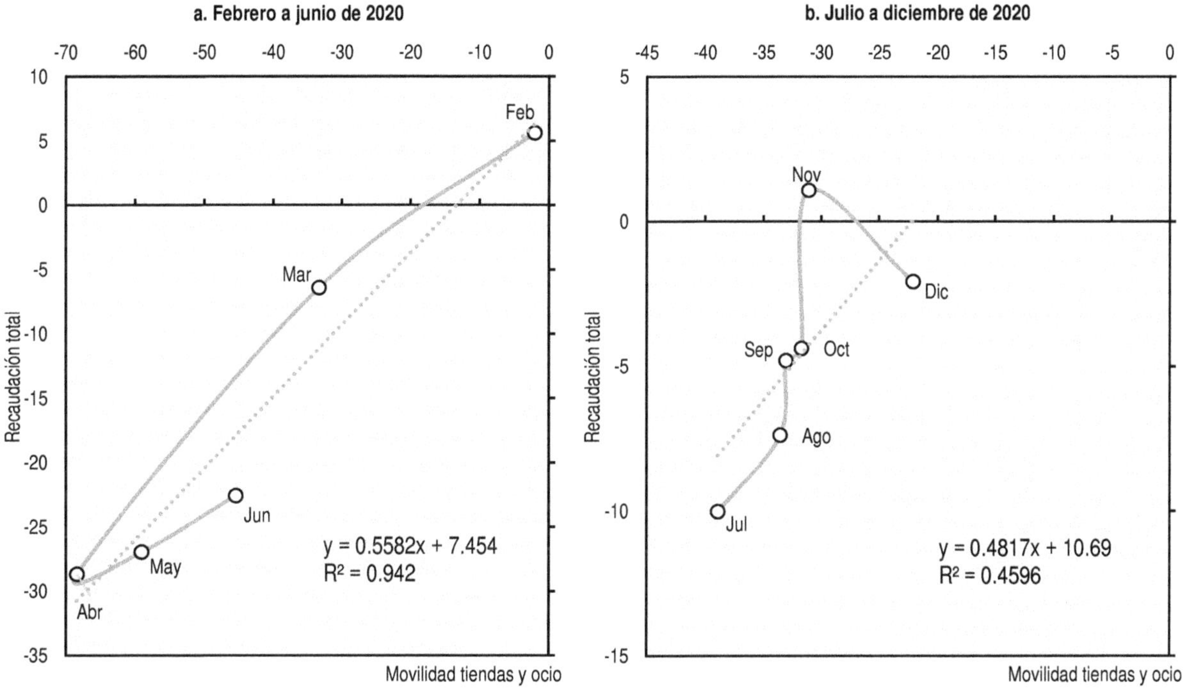


*Fuente:* Elaboración propia basada en Google LLC "Google COVID-19 Community Mobility Reports", *https://www.google.com/covid19/mobility/* (Consultado: 1 de marzo de 2021) y la Base de datos del RRC (CIAT).

StatLink *https://doi.org/10.1787/888934308827*

En el segundo período se observa un cambio, la relación entre la recaudación y las restricciones a la movilidad se debilita en los impuestos sobre la renta y los impuestos selectivos, con parámetros estimados que no difieren significativamente de los niveles de ajuste cero y reducidos. Esto se debe probablemente a una combinación de factores, como la reversión de los aplazamientos del pago de impuestos (especialmente en el caso del impuesto sobre la renta), la adaptación gradual del comportamiento de los consumidores y productores y el crecimiento de la actividad económica digital.

Dicho esto, cabe señalar que la relación se mantuvo clara e incluso fortalecida durante el segundo período en el caso del IVA: el ajuste fue del 68% en el segundo período frente al 56% en el primero, y el 66% de la variación de la movilidad en el segundo período se transfirió a ingresos frente al 44% en el primer período. Dado el peso del IVA en la estructura tributaria de la mayoría de los países, especialmente en la región de América Latina y el Caribe, estos datos facilitan proyecciones a corto plazo para la recaudación de ingresos basados en la trayectoria de la pandemia y las restricciones a la movilidad asociadas con su contención.

Gráfico 3.6. **Movilidad (tiendas y ocio) y recaudación resultados de estimación por datos de panel**

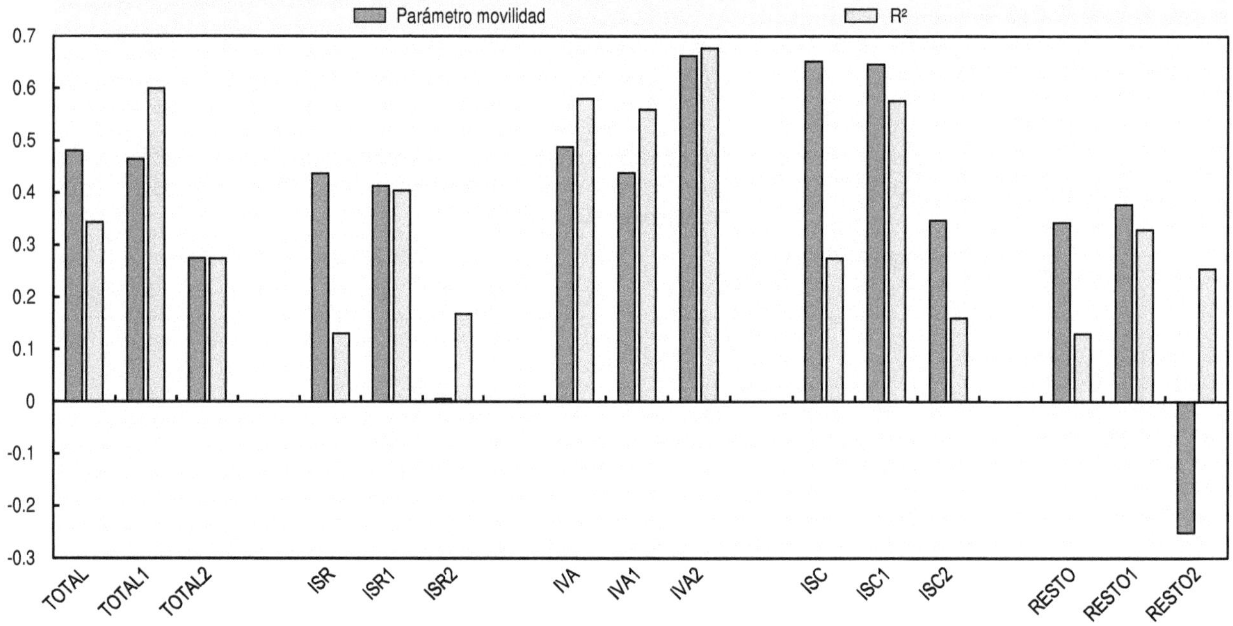


*Nota:* Estimación de datos de panel con Gretl (21 países; 11 meses; dividido en dos períodos para estimaciones parciales 1: Febrero-Junio; 2: Julio-diciembre); efectos fijos y estimación robusta de errores estándar (con respecto a heterocedasticidad y autocorrelación). La estimación se considera condicionada a la selección de los países utilizados (no a la muestra aleatoria). Considera la heterogeneidad entre países (diferentes constantes o intercepciones).

*Fuente:* Elaboración propia basada en Google LLC "Google COVID-19 Community Mobility Reports", *https://www.google.com/covid19/mobility/* (Consultado: 1 de marzo de 2021) y la Base de datos del CRR (CIAT).

StatLink https://doi.org/10.1787/888934308846

## Conclusiones y primeros resultados de 2021

El seguimiento mensual de los ingresos fiscales es una herramienta útil para monitorear los efectos de la crisis del COVID-19 en las finanzas públicas en toda la región de América Latina y el Caribe, diferenciando entre países, subregiones y categorías impositivas. Los efectos de las medidas de distanciamiento social en la movilidad ayudan a explicar las variaciones en los ingresos, que a su vez facilitaron mejoras en las previsiones de ingresos a corto plazo durante la pandemia, especialmente en el primer semestre de 2020. Estos datos podrían utilizarse para desarrollar nuevas investigaciones sobre la eficacia de las medidas adoptadas durante esta crisis extraordinaria y para aprender a hacer frente a futuros acontecimientos.

Mientras continúe la crisis, las estadísticas tributarias mensuales seguirán siendo útiles. Los últimos datos de los Reportes de Recaudación COVID-19 del CIAT muestran la recuperación que está teniendo lugar en toda la región durante los primeros ocho meses de 2021. En promedio, los ingresos de ALC aumentaron un 21.3% acumulado entre enero y agosto de 2021 con respecto al mismo período de 2020 en términos reales (Gráfico 3.7a).

Como siempre –y especialmente en medio de una de las mayores crisis económicas de los últimos siglos-, es necesario ser cautelosos al interpretar estos resultados. En primer lugar, porque los ritmos de la recuperación son muy diferentes entre las regiones y los países (por ejemplo, la región de América Central lidera la recuperación, con la excepción de Panamá). En segundo lugar, porque la serie temporal se ha visto muy perturbada por la extraordinaria caída de los ingresos fiscales y el PIB durante el año 2020.

Gráfico 3.7. **Evolución media de la recaudación acumulada de impuestos por tipo de impuesto en 2021 (cambios interanuales, en comparación con 2020 (a) y 2019 (b); precios constantes; en porcentajes)**

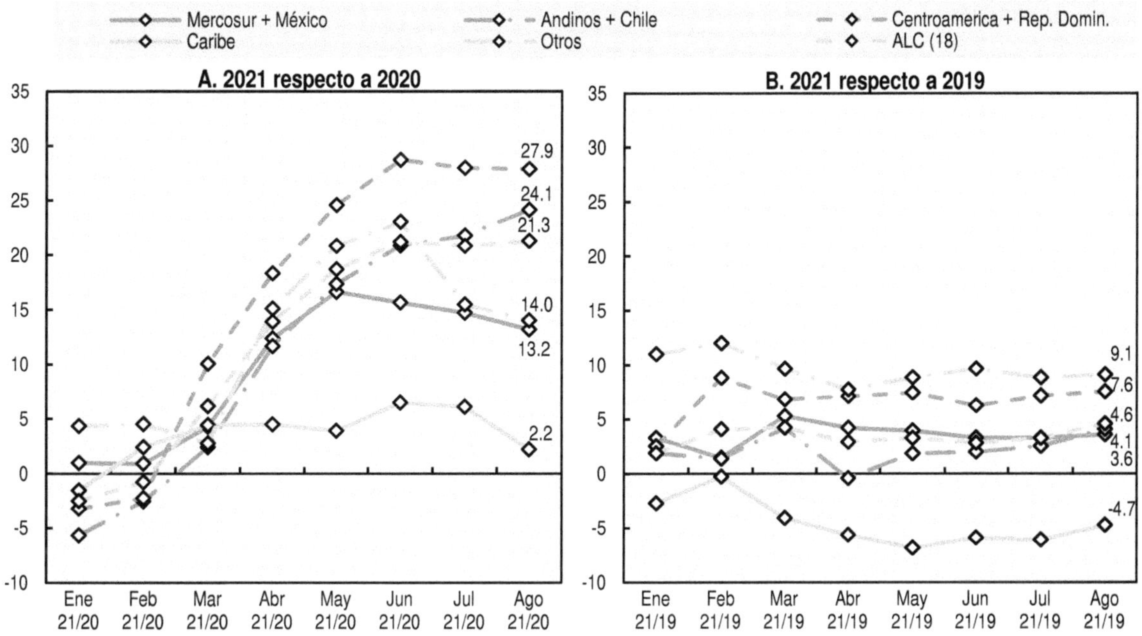


*Nota:* Mercosur incluye Argentina, Brasil, Paraguay y Uruguay; Andinos incluye Ecuador, Colombia y Perú; Caribe incluye Jamaica, y Trinidad y Tobago; Centroamerica incluye Costa Rica, El Salvador, Guatemala, Honduras, Nicaragua y Panamá; otros incluyen EEUU, España, Italia y Marruecos; ALC (18) incluye Argentina, Brasil, Chile, Colombia, Costa Rica, Ecuador, El Salvador, Guatemala, Honduras, Jamaica, México, Nicaragua, Panamá, Paraguay, Perú, República Dominicana, Trinidad y Tobago, Uruguay.

*Fuente:* Cálculos de los autores basados en información oficial de las administraciones tributarias.

StatLink https://doi.org/10.1787/888934308865

En este contexto, comparar el rendimiento acumulado durante los primeros ocho meses de 2021 con el mismo período de 2019 es una mejor guía en cuanto a la fortaleza de la recuperación. Esta comparativa muestra un aumento menos pronunciado, pero, en todo caso, alentador, de los ingresos fiscales: en términos acumulados, los ingresos para el promedio de ALC (18) de enero a agosto aumentaron un 4.6% con respecto al período equivalente en 2019 (Gráfico 3.7b).

## Notas

1. Aunque México podría agruparse con los países centroamericanos debido a su ubicación geográfica, sus características macroeconómicas y fiscales lo hacen más comparable a los países del Mercosur, especialmente Argentina y Brasil.
2. Bolivia también estaría incluida en este grupo, pero se ha excluido para evitar sesgos en los valores medios, dadas las extraordinarias variaciones observadas en su recaudación a lo largo del período para el que se dispone de información oficial.
3. Según el discurso pronunciado el 11 de marzo de 2020 por el Director de la OMS (Dr. T. A. Ghebreyesus).

4. Los datos muestran la tasa de cambio en el número de visitantes a los sitios categorizados (o el tiempo de permanencia en ellos) en comparación con un "día de referencia", que representa un valor normal en ese día de la semana y se calcula como el valor medio para el período de cinco semanas comprendido entre el 3 de enero y el 6 de febrero de 2020. En este trabajo se considera el promedio mensual de los datos diarios de cada uno de los países analizados por el CIAT.
5. A corto plazo, "Tiendas y Ocio" sirve como un mejor indicador de la actividad económica general y la recaudación de impuestos que solo los productos básicos (Comestibles y Farmacia) o la movilidad física a estaciones de tránsito o lugares de trabajo (teniendo en cuenta el teletrabajo). Sin embargo, la evolución de los diferentes índices es paralela, por lo que las conclusiones básicas del análisis no cambian.

*Chapter 4*

# Tax levels and tax structures, 1990-2020

*Capítulo 4*

# Niveles impositivos y estructuras tributarias, 1990-2020

# Chapter 4 / Capítulo 4

## 4.1. Comparative tables, 1990-2020

In all of the following tables a (..) indicates not available. The main series in this volume cover the years 1990 to 2020.

Figures referring to 1991-99, 2001-06, 2008-09 and 2011-14 in Tables 4.1 to 4.2 and Tables 4.15 to 4.17, figures relating to 1991-99, 2001-09 and 2011-18 in Tables 4.5 to 4.10 and figures relating to 1990-94, 1996-99 and 2001-19 in Tables 4.11 to 4.13 have been omitted because of lack of space. Complete series are, however, available on line at *www.latameconomy.org* and in the database OECD (2022), "Revenue Statistics in Latin America: Comparative tables", *OECD Tax Statistics*, *http://dx.doi.org/10.1787/data-00641-en*.

## 4.2. Cuadros comparativos, 1990-2020

En todos los cuadros siguientes, (..) indica dato indisponible. Las principales series de datos de esta sección cubren el periodo que va de 1990 a 2020.

Las cifras relativas a 1991-99, 2001-06, 2008-09 y a 2011-14 en Cuadros 4.1 hasta 4.2 y Cuadros 4.15 hasta 4.17 y las cifras relativas a 1991-99, 2001-09 y 2011-18 en Cuadros 4.5 hasta 4.10 y las cifras relativas a 1990-94, 1996-99 y 2001-19 en Cuadros 4.11 hasta 4.13 se han omitido por falta de espacio. Sin embargo, las series completas están disponibles en línea en *www.latameconomy.org* y en la base de datos OCDE (2022), "Revenue Statistics in Latin America: Comparative tables", *OECD Tax Statistics*, *http://dx.doi.org/10.1787/data-00641-en*.

## Table 4.1. **Total tax revenue as % of GDP, 1990-2020**
## Cuadro 4.1. **Total de ingresos tributarios en % del PIB, 1990-2020**

| | 1990 | 2000 | 2007 | 2010 | 2015 | 2016 | 2017 | 2018 | 2019 | 2020 |
|---|---|---|---|---|---|---|---|---|---|---|
| Antigua and Barbuda / Antigua y Barbuda[1] | .. | 12.0 | 21.5 | 21.3 | 20.4 | 19.6 | 19.6 | 19.0 | 18.0 | 19.8 |
| Argentina | 13.3 | 19.2 | 26.4 | 29.1 | 31.5 | 30.7 | 30.0 | 28.5 | 28.2 | 29.4 |
| Bahamas[1] | 9.7 | 12.2 | 13.1 | 12.7 | 15.4 | 16.2 | 17.1 | 16.8 | 18.8 | 18.6 |
| Barbados | 25.3 | 30.9 | 30.0 | 30.0 | 30.5 | 31.1 | 32.8 | 33.4 | 33.9 | 35.2 |
| Belize / Belice | 21.6 | 19.1 | 25.7 | 26.9 | 27.5 | 28.1 | 28.4 | 29.5 | 29.1 | 26.1 |
| Bolivia | 6.5 | 17.6 | 19.8 | 22.9 | 29.5 | 27.9 | 25.9 | 25.0 | 24.7 | 22.4 |
| Brazil / Brasil | 27.8 | 29.4 | 33.6 | 32.4 | 32.0 | 32.2 | 32.3 | 32.6 | 32.5 | 31.6 |
| Chile | 16.9 | 18.8 | 22.7 | 19.6 | 20.4 | 20.1 | 20.2 | 21.1 | 20.9 | 19.3 |
| Colombia | 11.3 | 15.7 | 19.3 | 18.1 | 19.9 | 19.1 | 19.0 | 19.3 | 19.7 | 18.7 |
| Costa Rica | 22.5 | 21.1 | 23.1 | 22.1 | 22.9 | 23.5 | 23.0 | 23.2 | 23.6 | 22.9 |
| Cuba | 31.9 | 37.2 | 44.0 | 37.2 | 38.1 | 41.1 | 42.4 | 42.3 | 42.1 | 37.5 |
| Dominican Republic / República Dominicana | 8.3 | 12.3 | 15.0 | 12.4 | 13.0 | 13.1 | 13.2 | 13.2 | 13.5 | 12.6 |
| Ecuador | 7.1 | 11.6 | 15.1 | 16.8 | 21.7 | 19.9 | 19.9 | 20.7 | 20.0 | 19.1 |
| El Salvador | 11.3 | 14.2 | 18.8 | 18.7 | 19.9 | 20.5 | 20.9 | 21.3 | 20.9 | 21.9 |
| Guatemala | 7.6 | 11.7 | 14.0 | 12.5 | 12.8 | 13.2 | 13.2 | 13.2 | 13.0 | 12.4 |
| Guyana | 15.2 | 15.7 | 15.6 | 16.0 | 18.1 | 18.4 | 19.5 | 22.2 | 23.2 | 21.3 |
| Honduras | 12.4 | 17.2 | 19.8 | 18.2 | 20.6 | 22.2 | 21.7 | 21.9 | 21.5 | 19.2 |
| Jamaica | 20.3 | 22.2 | 24.8 | 24.9 | 25.8 | 26.5 | 27.3 | 27.7 | 28.6 | 27.7 |
| Mexico / México | 12.1 | 11.5 | 12.0 | 12.8 | 15.9 | 16.6 | 16.1 | 16.1 | 16.3 | 17.9 |
| Nicaragua[1] | .. | 14.3 | 18.8 | 19.3 | 22.3 | 23.3 | 23.8 | 23.2 | 25.7 | 25.4 |
| Panama / Panamá | 16.6 | 15.5 | 15.5 | 16.4 | 15.1 | 15.5 | 15.1 | 14.8 | 14.0 | 13.7 |
| Paraguay | 8.5 | 11.6 | 10.8 | 12.1 | 13.7 | 13.4 | 14.0 | 13.9 | 14.0 | 13.4 |
| Peru / Perú | 12.0 | 15.2 | 18.5 | 17.8 | 17.4 | 16.2 | 15.3 | 16.4 | 16.6 | 15.2 |
| Saint Lucia / Santa Lucía | .. | 19.6 | 20.8 | 20.3 | 21.2 | 21.3 | 20.4 | 20.6 | 20.6 | 20.5 |
| Trinidad and Tobago / Trinidad y Tobago | 23.3 | 21.9 | 27.8 | 28.7 | 28.5 | 22.4 | 20.6 | 23.3 | 24.4 | 21.1 |
| Uruguay[1] | 18.4 | 21.4 | 23.6 | 24.3 | 25.2 | 25.6 | 26.9 | 27.0 | 26.6 | 26.6 |
| Venezuela[2] | 21.2 | 13.5 | 17.0 | 11.8 | .. | .. | .. | .. | .. | .. |
| *Unweighted average / Promedio no ponderado* | | | | | | | | | | |
| LAC / ALC[3] | 15.6 | 18.0 | 21.2 | 20.9 | 22.3 | 22.2 | 22.3 | 22.5 | 22.7 | 21.9 |
| OECD / OCDE[4] | 30.8 | 33.0 | 32.9 | 31.6 | 32.9 | 33.6 | 33.4 | 33.5 | 33.4 | 33.5 |

.. Not available

*Note:* The figures exclude local government revenues for Antigua and Barbuda, Argentina (but include provincial revenues), the Bahamas, Barbados, Cuba (except for 2002-2012), the Dominican Republic, Saint Lucia, Trinidad and Tobago and Venezuela as the data are not available. Local government revenue data have been available since 1991 for Nicaragua, since 1994 for Bolivia, since 1995 for Guatemala, since 1998 for Jamaica, since 1999 for Panama, since 2000 for Peru, since 2002 for El Salvador and Guyana, since 2006 for Paraguay and since 1990 for all other countries.

1. The data include the following estimations: Antigua and Barbuda (social security contributions for 2019 and 2020), Bahamas (social security contributions for 2019 and 2020), Nicaragua (local tax revenues for 2020) and Uruguay (local tax revenues for 2020). See the corresponding country tables for more information.
2. Some tax revenue data are not available between 2014 and 2017 and therefore total figures have not been included. Data since 2018 have not been available.
3. Represents the group of 26 Latin American and Caribbean countries included in this publication and excludes Venezuela due to data availability issues. Chile, Colombia, Costa Rica and Mexico are also part of the OECD (38) group.
4. Calculated by applying the unweighted average percentage change for 2020 in the 36 countries providing data for that year to the overall average tax to GDP ratio in 2019.

.. Non disponible

*Nota:* Las cifras excluyen los ingresos subnacionales para Antigua y Barbuda, Argentina (pero se incluyen los ingresos de las provincias), Las Bahamas, Barbados, Cuba (excepto 2002-2012), República Dominicana, Santa Lucía, Trinidad y Tobago y Venezuela, dado que los datos no están disponibles. Los datos de ingresos subnacionales están disponibles desde 1991 para Nicaragua, desde 1994 para Bolivia, desde 1995 para Guatemala, desde 1998 para Jamaica, desde 1999 para Panamá, desde 2000 para Perú, desde 2002 para El Salvador y Guyana, desde 2006 para Paraguay y desde 1990 para todos los demás países.

1. Los datos incluyen las siguientes estimaciones: Antigua y Barbuda (contribuciones a la seguridad social para 2019 y 2020), Bahamas (contribuciones a la seguridad social para 2019 y 2020), Nicaragua (ingresos tributarios locales para 2020) y Uruguay (ingresos tributarios locales para 2020). Consulte las tablas de países correspondientes para obtener más información.
2. Algunos datos de ingresos tributarios no están disponibles entre 2014 y 2017 y, por lo tanto, no se han incluido las cifras totales. Los datos para 2018 y 2019 no están disponibles.
3. Representa al grupo de 26 países de América Latina y el Caribe incluidos en esta publicación y excluye a Venezuela debido a problemas de disponibilidad de datos. Chile, Colombia, Costa Rica y México también forman parte del grupo OCDE (38).
4. Calculado mediante la aplicación del cambio porcentual promedio no ponderado para 2020 en los 36 países que proporcionan datos para ese año al promedio del recaudación tributario sobre PIB en 2019.

StatLink https://doi.org/10.1787/888934309036

## Table 4.2. **Total tax revenue in millions of USD at market exchange rates, 1990-2020**
## Cuadro 4.2. **Total de ingresos tributarios en millones de US dólares a tipos de cambio de mercado, 1990-2020**

| | 1990 | 2000 | 2007 | 2010 | 2015 | 2016 | 2017 | 2018 | 2019 | 2020 |
|---|---|---|---|---|---|---|---|---|---|---|
| Antigua and Barbuda / Antigua y Barbuda[1] | .. | 99 | 283 | 244 | 272 | 281 | 287 | 305 | 305 | 271 |
| Argentina | 20 952 | 61 084 | 75 919 | 123 456 | 202 079 | 170 714 | 193 442 | 149 532 | 127 386 | 114 412 |
| Bahamas[1] | 505 | 965 | 1 360 | 1 277 | 1 761 | 1 937 | 2 106 | 2 115 | 2 486 | 2 104 |
| Barbados | 513 | 946 | 1 412 | 1 368 | 1 447 | 1 513 | 1 640 | 1 717 | 1 721 | 1 491 |
| Belize / Belice | 89 | 159 | 326 | 370 | 473 | 503 | 527 | 565 | 577 | 445 |
| Bolivia | 317 | 1 478 | 2 620 | 4 527 | 9 805 | 9 547 | 9 777 | 10 136 | 10 173 | 8 234 |
| Brazil / Brasil | 133 077 | 192 661 | 468 987 | 715 679 | 576 176 | 578 290 | 665 542 | 625 649 | 609 494 | 456 611 |
| Chile | 5 829 | 14 650 | 39 444 | 42 836 | 49 719 | 50 448 | 55 902 | 62 806 | 58 332 | 48 940 |
| Colombia | 5 136 | 14 655 | 39 791 | 51 858 | 58 412 | 53 960 | 59 206 | 64 384 | 63 725 | 50 791 |
| Costa Rica | 1 285 | 3 174 | 6 220 | 8 334 | 12 952 | 13 821 | 13 909 | 14 455 | 15 079 | 14 080 |
| Cuba | 6 870 | 11 367 | 25 787 | 23 949 | 33 182 | 37 597 | 41 021 | 42 307 | 43 379 | 36 003 |
| Dominican Republic / República Dominicana | 664 | 2 986 | 6 614 | 6 670 | 9 260 | 9 905 | 10 603 | 11 340 | 12 056 | 9 909 |
| Ecuador | 1 078 | 2 125 | 7 698 | 11 693 | 21 591 | 19 897 | 20 759 | 22 290 | 21 665 | 18 908 |
| El Salvador | 543 | 1 669 | 3 192 | 3 447 | 4 659 | 4 963 | 5 231 | 5 539 | 5 629 | 5 392 |
| Guatemala | 573 | 2 129 | 4 782 | 5 153 | 7 944 | 8 734 | 9 481 | 9 643 | 10 018 | 9 652 |
| Guyana | 104 | 234 | 425 | 549 | 774 | 825 | 927 | 1 061 | 1 200 | 1 168 |
| Honduras | 515 | 1 233 | 2 443 | 2 887 | 4 315 | 4 827 | 5 009 | 5 274 | 5 386 | 4 574 |
| Jamaica | 1 027 | 1 998 | 3 192 | 3 286 | 3 647 | 3 744 | 4 026 | 4 338 | 4 514 | 3 841 |
| Mexico / México | 35 908 | 81 160 | 126 466 | 135 866 | 186 055 | 179 484 | 186 897 | 198 032 | 207 926 | 193 750 |
| Nicaragua[1] | .. | 733 | 1 399 | 1 693 | 2 846 | 3 092 | 3 288 | 3 025 | 3 244 | 3 202 |
| Panama / Panamá | 948 | 1 942 | 3 298 | 4 815 | 8 193 | 9 004 | 9 366 | 9 631 | 9 382 | 7 238 |
| Paraguay | 494 | 1 029 | 1 921 | 3 286 | 4 967 | 4 844 | 5 469 | 5 575 | 5 289 | 4 791 |
| Peru / Perú | 3 389 | 7 674 | 18 919 | 26 478 | 33 337 | 31 415 | 32 822 | 37 067 | 38 355 | 31 301 |
| Saint Lucia / Santa Lucía | .. | 178 | 283 | 307 | 387 | 404 | 410 | 429 | 437 | 336 |
| Trinidad and Tobago / Trinidad y Tobago | 1 158 | 1 746 | 5 893 | 6 261 | 7 339 | 5 188 | 4 617 | 5 449 | 5 686 | 4 630 |
| Uruguay[1] | 2 051 | 5 307 | 6 026 | 10 614 | 14 574 | 14 650 | 17 258 | 17 464 | 16 457 | 15 067 |
| Venezuela[2] | 10 259 | 12 758 | 39 055 | 38 220 | .. | .. | .. | .. | .. | .. |

.. Not available

*Note:* The figures exclude local government revenues for Antigua and Barbuda, Argentina (but include provincial revenues), the Bahamas, Barbados, Cuba (except for 2002-2012), the Dominican Republic, Saint Lucia, Trinidad and Tobago and Venezuela as the data are not available. Local government revenue data have been available since 1991 for Nicaragua, since 1994 for Bolivia, since 1995 for Guatemala, since 1998 for Jamaica, since 1999 for Panama, since 2000 for Peru, since 2002 for El Salvador and Guyana, since 2006 for Paraguay and since 1990 for all other countries.

1. The data include the following estimations: Antigua and Barbuda (social security contributions for 2019 and 2020), Bahamas (social security contributions for 2019 and 2020), Nicaragua (local tax revenues for 2020) and Uruguay (local tax revenues for 2020). See the corresponding country tables for more information.
2. Some tax revenue data are not available between 2014 and 2017 and therefore total figures have not been included. Data since 2018 have not been available.

.. Non disponible

*Nota:* Las cifras excluyen los ingresos subnacionales para Antigua y Barbuda, Argentina (pero se incluyen los ingresos de las provincias), Las Bahamas, Barbados, Cuba (excepto 2002-2012), República Dominicana, Santa Lucía, Trinidad y Tobago y Venezuela, dado que los datos no están disponibles. Los datos de ingresos subnacionales están disponibles desde 1991 para Nicaragua, desde 1994 para Bolivia, desde 1995 para Guatemala, desde 1998 para Jamaica, desde 1999 para Panamá, desde 2000 para Perú, desde 2002 para El Salvador y Guyana, desde 2006 para Paraguay y desde 1990 para todos los demás países.

1. Los datos incluyen las siguientes estimaciones: Antigua y Barbuda (contribuciones a la seguridad social para 2019 y 2020), Bahamas (contribuciones a la seguridad social para 2019 y 2020), Nicaragua (ingresos tributarios locales para 2020) y Uruguay (ingresos tributarios locales para 2020). Consulte las tablas de países correspondientes para obtener más información.
2. Algunos datos de ingresos tributarios no están disponibles entre 2014 y 2017 y, por lo tanto, no se han incluido las cifras totales. Los datos para 2018 y 2019 no están disponibles.

StatLink https://doi.org/10.1787/888934309055

## Table 4.3. **Tax revenue of main headings as % of GDP, 2020**
## Cuadro 4.3. **Ingresos tributarios en las principales partidas en % del PIB, 2020**

| | 1000 Income & profits / Ingresos y utilidades | 2000 Social security / Seguridad social | 3000 Payroll / Nómina | 4000 Property / Propiedad | 5000 Goods and services / Bienes y servicios | 6000 Others / Otros |
|---|---|---|---|---|---|---|
| Antigua and Barbuda / Antigua y Barbuda[1] | 2.4 | 3.3 | 0.0 | 1.5 | 12.6 | 0.0 |
| Argentina | 5.4 | 5.6 | 0.0 | 3.2 | 15.0 | 0.2 |
| Bahamas[1] | 0.0 | 2.2 | 0.0 | 1.5 | 14.9 | 0.0 |
| Barbados | 11.5 | 7.0 | 0.0 | 2.2 | 14.4 | 0.0 |
| Belize / Belice | 6.4 | 3.2 | 0.0 | 0.9 | 15.6 | 0.0 |
| Bolivia | 2.9 | 6.7 | 0.0 | 0.2 | 10.2 | 2.3 |
| Brazil / Brasil | 7.1 | 8.2 | 0.5 | 1.2 | 13.9 | 0.6 |
| Chile | 6.3 | 1.5 | 0.0 | 1.0 | 10.6 | -0.1 |
| Colombia | 6.2 | 1.9 | 0.4 | 1.8 | 7.8 | 0.8 |
| Costa Rica | 4.6 | 8.3 | 1.5 | 0.5 | 7.6 | 0.5 |
| Cuba | 10.6 | 6.0 | 1.5 | 0.0 | 17.4 | 2.0 |
| Dominican Republic / República Dominicana | 4.2 | 0.1 | 0.1 | 0.6 | 7.6 | 0.0 |
| Ecuador | 4.6 | 5.5 | 0.0 | 0.3 | 8.7 | 0.0 |
| El Salvador | 7.9 | 2.8 | 0.1 | 0.1 | 10.5 | 0.4 |
| Guatemala | 2.8 | 2.1 | 0.1 | 0.2 | 6.3 | 0.8 |
| Guyana | 9.3 | 2.2 | 0.0 | 0.4 | 9.4 | 0.2 |
| Honduras | 4.4 | 4.0 | 0.2 | 0.5 | 9.5 | 0.7 |
| Jamaica | 7.9 | 1.3 | 1.6 | 0.8 | 16.0 | 0.1 |
| Mexico / México | 7.6 | 2.5 | 0.5 | 0.3 | 6.7 | 0.4 |
| Nicaragua[1] | 7.5 | 6.7 | 0.0 | 0.2 | 10.7 | 0.2 |
| Panama / Panamá | 3.6 | 6.1 | 0.2 | 0.2 | 3.6 | 0.0 |
| Paraguay | 2.5 | 3.7 | 0.0 | 0.2 | 7.0 | 0.1 |
| Peru / Perú | 5.6 | 2.0 | 0.0 | 0.3 | 7.1 | 0.1 |
| Saint Lucia / Santa Lucía | 4.8 | 2.6 | 0.0 | 0.4 | 12.7 | 0.0 |
| Trinidad and Tobago / Trinidad y Tobago | 10.3 | 3.2 | 0.0 | 0.2 | 7.4 | 0.0 |
| Uruguay[1] | 7.1 | 6.7 | 0.0 | 2.1 | 10.7 | 0.2 |
| Venezuela[2] | .. | .. | .. | .. | .. | .. |
| *Unweighted average / Promedio no ponderado* | | | | | | |
| LAC / ALC[3] | 5.9 | 4.0 | 0.3 | 0.8 | 10.5 | 0.4 |
| OECD / OCDE[4] | 11.3 | 8.9 | 0.5 | 1.8 | 10.8 | 0.2 |

.. Not available

*Note:* The figures exclude local government revenues for Antigua and Barbuda, Argentina (but include provincial revenues), the Bahamas, Barbados, Cuba (except for 2002-2012), the Dominican Republic, Saint Lucia, Trinidad and Tobago and Venezuela as the data are not available. Local government revenue data have been available since 1991 for Nicaragua, since 1994 for Bolivia, since 1995 for Guatemala, since 1998 for Jamaica, since 1999 for Panama, since 2000 for Peru, since 2002 for El Salvador and Guyana, since 2006 for Paraguay and since 1990 for all other countries.

1. The data include the following estimations: Antigua and Barbuda (social security contributions for 2019 and 2020), Bahamas (social security contributions for 2019 and 2020), Nicaragua (local tax revenues for 2020) and Uruguay (local tax revenues for 2020). See the corresponding country tables for more information.
2. Data for 2018 and subsequent years are not available.
3. Represents the group of 26 Latin American and Caribbean countries included in this publication and excludes Venezuela due to data availability issues. Chile, Colombia, Costa Rica and Mexico are also part of the OECD (38) group.
4. Represents the unweighted average for OECD member countries. Data for 2019 are used as data for 2020 were not available at the time of publication.

.. Non disponible

*Nota:* Las cifras excluyen los ingresos subnacionales para Antigua y Barbuda, Argentina (pero se incluyen los ingresos de las provincias), Las Bahamas, Barbados, Cuba (excepto 2002-2012), República Dominicana, Santa Lucía, Trinidad y Tobago y Venezuela, dado que los datos no están disponibles. Los datos de ingresos subnacionales están disponibles desde 1991 para Nicaragua, desde 1994 para Bolivia, desde 1995 para Guatemala, desde 1998 para Jamaica, desde 1999 para Panamá, desde 2000 para Perú, desde 2002 para El Salvador y Guyana, desde 2006 para Paraguay y desde 1990 para todos los demás países.

1. Los datos incluyen las siguientes estimaciones: Antigua y Barbuda (contribuciones a la seguridad social para 2019 y 2020), Bahamas (contribuciones a la seguridad social para 2019 y 2020), Nicaragua (ingresos tributarios locales para 2020) y Uruguay (ingresos tributarios locales para 2020). Consulte las tablas de países correspondientes para obtener más información.
2. Los datos de 2018 y años posteriores no están disponibles.
3. Representa al grupo de 26 países de América Latina y el Caribe incluidos en esta publicación y excluye a Venezuela debido a problemas de disponibilidad de datos. Chile, Colombia, Costa Rica y México también forman parte del grupo OCDE (38).
4. Representa el promedio no ponderado de los países miembros de la OCDE. Se utilizan los datos de 2019 porque los datos de 2020 no estaban disponibles en el momento de la publicación.

StatLink https://doi.org/10.1787/888934309074

## Table 4.4. **Tax revenue of main headings as % of total tax revenue, 2020**
## Cuadro 4.4. **Ingresos tributarios en las principales partidas en % del total de ingresos tributarios, 2020**

| | 1000 Income & profits / Ingresos y utilidades | 2000 Social security / Seguridad social | 3000 Payroll / Nómina | 4000 Property / Propiedad | 5000 Goods and services / Bienes y servicios | 6000 Others / Otros |
|---|---|---|---|---|---|---|
| Antigua and Barbuda / Antigua y Barbuda[1] | 11.9 | 16.7 | 0.0 | 7.6 | 63.8 | 0.0 |
| Argentina | 18.2 | 19.2 | 0.0 | 10.9 | 51.0 | 0.7 |
| Bahamas[1] | 0.0 | 11.7 | 0.0 | 8.2 | 80.1 | 0.0 |
| Barbados | 32.7 | 19.9 | 0.0 | 6.3 | 41.0 | 0.0 |
| Belize / Belice | 24.4 | 12.4 | 0.0 | 3.4 | 59.8 | 0.0 |
| Bolivia | 13.1 | 29.9 | 0.0 | 0.7 | 45.8 | 10.5 |
| Brazil / Brasil | 22.3 | 26.0 | 1.7 | 3.9 | 44.1 | 2.0 |
| Chile | 32.4 | 8.0 | 0.0 | 5.2 | 54.9 | -0.5 |
| Colombia | 32.9 | 9.9 | 2.0 | 9.7 | 41.4 | 4.1 |
| Costa Rica | 20.1 | 36.1 | 6.5 | 2.0 | 33.3 | 2.0 |
| Cuba | 28.3 | 16.0 | 4.0 | 0.0 | 46.4 | 5.4 |
| Dominican Republic / República Dominicana | 33.7 | 0.5 | 0.6 | 4.5 | 60.8 | 0.0 |
| Ecuador | 23.8 | 28.8 | 0.0 | 1.8 | 45.5 | 0.1 |
| El Salvador | 36.2 | 13.0 | 0.7 | 0.5 | 47.9 | 1.7 |
| Guatemala | 22.5 | 17.1 | 1.2 | 1.5 | 51.0 | 6.8 |
| Guyana | 43.4 | 10.1 | 0.0 | 1.8 | 43.8 | 0.8 |
| Honduras | 22.8 | 20.6 | 0.8 | 2.6 | 49.4 | 3.8 |
| Jamaica | 28.6 | 4.6 | 5.7 | 2.9 | 57.9 | 0.3 |
| Mexico / México | 42.7 | 13.9 | 2.5 | 1.6 | 37.2 | 2.1 |
| Nicaragua[1] | 29.5 | 26.4 | 0.0 | 0.9 | 42.3 | 0.8 |
| Panama / Panamá | 26.0 | 44.6 | 1.4 | 1.7 | 26.0 | 0.3 |
| Paraguay | 18.5 | 27.6 | 0.0 | 1.2 | 52.2 | 0.5 |
| Peru / Perú | 36.7 | 13.4 | 0.1 | 2.2 | 46.8 | 0.8 |
| Saint Lucia / Santa Lucía | 23.5 | 12.7 | 0.0 | 2.1 | 61.7 | 0.0 |
| Trinidad and Tobago / Trinidad y Tobago | 49.1 | 15.0 | 0.0 | 0.8 | 35.1 | 0.0 |
| Uruguay[1] | 26.6 | 25.0 | 0.0 | 7.7 | 40.0 | 0.6 |
| Venezuela[2] | .. | .. | .. | .. | .. | .. |
| *Unweighted average / Promedio no ponderado* | | | | | | |
| LAC / ALC[3] | 26.9 | 18.4 | 1.0 | 3.5 | 48.4 | 1.6 |
| OECD / OCDE[4] | 34.0 | 25.9 | 1.3 | 5.5 | 32.6 | 0.5 |

.. Not available

*Note:* The figures exclude local government revenues for Antigua and Barbuda, Argentina (but include provincial revenues), the Bahamas, Barbados, Cuba (except for 2002-2012), the Dominican Republic, Saint Lucia, Trinidad and Tobago and Venezuela as the data are not available. Local government revenue data have been available since 1991 for Nicaragua, since 1994 for Bolivia, since 1995 for Guatemala, since 1998 for Jamaica, since 1999 for Panama, since 2000 for Peru, since 2002 for El Salvador and Guyana, since 2006 for Paraguay and since 1990 for all other countries.

1. The data include the following estimations: Antigua and Barbuda (social security contributions for 2019 and 2020), Bahamas (social security contributions for 2019 and 2020), Nicaragua (local tax revenues for 2020) and Uruguay (local tax revenues for 2020). See the corresponding country tables for more information.
2. Data for 2018 and subsequent years are not available.
3. Represents the group of 26 Latin American and Caribbean countries included in this publication and excludes Venezuela due to data availability issues. Chile, Colombia, Costa Rica and Mexico are also part of the OECD (38) group.
4. Represents the unweighted average for OECD member countries. Data for 2019 are used as data for 2020 were not available at the time of publication.

.. Non disponible

*Nota:* Las cifras excluyen los ingresos subnacionales para Antigua y Barbuda, Argentina (pero se incluyen los ingresos de las provincias), Las Bahamas, Barbados, Cuba (excepto 2002-2012), República Dominicana, Santa Lucía, Trinidad y Tobago y Venezuela, dado que los datos no están disponibles. Los datos de ingresos subnacionales están disponibles desde 1991 para Nicaragua, desde 1994 para Bolivia, desde 1995 para Guatemala, desde 1998 para Jamaica, desde 1999 para Panamá, desde 2000 para Perú, desde 2002 para El Salvador y Guyana, desde 2006 para Paraguay y desde 1990 para todos los demás países.

1. Los datos incluyen las siguientes estimaciones: Antigua y Barbuda (contribuciones a la seguridad social para 2019 y 2020), Bahamas (contribuciones a la seguridad social para 2019 y 2020), Nicaragua (ingresos tributarios locales para 2020) y Uruguay (ingresos tributarios locales para 2020). Consulte las tablas de países correspondientes para obtener más información.
2. Los datos de 2018 y años posteriores no están disponibles.
3. Representa al grupo de 26 países de América Latina y el Caribe incluidos en esta publicación y excluye a Venezuela debido a problemas de disponibilidad de datos. Chile, Colombia, Costa Rica y México también forman parte del grupo OCDE (38).
4. Representa el promedio no ponderado de los países miembros de la OCDE. Se utilizan los datos de 2019 porque los datos de 2020 no estaban disponibles en el momento de la publicación.

StatLink https://doi.org/10.1787/888934309093

## Table 4.5. **Taxes on income and profits (1000) as % of GDP and as % of total tax revenue**
## Cuadro 4.5. **Impuestos sobre la renta y las utilidades (1000) en % del PIB y del total de ingresos tributarios**

| | % of GDP / % del PIB | | | | | % of total tax revenue / % del total de ingresos tributarios | | | | |
|---|---|---|---|---|---|---|---|---|---|---|
| | 1990 | 2000 | 2010 | 2019 | 2020 | 1990 | 2000 | 2010 | 2019 | 2020 |
| Antigua and Barbuda / Antigua y Barbuda | .. | 1.7 | 3.0 | 1.7 | 2.4 | .. | 14.0 | 14.0 | 9.6 | 11.9 |
| Argentina | 0.7 | 3.6 | 4.7 | 5.1 | 5.4 | 5.3 | 18.5 | 16.2 | 17.9 | 18.2 |
| Bahamas | 0.0 | 0.0 | 0.0 | 0.0 | 0.0 | 0.0 | 0.0 | 0.0 | 0.0 | 0.0 |
| Barbados | 6.1 | 9.8 | 8.4 | 8.1 | 11.5 | 24.3 | 31.7 | 28.0 | 23.9 | 32.7 |
| Belize / Belice | 4.5 | 4.6 | 9.0 | 7.3 | 6.4 | 20.9 | 23.9 | 33.6 | 25.3 | 24.4 |
| Bolivia | 0.4 | 2.3 | 4.6 | 4.0 | 2.9 | 6.7 | 13.2 | 20.0 | 16.3 | 13.1 |
| Brazil / Brasil | 5.1 | 5.7 | 6.7 | 7.3 | 7.1 | 18.3 | 19.5 | 20.5 | 22.4 | 22.3 |
| Chile | 3.9 | 4.4 | 7.5 | 7.3 | 6.3 | 23.2 | 23.3 | 38.1 | 34.8 | 32.4 |
| Colombia | 3.4 | 3.6 | 4.8 | 6.4 | 6.2 | 29.9 | 23.2 | 26.6 | 32.3 | 32.9 |
| Costa Rica | 2.3 | 2.8 | 3.8 | 4.9 | 4.6 | 10.0 | 13.2 | 17.1 | 20.9 | 20.1 |
| Cuba | 0.1 | 6.0 | 5.6 | 11.9 | 10.6 | 0.2 | 16.1 | 15.0 | 28.2 | 28.3 |
| Dominican Republic / República Dominicana | 2.1 | 2.7 | 2.7 | 4.3 | 4.2 | 25.7 | 22.2 | 21.8 | 31.4 | 33.7 |
| Ecuador | 0.9 | 1.5 | 4.2 | 4.3 | 4.6 | 12.9 | 12.6 | 25.0 | 21.6 | 23.8 |
| El Salvador | 2.0 | 3.6 | 5.4 | 7.3 | 7.9 | 17.6 | 25.7 | 28.9 | 34.8 | 36.2 |
| Guatemala | 1.5 | 2.3 | 2.3 | 2.9 | 2.8 | 19.7 | 19.9 | 18.6 | 22.2 | 22.5 |
| Guyana | 5.1 | 5.9 | 5.7 | 8.8 | 9.3 | 33.5 | 37.8 | 35.4 | 37.8 | 43.4 |
| Honduras | 2.5 | 2.7 | 4.4 | 5.6 | 4.4 | 20.3 | 15.9 | 24.3 | 26.2 | 22.8 |
| Jamaica | 9.5 | 9.0 | 9.2 | 7.4 | 7.9 | 47.0 | 40.4 | 36.9 | 25.7 | 28.6 |
| Mexico / México | 4.1 | 4.1 | 5.1 | 6.9 | 7.6 | 34.0 | 36.0 | 39.8 | 42.4 | 42.7 |
| Nicaragua | .. | 1.8 | 4.5 | 7.9 | 7.5 | .. | 12.3 | 23.1 | 30.8 | 29.5 |
| Panama / Panamá | 3.8 | 3.9 | 4.5 | 3.7 | 3.6 | 22.9 | 25.0 | 27.4 | 26.1 | 26.0 |
| Paraguay | 1.0 | 1.5 | 1.6 | 2.5 | 2.5 | 12.1 | 13.1 | 13.4 | 18.2 | 18.5 |
| Peru / Perú | 0.7 | 2.9 | 6.5 | 6.1 | 5.6 | 5.8 | 19.0 | 36.5 | 36.5 | 36.7 |
| Saint Lucia / Santa Lucía | .. | 5.6 | 5.5 | 4.5 | 4.8 | .. | 28.6 | 27.1 | 21.9 | 23.5 |
| Trinidad and Tobago / Trinidad y Tobago | 12.3 | 12.4 | 19.6 | 14.2 | 10.3 | 52.7 | 56.8 | 68.5 | 58.3 | 49.1 |
| Uruguay | 0.9 | 2.9 | 4.9 | 6.9 | 7.1 | 4.7 | 13.6 | 20.0 | 26.1 | 26.6 |
| Venezuela[1] | 17.7 | 5.8 | 3.6 | .. | .. | 83.7 | 43.2 | 30.7 | .. | .. |
| *Unweighted average / Promedio no ponderado* | | | | | | | | | | |
| LAC / ALC[2] | 3.2 | 4.1 | 5.5 | 6.0 | 5.9 | 19.5 | 22.1 | 26.0 | 26.6 | 26.9 |
| OECD / OCDE[3] | 11.5 | 11.5 | 10.2 | 11.3 | .. | 36.2 | 33.9 | 32.2 | 34.0 | .. |

.. Not available

*Note:* The figures exclude local government revenues for Antigua and Barbuda, Argentina (but include provincial revenues), the Bahamas, Barbados, Cuba (except for 2002-2012), the Dominican Republic, Saint Lucia, Trinidad and Tobago and Venezuela as the data are not available. Local government revenue data have been available since 1991 for Nicaragua, since 1994 for Bolivia, since 1995 for Guatemala, since 1998 for Jamaica, since 1999 for Panama, since 2000 for Peru, since 2002 for El Salvador and Guyana, since 2006 for Paraguay and since 1990 for all other countries.

1. Some tax revenue data between 2014 and 2017 are not available. In those years data as % of total tax revenue cannot be calculated. Data for 2018 and subsequent years are not available.
2. Represents the group of 26 Latin American and Caribbean countries included in this publication and excludes Venezuela due to data availability issues. Chile, Colombia, Costa Rica and Mexico are also part of the OECD (38) group.
3. Represents the unweighted average for OECD member countries.

.. Non disponible

*Nota:* Las cifras excluyen los ingresos subnacionales para Antigua y Barbuda, Argentina (pero se incluyen los ingresos de las provincias), Las Bahamas, Barbados, Cuba (excepto 2002-2012), República Dominicana, Santa Lucía, Trinidad y Tobago y Venezuela, dado que los datos no están disponibles. Los datos de ingresos subnacionales están disponibles desde 1991 para Nicaragua, desde 1994 para Bolivia, desde 1995 para Guatemala, desde 1998 para Jamaica, desde 1999 para Panamá, desde 2000 para Perú, desde 2002 para El Salvador y Guyana, desde 2006 para Paraguay y desde 1990 para todos los demás países.

1. Algunos datos de ingresos tributarios entre 2014 y 2017 no están disponibles. Para esos años, no se pueden calcular los ingresos como porcentaje de los ingresos tributarios totales. Los datos de 2018 y años posteriores no están disponibles.
2. Representa al grupo de 26 países de América Latina y el Caribe incluidos en esta publicación y excluye a Venezuela debido a problemas de disponibilidad de datos. Chile, Colombia, Costa Rica y México también forman parte del grupo OCDE (38).
3. Representa el promedio no ponderado para los países miembros de la OCDE.

StatLink https://doi.org/10.1787/888934309112

## Table 4.6. **Social security contributions (2000) as % of GDP and as % of total tax revenue**

## Cuadro 4.6. **Contribuciones a la seguridad social (2000) en % del PIB y del total de ingresos tributarios**

| | % of GDP / % del PIB | | | | | % of total tax revenue / % del total de ingresos tributarios | | | | |
|---|---|---|---|---|---|---|---|---|---|---|
| | 1990 | 2000 | 2010 | 2019 | 2020 | 1990 | 2000 | 2010 | 2019 | 2020 |
| Antigua and Barbuda / Antigua y Barbuda[1] | .. | .. | 2.7 | 3.3 | 3.3 | .. | .. | 12.6 | 18.3 | 16.7 |
| Argentina | 3.4 | 3.0 | 6.2 | 5.6 | 5.6 | 25.3 | 15.8 | 21.2 | 19.9 | 19.2 |
| Bahamas[1] | 1.3 | 1.5 | 1.7 | 2.2 | 2.2 | 13.2 | 11.9 | 13.1 | 11.6 | 11.7 |
| Barbados | 3.3 | 4.8 | 6.2 | 6.6 | 7.0 | 13.1 | 15.6 | 20.6 | 19.5 | 19.9 |
| Belize / Belice | 1.2 | 1.1 | 2.2 | 2.5 | 3.2 | 5.7 | 5.8 | 8.2 | 8.7 | 12.4 |
| Bolivia | 0.0 | 1.3 | 3.8 | 6.2 | 6.7 | 0.0 | 7.3 | 16.7 | 25.1 | 29.9 |
| Brazil / Brasil | 6.8 | 7.0 | 8.1 | 8.4 | 8.2 | 24.3 | 23.7 | 25.1 | 25.9 | 26.0 |
| Chile | 1.5 | 1.4 | 1.3 | 1.5 | 1.5 | 9.0 | 7.3 | 6.8 | 7.3 | 8.0 |
| Colombia | 0.9 | 2.6 | 2.1 | 1.9 | 1.9 | 7.9 | 16.3 | 11.7 | 9.5 | 9.9 |
| Costa Rica | 6.5 | 6.4 | 7.3 | 8.1 | 8.3 | 28.9 | 30.4 | 33.1 | 34.2 | 36.1 |
| Cuba | 3.5 | 3.9 | 4.6 | 5.5 | 6.0 | 11.0 | 10.4 | 12.4 | 13.2 | 16.0 |
| Dominican Republic / República Dominicana | 0.1 | 0.1 | 0.1 | 0.1 | 0.1 | 0.8 | 1.0 | 0.8 | 0.4 | 0.5 |
| Ecuador | 1.6 | 1.2 | 3.7 | 5.4 | 5.5 | 22.5 | 10.7 | 21.7 | 27.1 | 28.8 |
| El Salvador | 2.2 | 2.8 | 2.5 | 2.7 | 2.8 | 19.2 | 19.5 | 13.6 | 12.8 | 13.0 |
| Guatemala | 1.3 | 1.8 | 1.9 | 2.2 | 2.1 | 17.0 | 15.5 | 15.2 | 16.8 | 17.1 |
| Guyana | 0.6 | 1.8 | 1.4 | 2.2 | 2.2 | 3.7 | 11.4 | 9.0 | 9.5 | 10.1 |
| Honduras | 1.0 | 1.6 | 2.9 | 3.4 | 4.0 | 8.5 | 9.4 | 15.9 | 16.0 | 20.6 |
| Jamaica | .. | .. | 0.7 | 1.2 | 1.3 | .. | .. | 2.9 | 4.1 | 4.6 |
| Mexico / México | 2.0 | 2.1 | 2.1 | 2.3 | 2.5 | 16.8 | 18.0 | 16.2 | 13.8 | 13.9 |
| Nicaragua | .. | 2.6 | 4.3 | 6.6 | 6.7 | .. | 18.0 | 22.4 | 25.7 | 26.4 |
| Panama / Panamá | 5.7 | 5.9 | 5.6 | 5.8 | 6.1 | 34.2 | 38.2 | 34.0 | 41.5 | 44.6 |
| Paraguay | 0.4 | 3.0 | 2.8 | 3.7 | 3.7 | 4.8 | 25.6 | 22.7 | 26.4 | 27.6 |
| Peru / Perú | 0.9 | 1.8 | 1.9 | 2.0 | 2.0 | 7.8 | 11.9 | 10.6 | 12.1 | 13.4 |
| Saint Lucia / Santa Lucía | .. | 2.0 | 2.3 | 2.2 | 2.6 | .. | 10.0 | 11.1 | 10.7 | 12.7 |
| Trinidad and Tobago / Trinidad y Tobago | 0.9 | 1.4 | 1.9 | 3.0 | 3.2 | 3.7 | 6.4 | 6.7 | 12.3 | 15.0 |
| Uruguay[2] | 5.5 | 5.9 | 5.7 | 7.0 | 6.7 | 29.9 | 27.5 | 23.4 | 26.4 | 25.0 |
| Venezuela[3] | 1.0 | 0.7 | 1.0 | .. | .. | 4.9 | 5.4 | 8.1 | .. | .. |
| *Unweighted average / Promedio no ponderado* | | | | | | | | | | |
| LAC / ALC[4] | 2.3 | 2.8 | 3.3 | 3.9 | 4.0 | 14.0 | 15.3 | 15.7 | 17.3 | 18.4 |
| OECD / OCDE[5] | 7.1 | 8.4 | 8.6 | 8.9 | .. | 21.8 | 24.9 | 26.6 | 25.9 | .. |

.. Not available

*Note:* The figures exclude local government revenues for Antigua and Barbuda, Argentina (but include provincial revenues), the Bahamas, Barbados, Cuba (except for 2002-2012), the Dominican Republic, Saint Lucia, Trinidad and Tobago and Venezuela as the data are not available. Local government revenue data have been available since 1991 for Nicaragua, since 1994 for Bolivia, since 1995 for Guatemala, since 1998 for Jamaica, since 1999 for Panama, since 2000 for Peru, since 2002 for El Salvador and Guyana, since 2006 for Paraguay and since 1990 for all other countries.

1. Revenues from social security contributions are estimated in the following countries: Antigua and Barbuda (2019 and 2020) and Bahamas (2019 and 2020).
2. Figures for 1990-98 are estimated by the Direction General of Taxes as the methodology they use to calculate social security contributions was not employed until 1999.
3. Some tax revenue data between 2014 and 2017 are not available. In those years data as % of total tax revenue cannot be calculated. Data for 2018 and subsequent years are not available.
4. Represents the group of 26 Latin American and Caribbean countries included in this publication and excludes Venezuela due to data availability issues. Chile, Colombia, Costa Rica and Mexico are also part of the OECD (38) group.
5. Represents the unweighted average for OECD member countries.

.. Non disponible

*Nota:* Las cifras excluyen los ingresos subnacionales para Antigua y Barbuda, Argentina (pero se incluyen los ingresos de las provincias), Las Bahamas, Barbados, Cuba (excepto 2002-2012), República Dominicana, Santa Lucía, Trinidad y Tobago y Venezuela, dado que los datos no están disponibles. Los datos de ingresos subnacionales están disponibles desde 1991 para Nicaragua, desde 1994 para Bolivia, desde 1995 para Guatemala, desde 1998 para Jamaica, desde 1999 para Panamá, desde 2000 para Perú, desde 2002 para El Salvador y Guyana, desde 2006 para Paraguay y desde 1990 para todos los demás países.

1. Los ingresos por las cotizaciones a la seguridad social se estiman en los siguientes países: Antigua y Barbuda (2019 y 2020) y Bahamas (2019 y 2020).

## Table 4.6. **Social security contributions (2000) as % of GDP and as % of total tax revenue** *(cont.)*
## Cuadro 4.6. **Contribuciones a la seguridad social (2000) en % del PIB y del total de ingresos tributarios** *(cont.)*

2. Las cifras de 1990-98 son estimaciones de la Dirección General de Impuestos dado que el empleo de la metodología actual utilizada para calcular las contribuciones a la seguridad social tuvo lugar en 1999.
3. Algunos datos de ingresos tributarios entre 2014 y 2017 no están disponibles. Para esos años, no se pueden calcular los ingresos como porcentaje de los ingresos tributarios totales. Los datos de 2018 y años posteriores no están disponibles.
4. Representa al grupo de 26 países de América Latina y el Caribe incluidos en esta publicación y excluye a Venezuela debido a problemas de disponibilidad de datos. Chile, Colombia, Costa Rica y México también forman parte del grupo OCDE (38).
5. Representa el promedio no ponderado para los países miembros de la OCDE.

StatLink https://doi.org/10.1787/888934309131

## Table 4.7. **Taxes on payroll (3000) as % of GDP and as % of total tax revenue**
## Cuadro 4.7. **Impuestos sobre la nómina (3000) en % del PIB y del total ingresos tributarios**

| | % of GDP / % del PIB | | | | | % of total tax revenue / % del total de ingresos tributarios | | | | |
|---|---|---|---|---|---|---|---|---|---|---|
| | 1990 | 2000 | 2010 | 2019 | 2020 | 1990 | 2000 | 2010 | 2019 | 2020 |
| Antigua and Barbuda / Antigua y Barbuda | .. | 0.0 | 0.0 | 0.0 | 0.0 | .. | 0.0 | 0.0 | 0.0 | 0.0 |
| Argentina | 0.0 | 0.0 | 0.0 | 0.0 | 0.0 | 0.0 | 0.0 | 0.0 | 0.0 | 0.0 |
| Bahamas | 0.0 | 0.0 | 0.0 | 0.0 | 0.0 | 0.0 | 0.0 | 0.0 | 0.0 | 0.0 |
| Barbados | 0.0 | 0.0 | 0.0 | 0.0 | 0.0 | 0.0 | 0.0 | 0.0 | 0.0 | 0.0 |
| Belize / Belice | 0.0 | 0.0 | 0.0 | 0.0 | 0.0 | 0.0 | 0.0 | 0.0 | 0.0 | 0.0 |
| Bolivia | 0.0 | 0.0 | 0.0 | 0.0 | 0.0 | 0.0 | 0.0 | 0.0 | 0.0 | 0.0 |
| Brazil / Brasil | 0.4 | 0.5 | 0.5 | 0.6 | 0.5 | 1.6 | 1.5 | 1.7 | 1.8 | 1.7 |
| Chile | 0.0 | 0.0 | 0.0 | 0.0 | 0.0 | 0.0 | 0.0 | 0.0 | 0.0 | 0.0 |
| Colombia | 0.0 | 0.7 | 0.7 | 0.3 | 0.4 | 0.0 | 4.2 | 4.1 | 1.7 | 2.0 |
| Costa Rica | 1.4 | 1.3 | 1.3 | 1.4 | 1.5 | 6.4 | 6.3 | 5.9 | 5.9 | 6.5 |
| Cuba | 0.0 | 3.2 | 6.9 | 1.4 | 1.5 | 0.0 | 8.5 | 18.4 | 3.3 | 4.0 |
| Dominican Republic / República Dominicana | 0.0 | 0.0 | 0.1 | 0.1 | 0.1 | 0.0 | 0.0 | 0.6 | 0.6 | 0.6 |
| Ecuador | 0.0 | 0.0 | 0.0 | 0.0 | 0.0 | 0.0 | 0.0 | 0.0 | 0.0 | 0.0 |
| El Salvador | 0.0 | 0.0 | 0.1 | 0.1 | 0.1 | 0.0 | 0.0 | 0.6 | 0.7 | 0.7 |
| Guatemala | 0.0 | 0.0 | 0.1 | 0.2 | 0.1 | 0.0 | 0.0 | 1.1 | 1.2 | 1.2 |
| Guyana | 0.0 | 0.0 | 0.0 | 0.0 | 0.0 | 0.0 | 0.0 | 0.0 | 0.0 | 0.0 |
| Honduras | 0.0 | 0.0 | 0.2 | 0.2 | 0.2 | 0.0 | 0.0 | 0.9 | 0.8 | 0.8 |
| Jamaica | 0.8 | 1.0 | 1.1 | 1.5 | 1.6 | 3.9 | 4.4 | 4.5 | 5.2 | 5.7 |
| Mexico / México | 0.2 | 0.2 | 0.3 | 0.4 | 0.5 | 1.8 | 1.5 | 2.2 | 2.5 | 2.5 |
| Nicaragua | .. | 0.0 | 0.0 | 0.0 | 0.0 | .. | 0.0 | 0.0 | 0.0 | 0.0 |
| Panama / Panamá | 0.0 | 0.3 | 0.2 | 0.2 | 0.2 | 0.0 | 1.9 | 1.2 | 1.5 | 1.4 |
| Paraguay | 0.0 | 0.0 | 0.0 | 0.0 | 0.0 | 0.0 | 0.0 | 0.0 | 0.0 | 0.0 |
| Peru / Perú | 0.0 | 0.7 | 0.0 | 0.0 | 0.0 | 0.0 | 4.4 | 0.1 | 0.1 | 0.1 |
| Saint Lucia / Santa Lucía | .. | 0.0 | 0.0 | 0.0 | 0.0 | .. | 0.0 | 0.0 | 0.0 | 0.0 |
| Trinidad and Tobago / Trinidad y Tobago | 0.0 | 0.0 | 0.0 | 0.0 | 0.0 | 0.0 | 0.0 | 0.0 | 0.0 | 0.0 |
| Uruguay | 0.0 | 0.0 | 0.0 | 0.0 | 0.0 | 0.0 | 0.0 | 0.0 | 0.0 | 0.0 |
| Venezuela[1] | 0.0 | 0.0 | 0.0 | .. | .. | 0.0 | 0.0 | 0.0 | .. | .. |
| *Unweighted average / Promedio no ponderado* | | | | | | | | | | |
| LAC / ALC[2] | 0.1 | 0.3 | 0.4 | 0.2 | 0.3 | 0.6 | 1.3 | 1.6 | 1.0 | 1.0 |
| OECD / OCDE[3] | 0.4 | 0.4 | 0.4 | 0.5 | .. | 1.2 | 1.2 | 1.2 | 1.3 | .. |

.. Not available

*Note:* The figures exclude local government revenues for Antigua and Barbuda, Argentina (but include provincial revenues), the Bahamas, Barbados, Cuba (except for 2002-2012), the Dominican Republic, Saint Lucia, Trinidad and Tobago and Venezuela as the data are not available. Local government revenue data have been available since 1991 for Nicaragua, since 1994 for Bolivia, since 1995 for Guatemala, since 1998 for Jamaica, since 1999 for Panama, since 2000 for Peru, since 2002 for El Salvador and Guyana, since 2006 for Paraguay and since 1990 for all other countries.

1. Some tax revenue data between 2014 and 2017 are not available. In those years data as % of total tax revenue cannot be calculated. Data for 2018 and subsequent years are not available.
2. Represents the group of 26 Latin American and Caribbean countries included in this publication and excludes Venezuela due to data availability issues. Chile, Colombia, Costa Rica and Mexico are also part of the OECD (38) group.
3. Represents the unweighted average for OECD member countries.

.. Non disponible

*Nota:* Las cifras excluyen los ingresos subnacionales para Antigua y Barbuda, Argentina (pero se incluyen los ingresos de las provincias), Las Bahamas, Barbados, Cuba (excepto 2002-2012), República Dominicana, Santa Lucía, Trinidad y Tobago y Venezuela, dado que los datos no están disponibles. Los datos de ingresos subnacionales están disponibles desde 1991 para Nicaragua, desde 1994 para Bolivia, desde 1995 para Guatemala, desde 1998 para Jamaica, desde 1999 para Panamá, desde 2000 para Perú, desde 2002 para El Salvador y Guyana, desde 2006 para Paraguay y desde 1990 para todos los demás países.

1. Algunos datos de ingresos tributarios entre 2014 y 2017 no están disponibles. Para esos años, no se pueden calcular los ingresos como porcentaje de los ingresos tributarios totales. Los datos de 2018 y años posteriores no están disponibles.
2. Representa al grupo de 26 países de América Latina y el Caribe incluidos en esta publicación y excluye a Venezuela debido a problemas de disponibilidad de datos. Chile, Colombia, Costa Rica y México también forman parte del grupo OCDE (38).
3. Representa el promedio no ponderado para los países miembros de la OCDE.

StatLink https://doi.org/10.1787/888934309150

## Table 4.8. **Taxes on property (4000) as % of GDP and as % of total tax revenue**
## Cuadro 4.8. **Impuestos sobre la propiedad (4000) en % del PIB y del total de ingresos tributarios**

| | % of GDP / % del PIB | | | | | % of total tax revenue / % del total de ingresos tributarios | | | | |
|---|---|---|---|---|---|---|---|---|---|---|
| | 1990 | 2000 | 2010 | 2019 | 2020 | 1990 | 2000 | 2010 | 2019 | 2020 |
| Antigua and Barbuda / Antigua y Barbuda | .. | 0.6 | 1.6 | 1.6 | 1.5 | .. | 4.9 | 7.5 | 8.7 | 7.6 |
| Argentina | 1.5 | 1.2 | 2.6 | 2.6 | 3.2 | 11.4 | 6.3 | 9.0 | 9.1 | 10.9 |
| Bahamas | 1.1 | 2.6 | 2.7 | 2.6 | 1.5 | 11.2 | 21.6 | 21.1 | 13.9 | 8.2 |
| Barbados | 3.6 | 1.8 | 1.4 | 2.2 | 2.2 | 14.4 | 5.7 | 4.8 | 6.6 | 6.3 |
| Belize / Belice | 4.2 | 0.8 | 0.8 | 1.0 | 0.9 | 19.2 | 4.2 | 3.1 | 3.4 | 3.4 |
| Bolivia | 0.0 | 0.0 | 0.3 | 0.2 | 0.2 | 0.1 | 0.0 | 1.2 | 0.7 | 0.7 |
| Brazil / Brasil | 1.6 | 2.0 | 1.4 | 1.5 | 1.2 | 5.9 | 6.7 | 4.2 | 4.7 | 3.9 |
| Chile | 1.0 | 1.3 | 0.8 | 1.1 | 1.0 | 6.2 | 7.0 | 4.1 | 5.5 | 5.2 |
| Colombia | 0.2 | 1.0 | 1.6 | 1.8 | 1.8 | 2.2 | 6.6 | 8.7 | 9.1 | 9.7 |
| Costa Rica | 0.3 | 0.2 | 0.3 | 0.4 | 0.5 | 1.3 | 0.9 | 1.5 | 1.9 | 2.0 |
| Cuba | 0.0 | 0.0 | 0.0 | 0.0 | 0.0 | 0.0 | 0.0 | 0.0 | 0.0 | 0.0 |
| Dominican Republic / República Dominicana | 0.1 | 0.2 | 0.7 | 0.6 | 0.6 | 1.2 | 1.4 | 5.4 | 4.8 | 4.5 |
| Ecuador | 0.1 | 0.1 | 0.2 | 0.3 | 0.3 | 1.5 | 0.8 | 1.4 | 1.6 | 1.8 |
| El Salvador | 0.5 | 0.1 | 0.1 | 0.2 | 0.1 | 4.8 | 0.7 | 0.6 | 0.8 | 0.5 |
| Guatemala | 0.4 | 0.2 | 0.4 | 0.2 | 0.2 | 5.8 | 2.1 | 2.9 | 1.5 | 1.5 |
| Guyana | 0.2 | 0.3 | 0.3 | 0.5 | 0.4 | 1.0 | 1.6 | 1.8 | 2.0 | 1.8 |
| Honduras | 0.1 | 0.3 | 0.3 | 0.6 | 0.5 | 0.7 | 1.5 | 1.8 | 2.6 | 2.6 |
| Jamaica | 2.5 | 1.1 | 0.9 | 0.9 | 0.8 | 12.5 | 4.9 | 3.5 | 3.2 | 2.9 |
| Mexico / México | 0.2 | 0.2 | 0.3 | 0.3 | 0.3 | 1.9 | 1.8 | 2.3 | 2.0 | 1.6 |
| Nicaragua | .. | 0.0 | 0.2 | 0.3 | 0.2 | .. | 0.1 | 1.2 | 1.1 | 0.9 |
| Panama / Panamá | 0.6 | 0.3 | 0.5 | 0.3 | 0.2 | 3.4 | 2.2 | 2.9 | 1.8 | 1.7 |
| Paraguay | 0.2 | 0.2 | 0.2 | 0.2 | 0.2 | 2.8 | 2.0 | 1.8 | 1.3 | 1.2 |
| Peru / Perú | 1.6 | 0.2 | 0.5 | 0.4 | 0.3 | 13.6 | 1.2 | 3.0 | 2.4 | 2.2 |
| Saint Lucia / Santa Lucía | .. | 0.4 | 0.5 | 0.4 | 0.4 | .. | 2.2 | 2.3 | 2.1 | 2.1 |
| Trinidad and Tobago / Trinidad y Tobago | 0.4 | 0.3 | 0.1 | 0.3 | 0.2 | 1.8 | 1.6 | 0.5 | 1.1 | 0.8 |
| Uruguay | 1.6 | 1.8 | 2.2 | 2.0 | 2.1 | 8.9 | 8.6 | 8.9 | 7.7 | 7.7 |
| Venezuela[1] | 0.1 | 0.5 | 0.0 | .. | .. | 0.3 | 3.7 | 0.2 | .. | .. |
| *Unweighted average / Promedio no ponderado* | | | | | | | | | | |
| LAC / ALC[2] | 1.0 | 0.7 | 0.8 | 0.9 | 0.8 | 5.7 | 3.7 | 4.0 | 3.8 | 3.5 |
| OECD / OCDE[3] | 1.7 | 1.7 | 1.6 | 1.8 | .. | 5.5 | 5.3 | 5.4 | 5.5 | .. |

.. Not available

*Note:* The figures exclude local government revenues for Antigua and Barbuda, Argentina (but include provincial revenues), the Bahamas, Barbados, Cuba (except for 2002-2012), the Dominican Republic, Saint Lucia, Trinidad and Tobago and Venezuela as the data are not available. Local government revenue data have been available since 1991 for Nicaragua, since 1994 for Bolivia, since 1995 for Guatemala, since 1998 for Jamaica, since 1999 for Panama, since 2000 for Peru, since 2002 for El Salvador and Guyana, since 2006 for Paraguay and since 1990 for all other countries.

1. Some tax revenue data between 2014 and 2017 are not available. In those years data as % of total tax revenue cannot be calculated. Data for 2018 and subsequent years are not available.
2. Represents the group of 26 Latin American and Caribbean countries included in this publication and excludes Venezuela due to data availability issues. Chile, Colombia, Costa Rica and Mexico are also part of the OECD (38) group.
3. Represents the unweighted average for OECD member countries.

.. Non disponible

*Nota:* Las cifras excluyen los ingresos subnacionales para Antigua y Barbuda, Argentina (pero se incluyen los ingresos de las provincias), Las Bahamas, Barbados, Cuba (excepto 2002-2012), República Dominicana, Santa Lucía, Trinidad y Tobago y Venezuela, dado que los datos no están disponibles. Los datos de ingresos subnacionales están disponibles desde 1991 para Nicaragua, desde 1994 para Bolivia, desde 1995 para Guatemala, desde 1998 para Jamaica, desde 1999 para Panamá, desde 2000 para Perú, desde 2002 para El Salvador y Guyana, desde 2006 para Paraguay y desde 1990 para todos los demás países.

1. Algunos datos de ingresos tributarios entre 2014 y 2017 no están disponibles. Para esos años, no se pueden calcular los ingresos como porcentaje de los ingresos tributarios totales. Los datos de 2018 y años posteriores no están disponibles.
2. Representa al grupo de 26 países de América Latina y el Caribe incluidos en esta publicación y excluye a Venezuela debido a problemas de disponibilidad de datos. Chile, Colombia, Costa Rica y México también forman parte del grupo OCDE (38).
3. Representa el promedio no ponderado para los países miembros de la OCDE.

StatLink https://doi.org/10.1787/888934309169

## Table 4.9. **Taxes on goods and services (5000) as % of GDP and as % of total tax revenue**

## Cuadro 4.9. **Impuestos sobre bienes y servicios (5000) en % del PIB y del total de ingresos tributarios**

| | % of GDP / % del PIB | | | | | % of total tax revenue / % del total de ingresos tributarios | | | | |
|---|---|---|---|---|---|---|---|---|---|---|
| | 1990 | 2000 | 2010 | 2019 | 2020 | 1990 | 2000 | 2010 | 2019 | 2020 |
| Antigua and Barbuda / Antigua y Barbuda | .. | 9.7 | 14.0 | 11.4 | 12.6 | .. | 81.1 | 65.9 | 63.4 | 63.8 |
| Argentina | 7.3 | 10.9 | 15.2 | 14.7 | 15.0 | 55.2 | 56.5 | 52.4 | 52.2 | 51.0 |
| Bahamas | 7.4 | 7.9 | 7.8 | 14.0 | 14.9 | 76.4 | 64.3 | 61.1 | 74.6 | 80.1 |
| Barbados | 12.2 | 14.5 | 14.0 | 17.0 | 14.4 | 48.2 | 47.0 | 46.6 | 50.0 | 41.0 |
| Belize / Belice | 11.7 | 12.7 | 14.8 | 18.2 | 15.6 | 54.1 | 66.1 | 55.2 | 62.7 | 59.8 |
| Bolivia | 5.9 | 12.8 | 12.9 | 12.1 | 10.2 | 90.2 | 72.7 | 56.4 | 49.0 | 45.8 |
| Brazil / Brasil | 13.5 | 14.1 | 15.0 | 14.2 | 13.9 | 48.7 | 48.0 | 46.3 | 43.6 | 44.1 |
| Chile | 10.6 | 12.0 | 10.0 | 11.1 | 10.6 | 62.9 | 63.8 | 51.2 | 53.0 | 54.9 |
| Colombia | 6.1 | 7.3 | 8.2 | 8.5 | 7.8 | 53.8 | 46.3 | 45.1 | 43.0 | 41.4 |
| Costa Rica | 10.2 | 9.9 | 8.9 | 8.2 | 7.6 | 45.5 | 46.7 | 40.3 | 34.8 | 33.3 |
| Cuba | 27.7 | 22.0 | 19.1 | 20.3 | 17.4 | 86.9 | 59.2 | 51.3 | 48.3 | 46.4 |
| Dominican Republic / República Dominicana | 5.8 | 9.1 | 8.8 | 8.5 | 7.6 | 69.9 | 74.4 | 71.5 | 62.8 | 60.8 |
| Ecuador | 4.5 | 8.8 | 8.7 | 10.0 | 8.7 | 63.0 | 75.7 | 51.9 | 49.7 | 45.5 |
| El Salvador | 5.4 | 7.7 | 10.2 | 10.3 | 10.5 | 47.7 | 54.1 | 54.5 | 49.3 | 47.9 |
| Guatemala | 4.4 | 7.3 | 7.0 | 6.8 | 6.3 | 57.5 | 62.4 | 56.0 | 52.0 | 51.0 |
| Guyana | 6.4 | 7.6 | 8.5 | 11.6 | 9.4 | 42.0 | 48.6 | 53.0 | 49.9 | 43.8 |
| Honduras | 8.2 | 11.7 | 9.7 | 10.9 | 9.5 | 66.2 | 68.0 | 53.1 | 50.6 | 49.4 |
| Jamaica | 7.4 | 11.1 | 13.0 | 17.5 | 16.0 | 36.4 | 50.1 | 52.1 | 61.5 | 57.9 |
| Mexico / México | 5.3 | 4.8 | 4.9 | 6.2 | 6.7 | 44.0 | 41.7 | 38.0 | 37.6 | 37.2 |
| Nicaragua | .. | 8.6 | 10.1 | 10.7 | 10.7 | .. | 60.0 | 52.4 | 41.6 | 42.3 |
| Panama / Panamá | 6.1 | 4.9 | 5.5 | 4.1 | 3.6 | 36.8 | 31.3 | 33.7 | 28.8 | 26.0 |
| Paraguay | 6.1 | 6.7 | 7.3 | 7.4 | 7.0 | 72.1 | 58.0 | 60.5 | 53.4 | 52.2 |
| Peru / Perú | 8.5 | 9.2 | 8.6 | 7.8 | 7.1 | 71.4 | 60.8 | 48.6 | 47.2 | 46.8 |
| Saint Lucia / Santa Lucía | .. | 11.6 | 12.1 | 13.5 | 12.7 | .. | 59.1 | 59.5 | 65.3 | 61.7 |
| Trinidad and Tobago / Trinidad y Tobago | 9.7 | 7.7 | 7.0 | 6.9 | 7.4 | 41.7 | 35.2 | 24.3 | 28.4 | 35.1 |
| Uruguay | 10.4 | 10.7 | 11.4 | 10.4 | 10.7 | 56.6 | 50.1 | 47.1 | 39.1 | 40.0 |
| Venezuela[1] | 2.4 | 6.4 | 7.2 | .. | .. | 11.1 | 47.7 | 61.1 | .. | .. |
| *Unweighted average / Promedio no ponderado* | | | | | | | | | | |
| LAC / ALC[2] | 8.7 | 10.1 | 10.5 | 11.2 | 10.5 | 57.7 | 57.0 | 51.1 | 49.7 | 48.4 |
| OECD / OCDE[3] | 9.9 | 10.8 | 10.5 | 10.8 | .. | 33.7 | 33.9 | 34.0 | 32.6 | .. |

.. Not available

*Note:* The figures exclude local government revenues for Antigua and Barbuda, Argentina (but include provincial revenues), the Bahamas, Barbados, Cuba (except for 2002-2012), the Dominican Republic, Saint Lucia, Trinidad and Tobago and Venezuela as the data are not available. Local government revenue data have been available since 1991 for Nicaragua, since 1994 for Bolivia, since 1995 for Guatemala, since 1998 for Jamaica, since 1999 for Panama, since 2000 for Peru, since 2002 for El Salvador and Guyana, since 2006 for Paraguay and since 1990 for all other countries.

1. Some tax revenue data between 2014 and 2017 are not available. In those years data as % of total tax revenue cannot be calculated. Data for 2018 and subsequent years are not available.
2. Represents the group of 26 Latin American and Caribbean countries included in this publication and excludes Venezuela due to data availability issues. Chile, Colombia, Costa Rica and Mexico are also part of the OECD (38) group.
3. Represents the unweighted average for OECD member countries.

.. Non disponible

*Nota:* Las cifras excluyen los ingresos subnacionales para Antigua y Barbuda, Argentina (pero se incluyen los ingresos de las provincias), Las Bahamas, Barbados, Cuba (excepto 2002-2012), República Dominicana, Santa Lucía, Trinidad y Tobago y Venezuela, dado que los datos no están disponibles. Los datos de ingresos subnacionales están disponibles desde 1991 para Nicaragua, desde 1994 para Bolivia, desde 1995 para Guatemala, desde 1998 para Jamaica, desde 1999 para Panamá, desde 2000 para Perú, desde 2002 para El Salvador y Guyana, desde 2006 para Paraguay y desde 1990 para todos los demás países.

1. Algunos datos de ingresos tributarios entre 2014 y 2017 no están disponibles. Para esos años, no se pueden calcular los ingresos como porcentaje de los ingresos tributarios totales. Los datos de 2018 y años posteriores no están disponibles.
2. Representa al grupo de 26 países de América Latina y el Caribe incluidos en esta publicación y excluye a Venezuela debido a problemas de disponibilidad de datos. Chile, Colombia, Costa Rica y México también forman parte del grupo OCDE (38).
3. Representa el promedio no ponderado para los países miembros de la OCDE.

StatLink https://doi.org/10.1787/888934309188

## Table 4.10. **Value added taxes (5111) as % of GDP and as % of total tax revenue**
## Cuadro 4.10. **Impuesto al valor agregado (5111) en % del PIB y del total de ingresos tributarios**

| | % of GDP / % del PIB | | | | | % of total tax revenue / % del total de ingresos tributarios | | | | |
|---|---|---|---|---|---|---|---|---|---|---|
| | 1990 | 2000 | 2010 | 2019 | 2020 | 1990 | 2000 | 2010 | 2019 | 2020 |
| Antigua and Barbuda / Antigua y Barbuda | .. | .. | 5.8 | 5.5 | 5.6 | .. | .. | 27.2 | 30.7 | 28.2 |
| Argentina | 2.1 | 6.0 | 7.0 | 7.0 | 6.9 | 15.6 | 31.1 | 24.1 | 24.9 | 23.6 |
| Bahamas | 0.0 | 0.0 | 0.0 | 6.8 | 7.8 | 0.0 | 0.0 | 0.0 | 36.1 | 41.8 |
| Barbados | 0.0 | 8.0 | 8.4 | 9.5 | 8.3 | 0.0 | 26.0 | 28.1 | 28.1 | 23.7 |
| Belize / Belice | 0.0 | 0.0 | 7.2 | 8.1 | 6.8 | 0.0 | 0.0 | 26.9 | 28.0 | 26.1 |
| Bolivia | 2.8 | 5.7 | 7.4 | 7.2 | 6.0 | 43.0 | 32.2 | 32.5 | 29.2 | 26.8 |
| Brazil / Brasil | 8.0 | 6.9 | 6.9 | 6.9 | 7.0 | 28.7 | 23.3 | 21.3 | 21.2 | 22.2 |
| Chile | 6.3 | 7.9 | 7.5 | 8.3 | 8.0 | 37.4 | 41.8 | 38.5 | 39.9 | 41.2 |
| Colombia | 2.6 | 4.3 | 5.3 | 5.8 | 5.4 | 22.6 | 27.6 | 29.3 | 29.6 | 28.7 |
| Costa Rica | 4.1 | 4.8 | 4.6 | 4.4 | 4.5 | 18.1 | 22.8 | 21.0 | 18.5 | 19.7 |
| Cuba | 0.0 | 0.0 | 0.0 | 0.0 | 0.0 | 0.0 | 0.0 | 0.0 | 0.0 | 0.0 |
| Dominican Republic / República Dominicana | 1.3 | 2.5 | 4.1 | 4.7 | 4.4 | 15.1 | 20.5 | 33.1 | 34.7 | 34.7 |
| Ecuador | 2.0 | 5.0 | 5.4 | 6.0 | 5.5 | 28.0 | 43.5 | 32.1 | 30.2 | 28.5 |
| El Salvador | 0.0 | 6.1 | 7.8 | 7.8 | 8.3 | 0.0 | 42.8 | 41.6 | 37.5 | 37.7 |
| Guatemala | 2.3 | 4.4 | 5.1 | 5.0 | 4.8 | 29.7 | 37.9 | 40.9 | 38.8 | 38.6 |
| Guyana | 0.0 | 0.0 | 3.9 | 4.9 | 4.4 | 0.0 | 0.0 | 24.2 | 21.1 | 20.5 |
| Honduras | 2.0 | 4.8 | 5.4 | 7.0 | 6.1 | 16.2 | 28.1 | 29.4 | 32.5 | 31.9 |
| Jamaica | 0.8 | 5.7 | 7.1 | 9.4 | 8.8 | 3.8 | 25.5 | 28.7 | 33.0 | 31.9 |
| Mexico / México | 3.2 | 2.8 | 3.8 | 3.8 | 4.3 | 26.1 | 24.7 | 29.4 | 23.4 | 23.8 |
| Nicaragua | .. | 4.5 | 5.5 | 5.8 | 5.8 | .. | 31.5 | 28.6 | 22.5 | 22.7 |
| Panama / Panamá | 1.4 | 0.6 | 2.6 | 2.2 | 1.8 | 8.5 | 3.6 | 15.9 | 15.3 | 13.3 |
| Paraguay | 0.0 | 3.7 | 4.6 | 5.0 | 4.9 | 0.0 | 32.1 | 38.3 | 35.7 | 36.3 |
| Peru / Perú | 2.1 | 5.5 | 6.9 | 6.4 | 5.9 | 17.1 | 36.0 | 38.9 | 38.4 | 38.7 |
| Saint Lucia / Santa Lucía | .. | 0.0 | 0.0 | 5.9 | 5.4 | .. | 0.0 | 0.0 | 28.8 | 26.5 |
| Trinidad and Tobago / Trinidad y Tobago | 4.4 | 3.8 | 4.4 | 3.7 | 4.5 | 18.8 | 17.3 | 15.2 | 15.2 | 21.4 |
| Uruguay | 5.1 | 6.0 | 8.0 | 6.8 | 7.0 | 27.5 | 28.0 | 32.8 | 25.4 | 26.3 |
| Venezuela[1] | 0.0 | 4.1 | 5.5 | .. | .. | 0.0 | 30.2 | 46.7 | .. | .. |
| *Unweighted average / Promedio no ponderado* | | | | | | | | | | |
| LAC / ALC[2] | 2.2 | 4.0 | 5.2 | 5.9 | 5.7 | 15.5 | 23.1 | 26.1 | 27.6 | 27.5 |
| OECD / OCDE[3] | 5.1 | 6.3 | 6.4 | 6.7 | .. | 17.0 | 19.6 | 20.5 | 20.3 | .. |

.. Not available

*Note:* The figures exclude local government revenues for Antigua and Barbuda, Argentina (but include provincial revenues), the Bahamas, Barbados, Cuba (except for 2002-2012), the Dominican Republic, Saint Lucia, Trinidad and Tobago and Venezuela as the data are not available. Local government revenue data have been available since 1991 for Nicaragua, since 1994 for Bolivia, since 1995 for Guatemala, since 1998 for Jamaica, since 1999 for Panama, since 2000 for Peru, since 2002 for El Salvador and Guyana, since 2006 for Paraguay and since 1990 for all other countries.

1. Some tax revenue data between 2014 and 2017 are not available. In those years data as % of total tax revenue cannot be calculated. Data for 2018 and subsequent years are not available.
2. Represents the group of 26 Latin American and Caribbean countries included in this publication and excludes Venezuela due to data availability issues. Chile, Colombia, Costa Rica and Mexico are also part of the OECD (38) group.
3. Represents the unweighted average for OECD member countries.

.. Non disponible

*Nota:* Las cifras excluyen los ingresos subnacionales para Antigua y Barbuda, Argentina (pero se incluyen los ingresos de las provincias), Las Bahamas, Barbados, Cuba (excepto 2002-2012), República Dominicana, Santa Lucía, Trinidad y Tobago y Venezuela, dado que los datos no están disponibles. Los datos de ingresos subnacionales están disponibles desde 1991 para Nicaragua, desde 1994 para Bolivia, desde 1995 para Guatemala, desde 1998 para Jamaica, desde 1999 para Panamá, desde 2000 para Perú, desde 2002 para El Salvador y Guyana, desde 2006 para Paraguay y desde 1990 para todos los demás países.

1. Algunos datos de ingresos tributarios entre 2014 y 2017 no están disponibles. Para esos años, no se pueden calcular los ingresos como porcentaje de los ingresos tributarios totales. Los datos de 2018 y años posteriores no están disponibles.
2. Representa al grupo de 26 países de América Latina y el Caribe incluidos en esta publicación y excluye a Venezuela debido a problemas de disponibilidad de datos. Chile, Colombia, Costa Rica y México también forman parte del grupo OCDE (38).
3. Representa el promedio no ponderado para los países miembros de la OCDE.

StatLink https://doi.org/10.1787/888934309207

## Table 4.11. **Tax revenues of sub-sectors of general government as % of total tax revenue**
## Cuadro 4.11. **Ingresos tributarios por subsector del gobierno general, en % del total de ingresos tributarios**

| | Central government / Gobierno central | | | State or Regional government / Gobierno estatal o regional | | | Local government / Gobierno local | | | Social Security Funds / Fondos de seguridad social | | |
|---|---|---|---|---|---|---|---|---|---|---|---|---|
| | 1995 | 2000 | 2020 | 1995 | 2000 | 2020 | 1995 | 2000 | 2020 | 1995 | 2000 | 2020 |
| **Federal countries / Países federales** | | | | | | | | | | | | |
| Argentina | 59.0 | 66.4 | 64.1 | 17.5 | 17.8 | 16.8 | .. | .. | .. | 23.4 | 15.8 | 19.2 |
| Brazil / Brasil | 44.8 | 47.9 | 42.4 | 26.5 | 25.0 | 25.6 | 3.7 | 3.4 | 6.1 | 25.0 | 23.7 | 26.0 |
| Mexico / México | 73.9 | 78.3 | 80.7 | 2.8 | 2.7 | 3.9 | 1.5 | 1.0 | 1.5 | 21.8 | 18.0 | 13.9 |
| Venezuela[1] | 94.6 | 94.6 | .. | .. | .. | .. | .. | .. | .. | 5.4 | 5.4 | .. |
| **Regional country / País régional** | | | | | | | | | | | | |
| Colombia | 63.2 | 68.7 | 71.9 | 5.5 | 5.6 | 4.8 | 8.6 | 9.4 | 13.3 | 22.7 | 16.3 | 9.9 |
| **Unitary countries / Países unitarios** | | | | | | | | | | | | |
| Antigua and Barbuda / Antigua y Barbuda[2] | 100.0 | 100.0 | 83.3 | .. | .. | .. | .. | .. | .. | .. | .. | 16.7 |
| Bahamas[2] | 89.1 | 88.1 | 88.3 | .. | .. | .. | .. | .. | .. | 10.9 | 11.9 | 11.7 |
| Barbados | 85.6 | 84.4 | 80.1 | .. | .. | .. | .. | .. | .. | 14.4 | 15.6 | 19.9 |
| Belize / Belice | 93.2 | 93.5 | 86.9 | .. | .. | .. | 0.5 | 0.7 | 0.7 | 6.3 | 5.8 | 12.4 |
| Bolivia | 94.3 | 86.4 | 65.3 | .. | .. | .. | 5.7 | 6.3 | 4.8 | .. | 7.3 | 29.9 |
| Chile | 89.9 | 87.8 | 84.7 | .. | .. | .. | 6.5 | 7.9 | 8.6 | 3.6 | 4.4 | 6.7 |
| Costa Rica | 65.5 | 63.3 | 55.2 | .. | .. | .. | 1.6 | 1.9 | 3.1 | 33.0 | 34.8 | 41.6 |
| Cuba | .. | .. | .. | .. | .. | .. | .. | .. | .. | 11.3 | 10.4 | 16.0 |
| Dominican Republic / República Dominicana | 99.3 | 99.0 | 99.5 | .. | .. | .. | .. | .. | .. | 0.7 | 1.0 | 0.5 |
| Ecuador | 70.5 | 87.7 | 68.4 | .. | .. | .. | 4.0 | 1.6 | 2.8 | 25.5 | 10.7 | 28.8 |
| El Salvador | 80.9 | 80.5 | 85.0 | .. | .. | .. | .. | .. | 2.0 | 19.1 | 19.5 | 13.0 |
| Guatemala | 83.3 | 83.6 | 82.0 | .. | .. | .. | 0.7 | 0.9 | 1.0 | 16.1 | 15.5 | 17.1 |
| Guyana | 92.6 | 88.6 | 89.8 | .. | .. | .. | .. | .. | 0.0 | 7.4 | 11.4 | 10.1 |
| Honduras | 86.1 | 85.3 | 75.6 | .. | .. | .. | 4.4 | 5.2 | 3.8 | 9.5 | 9.4 | 20.6 |
| Jamaica | 100.0 | 99.3 | 93.9 | .. | .. | .. | .. | 0.7 | 1.5 | .. | .. | 4.6 |
| Nicaragua[2] | 78.0 | 72.5 | 67.6 | .. | .. | .. | 5.1 | 9.5 | 6.1 | 16.9 | 18.0 | 26.4 |
| Panama / Panamá | 67.2 | 59.6 | 53.8 | .. | .. | .. | .. | 2.2 | 1.6 | 32.8 | 38.2 | 44.6 |
| Paraguay | 92.0 | 74.4 | 69.8 | .. | .. | .. | .. | .. | 2.6 | 8.0 | 25.6 | 27.6 |
| Peru / Perú | 88.7 | 86.5 | 84.2 | .. | .. | .. | .. | 1.6 | 2.3 | 11.3 | 11.9 | 13.4 |
| Saint Lucia / Santa Lucía | 100.0 | 90.0 | 87.3 | .. | .. | .. | .. | .. | .. | .. | 10.0 | 12.7 |
| Trinidad and Tobago / Trinidad y Tobago | 96.8 | 93.6 | 85.0 | .. | .. | .. | .. | .. | .. | 3.2 | 6.4 | 15.0 |
| Uruguay[2] | 61.7 | 63.6 | 69.3 | .. | .. | .. | 8.8 | 8.9 | 5.6 | 29.5 | 27.5 | 25.0 |

.. Not available

*Note:* The figures exclude local government revenues for Antigua and Barbuda, Argentina (but include provincial revenues), the Bahamas, Barbados, Cuba (except for 2002-2012), the Dominican Republic, Saint Lucia, Trinidad and Tobago and Venezuela as the data are not available. Local government revenue data have been available since 1991 for Nicaragua, since 1994 for Bolivia, since 1995 for Guatemala, since 1998 for Jamaica, since 1999 for Panama, since 2000 for Peru, since 2002 for El Salvador and Guyana, since 2006 for Paraguay and since 1990 for all other countries.

1. Some tax revenue data between 2014 and 2017 and data for 2018 and subsequent years are not available. The breakdown by sub-sectors of general government is not available for those years.
2. The data include the following estimations: Antigua and Barbuda (social security contributions for 2019 and 2020), Bahamas (social security contributions for 2019 and 2020), Nicaragua (local tax revenues for 2020) and Uruguay (local tax revenues for 2020). See the corresponding country tables for more information.

.. Non disponible

*Nota:* Las cifras excluyen los ingresos subnacionales para Antigua y Barbuda, Argentina (pero se incluyen los ingresos de las provincias), Las Bahamas, Barbados, Cuba (excepto 2002-2012), República Dominicana, Santa Lucía, Trinidad y Tobago y Venezuela, dado que los datos no están disponibles. Los datos de ingresos subnacionales están disponibles desde 1991 para Nicaragua, desde 1994 para Bolivia, desde 1995 para Guatemala, desde 1998 para Jamaica, desde 1999 para Panamá, desde 2000 para Perú, desde 2002 para El Salvador y Guyana, desde 2006 para Paraguay y desde 1990 para todos los demás países.

1. Algunos datos de ingresos tributarios entre 2014 y 2017 y tos datos de 2018 y años posteriores no están disponibles. El desglose por subsectores del gobierno general no está disponible para esos años.
2. Los datos incluyen las siguientes estimaciones: Antigua y Barbuda (contribuciones a la seguridad social para 2019 y 2020), Bahamas (contribuciones a la seguridad social para 2019 y 2020), Nicaragua (ingresos tributarios locales para 2020) y Uruguay (ingresos tributarios locales para 2020). Consulte las tablas de países correspondientes para obtener más información.

StatLink https://doi.org/10.1787/888934309226

## Table 4.12. Main central government taxes as % of total tax revenues of central government, 2020

## Cuadro 4.12. Impuestos principales del gobierno central en % del total de ingresos tributarios del gobierno central, 2020

| | 1000 Income & profits / Ingresos y utilidades | 2000 Social security / Seguridad social | 3000 Payroll / Nómina | 4000 Property / Propiedad | 5000 Goods and services / Bienes y servicios | 6000 Others / Otros |
|---|---|---|---|---|---|---|
| **Federal countries / Países federales** | | | | | | |
| Argentina | 28.4 | 0.0 | 0.0 | 12.9 | 58.0 | 0.7 |
| Brazil / Brasil | 52.7 | 0.0 | 4.0 | 2.4 | 39.0 | 1.9 |
| Mexico / México | 52.8 | 0.0 | 0.0 | 0.0 | 45.5 | 1.7 |
| Venezuela | .. | .. | .. | .. | .. | .. |
| **Regional country / País régional** | | | | | | |
| Colombia | 45.8 | 0.0 | 2.7 | 6.7 | 44.5 | 0.2 |
| **Unitary countries / Países unitarios** | | | | | | |
| Antigua and Barbuda / Antigua y Barbuda | 14.3 | 0.0 | 0.0 | 9.1 | 76.6 | 0.0 |
| Bahamas | 0.0 | 0.0 | 0.0 | 9.3 | 90.7 | 0.0 |
| Barbados | 40.9 | 0.0 | 0.0 | 7.9 | 51.2 | 0.0 |
| Belize / Belice | 28.0 | 0.0 | 0.0 | 3.2 | 68.8 | 0.0 |
| Bolivia | 20.1 | 0.0 | 0.0 | 1.1 | 70.1 | 8.7 |
| Chile | 38.2 | 1.6 | 0.0 | 1.6 | 59.2 | -0.5 |
| Costa Rica | 36.3 | 1.7 | 0.0 | 0.9 | 57.4 | 3.7 |
| Cuba | .. | .. | .. | .. | .. | .. |
| Dominican Republic / República Dominicana | 33.8 | 0.0 | 0.6 | 4.5 | 61.1 | 0.0 |
| Ecuador | 34.4 | 0.0 | 0.0 | 0.4 | 65.0 | 0.2 |
| El Salvador | 42.6 | 0.0 | 0.8 | 0.5 | 56.1 | 0.0 |
| Guatemala | 27.4 | 0.0 | 1.4 | 0.7 | 62.2 | 8.3 |
| Guyana | 48.4 | 0.0 | 0.0 | 2.0 | 48.8 | 0.9 |
| Honduras | 30.1 | 0.0 | 1.1 | 3.5 | 65.3 | 0.0 |
| Jamaica | 30.4 | 0.0 | 6.0 | 1.5 | 61.7 | 0.4 |
| Nicaragua | 43.7 | 0.0 | 0.0 | 0.1 | 56.2 | 0.0 |
| Panama / Panamá | 48.3 | 0.0 | 2.6 | 3.2 | 45.3 | 0.5 |
| Paraguay | 26.5 | 0.0 | 0.0 | 0.0 | 73.0 | 0.4 |
| Peru / Perú | 43.5 | 0.0 | 0.1 | 0.2 | 55.2 | 0.9 |
| Saint Lucia / Santa Lucía | 26.9 | 0.0 | 0.0 | 2.4 | 70.7 | 0.0 |
| Trinidad and Tobago / Trinidad y Tobago | 57.7 | 0.0 | 0.0 | 1.0 | 41.3 | 0.0 |
| Uruguay | 38.4 | 0.0 | 0.0 | 6.7 | 54.6 | 0.2 |

.. Not available

*Note:* Excluding social security contributions collected by social security funds.

.. Non disponible

*Nota:* Se excluyen las contribuciones a la seguridad social recaudadas por los fondos de la seguridad social.

StatLink https://doi.org/10.1787/888934309245

## Table 4.13. **Main state government taxes as % of total tax revenues of state government, 2020**
## Cuadro 4.13. **Impuestos principales del gobierno estatal en % del total de ingresos tributarios del gobierno estatal, 2020**

| | 1000 Income & profits / Ingresos y utilidades | 2000 Social security / Seguridad social | 3000 Payroll / Nómina | 4000 Property / Propiedad | 5000 Goods and services / Bienes y servicios | 6000 Others / Otros |
|---|---|---|---|---|---|---|
| **Federal countries / Países federales** | | | | | | |
| Argentina | 0.0 | 0.0 | 0.0 | 15.6 | 82.5 | 1.8 |
| Brazil / Brasil | 0.0 | 0.0 | 0.0 | 1.6 | 95.2 | 3.2 |
| Mexico / México | 0.0 | 0.0 | 65.4 | 16.4 | 13.1 | 5.0 |
| Venezuela | .. | .. | .. | .. | .. | .. |
| **Regional country / País régional** | | | | | | |
| Colombia | 0.0 | 0.0 | 0.0 | 0.0 | 72.3 | 27.7 |
| **Unitary countries / Países unitarios** | | | | | | |
| Antigua and Barbuda / Antigua y Barbuda | .. | .. | .. | .. | .. | .. |
| Bahamas | .. | .. | .. | .. | .. | .. |
| Barbados | .. | .. | .. | .. | .. | .. |
| Belize / Belice | .. | .. | .. | .. | .. | .. |
| Bolivia | .. | .. | .. | .. | .. | .. |
| Chile | .. | .. | .. | .. | .. | .. |
| Costa Rica | .. | .. | .. | .. | .. | .. |
| Cuba | .. | .. | .. | .. | .. | .. |
| Dominican Republic / República Dominicana | .. | .. | .. | .. | .. | .. |
| Ecuador | .. | .. | .. | .. | .. | .. |
| El Salvador | .. | .. | .. | .. | .. | .. |
| Guatemala | .. | .. | .. | .. | .. | .. |
| Guyana | .. | .. | .. | .. | .. | .. |
| Honduras | .. | .. | .. | .. | .. | .. |
| Jamaica | .. | .. | .. | .. | .. | .. |
| Nicaragua | .. | .. | .. | .. | .. | .. |
| Panama / Panamá | .. | .. | .. | .. | .. | .. |
| Paraguay | .. | .. | .. | .. | .. | .. |
| Peru / Perú | .. | .. | .. | .. | .. | .. |
| Saint Lucia / Santa Lucía | .. | .. | .. | .. | .. | .. |
| Trinidad and Tobago / Trinidad y Tobago | .. | .. | .. | .. | .. | .. |
| Uruguay | .. | .. | .. | .. | .. | .. |

.. Not available
.. Non disponible

StatLink https://doi.org/10.1787/888934309264

## Table 4.14. **Main local government taxes as % of total tax revenues of local government, 2020**
## Cuadro 4.14. **Impuestos principales del gobierno local en % del total de ingresos tributarios del gobierno local, 2020**

| | 1000 Income & profits / Ingresos y utilidades | 2000 Social security / Seguridad social | 3000 Payroll / Nómina | 4000 Property / Propiedad | 5000 Goods and services / Bienes y servicios | 6000 Others / Otros |
|---|---|---|---|---|---|---|
| **Federal countries / Países federales** | | | | | | |
| Argentina | .. | .. | .. | .. | .. | .. |
| Brazil / Brasil | 0.0 | 0.0 | 0.0 | 40.7 | 53.3 | 6.0 |
| Mexico / México | 0.0 | 0.0 | 0.0 | 65.3 | 1.3 | 33.4 |
| Venezuela | .. | .. | .. | .. | .. | .. |
| **Regional country / País régional** | | | | | | |
| Colombia | 0.0 | 0.0 | 0.0 | 36.4 | 44.2 | 19.3 |
| **Unitary countries / Países unitarios** | | | | | | |
| Antigua and Barbuda / Antigua y Barbuda | .. | .. | .. | .. | .. | .. |
| Bahamas | .. | .. | .. | .. | .. | .. |
| Barbados | .. | .. | .. | .. | .. | .. |
| Belize / Belice | 0.0 | 0.0 | 0.0 | 100.0 | 0.0 | 0.0 |
| Bolivia | 0.0 | 0.0 | 0.0 | 0.0 | 0.0 | 100.0 |
| Chile | 0.0 | 0.0 | 0.0 | 44.5 | 55.5 | 0.0 |
| Costa Rica | 0.0 | 0.0 | 0.0 | 47.9 | 52.1 | 0.0 |
| Cuba | .. | .. | .. | .. | .. | .. |
| Dominican Republic / República Dominicana | .. | .. | .. | .. | .. | .. |
| Ecuador | 9.3 | 0.0 | 0.0 | 52.0 | 38.6 | 0.0 |
| El Salvador | 0.0 | 0.0 | 0.0 | 5.5 | 9.4 | 85.1 |
| Guatemala | 0.0 | 0.0 | 0.0 | 100.0 | 0.0 | 0.0 |
| Guyana | 0.0 | 0.0 | 0.0 | 0.0 | 0.0 | 100.0 |
| Honduras | 0.0 | 0.0 | 0.0 | 0.0 | 0.0 | 100.0 |
| Jamaica | 0.0 | 0.0 | 0.0 | 100.0 | 0.0 | 0.0 |
| Nicaragua | 0.0 | 0.0 | 0.0 | 14.7 | 71.5 | 13.7 |
| Panama / Panamá | 0.0 | 0.0 | 0.0 | 0.0 | 100.0 | 0.0 |
| Paraguay | 0.0 | 0.0 | 0.0 | 48.3 | 45.9 | 5.8 |
| Peru / Perú | 0.0 | 0.0 | 0.0 | 86.1 | 12.1 | 1.8 |
| Saint Lucia / Santa Lucía | .. | .. | .. | .. | .. | .. |
| Trinidad and Tobago / Trinidad y Tobago | .. | .. | .. | .. | .. | .. |
| Uruguay | 0.0 | 0.0 | 0.0 | 54.2 | 38.3 | 7.5 |

.. Not available
.. Non disponible

StatLink https://doi.org/10.1787/888934309283

## Table 4.15. **Gross domestic product for tax reporting years at market prices, in millions of national currency**

## Cuadro 4.15. **Producto interno bruto para los años fiscales a precios de mercado, en millones de moneda local**

| | | 1990 | 2000 | 2007 | 2010 | 2015 | 2016 | 2017 | 2018 | 2019 | 2020 |
|---|---|---|---|---|---|---|---|---|---|---|---|
| Antigua and Barbuda / Antigua y Barbuda | XCD | 1 241 | 2 231 | 3 544 | 3 101 | 3 609 | 3 879 | 3 964 | 4 336 | 4 556 | 3 700 |
| Argentina | ARS | 77 060 | 317 759 | 896 980 | 1 661 721 | 5 954 511 | 8 228 160 | 10 660 228 | 14 744 811 | 21 802 256 | 27 481 440 |
| Bahamas | BSD | 5 218 | 7 880 | 10 393 | 10 039 | 11 411 | 11 986 | 12 283 | 12 593 | 13 205 | 11 301 |
| Barbados | BBD | 4 059 | 6 116 | 9 403 | 9 124 | 9 488 | 9 734 | 10 011 | 10 279 | 10 156 | 8 476 |
| Belize / Belice | BZD | 824 | 1 664 | 2 543 | 2 754 | 3 443 | 3 579 | 3 717 | 3 832 | 3 965 | 3 413 |
| Bolivia | BOB | 15 443 | 51 928 | 103 009 | 137 876 | 228 031 | 234 533 | 259 185 | 278 388 | 282 587 | 252 718 |
| Brazil / Brasil | BRL | 12 | 1 199 092 | 2 720 263 | 3 885 847 | 5 995 787 | 6 269 328 | 6 585 479 | 7 004 141 | 7 407 024 | 7 447 858 |
| Chile | CLP | 10 522 684 | 42 005 194 | 90 702 903 | 111 508 611 | 159 553 348 | 169 537 388 | 179 749 461 | 190 825 823 | 196 379 333 | 200 512 436 |
| Colombia | COP | 22 731 433 | 195 108 574 | 428 506 000 | 544 060 000 | 804 692 000 | 863 782 000 | 920 471 000 | 987 791 000 | 1 061 119 000 | 1 002 587 200 |
| Costa Rica | CRC | 523 319 | 4 627 051 | 13 889 053 | 19 802 011 | 30 171 919 | 32 056 288 | 34 343 647 | 35 966 118 | 37 558 144 | 35 983 495 |
| Cuba | CUP | 19 645 | 30 565 | 58 604 | 64 328 | 87 133 | 91 370 | 96 851 | 100 050 | 103 428 | 107 352 |
| Dominican Republic / República Dominicana | DOP | 77 344 | 393 303 | 1 458 417 | 1 983 202 | 3 205 655 | 3 487 293 | 3 802 656 | 4 235 847 | 4 562 235 | 4 456 657 |
| Ecuador | USD | 15 232 | 18 319 | 51 008 | 69 555 | 99 290 | 99 938 | 104 296 | 107 562 | 108 108 | 98 808 |
| El Salvador | USD | 4 818 | 11 785 | 17 012 | 18 448 | 23 438 | 24 191 | 24 979 | 26 021 | 26 897 | 24 639 |
| Guatemala | GTQ | 33 613 | 140 702 | 261 760 | 333 093 | 476 023 | 502 002 | 526 507 | 550 470 | 592 800 | 599 236 |
| Guyana | GYD | 34 523 | 273 054 | 552 603 | 699 064 | 883 787 | 925 677 | 980 498 | 994 472 | 1 078 729 | 1 140 757 |
| Honduras | HNL | 17 141 | 106 654 | 233 567 | 299 286 | 460 405 | 495 922 | 543 403 | 575 285 | 614 918 | 585 734 |
| Jamaica | JMD | 38 145 | 395 009 | 885 632 | 1 152 781 | 1 659 677 | 1 760 976 | 1 895 025 | 2 027 251 | 2 110 433 | 1 966 928 |
| Mexico / México | MXN | 843 623 | 6 693 683 | 11 504 076 | 13 366 377 | 18 572 109 | 20 129 057 | 21 934 168 | 23 523 247 | 24 443 014 | 23 122 023 |
| Nicaragua | NIO | 519 | 64 812 | 136 950 | 187 053 | 347 707 | 380 261 | 414 279 | 410 988 | 417 705 | 433 448 |
| Panama / Panamá | PAB | 5 723 | 12 502 | 21 296 | 29 440 | 54 092 | 57 908 | 62 203 | 64 928 | 66 788 | 52 938 |
| Paraguay | PYG | 7 147 738 | 30 874 088 | 89 866 049 | 129 092 883 | 188 477 327 | 204 647 273 | 219 122 277 | 230 576 477 | 236 566 704 | 241 527 086 |
| Peru / Perú | PEN | 5 322 | 175 862 | 319 693 | 420 420 | 609 145 | 655 759 | 698 244 | 740 817 | 770 388 | 718 189 |
| Saint Lucia / Santa Lucía | XCD | 1 559 | 2 446 | 3 676 | 4 075 | 4 924 | 5 125 | 5 437 | 5 612 | 5 721 | 4 432 |
| Trinidad and Tobago / Trinidad y Tobago | TTD | 21 105 | 50 098 | 133 468 | 138 557 | 163 633 | 151 765 | 151 145 | 158 189 | 157 650 | 148 490 |
| Uruguay | UYU | 13 047 | 299 995 | 596 911 | 877 848 | 1 581 546 | 1 726 406 | 1 841 999 | 1 982 247 | 2 158 728 | 2 253 124 |
| Venezuela | VES | 0 | 1 | 5 | 10 | 80 | 281 | 2 009 | 1 057 236 | 137 482 062 | 2 362 770 937 |

*Source:* OECD National Accounts data for Chile, Colombia, Costa Rica and Mexico, the World Economic Outlook (IMF) for Barbados, Belize, Saint Lucia, Trinidad & Tobago and Uruguay, and official National Accounts data for Antigua and Barbuda, Bolivia, Brazil, Ecuador, Paraguay and Peru. For Argentina, Bahamas, Dominican Republic, El Salvador, Guatemala, Guyana, Honduras, Jamaica, Nicaragua, Panama and Venezuela, official national sources were used where available, together with data from the IMF. For Cuba, figures since 1996 have come from Oficina Nacional de Estadística e Información (ONEI), while data before 1996 come from ECLAC/CEPAL. For Bahamas, Barbados, Belize, Saint Lucia and Trinidad and Tobago, GDP figures are reported on a fiscal year basis. For Jamaica, GDP for 1990-2003 are reported on a fiscal year basis, while for other years, they are reported on a calendar year basis.

*Fuente:* Datos de las Cuentas Nacionales de la OCDE para Chile, Colombia, Costa Rica y México, Perspectivas de la economía mundial (FMI) para Barbados, Belice, Santa Lucía, Trinidad y Tobago y Uruguay, y datos de cuentas nacionales para Antigua y Barbuda, Bolivia, Brasil, Ecuador, Paraguay y Perú. Para Argentina, Bahamas, República Dominicana, El Salvador, Guatemala, Guyana, Honduras, Jamaica, Nicaragua, Panamá y Venezuela, se utilizan fuentes nacionales oficiales donde los datos están disponibles, junto con los datos del FMI. Para Cuba, los datos anteriores a 1996 proceden de la CEPAL. Para Bahamas, Barbados, Belice, Santa Lucía y Trinidad y Tobago, las cifras del PIB se informan sobre la base del año fiscal. Para Jamaica, el PIB reportado para 1990-2003 se presenta sobre una base de año fiscal, mientras que para otros años, se presenta sobre una base de año calendario.

StatLink https://doi.org/10.1787/888934309302

## Table 4.16. **Gross domestic product for tax reporting years at market prices, in USD million**
## Cuadro 4.16. **Producto interno bruto para los años fiscales a precios de mercado, en millones de US dólares**

| | 1990 | 2000 | 2007 | 2010 | 2015 | 2016 | 2017 | 2018 | 2019 | 2020 |
|---|---|---|---|---|---|---|---|---|---|---|
| Antigua and Barbuda / Antigua y Barbuda | 459 | 826 | 1 313 | 1 149 | 1 337 | 1 437 | 1 468 | 1 606 | 1 688 | 1 370 |
| Argentina | 158 024 | 317 759 | 287 921 | 424 729 | 642 464 | 556 774 | 643 861 | 524 431 | 451 815 | 389 064 |
| Bahamas | 5 218 | 7 880 | 10 393 | 10 039 | 11 411 | 11 986 | 12 283 | 12 593 | 13 205 | 11 301 |
| Barbados | 2 030 | 3 058 | 4 702 | 4 562 | 4 744 | 4 867 | 5 006 | 5 140 | 5 078 | 4 238 |
| Belize / Belice | 412 | 832 | 1 272 | 1 377 | 1 722 | 1 790 | 1 859 | 1 916 | 1 983 | 1 707 |
| Bolivia | 4 868 | 8 385 | 13 216 | 19 786 | 33 241 | 34 189 | 37 782 | 40 581 | 41 193 | 36 839 |
| Brazil / Brasil | 478 052 | 655 453 | 1 397 114 | 2 208 704 | 1 800 046 | 1 796 622 | 2 063 518 | 1 916 934 | 1 877 822 | 1 444 718 |
| Chile | 34 512 | 77 876 | 173 684 | 218 652 | 243 845 | 250 595 | 277 102 | 297 285 | 279 223 | 253 263 |
| Colombia | 45 258 | 93 447 | 206 182 | 286 563 | 293 482 | 282 825 | 311 884 | 334 198 | 323 430 | 271 347 |
| Costa Rica | 5 714 | 15 014 | 26 885 | 37 659 | 56 442 | 58 847 | 60 516 | 62 336 | 63 951 | 61 521 |
| Cuba | 21 541 | 30 565 | 58 604 | 64 328 | 87 133 | 91 370 | 96 851 | 100 050 | 103 131 | 95 994 |
| Dominican Republic / República Dominicana | 7 995 | 24 306 | 44 067 | 53 921 | 71 254 | 75 777 | 80 082 | 85 630 | 89 032 | 78 923 |
| Ecuador | 15 232 | 18 319 | 51 008 | 69 555 | 99 290 | 99 938 | 104 296 | 107 562 | 108 108 | 98 808 |
| El Salvador | 4 818 | 11 785 | 17 012 | 18 448 | 23 438 | 24 191 | 24 979 | 26 021 | 26 897 | 24 639 |
| Guatemala | 7 493 | 18 124 | 34 108 | 41 327 | 62 180 | 66 034 | 71 624 | 73 212 | 77 004 | 77 603 |
| Guyana | 685 | 1 497 | 2 732 | 3 432 | 4 280 | 4 483 | 4 748 | 4 788 | 5 174 | 5 471 |
| Honduras | 4 169 | 7 187 | 12 361 | 15 839 | 20 980 | 21 718 | 23 136 | 24 068 | 25 090 | 23 828 |
| Jamaica | 5 058 | 8 997 | 12 881 | 13 193 | 14 154 | 14 108 | 14 755 | 15 648 | 15 808 | 13 884 |
| Mexico / México | 296 972 | 708 096 | 1 052 654 | 1 058 146 | 1 169 956 | 1 080 616 | 1 162 291 | 1 226 564 | 1 271 964 | 1 080 425 |
| Nicaragua | 519 | 5 109 | 7 423 | 8 759 | 12 757 | 13 286 | 13 786 | 13 025 | 12 625 | 12 620 |
| Panama / Panamá | 5 723 | 12 502 | 21 296 | 29 440 | 54 092 | 57 908 | 62 203 | 64 928 | 66 788 | 52 938 |
| Paraguay | 5 812 | 8 856 | 17 856 | 27 129 | 36 211 | 36 090 | 38 997 | 40 225 | 37 907 | 35 670 |
| Peru / Perú | 28 326 | 50 414 | 102 187 | 148 819 | 191 247 | 194 266 | 214 128 | 225 369 | 230 865 | 205 458 |
| Saint Lucia / Santa Lucía | 577 | 906 | 1 361 | 1 509 | 1 824 | 1 898 | 2 014 | 2 079 | 2 119 | 1 641 |
| Trinidad and Tobago / Trinidad y Tobago | 4 966 | 7 986 | 21 199 | 21 841 | 25 791 | 23 168 | 22 394 | 23 413 | 23 334 | 21 996 |
| Uruguay | 11 156 | 24 804 | 25 486 | 43 763 | 57 874 | 57 237 | 64 234 | 64 766 | 61 931 | 56 577 |
| Venezuela | 48 391 | 94 665 | 229 896 | 323 200 | 325 122 | 279 160 | 143 834 | 98 400 | 63 960 | 47 255 |

*Source:* The figures are derived by dividing the GDP data in Table 4.15 by the exchange rate in Table 4.17.
*Fuente:* Las cifras se obtienen de la división de los datos del PIB en el Cuadro 4.15 por el tipo de cambio en el Cuadro 4.17.

StatLink https://doi.org/10.1787/888934309321

## Table 4.17. **Exchange rates used, national currency per US dollar at market exchange rates**
## Cuadro 4.17. **Tasas de cambio utilizadas, moneda local por US dólares a precios de mercado**

| | | 1990 | 2000 | 2007 | 2010 | 2015 | 2016 | 2017 | 2018 | 2019 | 2020 |
|---|---|---|---|---|---|---|---|---|---|---|---|
| Antigua and Barbuda / Antigua y Barbuda | XCD | 2.704 | 2.701 | 2.699 | 2.699 | 2.699 | 2.699 | 2.700 | 2.700 | 2.699 | 2.700 |
| Argentina | ARS | 0.488 | 1.000 | 3.115 | 3.912 | 9.268 | 14.778 | 16.557 | 28.116 | 48.255 | 70.635 |
| Bahamas | BSD | 1.000 | 1.000 | 1.000 | 1.000 | 1.000 | 1.000 | 1.000 | 1.000 | 1.000 | 1.000 |
| Barbados | BBD | 2.000 | 2.000 | 2.000 | 2.000 | 2.000 | 2.000 | 2.000 | 2.000 | 2.000 | 2.000 |
| Belize / Belice | BZD | 2.000 | 2.000 | 2.000 | 2.000 | 2.000 | 2.000 | 2.000 | 2.000 | 2.000 | 2.000 |
| Bolivia | BOB | 3.172 | 6.193 | 7.794 | 6.968 | 6.860 | 6.860 | 6.860 | 6.860 | 6.860 | 6.860 |
| Brazil / Brasil | BRL | 0.000 | 1.829 | 1.947 | 1.759 | 3.331 | 3.490 | 3.191 | 3.654 | 3.944 | 5.155 |
| Chile | CLP | 304.903 | 539.388 | 522.228 | 509.982 | 654.322 | 676.541 | 648.677 | 641.896 | 703.308 | 791.715 |
| Colombia | COP | 502.259 | 2 087.904 | 2 078.292 | 1 898.570 | 2 741.881 | 3 054.122 | 2 951.327 | 2 955.704 | 3 280.832 | 3 694.854 |
| Costa Rica | CRC | 91.579 | 308.187 | 516.617 | 525.829 | 534.566 | 544.739 | 567.513 | 576.973 | 587.295 | 584.901 |
| Cuba | CUP | 0.912 | 1.000 | 1.000 | 1.000 | 1.000 | 1.000 | 1.000 | 1.000 | 1.003 | 1.118 |
| Dominican Republic / República Dominicana | DOP | 9.674 | 16.181 | 33.095 | 36.780 | 44.989 | 46.020 | 47.485 | 49.467 | 51.243 | 56.468 |
| Ecuador | USD | 1.000 | 1.000 | 1.000 | 1.000 | 1.000 | 1.000 | 1.000 | 1.000 | 1.000 | 1.000 |
| El Salvador | USD | 1.000 | 1.000 | 1.000 | 1.000 | 1.000 | 1.000 | 1.000 | 1.000 | 1.000 | 1.000 |
| Guatemala | GTQ | 4.486 | 7.763 | 7.675 | 8.060 | 7.656 | 7.602 | 7.351 | 7.519 | 7.698 | 7.722 |
| Guyana | GYD | 50.399 | 182.401 | 202.239 | 203.670 | 206.492 | 206.486 | 206.508 | 207.701 | 208.490 | 208.510 |
| Honduras | HNL | 4.112 | 14.840 | 18.895 | 18.896 | 21.945 | 22.835 | 23.487 | 23.902 | 24.508 | 24.582 |
| Jamaica | JMD | 7.541 | 43.907 | 68.755 | 87.378 | 117.259 | 124.821 | 128.433 | 129.553 | 133.504 | 141.664 |
| Mexico / México | MXN | 2.841 | 9.453 | 10.929 | 12.632 | 15.874 | 18.627 | 18.871 | 19.178 | 19.217 | 21.401 |
| Nicaragua | NIO | 1.000 | 12.686 | 18.449 | 21.356 | 27.256 | 28.621 | 30.051 | 31.554 | 33.086 | 34.346 |
| Panama / Panamá | PAB | 1.000 | 1.000 | 1.000 | 1.000 | 1.000 | 1.000 | 1.000 | 1.000 | 1.000 | 1.000 |
| Paraguay | PYG | 1 229.845 | 3 486.234 | 5 032.821 | 4 758.483 | 5 204.974 | 5 670.470 | 5 618.952 | 5 732.168 | 6 240.713 | 6 771.155 |
| Peru / Perú | PEN | 0.188 | 3.488 | 3.129 | 2.825 | 3.185 | 3.376 | 3.261 | 3.287 | 3.337 | 3.496 |
| Saint Lucia / Santa Lucía | XCD | 2.700 | 2.700 | 2.700 | 2.700 | 2.700 | 2.700 | 2.700 | 2.700 | 2.700 | 2.700 |
| Trinidad and Tobago / Trinidad y Tobago | TTD | 4.250 | 6.273 | 6.296 | 6.344 | 6.344 | 6.551 | 6.749 | 6.756 | 6.756 | 6.751 |
| Uruguay | UYU | 1.170 | 12.095 | 23.421 | 20.059 | 27.327 | 30.162 | 28.676 | 30.606 | 34.857 | 39.824 |
| Venezuela | VES | 0.000 | 0.000 | 0.000 | 0.000 | 0.000 | 0.001 | 0.014 | 10.744 | 2 149.501 | 50 000.443 |

*Note:* Annual average market exchange rates.
*Source:* World Economic Outlook (IMF), October 2021.
*Nota:* Se utilizan tasas de cambio de promedio anual de mercados.
*Fuente:* Perspectivas de la economía mundial (FMI), octubre de 2021

StatLink https://doi.org/10.1787/888934309340

*Chapter 5*

# Country tables, 1990-2020 – Tax revenues

*Capítulo 5*

# Cuadros país, 1990-2020 – Ingresos tributarios

## Table 5.1. **Antigua and Barbuda / Antigua y Barbuda**

Details of tax revenue / Ingresos tributarios detallados

*Million XCD*

| | 1990 | 2000 | 2007 | 2010 | 2015 | 2016 | 2017 | 2018 | 2019 | 2020 |
|---|---|---|---|---|---|---|---|---|---|---|
| **Total tax revenue** | .. | **268** | **763** | **660** | **735** | **760** | **776** | **823** | **822** | **732** |
| **1000 Taxes on income, profits and capital gains** | .. | **38** | **100** | **92** | **89** | **76** | **74** | **78** | **79** | **87** |
| 1100 Taxes Of individuals | .. | 0 | 50 | 33 | 37 | 26 | 2 | 0 | 1 | 0 |
| 1110 On income and profits | .. | 0 | 50 | 33 | 37 | 26 | 2 | 0 | 1 | 0 |
| 1120 On capital gains | .. | .. | .. | .. | .. | .. | .. | .. | .. | .. |
| 1200 Corporate | .. | 37 | 50 | 59 | 52 | 50 | 72 | 78 | 79 | 87 |
| 1210 On profits | .. | 37 | 50 | 59 | 52 | 50 | 72 | 78 | 79 | 87 |
| 1220 On capital gains of corporates | .. | .. | .. | .. | .. | .. | .. | .. | .. | .. |
| 1300 Unallocable between 1100 and 1200 | .. | 0 | 0 | 0 | 0 | 0 | 0 | 0 | 0 | 0 |
| **2000 Social security contributions (SSC)** | .. | .. | **78** | **83** | **113** | **119** | **140** | **143** | **150** | **122** |
| 2100 Employees SSC | .. | .. | .. | .. | .. | .. | .. | .. | .. | .. |
| 2110 On a payroll basis | .. | .. | .. | .. | .. | .. | .. | .. | .. | .. |
| 2120 On an income tax basis | .. | .. | .. | .. | .. | .. | .. | .. | .. | .. |
| 2200 Employers | .. | .. | .. | .. | .. | .. | .. | .. | .. | .. |
| 2210 On a payroll | .. | .. | .. | .. | .. | .. | .. | .. | .. | .. |
| 2220 On an income tax basis | .. | .. | .. | .. | .. | .. | .. | .. | .. | .. |
| 2300 Self-employed or non-employed | .. | .. | .. | .. | .. | .. | .. | .. | .. | .. |
| 2310 On a payroll basis | .. | .. | .. | .. | .. | .. | .. | .. | .. | .. |
| 2320 On an income tax basis | .. | .. | .. | .. | .. | .. | .. | .. | .. | .. |
| 2400 Unallocable between 2100, 2200 and 2300 | .. | .. | 78 | 83 | 113 | 119 | 140 | 143 | 150 | 122 |
| 2410 On a payroll basis | .. | .. | 78 | 83 | 113 | 119 | 140 | 143 | 150 | 122 |
| 2420 On an income tax basis | .. | .. | 0 | 0 | 0 | 0 | 0 | 0 | 0 | 0 |
| **3000 Taxes on payroll and workforce** | .. | **0** | **0** | **0** | **0** | **0** | **0** | **0** | **0** | **0** |
| **4000 Taxes on property** | .. | **13** | **55** | **49** | **52** | **60** | **70** | **62** | **72** | **56** |
| 4100 Recurrent taxes on immovable property | .. | 0 | 9 | 18 | 18 | 18 | 20 | 21 | 29 | 18 |
| 4110 Households | .. | .. | 9 | 18 | 18 | 18 | 20 | 21 | 29 | 18 |
| Property tax | .. | .. | 9 | 18 | 18 | 17 | 19 | 20 | 24 | 18 |
| Land tax | .. | .. | 0 | 0 | 0 | 1 | 2 | 1 | 2 | 0 |
| Non-Citizens Undeveloped Land Tax | .. | .. | 0 | 0 | 0 | 0 | 0 | 0 | 3 | 0 |
| 4120 Others | .. | .. | 0 | 0 | 0 | 0 | 0 | 0 | 0 | 0 |
| 4200 Recurrent taxes on net wealth | .. | 0 | 0 | 0 | 0 | 0 | 0 | 0 | 0 | 0 |
| 4210 Individual | .. | .. | .. | .. | .. | .. | .. | .. | .. | .. |
| 4220 Corporate | .. | .. | .. | .. | .. | .. | .. | .. | .. | .. |
| 4300 Estate, inheritance and gift taxes | .. | 0 | 0 | 0 | 0 | 0 | 0 | 0 | 0 | 0 |
| 4310 Estate and inheritance taxes | .. | .. | .. | .. | .. | .. | .. | .. | .. | .. |
| 4320 Gift taxes | .. | .. | .. | .. | .. | .. | .. | .. | .. | .. |
| 4400 Taxes on financial and capital transactions | .. | 13 | 46 | 32 | 34 | 42 | 50 | 41 | 43 | 38 |
| Stamp duties | .. | 13 | 45 | 31 | 34 | 42 | 50 | 41 | 43 | 38 |
| Other taxes on transactions | .. | 0 | 1 | 0 | 0 | 0 | 0 | 0 | 0 | 0 |
| 4500 Non-recurrent taxes | .. | 0 | 0 | 0 | 0 | 0 | 0 | 0 | 0 | 0 |
| 4510 On net wealth | .. | .. | .. | .. | .. | .. | .. | .. | .. | .. |
| 4520 Other non-recurrent taxes | .. | .. | .. | .. | .. | .. | .. | .. | .. | .. |
| 4600 Other recurrent taxes on property | .. | 0 | 0 | 0 | 0 | 0 | 0 | 0 | 0 | 0 |
| **5000 Taxes on goods and services** | .. | **217** | **530** | **435** | **481** | **506** | **492** | **539** | **521** | **467** |
| 5100 Taxes on production, sale, transfer, etc | .. | 217 | 512 | 429 | 478 | 503 | 489 | 535 | 517 | 464 |
| 5110 General taxes | .. | 0 | 202 | 179 | 307 | 325 | 312 | 362 | 333 | 273 |
| 5111 Value added taxes | .. | .. | 202 | 179 | 232 | 251 | 237 | 278 | 253 | 207 |
| 5112 Sales tax | .. | .. | 0 | 0 | 75 | 74 | 75 | 84 | 80 | 66 |
| 5113 Other | .. | .. | 0 | 0 | 0 | 0 | 0 | 0 | 0 | 0 |
| 5120 Taxes on specific goods and services | .. | 217 | 310 | 250 | 171 | 178 | 177 | 173 | 185 | 191 |
| 5121 Excises | .. | 72 | 66 | 34 | 69 | 81 | 68 | 56 | 67 | 83 |
| Consumption duties | .. | 72 | 58 | 31 | 64 | 78 | 64 | 53 | 64 | 79 |
| Environmental tax | .. | 0 | 8 | 3 | 5 | 4 | 3 | 3 | 3 | 4 |
| 5122 Profits of fiscal monopolies | .. | 0 | 0 | 0 | 0 | 0 | 0 | 0 | 0 | 0 |
| 5123 Customs and import duties | .. | 83 | 187 | 96 | 88 | 84 | 93 | 101 | 102 | 86 |
| Import duties | .. | 57 | 93 | 79 | 82 | 82 | 88 | 97 | 98 | 82 |
| Throughput Levy on Fuel Products | .. | 0 | 0 | 12 | 5 | 2 | 5 | 4 | 4 | 4 |
| Other customs charges | .. | 26 | 94 | 5 | 0 | 0 | 0 | 0 | 0 | 0 |
| 5124 Taxes on exports | .. | 0 | 0 | 0 | 0 | 0 | 0 | 0 | 0 | 0 |
| 5125 Taxes on investment goods | .. | 0 | 0 | 0 | 0 | 0 | 0 | 0 | 0 | 0 |
| 5126 Taxes on specific services | .. | 53 | 57 | 54 | 14 | 13 | 17 | 16 | 15 | 22 |
| Travel tax | .. | 4 | 7 | 4 | 6 | 5 | 6 | 7 | 7 | 3 |
| Insurance levy | .. | 0 | 4 | 4 | 4 | 4 | 7 | 5 | 5 | 7 |
| Money transfer levy | .. | 0 | 1 | 1 | 2 | 2 | 2 | 2 | 1 | 1 |
| Other taxes on hospitality, transport and telecommunication services | .. | 49 | 44 | 44 | 2 | 1 | 2 | 2 | 2 | 11 |
| 5127 Other taxes on internat. trade and transactions | .. | 9 | 0 | 66 | 0 | 0 | 0 | 0 | 0 | 0 |
| 5128 Other taxes | .. | 0 | 0 | 0 | 0 | 0 | 0 | 0 | 0 | 0 |
| 5130 Unallocable between 5110 and 5120 | .. | 0 | 0 | 0 | 0 | 0 | 0 | 0 | 0 | 0 |
| 5200 Taxes on use of goods and perform activities | .. | 0 | 17 | 6 | 3 | 3 | 3 | 3 | 4 | 3 |

## Table 5.1. **Antigua and Barbuda / Antigua y Barbuda** *(cont.)*

Details of tax revenue / Ingresos tributarios detallados

*Million XCD*

| | 1990 | 2000 | 2007 | 2010 | 2015 | 2016 | 2017 | 2018 | 2019 | 2020 |
|---|---|---|---|---|---|---|---|---|---|---|
| 5210 Recurrent taxes | .. | .. | 17 | 6 | 3 | 3 | 3 | 3 | 4 | 3 |
| 5211 Paid by households: motor vehicles | .. | .. | 0 | 0 | 0 | 0 | 0 | 0 | 0 | 0 |
| 5212 Paid by others: motor vehicles | .. | .. | 15 | 3 | 2 | 2 | 2 | 2 | 2 | 2 |
| 5213 Paid in respect of other goods | .. | .. | 2 | 2 | 1 | 1 | 1 | 1 | 2 | 1 |
| 5220 Non-recurrent taxes | .. | .. | 0 | 0 | 0 | 0 | 0 | 0 | 0 | 0 |
| 5300 Unallocable between 5100 and 5200 | .. | 0 | 1 | 0 | 0 | 0 | 0 | 0 | 0 | 0 |
| **6000 Other taxes** | **..** | **0** | **0** | **0** | **0** | **0** | **0** | **0** | **0** | **0** |
| 6100 Paid solely by business | .. | .. | .. | .. | .. | .. | .. | .. | .. | .. |
| 6200 Other | .. | .. | .. | .. | .. | .. | .. | .. | .. | .. |

.. Not available

*Note:* Year ending 31st December.

The data are on a cash basis.

The figures do not include local tax revenues because data are not available.

Heading 2000: Social security contributions for 2019 and 2020 are estimated.

Heading 5112: The Revenue Recovery Charge, levied on all goods imported into or manufactured in Antigua and Barbuda, is classified under this heading according to the OECD classification described in the Interpretative Guide.

Heading 5121: The environmental tax, levied on specific goods imported into or manufactured in Antigua and Barbuda, is classified under this heading according to the OECD classification described in the Interpretative Guide.

*Source:* Ministry of Finance; Corporate Governance and Social Security Board.

StatLink https://doi.org/10.1787/888934309359

# Table 5.2. **Argentina**

Details of tax revenue / Ingresos tributarios detallados

*Million ARS*

| | 1990 | 2000 | 2007 | 2010 | 2015 | 2016 | 2017 | 2018 | 2019 | 2020 |
|---|---|---|---|---|---|---|---|---|---|---|
| **Total tax revenue** | **10 217** | **61 084** | **236 516** | **483 014** | **1 872 915** | **2 522 854** | **3 202 762** | **4 204 218** | **6 147 006** | **8 081 483** |
| **1000 Taxes on income, profits and capital gains** | **542** | **11 303** | **44 226** | **78 427** | **384 536** | **436 927** | **559 755** | **746 994** | **1 102 982** | **1 470 348** |
| 1100 Of individuals | 141 | 3 937 | 12 777 | 23 980 | 188 218 | 174 483 | 236 284 | 297 200 | 433 621 | 634 425 |
| 1110 On income and profits | 130 | 3 854 | 12 715 | 23 858 | 187 663 | 173 721 | 234 117 | 294 320 | 429 882 | 632 276 |
| 1120 On capital gains | 11 | 82 | 62 | 122 | 555 | 762 | 2 167 | 2 880 | 3 739 | 2 150 |
| 1200 Corporate | 357 | 6 575 | 29 145 | 50 664 | 185 725 | 236 286 | 297 111 | 401 270 | 589 993 | 756 440 |
| 1210 On profits | 357 | 6 575 | 29 145 | 50 664 | 185 725 | 236 286 | 297 111 | 401 270 | 589 993 | 756 440 |
| Corporate income taxes | 198 | 5 956 | 27 837 | 49 012 | 183 207 | 233 028 | 294 546 | 399 210 | 587 272 | 755 545 |
| Tax on assets | 160 | 19 | 9 | 4 | 4 | 12 | 5 | 5 | 5 | 2 |
| Tax on assumed minimum income | 0 | 600 | 1 299 | 1 648 | 2 513 | 3 246 | 2 560 | 2 055 | 2 716 | 893 |
| 1220 On capital gains of corporates | .. | .. | .. | .. | .. | .. | .. | .. | .. | .. |
| 1300 Unallocable between 1100 and 1200 | 43 | 792 | 2 304 | 3 783 | 10 593 | 26 159 | 26 360 | 48 524 | 79 367 | 79 483 |
| Non resident taxpayers | 11 | 792 | 2 304 | 3 783 | 10 593 | 26 159 | 26 360 | 48 524 | 79 367 | 79 483 |
| Other | 33 | 0 | 0 | 0 | 0 | 0 | 0 | 0 | 0 | 0 |
| **2000 Social security contributions** | **2 583** | **9 670** | **36 612** | **102 460** | **415 410** | **556 067** | **733 527** | **914 436** | **1 225 664** | **1 548 052** |
| 2100 Employees | .. | 2 486 | 7 052 | 37 990 | 163 590 | 219 446 | 288 985 | 364 291 | 481 007 | 626 400 |
| 2110 On a payroll basis | .. | 2 486 | 7 052 | 37 990 | 163 590 | 219 446 | 288 985 | 364 291 | 481 007 | 626 400 |
| 2120 On an income tax basis | .. | 0 | 0 | 0 | 0 | 0 | 0 | 0 | 0 | 0 |
| 2200 Employers | .. | 6 069 | 23 939 | 54 713 | 235 610 | 314 628 | 413 212 | 512 615 | 699 601 | 864 329 |
| 2210 On a payroll basis | .. | 6 069 | 23 939 | 54 713 | 235 610 | 314 628 | 413 212 | 512 615 | 699 601 | 864 329 |
| 2220 On an income tax basis | .. | 0 | 0 | 0 | 0 | 0 | 0 | 0 | 0 | 0 |
| 2300 Self-employed or non-employed | 98 | 1 115 | 5 620 | 9 757 | 16 210 | 21 994 | 31 330 | 37 529 | 45 056 | 57 323 |
| 2310 On a payroll basis | 98 | 1 115 | 5 620 | 9 757 | 16 210 | 21 994 | 31 330 | 37 529 | 45 056 | 57 323 |
| 2320 On an income tax basis | 0 | 0 | 0 | 0 | 0 | 0 | 0 | 0 | 0 | 0 |
| 2400 Unallocable between 2100, 2200 and 2300 | 2 485 | 0 | 0 | 0 | 0 | 0 | 0 | 0 | 0 | 0 |
| 2410 On a payroll basis | 2 485 | .. | .. | .. | .. | .. | .. | .. | .. | .. |
| 2420 On an income tax basis | 0 | .. | .. | .. | .. | .. | .. | .. | .. | .. |
| **3000 Taxes on payroll and workforce** | **0** | **0** | **0** | **0** | **0** | **0** | **0** | **0** | **0** | **0** |
| **4000 Taxes on property** | **1 164** | **3 867** | **23 978** | **43 538** | **166 182** | **224 193** | **303 382** | **395 484** | **560 204** | **879 143** |
| 4100 Recurrent taxes on immovable property | 419 | 1 809 | 3 025 | 5 035 | 21 738 | 32 770 | 44 236 | 66 035 | 85 695 | 113 243 |
| 4110 Households | 0 | 0 | 0 | 0 | 0 | 0 | 0 | 0 | 0 | 0 |
| 4120 Others | 419 | 1 809 | 3 025 | 5 035 | 21 738 | 32 770 | 44 236 | 66 035 | 85 695 | 113 243 |
| 4200 Recurrent taxes on net wealth | 246 | 1 084 | 2 557 | 5 248 | 18 538 | 19 976 | 22 786 | 15 296 | 32 383 | 209 929 |
| 4210 Individual | 3 | 1 024 | 2 492 | 5 147 | 18 210 | 19 541 | 22 165 | 14 517 | 31 184 | 207 382 |
| Personal assets | 0 | 1 024 | 2 492 | 5 147 | 18 210 | 19 541 | 22 165 | 14 517 | 31 184 | 207 382 |
| Recurrent taxes on net wealth | 3 | 0 | 0 | 0 | 0 | 0 | 0 | 0 | 0 | 0 |
| 4220 Corporate | 242 | 60 | 65 | 101 | 327 | 435 | 621 | 778 | 1 199 | 2 547 |
| 4300 Estate, inheritance and gift taxes | 0 | 0 | 0 | 0 | 0 | 0 | 0 | 0 | 0 | 0 |
| 4310 Estate and inheritance taxes | .. | .. | .. | .. | .. | .. | .. | .. | .. | .. |
| 4320 Gift taxes | .. | .. | .. | .. | .. | .. | .. | .. | .. | .. |
| 4400 Taxes on financial and capital transactions | 459 | 904 | 18 390 | 33 252 | 125 906 | 171 447 | 236 360 | 314 153 | 442 125 | 555 971 |
| Immovable property transfers | 0 | 54 | 382 | 539 | 1 256 | 2 052 | 4 091 | 5 935 | 5 575 | 4 958 |
| Movable property transfers | 44 | 0 | 0 | 0 | 0 | 0 | 0 | 0 | 0 | 0 |
| Bank accounts' credits and debits | 205 | 0 | 15 065 | 26 885 | 97 480 | 131 669 | 172 838 | 234 300 | 349 559 | 452 459 |
| Stamp taxes | 211 | 850 | 2 942 | 5 829 | 27 170 | 37 726 | 59 431 | 73 918 | 86 991 | 98 554 |
| 4500 Non-recurrent taxes | 40 | 70 | 6 | 3 | 0 | 0 | 0 | 0 | 0 | 0 |
| 4510 On net wealth | 0 | 0 | 0 | 0 | .. | .. | .. | .. | .. | .. |
| 4520 Other non-recurrent taxes | 40 | 70 | 6 | 3 | .. | .. | .. | .. | .. | .. |
| 4600 Other recurrent taxes on property | 0 | 0 | 0 | 0 | 0 | 0 | 0 | 0 | 0 | 0 |
| **5000 Taxes on goods and services** | **5 636** | **34 539** | **128 329** | **253 092** | **889 323** | **1 176 337** | **1 531 220** | **2 119 852** | **3 210 001** | **4 123 803** |
| 5100 Taxes on production, sale, transfer, etc | 5 462 | 34 288 | 128 321 | 252 550 | 881 120 | 1 167 379 | 1 520 300 | 2 112 824 | 3 181 551 | 4 083 236 |
| 5110 General taxes | 2 384 | 25 123 | 86 803 | 167 534 | 671 297 | 901 584 | 1 188 317 | 1 671 105 | 2 318 190 | 2 951 468 |
| 5111 Value added taxes | 1 594 | 19 009 | 62 669 | 116 386 | 433 076 | 583 217 | 765 336 | 1 104 580 | 1 532 597 | 1 905 385 |
| 5112 Sales tax | 0 | 0 | 0 | 0 | 0 | 0 | 0 | 0 | 0 | 0 |
| 5113 Other | 791 | 6 114 | 24 134 | 51 148 | 238 221 | 318 367 | 422 981 | 566 524 | 785 593 | 1 046 083 |
| 5120 Taxes on specific goods and services | 3 077 | 9 166 | 41 517 | 85 016 | 209 822 | 265 795 | 331 983 | 441 719 | 863 362 | 1 131 767 |
| 5121 Excises | 1 866 | 5 850 | 13 164 | 26 208 | 92 349 | 129 790 | 182 818 | 204 999 | 282 964 | 395 867 |
| Alcoholic beverages | 25 | 36 | 95 | 238 | 985 | 1 163 | 1 591 | 2 147 | 2 558 | 4 639 |
| Non alcoholic beverages | 25 | 90 | 312 | 501 | 2 168 | 2 477 | 3 136 | 3 627 | 4 006 | 5 296 |
| Beers | 0 | 50 | 149 | 212 | 1 384 | 1 171 | 2 811 | 4 729 | 1 339 | 3 877 |
| Tobacco products | 425 | 1 875 | 3 881 | 6 884 | 26 152 | 42 183 | 60 249 | 67 264 | 90 857 | 132 703 |
| Liquid fuels and gas | 1 073 | 3 478 | 7 466 | 15 269 | 56 478 | 75 664 | 102 846 | 116 409 | 161 666 | 195 659 |
| Electricity | 72 | 205 | 538 | 591 | 590 | 637 | 1 768 | 2 174 | 7 818 | 7 139 |
| Motor vehicles | 59 | 20 | 0 | 27 | 88 | 265 | 476 | 337 | 443 | 2 634 |
| Other | 189 | 96 | 724 | 2 485 | 4 503 | 6 229 | 9 942 | 8 311 | 14 275 | 43 921 |
| 5122 Profits of fiscal monopolies | 0 | 0 | 0 | 0 | 0 | 0 | 0 | 0 | 0 | 0 |
| 5123 Customs and import duties | 219 | 1 976 | 7 015 | 11 428 | 35 512 | 56 365 | 70 635 | 107 178 | 163 076 | 199 737 |
| Import duties | 166 | 1 938 | 6 859 | 11 183 | 34 822 | 55 305 | 69 259 | 104 991 | 132 405 | 164 888 |
| Import fees | 53 | 38 | 156 | 246 | 691 | 1 060 | 1 376 | 2 187 | 30 671 | 34 848 |
| 5124 Taxes on exports | 724 | 32 | 20 450 | 45 547 | 75 939 | 71 509 | 66 121 | 114 160 | 398 312 | 387 643 |

## Table 5.2. **Argentina** *(cont.)*

Details of tax revenue / Ingresos tributarios detallados

*Million ARS*

| | 1990 | 2000 | 2007 | 2010 | 2015 | 2016 | 2017 | 2018 | 2019 | 2020 |
|---|---|---|---|---|---|---|---|---|---|---|
| 5125 Taxes on investment goods | 0 | 0 | 0 | 0 | 0 | 0 | 0 | 0 | 0 | 0 |
| 5126 Taxes on specific services | 163 | 1 233 | 674 | 1 429 | 4 420 | 5 782 | 7 792 | 9 293 | 9 729 | 10 127 |
| Insurance services | 42 | 194 | 11 | 21 | 88 | 118 | 167 | 198 | 289 | 376 |
| Financial services | 32 | 855 | 1 | 0 | 0 | 0 | 0 | 0 | 0 | 0 |
| Telephone services | 82 | 33 | 417 | 936 | 2 301 | 2 911 | 4 061 | 4 626 | 3 350 | 2 942 |
| Other specific services | 7 | 151 | 246 | 472 | 2 031 | 2 753 | 3 564 | 4 469 | 6 090 | 6 809 |
| 5127 Other taxes on internat. trade and transactions | 98 | 74 | 214 | 404 | 1 601 | 2 349 | 4 616 | 6 089 | 9 281 | 138 394 |
| 5128 Other taxes | 8 | 0 | 0 | 0 | 0 | 0 | 0 | 0 | 0 | 0 |
| 5130 Unallocable between 5110 and 5120 | 0 | 0 | 0 | 0 | 0 | 0 | 0 | 0 | 0 | 0 |
| 5200 Taxes on use of goods and perform activities | 177 | 833 | 1 921 | 3 598 | 17 035 | 23 941 | 35 873 | 41 628 | 57 720 | 72 748 |
| 5210 Recurrent taxes | 177 | 833 | 1 921 | 3 598 | 17 035 | 23 941 | 35 873 | 41 628 | 57 720 | 72 748 |
| 5211 Paid by households: motor vehicles | 177 | 833 | 1 921 | 3 598 | 17 035 | 23 941 | 35 873 | 41 628 | 57 720 | 72 748 |
| 5212 Paid by others: motor vehicles | 0 | 0 | 0 | 0 | 0 | 0 | 0 | 0 | 0 | 0 |
| 5213 Paid in respect of other goods | 0 | 0 | 0 | 0 | 0 | 0 | 0 | 0 | 0 | 0 |
| 5220 Non-recurrent taxes | 0 | 0 | 0 | 0 | 0 | 0 | 0 | 0 | 0 | 0 |
| 5300 Unallocable between 5100 and 5200 | -3 | -583 | -1 912 | -3 056 | -8 831 | -14 983 | -24 953 | -34 600 | -29 270 | -32 182 |
| **6000 Other taxes** | **292** | **1 704** | **3 371** | **5 497** | **17 463** | **129 330** | **74 878** | **27 452** | **48 156** | **60 137** |
| 6100 Paid solely by business | 0 | 354 | 1 063 | 2 093 | 5 624 | 6 873 | 10 544 | 16 052 | 20 635 | 29 169 |
| Simplified system for small taxpayers | .. | 354 | 1 063 | 2 093 | 5 624 | 6 873 | 10 544 | 16 052 | 20 635 | 29 169 |
| 6200 Other | 292 | 1 351 | 2 308 | 3 404 | 11 839 | 122 457 | 64 334 | 11 399 | 27 521 | 30 968 |
| Tax debt payments | 135 | 24 | 38 | 293 | 1 306 | 110 721 | 46 131 | -8 646 | -1 070 | 6 215 |
| Special payments | 79 | 6 | 0 | 0 | 0 | 0 | 0 | 0 | 0 | 0 |
| Other national level | 0 | 12 | 0 | 0 | 0 | 0 | 0 | 0 | 0 | 0 |
| Other provincial level | 78 | 1 309 | 2 269 | 3 110 | 10 533 | 11 736 | 18 202 | 20 045 | 28 591 | 24 753 |

.. Not available

*Note:* Year ending 31st December.

The data are on a cash basis.

The figures exclude local government tax revenues as the data are not available (but include provincial revenues).

Heading 2000: The figures may be under-estimated as they exclude certain types of social security contributions for which data are not readily available.

Heading 5212: In ECLAC data, property tax on motor vehicles is classified in category 4000.

Heading 5300: The figures are negative as they represent general reimbursements of exports and specific taxes on goods and services.

Heading 6200: The tax debt payments from 2016 include revenue following the implementation of a new voluntary disclosure regime in July 2016 (Law 27260).

*Source:* Subsecretaría de Ingresos Públicos, Dirección Nacional de Investigaciones y Análisis Fiscal, Ministerio de Hacienda (Undersecretary of Public Revenue, National Direction of Research and Fiscal Analysis, Ministry of Finance).

StatLink https://doi.org/10.1787/888934309378

## Table 5.3. **Bahamas**

Details of tax revenue / Ingresos tributarios detallados

*Million BSD*

| | 1990 | 2000 | 2007 | 2010 | 2015 | 2016 | 2017 | 2018 | 2019 | 2020 |
|---|---|---|---|---|---|---|---|---|---|---|
| **Total tax revenue** | **505** | **965** | **1 360** | **1 277** | **1 761** | **1 937** | **2 106** | **2 115** | **2 486** | **2 104** |
| **1000 Taxes on income, profits and capital gains** | **0** | **0** | **0** | **0** | **0** | **0** | **0** | **0** | **0** | **0** |
| 1100 Of individuals | 0 | 0 | 0 | 0 | 0 | 0 | 0 | 0 | 0 | 0 |
| 1110 On income and profits | .. | .. | .. | .. | .. | .. | .. | .. | .. | .. |
| 1120 On capital gains | .. | .. | .. | .. | .. | .. | .. | .. | .. | .. |
| 1200 Corporate | 0 | 0 | 0 | 0 | 0 | 0 | 0 | 0 | 0 | 0 |
| 1210 On profits | .. | .. | .. | .. | .. | .. | .. | .. | .. | .. |
| 1220 On capital gains of corporates | .. | .. | .. | .. | .. | .. | .. | .. | .. | .. |
| 1300 Unallocable between 1100 and 1200 | 0 | 0 | 0 | 0 | 0 | 0 | 0 | 0 | 0 | 0 |
| **2000 Social security contributions** | **66** | **115** | **155** | **167** | **260** | **258** | **265** | **279** | **287** | **246** |
| 2100 Employees | .. | .. | .. | 60 | 98 | .. | .. | .. | .. | .. |
| 2110 On a payroll basis | .. | .. | .. | .. | .. | .. | .. | .. | .. | .. |
| 2120 On an income tax basis | .. | .. | .. | .. | .. | .. | .. | .. | .. | .. |
| 2200 Employers | .. | .. | .. | 104 | 157 | .. | .. | .. | .. | .. |
| 2210 On a payroll basis | .. | .. | .. | .. | .. | .. | .. | .. | .. | .. |
| 2220 On an income tax basis | .. | .. | .. | .. | .. | .. | .. | .. | .. | .. |
| 2300 Self-employed or non-employed | .. | .. | .. | 3 | 6 | .. | .. | .. | .. | .. |
| 2310 On a payroll basis | .. | .. | .. | .. | .. | .. | .. | .. | .. | .. |
| 2320 On an income tax basis | .. | .. | .. | .. | .. | .. | .. | .. | .. | .. |
| 2400 Unallocable between 2100, 2200 and 2300 | 66 | 115 | 155 | 0 | -1 | 258 | 265 | 279 | 287 | 246 |
| 2410 On a payroll basis | .. | .. | .. | .. | .. | .. | .. | .. | .. | .. |
| 2420 On an income tax basis | .. | .. | .. | .. | .. | .. | .. | .. | .. | .. |
| **3000 Taxes on payroll and workforce** | **0** | **0** | **0** | **0** | **0** | **0** | **0** | **0** | **0** | **0** |
| **4000 Taxes on property** | **56** | **208** | **450** | **269** | **298** | **204** | **233** | **237** | **345** | **173** |
| 4100 Recurrent taxes on immovable property | 19 | 32 | 79 | 92 | 107 | 104 | 121 | 124 | 109 | 99 |
| 4110 Households | 0 | 0 | 0 | 0 | 0 | 0 | 0 | 0 | 0 | 0 |
| 4120 Others | 19 | 32 | 79 | 92 | 107 | 104 | 121 | 124 | 109 | 99 |
| 4200 Recurrent taxes on net wealth | 0 | 0 | 0 | 0 | 0 | 0 | 0 | 0 | 0 | 0 |
| 4210 Individual | .. | .. | .. | .. | .. | .. | .. | .. | .. | .. |
| 4220 Corporate | .. | .. | .. | .. | .. | .. | .. | .. | .. | .. |
| 4300 Estate, inheritance and gift taxes | 0 | 0 | 0 | 0 | 0 | 0 | 0 | 0 | 0 | 0 |
| 4310 Estate and inheritance taxes | .. | .. | .. | .. | .. | .. | .. | .. | .. | .. |
| 4320 Gift taxes | .. | .. | .. | .. | .. | .. | .. | .. | .. | .. |
| 4400 Taxes on financial and capital transactions | 37 | 176 | 371 | 177 | 191 | 100 | 112 | 114 | 235 | 74 |
| Stamp Tax from Imports | 0 | 102 | 143 | 15 | 0 | 0 | 0 | 0 | 0 | 0 |
| Stamp Tax from Exports | 0 | 0 | 0 | 0 | 0 | 0 | 0 | 0 | 0 | 0 |
| All Other Stamp Tax | 37 | 74 | 228 | 162 | 191 | 100 | 112 | 114 | 235 | 74 |
| 4500 Non-recurrent taxes | 0 | 0 | 0 | 0 | 0 | 0 | 0 | 0 | 0 | 0 |
| 4510 On net wealth | .. | .. | .. | .. | .. | .. | .. | .. | .. | .. |
| 4520 Other non-recurrent taxes | .. | .. | .. | .. | .. | .. | .. | .. | .. | .. |
| 4600 Other recurrent taxes on property | 0 | 0 | 0 | 0 | 0 | 0 | 0 | 0 | 0 | 0 |
| **5000 Taxes on goods and services** | **386** | **620** | **737** | **780** | **1 203** | **1 475** | **1 608** | **1 598** | **1 854** | **1 686** |
| 5100 Taxes on production, sale, transfer, etc | 354 | 552 | 638 | 657 | 993 | 1 297 | 1 386 | 1 407 | 1 623 | 1 533 |
| 5110 General taxes | 0 | 0 | 0 | 0 | 219 | 628 | 638 | 681 | 897 | 880 |
| 5111 Value added taxes | 0 | 0 | 0 | 0 | 219 | 628 | 638 | 681 | 897 | 880 |
| 5112 Sales tax | .. | .. | .. | .. | 0 | 0 | 0 | 0 | 0 | 0 |
| 5113 Other | .. | .. | .. | .. | 0 | 0 | 0 | 0 | 0 | 0 |
| 5120 Taxes on specific goods and services | 354 | 552 | 638 | 657 | 775 | 669 | 747 | 726 | 727 | 654 |
| 5121 Excises | 0 | 0 | 0 | 188 | 262 | 231 | 289 | 257 | 242 | 208 |
| Fuel surcharges | .. | .. | .. | .. | .. | 1 | 1 | 1 | 1 | 1 |
| Other excises | .. | .. | .. | .. | .. | 230 | 287 | 255 | 241 | 207 |
| 5122 Profits of fiscal monopolies | 0 | 0 | 0 | 0 | 0 | 0 | 0 | 0 | 0 | 0 |
| 5123 Customs and import duties | 289 | 435 | 507 | 348 | 307 | 263 | 286 | 270 | 284 | 227 |
| 5124 Taxes on exports | 6 | 13 | 14 | 14 | 9 | 13 | 9 | 18 | 13 | 53 |
| 5125 Taxes on investment goods | 0 | 0 | 0 | 0 | 0 | 0 | 0 | 0 | 0 | 0 |
| 5126 Taxes on specific services | 59 | 104 | 117 | 106 | 197 | 162 | 163 | 180 | 187 | 165 |
| Departure tax | 27 | 64 | 77 | 70 | 147 | 135 | 135 | 143 | 147 | 125 |
| Gaming tax | 27 | 20 | 14 | 10 | 25 | 26 | 27 | 37 | 40 | 40 |
| Hotel occupancy tax | 5 | 20 | 26 | 25 | 25 | 1 | 1 | 0 | 0 | 0 |
| 5127 Other taxes on internat. trade and transactions | 0 | 0 | 0 | 0 | 0 | 0 | 0 | 0 | 0 | 0 |
| 5128 Other taxes | 0 | 0 | 0 | 0 | 0 | 0 | 0 | 0 | 0 | 0 |
| 5130 Unallocable between 5110 and 5120 | 0 | 0 | 0 | 0 | 0 | 0 | 0 | 0 | 0 | 0 |
| 5200 Taxes on use of goods and perform activities | 32 | 69 | 99 | 123 | 209 | 178 | 222 | 192 | 231 | 152 |
| 5210 Recurrent taxes | 32 | 69 | 99 | 123 | 209 | 178 | 222 | 192 | 231 | 152 |
| Motor vehicle tax | 10 | 14 | 20 | 21 | 29 | 29 | 30 | 37 | 35 | 31 |
| 5211 Paid by households: motor vehicles | .. | .. | .. | .. | .. | .. | .. | .. | .. | .. |
| 5212 Paid by others: motor vehicles | .. | .. | .. | .. | .. | .. | .. | .. | .. | .. |

## Table 5.3. **Bahamas** *(cont.)*

Details of tax revenue / Ingresos tributarios detallados

*Million BSD*

| | 1990 | 2000 | 2007 | 2010 | 2015 | 2016 | 2017 | 2018 | 2019 | 2020 |
|---|---|---|---|---|---|---|---|---|---|---|
| 5213 Paid in respect of other goods | 22 | 55 | 78 | 102 | 180 | 149 | 193 | 155 | 195 | 122 |
| Company fees and registration | 0 | 5 | 5 | 5 | 5 | 0 | 0 | 0 | 0 | 0 |
| International business companies | 0 | 17 | 20 | 19 | 16 | 0 | 0 | 0 | 0 | 0 |
| Others | 22 | 33 | 54 | 78 | 159 | 149 | 193 | 155 | 195 | 122 |
| 5220 Non-recurrent taxes | 0 | 0 | 0 | 0 | 0 | 0 | 0 | 0 | 0 | 0 |
| 5300 Unallocable between 5100 and 5200 | 0 | 0 | 0 | 0 | 0 | 0 | 0 | 0 | 0 | 0 |
| **6000 Other taxes** | **-4** | **21** | **17** | **60** | **0** | **0** | **0** | **0** | **0** | **0** |
| 6100 Paid solely by business | 0 | 0 | 0 | 0 | 0 | 0 | .. | .. | .. | .. |
| 6200 Other | -4 | 21 | 17 | 60 | 0 | 0 | .. | .. | .. | .. |
| Incentive acts and other refunds | -8 | 14 | -5 | 11 | 0 | .. | .. | .. | .. | .. |
| Other taxes | 4 | 7 | 22 | 49 | 0 | .. | .. | .. | .. | .. |

.. Not available

*Note:* Fiscal year ending on 30th June. For example, the data for 2020 represent July 2019 to June 2020.
The data are on a cash basis.
The figures exclude local government tax revenues as the data are not available.
Heading 2000: The data are estimated for 2019 and 2020.
Heading 2400: This heading includes refunds of social security contributions as reported by the National Insurance Board (NIB) before 2016. The figures refer to the aggregate social security contributions between 2016 and 2020.
Heading 4400: This heading includes all stamp taxes.
Heading 5111: A value added tax was enforced on 1st January 2015.

*Source:* The Central Bank of The Bahamas; Ministry of Finance of The Bahamas; National Insurance Board of The Bahamas; Centro Interamericano de Administraciones Tributarias (Inter-American Center of Tax Administrations).

StatLink https://doi.org/10.1787/888934309397

## Table 5.4. **Barbados**

Details of tax revenue / Ingresos tributarios detallados

*Million BBD*

| | 1990 | 2000 | 2007 | 2010 | 2015 | 2016 | 2017 | 2018 | 2019 | 2020 |
|---|---|---|---|---|---|---|---|---|---|---|
| **Total tax revenue** | **1 026** | **1 892** | **2 824** | **2 736** | **2 893** | **3 027** | **3 280** | **3 434** | **3 442** | **2 982** |
| **1000 Taxes on income, profits and capital gains** | **250** | **599** | **947** | **766** | **714** | **802** | **783** | **921** | **823** | **976** |
| 1100 Of individuals | 140 | 293 | 335 | 395 | 433 | 492 | 463 | 482 | 455 | 308 |
| 1110 On income and profits | 140 | 293 | 335 | 395 | 433 | 492 | 463 | 482 | 455 | 308 |
| Personal income tax | 140 | 293 | 335 | 395 | 397 | 488 | 463 | 482 | 455 | 308 |
| Consolidation tax | 0 | 0 | 0 | 0 | 36 | 3 | 0 | 0 | 0 | 0 |
| 1120 On capital gains | .. | .. | .. | .. | .. | .. | .. | .. | .. | .. |
| 1200 Corporate | 95 | 269 | 521 | 294 | 215 | 248 | 275 | 355 | 309 | 613 |
| 1210 On profits | 95 | 269 | 521 | 294 | 215 | 248 | 275 | 355 | 309 | 613 |
| 1220 On capital gains of corporates | .. | .. | .. | .. | .. | .. | .. | .. | .. | .. |
| 1300 Unallocable between 1100 and 1200 | 15 | 37 | 91 | 76 | 66 | 63 | 45 | 83 | 59 | 55 |
| **2000 Social security contributions** | **134** | **295** | **487** | **565** | **627** | **532** | **624** | **621** | **671** | **595** |
| 2100 Employees | .. | .. | .. | .. | .. | .. | .. | .. | .. | .. |
| 2110 On a payroll basis | .. | .. | .. | .. | .. | .. | .. | .. | .. | .. |
| 2120 On an income tax basis | .. | .. | .. | .. | .. | .. | .. | .. | .. | .. |
| 2200 Employers | .. | .. | .. | .. | .. | .. | .. | .. | .. | .. |
| 2210 On a payroll basis | .. | .. | .. | .. | .. | .. | .. | .. | .. | .. |
| 2220 On an income tax basis | .. | .. | .. | .. | .. | .. | .. | .. | .. | .. |
| 2300 Self-employed or non-employed | .. | .. | .. | .. | .. | .. | .. | .. | .. | .. |
| 2310 On a payroll basis | .. | .. | .. | .. | .. | .. | .. | .. | .. | .. |
| 2320 On an income tax basis | .. | .. | .. | .. | .. | .. | .. | .. | .. | .. |
| 2400 Unallocable between 2100, 2200 and 2300 | 134 | 295 | 487 | 565 | 627 | 532 | 624 | 621 | 671 | 595 |
| 2410 On a payroll basis | .. | .. | .. | .. | .. | .. | .. | .. | .. | .. |
| 2420 On an income tax basis | .. | .. | .. | .. | .. | .. | .. | .. | .. | .. |
| **3000 Taxes on payroll and workforce** | **0** | **0** | **0** | **0** | **0** | **0** | **0** | **0** | **0** | **0** |
| **4000 Taxes on property** | **147** | **108** | **125** | **130** | **143** | **145** | **148** | **172** | **226** | **189** |
| 4100 Recurrent taxes on immovable property | 46 | 95 | 103 | 118 | 133 | 135 | 138 | 161 | 215 | 182 |
| Property tax | 46 | 95 | 103 | 118 | 133 | 135 | 138 | 161 | 215 | 182 |
| Municipal solid waste tax | 0 | 0 | 0 | 0 | 0 | 0 | 0 | 0 | 0 | 0 |
| 4110 Households | .. | .. | .. | .. | .. | .. | .. | .. | .. | .. |
| 4120 Others | .. | .. | .. | .. | .. | .. | .. | .. | .. | .. |
| 4200 Recurrent taxes on net wealth | 0 | 0 | 0 | 0 | 0 | 0 | 0 | 0 | 0 | 0 |
| 4210 Individual | .. | .. | .. | .. | .. | .. | .. | .. | .. | .. |
| 4220 Corporate | .. | .. | .. | .. | .. | .. | .. | .. | .. | .. |
| 4300 Estate, inheritance and gift taxes | 0 | 0 | 0 | 0 | 0 | 0 | 0 | 0 | 0 | 0 |
| 4310 Estate and inheritance taxes | .. | .. | .. | .. | .. | .. | .. | .. | .. | .. |
| 4320 Gift taxes | .. | .. | .. | .. | .. | .. | .. | .. | .. | .. |
| 4400 Taxes on financial and capital transactions | 101 | 13 | 22 | 12 | 10 | 9 | 11 | 11 | 11 | 8 |
| Stamp duties | 101 | 13 | 22 | 12 | 10 | 9 | 11 | 11 | 11 | 8 |
| 4500 Non-recurrent taxes | 0 | 0 | 0 | 0 | 0 | 0 | 0 | 0 | 0 | 0 |
| 4510 On net wealth | .. | .. | .. | .. | .. | .. | .. | .. | .. | .. |
| 4520 Other non-recurrent taxes | .. | .. | .. | .. | .. | .. | .. | .. | .. | .. |
| 4600 Other recurrent taxes on property | 0 | 0 | 0 | 0 | 0 | 0 | 0 | 0 | 0 | 0 |
| **5000 Taxes on goods and services** | **495** | **889** | **1 265** | **1 276** | **1 410** | **1 547** | **1 726** | **1 719** | **1 723** | **1 223** |
| 5100 Taxes on production, sale, transfer, etc | 424 | 788 | 1 151 | 1 105 | 1 291 | 1 423 | 1 610 | 1 599 | 1 607 | 1 171 |
| 5110 General taxes | 197 | 492 | 790 | 768 | 861 | 920 | 1 039 | 990 | 967 | 706 |
| 5111 Value added taxes | 0 | 492 | 790 | 768 | 861 | 890 | 887 | 941 | 967 | 706 |
| 5112 Sales tax | 197 | 0 | 0 | 0 | 0 | 29 | 152 | 49 | 0 | 0 |
| Social responsibility levy | 0 | 0 | .. | .. | .. | 29 | 152 | 49 | 0 | .. |
| Consumption tax | 197 | 0 | .. | .. | .. | 0 | 0 | 0 | 0 | .. |
| 5113 Other | 0 | 0 | 0 | 0 | 0 | 0 | 0 | 0 | 0 | 0 |
| 5120 Taxes on specific goods and services | 227 | 296 | 362 | 337 | 430 | 503 | 570 | 608 | 640 | 465 |
| 5121 Excises | 91 | 175 | 164 | 146 | 169 | 226 | 303 | 271 | 251 | 154 |
| Excises | 0 | 160 | 164 | 146 | 169 | 226 | 303 | 271 | 251 | 154 |
| Levies | 91 | 15 | 0 | 0 | 0 | 0 | 0 | 0 | 0 | 0 |
| 5122 Profits of fiscal monopolies | 0 | 0 | 0 | 0 | 0 | 0 | 0 | 0 | 0 | 0 |
| 5123 Customs and import duties | 118 | 121 | 197 | 191 | 232 | 245 | 219 | 282 | 314 | 256 |
| Import duties | 118 | 121 | 197 | 191 | 232 | 245 | 219 | 214 | 232 | 192 |
| Fuel tax | 0 | 0 | 0 | 0 | 0 | 0 | 0 | 69 | 82 | 64 |
| 5124 Taxes on exports | 0 | 0 | 0 | 0 | 0 | 0 | 0 | 0 | 0 | 0 |
| 5125 Taxes on investment goods | 0 | 0 | 0 | 0 | 0 | 0 | 0 | 0 | 0 | 0 |
| 5126 Taxes on specific services | 17 | 1 | 0 | 0 | 29 | 33 | 49 | 55 | 76 | 55 |
| Hotel and restaurant tax | 17 | 1 | .. | .. | 0 | 0 | 0 | 0 | 0 | 0 |
| Banks and other asset tax | 0 | 0 | .. | .. | 29 | 33 | 49 | 45 | 47 | 46 |
| Room rate levy | 0 | 0 | .. | .. | 0 | 0 | 0 | 10 | 28 | 10 |
| 5127 Other taxes on internat. trade and transactions | 0 | 0 | 0 | 0 | 0 | 0 | 0 | 0 | 0 | 0 |
| 5128 Other taxes | 0 | 0 | 0 | 0 | 0 | 0 | 0 | 0 | 0 | 0 |
| 5130 Unallocable between 5110 and 5120 | 0 | 0 | 0 | 0 | 0 | 0 | 0 | 0 | 0 | 0 |
| 5200 Taxes on use of goods and perform activities | 71 | 101 | 114 | 171 | 119 | 124 | 116 | 121 | 115 | 52 |
| 5210 Recurrent taxes | 71 | 101 | 114 | 171 | 119 | 124 | 116 | 121 | 115 | 52 |

## Table 5.4. **Barbados** *(cont.)*

Details of tax revenue / Ingresos tributarios detallados

*Million BBD*

| | 1990 | 2000 | 2007 | 2010 | 2015 | 2016 | 2017 | 2018 | 2019 | 2020 |
|---|---|---|---|---|---|---|---|---|---|---|
| 5211 Paid by households: motor vehicles | 0 | 0 | 0 | 0 | 0 | 0 | 0 | 0 | 0 | 0 |
| 5212 Paid by others: motor vehicles | 0 | 0 | 0 | 0 | 0 | 0 | 0 | 0 | 0 | 0 |
| 5213 Paid in respect of other goods | 71 | 101 | 114 | 171 | 119 | 124 | 116 | 121 | 115 | 52 |
| 5220 Non-recurrent taxes | 0 | 0 | 0 | 0 | 0 | 0 | 0 | 0 | 0 | 0 |
| 5300 Unallocable between 5100 and 5200 | 0 | 0 | 0 | 0 | 0 | 0 | 0 | 0 | 0 | 0 |
| **6000 Other taxes** | **0** | **0** | **0** | **0** | **0** | **0** | **0** | **0** | **0** | **0** |
| 6100 Paid solely by business | .. | .. | .. | .. | .. | .. | .. | .. | .. | .. |
| 6200 Other | .. | .. | .. | .. | .. | .. | .. | .. | .. | .. |

.. Not available

*Note:* Year ending 31st March. For example, the data for 2020 represent April 2020 to March 2021.

The data are on a cash basis, except for social security contributions which are on an accrual basis.

The figures exclude local government tax revenues as the data are not available.

Heading 1300: This heading includes withholding taxes levied on both individuals and corporate entities.

Heading 2000: Social security contributions refer to contribution income of National Insurance Scheme.

Heading 5213: This heading includes miscellaneous indirect taxes levied on a recurrent basis such as revenues from various licences.

*Source:* The Central Bank of Barbados; National Insurance Board of Barbados.

StatLink https://doi.org/10.1787/888934309416

## Table 5.5. **Belize / Belice**

Details of tax revenue / Ingresos tributarios detallados

*Million BZD*

| | 1990 | 2000 | 2007 | 2010 | 2015 | 2016 | 2017 | 2018 | 2019 | 2020 |
|---|---|---|---|---|---|---|---|---|---|---|
| **Total tax revenue** | **178** | **318** | **652** | **740** | **947** | **1 005** | **1 054** | **1 129** | **1 153** | **890** |
| **1000 Taxes on income, profits and capital gains** | **37** | **76** | **180** | **248** | **254** | **261** | **269** | **286** | **291** | **217** |
| 1100 Of individuals | 21 | 19 | 45 | 52 | 82 | 88 | 93 | 101 | 105 | 87 |
| 1110 On income and profits | 21 | 19 | 45 | 52 | 82 | 88 | 93 | 101 | 105 | 87 |
| Income tax (PAYE) | 20 | 19 | 45 | 52 | 82 | 88 | 93 | 101 | 105 | 87 |
| Income tax on individuals | 1 | 0 | 0 | 0 | 0 | 0 | 0 | 0 | 0 | 0 |
| 1120 On capital gains | .. | .. | .. | .. | .. | .. | .. | .. | .. | .. |
| 1200 Corporate | 12 | 51 | 127 | 189 | 159 | 162 | 166 | 173 | 174 | 121 |
| Income tax (companies) | 12 | 1 | 11 | 51 | 1 | 0 | 0 | 3 | 3 | 1 |
| Income tax (business tax) | 0 | 51 | 115 | 138 | 158 | 162 | 166 | 170 | 171 | 119 |
| Income tax (supplemental petroleum tax) | 0 | 0 | 0 | 0 | 0 | 0 | 0 | 0 | 0 | 0 |
| 1210 On profits | .. | .. | .. | .. | .. | .. | .. | .. | .. | .. |
| 1220 On capital gains of corporates | .. | .. | .. | .. | .. | .. | .. | .. | .. | .. |
| 1300 Unallocable between 1100 and 1200 | 4 | 6 | 9 | 7 | 13 | 11 | 10 | 12 | 12 | 10 |
| Income tax (arrears) | 4 | 3 | 5 | 1 | 2 | 2 | 2 | 3 | 2 | 2 |
| Income tax (withholding) | 0 | 3 | 4 | 6 | 11 | 9 | 8 | 10 | 10 | 8 |
| **2000 Social security contributions** | **10** | **18** | **53** | **60** | **77** | **80** | **83** | **87** | **100** | **110** |
| 2100 Employees | .. | .. | .. | .. | .. | .. | .. | .. | .. | .. |
| 2110 On a payroll basis | .. | .. | .. | .. | .. | .. | .. | .. | .. | .. |
| 2120 On an income tax basis | .. | .. | .. | .. | .. | .. | .. | .. | .. | .. |
| 2200 Employers | .. | .. | .. | .. | .. | .. | .. | .. | .. | .. |
| 2210 On a payroll basis | .. | .. | .. | .. | .. | .. | .. | .. | .. | .. |
| 2220 On an income tax basis | .. | .. | .. | .. | .. | .. | .. | .. | .. | .. |
| 2300 Self-employed or non-employed | .. | .. | .. | .. | .. | .. | .. | .. | .. | .. |
| 2310 On a payroll basis | .. | .. | .. | .. | .. | .. | .. | .. | .. | .. |
| 2320 On an income tax basis | .. | .. | .. | .. | .. | .. | .. | .. | .. | .. |
| 2400 Unallocable between 2100, 2200 and 2300 | 10 | 18 | 53 | 60 | 77 | 80 | 83 | 87 | 100 | 110 |
| 2410 On a payroll basis | .. | .. | .. | .. | .. | .. | .. | .. | .. | .. |
| 2420 On an income tax basis | .. | .. | .. | .. | .. | .. | .. | .. | .. | .. |
| **3000 Taxes on payroll and workforce** | **0** | **0** | **0** | **0** | **0** | **0** | **0** | **0** | **0** | **0** |
| **4000 Taxes on property** | **34** | **13** | **31** | **23** | **35** | **31** | **32** | **49** | **39** | **31** |
| 4100 Recurrent taxes on immovable property | 1 | 2 | 7 | 7 | 5 | 7 | 6 | 6 | 7 | 6 |
| 4110 Households | 1 | 2 | 7 | 7 | 5 | 7 | 6 | 6 | 7 | 6 |
| 4120 Others | 0 | 0 | 0 | 0 | 0 | 0 | 0 | 0 | 0 | 0 |
| 4200 Recurrent taxes on net wealth | 0 | 0 | 0 | 0 | 0 | 0 | 0 | 0 | 0 | 0 |
| 4210 Individual | .. | .. | .. | .. | .. | .. | .. | .. | .. | .. |
| 4220 Corporate | .. | .. | .. | .. | .. | .. | .. | .. | .. | .. |
| 4300 Estate, inheritance and gift taxes | 0 | 0 | 0 | 0 | 0 | 0 | 0 | 0 | 0 | 0 |
| 4310 Estate and inheritance taxes | .. | 0 | 0 | 0 | 0 | 0 | 0 | 0 | 0 | 0 |
| 4320 Gift taxes | .. | 0 | 0 | 0 | 0 | 0 | 0 | 0 | 0 | 0 |
| 4400 Taxes on financial and capital transactions | 33 | 11 | 24 | 16 | 29 | 25 | 26 | 44 | 32 | 25 |
| Stamp duties on customs | 28 | 0 | 0 | 0 | 0 | 0 | 0 | 0 | 0 | 0 |
| Stamp duties (other departments) | 5 | 11 | 24 | 16 | 29 | 25 | 26 | 44 | 14 | 3 |
| Stamp duties (land transactions) | 0 | 0 | 0 | 0 | 0 | 0 | 0 | 0 | 18 | 22 |
| 4500 Non-recurrent taxes | 0 | 0 | 0 | 0 | 0 | 0 | 0 | 0 | 0 | 0 |
| 4510 On net wealth | .. | .. | .. | .. | .. | .. | .. | .. | .. | .. |
| 4520 Other non-recurrent taxes | .. | .. | .. | .. | .. | .. | .. | .. | .. | .. |
| 4600 Other recurrent taxes on property | 0 | 0 | 0 | 0 | 0 | 0 | 0 | 0 | 0 | 0 |
| **5000 Taxes on goods and services** | **97** | **211** | **389** | **409** | **580** | **633** | **670** | **707** | **723** | **532** |
| 5100 Taxes on production, sale, transfer, etc. | 94 | 207 | 380 | 400 | 571 | 630 | 662 | 696 | 712 | 526 |
| 5110 General taxes | 0 | 82 | 175 | 199 | 275 | 292 | 292 | 317 | 323 | 232 |
| 5111 Value added taxes | 0 | 0 | 174 | 199 | 275 | 292 | 292 | 317 | 323 | 232 |
| 5112 Sales tax | .. | 82 | 0 | 0 | 0 | 0 | 0 | 0 | 0 | 0 |
| 5113 Other | .. | 0 | 0 | 0 | 0 | 0 | 0 | 0 | 0 | 0 |
| 5120 Taxes on specific goods and services | 94 | 125 | 205 | 200 | 296 | 338 | 369 | 379 | 389 | 294 |
| 5121 Excises | 35 | 47 | 72 | 31 | 39 | 159 | 187 | 193 | 194 | 150 |
| Revenue replacement duty | 18 | 39 | 49 | 7 | 15 | 1 | 1 | 1 | 1 | 1 |
| Excise duties | 17 | 8 | 22 | 22 | 23 | 157 | 186 | 191 | 192 | 145 |
| Excise on locally refined petroleum products | 0 | 0 | 0 | 0 | 1 | 0 | 0 | 1 | 0 | 4 |
| Excise on locally extracted crude oil | 0 | 0 | 0 | 1 | 0 | 1 | 1 | 1 | 1 | 0 |
| 5122 Profits of fiscal monopolies | 0 | 0 | 0 | 0 | 0 | 0 | 0 | 0 | 0 | 0 |
| 5123 Customs and import duties | 50 | 64 | 113 | 144 | 221 | 154 | 139 | 139 | 137 | 100 |
| Import duties | 50 | 64 | 92 | 123 | 190 | 123 | 98 | 98 | 95 | 68 |
| Environmental tax | 0 | 0 | 21 | 21 | 31 | 31 | 40 | 41 | 42 | 32 |
| Imports into EPZs | 0 | 0 | 0 | 0 | 0 | 0 | 0 | 0 | 0 | 0 |
| 5124 Taxes on exports | 0 | 0 | 0 | 0 | 0 | 0 | 0 | 0 | 0 | 3 |
| 5125 Taxes on investment goods | 0 | 0 | 0 | 0 | 0 | 0 | 0 | 0 | 0 | 0 |
| 5126 Taxes on specific services | 0 | 0 | 0 | 0 | 0 | 0 | 0 | 0 | 0 | 0 |

## Table 5.5. **Belize / Belice** *(cont.)*

Details of tax revenue / Ingresos tributarios detallados

*Million BZD*

| | 1990 | 2000 | 2007 | 2010 | 2015 | 2016 | 2017 | 2018 | 2019 | 2020 |
|---|---|---|---|---|---|---|---|---|---|---|
| 5127 Other taxes on internat. trade and transactions | 8 | 14 | 21 | 25 | 35 | 24 | 43 | 47 | 59 | 41 |
| Goods in transit - administration charge | 3 | 1 | 1 | 1 | 1 | 1 | 1 | 1 | 1 | 1 |
| Goods in transit - social fee | 0 | 5 | 6 | 8 | 11 | 10 | 17 | 23 | 22 | 17 |
| Taxes on foreign currency transactions | 6 | 8 | 14 | 16 | 23 | 13 | 25 | 23 | 35 | 23 |
| 5128 Other taxes | 0 | 0 | 0 | 0 | 0 | 0 | 0 | 0 | 0 | 0 |
| 5130 Unallocable between 5110 and 5120 | 0 | 0 | 0 | 0 | 0 | 0 | 0 | 0 | 0 | 0 |
| 5200 Taxes on use of goods and perform activities | 3 | 4 | 8 | 9 | 9 | 3 | 9 | 11 | 11 | 6 |
| 5210 Recurrent taxes | 3 | 4 | 8 | 9 | 9 | 3 | 9 | 11 | 11 | 6 |
| 5211 Paid by households: motor vehicles | 2 | 3 | 6 | 3 | 4 | 0 | 5 | 5 | 5 | 5 |
| 5212 Paid by others: motor vehicles | 0 | 0 | 0 | 0 | 0 | 0 | 0 | 0 | 0 | 0 |
| 5213 Paid in respect of other goods | 1 | 1 | 3 | 6 | 5 | 3 | 4 | 6 | 5 | 2 |
| 5220 Non-recurrent taxes | 0 | 0 | 0 | 0 | 0 | 0 | 0 | 0 | 0 | 0 |
| 5300 Unallocable between 5100 and 5200 | 0 | 0 | 0 | 0 | 0 | 0 | 0 | 0 | 0 | 0 |
| **6000 Other taxes** | **0** | **0** | **0** | **0** | **0** | **0** | **0** | **0** | **0** | **0** |
| 6100 Paid solely by business | .. | .. | .. | .. | .. | .. | .. | .. | .. | .. |
| 6200 Other | .. | .. | .. | .. | .. | .. | .. | .. | .. | .. |

.. Not available

*Note:* Year ending 31st March. For example, the data for 2020 represent April 2020 to March 2021.

The data are on a cash basis.

The data for 2020 represent the revised estimates for the 2020/21 fiscal year reported in the Approved Estimates of Revenue and Expenditure for Fiscal Year 2021/2022.

Heading 2000: Social security contributions refer to total contributions to the Social Security Fund excluding government contributions to the National Health Insurance (NHI) fund. The government contributions are government subsidies to the social security system and hence are not considered as tax revenues according to the OECD classification described in the Interpretative Guide.

Heading 4400: This heading includes all stamp duties.

*Source:* Ministry of Finance of Belize; Social Security Board Belize.

StatLink https://doi.org/10.1787/888934309435

## Table 5.6. **Bolivia**

Details of tax revenue / Ingresos tributarios detallados

*Million BOB*

| | 1990 | 2000 | 2007 | 2010 | 2015 | 2016 | 2017 | 2018 | 2019 | 2020 |
|---|---|---|---|---|---|---|---|---|---|---|
| **Total tax revenue** | **1 005** | **9 151** | **20 423** | **31 549** | **67 264** | **65 492** | **67 072** | **69 535** | **69 785** | **56 486** |
| **1000 Taxes on income, profits and capital gains** | **68** | **1 209** | **3 433** | **6 294** | **12 809** | **10 876** | **10 152** | **10 591** | **11 356** | **7 402** |
| 1100 Of individuals | 68 | 214 | 217 | 263 | 508 | 496 | 502 | 525 | 518 | 470 |
| 1110 On income and profits | 68 | 214 | 217 | 263 | 508 | 496 | 502 | 525 | 518 | 470 |
| Value added supplementary scheme | 62 | 161 | 195 | 237 | 461 | 442 | 441 | 475 | 464 | 426 |
| Fiscal notes on value added supplementary scheme | 6 | 52 | 23 | 26 | 47 | 55 | 61 | 50 | 53 | 44 |
| 1120 On capital gains | .. | .. | .. | .. | .. | .. | .. | .. | .. | .. |
| 1200 Corporate | 0 | 995 | 3 215 | 6 031 | 12 302 | 10 379 | 9 650 | 10 066 | 10 838 | 6 931 |
| 1210 On profits | .. | 995 | 3 215 | 6 031 | 12 302 | 10 379 | 9 650 | 10 066 | 10 838 | 6 931 |
| Corporate tax | .. | 804 | 2 922 | 5 089 | 10 260 | 8 638 | 8 655 | 9 165 | 9 724 | 6 465 |
| Fiscal notes on corporate tax | .. | 191 | 293 | 942 | 2 041 | 1 742 | 995 | 901 | 1 115 | 467 |
| 1220 On capital gains of corporates | .. | .. | .. | .. | .. | .. | .. | .. | .. | .. |
| 1300 Unallocable between 1100 and 1200 | 0 | 0 | 0 | 0 | 0 | 0 | 0 | 0 | 0 | 0 |
| **2000 Social security contributions** | **0** | **666** | **1 109** | **5 265** | **14 235** | **14 828** | **15 915** | **16 767** | **17 500** | **16 893** |
| 2100 Employees | .. | .. | .. | .. | .. | .. | .. | .. | .. | .. |
| 2110 On a payroll basis | .. | .. | .. | .. | .. | .. | .. | .. | .. | .. |
| 2120 On an income tax basis | .. | .. | .. | .. | .. | .. | .. | .. | .. | .. |
| 2200 Employers | .. | .. | .. | .. | .. | .. | .. | .. | .. | .. |
| 2210 On a payroll basis | .. | .. | .. | .. | .. | .. | .. | .. | .. | .. |
| 2220 On an income tax basis | .. | .. | .. | .. | .. | .. | .. | .. | .. | .. |
| 2300 Self-employed or non-employed | .. | .. | .. | .. | .. | .. | .. | .. | .. | .. |
| 2310 On a payroll basis | .. | .. | .. | .. | .. | .. | .. | .. | .. | .. |
| 2320 On an income tax basis | .. | .. | .. | .. | .. | .. | .. | .. | .. | .. |
| 2400 Unallocable between 2100, 2200 and 2300 | .. | 666 | 1 109 | 5 265 | 14 235 | 14 828 | 15 915 | 16 767 | 17 500 | 16 893 |
| 2410 On a payroll basis | .. | 666 | 1 109 | 5 265 | 14 235 | 14 828 | 15 915 | 16 767 | 17 500 | 16 893 |
| 2420 On an income tax basis | .. | 0 | 0 | 0 | 0 | 0 | 0 | 0 | 0 | 0 |
| **3000 Taxes on payroll and workforce** | **0** | **0** | **0** | **0** | **0** | **0** | **0** | **0** | **0** | **0** |
| **4000 Taxes on property** | **1** | **3** | **334** | **367** | **424** | **455** | **492** | **543** | **522** | **421** |
| 4100 Recurrent taxes on immovable property | 0 | 0 | 0 | 0 | 0 | 0 | 0 | 0 | 0 | 0 |
| 4110 Households | .. | .. | .. | .. | .. | .. | .. | .. | .. | .. |
| 4120 Others | .. | .. | .. | .. | .. | .. | .. | .. | .. | .. |
| 4200 Recurrent taxes on net wealth | 0 | 0 | 0 | 0 | 0 | 0 | 0 | 0 | 0 | 0 |
| 4210 Individual | .. | .. | .. | .. | .. | .. | .. | .. | .. | .. |
| 4220 Corporate | .. | .. | .. | .. | .. | .. | .. | .. | .. | .. |
| 4300 Estate, inheritance and gift taxes | 1 | 3 | 11 | 20 | 36 | 15 | 1 | 0 | 0 | 0 |
| 4310 Estate and inheritance taxes | 1 | 3 | 11 | 20 | 36 | 15 | 1 | 0 | 0 | .. |
| 4320 Gift taxes | 0 | 0 | 0 | 0 | 0 | 0 | 0 | 0 | 0 | .. |
| 4400 Taxes on financial and capital transactions | 0 | 0 | 324 | 347 | 388 | 439 | 491 | 543 | 522 | 421 |
| 4500 Non-recurrent taxes | 0 | 0 | 0 | 0 | 0 | 0 | 0 | 0 | 0 | 0 |
| 4510 On net wealth | .. | .. | .. | .. | .. | .. | .. | .. | .. | .. |
| 4520 Other non-recurrent taxes | .. | .. | .. | .. | .. | .. | .. | .. | .. | .. |
| 4600 Other recurrent taxes on property | 0 | 0 | 0 | 0 | 0 | 0 | 0 | 0 | 0 | 0 |
| **5000 Taxes on goods and services** | **907** | **6 656** | **14 261** | **17 791** | **34 759** | **33 441** | **34 022** | **35 215** | **34 187** | **25 866** |
| 5100 Taxes on production, sale, transfer, etc. | 907 | 6 656 | 14 261 | 17 791 | 34 759 | 33 441 | 34 022 | 35 215 | 34 187 | 25 866 |
| 5110 General taxes | 584 | 3 953 | 9 568 | 12 541 | 25 247 | 24 327 | 24 591 | 25 615 | 25 405 | 19 124 |
| 5111 Value added taxes | 432 | 2 949 | 7 487 | 10 259 | 20 756 | 19 902 | 20 199 | 20 977 | 20 391 | 15 146 |
| VAT (internal market) | 178 | 1 204 | 3 001 | 4 100 | 9 914 | 10 318 | 9 910 | 10 155 | 10 000 | 7 692 |
| VAT (imports) | 178 | 1 445 | 3 734 | 5 193 | 9 738 | 8 458 | 9 154 | 9 387 | 8 594 | 6 522 |
| VAT fiscal notes (internal market) | 56 | 223 | 654 | 581 | 666 | 622 | 439 | 411 | 271 | 336 |
| VAT fiscal notes (imports) | 20 | 76 | 99 | 385 | 438 | 504 | 696 | 1 024 | 1 526 | 596 |
| 5112 Sales tax | 0 | 0 | 0 | 0 | 0 | 0 | 0 | 0 | 0 | 0 |
| 5113 Other | 151 | 1 005 | 2 081 | 2 282 | 4 491 | 4 425 | 4 392 | 4 638 | 5 014 | 3 978 |
| Transactions tax | 136 | 943 | 1 905 | 2 174 | 4 463 | 4 386 | 4 323 | 4 547 | 4 652 | 3 446 |
| Fiscal note on transactions tax | 15 | 62 | 176 | 107 | 28 | 39 | 69 | 92 | 362 | 531 |
| 5120 Taxes on specific goods and services | 324 | 2 702 | 4 693 | 5 250 | 9 511 | 9 114 | 9 430 | 9 600 | 8 782 | 6 742 |
| 5121 Excises | 118 | 2 047 | 3 546 | 3 658 | 5 853 | 6 040 | 6 032 | 6 191 | 5 187 | 4 563 |
| Excises (internal market) | 61 | 244 | 598 | 933 | 1 486 | 1 687 | 1 450 | 1 649 | 1 456 | 1 225 |
| Excises (Imports) | 22 | 298 | 485 | 379 | 1 109 | 917 | 953 | 1 091 | 785 | 561 |
| Special tax on hydrocarbons and derivatives | 0 | 1 348 | 2 073 | 1 070 | 2 581 | 2 695 | 3 105 | 3 076 | 1 911 | 1 697 |
| Fiscal notes on excises | 35 | 118 | 119 | 155 | 262 | 103 | 442 | 272 | 442 | 315 |
| Fiscal notes on special tax on hydrocarb. and deriv. | 0 | 40 | 271 | 1 121 | 415 | 638 | 82 | 103 | 594 | 765 |
| 5122 Profits of fiscal monopolies | 0 | 0 | 0 | 0 | 0 | 0 | 0 | 0 | 0 | 0 |
| 5123 Customs and import duties | 204 | 640 | 1 114 | 1 545 | 3 254 | 2 893 | 3 198 | 3 185 | 3 376 | 2 091 |
| Customs and import duties | 163 | 616 | 1 079 | 1 504 | 3 057 | 2 786 | 3 043 | 2 937 | 2 976 | 1 998 |
| Fiscal notes on customs and import duties | 41 | 24 | 34 | 41 | 197 | 107 | 155 | 248 | 399 | 93 |
| 5124 Taxes on exports | 0 | 0 | 0 | 0 | 0 | 0 | 0 | 0 | 0 | 0 |
| 5125 Taxes on investment goods | 0 | 0 | 0 | 0 | 0 | 0 | 0 | 0 | 0 | 0 |
| 5126 Taxes on specific services | 2 | 15 | 33 | 47 | 127 | 175 | 200 | 224 | 218 | 89 |
| Air departure tax | 2 | 15 | 33 | 47 | 102 | 116 | 122 | 128 | 130 | 42 |
| Tax on gambling | 0 | 0 | 0 | 0 | 25 | 59 | 78 | 96 | 88 | 47 |

## Table 5.6. **Bolivia** *(cont.)*

Details of tax revenue / Ingresos tributarios detallados

*Million BOB*

| | 1990 | 2000 | 2007 | 2010 | 2015 | 2016 | 2017 | 2018 | 2019 | 2020 |
|---|---|---|---|---|---|---|---|---|---|---|
| 5127 Other taxes on internat. trade and transactions | 0 | 0 | 0 | 0 | 277 | 6 | 0 | 0 | 0 | 0 |
| 5128 Other taxes | 0 | 0 | 0 | 0 | 0 | 0 | 0 | 0 | 0 | 0 |
| 5130 Unallocable between 5110 and 5120 | 0 | 0 | 0 | 0 | 0 | 0 | 0 | 0 | 0 | 0 |
| 5200 Taxes on use of goods and perform activities | 0 | 0 | 0 | 0 | 0 | 0 | 0 | 0 | 0 | 0 |
| 5210 Recurrent taxes | .. | .. | .. | .. | .. | .. | .. | .. | .. | .. |
| 5211 Paid by households: motor vehicles | .. | .. | .. | .. | .. | .. | .. | .. | .. | .. |
| 5212 Paid by others: motor vehicles | .. | .. | .. | .. | .. | .. | .. | .. | .. | .. |
| 5213 Paid in respect of other goods | .. | .. | .. | .. | .. | .. | .. | .. | .. | .. |
| 5220 Non-recurrent taxes | .. | .. | .. | .. | .. | .. | .. | .. | .. | .. |
| 5300 Unallocable between 5100 and 5200 | 0 | 0 | 0 | 0 | 0 | 0 | 0 | 0 | 0 | 0 |
| **6000 Other taxes** | **30** | **617** | **1 286** | **1 832** | **5 037** | **5 893** | **6 491** | **6 419** | **6 220** | **5 905** |
| 6100 Paid solely by business | 4 | 6 | 8 | 12 | 25 | 35 | 30 | 33 | 36 | 25 |
| Simplified tax regime | 3 | 6 | 8 | 12 | 25 | 35 | 30 | 33 | 36 | 25 |
| Integrated tax system | 1 | 0 | 0 | 0 | 0 | 0 | 0 | 0 | 0 | 0 |
| 6200 Other | 26 | 611 | 1 278 | 1 819 | 5 012 | 5 858 | 6 461 | 6 386 | 6 184 | 5 880 |
| Municipal taxes | 0 | 575 | 961 | 1 381 | 2 585 | 3 073 | 3 737 | 3 561 | 3 203 | 2 715 |
| Other taxes | 20 | 35 | 279 | 422 | 2 378 | 2 696 | 2 685 | 2 784 | 2 866 | 3 107 |
| Fiscal notes on other taxes | 3 | 0 | 31 | 3 | 23 | 63 | 8 | 9 | 88 | 32 |
| Unified agricultural regime | 2 | 1 | 7 | 14 | 26 | 27 | 31 | 32 | 28 | 27 |

.. Not available

*Note:* Year ending 31st December.

The data are on a cash basis.

The figures exclude local government tax revenues for the period 1990-1993 as the data are not available.

Heading 1210: Corporate tax under heading 1210 includes revenues from IUE (corporate tax), IUE-RE (corporate tax remittances) and IUM (mining profits). Fiscal notes on corporate tax include fiscal notes on IUE and IUM.

Heading 2000: The figures include social security contributions to Bolivia's pension system and healthcare related funds. Contributions to the pension system between 1997 and 2009 have been removed in this edition because Bolivia's pension system was private during this period.

Heading 5113: This heading includes both IT (transactions tax) and its fiscal notes. Special Integrated System of Transition for Entrepreneurs (SIETE-RG) has also been added under heading 5113 in this edition. SIETE-RG was introduced in 2020 to consolidate the payments of value added tax (VAT), transaction tax and corporate income tax for some businesses in order to promote entrepreneurial activity and was levied on 5% of their gross sales.

Heading 5127: This heading includes IVME (tax on the sales of foreign currency).

Heading 6200: Other taxes include revenues from "conceptos varios" (miscellaneous concepts), programa transitorio (transitional programme) and otros ingresos en efectivo (other cash revenue). Fiscal notes on other taxes include fiscal notes on "conceptos varios".

*Source:* Ministerio de Economía y Finanzas Públicas de Bolivia (Ministry of Economy and Public Finance of Bolivia); Servicio de Impuestos Nacionales (National Tax Service); Aduana Nacional de Bolivia (National Customs of Bolivia); Caja Nacional de Salud (National Health Fund).

StatLink https://doi.org/10.1787/888934309454

# Table 5.7. **Brazil / Brasil**

Details of tax revenue / Ingresos tributarios detallados

*Million BRL*

| | 1990 | 2000 | 2007 | 2010 | 2015 | 2016 | 2017 | 2018 | 2019 | 2020 |
|---|---|---|---|---|---|---|---|---|---|---|
| **Total tax revenue** | **3** | **352 456** | **913 145** | **1 259 118** | **1 919 188** | **2 017 949** | **2 123 999** | **2 286 010** | **2 404 134** | **2 353 938** |
| **1000 Taxes on income, profits and capital gains** | **1** | **68 667** | **193 054** | **258 738** | **400 993** | **453 127** | **458 312** | **490 793** | **537 937** | **525 627** |
| 1100 Of individuals | 0 | 3 406 | 60 336 | 87 828 | 148 739 | 161 833 | 177 377 | 196 314 | 221 773 | 224 582 |
| 1110 On income and profits | 0 | 3 406 | 60 336 | 87 828 | 148 739 | 161 833 | 177 377 | 196 314 | 221 773 | 224 582 |
| Withholding income tax (IRRF) | 0 | 0 | 47 631 | 71 579 | 121 540 | 133 549 | 146 872 | 163 801 | 184 073 | 184 881 |
| Other personal income taxes | 0 | 3 406 | 12 706 | 16 248 | 27 199 | 28 284 | 30 504 | 32 513 | 37 700 | 39 701 |
| 1120 On capital gains | .. | .. | .. | .. | .. | .. | .. | .. | .. | .. |
| 1200 Corporate | 0 | 25 430 | 99 062 | 128 255 | 164 057 | 197 941 | 184 501 | 194 814 | 207 505 | 200 032 |
| 1210 On profits | 0 | 25 430 | 99 062 | 128 255 | 164 057 | 197 941 | 184 501 | 194 814 | 207 505 | 200 032 |
| Corporate income tax | 0 | 16 680 | 65 767 | 82 474 | 104 910 | 131 181 | 113 815 | 119 063 | 127 130 | 122 679 |
| Social contribution on net profits (CSLL) | 0 | 8 750 | 33 295 | 45 780 | 59 147 | 66 760 | 70 686 | 75 751 | 80 374 | 77 352 |
| 1220 On capital gains of corporates | .. | .. | .. | .. | .. | .. | .. | .. | .. | .. |
| 1300 Unallocable between 1100 and 1200 | 0 | 39 831 | 33 656 | 42 656 | 88 196 | 93 353 | 96 434 | 99 666 | 108 659 | 101 014 |
| Withholding tax on non-resident income (remittances abroad) | .. | .. | 7 868 | 11 537 | 24 669 | 24 892 | 27 270 | 35 331 | 39 293 | 39 593 |
| Withholding tax on capital income | .. | .. | 21 384 | 24 887 | 53 692 | 59 404 | 59 470 | 53 585 | 57 184 | 48 346 |
| Withholding tax on other income | .. | .. | 4 404 | 6 232 | 9 836 | 9 057 | 9 694 | 10 749 | 12 182 | 13 075 |
| **2000 Social security contributions** | **1** | **83 469** | **214 508** | **316 530** | **503 222** | **528 423** | **556 408** | **585 684** | **621 821** | **611 542** |
| 2100 Employees | .. | .. | 51 984 | 75 509 | 114 653 | 121 969 | 128 517 | 139 970 | 149 373 | .. |
| 2110 On a payroll basis | .. | .. | 51 984 | 75 509 | 114 653 | 121 969 | 128 517 | 139 970 | 149 373 | .. |
| 2120 On an income tax basis | .. | .. | 0 | 0 | 0 | 0 | 0 | 0 | 0 | .. |
| 2200 Employers | 0 | 18 709 | 161 934 | 240 280 | 369 094 | 389 923 | 408 005 | 430 521 | 460 699 | 127 503 |
| 2210 On a payroll basis | 0 | 18 709 | 161 934 | 240 280 | 369 094 | 389 923 | 408 005 | 430 521 | 460 699 | 127 503 |
| 2220 On an income tax basis | 0 | 0 | 0 | 0 | 0 | 0 | 0 | 0 | 0 | 0 |
| 2300 Self-employed or non-employed | .. | .. | .. | .. | .. | .. | .. | .. | .. | .. |
| 2310 On a payroll basis | .. | .. | .. | .. | .. | .. | .. | .. | .. | .. |
| 2320 On an income tax basis | .. | .. | .. | .. | .. | .. | .. | .. | .. | .. |
| 2400 Unallocable between 2100, 2200 and 2300 | 1 | 64 760 | 590 | 741 | 19 474 | 16 531 | 19 885 | 15 192 | 11 749 | 484 039 |
| 2410 On a payroll basis | 1 | 64 760 | 590 | 741 | 19 474 | 16 531 | 19 885 | 15 192 | 11 749 | 484 039 |
| 2420 On an income tax basis | 0 | 0 | 0 | 0 | 0 | 0 | 0 | 0 | 0 | 0 |
| **3000 Taxes on payroll and workforce** | **0** | **5 437** | **13 985** | **21 348** | **37 891** | **38 629** | **39 824** | **42 223** | **42 907** | **40 056** |
| Payroll-based contribution to education | 0 | 2 791 | 7 089 | 11 049 | 19 039 | 19 473 | 20 010 | 21 979 | 21 977 | 21 086 |
| "S" System contributions | 0 | 2 646 | 6 592 | 9 925 | 18 153 | 18 428 | 19 075 | 19 820 | 20 549 | 18 970 |
| Other payroll taxes | 0 | 0 | 304 | 374 | 699 | 728 | 739 | 423 | 381 | 0 |
| **4000 Taxes on property** | **0** | **23 524** | **61 870** | **53 285** | **84 365** | **86 721** | **92 482** | **100 789** | **111 784** | **91 590** |
| 4100 Recurrent taxes on immovable property | 0 | 4 753 | 13 140 | 18 367 | 33 313 | 36 249 | 40 495 | 45 828 | 49 680 | 47 830 |
| Tax on rural land property (ITR) | 0 | 234 | 317 | 485 | 1 105 | 1 126 | 1 273 | 1 419 | 1 630 | 1 761 |
| Tax on urban land property (IPTU) | 0 | 4 519 | 12 822 | 17 882 | 32 208 | 35 123 | 39 222 | 44 409 | 48 051 | 46 069 |
| 4110 Households | .. | .. | .. | .. | .. | .. | .. | .. | .. | .. |
| 4120 Others | .. | .. | .. | .. | .. | .. | .. | .. | .. | .. |
| 4200 Recurrent taxes on net wealth | 0 | 0 | 0 | 0 | 0 | 0 | 0 | 0 | 0 | 0 |
| 4210 Individual | .. | .. | .. | .. | .. | .. | .. | .. | .. | .. |
| 4220 Corporate | .. | .. | .. | .. | .. | .. | .. | .. | .. | .. |
| 4300 Estate, inheritance and gift taxes | 0 | 329 | 1 207 | 2 518 | 6 461 | 7 345 | 7 242 | 7 330 | 8 625 | 8 521 |
| 4310 Estate and inheritance taxes | .. | .. | .. | .. | .. | .. | .. | .. | .. | .. |
| 4320 Gift taxes | .. | .. | .. | .. | .. | .. | .. | .. | .. | .. |
| 4400 Taxes on financial and capital transactions | 0 | 18 442 | 47 523 | 32 400 | 44 591 | 43 126 | 44 745 | 47 630 | 53 479 | 35 239 |
| Tax on financial operations (IOF) | 0 | 3 096 | 7 818 | 26 571 | 34 681 | 33 645 | 34 660 | 36 615 | 40 945 | 21 949 |
| Tax on real estate property transfers (ITBI) | 0 | 950 | 3 383 | 5 840 | 9 904 | 9 482 | 10 062 | 11 013 | 12 568 | 13 290 |
| Other | 0 | 14 396 | 36 323 | -12 | 5 | 0 | 23 | 3 | -34 | 0 |
| 4500 Non-recurrent taxes | 0 | 0 | 0 | 0 | 0 | 0 | 0 | 0 | 0 | 0 |
| 4510 On net wealth | .. | .. | .. | .. | .. | .. | .. | .. | .. | .. |
| 4520 Other non-recurrent taxes | .. | .. | .. | .. | .. | .. | .. | .. | .. | .. |
| 4600 Other recurrent taxes on property | 0 | 0 | 0 | 0 | 0 | 0 | 0 | 0 | 0 | 0 |
| **5000 Taxes on goods and services** | **2** | **169 181** | **406 743** | **582 552** | **852 129** | **864 758** | **928 305** | **1 020 683** | **1 048 269** | **1 038 683** |
| 5100 Taxes on production, sale, transfer, etc | 2 | 163 887 | 388 675 | 555 787 | 807 132 | 817 200 | 880 218 | 968 294 | 996 335 | 990 331 |
| 5110 General taxes | 1 | 136 743 | 335 395 | 484 000 | 705 879 | 725 724 | 782 480 | 854 999 | 881 437 | 871 293 |
| 5111 Value added taxes | 1 | 82 279 | 187 190 | 268 117 | 396 428 | 413 175 | 441 039 | 479 310 | 508 832 | 522 690 |
| Tax on the circulation of goods and services (ICMS) | 1 | 82 279 | 187 190 | 268 117 | 396 428 | 413 175 | 441 039 | 479 310 | 508 832 | 522 690 |
| 5112 Sales tax | 0 | 0 | 0 | 0 | 0 | 0 | 0 | 0 | 0 | 0 |
| 5113 Other | 0 | 54 464 | 148 205 | 215 883 | 309 450 | 312 549 | 341 441 | 375 689 | 372 605 | 348 602 |
| Contribution to COFINS | 0 | 38 707 | 100 946 | 140 939 | 199 876 | 201 517 | 221 670 | 244 287 | 237 372 | 218 602 |
| Contribution to PIS | 0 | 8 339 | 21 813 | 30 714 | 42 632 | 44 797 | 49 380 | 54 461 | 51 390 | 46 626 |
| Contribution to PASEP | 0 | 1 312 | 4 049 | 9 880 | 9 958 | 10 026 | 11 395 | 12 066 | 12 626 | 14 686 |
| Tax on general services (ISS) | 0 | 6 106 | 20 673 | 33 696 | 56 094 | 55 382 | 58 074 | 63 837 | 70 150 | 68 688 |
| Others | 0 | 0 | 723 | 656 | 890 | 826 | 922 | 1 038 | 1 067 | 0 |
| 5120 Taxes on specific goods and services | 0 | 27 144 | 53 280 | 71 786 | 101 254 | 91 476 | 97 739 | 113 294 | 114 898 | 119 039 |

## Table 5.7. **Brazil / Brasil** (*cont.*)

Details of tax revenue / Ingresos tributarios detallados

*Million BRL*

| | 1990 | 2000 | 2007 | 2010 | 2015 | 2016 | 2017 | 2018 | 2019 | 2020 |
|---|---|---|---|---|---|---|---|---|---|---|
| 5121 Excises | 0 | 18 699 | 39 241 | 48 170 | 57 437 | 55 279 | 60 570 | 66 870 | 65 277 | 67 417 |
| Vehicles | .. | .. | 5 238 | 5 787 | 4 367 | 3 299 | 4 467 | 5 713 | 5 639 | 3 446 |
| Beverages | .. | .. | 2 595 | 2 431 | 2 599 | 2 684 | 2 944 | 2 768 | 3 641 | 2 985 |
| Tobacco | .. | .. | 2 806 | 3 704 | 5 692 | 5 718 | 5 210 | 5 208 | 5 559 | 5 975 |
| Fuels | .. | .. | 7 943 | 7 759 | 3 271 | 6 001 | 5 821 | 3 928 | 2 776 | 1 986 |
| Other excises | .. | .. | 20 660 | 28 489 | 41 508 | 37 577 | 42 128 | 49 253 | 47 662 | 53 025 |
| 5122 Profits of fiscal monopolies | 0 | 0 | 0 | 0 | 0 | 0 | 0 | 0 | 0 | 0 |
| 5123 Customs and import duties | 0 | 8 445 | 12 157 | 21 072 | 38 870 | 31 308 | 32 284 | 40 575 | 42 842 | 45 671 |
| 5124 Taxes on exports | 0 | 0 | 61 | 47 | 99 | 139 | 66 | 129 | 91 | 51 |
| 5125 Taxes on investment goods | 0 | 0 | 0 | 0 | 0 | 0 | 0 | 0 | 0 | 0 |
| 5126 Taxes on specific services | 0 | 0 | 1 017 | 1 286 | 1 863 | 1 809 | 1 807 | 1 623 | 1 561 | 0 |
| Contribution on revenues of telecom companies | .. | .. | 935 | 1 186 | 1 657 | 1 608 | 1 610 | 1 440 | 1 392 | .. |
| Contribution on billing of IT companies | .. | .. | 80 | 100 | 206 | 200 | 196 | 182 | 168 | .. |
| Other taxes on specific services | .. | .. | 1 | 1 | 1 | 0 | 1 | 1 | 1 | .. |
| 5127 Other taxes on internat. trade and transactions | 0 | 0 | 805 | 1 212 | 2 983 | 2 940 | 3 011 | 4 097 | 5 127 | 5 900 |
| CIDE on remittances abroad | .. | .. | 805 | 1 212 | 2 983 | 2 940 | 3 011 | 4 097 | 5 127 | 5 900 |
| 5128 Other taxes | 0 | 0 | 0 | 0 | 0 | 0 | 0 | 0 | 0 | 0 |
| 5130 Unallocable between 5110 and 5120 | 0 | 0 | 0 | 0 | 0 | 0 | 0 | 0 | 0 | 0 |
| 5200 Taxes on use of goods and perform activities | 0 | 5 294 | 18 068 | 26 765 | 44 997 | 47 559 | 48 087 | 52 389 | 51 934 | 48 351 |
| 5210 Recurrent taxes | 0 | 5 294 | 16 687 | 24 417 | 41 992 | 44 817 | 45 225 | 48 668 | 48 704 | 48 351 |
| 5211 Paid by households: motor vehicles | 0 | 5 294 | 16 523 | 24 197 | 40 460 | 43 336 | 43 810 | 45 432 | 47 241 | 48 351 |
| Motor vehicle property tax (IPVA) | 0 | 5 294 | 14 627 | 21 367 | 36 219 | 39 093 | 40 509 | 43 120 | 46 213 | 48 178 |
| Contributions to DPVAT | 0 | 0 | 1 896 | 2 830 | 4 242 | 4 243 | 3 302 | 2 312 | 1 027 | 173 |
| 5212 Paid by others: motor vehicles | 0 | 0 | 0 | 0 | 0 | 0 | 0 | 0 | 0 | 0 |
| 5213 Paid in respect of other goods | 0 | 0 | 164 | 220 | 1 531 | 1 481 | 1 415 | 3 235 | 1 463 | 0 |
| CONDECINE | .. | .. | 39 | 49 | 1 062 | 1 225 | 1 133 | 1 084 | 1 061 | .. |
| Others | .. | .. | 125 | 170 | 469 | 256 | 281 | 2 151 | 402 | .. |
| 5220 Non-recurrent taxes | 0 | 0 | 1 381 | 2 349 | 3 005 | 2 741 | 2 862 | 3 722 | 3 231 | 0 |
| AFRMM | .. | .. | 1 381 | 2 349 | 3 005 | 2 741 | 2 862 | 3 722 | 3 231 | .. |
| 5300 Unallocable between 5100 and 5200 | 0 | 0 | 0 | 0 | 0 | 0 | 0 | 0 | 0 | 0 |
| **6000 Other taxes** | **0** | **2 178** | **22 986** | **26 666** | **40 589** | **46 292** | **48 667** | **45 838** | **41 416** | **46 439** |
| 6100 Paid solely by business | 0 | 0 | 0 | 0 | 0 | 0 | 0 | 0 | 0 | 0 |
| 6200 Other | 0 | 2 178 | 22 986 | 26 666 | 40 589 | 46 292 | 48 667 | 45 838 | 41 416 | 46 439 |

.. Not available

*Note:* Year ending 31st December.

The data are on a cash basis.

Data in 2019 have been updated with detailed information from Carga Tributária no Brasil by the Secretaria da Receita Federal do Brasil. Data for 2020 are sourced from latest reports of Secretaria do Tesouro Nacional.

Heading 2000: Social security contributions include contributions to the General Social Security Regime (RGPS), contributions to the Own Social Security Schemes (RPPS), contributions to the Severance Indemnity Fund (FGTS) and contributions to the health fund for military police and fire department.

Heading 4100: Tax on urban land property (IPTU) under state governments has been identified and classified under heading 4100 between 2010 and 2020 in this edition. It was previously under heading 6200.

Heading 5113: Tax on general services (ISS) under state governments has been identified and classified under heading 5113 between 2010 and 2020 in this edition. It was previously under heading 6200. Contributions to PASEP are included in contributions to PIS before 2000 as they cannot be distinguished.

Heading 5121: Contribution to the Funding of the Public Lighting Service (COSIP) under municipal governments has been identified and classified under heading 5121 between 2010 and 2020 in this edition. It was previously under heading 6200. COSIP is levied monthly on consumers of electricity and the amount is based on energy consumption.

Heading 5123: This heading includes tax on exports before 2002.

*Source:* Secretaria da Receita Federal do Brasil, Ministério da Economia (Special Department of Federal Revenue of Brazil under Ministry of Economy); Secretaria do Tesouro Nacional, Ministério da Economia (National Treasury Secretariat under Ministry of Economy).

StatLink https://doi.org/10.1787/888934309473

# Table 5.8. **Chile**

Details of tax revenue / Ingresos tributarios detallados

*Million CLP*

| | 1990 | 2000 | 2007 | 2010 | 2015 | 2016 | 2017 | 2018 | 2019 | 2020 |
|---|---|---|---|---|---|---|---|---|---|---|
| **Total tax revenue** | **1 777 218** | **7 901 998** | **20 598 963** | **21 845 693** | **32 532 354** | **34 129 982** | **36 262 036** | **40 314 703** | **41 025 508** | **38 746 799** |
| **1000 Taxes on income, profits and capital gains** | **412 974** | **1 841 630** | **9 412 056** | **8 329 060** | **11 840 521** | **11 445 244** | **12 516 154** | **14 418 859** | **14 283 183** | **12 540 335** |
| 1100 Of individuals | 99 154 | 604 100 | 989 348 | 1 492 837 | 3 199 876 | 2 990 653 | 3 500 023 | 2 701 416 | 2 937 532 | 3 976 009 |
| Second category tax | 65 552 | 490 980 | 993 129 | 1 449 099 | 2 350 120 | 2 458 249 | 2 585 694 | 2 848 205 | 3 015 794 | 3 051 177 |
| Global complementary tax | 33 603 | 113 120 | -3 781 | 43 738 | -36 757 | -213 365 | 50 495 | -146 789 | -78 261 | 132 551 |
| Others | 0 | 0 | 0 | 0 | 886 513 | 745 769 | 863 834 | 0 | 0 | 792 281 |
| 1110 On income and profits | .. | .. | .. | .. | .. | .. | .. | .. | .. | .. |
| 1120 On capital gains | .. | .. | .. | .. | .. | .. | .. | .. | .. | .. |
| 1200 Corporate | 219 586 | 882 896 | 6 054 487 | 4 448 745 | 6 839 133 | 7 147 331 | 7 658 420 | 8 920 497 | 9 597 472 | 9 429 787 |
| First category tax | 200 891 | 815 747 | 5 084 996 | 3 913 870 | 6 183 830 | 6 688 868 | 7 049 471 | 7 836 379 | 8 880 080 | 8 745 612 |
| Surtax on state owned enterprises | 16 074 | 47 634 | 113 334 | 194 203 | 132 352 | 88 362 | 193 058 | 184 442 | 122 054 | 203 416 |
| Mining tax | 0 | 0 | 835 452 | 298 558 | 323 507 | 106 560 | 101 970 | 184 382 | 277 861 | 267 544 |
| Other | 2 621 | 19 516 | 20 705 | 42 114 | 199 444 | 263 541 | 313 921 | 715 293 | 317 477 | 213 216 |
| 1210 On profits | .. | .. | .. | .. | .. | .. | .. | .. | .. | .. |
| 1220 On capital gains of corporates | .. | .. | .. | .. | .. | .. | .. | .. | .. | .. |
| 1300 Unallocable between 1100 and 1200 | 94 233 | 354 634 | 2 368 221 | 2 387 478 | 1 801 512 | 1 307 260 | 1 357 711 | 2 796 947 | 1 748 179 | -865 461 |
| Additional tax | 59 082 | 350 301 | 1 462 715 | 1 414 057 | 1 429 758 | 1 331 564 | 1 453 577 | 2 127 948 | 1 902 585 | 2 063 149 |
| Other | 35 151 | 4 332 | 905 507 | 973 421 | 371 755 | -24 304 | -95 865 | 668 998 | -154 406 | -2 928 610 |
| **2000 Social security contributions** | **159 559** | **576 758** | **1 148 647** | **1 493 987** | **2 252 489** | **2 441 419** | **2 627 558** | **2 786 173** | **2 994 906** | **3 104 866** |
| 2100 Employees | 154 021 | 553 937 | 1 098 620 | 1 433 159 | 2 188 575 | 2 373 777 | 2 553 916 | 2 703 261 | 2 894 725 | 2 994 036 |
| 2110 On a payroll basis | 154 021 | 553 937 | 1 098 620 | 1 433 159 | 2 188 575 | 2 373 777 | 2 553 916 | 2 703 261 | 2 894 725 | 2 994 036 |
| 2120 On an income tax basis | 0 | 0 | 0 | 0 | 0 | 0 | 0 | 0 | 0 | 0 |
| 2200 Employers | 5 538 | 22 821 | 50 027 | 60 828 | 63 914 | 67 642 | 73 643 | 82 912 | 100 181 | 110 830 |
| 2210 On a payroll basis | 5 538 | 22 821 | 50 027 | 60 828 | 63 914 | 67 642 | 73 643 | 82 912 | 100 181 | 110 830 |
| 2220 On an income tax basis | 0 | 0 | 0 | 0 | 0 | 0 | 0 | 0 | 0 | 0 |
| 2300 Self-employed or non-employed | 0 | 0 | 0 | 0 | 0 | 0 | 0 | 0 | 0 | 0 |
| 2310 On a payroll basis | .. | .. | .. | .. | .. | .. | .. | .. | .. | .. |
| 2320 On an income tax basis | .. | .. | .. | .. | .. | .. | .. | .. | .. | .. |
| 2400 Unallocable between 2100, 2200 and 2300 | 0 | 0 | 0 | 0 | 0 | 0 | 0 | 0 | 0 | 0 |
| 2410 On a payroll basis | .. | .. | .. | .. | .. | .. | .. | .. | .. | .. |
| 2420 On an income tax basis | .. | .. | .. | .. | .. | .. | .. | .. | .. | .. |
| **3000 Taxes on payroll and workforce** | **0** | **0** | **0** | **0** | **0** | **0** | **0** | **0** | **0** | **0** |
| **4000 Taxes on property** | **109 319** | **554 037** | **1 013 571** | **898 607** | **1 421 274** | **1 731 723** | **1 969 157** | **2 086 866** | **2 242 561** | **2 011 004** |
| 4100 Recurrent taxes on immovable property | 59 968 | 302 244 | 496 311 | 662 368 | 1 056 920 | 1 171 399 | 1 248 136 | 1 373 495 | 1 507 182 | 1 501 400 |
| 4110 Households | .. | .. | .. | .. | .. | .. | .. | .. | .. | .. |
| 4120 Others | .. | .. | .. | .. | .. | .. | .. | .. | .. | .. |
| 4200 Recurrent taxes on net wealth | 0 | 0 | 0 | 0 | 0 | 0 | 0 | 0 | 0 | 0 |
| 4210 Individual | .. | .. | .. | .. | .. | .. | .. | .. | .. | .. |
| 4220 Corporate | .. | .. | .. | .. | .. | .. | .. | .. | .. | .. |
| 4300 Estate, inheritance and gift taxes | 3 444 | 10 906 | 28 501 | 39 338 | 92 236 | 100 490 | 202 376 | 125 649 | 62 824 | 155 433 |
| 4310 Estate and inheritance taxes | .. | .. | .. | .. | .. | .. | .. | .. | .. | .. |
| 4320 Gift taxes | .. | .. | .. | .. | .. | .. | .. | .. | .. | .. |
| 4400 Taxes on financial and capital transactions | 45 907 | 240 886 | 488 759 | 196 901 | 272 118 | 459 834 | 518 645 | 587 721 | 672 555 | 354 171 |
| 4500 Non-recurrent taxes | 0 | 0 | 0 | 0 | 0 | 0 | 0 | 0 | 0 | 0 |
| 4510 On net wealth | .. | .. | .. | .. | .. | .. | .. | .. | .. | .. |
| 4520 Other non-recurrent taxes | .. | .. | .. | .. | .. | .. | .. | .. | .. | .. |
| 4600 Other recurrent taxes on property | 0 | 0 | 0 | 0 | 0 | 0 | 0 | 0 | 0 | 0 |
| **5000 Taxes on goods and services** | **1 118 722** | **5 041 769** | **9 023 666** | **11 185 156** | **17 597 378** | **18 629 617** | **19 863 420** | **21 470 498** | **21 755 381** | **21 265 611** |
| 5100 Taxes on production, sale, transfer, etc | 1 074 009 | 4 789 827 | 8 578 636 | 10 532 904 | 16 515 485 | 17 449 222 | 18 599 503 | 19 953 036 | 20 167 012 | 19 609 059 |
| 5110 General taxes | 664 421 | 3 306 350 | 6 781 501 | 8 399 926 | 13 273 958 | 14 073 050 | 15 069 540 | 16 211 646 | 16 348 944 | 15 963 032 |
| 5111 Value added taxes | 664 421 | 3 306 350 | 6 781 501 | 8 399 926 | 13 273 958 | 14 073 050 | 15 069 540 | 16 211 646 | 16 348 944 | 15 963 032 |
| 5112 Sales tax | 0 | 0 | 0 | 0 | 0 | 0 | 0 | 0 | 0 | 0 |
| 5113 Other | 0 | 0 | 0 | 0 | 0 | 0 | 0 | 0 | 0 | 0 |
| 5120 Taxes on specific goods and services | 409 588 | 1 483 477 | 1 797 135 | 2 132 978 | 3 241 527 | 3 376 172 | 3 529 963 | 3 741 389 | 3 818 068 | 3 646 028 |
| 5121 Excises | 166 050 | 816 160 | 1 299 844 | 1 561 205 | 2 412 773 | 2 568 863 | 2 682 659 | 2 796 033 | 2 862 327 | 2 900 245 |
| Cigarettes and tobacco | 60 604 | 283 275 | 455 595 | 647 637 | 981 422 | 1 009 034 | 978 696 | 981 456 | 973 335 | 1 021 917 |
| Gasoline and diesel | 105 445 | 532 885 | 844 249 | 913 568 | 1 388 218 | 1 502 039 | 1 629 561 | 1 727 392 | 1 811 132 | 1 799 846 |
| Oil stabilisation fund | 0 | 0 | 0 | 0 | 0 | 0 | 0 | 0 | 0 | 0 |
| Fisheries Law Extraction Rights | 0 | 0 | 0 | 0 | 8 558 | 9 998 | 11 749 | 19 623 | 17 662 | 33 104 |
| Additional tax on new motor vehicles | 0 | 0 | 0 | 0 | 34 575 | 47 792 | 62 654 | 67 561 | 60 197 | 45 379 |
| 5122 Profits of fiscal monopolies | 0 | 0 | 0 | 0 | 0 | 0 | 0 | 0 | 0 | 0 |
| 5123 Customs and import duties | 222 486 | 548 571 | 300 416 | 267 331 | 343 491 | 308 871 | 321 156 | 347 555 | 331 846 | 294 204 |
| 5124 Taxes on exports | 0 | 0 | 0 | 0 | 0 | 0 | 0 | 0 | 0 | 0 |
| 5125 Taxes on investment goods | 0 | 0 | 0 | 0 | 0 | 0 | 0 | 0 | 0 | 0 |
| 5126 Taxes on specific services | 21 052 | 118 746 | 196 875 | 304 442 | 485 263 | 498 438 | 526 147 | 597 802 | 623 895 | 451 579 |
| 5127 Other taxes on internat. trade and transactions | 0 | 0 | 0 | 0 | 0 | 0 | 0 | 0 | 0 | 0 |
| 5128 Other taxes | 0 | 0 | 0 | 0 | 0 | 0 | 0 | 0 | 0 | 0 |
| 5130 Unallocable between 5110 and 5120 | 0 | 0 | 0 | 0 | 0 | 0 | 0 | 0 | 0 | 0 |
| 5200 Taxes on use of goods and perform activities | 44 714 | 251 942 | 445 030 | 652 252 | 1 081 893 | 1 180 395 | 1 263 917 | 1 517 462 | 1 588 369 | 1 656 551 |

## Table 5.8. **Chile** *(cont.)*

Details of tax revenue / Ingresos tributarios detallados

*Million CLP*

| | 1990 | 2000 | 2007 | 2010 | 2015 | 2016 | 2017 | 2018 | 2019 | 2020 |
|---|---|---|---|---|---|---|---|---|---|---|
| 5210 Recurrent taxes | 44 714 | 251 942 | 445 030 | 652 252 | 1 081 893 | 1 180 395 | 1 263 917 | 1 402 110 | 1 461 686 | 1 498 957 |
| Motor vehicles | 24 469 | 93 880 | 155 158 | 218 219 | 397 608 | 434 137 | 482 916 | 539 918 | 592 327 | 582 616 |
| 5211 Paid by households: motor vehicles | 0 | 0 | 0 | 0 | 0 | 0 | 0 | 0 | 0 | 0 |
| 5212 Paid by others: motor vehicles | 0 | 0 | 0 | 0 | 0 | 0 | 0 | 0 | 0 | 0 |
| 5213 Paid in respect of other goods | 20 245 | 158 062 | 289 872 | 434 033 | 684 285 | 746 258 | 781 001 | 862 192 | 869 359 | 916 341 |
| Municipal permits | 18 401 | 136 138 | 263 996 | 396 944 | 630 943 | 692 974 | 727 246 | 806 734 | 813 159 | 860 414 |
| Mining patents | 3 374 | 34 730 | 25 184 | 36 213 | 51 767 | 51 641 | 52 254 | 53 854 | 54 696 | 54 932 |
| Other | -1 530 | -12 806 | 692 | 876 | 1 575 | 1 643 | 1 501 | 1 604 | 1 504 | 995 |
| 5220 Non-recurrent taxes | 0 | 0 | 0 | 0 | 0 | 0 | 0 | 115 352 | 126 683 | 157 594 |
| Tax on polluting fixed sources | .. | .. | .. | .. | .. | .. | .. | 115 352 | 126 683 | 157 594 |
| 5300 Unallocable between 5100 and 5200 | 0 | 0 | 0 | 0 | 0 | 0 | 0 | 0 | 0 | 0 |
| **6000 Other taxes** | **-23 356** | **-112 195** | **1 023** | **-61 117** | **-579 308** | **-118 021** | **-714 253** | **-447 692** | **-250 523** | **-175 017** |
| 6100 Paid solely by business | 0 | 0 | 0 | 0 | 0 | 0 | 0 | 0 | 0 | 0 |
| 6200 Other | -23 356 | -112 195 | 1 023 | -61 117 | -579 308 | -118 021 | -714 253 | -447 692 | -250 523 | -175 017 |

.. Not available

*Note:* Year ending 31st December.

The data are on a cash basis.

Heading 5121: In ECLAC data, figures from the Oil Prices Stabilisation Fund (FEPP) are considered as non-tax revenues.

*Source:* Servicio de Impuestos Internos (Chile's Tax Service).

StatLink https://doi.org/10.1787/888934309492

# Table 5.9. **Colombia**

Details of tax revenue / Ingresos tributarios detallados

*Million COP*

| | 1990 | 2000 | 2007 | 2010 | 2015 | 2016 | 2017 | 2018 | 2019 | 2020 |
|---|---|---|---|---|---|---|---|---|---|---|
| **Total tax revenue** | **2 579 426** | **30 598 630** | **82 697 457** | **98 455 335** | **160 157 693** | **164 800 001** | **174 735 823** | **190 299 911** | **209 071 314** | **187 664 589** |
| **1000 Taxes on income, profits and capital gains** | **771 694** | **7 103 525** | **24 010 404** | **26 218 852** | **52 656 876** | **54 326 726** | **57 615 236** | **64 043 928** | **67 519 599** | **61 812 525** |
| 1100 Of individuals | 47 210 | 1 499 345 | 4 751 580 | 5 192 384 | 9 215 137 | 9 843 974 | 10 391 187 | 12 235 324 | 14 155 111 | 12 977 788 |
| 1110 On income and profits | 47 210 | 1 499 345 | 4 751 580 | 5 192 384 | 9 215 137 | 9 843 974 | 10 391 187 | 12 235 324 | 14 155 111 | 12 977 788 |
| Income tax | 47 210 | 1 499 345 | 4 751 580 | 5 192 384 | 9 215 137 | 9 843 974 | 10 391 187 | 12 235 324 | 14 148 562 | 12 942 190 |
| Simple tax regime | 0 | 0 | 0 | 0 | 0 | 0 | 0 | 0 | 6 549 | 35 598 |
| 1120 On capital gains | .. | .. | .. | .. | .. | .. | .. | .. | .. | .. |
| 1200 Corporate | 359 758 | 5 119 828 | 18 427 899 | 20 405 209 | 41 401 857 | 42 364 674 | 44 974 479 | 48 628 587 | 50 242 515 | 45 978 957 |
| 1210 On profits | 359 758 | 5 119 828 | 18 427 899 | 20 405 209 | 41 401 857 | 42 364 674 | 44 974 479 | 48 628 587 | 50 242 515 | 45 978 957 |
| Income tax | 359 758 | 5 119 828 | 18 427 899 | 20 405 209 | 27 475 688 | 28 253 940 | 40 128 289 | 48 495 864 | 50 126 648 | 45 852 617 |
| Pro Equity Income Tax - CREE | 0 | 0 | 0 | 0 | 13 926 169 | 14 110 734 | 4 846 190 | 132 723 | 99 798 | 39 871 |
| Simple tax regime | 0 | 0 | 0 | 0 | 0 | 0 | 0 | 0 | 16 068 | 86 469 |
| 1220 On capital gains of corporates | .. | .. | .. | .. | .. | .. | .. | .. | .. | .. |
| 1300 Unallocable between 1100 and 1200 | 364 726 | 484 352 | 830 925 | 621 258 | 2 039 882 | 2 118 078 | 2 249 569 | 3 180 016 | 3 121 974 | 2 855 780 |
| Income tax | 364 726 | 484 352 | 830 925 | 621 258 | 2 039 882 | 2 118 078 | 2 249 569 | 3 180 016 | 3 121 974 | 2 855 780 |
| Pro Equity Income Tax - CREE | 0 | 0 | 0 | 0 | 0 | 0 | 0 | 0 | 0 | 0 |
| **2000 Social security contributions** | **203 596** | **4 989 000** | **9 694 000** | **11 478 085** | **13 585 138** | **15 443 016** | **13 351 711** | **18 192 049** | **19 875 398** | **18 615 408** |
| 2100 Employees | .. | .. | .. | .. | .. | .. | .. | .. | .. | .. |
| 2110 On a payroll basis | .. | .. | .. | .. | .. | .. | .. | .. | .. | .. |
| 2120 On an income tax basis | .. | .. | .. | .. | .. | .. | .. | .. | .. | .. |
| 2200 Employers | .. | .. | .. | .. | .. | .. | .. | .. | .. | .. |
| 2210 On a payroll basis | .. | .. | .. | .. | .. | .. | .. | .. | .. | .. |
| 2220 On an income tax basis | .. | .. | .. | .. | .. | .. | .. | .. | .. | .. |
| 2300 Self-employed or non-employed | .. | .. | .. | .. | .. | .. | .. | .. | .. | .. |
| 2310 On a payroll basis | .. | .. | .. | .. | .. | .. | .. | .. | .. | .. |
| 2320 On an income tax basis | .. | .. | .. | .. | .. | .. | .. | .. | .. | .. |
| 2400 Unallocable between 2100, 2200 and 2300 | 203 596 | 4 989 000 | 9 694 000 | 11 478 085 | 13 585 138 | 15 443 016 | 13 351 711 | 18 192 049 | 19 875 398 | 18 615 408 |
| 2410 On a payroll basis | 203 596 | 4 989 000 | 9 694 000 | 11 478 085 | 13 585 138 | 15 443 016 | 13 351 711 | 18 192 049 | 19 875 398 | 18 615 408 |
| 2420 On an income tax basis | 0 | 0 | 0 | 0 | 0 | 0 | 0 | 0 | 0 | 0 |
| **3000 Taxes on payroll and workforce** | **0** | **1 286 803** | **2 798 906** | **4 022 503** | **2 797 308** | **2 998 237** | **3 200 238** | **3 461 352** | **3 604 071** | **3 670 490** |
| **4000 Taxes on property** | **56 160** | **2 027 654** | **6 459 259** | **8 535 238** | **18 156 105** | **18 090 331** | **17 950 494** | **15 265 472** | **18 984 414** | **18 167 358** |
| 4100 Recurrent taxes on immovable property | 56 160 | 991 070 | 2 298 829 | 3 338 935 | 6 061 965 | 6 571 134 | 7 310 244 | 7 981 989 | 8 743 115 | 9 109 598 |
| 4110 Households | 0 | 0 | 0 | 0 | 0 | 0 | 0 | 0 | 0 | 0 |
| 4120 Others | 56 160 | 991 070 | 2 298 829 | 3 338 935 | 6 061 965 | 6 571 134 | 7 310 244 | 7 981 989 | 8 743 115 | 9 109 598 |
| 4200 Recurrent taxes on net wealth | 0 | 0 | 1 170 908 | 1 970 530 | 5 352 940 | 4 440 142 | 3 868 595 | 467 925 | 923 255 | 957 137 |
| 4210 Individual | .. | .. | 1 170 908 | 1 970 530 | 5 352 940 | 4 440 142 | 3 868 595 | 467 925 | 923 255 | 957 137 |
| 4220 Corporate | .. | .. | 0 | 0 | 0 | 0 | 0 | 0 | 0 | 0 |
| 4300 Estate, inheritance and gift taxes | 0 | 0 | 0 | 0 | 0 | 0 | 0 | 0 | 0 | 0 |
| 4310 Estate and inheritance taxes | .. | .. | .. | .. | .. | .. | .. | .. | .. | .. |
| 4320 Gift taxes | .. | .. | .. | .. | .. | .. | .. | .. | .. | .. |
| 4400 Taxes on financial and capital transactions | 0 | 1 036 584 | 2 989 522 | 3 225 773 | 6 741 200 | 7 079 055 | 6 771 655 | 6 815 558 | 8 190 516 | 7 476 295 |
| 4500 Non-recurrent taxes | 0 | 0 | 0 | 0 | 0 | 0 | 0 | 0 | 1 127 528 | 624 327 |
| 4510 On net wealth | .. | .. | .. | .. | .. | .. | .. | .. | 0 | 0 |
| 4520 Other non-recurrent taxes | .. | .. | .. | .. | .. | .. | .. | .. | 1 127 528 | 624 327 |
| 4600 Other recurrent taxes on property | 0 | 0 | 0 | 0 | 0 | 0 | 0 | 0 | 0 | 0 |
| **5000 Taxes on goods and services** | **1 388 653** | **14 180 450** | **36 766 741** | **44 411 642** | **65 716 566** | **66 962 420** | **75 381 123** | **81 408 789** | **89 797 927** | **77 752 543** |
| 5100 Taxes on production, sale, transfer, etc | 1 388 653 | 14 048 655 | 36 447 297 | 44 038 074 | 64 688 081 | 65 786 951 | 74 003 567 | 79 935 336 | 88 064 087 | 75 960 351 |
| 5110 General taxes | 672 368 | 9 585 866 | 26 910 512 | 33 333 802 | 48 684 900 | 49 355 123 | 58 565 799 | 64 316 019 | 71 235 138 | 62 866 653 |
| 5111 Value added taxes | 583 078 | 8 445 776 | 23 377 821 | 28 811 682 | 41 659 696 | 41 878 886 | 50 619 849 | 55 879 110 | 61 936 282 | 53 912 648 |
| 5112 Sales tax | 89 290 | 1 140 090 | 3 532 691 | 4 522 121 | 7 025 204 | 7 476 238 | 7 945 950 | 8 436 909 | 9 298 856 | 8 954 004 |
| Industry and commerce tax (State) | 89 290 | 1 140 090 | 3 532 691 | 4 522 121 | 7 025 204 | 7 476 238 | 7 945 950 | 8 436 909 | 9 298 856 | 8 954 004 |
| 5113 Other | 0 | 0 | 0 | 0 | 0 | 0 | 0 | 0 | 0 | 0 |
| 5120 Taxes on specific goods and services | 716 285 | 4 462 789 | 9 536 785 | 10 704 271 | 16 003 181 | 16 431 827 | 15 437 768 | 15 619 317 | 16 828 948 | 13 093 698 |
| 5121 Excises | 404 699 | 2 718 692 | 5 276 999 | 6 052 273 | 11 412 250 | 12 318 641 | 11 616 844 | 12 061 132 | 12 995 955 | 10 159 930 |
| Oil | 141 270 | 833 004 | 1 211 511 | 1 418 766 | 3 297 392 | 3 335 157 | 1 352 793 | 1 517 546 | 1 585 141 | 1 205 806 |
| Tobacco (State) | 52 898 | 213 412 | 330 016 | 390 472 | 524 357 | 595 476 | 887 534 | 1 145 879 | 1 278 561 | 1 239 269 |
| Beer (State) | 85 722 | 471 135 | 1 203 838 | 1 432 453 | 2 305 895 | 2 549 949 | 2 572 771 | 2 637 674 | 2 611 466 | 2 243 811 |
| Liquors (State) | 124 808 | 520 394 | 834 390 | 929 328 | 1 253 466 | 1 574 864 | 1 907 802 | 1 800 605 | 2 146 818 | 1 675 472 |
| Restaurant, vehicles sale and mobile telephony | 0 | 0 | 0 | 0 | 1 684 179 | 1 700 069 | 1 948 718 | 2 047 419 | 2 208 669 | 1 226 863 |
| Carbon | 0 | 0 | 0 | 0 | 0 | 0 | 474 596 | 288 373 | 436 914 | 281 911 |
| Plastic bags | 0 | 0 | 0 | 0 | 0 | 0 | 6 546 | 28 099 | 37 331 | 43 777 |
| Medicinal cannabis | 0 | 0 | 0 | 0 | 0 | 0 | 10 | 3 | 145 | 972 |
| Diesel surcharge | 0 | 85 716 | 388 091 | 500 405 | 598 993 | 590 233 | 546 243 | 579 613 | 599 600 | 505 000 |
| Petrol surcharge | 0 | 595 031 | 1 309 154 | 1 380 848 | 1 747 969 | 1 972 893 | 1 919 830 | 2 015 922 | 2 091 310 | 1 737 050 |
| 5122 Profits of fiscal monopolies | 0 | 0 | 0 | 0 | 0 | 0 | 0 | 0 | 0 | 0 |
| 5123 Customs and import duties | 311 586 | 1 744 097 | 4 259 786 | 4 651 999 | 4 590 931 | 4 113 187 | 3 820 924 | 3 558 185 | 3 832 994 | 2 933 768 |
| Custom duties | 180 989 | 1 744 097 | 4 259 786 | 4 651 999 | 4 590 931 | 4 113 187 | 3 820 924 | 3 558 185 | 3 832 994 | 2 933 768 |
| Imports surcharge | 130 597 | 0 | 0 | 0 | 0 | 0 | 0 | 0 | 0 | 0 |
| 5124 Taxes on exports | 0 | 0 | 0 | 0 | 0 | 0 | 0 | 0 | 0 | 0 |
| 5125 Taxes on investment goods | 0 | 0 | 0 | 0 | 0 | 0 | 0 | 0 | 0 | 0 |

## Table 5.9. **Colombia** *(cont.)*

Details of tax revenue / Ingresos tributarios detallados

*Million COP*

| | 1990 | 2000 | 2007 | 2010 | 2015 | 2016 | 2017 | 2018 | 2019 | 2020 |
|---|---|---|---|---|---|---|---|---|---|---|
| 5126 Taxes on specific services | 0 | 0 | 0 | 0 | 0 | 0 | 0 | 0 | 0 | 0 |
| 5127 Other taxes on internat. trade and transactions | 0 | 0 | 0 | 0 | 0 | 0 | 0 | 0 | 0 | 0 |
| 5128 Other taxes | 0 | 0 | 0 | 0 | 0 | 0 | 0 | 0 | 0 | 0 |
| 5130 Unallocable between 5110 and 5120 | 0 | 0 | 0 | 0 | 0 | 0 | 0 | 0 | 0 | 0 |
| 5200 Taxes on use of goods and perform activities | 0 | 131 795 | 319 444 | 373 568 | 1 028 485 | 1 175 469 | 1 377 556 | 1 473 453 | 1 733 840 | 1 792 192 |
| 5210 Recurrent taxes | .. | 131 795 | 319 444 | 373 568 | 1 028 485 | 1 175 469 | 1 377 556 | 1 473 453 | 1 733 840 | 1 792 192 |
| 5211 Paid by households: motor vehicles | .. | 131 795 | 319 444 | 373 568 | 1 028 485 | 1 175 469 | 1 377 556 | 1 473 453 | 1 733 840 | 1 792 192 |
| Tax on motor vehicle ownership | .. | 131 795 | 319 444 | 373 568 | 1 028 485 | 1 175 469 | 1 377 556 | 1 473 453 | 1 733 840 | 1 792 192 |
| 5212 Paid by others: motor vehicles | .. | .. | .. | .. | .. | .. | .. | .. | .. | .. |
| 5213 Paid in respect of other goods | .. | .. | .. | .. | .. | .. | .. | .. | .. | .. |
| 5220 Non-recurrent taxes | .. | .. | .. | .. | .. | .. | .. | .. | .. | .. |
| 5300 Unallocable between 5100 and 5200 | 0 | 0 | 0 | 0 | 0 | 0 | 0 | 0 | 0 | 0 |
| **6000 Other taxes** | **159 323** | **1 011 197** | **2 968 147** | **3 789 014** | **7 245 701** | **6 979 271** | **7 237 021** | **7 928 320** | **9 289 906** | **7 646 264** |
| 6100 Paid solely by business | 0 | 0 | 0 | 0 | 0 | 0 | 0 | 0 | 0 | 0 |
| 6200 Other | 159 323 | 1 011 197 | 2 968 147 | 3 789 014 | 7 245 701 | 6 979 271 | 7 237 021 | 7 928 320 | 9 289 906 | 7 646 264 |
| Stamp tax | 0 | 401 497 | 759 787 | 357 160 | 101 668 | 97 492 | 75 493 | 79 868 | 85 799 | 41 373 |
| Other | 78 306 | 79 287 | 86 297 | 126 602 | 318 271 | 357 863 | 403 473 | 461 160 | 533 852 | 245 541 |
| Other (sub-national) | 81 017 | 530 413 | 2 122 062 | 3 305 252 | 6 825 762 | 6 523 916 | 6 758 055 | 7 387 293 | 8 670 255 | 7 359 350 |

.. Not available

*Note:* Year ending 31st December.

The data are on a cash basis.

Includes the reported consolidated revenues of the territorial entities (departments and municipalities).

Heading 1000: The income tax figures in 2020 under headings 1100, 1200 and 1300 are estimated.

Heading 2000: Before 2013, social security contributions did not include all the contributions entering FOSYGA (Solidarity and Guarantee Fund). Only the portion of the contributions used to finance the subsidised regime (up to 1.5 pp of the 12.5% of the monthly wage paid by employers and employees as an obligatory health contribution) was included. The part of the contributions entering FOSYGA to finance the contributory regime was classified in the social security sector as "other incomes". From 2013 onwards, all of the health contributions entering FOSYGA are classified as social security contributions. The portion of the contributions not entering FOSYGA that is both collected and spent by the health insurers – EPS - is not part of the fiscal accounts.

*Source:* Dirección de Impuestos y Aduanas Nacionales de Colombia, Ministerio de Hacienda y Crédito Público y Banco Central de Colombia. (National Tax and Customs Administration, Ministry of Finance and Public Credit and Central Bank of Colombia).

StatLink https://doi.org/10.1787/888934309511

## Table 5.10. **Costa Rica**

Details of tax revenue / Ingresos tributarios detallados

*Million CRC*

| | 1990 | 2000 | 2007 | 2010 | 2015 | 2016 | 2017 | 2018 | 2019 | 2020 |
|---|---|---|---|---|---|---|---|---|---|---|
| **Total tax revenue** | **117 711** | **978 114** | **3 213 401** | **4 382 367** | **6 923 575** | **7 528 752** | **7 893 642** | **8 339 991** | **8 855 885** | **8 235 528** |
| **1000 Taxes on income, profits and capital gains** | **11 820** | **128 805** | **531 552** | **748 093** | **1 247 308** | **1 416 218** | **1 562 063** | **1 699 258** | **1 854 866** | **1 651 249** |
| 1100 Of individuals | .. | .. | 123 194 | 202 849 | 386 241 | 414 247 | 446 519 | 483 645 | 540 954 | 556 084 |
| 1110 On income and profits | .. | .. | 123 194 | 202 849 | 386 241 | 414 247 | 446 519 | 483 645 | 535 412 | 554 486 |
| 1120 On capital gains | .. | .. | 0 | 0 | 0 | 0 | 0 | 0 | 5 542 | 1 598 |
| 1200 Corporate | .. | .. | 348 826 | 450 312 | 659 951 | 742 011 | 843 879 | 915 284 | 1 058 086 | 692 551 |
| 1210 On profits | .. | .. | 348 826 | 450 312 | 659 951 | 742 011 | 843 879 | 915 284 | 955 908 | 685 470 |
| 1220 On capital gains of corporates | .. | .. | 0 | 0 | 0 | 0 | 0 | 0 | 102 177 | 7 081 |
| 1300 Unallocable between 1100 and 1200 | 11 820 | 128 805 | 59 531 | 94 932 | 201 116 | 259 961 | 271 664 | 300 330 | 255 827 | 402 613 |
| **2000 Social security contributions** | **33 990** | **297 069** | **885 053** | **1 450 531** | **2 305 133** | **2 539 755** | **2 640 785** | **2 859 467** | **3 026 691** | **2 971 589** |
| 2100 Employees | .. | .. | .. | .. | .. | .. | .. | .. | .. | .. |
| 2110 On a payroll basis | .. | .. | .. | .. | .. | .. | .. | .. | .. | .. |
| 2120 On an income tax basis | .. | .. | .. | .. | .. | .. | .. | .. | .. | .. |
| 2200 Employers | 3 447 | 37 313 | 107 398 | 207 206 | 318 652 | 331 124 | 361 161 | 368 865 | 381 940 | 387 840 |
| Government contributions | 3 447 | 37 313 | 107 398 | 207 206 | 318 652 | 331 124 | 361 161 | 368 865 | 381 940 | 387 840 |
| 2210 On a payroll basis | .. | .. | .. | .. | .. | .. | .. | .. | .. | .. |
| 2220 On an income tax basis | .. | .. | .. | .. | .. | .. | .. | .. | .. | .. |
| 2300 Self-employed or non-employed | .. | .. | .. | .. | .. | .. | .. | .. | .. | .. |
| 2310 On a payroll basis | .. | .. | .. | .. | .. | .. | .. | .. | .. | .. |
| 2320 On an income tax basis | .. | .. | .. | .. | .. | .. | .. | .. | .. | .. |
| 2400 Unallocable between 2100, 2200 and 2300 | 30 543 | 259 756 | 777 654 | 1 243 325 | 1 986 481 | 2 208 631 | 2 279 624 | 2 490 602 | 2 644 751 | 2 583 749 |
| Contributions by employees and non-government employers | 30 543 | 249 182 | 727 844 | 1 139 265 | 1 785 522 | 1 985 151 | 1 971 472 | 2 157 256 | 2 274 644 | 2 212 249 |
| Contributions for the special regimes | 0 | 10 574 | 49 811 | 104 060 | 200 959 | 223 480 | 237 004 | 247 939 | 292 634 | 292 072 |
| 2410 On a payroll basis | .. | .. | .. | .. | .. | .. | .. | .. | .. | .. |
| 2420 On an income tax basis | .. | .. | .. | .. | .. | .. | .. | .. | .. | .. |
| **3000 Taxes on payroll and workforce** | **7 575** | **61 796** | **170 996** | **260 664** | **423 616** | **453 369** | **471 206** | **498 577** | **522 529** | **537 654** |
| Contributions by non-government employers | 7 484 | 59 129 | 165 677 | 248 259 | 406 296 | 435 328 | 453 128 | 478 523 | 501 734 | 515 624 |
| Contributions by government employers | 91 | 2 666 | 5 320 | 12 405 | 17 321 | 18 041 | 18 078 | 20 054 | 20 795 | 22 030 |
| **4000 Taxes on property** | **1 566** | **8 396** | **42 658** | **63 706** | **123 261** | **134 332** | **145 955** | **149 310** | **167 952** | **162 950** |
| 4100 Recurrent taxes on immovable property | 1 200 | 5 390 | 23 293 | 48 963 | 90 003 | 97 869 | 107 156 | 113 586 | 125 398 | 127 625 |
| Land tax | 0 | 0 | 0 | 0 | 0 | 0 | 0 | 0 | 0 | 0 |
| Additional land tax | 0 | 0 | 0 | 0 | 0 | 0 | 0 | 0 | 0 | 0 |
| Tax on sumptuary constructions | 0 | 0 | 0 | 0 | 0 | 0 | 0 | 0 | 0 | 0 |
| Immovable property tax | 0 | 0 | 0 | 3 527 | 4 076 | 4 098 | 4 255 | 4 468 | 4 699 | 4 655 |
| Municipal immovable property tax | 1 200 | 5 390 | 23 293 | 45 436 | 85 927 | 93 771 | 102 901 | 109 119 | 120 698 | 122 970 |
| 4110 Households | .. | .. | .. | .. | .. | .. | .. | .. | .. | .. |
| 4120 Others | .. | .. | .. | .. | .. | .. | .. | .. | .. | .. |
| 4200 Recurrent taxes on net wealth | 0 | 0 | 0 | 0 | 0 | 0 | 0 | 0 | 0 | 0 |
| 4210 Individual | .. | .. | .. | .. | .. | .. | .. | .. | .. | .. |
| 4220 Corporate | .. | .. | .. | .. | .. | .. | .. | .. | .. | .. |
| 4300 Estate, inheritance and gift taxes | 0 | 0 | 0 | 0 | 0 | 0 | 0 | 0 | 0 | 0 |
| 4310 Estate and inheritance taxes | .. | .. | .. | .. | .. | .. | .. | .. | .. | .. |
| 4320 Gift taxes | .. | .. | .. | .. | .. | .. | .. | .. | .. | .. |
| 4400 Taxes on financial and capital transactions | 366 | 3 007 | 19 366 | 14 743 | 33 258 | 36 462 | 38 799 | 35 724 | 42 554 | 35 300 |
| 4500 Non-recurrent taxes | 0 | 0 | 0 | 0 | 0 | 0 | 0 | 0 | 0 | 24 |
| 4510 On net wealth | .. | .. | .. | .. | .. | .. | .. | .. | .. | .. |
| 4520 Other non-recurrent taxes | .. | .. | .. | .. | .. | .. | .. | .. | .. | .. |
| 4600 Other recurrent taxes on property | 0 | 0 | 0 | 0 | 0 | 0 | 0 | 0 | 0 | 0 |
| **5000 Taxes on goods and services** | **53 509** | **456 851** | **1 505 510** | **1 766 914** | **2 661 902** | **2 794 229** | **2 875 333** | **2 918 471** | **3 081 941** | **2 745 118** |
| 5100 Taxes on production, sale, transfer, etc | 49 867 | 425 713 | 1 406 100 | 1 600 302 | 2 388 900 | 2 508 186 | 2 575 411 | 2 608 864 | 2 756 759 | 2 500 510 |
| 5110 General taxes | 21 326 | 222 775 | 797 850 | 920 298 | 1 368 601 | 1 420 938 | 1 466 986 | 1 513 677 | 1 662 503 | 1 649 531 |
| 5111 Value added taxes | 21 326 | 222 775 | 797 850 | 920 298 | 1 336 075 | 1 414 358 | 1 453 348 | 1 487 620 | 1 634 986 | 1 623 695 |
| 5112 Sales tax | 0 | 0 | 0 | 0 | 0 | 0 | 0 | 0 | 0 | 0 |
| 5113 Other | 0 | 0 | 0 | 0 | 32 526 | 6 580 | 13 638 | 26 057 | 27 517 | 25 836 |
| 5120 Taxes on specific goods and services | 28 541 | 202 939 | 608 250 | 680 004 | 1 020 299 | 1 087 248 | 1 108 425 | 1 095 187 | 1 094 256 | 850 979 |
| 5121 Excises | 11 096 | 157 204 | 447 168 | 523 617 | 798 412 | 846 864 | 870 225 | 858 424 | 864 985 | 688 784 |
| Fuels and energy | 0 | 0 | 250 577 | 320 638 | 457 827 | 472 644 | 510 260 | 517 666 | 552 017 | 436 384 |
| Alcoholic beverages | 0 | 8 229 | 23 802 | 28 035 | 43 095 | 43 400 | 43 176 | 45 610 | 43 849 | 44 373 |
| Non alcoholic beverages | 0 | 0 | 18 263 | 26 566 | 36 353 | 39 764 | 39 781 | 40 182 | 41 247 | 38 510 |
| Soaps | 0 | 0 | 883 | 1 317 | 2 562 | 2 912 | 2 332 | 2 712 | 3 020 | 3 052 |
| Cement | 0 | 0 | 0 | 227 | 304 | 267 | 311 | 289 | 216 | 123 |
| Tobacco | 0 | 0 | 0 | 0 | 33 681 | 32 560 | 30 590 | 30 766 | 27 185 | 23 896 |
| Abolished specific taxes on production and consumption | 0 | 0 | 0 | 0 | 0 | 0 | 0 | 0 | 0 | 0 |
| Other specific taxes on consumption | 11 096 | 148 975 | 153 643 | 146 834 | 224 590 | 255 317 | 243 775 | 221 200 | 197 452 | 142 447 |
| 5122 Profits of fiscal monopolies | 0 | 0 | 0 | 0 | 0 | 0 | 0 | 0 | 0 | 0 |

## Table 5.10. **Costa Rica** *(cont.)*

Details of tax revenue / Ingresos tributarios detallados

*Million CRC*

| | 1990 | 2000 | 2007 | 2010 | 2015 | 2016 | 2017 | 2018 | 2019 | 2020 |
|---|---|---|---|---|---|---|---|---|---|---|
| 5123 Customs and import duties | 15 052 | 40 485 | 134 576 | 126 134 | 174 568 | 185 544 | 179 188 | 175 368 | 164 224 | 133 733 |
| Import duties | 13 977 | 32 336 | 107 565 | 103 851 | 148 666 | 158 559 | 152 756 | 149 017 | 140 919 | 114 777 |
| Custom duties | 1 075 | 8 149 | 27 011 | 22 284 | 25 902 | 26 986 | 26 432 | 26 351 | 23 305 | 18 956 |
| Import duties on animals | 0 | 0 | 0 | 0 | 0 | 0 | 0 | 0 | 0 | 0 |
| 5124 Taxes on exports | 2 113 | 2 238 | 2 432 | 3 973 | 4 468 | 5 073 | 5 638 | 5 468 | 5 412 | 5 471 |
| Export duties | 2 113 | 2 088 | 2 260 | 3 816 | 2 701 | 3 250 | 3 673 | 3 594 | 3 502 | 3 777 |
| Export duties Law 133 | 0 | 0 | 0 | 0 | 0 | 0 | 0 | 0 | 0 | 0 |
| Export duties Law 5519 | 0 | 0 | 0 | 0 | 0 | 0 | 0 | 0 | 0 | 0 |
| Tax on banana exports | 0 | 150 | 172 | 157 | 156 | 184 | 199 | 193 | 184 | 199 |
| Export duties on ground transportation | 0 | 0 | 0 | 0 | 1 611 | 1 638 | 1 766 | 1 682 | 1 726 | 1 494 |
| 5125 Taxes on investment goods | 0 | 0 | 0 | 0 | 0 | 0 | 0 | 0 | 0 | 0 |
| 5126 Taxes on specific services | 280 | 2 929 | 23 242 | 24 767 | 38 687 | 44 934 | 48 290 | 50 554 | 54 556 | 18 463 |
| Casinos and gambling | 0 | 225 | 442 | 445 | 1 455 | 1 609 | 891 | 1 060 | 1 241 | 378 |
| Port cargo movements | 0 | 6 | 0 | 0 | 0 | 0 | 0 | 0 | 0 | 0 |
| Overseas departure tax | 0 | 0 | 22 799 | 24 322 | 37 232 | 43 325 | 47 399 | 49 494 | 53 315 | 18 085 |
| 10% on public shows | 0 | 0 | 0 | 0 | 0 | 0 | 0 | 0 | 0 | 0 |
| Pro-national airport's stamp tax | 0 | 0 | 0 | 0 | 0 | 0 | 0 | 0 | 0 | 0 |
| Stamp tax on the use of borders and ports | 280 | 2 697 | 0 | 0 | 0 | 0 | 0 | 0 | 0 | 0 |
| 5127 Other taxes on internat. trade and transactions | 0 | 83 | 832 | 1 513 | 3 093 | 3 512 | 3 695 | 3 785 | 3 841 | 3 304 |
| 5128 Other taxes | 0 | 0 | 0 | 0 | 1 071 | 1 320 | 1 389 | 1 589 | 1 238 | 1 225 |
| 5130 Unallocable between 5110 and 5120 | 0 | 0 | 0 | 0 | 0 | 0 | 0 | 0 | 0 | 0 |
| 5200 Taxes on use of goods and perform activities | 3 642 | 31 138 | 99 410 | 166 612 | 273 003 | 286 044 | 299 922 | 309 607 | 325 182 | 244 608 |
| 5210 Recurrent taxes | 3 642 | 31 138 | 99 410 | 166 612 | 273 003 | 286 044 | 299 922 | 309 607 | 325 182 | 244 608 |
| 5211 Paid by households: motor vehicles | 0 | 0 | 0 | 0 | 0 | 0 | 0 | 0 | 0 | 0 |
| 5212 Paid by others: motor vehicles | 1 425 | 15 374 | 52 511 | 94 102 | 145 894 | 156 517 | 164 034 | 171 523 | 181 198 | 108 198 |
| Property tax on vehicles, aircraft and boats | 1 425 | 15 374 | 52 511 | 94 102 | 145 894 | 156 517 | 164 034 | 171 523 | 181 198 | 108 198 |
| 5213 Paid in respect of other goods | 2 217 | 15 763 | 46 899 | 72 510 | 127 109 | 129 527 | 135 888 | 138 084 | 143 984 | 136 410 |
| Local taxes | 1 262 | 11 898 | 43 874 | 68 808 | 122 248 | 124 862 | 130 639 | 132 514 | 137 979 | 130 332 |
| Hunting and fishing licences | 0 | 0 | 0 | 0 | 0 | 0 | 0 | 0 | 0 | 0 |
| Spirits licence | 0 | 0 | 0 | 0 | 0 | 0 | 0 | 0 | 0 | 0 |
| Revenue stamps | 955 | 3 866 | 3 025 | 3 702 | 4 861 | 4 664 | 5 249 | 5 571 | 6 004 | 6 078 |
| Sport stamp tax | 0 | 0 | 0 | 0 | 0 | 0 | 0 | 0 | 0 | 0 |
| 5220 Non-recurrent taxes | 0 | 0 | 0 | 0 | 0 | 0 | 0 | 0 | 0 | 0 |
| 5300 Unallocable between 5100 and 5200 | 0 | 0 | 0 | 0 | 0 | 0 | 0 | 0 | 0 | 0 |
| **6000 Other taxes** | **9 251** | **25 198** | **77 632** | **92 460** | **162 355** | **190 850** | **198 300** | **214 908** | **201 906** | **166 969** |
| 6100 Paid solely by business | 0 | 0 | 0 | 0 | 0 | 0 | 0 | 0 | 0 | 0 |
| 6200 Other | 9 251 | 25 198 | 77 632 | 92 460 | 162 355 | 190 850 | 198 300 | 214 908 | 201 906 | 166 969 |
| Transfers of vehicles, aircraft and boats | 497 | 2 530 | 9 937 | 12 311 | 20 999 | 23 022 | 21 872 | 22 265 | 23 223 | 22 593 |
| Tax revenue from decentralised units | 2 764 | 15 048 | 22 257 | 29 969 | 49 334 | 67 584 | 68 127 | 63 329 | 67 968 | 60 054 |
| Other taxes | 5 990 | 7 620 | 45 438 | 50 180 | 92 022 | 100 243 | 108 181 | 129 268 | 110 654 | 84 266 |

.. Not available

*Note:* Year ending 31st December.

The data are on a cash basis.

Heading 2000: The data include social security contributions paid by the governments for their employees as well as the contributions for special regimes (teachers and magistrates). In ECLAC data, social security contributions also include INA (National Institute of Apprenticeship), IMAS (Joint Social Aid Institute) and FODESAF (Social Development and Family Allowances Fund).

Heading 3000: In Costa Rica and for ECLAC, social security contributions from decentralised institutions are classified under heading 2000.

Heading 5212: In ECLAC data, tax on ownership of vehicles, aircraft and boats is classified in category 4000.

Heading 6200: The figures include the tax revenue of decentralised bodies (other than social security contributions). The tax revenue of decentralised bodies is classified under central government. In Costa Rica this revenue is classified under a separate unit (decentralised) considered to be separate from the central government.

In ECLAC data, the tax on the transfer of used vehicles Law No. 7088 of 30/11/87 is classified as a property tax.

*Source:* Secretaría Técnica de la Autoridad Presupuestaria, Ministerio de Finanzas y Contraloría General de la República (Technical Secretary of the Budgeting Authority, Ministry of Finance and National General Comptroller).

StatLink https://doi.org/10.1787/888934309530

## Table 5.11. **Cuba**

Details of tax revenue / Ingresos tributarios detallados

*Million CUP*

| | 1990 | 2000 | 2007 | 2010 | 2015 | 2016 | 2017 | 2018 | 2019 | 2020 |
|---|---|---|---|---|---|---|---|---|---|---|
| **Total tax revenue** | **6 265** | **11 367** | **25 787** | **23 949** | **33 182** | **37 597** | **41 021** | **42 307** | **43 504** | **40 263** |
| **1000 Taxes on income, profits and capital gains** | **14** | **1 826** | **3 403** | **3 603** | **6 676** | **8 018** | **9 931** | **11 094** | **12 257** | **11 383** |
| 1100 Of individuals | 14 | 291 | 404 | 554 | 1 848 | 2 343 | 3 279 | 4 002 | 4 762 | 4 587 |
| 1110 On income and profits | .. | .. | .. | .. | .. | .. | .. | .. | .. | .. |
| 1120 On capital gains | .. | .. | .. | .. | .. | .. | .. | .. | .. | .. |
| 1200 Corporate | 0 | 1 535 | 2 999 | 3 049 | 4 828 | 5 675 | 6 651 | 7 092 | 7 495 | 6 797 |
| 1210 On profits | .. | .. | .. | .. | .. | .. | .. | .. | .. | .. |
| 1220 On capital gains of corporates | .. | .. | .. | .. | .. | .. | .. | .. | .. | .. |
| 1300 Unallocable between 1100 and 1200 | 0 | 0 | 0 | 0 | 0 | 0 | 0 | 0 | 0 | 0 |
| **2000 Social security contributions** | **691** | **1 181** | **2 412** | **2 974** | **4 322** | **4 710** | **5 108** | **5 206** | **5 727** | **6 433** |
| 2100 Employees | .. | .. | .. | .. | .. | .. | .. | .. | .. | .. |
| 2110 On a payroll basis | .. | .. | .. | .. | .. | .. | .. | .. | .. | .. |
| 2120 On an income tax basis | .. | .. | .. | .. | .. | .. | .. | .. | .. | .. |
| 2200 Employers | .. | .. | .. | .. | .. | .. | .. | .. | .. | .. |
| 2210 On a payroll basis | .. | .. | .. | .. | .. | .. | .. | .. | .. | .. |
| 2220 On an income tax basis | .. | .. | .. | .. | .. | .. | .. | .. | .. | .. |
| 2300 Self-employed or non-employed | .. | .. | .. | .. | .. | .. | .. | .. | .. | .. |
| 2310 On a payroll basis | .. | .. | .. | .. | .. | .. | .. | .. | .. | .. |
| 2320 On an income tax basis | .. | .. | .. | .. | .. | .. | .. | .. | .. | .. |
| 2400 Unallocable between 2100, 2200 and 2300 | 691 | 1 181 | 2 412 | 2 974 | 4 322 | 4 710 | 5 108 | 5 206 | 5 727 | 6 433 |
| 2410 On a payroll basis | 691 | 1 181 | 2 412 | 2 974 | 4 322 | 4 710 | 5 108 | 5 206 | 5 727 | 6 433 |
| 2420 On an income tax basis | 0 | 0 | 0 | 0 | 0 | 0 | 0 | 0 | 0 | 0 |
| **3000 Taxes on payroll and workforce** | **0** | **970** | **3 417** | **4 414** | **2 753** | **2 411** | **1 385** | **1 273** | **1 415** | **1 605** |
| **4000 Taxes on property** | **0** | **0** | **0** | **0** | **0** | **0** | **0** | **0** | **0** | **0** |
| 4100 Recurrent taxes on immovable property | .. | .. | .. | .. | .. | .. | .. | .. | .. | .. |
| 4110 Households | .. | .. | .. | .. | .. | .. | .. | .. | .. | .. |
| 4120 Others | .. | .. | .. | .. | .. | .. | .. | .. | .. | .. |
| 4200 Recurrent taxes on net wealth | .. | .. | .. | .. | .. | .. | .. | .. | .. | .. |
| 4210 Individual | .. | .. | .. | .. | .. | .. | .. | .. | .. | .. |
| 4220 Corporate | .. | .. | .. | .. | .. | .. | .. | .. | .. | .. |
| 4300 Estate, inheritance and gift taxes | .. | .. | .. | .. | .. | .. | .. | .. | .. | .. |
| 4310 Estate and inheritance taxes | .. | .. | .. | .. | .. | .. | .. | .. | .. | .. |
| 4320 Gift taxes | .. | .. | .. | .. | .. | .. | .. | .. | .. | .. |
| 4400 Taxes on financial and capital transactions | .. | .. | .. | .. | .. | .. | .. | .. | .. | .. |
| 4500 Non-recurrent taxes | .. | .. | .. | .. | .. | .. | .. | .. | .. | .. |
| 4510 On net wealth | .. | .. | .. | .. | .. | .. | .. | .. | .. | .. |
| 4520 Other non-recurrent taxes | .. | .. | .. | .. | .. | .. | .. | .. | .. | .. |
| 4600 Other recurrent taxes on property | .. | .. | .. | .. | .. | .. | .. | .. | .. | .. |
| **5000 Taxes on goods and services** | **5 443** | **6 732** | **15 875** | **12 283** | **17 742** | **20 309** | **22 055** | **21 969** | **20 995** | **18 673** |
| 5100 Taxes on production, sale, transfer, etc | 5 443 | 6 732 | 15 875 | 12 283 | 17 742 | 20 309 | 22 055 | 21 969 | 20 995 | 18 673 |
| 5110 General taxes | 5 017 | 6 131 | 14 464 | 10 525 | 15 611 | 17 690 | 17 961 | 17 623 | 16 619 | 14 498 |
| 5111 Value added taxes | 0 | 0 | 0 | 0 | 0 | 0 | 0 | 0 | 0 | 0 |
| 5112 Sales tax | 5 017 | 6 131 | 14 464 | 10 525 | 15 611 | 17 690 | 17 961 | 17 623 | 16 619 | 14 498 |
| 5113 Other | 0 | 0 | 0 | 0 | 0 | 0 | 0 | 0 | 0 | 0 |
| 5120 Taxes on specific goods and services | 426 | 602 | 1 412 | 1 758 | 2 131 | 2 618 | 4 094 | 4 346 | 4 376 | 4 175 |
| 5121 Excises | .. | .. | .. | .. | .. | .. | .. | .. | .. | .. |
| 5122 Profits of fiscal monopolies | .. | .. | .. | .. | .. | .. | .. | .. | .. | .. |
| 5123 Customs and import duties | .. | .. | .. | .. | .. | .. | .. | .. | .. | .. |
| 5124 Taxes on exports | .. | .. | .. | .. | .. | .. | .. | .. | .. | .. |
| 5125 Taxes on investment goods | .. | .. | .. | .. | .. | .. | .. | .. | .. | .. |
| 5126 Taxes on specific services | .. | .. | .. | .. | .. | .. | .. | .. | .. | .. |
| 5127 Other taxes on internat. trade and transactions | .. | .. | .. | .. | .. | .. | .. | .. | .. | .. |
| 5128 Other taxes | .. | .. | .. | .. | .. | .. | .. | .. | .. | .. |
| 5130 Unallocable between 5110 and 5120 | 0 | 0 | 0 | 0 | 0 | 0 | 0 | 0 | 0 | 0 |
| 5200 Taxes on use of goods and perform activities | 0 | 0 | 0 | 0 | 0 | 0 | 0 | 0 | 0 | 0 |
| 5210 Recurrent taxes | .. | .. | .. | .. | .. | .. | .. | .. | .. | .. |
| 5211 Paid by households: motor vehicles | .. | .. | .. | .. | .. | .. | .. | .. | .. | .. |
| 5212 Paid by others: motor vehicles | .. | .. | .. | .. | .. | .. | .. | .. | .. | .. |
| 5213 Paid in respect of other goods | .. | .. | .. | .. | .. | .. | .. | .. | .. | .. |
| 5220 Non-recurrent taxes | .. | .. | .. | .. | .. | .. | .. | .. | .. | .. |
| 5300 Unallocable between 5100 and 5200 | 0 | 0 | 0 | 0 | 0 | 0 | 0 | 0 | 0 | 0 |
| **6000 Other taxes** | **117** | **657** | **681** | **675** | **1 690** | **2 149** | **2 543** | **2 766** | **3 110** | **2 169** |
| 6100 Paid solely by business | .. | .. | .. | .. | .. | .. | .. | .. | .. | .. |
| 6200 Other | .. | .. | .. | .. | .. | .. | .. | .. | .. | .. |

## Table 5.11. **Cuba** *(cont.)*

Details of tax revenue / Ingresos tributarios detallados

.. Not available

*Note:* Year ending 31st December.

The data are on a cash basis.

The figures for the sub-categories under the heading 5120 are not available.

Central and local government tax revenues are only available between 2002 and 2012.

There are discrepancies between national tax revenue data and the sum of central and local tax revenues mainly due to rounding.

*Source:* Ministerio de Finanzas y Precios de la República de Cuba (Ministry of Finance and Prices of the Republic of Cuba); Oficina Nacional de Estadísticas de Cuba (National Statistics Office of Cuba).

StatLink https://doi.org/10.1787/888934309549

## Table 5.12. **Dominican Republic / República Dominicana**

Details of tax revenue / Ingresos tributarios detallados

*Million DOP*

| | 1990 | 2000 | 2007 | 2010 | 2015 | 2016 | 2017 | 2018 | 2019 | 2020 |
|---|---|---|---|---|---|---|---|---|---|---|
| **Total tax revenue** | **6 424** | **48 310** | **218 887** | **245 327** | **416 611** | **455 827** | **503 494** | **560 962** | **617 802** | **559 572** |
| **1000 Taxes on income, profits and capital gains** | **1 650** | **10 708** | **55 093** | **53 492** | **119 580** | **135 416** | **154 762** | **170 561** | **194 281** | **188 486** |
| 1100 Of individuals | .. | 4 088 | 14 665 | 17 088 | 35 549 | 40 193 | 43 553 | 51 425 | 59 448 | 58 747 |
| 1110 On income and profits | .. | 4 070 | 14 577 | 16 901 | 35 187 | 39 775 | 43 097 | 51 031 | 58 842 | 58 355 |
| 1120 On capital gains | .. | 18 | 87 | 187 | 361 | 418 | 456 | 394 | 606 | 392 |
| 1200 Corporate | .. | 4 605 | 29 063 | 21 325 | 61 455 | 69 079 | 82 785 | 88 079 | 96 181 | 90 442 |
| 1210 On profits | .. | 4 605 | 29 063 | 21 325 | 61 455 | 69 079 | 82 785 | 88 079 | 96 181 | 90 442 |
| 1220 On capital gains of corporates | .. | .. | .. | .. | .. | .. | .. | .. | .. | .. |
| 1300 Unallocable between 1100 and 1200 | 1 670 | 2 015 | 11 365 | 15 080 | 22 576 | 26 144 | 28 425 | 31 057 | 38 652 | 39 297 |
| **2000 Social security contributions** | **53** | **490** | **860** | **1 845** | **1 483** | **1 550** | **2 635** | **2 514** | **2 553** | **2 661** |
| 2100 Employees | .. | .. | 775 | 1 720 | 1 321 | 1 392 | 1 535 | .. | .. | .. |
| 2110 On a payroll basis | .. | .. | .. | .. | .. | .. | .. | .. | .. | .. |
| 2120 On an income tax basis | .. | .. | .. | .. | .. | .. | .. | .. | .. | .. |
| 2200 Employers | .. | .. | 85 | 125 | 163 | 158 | 1 099 | .. | .. | .. |
| 2210 On a payroll basis | .. | .. | .. | .. | .. | .. | .. | .. | .. | .. |
| 2220 On an income tax basis | .. | .. | .. | .. | .. | .. | .. | .. | .. | .. |
| 2300 Self-employed or non-employed | .. | .. | 0 | 0 | 0 | 0 | 0 | .. | .. | .. |
| 2310 On a payroll basis | .. | .. | .. | .. | .. | .. | .. | .. | .. | .. |
| 2320 On an income tax basis | .. | .. | .. | .. | .. | .. | .. | .. | .. | .. |
| 2400 Unallocable between 2100, 2200 and 2300 | 53 | 490 | 0 | 0 | 0 | 0 | 0 | 2 514 | 2 553 | 2 661 |
| 2410 On a payroll basis | 53 | 490 | .. | .. | .. | .. | .. | 2 514 | 2 553 | 2 661 |
| 2420 On an income tax basis | 0 | 0 | .. | .. | .. | .. | .. | 0 | 0 | 0 |
| **3000 Taxes on payroll and workforce** | **0** | **0** | **927** | **1 385** | **2 366** | **2 636** | **2 912** | **3 282** | **3 502** | **3 141** |
| **4000 Taxes on property** | **74** | **689** | **9 996** | **13 315** | **19 044** | **20 717** | **22 942** | **25 716** | **29 564** | **25 252** |
| 4100 Recurrent taxes on immovable property | 9 | 115 | 594 | 555 | 1 755 | 1 871 | 2 166 | 2 527 | 2 904 | 2 857 |
| 4110 Households | 9 | 115 | 594 | 555 | 1 755 | 1 871 | 2 166 | 2 527 | 2 904 | 2 857 |
| 4120 Others | 0 | 0 | 0 | 0 | 0 | 0 | 0 | 0 | 0 | 0 |
| 4200 Recurrent taxes on net wealth | 0 | 0 | 1 281 | 2 449 | 3 445 | 3 544 | 4 113 | 4 609 | 5 155 | 4 522 |
| Tax on assets | .. | .. | 1 281 | 2 449 | 3 445 | 3 544 | 4 113 | 4 609 | 5 155 | 4 522 |
| 4210 Individual | .. | .. | .. | .. | .. | .. | .. | .. | .. | .. |
| 4220 Corporate | .. | .. | .. | .. | .. | .. | .. | .. | .. | .. |
| 4300 Estate, inheritance and gift taxes | 11 | 96 | 143 | 231 | 418 | 388 | 455 | 526 | 715 | 523 |
| 4310 Estate and inheritance taxes | .. | .. | .. | .. | .. | .. | .. | .. | .. | .. |
| 4320 Gift taxes | .. | .. | .. | .. | .. | .. | .. | .. | .. | .. |
| 4400 Taxes on financial and capital transactions | 40 | 377 | 7 375 | 8 658 | 12 067 | 13 265 | 13 995 | 15 675 | 17 594 | 15 634 |
| Tax on checks | 0 | 0 | 3 833 | 4 262 | 5 951 | 6 591 | 7 117 | 8 139 | 8 646 | 8 644 |
| Real estate operations | 22 | 217 | 3 291 | 3 864 | 5 169 | 5 668 | 5 802 | 6 320 | 7 526 | 5 910 |
| Tax on the transfer of immovable property | 18 | 160 | 252 | 533 | 947 | 1 005 | 1 076 | 1 215 | 1 422 | 1 080 |
| 4500 Non-recurrent taxes | 3 | 32 | 270 | 488 | 591 | 681 | 711 | 553 | 931 | 779 |
| 4510 On net wealth | 3 | 32 | 270 | 488 | 591 | 681 | 711 | 553 | 931 | 779 |
| 4520 Other non-recurrent taxes | 0 | 0 | 0 | 0 | 0 | 0 | 0 | 0 | 0 | 0 |
| 4600 Other recurrent taxes on property | 11 | 70 | 333 | 934 | 769 | 969 | 1 503 | 1 827 | 2 266 | 936 |
| **5000 Taxes on goods and services** | **4 487** | **35 927** | **150 465** | **175 290** | **274 137** | **295 506** | **320 242** | **358 888** | **387 900** | **340 031** |
| 5100 Taxes on production, sale, transfer, etc | 4 418 | 35 209 | 144 024 | 168 791 | 263 675 | 282 571 | 306 942 | 344 706 | 370 718 | 328 258 |
| 5110 General taxes | 970 | 9 912 | 66 613 | 81 226 | 147 039 | 159 212 | 169 629 | 194 725 | 214 324 | 194 408 |
| 5111 Value added taxes | 970 | 9 912 | 66 613 | 81 226 | 147 039 | 159 212 | 169 629 | 194 725 | 214 324 | 194 408 |
| 5112 Sales tax | 0 | 0 | 0 | 0 | 0 | 0 | 0 | 0 | 0 | 0 |
| 5113 Other | 0 | 0 | 0 | 0 | 0 | 0 | 0 | 0 | 0 | 0 |
| 5120 Taxes on specific goods and services | 3 449 | 25 297 | 77 411 | 87 566 | 116 636 | 123 359 | 137 313 | 149 981 | 156 394 | 133 851 |
| 5121 Excises | 495 | 6 614 | 47 888 | 56 024 | 74 586 | 78 105 | 89 681 | 97 278 | 102 087 | 86 459 |
| Alcoholic beverages | 251 | 2 451 | 13 101 | 15 054 | 22 371 | 23 617 | 25 694 | 28 882 | 30 610 | 29 336 |
| Tobacco products | 102 | 469 | 3 284 | 4 529 | 4 532 | 4 117 | 5 120 | 4 355 | 3 923 | 3 507 |
| Petroleum products | 89 | 3 143 | 29 985 | 34 598 | 43 315 | 45 698 | 53 075 | 57 053 | 60 828 | 47 854 |
| Other excises | 52 | 551 | 1 518 | 1 843 | 4 367 | 4 674 | 5 792 | 6 988 | 6 725 | 5 762 |
| 5122 Profits of fiscal monopolies | 0 | 0 | 0 | 0 | 0 | 0 | 0 | 0 | 0 | 0 |
| 5123 Customs and import duties | 1 548 | 13 459 | 19 337 | 19 455 | 25 212 | 27 286 | 28 703 | 32 096 | 32 478 | 29 630 |
| Import duties | 615 | 13 456 | 19 336 | 19 455 | 24 378 | 26 397 | 27 276 | 30 931 | 32 478 | 29 630 |
| Others | 933 | 3 | 1 | 0 | 834 | 889 | 1 426 | 1 165 | 0 | 0 |
| 5124 Taxes on exports | 6 | 4 | 83 | 146 | 8 | 0 | 0 | 0 | 0 | 0 |
| 5125 Taxes on investment goods | 0 | 0 | 0 | 0 | 0 | 0 | 0 | 0 | 0 | 0 |
| 5126 Taxes on specific services | 364 | 1 664 | 9 350 | 11 562 | 16 485 | 17 644 | 18 549 | 20 173 | 21 318 | 17 551 |
| Telecommunications | 85 | 0 | 3 867 | 4 886 | 6 375 | 6 607 | 6 781 | 7 146 | 7 313 | 7 494 |
| Insurance premiums | 33 | 584 | 2 211 | 3 088 | 4 301 | 4 828 | 5 236 | 5 976 | 6 782 | 7 128 |
| Departure tax | 204 | 809 | 3 131 | 3 428 | 5 535 | 5 892 | 6 252 | 6 933 | 7 180 | 2 894 |
| Hotels | 22 | 191 | 0 | 0 | 0 | 0 | 0 | 0 | 0 | 0 |
| Casinos | 16 | 59 | 140 | 151 | 184 | 228 | 237 | 0 | 0 | 0 |
| Racetracks | 4 | 15 | 0 | 0 | 0 | 0 | 0 | 0 | 0 | 0 |
| Phone gaming | 0 | 0 | 0 | 0 | 56 | 55 | 25 | 0 | 0 | 0 |
| Others | 0 | 7 | 2 | 9 | 35 | 34 | 18 | 119 | 43 | 35 |

## Table 5.12. **Dominican Republic / República Dominicana** *(cont.)*

Details of tax revenue / Ingresos tributarios detallados

*Million DOP*

| | 1990 | 2000 | 2007 | 2010 | 2015 | 2016 | 2017 | 2018 | 2019 | 2020 |
|---|---|---|---|---|---|---|---|---|---|---|
| 5127 Other taxes on internat. trade and transactions | 1 037 | 3 556 | 753 | 379 | 346 | 323 | 380 | 435 | 511 | 211 |
| Exchange commission | 857 | 3 412 | 233 | 70 | 0 | 0 | 0 | 0 | 0 | 0 |
| Consular fees | 77 | 32 | 342 | 132 | 137 | 149 | 153 | 153 | 156 | 72 |
| Others | 103 | 112 | 178 | 176 | 209 | 174 | 227 | 281 | 355 | 139 |
| 5128 Other taxes | 0 | 0 | 0 | 0 | 0 | 0 | 0 | 0 | 0 | 0 |
| 5130 Unallocable between 5110 and 5120 | 0 | 0 | 0 | 0 | 0 | 0 | 0 | 0 | 0 | 0 |
| 5200 Taxes on use of goods and perform activities | 69 | 718 | 6 441 | 6 498 | 10 463 | 12 935 | 13 300 | 14 182 | 17 183 | 11 773 |
| 5210 Recurrent taxes | 69 | 718 | 2 301 | 2 265 | 2 958 | 3 365 | 3 553 | 3 804 | 4 906 | 2 262 |
| 5211 Paid by households: motor vehicles | 45 | 268 | 1 391 | 1 277 | 1 558 | 1 932 | 2 081 | 2 310 | 3 407 | 1 189 |
| 5212 Paid by others: motor vehicles | 0 | 0 | 0 | 0 | 0 | 0 | 0 | 0 | 0 | 0 |
| 5213 Paid in respect of other goods | 24 | 450 | 910 | 988 | 1 400 | 1 433 | 1 472 | 1 494 | 1 499 | 1 072 |
| Licences to carry firearms | 17 | 237 | 316 | 296 | 171 | 190 | 176 | 192 | 182 | 162 |
| Licences to operate gambling houses | 0 | 114 | 217 | 211 | 1 208 | 1 210 | 1 250 | 1 262 | 1 268 | 885 |
| Licences to operate slot machines | 4 | 60 | 371 | 458 | 0 | 0 | 0 | 0 | 0 | 0 |
| Others | 4 | 39 | 7 | 24 | 21 | 34 | 46 | 41 | 49 | 26 |
| 5220 Non-recurrent taxes | 0 | 0 | 4 140 | 4 234 | 7 505 | 9 570 | 9 747 | 10 378 | 12 277 | 9 511 |
| Vehicle property registration | .. | .. | 4 140 | 4 234 | 6 990 | 8 903 | 9 072 | 9 667 | 11 442 | 8 882 |
| Ecological taxes | .. | .. | 0 | 0 | 515 | 667 | 675 | 711 | 835 | 629 |
| 5300 Unallocable between 5100 and 5200 | 0 | 0 | 0 | 0 | 0 | 0 | 0 | 0 | 0 | 0 |
| **6000 Other taxes** | **159** | **495** | **1 546** | **0** | **1** | **1** | **1** | **1** | **2** | **1** |
| 6100 Paid solely by business | 0 | 0 | 0 | .. | 0 | 0 | 0 | 0 | 0 | 0 |
| 6200 Other | 159 | 495 | 1 546 | .. | 1 | 1 | 1 | 1 | 2 | 1 |

.. Not available

*Note:* Year ending 31st December.

The data are on a cash basis.

The figures exclude local government tax revenues as the data are not available.

Heading 2000: The data exclude social security contributions to general government managed by the private sector. An additional breakdown has been available between 2006 and 2017 to distinguish between social security contributions paid by employees and those paid by employers.

Heading 3000: This heading includes the mandatory non-pensions contributions to the Instituto de Formacion Tecnico Profesinal (INFOTEP). The tax revenue is classified under the central government. In Dominican Republic this revenue is classified under a separate unit (decentralised) considered to be different to the central government.

Heading 5126: Tax on national racetracks, tax on gaming casinos and tax on telephone games have been classified under heading 5126 in this edition. They were previously under heading 1200.

Heading 5211: In ECLAC data, the vehicle transfer tax is classified as a property tax (4000).

*Source:* Ministerio de Hacienda (Ministry of Finance); Instituto Nacional de Formación Técnico Profesional (National Institute for Technical and Vocational Training).

StatLink https://doi.org/10.1787/888934309568

## Table 5.13. **Ecuador**

Details of tax revenue / Ingresos tributarios detallados

*Million USD*

| | 1990 | 2000 | 2007 | 2010 | 2015 | 2016 | 2017 | 2018 | 2019 | 2020 |
|---|---|---|---|---|---|---|---|---|---|---|
| **Total tax revenue** | **1 078** | **2 125** | **7 698** | **11 693** | **21 591** | **19 897** | **20 759** | **22 290** | **21 665** | **18 908** |
| **1000 Taxes on income, profits and capital gains** | **139** | **268** | **1 743** | **2 924** | **5 010** | **4 386** | **4 134** | **5 246** | **4 669** | **4 503** |
| 1100 Of individuals | .. | 10 | 39 | 80 | 192 | 224 | 180 | 193 | 197 | 155 |
| 1110 On income and profits | .. | 10 | 39 | 80 | 192 | 224 | 180 | 193 | 197 | 155 |
| Personal income tax | .. | 10 | 39 | 80 | 192 | 164 | 176 | 193 | 197 | 155 |
| Solidarity contribution on remuneration | .. | 0 | 0 | 0 | 0 | 60 | 5 | 0 | 0 | 0 |
| 1120 On capital gains | .. | .. | .. | 0 | 0 | 0 | 0 | 0 | 0 | 0 |
| 1200 Corporate | .. | 53 | 424 | 1 046 | 1 723 | 1 377 | 1 074 | 1 894 | 1 308 | 1 333 |
| 1210 On profits | .. | 53 | 424 | 1 046 | 1 723 | 1 377 | 1 074 | 1 894 | 1 308 | 1 333 |
| Corporate income tax | .. | 53 | 424 | 474 | 1 655 | 943 | 991 | 1 808 | 1 232 | 1 276 |
| Income tax on oil companies and others | .. | 0 | 0 | 572 | 68 | 79 | 63 | 81 | 75 | 57 |
| Solidarity contribution on profits | .. | 0 | 0 | 0 | 0 | 355 | 19 | 4 | 0 | 0 |
| 1220 On capital gains of corporates | .. | .. | .. | .. | .. | .. | .. | .. | .. | .. |
| 1300 Unallocable between 1100 and 1200 | 139 | 206 | 1 279 | 1 798 | 3 094 | 2 784 | 2 880 | 3 159 | 3 164 | 3 015 |
| Withholding tax | 0 | 190 | 1 047 | 1 560 | 2 753 | 2 411 | 2 578 | 2 858 | 2 847 | 2 787 |
| Income tax advances | 0 | 14 | 227 | 298 | 366 | 335 | 343 | 353 | 394 | 290 |
| Income tax refunds | 0 | 0 | 0 | -75 | -99 | -32 | -112 | -132 | -151 | -112 |
| Other income taxes (local) | 1 | 2 | 5 | 15 | 75 | 71 | 71 | 81 | 74 | 50 |
| **2000 Social security contributions** | **243** | **228** | **1 792** | **2 541** | **5 062** | **4 755** | **5 428** | **5 541** | **5 863** | **5 443** |
| 2100 Employees | .. | .. | .. | .. | .. | .. | .. | .. | .. | .. |
| 2110 On a payroll basis | .. | .. | .. | .. | .. | .. | .. | .. | .. | .. |
| 2120 On an income tax basis | .. | .. | .. | .. | .. | .. | .. | .. | .. | .. |
| 2200 Employers | .. | .. | .. | .. | .. | .. | .. | .. | .. | .. |
| 2210 On a payroll basis | .. | .. | .. | .. | .. | .. | .. | .. | .. | .. |
| 2220 On an income tax basis | .. | .. | .. | .. | .. | .. | .. | .. | .. | .. |
| 2300 Self-employed or non-employed | .. | .. | .. | .. | .. | .. | .. | .. | .. | .. |
| 2310 On a payroll basis | .. | .. | .. | .. | .. | .. | .. | .. | .. | .. |
| 2320 On an income tax basis | .. | .. | .. | .. | .. | .. | .. | .. | .. | .. |
| 2400 Unallocable between 2100, 2200 and 2300 | 243 | 228 | 1 792 | 2 541 | 5 062 | 4 755 | 5 428 | 5 541 | 5 863 | 5 443 |
| 2410 On a payroll basis | .. | .. | .. | .. | .. | .. | .. | .. | .. | .. |
| 2420 On an income tax basis | .. | .. | .. | .. | .. | .. | .. | .. | .. | .. |
| **3000 Taxes on payroll and workforce** | **0** | **0** | **0** | **0** | **0** | **0** | **0** | **0** | **0** | **0** |
| **4000 Taxes on property** | **16** | **17** | **91** | **159** | **304** | **639** | **347** | **372** | **353** | **334** |
| 4100 Recurrent taxes on immovable property | 13 | 8 | 48 | 68 | 134 | 142 | 162 | 192 | 185 | 172 |
| Rural land tax | 0 | 0 | 0 | 3 | 9 | 8 | 7 | 2 | 0 | 0 |
| 4110 Households | 0 | 0 | 0 | 0 | 0 | .. | .. | 0 | 0 | 0 |
| 4120 Others | 13 | 8 | 48 | 66 | 125 | 134 | 155 | 190 | 185 | 172 |
| Tax on urban properties | 12 | 7 | 40 | 55 | 106 | 113 | 129 | 162 | 158 | 145 |
| Tax on rural properties | 1 | 1 | 8 | 10 | 19 | 21 | 26 | 27 | 27 | 27 |
| 4200 Recurrent taxes on net wealth | 0 | 0 | 0 | 35 | 49 | 47 | 35 | 30 | 35 | 31 |
| 4210 Individual | .. | .. | .. | 0 | 0 | 0 | 0 | 0 | 0 | 0 |
| 4220 Corporate | .. | .. | .. | 35 | 49 | 47 | 35 | 30 | 35 | 31 |
| Tax on foreign assets | .. | .. | .. | 35 | 49 | 47 | 35 | 30 | 35 | 31 |
| 4300 Estate, inheritance and gift taxes | 0 | 0 | 3 | 5 | 29 | 15 | 26 | 27 | 24 | 24 |
| 4310 Estate and inheritance taxes | .. | .. | 3 | 5 | 29 | 15 | 26 | 27 | 24 | 24 |
| 4320 Gift taxes | .. | .. | 0 | 0 | 0 | 0 | 0 | 0 | 0 | 0 |
| 4400 Taxes on financial and capital transactions | 0 | 0 | 0 | 0 | 0 | 0 | 0 | 0 | 0 | 0 |
| 4500 Non-recurrent taxes | 0 | 0 | 0 | 0 | 0 | 343 | 19 | 7 | 0 | 0 |
| 4510 On net wealth | .. | .. | .. | .. | .. | 343 | 19 | 7 | .. | .. |
| Solidarity contribution on equity | .. | .. | .. | .. | .. | 202 | 16 | 6 | .. | .. |
| Solidarity contribution on foreign assets | .. | .. | .. | .. | .. | 141 | 3 | 1 | .. | .. |
| 4520 Other non-recurrent taxes | .. | .. | .. | .. | .. | 0 | 0 | 0 | .. | .. |
| 4600 Other recurrent taxes on property | 3 | 9 | 40 | 50 | 91 | 92 | 106 | 116 | 108 | 107 |
| **5000 Taxes on goods and services** | **679** | **1 609** | **4 072** | **6 066** | **11 205** | **10 098** | **10 830** | **11 110** | **10 760** | **8 609** |
| 5100 Taxes on production, sale, transfer, etc | 671 | 1 580 | 3 958 | 5 863 | 10 711 | 9 639 | 10 371 | 10 617 | 10 253 | 8 267 |
| 5110 General taxes | 306 | 928 | 2 819 | 3 801 | 6 547 | 6 116 | 6 718 | 6 716 | 6 622 | 5 459 |
| 5111 Value added taxes | 302 | 923 | 2 787 | 3 759 | 6 468 | 6 042 | 6 643 | 6 630 | 6 539 | 5 398 |
| VAT (internal operations) | .. | 557 | 1 518 | 2 506 | 4 894 | 4 375 | 4 672 | 4 789 | 4 885 | 4 093 |
| VAT (imports) | .. | 381 | 1 486 | 1 668 | 1 722 | 1 329 | 1 646 | 1 947 | 1 800 | 1 413 |
| 2% contribution on VAT | .. | 0 | 0 | 0 | 0 | 402 | 412 | 4 | 0 | 0 |
| VAT refunds | .. | -14 | -218 | -416 | -148 | -65 | -87 | -109 | -146 | -108 |
| Other VATs (local) | .. | 0 | 0 | 0 | 0 | 0 | 0 | 0 | 0 | 0 |
| 5112 Sales tax | 0 | 0 | 0 | 0 | 0 | 0 | 0 | 0 | 0 | 0 |
| 5113 Other | 4 | 5 | 32 | 41 | 79 | 74 | 75 | 85 | 83 | 61 |
| 5120 Taxes on specific goods and services | 365 | 652 | 1 139 | 2 062 | 4 164 | 3 524 | 3 653 | 3 901 | 3 631 | 2 808 |

## Table 5.13. **Ecuador** *(cont.)*

Details of tax revenue / Ingresos tributarios detallados

*Million USD*

| | 1990 | 2000 | 2007 | 2010 | 2015 | 2016 | 2017 | 2018 | 2019 | 2020 |
|---|---|---|---|---|---|---|---|---|---|---|
| 5121 Excises | 90 | 89 | 269 | 508 | 812 | 769 | 919 | 955 | 885 | 715 |
| Beer | .. | 29 | 81 | 119 | 190 | 194 | 237 | 239 | 246 | 209 |
| Cigarettes | .. | 30 | 74 | 117 | 195 | 158 | 126 | 112 | 103 | 71 |
| Fizzy drinks | .. | 9 | 16 | 40 | 62 | 109 | 103 | 94 | 93 | 79 |
| Vehicles | .. | 6 | 11 | 55 | 99 | 50 | 67 | 63 | 42 | 25 |
| Alcohol and alcoholic products | .. | 4 | 11 | 23 | 44 | 35 | 38 | 43 | 40 | 28 |
| Non-returnable plastic bottles | .. | 0 | 0 | 0 | 22 | 28 | 31 | 35 | 36 | 29 |
| Telephone | .. | 0 | 0 | 0 | 0 | 24 | 37 | 32 | 29 | 84 |
| Water heaters | .. | 0 | 0 | 0 | 3 | 14 | 32 | 26 | 2 | 1 |
| Perfumes | .. | 0 | 0 | 17 | 44 | 23 | 24 | 25 | 21 | 13 |
| Non-alcoholic drinks | .. | 0 | 0 | 0 | 0 | 8 | 11 | 11 | 11 | 11 |
| Other excises (internal operations) | .. | 0 | 0 | 0 | 13 | 2 | 4 | 5 | 5 | 4 |
| Excises on imports | .. | 10 | 76 | 138 | 142 | 124 | 209 | 271 | 257 | 162 |
| 5122 Profits of fiscal monopolies | 0 | 0 | 0 | 0 | 0 | 0 | 0 | 0 | 0 | 0 |
| 5123 Customs and import duties | 227 | 217 | 679 | 1 153 | 2 026 | 1 633 | 1 468 | 1 561 | 1 418 | 946 |
| 5124 Taxes on exports | 0 | 0 | 0 | 0 | 0 | 0 | 0 | 0 | 0 | 0 |
| 5125 Taxes on investment goods | 0 | 0 | 0 | 0 | 0 | 0 | 0 | 0 | 0 | 0 |
| 5126 Taxes on specific services | 26 | 343 | 192 | 30 | 146 | 157 | 169 | 179 | 188 | 183 |
| Contribution to comprehensive cancer care | 0 | 0 | 0 | 0 | 81 | 90 | 97 | 104 | 116 | 125 |
| Prepaid television services | 0 | 0 | 0 | 14 | 55 | 56 | 60 | 64 | 60 | 54 |
| Club membership fees | 0 | 0 | 0 | 0 | 1 | 1 | 1 | 1 | 1 | 0 |
| Casino services | 0 | 0 | 0 | 8 | 0 | 0 | 0 | 0 | 0 | 0 |
| Telecommunications | 0 | 0 | 188 | 0 | 0 | 0 | 0 | 0 | 0 | 0 |
| Capital circulation tax | 0 | 322 | 0 | 0 | 0 | 0 | 0 | 0 | 0 | 0 |
| Departure tax | 7 | 16 | 0 | 0 | 0 | 0 | 0 | 0 | 0 | 0 |
| Tax on credit operations | 18 | 2 | 0 | 1 | 0 | 0 | 0 | 0 | 0 | 0 |
| Other service taxes (local) | 1 | 2 | 4 | 7 | 10 | 9 | 10 | 10 | 11 | 3 |
| 5127 Other taxes on internat. trade and transactions | 22 | 4 | 0 | 371 | 1 180 | 965 | 1 098 | 1 206 | 1 140 | 964 |
| Foreign Currency Exit Tax (ISD) | 0 | 0 | .. | 371 | 1 180 | 965 | 1 098 | 1 206 | 1 140 | 964 |
| Tax on purchase of foreign currency | 22 | 4 | .. | 0 | 0 | 0 | 0 | 0 | 0 | 0 |
| 5128 Other taxes | 0 | 0 | 0 | 0 | 0 | 0 | 0 | 0 | 0 | 0 |
| 5130 Unallocable between 5110 and 5120 | 0 | 0 | 0 | 0 | 0 | 0 | 0 | 0 | 0 | 0 |
| 5200 Taxes on use of goods and perform activities | 8 | 29 | 114 | 203 | 493 | 459 | 460 | 493 | 507 | 342 |
| 5210 Recurrent taxes | 5 | 28 | 114 | 203 | 473 | 441 | 441 | 477 | 491 | 330 |
| 5211 Paid by households: motor vehicles | 5 | 23 | 85 | 168 | 358 | 328 | 323 | 354 | 364 | 215 |
| Motor vehicle tax | 5 | 23 | 85 | 168 | 245 | 216 | 212 | 234 | 242 | 208 |
| Environmental tax on vehicle pollution | 0 | 0 | 0 | 0 | 113 | 112 | 111 | 119 | 122 | 7 |
| 5212 Paid by others: motor vehicles | 0 | 0 | 0 | 0 | 0 | 0 | 0 | 0 | 0 | 0 |
| 5213 Paid in respect of other goods | 1 | 5 | 29 | 35 | 115 | 113 | 118 | 123 | 127 | 115 |
| 5220 Non-recurrent taxes | 2 | 1 | 0 | 0 | 20 | 18 | 18 | 16 | 16 | 11 |
| 5300 Unallocable between 5100 and 5200 | 0 | 0 | 0 | 0 | 0 | 0 | 0 | 0 | 0 | 0 |
| **6000 Other taxes** | **2** | **2** | **1** | **4** | **10** | **18** | **19** | **21** | **20** | **20** |
| 6100 Paid solely by business | 0 | 0 | 0 | 0 | 0 | 0 | 0 | 0 | 0 | 0 |
| 6200 Other | 2 | 2 | 1 | 4 | 10 | 18 | 19 | 21 | 20 | 20 |
| Simplified taxation system of Ecuador (RISE) | 0 | 0 | 0 | 6 | 20 | 19 | 22 | 23 | 22 | 20 |
| Other tax refunds | 0 | 0 | 0 | -2 | -10 | -1 | -3 | -2 | -2 | -1 |
| Other taxes (local) | 2 | 2 | 1 | 1 | 0 | 0 | 0 | 0 | 0 | 0 |

.. Not available

*Note:* Year ending 31st December.

The data are on a cash basis.

Central tax revenues mainly come from the Internal Revenue Service while some are from the Central Bank of Ecuador (see details below). Local tax revenues come from the Development Bank of Ecuador.

Heading 1200: Impuesto ingresos extraordinarios (tax on extraordinary income) has been identified and included under heading 1210 "income tax on oil companies and others" in this edition. This tax was imposed in 2010 and 2011 on certain profits from companies engaging in exploration and exploitation of non-renewable resources in Ecuador. Contribución única y temporal (one-time and temporary contribution) has been added under heading 1210 "corporate income tax" in this edition. This tax was introduced in 2020 and levied on the same tax base as corporate income tax on companies generating taxable income of one million US dollars and above in fiscal year 2018.

Heading 2000: The data are collected from non-financial public sector operations published by the Central Bank of Ecuador.

Heading 5121: Excise on plastic covers has been added under heading 5121 "other excises (internal operations)" in this edition.

Heading 5123: The data are collected from the general budget of the consolidated state government published by the Central Bank of Ecuador.

Heading 5126: This heading includes the tax on credit operations from the general budget of the consolidated state government published by the Central Bank of Ecuador.

Heading 5127: This heading includes the tax on purchase of foreign currency from the general budget of the consolidated state government published by the Central Bank of Ecuador.

*Source:* Servicio de Rentas Internas (Internal Revenue Service); Banco Central del Ecuador (Central Bank of Ecuador); Banco de Desarrollo de Ecuador (Development Bank of Ecuador).

StatLink https://doi.org/10.1787/888934309587

## Table 5.14. **El Salvador**

Details of tax revenue / Ingresos tributarios detallados

*Million USD*

| | 1990 | 2000 | 2007 | 2010 | 2015 | 2016 | 2017 | 2018 | 2019 | 2020 |
|---|---|---|---|---|---|---|---|---|---|---|
| **Total tax revenue** | **543** | **1 669** | **3 192** | **3 447** | **4 659** | **4 963** | **5 231** | **5 539** | **5 629** | **5 392** |
| **1000 Taxes on income, profits and capital gains** | **95** | **429** | **933** | **996** | **1 545** | **1 666** | **1 799** | **1 889** | **1 959** | **1 954** |
| 1100 Of individuals | .. | .. | 395 | 590 | 774 | 732 | 759 | 795 | 836 | 820 |
| 1110 On income and profits | .. | .. | 395 | 590 | 774 | 732 | 759 | 795 | 836 | 820 |
| 1120 On capital gains | .. | .. | .. | .. | .. | .. | .. | .. | .. | .. |
| 1200 Corporate | .. | .. | 573 | 420 | 622 | 770 | 870 | 914 | 922 | 934 |
| 1210 On profits | .. | .. | 573 | 420 | 622 | 770 | 870 | 914 | 922 | 934 |
| Corporate income tax | .. | .. | .. | .. | .. | .. | .. | .. | .. | .. |
| Special Contribution - Public security (large taxpayers) | .. | .. | 0 | 0 | 0 | 7 | 67 | 70 | 74 | 85 |
| 1220 On capital gains of corporates | .. | .. | .. | .. | .. | .. | .. | .. | .. | .. |
| 1300 Unallocable between 1100 and 1200 | 95 | 429 | -35 | -14 | 148 | 164 | 170 | 180 | 201 | 201 |
| Withholding income tax | .. | .. | 0 | 41 | 178 | 195 | 209 | 220 | 249 | 239 |
| Income tax refunds | .. | .. | -35 | -55 | -30 | -31 | -39 | -40 | -48 | -38 |
| **2000 Social security contributions** | **104** | **325** | **391** | **470** | **608** | **655** | **684** | **705** | **722** | **700** |
| 2100 Employees | .. | 75 | 137 | 165 | 214 | 228 | 239 | 246 | 251 | 246 |
| 2110 On a payroll basis | .. | 75 | 137 | 165 | 214 | 228 | 239 | 246 | 251 | 246 |
| 2120 On an income tax basis | .. | 0 | 0 | 0 | 0 | 0 | 0 | 0 | 0 | 0 |
| 2200 Employers | .. | 176 | 254 | 306 | 393 | 427 | 444 | 459 | 471 | 454 |
| 2210 On a payroll basis | .. | 176 | 254 | 306 | 393 | 427 | 444 | 459 | 471 | 454 |
| 2220 On an income tax basis | .. | 0 | 0 | 0 | 0 | 0 | 0 | 0 | 0 | 0 |
| 2300 Self-employed or non-employed | .. | 13 | 0 | 0 | 0 | 0 | 0 | 0 | 0 | 0 |
| 2310 On a payroll basis | .. | 13 | .. | .. | .. | .. | .. | .. | .. | .. |
| 2320 On an income tax basis | .. | 0 | .. | .. | .. | .. | .. | .. | .. | .. |
| 2400 Unallocable between 2100, 2200 and 2300 | 104 | 62 | 0 | 0 | 0 | 0 | 0 | 0 | 0 | 0 |
| 2410 On a payroll basis | 104 | 62 | .. | .. | .. | .. | .. | .. | .. | .. |
| 2420 On an income tax basis | 0 | 0 | .. | .. | .. | .. | .. | .. | .. | .. |
| **3000 Taxes on payroll and workforce** | **0** | **0** | **19** | **21** | **30** | **33** | **36** | **37** | **38** | **36** |
| **4000 Taxes on property** | **26** | **12** | **24** | **19** | **112** | **112** | **112** | **119** | **44** | **27** |
| 4100 Recurrent taxes on immovable property | 0 | 0 | 3 | 3 | 5 | 5 | 5 | 6 | 7 | 6 |
| 4110 Households | .. | .. | .. | .. | .. | .. | .. | .. | .. | .. |
| 4120 Others | .. | .. | .. | .. | .. | .. | .. | .. | .. | .. |
| 4200 Recurrent taxes on net wealth | 16 | 0 | 0 | 0 | 0 | 0 | 0 | 0 | 0 | 0 |
| 4210 Individual | .. | .. | .. | .. | .. | .. | .. | .. | .. | .. |
| 4220 Corporate | .. | .. | .. | .. | .. | .. | .. | .. | .. | .. |
| 4300 Estate, inheritance and gift taxes | 0 | 0 | 0 | 0 | 0 | 0 | 0 | 0 | 0 | 0 |
| 4310 Estate and inheritance taxes | .. | .. | .. | .. | .. | .. | .. | .. | .. | .. |
| 4320 Gift taxes | .. | .. | .. | .. | .. | .. | .. | .. | .. | .. |
| 4400 Taxes on financial and capital transactions | 10 | 12 | 21 | 16 | 107 | 107 | 108 | 113 | 37 | 21 |
| Property transfers | 10 | 12 | 21 | 16 | 20 | 23 | 23 | 24 | 29 | 21 |
| Checks and electronic transfers of funds | 0 | 0 | 0 | 0 | 55 | 54 | 53 | 56 | 5 | 0 |
| Withholding for liquidity control | 0 | 0 | 0 | 0 | 31 | 31 | 32 | 34 | 3 | 0 |
| 4500 Non-recurrent taxes | 0 | 0 | 0 | 0 | 0 | 0 | 0 | 0 | 0 | 0 |
| 4510 On net wealth | .. | .. | .. | .. | .. | .. | .. | .. | .. | .. |
| 4520 Other non-recurrent taxes | .. | .. | .. | .. | .. | .. | .. | .. | .. | .. |
| 4600 Other recurrent taxes on property | 0 | 0 | 0 | 0 | 0 | 0 | 0 | 0 | 0 | 0 |
| **5000 Taxes on goods and services** | **259** | **903** | **1 775** | **1 878** | **2 278** | **2 406** | **2 512** | **2 693** | **2 777** | **2 584** |
| 5100 Taxes on production, sale, transfer, etc | 259 | 903 | 1 770 | 1 863 | 2 254 | 2 379 | 2 484 | 2 663 | 2 747 | 2 561 |
| 5110 General taxes | 133 | 714 | 1 389 | 1 433 | 1 764 | 1 813 | 1 904 | 2 054 | 2 109 | 2 033 |
| 5111 Value added taxes | 0 | 714 | 1 389 | 1 433 | 1 764 | 1 813 | 1 904 | 2 054 | 2 109 | 2 033 |
| 5112 Sales tax | 0 | 0 | 0 | 0 | 0 | 0 | 0 | 0 | 0 | 0 |
| 5113 Other | 133 | 0 | 0 | 0 | 0 | 0 | 0 | 0 | 0 | 0 |
| 5120 Taxes on specific goods and services | 127 | 189 | 381 | 431 | 490 | 566 | 580 | 608 | 638 | 528 |
| 5121 Excises | 65 | 49 | 169 | 224 | 285 | 348 | 357 | 367 | 393 | 336 |
| Alcoholic beverages | .. | .. | 15 | 22 | 22 | 23 | 24 | 24 | 25 | 34 |
| Cigarettes | .. | .. | 27 | 38 | 29 | 28 | 27 | 24 | 24 | 25 |
| Soft drinks | .. | .. | 25 | 31 | 48 | 49 | 49 | 49 | 52 | 50 |
| Beer | .. | .. | 30 | 29 | 55 | 61 | 65 | 73 | 82 | 67 |
| Weapons, ammunition and explosives | .. | .. | 1 | 1 | 1 | 1 | 1 | 1 | 1 | 1 |
| Ad-valorem on fuels | .. | .. | 0 | 0 | 7 | 9 | 8 | 7 | 8 | 7 |
| Special contribution- Sugar | .. | .. | 1 | 1 | 1 | 1 | 1 | 1 | 1 | 1 |
| Special contribution- Public transportation | .. | .. | 0 | 35 | 40 | 43 | 45 | 47 | 48 | 23 |
| Special contribution- FOVIAL | .. | .. | 70 | 69 | 80 | 86 | 89 | 93 | 96 | 83 |
| Special contribution- Public security | .. | .. | 0 | 0 | 2 | 49 | 49 | 48 | 55 | 43 |
| 5122 Profits of fiscal monopolies | 0 | 0 | 0 | 0 | 0 | 0 | 0 | 0 | 0 | 0 |
| 5123 Customs and import duties | 61 | 141 | 204 | 151 | 194 | 206 | 211 | 227 | 232 | 187 |
| 5124 Taxes on exports | 0 | 0 | 0 | 0 | 0 | 0 | 0 | 0 | 0 | 0 |
| 5125 Taxes on investment goods | 0 | 0 | 0 | 0 | 0 | 0 | 0 | 0 | 0 | 0 |
| 5126 Taxes on specific services | 0 | 0 | 8 | 56 | 11 | 12 | 13 | 14 | 13 | 5 |
| 5127 Other taxes on internat. trade and transactions | 0 | 0 | 0 | 0 | 0 | 0 | 0 | 0 | 0 | 0 |
| 5128 Other taxes | 0 | 0 | 0 | 0 | 0 | 0 | 0 | 0 | 0 | 0 |

## Table 5.14. **El Salvador** *(cont.)*

Details of tax revenue / Ingresos tributarios detallados

*Million USD*

| | 1990 | 2000 | 2007 | 2010 | 2015 | 2016 | 2017 | 2018 | 2019 | 2020 |
|---|---|---|---|---|---|---|---|---|---|---|
| 5130 Unallocable between 5110 and 5120 | 0 | 0 | 0 | 0 | 0 | 0 | 0 | 0 | 0 | 0 |
| 5200 Taxes on use of goods and perform activities | 0 | 0 | 5 | 15 | 24 | 26 | 27 | 31 | 29 | 23 |
| 5210 Recurrent taxes | .. | .. | 5 | 7 | 12 | 12 | 14 | 16 | 13 | 10 |
| 5211 Paid by households: motor vehicles | .. | .. | 0 | 0 | 0 | 0 | 0 | 0 | 0 | 0 |
| 5212 Paid by others: motor vehicles | .. | .. | 0 | 0 | 0 | 0 | 0 | 0 | 0 | 0 |
| 5213 Paid in respect of other goods | .. | .. | 5 | 7 | 12 | 12 | 14 | 16 | 13 | 10 |
| 5220 Non-recurrent taxes | .. | .. | 0 | 7 | 12 | 14 | 14 | 15 | 16 | 12 |
| 5300 Unallocable between 5100 and 5200 | 0 | 0 | 0 | 0 | 0 | 0 | 0 | 0 | 0 | 0 |
| **6000 Other taxes** | **58** | **0** | **49** | **63** | **86** | **91** | **88** | **96** | **89** | **92** |
| 6100 Paid solely by business | 0 | 0 | 0 | 0 | 0 | 0 | 0 | 0 | 0 | 0 |
| 6200 Other | 58 | 0 | 49 | 63 | 86 | 91 | 88 | 96 | 89 | 92 |

.. Not available

*Note:* Year ending 31st December.

The data are on a cash basis.

Heading 1000: Disaggregated individual and corporate income taxes are not available before 2002. Special contribution to public security by large taxpayers has been classified under heading 1210 in this edition. It was previously under heading 5121.

Heading 2000: The figures include social security contributions paid to the Salvadoran Institute of Social Security (ISSS), National Public Employees Pension Institute (INPEP), Social Security Institute of the Armed Forces (IPSFA) and Salvadoran Institute of Teacher Welfare (ISBM). The figures exclude payments to privately managed pension funds (AFPs) and may include a small amount of voluntary contributions which is undistinguishable from the public social security contribution data.

Heading 3000: Vocational training contributions to the Instituto Salvadoreño de Formación Profesional (INSAFORP) are included in heading 3000. The tax revenue is classified under the central government. In El Salvador this revenue is classified under a separate unit considered to be different to the central government.

*Source:* Dirección General de Tesorería en Ministerio de Hacienda (General Treasury Directorate in Ministry of Finance); Dirección General de Contabilidad Gubernamental en Ministerio de Hacienda (General Directorate of Government Accounting in Ministry of Finance); Departamento de Análisis Financiero y Estadística en Ministerio de Hacienda (Department of Financial Analysis and Statistics in Ministry of Finance); Instituto Salvadoreño del Seguro Social (Salvadoran Social Security Institute); Centro Interamericano de Administraciones Tributarias (Inter-American Center of Tax Administrations).

StatLink https://doi.org/10.1787/888934309606

## Table 5.15. **Guatemala**

Details of tax revenue / Ingresos tributarios detallados

*Million GTQ*

| | 1990 | 2000 | 2007 | 2010 | 2015 | 2016 | 2017 | 2018 | 2019 | 2020 |
|---|---|---|---|---|---|---|---|---|---|---|
| **Total tax revenue** | **2 569** | **16 531** | **36 702** | **41 537** | **60 817** | **66 401** | **69 691** | **72 505** | **77 121** | **74 529** |
| **1000 Taxes on income, profits and capital gains** | **507** | **3 293** | **6 606** | **7 745** | **13 628** | **16 500** | **16 313** | **16 236** | **17 100** | **16 751** |
| 1100 Of individuals | 25 | 143 | 877 | 1 225 | 1 826 | 2 082 | 2 468 | 2 603 | 2 813 | 2 816 |
| 1110 On income and profits | 25 | 143 | 877 | 1 225 | 1 826 | 2 082 | 2 468 | 2 603 | 2 813 | 2 816 |
| 1120 On capital gains | .. | .. | .. | .. | .. | .. | .. | .. | .. | .. |
| 1200 Corporate | 482 | 3 149 | 5 729 | 6 520 | 11 801 | 14 418 | 13 846 | 13 633 | 14 287 | 13 935 |
| 1210 On profits | 482 | 3 149 | 5 729 | 6 520 | 11 801 | 14 418 | 13 846 | 13 633 | 14 287 | 13 935 |
| Corporate income tax | 482 | 1 858 | 5 720 | 6 518 | 11 801 | 14 417 | 13 839 | 13 633 | 14 285 | 13 933 |
| Commercial and agricultural enterprises | 0 | 1 291 | 9 | 2 | 0 | 1 | 6 | 0 | 2 | 2 |
| 1220 On capital gains of corporates | .. | .. | .. | .. | .. | .. | .. | .. | .. | .. |
| 1300 Unallocable between 1100 and 1200 | 0 | 0 | 0 | 0 | 0 | 0 | 0 | 0 | 0 | 0 |
| **2000 Social security contributions** | **436** | **2 569** | **5 069** | **6 312** | **9 778** | **10 974** | **11 523** | **12 102** | **12 957** | **12 742** |
| 2100 Employees | .. | .. | .. | .. | .. | .. | .. | .. | .. | .. |
| 2110 On a payroll basis | .. | .. | .. | .. | .. | .. | .. | .. | .. | .. |
| 2120 On an income tax basis | .. | .. | .. | .. | .. | .. | .. | .. | .. | .. |
| 2200 Employers | .. | .. | .. | .. | .. | .. | .. | .. | .. | .. |
| 2210 On a payroll basis | .. | .. | .. | .. | .. | .. | .. | .. | .. | .. |
| 2220 On an income tax basis | .. | .. | .. | .. | .. | .. | .. | .. | .. | .. |
| 2300 Self-employed or non-employed | .. | .. | .. | .. | .. | .. | .. | .. | .. | .. |
| 2310 On a payroll basis | .. | .. | .. | .. | .. | .. | .. | .. | .. | .. |
| 2320 On an income tax basis | .. | .. | .. | .. | .. | .. | .. | .. | .. | .. |
| 2400 Unallocable between 2100, 2200 and 2300 | 436 | 2 569 | 5 069 | 6 312 | 9 778 | 10 974 | 11 523 | 12 102 | 12 957 | 12 742 |
| 2410 On a payroll basis | 436 | 2 569 | 5 069 | 6 312 | 9 778 | 10 974 | 11 523 | 12 102 | 12 957 | 12 742 |
| 2420 On an income tax basis | 0 | 0 | 0 | 0 | 0 | 0 | 0 | 0 | 0 | 0 |
| **3000 Taxes on payroll and workforce** | **0** | **0** | **381** | **447** | **736** | **792** | **862** | **903** | **933** | **859** |
| Contributions to INTECAP | .. | .. | 199 | 233 | 384 | 414 | 449 | 469 | 484 | 448 |
| Contributions to IRTRA | .. | .. | 183 | 214 | 352 | 379 | 413 | 434 | 449 | 411 |
| **4000 Taxes on property** | **149** | **347** | **832** | **1 202** | **1 050** | **957** | **1 247** | **1 354** | **1 177** | **1 115** |
| 4100 Recurrent taxes on immovable property | 0 | 153 | 426 | 621 | 693 | 565 | 710 | 865 | 685 | 712 |
| 4110 Households | .. | 0 | 0 | 0 | 0 | 0 | 0 | 0 | 0 | 0 |
| 4120 Others | .. | 153 | 426 | 621 | 693 | 565 | 710 | 865 | 685 | 712 |
| Property tax | .. | 6 | 1 | 1 | 1 | 1 | 1 | 2 | 2 | 1 |
| Property tax (municipal) | .. | 147 | 426 | 620 | 692 | 564 | 709 | 863 | 683 | 711 |
| 4200 Recurrent taxes on net wealth | 0 | 0 | 0 | 0 | 0 | 0 | 0 | 0 | 0 | 0 |
| 4210 Individual | .. | .. | .. | .. | .. | .. | .. | .. | .. | .. |
| 4220 Corporate | .. | .. | .. | .. | .. | .. | .. | .. | .. | .. |
| 4300 Estate, inheritance and gift taxes | 0 | 0 | 0 | 0 | 0 | 0 | 0 | 0 | 0 | 0 |
| 4310 Estate and inheritance taxes | .. | .. | .. | .. | .. | .. | .. | .. | .. | .. |
| 4320 Gift taxes | .. | .. | .. | .. | .. | .. | .. | .. | .. | .. |
| 4400 Taxes on financial and capital transactions | 149 | 194 | 406 | 581 | 357 | 393 | 537 | 489 | 492 | 403 |
| Stamp duty | 104 | 182 | 392 | 572 | 336 | 370 | 508 | 463 | 451 | 392 |
| Tax on property transfer | 45 | 12 | 14 | 10 | 20 | 23 | 29 | 26 | 40 | 11 |
| 4500 Non-recurrent taxes | 0 | 0 | 0 | 0 | 0 | 0 | 0 | 0 | 0 | 0 |
| 4510 On net wealth | .. | .. | .. | .. | .. | .. | .. | .. | .. | .. |
| 4520 Other non-recurrent taxes | .. | .. | .. | .. | .. | .. | .. | .. | .. | .. |
| 4600 Other recurrent taxes on property | 0 | 0 | 0 | 0 | 0 | 0 | 0 | 0 | 0 | 0 |
| **5000 Taxes on goods and services** | **1 477** | **10 317** | **21 764** | **23 255** | **31 719** | **33 105** | **35 365** | **37 253** | **40 124** | **37 993** |
| 5100 Taxes on production, sale, transfer, etc | 1 449 | 10 131 | 21 411 | 22 750 | 31 002 | 32 323 | 34 539 | 36 372 | 39 215 | 37 090 |
| 5110 General taxes | 762 | 6 259 | 15 382 | 16 980 | 23 271 | 24 215 | 26 187 | 27 733 | 29 920 | 28 760 |
| 5111 Value added taxes | 762 | 6 259 | 15 382 | 16 980 | 23 271 | 24 215 | 26 187 | 27 733 | 29 920 | 28 760 |
| VAT domestic | 361 | 2 903 | 6 647 | 7 995 | 12 023 | 13 308 | 14 380 | 14 573 | 15 897 | 15 992 |
| VAT imports | 401 | 4 189 | 10 532 | 11 127 | 13 630 | 13 361 | 14 148 | 15 560 | 16 331 | 14 955 |
| Tax credit refunds | 0 | -834 | -1 797 | -2 142 | -2 381 | -2 455 | -2 342 | -2 401 | -2 307 | -2 187 |
| 5112 Sales tax | 0 | 0 | 0 | 0 | 0 | 0 | 0 | 0 | 0 | 0 |
| 5113 Other | 0 | 0 | 0 | 0 | 0 | 0 | 0 | 0 | 0 | 0 |
| 5120 Taxes on specific goods and services | 687 | 3 872 | 6 029 | 5 770 | 7 730 | 8 107 | 8 353 | 8 640 | 9 294 | 8 330 |
| 5121 Excises | 181 | 1 797 | 2 946 | 3 101 | 5 202 | 5 389 | 5 471 | 5 621 | 6 106 | 5 662 |
| Tobacco and derivatives | 76 | 205 | 355 | 347 | 369 | 365 | 348 | 337 | 363 | 299 |
| Beer | 0 | 97 | 144 | 159 | 293 | 306 | 314 | 322 | 365 | 387 |
| Alcoholic beverages | 0 | 77 | 87 | 97 | 88 | 90 | 96 | 103 | 109 | 104 |
| Soft drinks | 0 | 15 | 195 | 220 | 328 | 348 | 348 | 365 | 396 | 405 |
| Other beverages | 0 | 12 | 1 | 2 | 0 | 1 | 0 | 0 | 0 | 0 |
| Cement | 0 | 0 | 117 | 99 | 312 | 117 | 114 | 123 | 131 | 147 |
| Oil and derivatives | 105 | 1 389 | 2 047 | 2 179 | 2 899 | 3 195 | 3 296 | 3 417 | 3 743 | 3 485 |
| IPRIMA | 0 | 0 | 0 | 0 | 914 | 967 | 953 | 953 | 999 | 836 |
| 5122 Profits of fiscal monopolies | 0 | 0 | 0 | 0 | 0 | 0 | 0 | 0 | 0 | 0 |
| 5123 Customs and import duties | 506 | 1 806 | 2 654 | 2 368 | 2 157 | 2 323 | 2 455 | 2 576 | 2 712 | 2 487 |
| 5124 Taxes on exports | 0 | 0 | 0 | 0 | 0 | 0 | 0 | 0 | 0 | 0 |
| 5125 Taxes on investment goods | 0 | 0 | 0 | 0 | 0 | 0 | 0 | 0 | 0 | 0 |

## Table 5.15. **Guatemala** *(cont.)*

Details of tax revenue / Ingresos tributarios detallados

*Million GTQ*

| | 1990 | 2000 | 2007 | 2010 | 2015 | 2016 | 2017 | 2018 | 2019 | 2020 |
|---|---|---|---|---|---|---|---|---|---|---|
| 5126 Taxes on specific services | 0 | 269 | 429 | 301 | 370 | 396 | 427 | 443 | 477 | 181 |
| Departure tax | .. | 135 | 229 | 224 | 263 | 280 | 300 | 312 | 338 | 117 |
| INGUATE | .. | 40 | 78 | 73 | 104 | 110 | 120 | 125 | 132 | 57 |
| Transportation and communications | .. | 94 | 122 | 3 | 4 | 5 | 7 | 6 | 7 | 7 |
| 5127 Other taxes on internat. trade and transactions | 0 | 0 | 0 | 0 | 0 | 0 | 0 | 0 | 0 | 0 |
| 5128 Other taxes | 0 | 0 | 0 | 0 | 0 | 0 | 0 | 0 | 0 | 0 |
| 5130 Unallocable between 5110 and 5120 | 0 | 0 | 0 | 0 | 0 | 0 | 0 | 0 | 0 | 0 |
| 5200 Taxes on use of goods and perform activities | 28 | 186 | 353 | 505 | 717 | 782 | 826 | 881 | 909 | 903 |
| 5210 Recurrent taxes | 28 | 186 | 353 | 505 | 717 | 782 | 826 | 881 | 909 | 903 |
| 5211 Paid by households: motor vehicles | 0 | 0 | 0 | 0 | 0 | 0 | 0 | 0 | 0 | 0 |
| 5212 Paid by others: motor vehicles | 28 | 186 | 353 | 505 | 717 | 782 | 826 | 881 | 909 | 903 |
| 5213 Paid in respect of other goods | 0 | 0 | 0 | 0 | 0 | 0 | 0 | 0 | 0 | 0 |
| 5220 Non-recurrent taxes | 0 | 0 | 0 | 0 | 0 | 0 | 0 | 0 | 0 | 0 |
| 5300 Unallocable between 5100 and 5200 | 0 | 0 | 0 | 0 | 0 | 0 | 0 | 0 | 0 | 0 |
| **6000 Other taxes** | **0** | **7** | **2 049** | **2 575** | **3 907** | **4 072** | **4 380** | **4 656** | **4 830** | **5 070** |
| 6100 Paid solely by business | .. | 0 | 0 | 0 | 0 | 0 | 0 | 0 | 0 | 0 |
| 6200 Other | .. | 7 | 2 049 | 2 575 | 3 907 | 4 072 | 4 380 | 4 656 | 4 830 | 5 070 |
| Extraordinary and temporary solidarity tax in support of peace agreements | .. | 0 | 2 047 | 44 | 1 | 1 | 28 | 10 | 63 | 3 |
| Solidarity tax | .. | 0 | 0 | 2 530 | 3 906 | 4 070 | 4 352 | 4 646 | 4 766 | 5 067 |
| Extraordinary and temporary solidarity tax | .. | 2 | 1 | 0 | 0 | 0 | 0 | 0 | 0 | 0 |
| Other indirect taxes | .. | 4 | 1 | 1 | 0 | 0 | 0 | 0 | 0 | 0 |

.. Not available

*Note:* Year ending 31st December.

The data are on a cash basis.

Local government tax revenues include revenues from the municipal property tax (IUSI).

Heading 1000: Personal and corporate income taxes also include taxes on income from financial products.

Heading 2000: Figures include contributions to the Guatemalan Social Security Institute (IGSS) and payments by public employees to the government's pension fund.

Heading 3000: Contributions to INTECAP and contributions to IRTRA are included in heading 3000. The tax revenues are classified under the central government. In Guatemala these revenues are classified under a separate unit considered to be different to the central government.

Heading 4400: Before 2000, tax on property transfer under heading 4400 also includes central government property tax under heading 4120 as they cannot be distinguished.

Heading 5121: Specific tax on the first registration of land motor vehicles (IPRIMA) is classified under heading 5121 in this edition. It was previously under heading 5211. Other beverages contain all alcoholic and non-alcoholic beverages before 2000.

Heading 6200: Solidarity taxes are classified under heading 6200 in this edition. They were previously under heading 1300.

*Source:* Superintendencia de Administración Tributaria (Superintendency of Tax Administration); Ministerio de Finanzas Públicas (Ministry of Public Finance); Contraloría General de Cuentas (General Comptroller's Office).

StatLink https://doi.org/10.1787/888934309625

# Table 5.16. **Guyana**

Details of tax revenue / Ingresos tributarios detallados

*Million GYD*

| | 1990 | 2000 | 2007 | 2010 | 2015 | 2016 | 2017 | 2018 | 2019 | 2020 |
|---|---|---|---|---|---|---|---|---|---|---|
| **Total tax revenue** | **5 232** | **42 750** | **85 991** | **111 906** | **159 895** | **170 305** | **191 513** | **220 421** | **250 240** | **243 507** |
| **1000 Taxes on income, profits and capital gains** | **1 752** | **16 179** | **29 520** | **39 561** | **55 011** | **61 127** | **68 088** | **78 956** | **94 504** | **105 756** |
| 1100 Of individuals | 333 | 7 734 | 12 832 | 17 816 | 23 300 | 26 773 | 26 564 | 32 037 | 35 249 | 39 711 |
| 1110 On income and profits | 333 | 7 734 | 12 832 | 17 816 | 23 300 | 26 773 | 26 564 | 32 037 | 35 249 | 39 711 |
| Personal | 306 | 7 157 | 12 832 | 15 419 | 19 894 | 22 727 | 21 669 | 25 808 | 29 213 | 34 688 |
| Self-employed | 27 | 577 | 0 | 2 397 | 3 407 | 4 045 | 4 895 | 6 229 | 6 036 | 5 024 |
| 1120 On capital gains | .. | .. | .. | .. | .. | .. | .. | .. | .. | .. |
| 1200 Corporate | 1 375 | 8 266 | 16 460 | 21 427 | 31 200 | 33 852 | 41 183 | 46 198 | 58 346 | 64 992 |
| 1210 On profits | 1 375 | 8 266 | 16 460 | 21 427 | 31 200 | 33 852 | 41 183 | 46 198 | 58 346 | 64 992 |
| 1220 On capital gains of corporates | .. | .. | .. | .. | .. | .. | .. | .. | .. | .. |
| 1300 Unallocable between 1100 and 1200 | 43 | 179 | 229 | 317 | 511 | 502 | 341 | 721 | 908 | 1 053 |
| **2000 Social security contributions** | **191** | **4 868** | **8 061** | **10 047** | **16 644** | **18 211** | **19 911** | **21 178** | **23 728** | **24 706** |
| 2100 Employees | .. | .. | .. | .. | .. | .. | .. | .. | .. | .. |
| 2110 On a payroll basis | .. | .. | .. | .. | .. | .. | .. | .. | .. | .. |
| 2120 On an income tax basis | .. | .. | .. | .. | .. | .. | .. | .. | .. | .. |
| 2200 Employers | .. | .. | .. | .. | .. | .. | .. | .. | .. | .. |
| 2210 On a payroll basis | .. | .. | .. | .. | .. | .. | .. | .. | .. | .. |
| 2220 On an income tax basis | .. | .. | .. | .. | .. | .. | .. | .. | .. | .. |
| 2300 Self-employed or non-employed | .. | .. | .. | .. | .. | .. | .. | .. | .. | .. |
| 2310 On a payroll basis | .. | .. | .. | .. | .. | .. | .. | .. | .. | .. |
| 2320 On an income tax basis | .. | .. | .. | .. | .. | .. | .. | .. | .. | .. |
| 2400 Unallocable between 2100, 2200 and 2300 | 191 | 4 868 | 8 061 | 10 047 | 16 644 | 18 211 | 19 911 | 21 178 | 23 728 | 24 706 |
| 2410 On a payroll basis | .. | .. | .. | .. | .. | .. | .. | .. | .. | .. |
| 2420 On an income tax basis | .. | .. | .. | .. | .. | .. | .. | .. | .. | .. |
| **3000 Taxes on payroll and workforce** | **0** | **0** | **0** | **0** | **0** | **0** | **0** | **0** | **0** | **0** |
| **4000 Taxes on property** | **53** | **701** | **962** | **2 068** | **3 676** | **3 572** | **4 027** | **4 875** | **4 917** | **4 390** |
| 4100 Recurrent taxes on immovable property | 40 | 681 | 943 | 1 562 | 3 201 | 3 172 | 3 579 | 4 377 | 4 312 | 3 847 |
| 4110 Households | 0 | 0 | 0 | 0 | 588 | 659 | 781 | 1 016 | 933 | 892 |
| 4120 Others | 40 | 681 | 943 | 1 562 | 2 613 | 2 513 | 2 798 | 3 361 | 3 379 | 2 956 |
| 4200 Recurrent taxes on net wealth | 0 | 0 | 0 | 0 | 0 | 0 | 0 | 0 | 0 | 0 |
| 4210 Individual | .. | .. | .. | .. | .. | .. | .. | .. | .. | .. |
| 4220 Corporate | .. | .. | .. | .. | .. | .. | .. | .. | .. | .. |
| 4300 Estate, inheritance and gift taxes | 13 | 20 | 19 | 31 | 37 | 37 | 39 | 44 | 41 | 44 |
| 4310 Estate and inheritance taxes | 13 | 20 | 19 | 31 | 37 | 37 | 39 | 44 | 41 | 44 |
| 4320 Gift taxes | 0 | 0 | 0 | 0 | 0 | 0 | 0 | 0 | 0 | 0 |
| 4400 Taxes on financial and capital transactions | 0 | 0 | 0 | 476 | 438 | 363 | 409 | 454 | 565 | 499 |
| Stamp duties | .. | .. | .. | 476 | 438 | 363 | 409 | 454 | 565 | 499 |
| 4500 Non-recurrent taxes | 0 | 0 | 0 | 0 | 0 | 0 | 0 | 0 | 0 | 0 |
| 4510 On net wealth | .. | .. | .. | .. | .. | .. | .. | .. | .. | .. |
| 4520 Other non-recurrent taxes | .. | .. | .. | .. | .. | .. | .. | .. | .. | .. |
| 4600 Other recurrent taxes on property | 0 | 0 | 0 | 0 | 0 | 0 | 0 | 0 | 0 | 0 |
| **5000 Taxes on goods and services** | **2 200** | **20 798** | **46 544** | **59 360** | **83 924** | **86 445** | **97 502** | **113 216** | **124 952** | **106 683** |
| 5100 Taxes on production, sale, transfer, etc | 2 162 | 20 530 | 45 937 | 58 846 | 83 227 | 85 499 | 96 386 | 111 770 | 123 710 | 105 489 |
| 5110 General taxes | 1 399 | 14 861 | 22 755 | 27 044 | 35 374 | 37 468 | 42 728 | 48 155 | 52 735 | 49 907 |
| 5111 Value added taxes | 0 | 0 | 21 329 | 27 044 | 35 374 | 36 268 | 42 423 | 48 036 | 52 676 | 49 844 |
| Imports | .. | .. | .. | 14 877 | 19 366 | 18 477 | 23 261 | 27 819 | 29 302 | 22 934 |
| Domestic supply | .. | .. | .. | 12 168 | 16 008 | 17 791 | 19 162 | 20 216 | 23 374 | 26 910 |
| 5112 Sales tax | 0 | 0 | 0 | 0 | 0 | 0 | 0 | 0 | 0 | 0 |
| 5113 Other | 1 399 | 14 861 | 1 426 | 0 | 0 | 1 200 | 305 | 119 | 60 | 63 |
| 5120 Taxes on specific goods and services | 763 | 5 669 | 23 182 | 31 802 | 47 853 | 48 031 | 53 659 | 63 615 | 70 975 | 55 582 |
| 5121 Excises | 32 | 609 | 16 057 | 22 070 | 33 827 | 31 083 | 35 162 | 41 659 | 45 979 | 35 941 |
| Motor vehicle (imports) | .. | .. | .. | 7 702 | 8 499 | 7 088 | 5 443 | 6 781 | 7 977 | 8 188 |
| Petroleum products (imports) | .. | .. | .. | 9 437 | 19 355 | 18 007 | 21 745 | 26 359 | 29 124 | 19 290 |
| Tobacco (imports) | .. | .. | .. | 1 077 | 1 224 | 1 063 | 1 078 | 1 204 | 1 427 | 1 256 |
| Alcoholic beverages (imports) | .. | .. | .. | 719 | 875 | 884 | 844 | 867 | 785 | 589 |
| Alcoholic beverages (domestic) | .. | .. | .. | 2 358 | 3 377 | 4 040 | 4 348 | 4 468 | 4 486 | 4 599 |
| Purchase tax - motor cars | .. | .. | .. | 0 | 0 | 0 | 0 | 0 | 0 | 0 |
| Environmental tax | .. | .. | .. | 777 | 496 | 0 | 1 703 | 1 979 | 2 179 | 2 019 |
| 5122 Profits of fiscal monopolies | 0 | 0 | 0 | 0 | 0 | 0 | 0 | 0 | 0 | 0 |
| 5123 Customs and import duties | 544 | 3 943 | 6 005 | 8 302 | 12 357 | 14 887 | 16 273 | 19 321 | 22 140 | 18 624 |
| 5124 Taxes on exports | 94 | 7 | 9 | 7 | 12 | 13 | 23 | 33 | 29 | 27 |
| 5125 Taxes on investment goods | 0 | 0 | 0 | 0 | 0 | 0 | 0 | 0 | 0 | 0 |
| 5126 Taxes on specific services | 92 | 1 110 | 1 112 | 1 423 | 1 658 | 2 048 | 2 201 | 2 603 | 2 827 | 990 |
| Entertainment tax | 12 | 27 | 1 | 0 | 0 | 0 | 0 | 0 | 0 | 0 |
| Travel tax | 80 | 1 084 | 1 112 | 1 423 | 1 658 | 2 048 | 2 201 | 2 603 | 2 827 | 990 |
| 5127 Other taxes on internat. trade and transactions | 0 | 0 | 0 | 0 | 0 | 0 | 0 | 0 | 0 | 0 |
| 5128 Other taxes | 0 | 0 | 0 | 0 | 0 | 0 | 0 | 0 | 0 | 0 |
| 5130 Unallocable between 5110 and 5120 | 0 | 0 | 0 | 0 | 0 | 0 | 0 | 0 | 0 | 0 |
| 5200 Taxes on use of goods and perform activities | 38 | 268 | 607 | 514 | 697 | 945 | 1 116 | 1 446 | 1 242 | 1 194 |
| 5210 Recurrent taxes | 38 | 268 | 607 | 514 | 697 | 945 | 1 116 | 1 446 | 1 242 | 1 194 |

## Table 5.16. **Guyana** *(cont.)*

Details of tax revenue / Ingresos tributarios detallados

*Million GYD*

| | 1990 | 2000 | 2007 | 2010 | 2015 | 2016 | 2017 | 2018 | 2019 | 2020 |
|---|---|---|---|---|---|---|---|---|---|---|
| 5211 Paid by households: motor vehicles | 27 | 239 | 306 | 475 | 653 | 868 | 1 039 | 1 095 | 1 150 | 1 135 |
| 5212 Paid by others: motor vehicles | 0 | 0 | 0 | 0 | 0 | 0 | 0 | 0 | 0 | 0 |
| 5213 Paid in respect of other goods | 12 | 29 | 301 | 39 | 44 | 78 | 77 | 352 | 92 | 60 |
| Other licences | 12 | 29 | 301 | 39 | 44 | 78 | 77 | 352 | 92 | 60 |
| 5220 Non-recurrent taxes | 0 | 0 | 0 | 0 | 0 | 0 | 0 | 0 | 0 | 0 |
| 5300 Unallocable between 5100 and 5200 | 0 | 0 | 0 | 0 | 0 | 0 | 0 | 0 | 0 | 0 |
| **6000 Other taxes** | **1 037** | **204** | **904** | **870** | **640** | **950** | **1 985** | **2 196** | **2 139** | **1 972** |
| 6100 Paid solely by business | 0 | 0 | 0 | 0 | 0 | 0 | 0 | 0 | 0 | 0 |
| 6200 Other | 1 037 | 204 | 904 | 870 | 640 | 950 | 1 985 | 2 196 | 2 139 | 1 972 |

.. Not available

*Note:* Year ending 31st December.

The data are on a cash basis.

Central government tax revenues are based on Budget Estimates by the Ministry of Finance. Data on local government tax revenues include payments of local taxes by public corporations and come from the Bank of Guyana.

Heading 2000: The figures include contributions to the National Insurance Scheme.

*Source:* Ministry of Finance; Bank of Guyana; National Insurance Scheme.

StatLink https://doi.org/10.1787/888934309644

# Table 5.17. **Honduras**

Details of tax revenue / Ingresos tributarios detallados

*Million HNL*

| | 1990 | 2000 | 2007 | 2010 | 2015 | 2016 | 2017 | 2018 | 2019 | 2020 |
|---|---|---|---|---|---|---|---|---|---|---|
| **Total tax revenue** | **2 118** | **18 299** | **46 161** | **54 544** | **94 699** | **110 229** | **117 659** | **126 062** | **131 995** | **112 448** |
| **1000 Taxes on income, profits and capital gains** | **431** | **2 907** | **11 833** | **13 232** | **25 003** | **29 584** | **33 055** | **36 071** | **34 533** | **25 587** |
| 1100 Of individuals | 157 | 992 | 3 919 | 4 528 | 8 147 | 9 566 | 10 533 | 11 368 | 11 365 | 11 214 |
| 1110 On income and profits | 157 | 992 | 3 919 | 4 528 | 8 147 | 9 566 | 10 533 | 11 368 | 11 365 | 11 214 |
| 1120 On capital gains | .. | .. | .. | .. | .. | .. | .. | .. | .. | .. |
| 1200 Corporate | 274 | 1 916 | 7 915 | 8 705 | 16 856 | 20 018 | 22 522 | 24 702 | 23 167 | 14 373 |
| 1210 On profits | 274 | 1 916 | 7 915 | 8 705 | 16 856 | 20 018 | 22 522 | 24 702 | 23 167 | 14 373 |
| Corporate income tax | 274 | 1 916 | 6 877 | 7 400 | 15 206 | 18 020 | 20 668 | 22 083 | 20 538 | 12 731 |
| Income tax surcharge | 0 | 0 | 1 038 | 1 305 | 1 637 | 1 985 | 1 841 | 2 601 | 2 612 | 1 620 |
| Special contribution of the cooperative sector | 0 | 0 | 0 | 0 | 13 | 13 | 14 | 19 | 17 | 21 |
| 1220 On capital gains of corporates | .. | .. | .. | .. | .. | .. | .. | .. | .. | .. |
| 1300 Unallocable between 1100 and 1200 | 0 | 0 | 0 | 0 | 0 | 0 | 0 | 0 | 0 | 0 |
| **2000 Social security contributions** | **179** | **1 727** | **6 037** | **8 671** | **13 524** | **15 550** | **17 911** | **19 302** | **21 068** | **23 138** |
| 2100 Employees | .. | .. | .. | .. | .. | .. | .. | .. | .. | .. |
| 2110 On a payroll basis | .. | .. | .. | .. | .. | .. | .. | .. | .. | .. |
| 2120 On an income tax basis | .. | .. | .. | .. | .. | .. | .. | .. | .. | .. |
| 2200 Employers | .. | .. | .. | .. | .. | .. | .. | .. | .. | .. |
| 2210 On a payroll basis | .. | .. | .. | .. | .. | .. | .. | .. | .. | .. |
| 2220 On an income tax basis | .. | .. | .. | .. | .. | .. | .. | .. | .. | .. |
| 2300 Self-employed or non-employed | .. | .. | .. | .. | .. | .. | .. | .. | .. | .. |
| 2310 On a payroll basis | .. | .. | .. | .. | .. | .. | .. | .. | .. | .. |
| 2320 On an income tax basis | .. | .. | .. | .. | .. | .. | .. | .. | .. | .. |
| 2400 Unallocable between 2100, 2200 and 2300 | 179 | 1 727 | 6 037 | 8 671 | 13 524 | 15 550 | 17 911 | 19 302 | 21 068 | 23 138 |
| 2410 On a payroll basis | 179 | 1 727 | 6 037 | 8 671 | 13 524 | 15 550 | 17 911 | 19 302 | 21 068 | 23 138 |
| 2420 On an income tax basis | 0 | 0 | 0 | 0 | 0 | 0 | 0 | 0 | 0 | 0 |
| **3000 Taxes on payroll and workforce** | **0** | **0** | **398** | **485** | **1 007** | **869** | **925** | **1 025** | **1 005** | **935** |
| **4000 Taxes on property** | **16** | **266** | **439** | **994** | **2 635** | **2 726** | **3 046** | **3 243** | **3 428** | **2 954** |
| 4100 Recurrent taxes on immovable property | 16 | 189 | 291 | 254 | 298 | 330 | 344 | 435 | 446 | 282 |
| 4110 Households | .. | .. | .. | .. | .. | .. | .. | .. | .. | .. |
| 4120 Others | .. | .. | .. | .. | .. | .. | .. | .. | .. | .. |
| 4200 Recurrent taxes on net wealth | 0 | 78 | 148 | 359 | 334 | 294 | 349 | 278 | 341 | 328 |
| 4210 Individual | .. | .. | .. | .. | .. | .. | .. | .. | .. | .. |
| 4220 Corporate | .. | .. | .. | .. | .. | .. | .. | .. | .. | .. |
| 4300 Estate, inheritance and gift taxes | 0 | 0 | 0 | 0 | 0 | 0 | 0 | 0 | 0 | 0 |
| 4310 Estate and inheritance taxes | .. | .. | .. | .. | .. | .. | .. | .. | .. | .. |
| 4320 Gift taxes | .. | .. | .. | .. | .. | .. | .. | .. | .. | .. |
| 4400 Taxes on financial and capital transactions | 0 | 0 | 0 | 0 | 2 003 | 2 102 | 2 353 | 2 531 | 2 641 | 2 344 |
| 4500 Non-recurrent taxes | 0 | 0 | 0 | 380 | 0 | 0 | 0 | 0 | 0 | 0 |
| 4510 On net wealth | .. | .. | 0 | 0 | .. | .. | .. | .. | .. | .. |
| 4520 Other non-recurrent taxes | .. | .. | 0 | 380 | .. | .. | .. | .. | .. | .. |
| 4600 Other recurrent taxes on property | 0 | 0 | 0 | 0 | 0 | 0 | 0 | 0 | 0 | 0 |
| **5000 Taxes on goods and services** | **1 401** | **12 436** | **25 985** | **28 937** | **50 027** | **56 364** | **60 580** | **64 017** | **66 742** | **55 520** |
| 5100 Taxes on production, sale, transfer, etc | 1 401 | 12 436 | 25 985 | 28 937 | 50 027 | 56 364 | 60 580 | 64 017 | 66 742 | 55 520 |
| 5110 General taxes | 344 | 5 146 | 14 170 | 16 050 | 32 273 | 36 521 | 39 228 | 41 562 | 42 891 | 35 815 |
| 5111 Value added taxes | 344 | 5 146 | 14 170 | 16 050 | 32 273 | 36 521 | 39 228 | 41 562 | 42 891 | 35 815 |
| 5112 Sales tax | 0 | 0 | 0 | 0 | 0 | 0 | 0 | 0 | 0 | 0 |
| 5113 Other | 0 | 0 | 0 | 0 | 0 | 0 | 0 | 0 | 0 | 0 |
| 5120 Taxes on specific goods and services | 1 057 | 7 290 | 11 815 | 12 887 | 17 754 | 19 844 | 21 352 | 22 454 | 23 851 | 19 705 |
| 5121 Excises | 256 | 4 592 | 7 606 | 8 458 | 13 349 | 14 953 | 16 405 | 17 011 | 18 285 | 15 598 |
| Beer | 70 | 376 | 358 | 376 | 668 | 824 | 974 | 1 150 | 1 339 | 1 164 |
| Soft drinks | 25 | 240 | 419 | 514 | 838 | 890 | 938 | 979 | 1 075 | 1 073 |
| Liquors | 32 | 48 | 80 | 121 | 194 | 190 | 192 | 227 | 217 | 206 |
| Petroleum products | 43 | 347 | 0 | 0 | 0 | 0 | 0 | 0 | 0 | 0 |
| Cigarettes | 57 | 369 | 582 | 607 | 598 | 564 | 563 | 565 | 514 | 471 |
| Fuel tax | 0 | 2 954 | 5 578 | 6 288 | 10 317 | 11 594 | 12 773 | 13 061 | 14 131 | 11 951 |
| Other | 28 | 258 | 589 | 551 | 735 | 890 | 965 | 1 028 | 1 010 | 733 |
| 5122 Profits of fiscal monopolies | 0 | 0 | 0 | 0 | 0 | 0 | 0 | 0 | 0 | 0 |
| 5123 Customs and import duties | 498 | 2 083 | 2 869 | 2 505 | 3 541 | 3 998 | 4 244 | 4 485 | 4 474 | 3 282 |
| Petroleum | 0 | 297 | 0 | 0 | 0 | 0 | 0 | 0 | 0 | 0 |
| Other | 498 | 1 786 | 2 869 | 2 505 | 3 541 | 3 998 | 4 244 | 4 485 | 4 474 | 3 282 |
| 5124 Taxes on exports | 217 | 6 | 0 | 0 | 84 | 72 | 79 | 90 | 18 | 10 |
| Bananas | 39 | 5 | .. | .. | 0 | 0 | 0 | 0 | 0 | 0 |
| Coffee | 1 | 0 | .. | .. | 0 | 0 | 0 | 0 | 0 | 0 |
| Temporary export tax | 163 | 0 | .. | .. | 0 | 0 | 0 | 0 | 0 | 0 |
| Special contribution of the mining sector | 0 | 0 | .. | .. | 84 | 72 | 79 | 90 | 18 | 10 |
| Other | 15 | 1 | .. | .. | 0 | 0 | 0 | 0 | 0 | 0 |
| 5125 Taxes on investment goods | 0 | 0 | 0 | 0 | 0 | 0 | 0 | 0 | 0 | 0 |

## Table 5.17. **Honduras** *(cont.)*

Details of tax revenue / Ingresos tributarios detallados

*Million HNL*

| | 1990 | 2000 | 2007 | 2010 | 2015 | 2016 | 2017 | 2018 | 2019 | 2020 |
|---|---|---|---|---|---|---|---|---|---|---|
| 5126 Taxes on specific services | 0 | 0 | 0 | 0 | 91 | 86 | 84 | 80 | 49 | 41 |
| Special contribution of mobile services | .. | .. | .. | .. | 67 | 60 | 55 | 49 | 35 | 36 |
| Special contribution of the food and services sector | .. | .. | .. | .. | 21 | 23 | 25 | 26 | 9 | 3 |
| Special contribution of casino games and slot machines | .. | .. | .. | .. | 3 | 3 | 4 | 4 | 5 | 2 |
| 5127 Other taxes on internat. trade and transactions | 0 | 0 | 0 | 0 | 0 | 0 | 0 | 0 | 0 | 0 |
| 5128 Other taxes | 87 | 610 | 1 340 | 1 924 | 690 | 734 | 539 | 789 | 1 025 | 774 |
| 5130 Unallocable between 5110 and 5120 | 0 | 0 | 0 | 0 | 0 | 0 | 0 | 0 | 0 | 0 |
| 5200 Taxes on use of goods and perform activities | 0 | 0 | 0 | 0 | 0 | 0 | 0 | 0 | 0 | 0 |
| 5210 Recurrent taxes | .. | .. | .. | .. | .. | .. | .. | .. | .. | .. |
| 5211 Paid by households: motor vehicles | .. | .. | .. | .. | .. | .. | .. | .. | .. | .. |
| 5212 Paid by others: motor vehicles | .. | .. | .. | .. | .. | .. | .. | .. | .. | .. |
| 5213 Paid in respect of other goods | .. | .. | .. | .. | .. | .. | .. | .. | .. | .. |
| 5220 Non-recurrent taxes | .. | .. | .. | .. | .. | .. | .. | .. | .. | .. |
| 5300 Unallocable between 5100 and 5200 | 0 | 0 | 0 | 0 | 0 | 0 | 0 | 0 | 0 | 0 |
| **6000 Other taxes** | **91** | **962** | **1 469** | **2 225** | **2 503** | **5 136** | **2 142** | **2 404** | **5 220** | **4 315** |
| 6100 Paid solely by business | 0 | 0 | 0 | 0 | 0 | 0 | 0 | 0 | 0 | 0 |
| 6200 Other | 91 | 962 | 1 469 | 2 225 | 2 503 | 5 136 | 2 142 | 2 404 | 5 220 | 4 315 |

.. Not available

*Note:* Year ending 31st December.

The data are on a cash basis.

Figures for local tax revenues may include non-tax revenues and central government transfers which are not considered as tax revenues according to the OECD classification, described in the Interpretative Guide, but it has not been possible to distinguish the different components within the aggregate data.

Heading 3000: The employer contributions to the National Institute of Vocational Training (INFOP) are included in heading 3000. The tax revenue is classified under the central government. In Honduras this revenue is classified under a separate unit considered to be different to the central government.

*Source:* Servicio de Administración de Rentas (Revenue Administration Service); Secretaría de Finanzas (Ministry of Finance).

StatLink https://doi.org/10.1787/888934309663

## Table 5.18. **Jamaica**

Details of tax revenue / Ingresos tributarios detallados

*Million JMD*

| | 1990 | 2000 | 2007 | 2010 | 2015 | 2016 | 2017 | 2018 | 2019 | 2020 |
|---|---|---|---|---|---|---|---|---|---|---|
| **Total tax revenue** | **7 748** | **87 713** | **219 435** | **287 139** | **427 640** | **467 350** | **517 091** | **562 009** | **602 592** | **544 129** |
| **1000 Taxes on income, profits and capital gains** | **3 639** | **35 457** | **88 026** | **105 917** | **129 233** | **135 564** | **129 925** | **144 581** | **155 140** | **155 632** |
| 1100 Of individuals | 1 687 | 17 441 | 48 220 | 54 798 | 74 538 | 72 175 | 60 306 | 62 644 | 69 323 | 72 692 |
| 1110 On income and profits | 1 687 | 17 441 | 48 220 | 54 798 | 74 538 | 72 175 | 60 306 | 62 644 | 69 323 | 72 692 |
| PAYE | 1 489 | 16 515 | 45 533 | 50 828 | 70 075 | 67 591 | 54 879 | 57 472 | 63 716 | 67 228 |
| Other individuals | 198 | 926 | 2 687 | 3 969 | 4 463 | 4 584 | 5 427 | 5 173 | 5 607 | 5 464 |
| 1120 On capital gains | .. | .. | .. | .. | .. | .. | .. | .. | .. | .. |
| 1200 Corporate | 1 280 | 7 627 | 19 758 | 33 091 | 40 198 | 47 530 | 61 401 | 62 504 | 67 623 | 61 823 |
| 1210 On profits | 1 280 | 7 627 | 19 758 | 33 091 | 40 198 | 47 530 | 61 401 | 62 504 | 67 623 | 61 823 |
| Bauxite/alumina | 134 | 430 | 1 626 | 866 | 0 | 0 | 0 | 0 | 0 | 0 |
| Other companies | 1 146 | 7 197 | 18 132 | 32 224 | 39 668 | 46 823 | 60 431 | 61 427 | 67 251 | 61 665 |
| Minimum business tax | 0 | 0 | 0 | 0 | 529 | 707 | 970 | 1 077 | 372 | 159 |
| 1220 On capital gains of corporates | .. | .. | .. | .. | .. | .. | .. | .. | .. | .. |
| 1300 Unallocable between 1100 and 1200 | 672 | 10 389 | 20 048 | 18 028 | 14 498 | 15 859 | 8 218 | 19 433 | 18 194 | 21 117 |
| Tax on dividends | 68 | 854 | 1 928 | 1 059 | 979 | 1 408 | 1 801 | 1 987 | 2 368 | 2 757 |
| Tax on interests | 605 | 9 535 | 18 120 | 16 970 | 13 519 | 14 451 | 6 417 | 17 446 | 15 827 | 18 360 |
| **2000 Social security contributions** | **..** | **..** | **6 349** | **8 199** | **16 449** | **17 978** | **19 249** | **21 033** | **24 569** | **24 994** |
| 2100 Employees | .. | .. | .. | .. | .. | .. | .. | .. | .. | .. |
| 2110 On a payroll basis | .. | .. | .. | .. | .. | .. | .. | .. | .. | .. |
| 2120 On an income tax basis | .. | .. | .. | .. | .. | .. | .. | .. | .. | .. |
| 2200 Employers | .. | .. | .. | .. | .. | .. | .. | .. | .. | .. |
| 2210 On a payroll basis | .. | .. | .. | .. | .. | .. | .. | .. | .. | .. |
| 2220 On an income tax basis | .. | .. | .. | .. | .. | .. | .. | .. | .. | .. |
| 2300 Self-employed or non-employed | .. | .. | .. | .. | .. | .. | .. | .. | .. | .. |
| 2310 On a payroll basis | .. | .. | .. | .. | .. | .. | .. | .. | .. | .. |
| 2320 On an income tax basis | .. | .. | .. | .. | .. | .. | .. | .. | .. | .. |
| 2400 Unallocable between 2100, 2200 and 2300 | .. | .. | 6 349 | 8 199 | 16 449 | 17 978 | 19 249 | 21 033 | 24 569 | 24 994 |
| 2410 On a payroll basis | .. | .. | .. | .. | .. | .. | .. | .. | .. | .. |
| 2420 On an income tax basis | .. | .. | .. | .. | .. | .. | .. | .. | .. | .. |
| **3000 Taxes on payroll and workforce** | **305** | **3 821** | **9 898** | **12 792** | **20 757** | **22 845** | **25 865** | **28 541** | **31 294** | **30 813** |
| **4000 Taxes on property** | **965** | **4 262** | **12 617** | **9 939** | **19 411** | **21 149** | **23 583** | **24 793** | **19 117** | **15 600** |
| 4100 Recurrent taxes on immovable property | 67 | 639 | 1 788 | 2 600 | 7 271 | 7 101 | 8 523 | 8 478 | 9 020 | 7 996 |
| 4110 Households | 67 | 639 | 1 788 | 2 600 | 7 271 | 7 101 | 8 523 | 8 478 | 9 020 | 7 996 |
| Municipal property tax | 0 | 639 | 1 788 | 2 600 | 7 271 | 7 101 | 8 523 | 8 478 | 9 020 | 7 996 |
| Other property taxes | 67 | 0 | 0 | 0 | 0 | 0 | 0 | 0 | 0 | 0 |
| 4120 Others | 0 | 0 | 0 | 0 | 0 | 0 | 0 | 0 | 0 | 0 |
| 4200 Recurrent taxes on net wealth | 0 | 0 | 0 | 0 | 0 | 0 | 0 | 0 | 0 | 0 |
| 4210 Individual | .. | .. | .. | .. | .. | .. | .. | .. | .. | .. |
| 4220 Corporate | .. | .. | .. | .. | .. | .. | .. | .. | .. | .. |
| 4300 Estate, inheritance and gift taxes | 0 | 0 | 0 | 0 | 0 | 0 | 0 | 0 | 0 | 0 |
| 4310 Estate and inheritance taxes | .. | .. | .. | .. | .. | .. | .. | .. | .. | .. |
| 4320 Gift taxes | .. | .. | .. | .. | .. | .. | .. | .. | .. | .. |
| 4400 Taxes on financial and capital transactions | 898 | 3 623 | 10 829 | 7 339 | 12 140 | 14 048 | 15 060 | 16 315 | 10 097 | 7 603 |
| Stamp duty | 898 | 3 623 | 10 829 | 7 339 | 12 140 | 14 048 | 15 060 | 16 315 | 10 097 | 7 603 |
| 4500 Non-recurrent taxes | 0 | 0 | 0 | 0 | 0 | 0 | 0 | 0 | 0 | 0 |
| 4510 On net wealth | .. | .. | .. | .. | .. | .. | .. | .. | .. | .. |
| 4520 Other non-recurrent taxes | .. | .. | .. | .. | .. | .. | .. | .. | .. | .. |
| 4600 Other recurrent taxes on property | 0 | 0 | 0 | 0 | 0 | 0 | 0 | 0 | 0 | 0 |
| **5000 Taxes on goods and services** | **2 824** | **43 907** | **101 639** | **149 544** | **240 795** | **268 569** | **316 601** | **340 651** | **370 321** | **315 268** |
| 5100 Taxes on production, sale, transfer, etc | 2 760 | 43 107 | 100 317 | 147 500 | 237 456 | 265 064 | 311 911 | 335 189 | 363 429 | 308 011 |
| 5110 General taxes | 297 | 22 356 | 65 030 | 84 409 | 138 501 | 149 111 | 171 584 | 187 576 | 203 297 | 177 354 |
| 5111 Value added taxes | 293 | 22 356 | 63 948 | 82 407 | 135 827 | 146 030 | 168 112 | 183 646 | 199 150 | 173 480 |
| General consumption tax | 293 | 22 356 | 63 948 | 82 407 | 135 827 | 146 030 | 168 112 | 183 646 | 199 150 | 173 480 |
| 5112 Sales tax | 4 | 0 | 0 | 0 | 0 | 0 | 0 | 0 | 0 | 0 |
| Sales tax on used cars | 4 | .. | .. | .. | .. | .. | .. | .. | .. | .. |
| 5113 Other | 0 | 0 | 1 082 | 2 002 | 2 674 | 3 081 | 3 472 | 3 930 | 4 147 | 3 873 |
| Environmental levy | .. | .. | 1 082 | 2 002 | 2 674 | 3 081 | 3 472 | 3 930 | 4 147 | 3 873 |
| 5120 Taxes on specific goods and services | 2 463 | 20 752 | 35 287 | 63 091 | 98 955 | 115 953 | 140 327 | 147 613 | 160 133 | 130 658 |
| 5121 Excises | 1 158 | 9 751 | 13 289 | 38 112 | 49 202 | 59 327 | 75 152 | 75 169 | 80 773 | 69 949 |
| Special consumption tax | 1 115 | 9 751 | 13 289 | 38 112 | 49 202 | 59 327 | 75 112 | 75 103 | 80 693 | 69 852 |
| Quarry tax | 0 | 0 | 0 | 0 | 0 | 0 | 39 | 66 | 80 | 97 |
| Other excises | 44 | 0 | 0 | 0 | 0 | 0 | 0 | 0 | 0 | 0 |
| 5122 Profits of fiscal monopolies | 0 | 0 | 0 | 0 | 0 | 0 | 0 | 0 | 0 | 0 |
| 5123 Customs and import duties | 782 | 8 498 | 18 640 | 19 959 | 28 771 | 34 033 | 37 737 | 41 243 | 44 809 | 40 420 |
| 5124 Taxes on exports | 0 | 0 | 0 | 0 | 0 | 0 | 0 | 0 | 0 | 0 |
| 5125 Taxes on investment goods | 0 | 0 | 0 | 0 | 0 | 0 | 0 | 0 | 0 | 0 |

# Table 5.18. **Jamaica** *(cont.)*

Details of tax revenue / Ingresos tributarios detallados

*Million JMD*

| | 1990 | 2000 | 2007 | 2010 | 2015 | 2016 | 2017 | 2018 | 2019 | 2020 |
|---|---|---|---|---|---|---|---|---|---|---|
| 5126 Taxes on specific services | 523 | 2 503 | 3 359 | 5 020 | 20 982 | 22 593 | 27 438 | 31 202 | 34 550 | 20 289 |
| Travel tax | 86 | 1 999 | 2 144 | 3 512 | 9 979 | 12 726 | 18 659 | 20 114 | 21 954 | 9 108 |
| Telephone call tax | 86 | 0 | 0 | 0 | 6 157 | 4 810 | 3 543 | 3 247 | 3 568 | 3 619 |
| Betting, gaming and lottery | 50 | 504 | 1 215 | 1 508 | 2 797 | 2 802 | 2 639 | 5 205 | 6 152 | 6 163 |
| Accommodation tax | 87 | 0 | 0 | 0 | 2 050 | 2 254 | 2 598 | 2 636 | 2 877 | 1 400 |
| Bank and trust | 204 | 0 | 0 | 0 | 0 | 0 | 0 | 0 | 0 | 0 |
| Entertainment tax | 11 | 0 | 0 | 0 | 0 | 0 | 0 | 0 | 0 | 0 |
| 5127 Other taxes on internat. trade and transactions | 0 | 0 | 0 | 0 | 0 | 0 | 0 | 0 | 0 | 0 |
| 5128 Other taxes | 0 | 0 | 0 | 0 | 0 | 0 | 0 | 0 | 0 | 0 |
| 5130 Unallocable between 5110 and 5120 | 0 | 0 | 0 | 0 | 0 | 0 | 0 | 0 | 0 | 0 |
| 5200 Taxes on use of goods and perform activities | 64 | 800 | 1 322 | 2 045 | 3 339 | 3 505 | 4 690 | 5 463 | 6 892 | 7 257 |
| 5210 Recurrent taxes | 64 | 800 | 1 322 | 2 045 | 3 339 | 3 505 | 4 690 | 5 463 | 6 892 | 7 257 |
| 5211 Paid by households: motor vehicles | 47 | 751 | 1 012 | 1 775 | 2 901 | 3 032 | 3 768 | 4 334 | 4 863 | 4 528 |
| 5212 Paid by others: motor vehicles | 0 | 0 | 0 | 0 | 0 | 0 | 0 | 0 | 0 | 0 |
| 5213 Paid in respect of other goods | 17 | 49 | 310 | 270 | 438 | 473 | 922 | 1 129 | 2 029 | 2 728 |
| 5220 Non-recurrent taxes | 0 | 0 | 0 | 0 | 0 | 0 | 0 | 0 | 0 | 0 |
| 5300 Unallocable between 5100 and 5200 | 0 | 0 | 0 | 0 | 0 | 0 | 0 | 0 | 0 | 0 |
| **6000 Other taxes** | **16** | **266** | **907** | **748** | **994** | **1 245** | **1 868** | **2 410** | **2 151** | **1 824** |
| 6100 Paid solely by business | 0 | 0 | 0 | 0 | 0 | 0 | 0 | 0 | 0 | 0 |
| 6200 Other | 16 | 266 | 907 | 748 | 994 | 1 245 | 1 868 | 2 410 | 2 151 | 1 824 |
| Contractors levy | 16 | 266 | 907 | 748 | 994 | 1 245 | 1 868 | 2 410 | 2 151 | 1 824 |

.. Not available

*Note:* Year ending 31st December, except for 1990-2003 which refer to fiscal year ending 31st March due to data availability.
The data are on a cash basis.
Heading 2000: The figures include contributions to National Insurance Scheme (NIS).
Heading 3000: Education tax has been classified under heading 3000 in this edition. It was previously under heading 1300. Education tax in Jamaica includes contributions from employees, employers and the self-employed calculated based on their emoluments. The employer contributions account for the majority of the total contributions.

*Source:* Ministry of Finance and the Public Service; Tax Administration Jamaica.

StatLink https://doi.org/10.1787/888934309682

## Table 5.19. **Mexico / México**

Details of tax revenue / Ingresos tributarios detallados

*Million MXN*

| | 1990 | 2000 | 2007 | 2010 | 2015 | 2016 | 2017 | 2018 | 2019 | 2020 |
|---|---|---|---|---|---|---|---|---|---|---|
| **Total tax revenue** | **102 005** | **767 216** | **1 382 103** | **1 716 243** | **2 953 480** | **3 343 314** | **3 527 032** | **3 797 888** | **3 995 654** | **4 146 414** |
| **1000 Taxes on income, profits and capital gains** | **34 673** | **276 548** | **554 099** | **683 604** | **1 230 555** | **1 427 114** | **1 571 954** | **1 671 513** | **1 694 143** | **1 768 639** |
| 1100 Of individuals | .. | .. | 238 938 | 313 473 | 609 384 | 681 784 | 754 109 | 804 236 | 829 501 | 872 598 |
| Tax on income of individuals | .. | .. | 238 938 | 313 473 | 609 384 | 681 784 | 754 109 | 804 236 | 829 501 | 872 598 |
| 1110 On income and profits | .. | .. | .. | .. | .. | .. | .. | .. | .. | .. |
| 1120 On capital gains | .. | .. | .. | .. | .. | .. | .. | .. | .. | .. |
| 1200 Corporate | .. | .. | 217 790 | 246 745 | 592 443 | 700 925 | 769 193 | 809 834 | 803 643 | 832 120 |
| Tax on income of corporations | .. | .. | 217 790 | 246 745 | 592 443 | 700 925 | 769 193 | 809 834 | 803 643 | 832 120 |
| 1210 On profits | .. | .. | .. | .. | .. | .. | .. | .. | .. | .. |
| 1220 On capital gains of corporates | .. | .. | .. | .. | .. | .. | .. | .. | .. | .. |
| 1300 Unallocable between 1100 and 1200 | 34 673 | 276 548 | 97 370 | 123 386 | 28 728 | 44 405 | 48 652 | 57 443 | 60 999 | 63 922 |
| Tax on income of other individuals and corporations | .. | 244 841 | 54 785 | 66 937 | 36 268 | 44 225 | 46 004 | 50 878 | 54 686 | 58 196 |
| Tax on asset | .. | 13 913 | 15 670 | -624 | -502 | -918 | -1 069 | -396 | -585 | -1 245 |
| Credit on salary | .. | 17 794 | 23 177 | 9 708 | 993 | 1 144 | 1 036 | 1 172 | 1 290 | 958 |
| Oil yields tax | .. | 0 | 3 738 | 2 296 | 0 | 0 | 0 | 0 | 0 | 0 |
| IETU | .. | 0 | 0 | 45 069 | -11 777 | -4 039 | -1 648 | 319 | -195 | -888 |
| Imposed by Activity Exploration and extraction of hydrocarbon | .. | 0 | 0 | 0 | 3 746 | 3 994 | 4 330 | 5 470 | 5 803 | 6 902 |
| **2000 Social security contributions** | **17 165** | **138 223** | **236 727** | **277 459** | **409 249** | **434 998** | **467 619** | **509 087** | **552 058** | **576 019** |
| 2100 Employees | .. | .. | .. | .. | .. | .. | .. | .. | .. | .. |
| 2110 On a payroll basis | .. | .. | .. | .. | .. | .. | .. | .. | .. | .. |
| 2120 On an income tax basis | .. | .. | .. | .. | .. | .. | .. | .. | .. | .. |
| 2200 Employers | .. | .. | .. | .. | .. | .. | .. | .. | .. | .. |
| 2210 On a payroll basis | .. | .. | .. | .. | .. | .. | .. | .. | .. | .. |
| 2220 On an income tax basis | .. | .. | .. | .. | .. | .. | .. | .. | .. | .. |
| 2300 Self-employed or non-employed | .. | .. | .. | .. | .. | .. | .. | .. | .. | .. |
| 2310 On a payroll basis | .. | .. | .. | .. | .. | .. | .. | .. | .. | .. |
| 2320 On an income tax basis | .. | .. | .. | .. | .. | .. | .. | .. | .. | .. |
| 2400 Unallocable between 2100, 2200 and 2300 | 17 165 | 138 223 | 236 727 | 277 459 | 409 249 | 434 998 | 467 619 | 509 087 | 552 058 | 576 019 |
| 2410 On a payroll basis | .. | 138 223 | 236 727 | 277 459 | 409 249 | 434 998 | 467 619 | 509 087 | 552 058 | 576 019 |
| 2420 On an income tax basis | .. | 0 | 0 | 0 | 0 | 0 | 0 | 0 | 0 | 0 |
| **3000 Taxes on payroll and workforce** | **1 797** | **11 217** | **28 071** | **36 911** | **70 221** | **76 762** | **84 099** | **93 303** | **101 284** | **105 456** |
| Substitute tax on salary | .. | 0 | 0 | 0 | 0 | 0 | 0 | 0 | 0 | 0 |
| Payroll tax | .. | 11 101 | 20 277 | 27 813 | 69 866 | 76 304 | 83 608 | 92 833 | 100 798 | 104 826 |
| Tax on remuneration to the personal work | .. | 65 | 7 578 | 8 841 | 152 | 225 | 246 | 270 | 298 | 407 |
| Tax on professions and fees | .. | 36 | 68 | 71 | 106 | 99 | 103 | 111 | 121 | 177 |
| Tax on operations by contract | .. | 15 | 148 | 186 | 96 | 134 | 141 | 90 | 67 | 46 |
| **4000 Taxes on property** | **1 914** | **13 964** | **33 161** | **38 955** | **57 673** | **63 273** | **67 836** | **77 110** | **79 262** | **66 460** |
| 4100 Recurrent taxes on immovable property | 1 036 | 9 948 | 19 425 | 25 724 | 37 961 | 40 357 | 44 680 | 49 445 | 50 540 | 43 906 |
| 4110 Households | 0 | 0 | 0 | 0 | 0 | 0 | 0 | 0 | 0 | 0 |
| 4120 Others | 1 036 | 9 948 | 19 425 | 25 724 | 37 961 | 40 357 | 44 680 | 49 445 | 50 540 | 43 906 |
| Property tax | .. | 9 948 | 19 425 | 25 724 | 37 961 | 40 357 | 44 680 | 49 445 | 50 540 | 43 906 |
| 4200 Recurrent taxes on net wealth | 0 | 0 | 0 | 0 | 0 | 0 | 0 | 0 | 0 | 0 |
| 4210 Individual | .. | .. | .. | .. | .. | .. | .. | .. | .. | .. |
| 4220 Corporate | .. | .. | .. | .. | .. | .. | .. | .. | .. | .. |
| 4300 Estate, inheritance and gift taxes | 8 | 0 | 0 | 0 | 0 | 0 | 0 | 0 | 0 | 0 |
| 4310 Estate and inheritance taxes | 8 | .. | .. | .. | .. | .. | .. | .. | .. | .. |
| 4320 Gift taxes | 0 | .. | .. | .. | .. | .. | .. | .. | .. | .. |
| 4400 Taxes on financial and capital transactions | 870 | 4 017 | 13 736 | 13 231 | 19 712 | 22 917 | 23 156 | 27 665 | 28 722 | 22 555 |
| Alienation of immovable property | .. | 1 763 | 1 076 | 1 122 | 1 595 | 1 723 | 1 623 | 1 823 | 1 939 | 1 982 |
| Transfer of ownership of real estate | .. | 2 236 | 8 147 | 5 027 | 6 671 | 9 593 | 7 016 | 8 658 | 8 385 | 7 766 |
| Purchasing property | .. | 18 | 4 513 | 7 082 | 11 447 | 11 600 | 14 516 | 17 184 | 18 397 | 12 807 |
| 4500 Non-recurrent taxes | 0 | 0 | 0 | 0 | 0 | 0 | 0 | 0 | 0 | 0 |
| 4510 On net wealth | .. | .. | .. | .. | .. | .. | .. | .. | .. | .. |
| 4520 Other non-recurrent taxes | .. | .. | .. | .. | .. | .. | .. | .. | .. | .. |
| 4600 Other recurrent taxes on property | 0 | 0 | 0 | 0 | 0 | 0 | 0 | 0 | 0 | 0 |
| **5000 Taxes on goods and services** | **44 837** | **319 612** | **513 140** | **651 915** | **1 141 170** | **1 295 653** | **1 283 049** | **1 381 659** | **1 504 252** | **1 544 243** |
| 5100 Taxes on production, sale, transfer, etc | 44 171 | 310 325 | 491 928 | 630 123 | 1 120 610 | 1 274 738 | 1 262 770 | 1 364 208 | 1 486 758 | 1 527 715 |
| 5110 General taxes | 26 635 | 189 606 | 409 013 | 504 509 | 707 213 | 791 700 | 816 048 | 922 238 | 933 327 | 987 525 |
| 5111 Value added taxes | 26 635 | 189 606 | 409 013 | 504 509 | 707 213 | 791 700 | 816 048 | 922 238 | 933 327 | 987 525 |
| 5112 Sales tax | 0 | 0 | 0 | 0 | 0 | 0 | 0 | 0 | 0 | 0 |
| 5113 Other | 0 | 0 | 0 | 0 | 0 | 0 | 0 | 0 | 0 | 0 |
| 5120 Taxes on specific goods and services | 17 519 | 120 720 | 82 915 | 125 614 | 413 397 | 483 038 | 446 722 | 441 970 | 553 432 | 540 191 |
| 5121 Excises | 10 072 | 86 163 | 47 008 | 86 098 | 361 538 | 420 448 | 378 537 | 358 577 | 470 993 | 469 040 |
| Special tax on production and services | .. | 81 544 | 41 532 | 81 427 | 354 294 | 411 390 | 367 834 | 347 436 | 460 496 | 460 674 |
| Tax on new automobiles | .. | 4 619 | 5 476 | 4 671 | 7 244 | 9 058 | 10 703 | 11 142 | 10 497 | 8 366 |
| Tax on luxury goods and services | .. | 0 | 0 | 0 | 0 | 0 | 0 | 0 | 0 | 0 |
| 5122 Profits of fiscal monopolies | 0 | 0 | 0 | 0 | 0 | 0 | 0 | 0 | 0 | 0 |

## Table 5.19. **Mexico / México** *(cont.)*

Details of tax revenue / Ingresos tributarios detallados

*Million MXN*

| | 1990 | 2000 | 2007 | 2010 | 2015 | 2016 | 2017 | 2018 | 2019 | 2020 |
|---|---|---|---|---|---|---|---|---|---|---|
| 5123 Customs and import duties | 6 998 | 33 285 | 33 344 | 26 602 | 45 366 | 51 889 | 53 793 | 67 232 | 66 295 | 59 247 |
| Step customs officer | .. | 423 | 1 156 | 2 071 | 1 270 | 1 336 | 1 463 | 1 690 | 1 554 | 1 309 |
| Import taxes | .. | 32 861 | 32 188 | 24 531 | 44 096 | 50 553 | 52 330 | 65 543 | 64 741 | 57 938 |
| 5124 Taxes on exports | 75 | 4 | 3 | 0 | 1 | 0 | 0 | 0 | 0 | 0 |
| Tax on exports | .. | 4 | 3 | 0 | 1 | 0 | 0 | 0 | 0 | 0 |
| 5125 Taxes on investment goods | 0 | 0 | 0 | 0 | 0 | 0 | 0 | 0 | 0 | 0 |
| 5126 Taxes on specific services | 132 | 1 042 | 2 146 | 10 958 | 1 763 | 5 630 | 7 778 | 8 692 | 9 196 | 5 666 |
| IDE | .. | 0 | 0 | 8 022 | -3 323 | -1 262 | -739 | -629 | -405 | -252 |
| Tax on lodging | .. | 504 | 1 059 | 1 384 | 2 561 | 3 009 | 3 598 | 3 945 | 4 254 | 2 500 |
| Public entertainment tax | .. | 240 | 365 | 462 | 689 | 858 | 839 | 909 | 924 | 471 |
| Tax on lotteries, raffles and gambling | .. | 267 | 705 | 923 | 1 416 | 1 828 | 2 717 | 2 947 | 3 403 | 2 064 |
| Tax on commercials | .. | 4 | 17 | 166 | 210 | 906 | 1 082 | 1 231 | 376 | 0 |
| Various indirect taxes | .. | 28 | 0 | 1 | 209 | 291 | 282 | 288 | 644 | 883 |
| 5127 Other taxes on internat. trade and transactions | 0 | 0 | 0 | 0 | 0 | 0 | 0 | 0 | 0 | 0 |
| 5128 Other taxes | 242 | 226 | 414 | 1 956 | 4 730 | 5 070 | 6 613 | 7 468 | 6 947 | 6 238 |
| Mining fees | .. | 226 | 414 | 1 956 | 4 730 | 5 070 | 6 613 | 7 468 | 6 947 | 6 238 |
| 5130 Unallocable between 5110 and 5120 | 17 | 0 | 0 | 0 | 0 | 0 | 0 | 0 | 0 | 0 |
| 5200 Taxes on use of goods and perform activities | 666 | 9 287 | 21 212 | 21 793 | 20 560 | 20 915 | 20 279 | 17 451 | 17 494 | 16 527 |
| 5210 Recurrent taxes | 666 | 9 287 | 21 212 | 21 793 | 20 560 | 20 915 | 20 279 | 17 451 | 17 494 | 16 527 |
| 5211 Paid by households: motor vehicles | 567 | 8 878 | 20 692 | 21 319 | 19 880 | 20 192 | 19 530 | 16 533 | 16 624 | 15 699 |
| Tax on motor vehicules | .. | 8 878 | 20 692 | 21 319 | 19 880 | 20 192 | 19 530 | 16 533 | 16 624 | 15 699 |
| 5212 Paid by others: motor vehicles | 0 | 301 | 275 | 281 | 439 | 503 | 554 | 640 | 645 | 437 |
| Tax on federal auto transport | .. | 301 | 275 | 281 | 439 | 503 | 554 | 640 | 645 | 437 |
| 5213 Paid in respect of other goods | 99 | 108 | 246 | 193 | 240 | 220 | 194 | 278 | 225 | 392 |
| Sport fishing | .. | 40 | 98 | 59 | 62 | 68 | 71 | 73 | 73 | 55 |
| Sport hunting | .. | 3 | 0 | 0 | 0 | 0 | 0 | 0 | 0 | 0 |
| Tax on commercial activities | .. | 63 | 147 | 50 | 64 | 46 | 28 | 115 | 41 | 318 |
| Trade in books and magazines | .. | 0 | 0 | 0 | 1 | 1 | 0 | 0 | 0 | 0 |
| Tax on industrial activities | .. | 2 | 0 | 82 | 93 | 78 | 77 | 73 | 92 | 0 |
| Mining | .. | 0 | 0 | 1 | 21 | 28 | 18 | 17 | 17 | 19 |
| 5220 Non-recurrent taxes | 0 | 0 | 0 | 0 | 0 | 0 | 0 | 0 | 0 | 0 |
| 5300 Unallocable between 5100 and 5200 | 0 | 0 | 0 | 0 | 0 | 0 | 0 | 0 | 0 | 0 |
| **6000 Other taxes** | **1 619** | **7 651** | **16 905** | **27 398** | **44 612** | **45 514** | **52 475** | **65 217** | **64 654** | **85 597** |
| 6100 Paid solely by business | 0 | 0 | 0 | 0 | 0 | 0 | 0 | 0 | 0 | 0 |
| 6200 Other | 1 619 | 7 651 | 16 905 | 27 398 | 44 612 | 45 514 | 52 475 | 65 217 | 64 654 | 85 597 |
| Accessories | .. | 5 504 | 12 403 | 22 206 | 23 211 | 28 480 | 32 153 | 45 864 | 41 063 | 56 793 |
| Unallocable between 1000 and 5000 caused in exercices fiscal previous liquidation slopes or of payment | .. | 374 | 222 | 30 | 4 168 | 329 | 281 | 400 | 79 | 218 |
| Additional state and local taxes | .. | 1 773 | 4 280 | 5 162 | 17 232 | 16 705 | 20 042 | 18 952 | 23 512 | 28 586 |

.. Not available

*Note:* Year ending 31st December.

The data are on a cash basis.

Heading 1000: In ECLAC data, income taxes are presented net of credit on salary figures.

Heading 2000: In ECLAC data, social security contributions are presented net of transfers from the Federal government for the payment of IMSS (Mexican Social Security Institute) pensions.

*Source:* Ministry of Finance, Economic Department.

StatLink https://doi.org/10.1787/888934309701

## Table 5.20. **Nicaragua**

Details of tax revenue / Ingresos tributarios detallados

*Million NIO*

| | 1990 | 2000 | 2007 | 2010 | 2015 | 2016 | 2017 | 2018 | 2019 | 2020 |
|---|---|---|---|---|---|---|---|---|---|---|
| **Total tax revenue** | .. | **9 300** | **25 811** | **36 162** | **77 567** | **88 483** | **98 803** | **95 457** | **107 333** | **109 985** |
| **1000 Taxes on income, profits and capital gains** | .. | **1 144** | **5 746** | **8 351** | **21 313** | **24 911** | **28 557** | **29 258** | **33 036** | **32 460** |
| 1100 Of individuals | .. | 299 | 1 488 | 1 857 | 4 432 | 5 396 | 6 468 | 6 780 | 6 561 | 6 447 |
| 1110 On income and profits | .. | 299 | 1 488 | 1 857 | 4 432 | 5 396 | 6 468 | 6 780 | 6 561 | 6 447 |
| 1120 On capital gains | .. | .. | .. | .. | .. | .. | .. | .. | .. | .. |
| 1200 Corporate | .. | 845 | 4 258 | 6 494 | 16 881 | 19 515 | 22 089 | 22 478 | 26 475 | 26 013 |
| 1210 On profits | .. | 845 | 4 258 | 6 494 | 16 881 | 19 515 | 22 089 | 22 478 | 26 475 | 26 013 |
| 1220 On capital gains of corporates | .. | .. | .. | .. | .. | .. | .. | .. | .. | .. |
| 1300 Unallocable between 1100 and 1200 | .. | 0 | 0 | 0 | 0 | 0 | 0 | 0 | 0 | 0 |
| **2000 Social security contributions** | .. | **1 678** | **4 921** | **8 090** | **18 194** | **21 296** | **23 868** | **24 624** | **27 586** | **29 014** |
| 2100 Employees | .. | .. | .. | .. | .. | .. | .. | .. | .. | .. |
| 2110 On a payroll basis | .. | .. | .. | .. | .. | .. | .. | .. | .. | .. |
| 2120 On an income tax basis | .. | .. | .. | .. | .. | .. | .. | .. | .. | .. |
| 2200 Employers | .. | .. | .. | .. | .. | .. | .. | .. | .. | .. |
| 2210 On a payroll basis | .. | .. | .. | .. | .. | .. | .. | .. | .. | .. |
| 2220 On an income tax basis | .. | .. | .. | .. | .. | .. | .. | .. | .. | .. |
| 2300 Self-employed or non-employed | .. | .. | .. | .. | .. | .. | .. | .. | .. | .. |
| 2310 On a payroll basis | .. | .. | .. | .. | .. | .. | .. | .. | .. | .. |
| 2320 On an income tax basis | .. | .. | .. | .. | .. | .. | .. | .. | .. | .. |
| 2400 Unallocable between 2100, 2200 and 2300 | .. | 1 678 | 4 921 | 8 090 | 18 194 | 21 296 | 23 868 | 24 624 | 27 586 | 29 014 |
| 2410 On a payroll basis | .. | 1 678 | 4 921 | 8 090 | 18 194 | 21 296 | 23 868 | 24 624 | 27 586 | 29 014 |
| 2420 On an income tax basis | .. | 0 | 0 | 0 | 0 | 0 | 0 | 0 | 0 | 0 |
| **3000 Taxes on payroll and workforce** | .. | **0** | **0** | **0** | **0** | **0** | **0** | **0** | **0** | **0** |
| **4000 Taxes on property** | .. | **11** | **338** | **423** | **771** | **834** | **896** | **961** | **1 196** | **1 037** |
| 4100 Recurrent taxes on immovable property | .. | 0 | 318 | 403 | 682 | 744 | 808 | 881 | 1 129 | 982 |
| 4110 Households | .. | .. | .. | .. | .. | .. | .. | .. | .. | .. |
| 4120 Others | .. | .. | .. | .. | .. | .. | .. | .. | .. | .. |
| 4200 Recurrent taxes on net wealth | .. | 0 | 0 | 0 | 0 | 0 | 0 | 0 | 0 | 0 |
| 4210 Individual | .. | .. | .. | .. | .. | .. | .. | .. | .. | .. |
| 4220 Corporate | .. | .. | .. | .. | .. | .. | .. | .. | .. | .. |
| 4300 Estate, inheritance and gift taxes | .. | 0 | 0 | 0 | 0 | 0 | 0 | 0 | 0 | 0 |
| 4310 Estate and inheritance taxes | .. | .. | .. | .. | .. | .. | .. | .. | .. | .. |
| 4320 Gift taxes | .. | .. | .. | .. | .. | .. | .. | .. | .. | .. |
| 4400 Taxes on financial and capital transactions | .. | 11 | 20 | 20 | 90 | 90 | 88 | 80 | 67 | 55 |
| Stamp duties | .. | 11 | 20 | 20 | 90 | 90 | 88 | 80 | 67 | 55 |
| 4500 Non-recurrent taxes | .. | 0 | 0 | 0 | 0 | 0 | 0 | 0 | 0 | 0 |
| 4510 On net wealth | .. | .. | .. | .. | .. | .. | .. | .. | .. | .. |
| 4520 Other non-recurrent taxes | .. | .. | .. | .. | .. | .. | .. | .. | .. | .. |
| 4600 Other recurrent taxes on property | .. | 0 | 0 | 0 | 0 | 0 | 0 | 0 | 0 | 0 |
| **5000 Taxes on goods and services** | .. | **5 584** | **14 522** | **18 951** | **36 599** | **40 697** | **44 563** | **39 815** | **44 608** | **46 559** |
| 5100 Taxes on production, sale, transfer, etc | .. | 5 584 | 14 283 | 18 608 | 35 798 | 39 855 | 43 619 | 38 780 | 43 674 | 45 543 |
| 5110 General taxes | .. | 2 931 | 9 155 | 11 932 | 23 787 | 26 273 | 29 201 | 25 791 | 27 933 | 29 040 |
| 5111 Value added taxes | .. | 2 931 | 8 025 | 10 353 | 20 714 | 22 822 | 25 551 | 21 905 | 24 116 | 24 990 |
| 5112 Sales tax | .. | 0 | 0 | 0 | 0 | 0 | 0 | 0 | 0 | 0 |
| 5113 Other | .. | 0 | 1 129 | 1 579 | 3 073 | 3 452 | 3 650 | 3 886 | 3 817 | 4 050 |
| 5120 Taxes on specific goods and services | .. | 2 653 | 5 128 | 6 676 | 12 011 | 13 581 | 14 419 | 12 990 | 15 741 | 16 503 |
| 5121 Excises | .. | 2 034 | 4 099 | 5 541 | 9 773 | 10 950 | 11 764 | 10 931 | 13 616 | 14 163 |
| Alcoholic beverages | .. | 84 | 144 | 198 | 264 | 305 | 355 | 353 | 583 | 702 |
| Beer | .. | 203 | 480 | 645 | 1 370 | 1 476 | 1 649 | 1 663 | 1 857 | 1 939 |
| Cigarettes | .. | 70 | 158 | 45 | 0 | 0 | 0 | 0 | 0 | 0 |
| Soft drinks | .. | 123 | 146 | 248 | 501 | 525 | 545 | 523 | 470 | 539 |
| Petroleum products | .. | 1 359 | 2 108 | 2 699 | 4 396 | 5 021 | 5 534 | 5 395 | 5 589 | 5 561 |
| Gaming machines | .. | 0 | 0 | 0 | 0 | 0 | 0 | 90 | 120 | 118 |
| Excises on imports | .. | 196 | 1 025 | 1 559 | 3 105 | 3 505 | 3 541 | 2 763 | 4 805 | 5 083 |
| Other excises | .. | -1 | 37 | 148 | 136 | 117 | 140 | 145 | 193 | 222 |
| 5122 Profits of fiscal monopolies | .. | 0 | 0 | 0 | 0 | 0 | 0 | 0 | 0 | 0 |
| 5123 Customs and import duties | .. | 619 | 1 030 | 1 135 | 2 238 | 2 631 | 2 654 | 2 058 | 2 125 | 2 340 |
| Custom duties | .. | 452 | 1 004 | 1 094 | 2 155 | 2 509 | 2 623 | 2 058 | 2 125 | 2 340 |
| Temporary protection duty | .. | 96 | 0 | 0 | 0 | 0 | 0 | 0 | 0 | 0 |
| On products originating in Colombia or Honduras | .. | 72 | 26 | 41 | 83 | 123 | 31 | 0 | 0 | 0 |
| 5124 Taxes on exports | .. | 0 | 0 | 0 | 0 | 0 | 0 | 0 | 0 | 0 |
| 5125 Taxes on investment goods | .. | 0 | 0 | 0 | 0 | 0 | 0 | 0 | 0 | 0 |
| 5126 Taxes on specific services | .. | 0 | 0 | 0 | 0 | 0 | 0 | 0 | 0 | 0 |
| 5127 Other taxes on internat. trade and transactions | .. | 0 | 0 | 0 | 0 | 0 | 0 | 0 | 0 | 0 |
| 5128 Other taxes | .. | 0 | 0 | 0 | 0 | 0 | 0 | 0 | 0 | 0 |
| 5130 Unallocable between 5110 and 5120 | .. | 0 | 0 | 0 | 0 | 0 | 0 | 0 | 0 | 0 |
| 5200 Taxes on use of goods and perform activities | .. | 0 | 239 | 343 | 801 | 842 | 943 | 1 035 | 934 | 1 016 |
| 5210 Recurrent taxes | .. | .. | 18 | 20 | 60 | 59 | 59 | 59 | 61 | 62 |
| 5211 Paid by households: motor vehicles | .. | .. | 18 | 20 | 60 | 59 | 59 | 59 | 61 | 62 |
| 5212 Paid by others: motor vehicles | .. | .. | 0 | 0 | 0 | 0 | 0 | 0 | 0 | 0 |

## Table 5.20. **Nicaragua** *(cont.)*

Details of tax revenue / Ingresos tributarios detallados

*Million NIO*

| | 1990 | 2000 | 2007 | 2010 | 2015 | 2016 | 2017 | 2018 | 2019 | 2020 |
|---|---|---|---|---|---|---|---|---|---|---|
| 5213 Paid in respect of other goods | .. | .. | 0 | 0 | 0 | 0 | 0 | 0 | 0 | 0 |
| 5220 Non-recurrent taxes | .. | .. | 221 | 323 | 741 | 783 | 884 | 976 | 874 | 954 |
| 5300 Unallocable between 5100 and 5200 | .. | 0 | 0 | 0 | 0 | 0 | 0 | 0 | 0 | 0 |
| **6000 Other taxes** | **..** | **0** | **284** | **347** | **690** | **745** | **919** | **798** | **907** | **915** |
| 6100 Paid solely by business | .. | .. | 0 | 0 | 0 | 0 | 0 | 0 | 0 | 0 |
| 6200 Other | .. | .. | 284 | 347 | 690 | 745 | 919 | 798 | 907 | 915 |

.. Not available

*Note:* Year ending 31st December.

The data are on a cash basis.

Comparable statistics for 1990 cannot be shown due to the devaluation of the Nicaraguan cordoba.

Figures for local tax revenues are estimated for 2020 as data are not available.

*Source:* Ministerio de Hacienda y Crédito Público (Ministry of Finance and Public Credit); Centro Interamericano de Administraciones Tributarias (Inter-American Centre of Tax Administrations).

StatLink https://doi.org/10.1787/888934309720

## Table 5.21. **Panama / Panamá**

Details of tax revenue / Ingresos tributarios detallados

*Million PAB*

| | 1990 | 2000 | 2007 | 2010 | 2015 | 2016 | 2017 | 2018 | 2019 | 2020 |
|---|---|---|---|---|---|---|---|---|---|---|
| **Total tax revenue** | **948** | **1 942** | **3 298** | **4 815** | **8 193** | **9 004** | **9 366** | **9 631** | **9 382** | **7 238** |
| **1000 Taxes on income, profits and capital gains** | **217** | **485** | **940** | **1 317** | **2 066** | **2 400** | **2 451** | **2 672** | **2 445** | **1 881** |
| 1100 Of individuals | 140 | 295 | 393 | 440 | 799 | 870 | 1 088 | 1 193 | 1 135 | 965 |
| 1110 On income and profits | 140 | 295 | 393 | 440 | 799 | 870 | 1 088 | 1 193 | 1 135 | 965 |
| Payroll | 115 | 222 | 303 | 353 | 689 | 733 | 931 | 1 049 | 992 | 839 |
| Personal income tax | 14 | 20 | 28 | 35 | 45 | 54 | 68 | 54 | 49 | 32 |
| Panama Canal Authority withholding | 10 | 53 | 62 | 52 | 65 | 83 | 89 | 90 | 94 | 94 |
| 1120 On capital gains | .. | .. | .. | .. | .. | .. | .. | .. | .. | .. |
| 1200 Corporate | 66 | 159 | 382 | 603 | 851 | 1 036 | 943 | 955 | 902 | 596 |
| 1210 On profits | 66 | 159 | 382 | 603 | 851 | 1 036 | 943 | 955 | 902 | 596 |
| Colón Free Zone | 5 | 3 | 12 | 20 | 36 | 36 | 41 | 53 | 45 | 30 |
| Corporate income tax | 61 | 155 | 370 | 584 | 815 | 1 000 | 902 | 901 | 857 | 566 |
| 1220 On capital gains of corporates | .. | .. | .. | .. | .. | .. | .. | .. | .. | .. |
| 1300 Unallocable between 1100 and 1200 | 11 | 31 | 164 | 273 | 416 | 494 | 420 | 524 | 407 | 320 |
| Dividends and complimentary tax | 11 | 31 | 89 | 166 | 265 | 282 | 253 | 307 | 266 | 218 |
| Capital gains | 0 | 0 | 75 | 107 | 151 | 212 | 167 | 217 | 142 | 102 |
| **2000 Social security contributions** | **325** | **742** | **1 104** | **1 637** | **3 152** | **3 426** | **3 654** | **3 797** | **3 894** | **3 225** |
| 2100 Employees | .. | .. | .. | .. | .. | .. | .. | .. | .. | .. |
| 2110 On a payroll basis | .. | .. | .. | .. | .. | .. | .. | .. | .. | .. |
| 2120 On an income tax basis | .. | .. | .. | .. | .. | .. | .. | .. | .. | .. |
| 2200 Employers | .. | .. | .. | .. | .. | .. | .. | .. | .. | .. |
| 2210 On a payroll basis | .. | .. | .. | .. | .. | .. | .. | .. | .. | .. |
| 2220 On an income tax basis | .. | .. | .. | .. | .. | .. | .. | .. | .. | .. |
| 2300 Self-employed or non-employed | .. | .. | .. | .. | .. | .. | .. | .. | .. | .. |
| 2310 On a payroll basis | .. | .. | .. | .. | .. | .. | .. | .. | .. | .. |
| 2320 On an income tax basis | .. | .. | .. | .. | .. | .. | .. | .. | .. | .. |
| 2400 Unallocable between 2100, 2200 and 2300 | 325 | 742 | 1 104 | 1 637 | 3 152 | 3 426 | 3 654 | 3 797 | 3 894 | 3 225 |
| 2410 On a payroll basis | .. | .. | .. | .. | .. | .. | .. | .. | .. | .. |
| 2420 On an income tax basis | .. | .. | .. | .. | .. | .. | .. | .. | .. | .. |
| **3000 Taxes on payroll and workforce** | **0** | **36** | **40** | **59** | **111** | **111** | **127** | **130** | **138** | **103** |
| Education insurance | .. | 36 | 40 | 59 | 111 | 111 | 127 | 130 | 138 | 103 |
| **4000 Taxes on property** | **32** | **43** | **119** | **138** | **199** | **209** | **251** | **244** | **169** | **126** |
| 4100 Recurrent taxes on immovable property | 28 | 34 | 74 | 108 | 151 | 168 | 207 | 209 | 134 | 104 |
| 4110 Households | 28 | 34 | 74 | 108 | 151 | 168 | 207 | 209 | 134 | 104 |
| 4120 Others | 0 | 0 | 0 | 0 | 0 | 0 | 0 | 0 | 0 | 0 |
| 4200 Recurrent taxes on net wealth | 0 | 0 | 0 | 0 | 0 | 0 | 0 | 0 | 0 | 0 |
| 4210 Individual | .. | .. | .. | .. | .. | .. | .. | .. | .. | .. |
| 4220 Corporate | .. | .. | .. | .. | .. | .. | .. | .. | .. | .. |
| 4300 Estate, inheritance and gift taxes | 0 | 0 | 0 | 0 | 0 | 0 | 0 | 0 | 0 | 0 |
| 4310 Estate and inheritance taxes | .. | .. | .. | .. | .. | .. | .. | .. | .. | .. |
| 4320 Gift taxes | .. | .. | .. | .. | .. | .. | .. | .. | .. | .. |
| 4400 Taxes on financial and capital transactions | 3 | 9 | 45 | 30 | 48 | 41 | 44 | 36 | 35 | 22 |
| 4500 Non-recurrent taxes | 0 | 0 | 0 | 0 | 0 | 0 | 0 | 0 | 0 | 0 |
| 4510 On net wealth | .. | .. | .. | .. | .. | .. | .. | .. | .. | .. |
| 4520 Other non-recurrent taxes | .. | .. | .. | .. | .. | .. | .. | .. | .. | .. |
| 4600 Other recurrent taxes on property | 0 | 0 | 0 | 0 | 0 | 0 | 0 | 0 | 0 | 0 |
| **5000 Taxes on goods and services** | **349** | **608** | **1 057** | **1 623** | **2 627** | **2 823** | **2 849** | **2 754** | **2 705** | **1 884** |
| 5100 Taxes on production, sale, transfer, etc | 332 | 546 | 961 | 1 473 | 2 376 | 2 555 | 2 570 | 2 474 | 2 425 | 1 657 |
| 5110 General taxes | 80 | 69 | 205 | 766 | 1 357 | 1 510 | 1 529 | 1 477 | 1 436 | 963 |
| 5111 Value added taxes | 80 | 69 | 205 | 766 | 1 357 | 1 510 | 1 529 | 1 477 | 1 436 | 963 |
| ITBMS on sales | 31 | 69 | 205 | 399 | 798 | 974 | 983 | 957 | 954 | 646 |
| ITBMS on imports | 49 | 0 | 0 | 367 | 559 | 536 | 546 | 519 | 482 | 317 |
| 5112 Sales tax | 0 | 0 | 0 | 0 | 0 | 0 | 0 | 0 | 0 | 0 |
| 5113 Other | 0 | 0 | 0 | 0 | 0 | 0 | 0 | 0 | 0 | 0 |
| 5120 Taxes on specific goods and services | 251 | 477 | 756 | 707 | 1 019 | 1 045 | 1 041 | 997 | 989 | 695 |
| 5121 Excises | 0 | 141 | 140 | 239 | 496 | 519 | 480 | 449 | 468 | 310 |
| Petroleum products | .. | 109 | 90 | 97 | 157 | 214 | 190 | 168 | 196 | 130 |
| Beer | .. | 18 | 25 | 31 | 48 | 49 | 49 | 53 | 54 | 47 |
| Cigarette | .. | 0 | 0 | 0 | 32 | 23 | 21 | 24 | 26 | 22 |
| Wine and liquor | .. | 12 | 11 | 11 | 15 | 10 | 6 | 18 | 17 | 12 |
| Soft drinks | .. | 2 | 4 | 6 | 7 | 6 | 7 | 11 | 11 | 7 |
| Automobiles | .. | 0 | 0 | 0 | 182 | 172 | 182 | 149 | 138 | 72 |
| Other excises | .. | 0 | 11 | 95 | 53 | 46 | 25 | 27 | 26 | 21 |
| 5122 Profits of fiscal monopolies | 0 | 0 | 0 | 0 | 0 | 0 | 0 | 0 | 0 | 0 |
| 5123 Customs and import duties | 125 | 298 | 574 | 390 | 391 | 355 | 358 | 338 | 319 | 215 |
| 5124 Taxes on exports | 13 | 0 | 0 | 0 | 0 | 0 | 0 | 0 | 0 | 0 |
| 5125 Taxes on investment goods | 0 | 0 | 0 | 0 | 0 | 0 | 0 | 0 | 0 | 0 |

## Table 5.21. **Panama / Panamá** *(cont.)*

Details of tax revenue / Ingresos tributarios detallados

*Million PAB*

| | 1990 | 2000 | 2007 | 2010 | 2015 | 2016 | 2017 | 2018 | 2019 | 2020 |
|---|---|---|---|---|---|---|---|---|---|---|
| 5126 Taxes on specific services | 1 | 37 | 41 | 78 | 133 | 171 | 203 | 211 | 203 | 169 |
| Insurance premiums | 0 | 17 | 24 | 47 | 46 | 52 | 86 | 90 | 86 | 89 |
| Cable and telecommunications | 0 | 16 | 8 | 17 | 39 | 41 | 40 | 42 | 40 | 39 |
| Gambling | 0 | 0 | 1 | 1 | 23 | 53 | 52 | 53 | 50 | 16 |
| Banks, financial institutions and exchange houses | 0 | 2 | 9 | 12 | 24 | 25 | 25 | 26 | 26 | 25 |
| Commercial activities and services | 1 | 3 | 0 | 0 | 0 | 0 | 0 | 0 | 0 | 0 |
| 5127 Other taxes on internat. trade and transactions | 0 | 0 | 0 | 0 | 0 | 0 | 0 | 0 | 0 | 0 |
| 5128 Other taxes | 0 | 0 | 0 | 0 | 0 | 0 | 0 | 0 | 0 | 0 |
| 5130 Unallocable between 5110 and 5120 | 0 | 0 | 0 | 0 | 0 | 0 | 0 | 0 | 0 | 0 |
| 5200 Taxes on use of goods and perform activities | 15 | 62 | 97 | 151 | 251 | 268 | 279 | 280 | 280 | 227 |
| Other indirect taxes | 0 | 0 | 0 | 36 | 59 | 65 | 69 | 66 | 61 | 42 |
| 5210 Recurrent taxes | 12 | 58 | 83 | 115 | 192 | 204 | 210 | 214 | 219 | 184 |
| 5211 Paid by households: motor vehicles | 0 | 7 | 10 | 0 | 0 | 0 | 0 | 0 | 0 | 0 |
| 5212 Paid by others: motor vehicles | 0 | 5 | 5 | 0 | 0 | 0 | 0 | 0 | 0 | 0 |
| 5213 Paid in respect of other goods | 12 | 46 | 68 | 115 | 192 | 204 | 210 | 214 | 219 | 184 |
| Commercial licences | 12 | 19 | 35 | 75 | 120 | 123 | 121 | 124 | 126 | 108 |
| Permission to conduct commercial and service activities | 0 | 25 | 31 | 38 | 69 | 77 | 84 | 86 | 89 | 73 |
| Permission to conduct industrial activities | 0 | 2 | 2 | 2 | 3 | 4 | 4 | 4 | 4 | 3 |
| Others | 0 | 0 | 0 | 0 | 0 | 0 | 0 | 0 | 0 | 0 |
| 5220 Non-recurrent taxes | 4 | 4 | 13 | 0 | 0 | 0 | 0 | 0 | 0 | 0 |
| Building and construction | 0 | 4 | 13 | .. | .. | .. | .. | .. | .. | .. |
| Ship registration | 4 | 0 | 0 | .. | .. | .. | .. | .. | .. | .. |
| 5300 Unallocable between 5100 and 5200 | 2 | 0 | 0 | 0 | 0 | 0 | 0 | 0 | 0 | 0 |
| **6000 Other taxes** | **26** | **27** | **38** | **41** | **37** | **35** | **34** | **34** | **30** | **20** |
| 6100 Paid solely by business | 0 | 0 | 0 | 0 | 0 | 0 | 0 | 0 | 0 | 0 |
| 6200 Other | 26 | 27 | 38 | 41 | 37 | 35 | 34 | 34 | 30 | 20 |
| Stamp duties | 17 | 27 | 38 | 41 | 37 | 35 | 34 | 34 | 30 | 20 |
| Others | 9 | 0 | 0 | 0 | 0 | 0 | 0 | 0 | 0 | 0 |

.. Not available

*Note:* Year ending 31st December.

The data are on a cash basis.

Tax revenue data are exclusive of documentos fiscales which are considered as wastable tax credits according to the OECD classification described in the Interpretative Guide.

Heading 2000: Social security contributions include regular and special contributions and professional risks premium collected by the Caja de Seguro Social (CSS).

Heading 3000: In ECLAC data, education insurance is classified as "Other taxes" (6000).

Heading 5126: In CIAT and ECLAC data, tax on banks, financial institutions and exchange houses is classified as a property tax (4000).

Heading 6200: Stamp duties before 2000 include tax on telephone calls and cables which cannot be distinguished due to data availability.

*Source:* Contraloría General de la República de Panamá (Comptroller General of the Republic of Panama); Ministerio de Economía y Finanzas de Panamá (Ministry of Economy and Finance of Panama); Caja de Seguro Social (Social Security Fund); Centro Interamericano de Administraciones Tributarias (Inter-American Centre of Tax Administrations).

StatLink https://doi.org/10.1787/888934309739

# Table 5.22. **Paraguay**

Details of tax revenue / Ingresos tributarios detallados

*Million PYG*

| | 1990 | 2000 | 2007 | 2010 | 2015 | 2016 | 2017 | 2018 | 2019 | 2020 |
|---|---|---|---|---|---|---|---|---|---|---|
| **Total tax revenue** | **608 021** | **3 587 445** | **9 669 201** | **15 638 531** | **25 855 185** | **27 466 261** | **30 731 221** | **31 954 693** | **33 008 733** | **32 441 314** |
| **1000 Taxes on income, profits and capital gains** | **73 726** | **470 388** | **1 228 684** | **2 096 498** | **3 922 384** | **4 429 169** | **5 086 803** | **5 265 609** | **6 022 875** | **6 010 196** |
| 1100 Of individuals | .. | 15 042 | 11 966 | 31 263 | 409 238 | 396 573 | 526 704 | 626 525 | 620 038 | 536 357 |
| 1110 On income and profits | .. | 15 042 | 11 966 | 31 263 | 409 238 | 396 573 | 526 704 | 626 525 | 620 038 | 536 357 |
| IRAGRO-IMAGRO | .. | 15 042 | 11 200 | 30 113 | 283 401 | 256 019 | 326 555 | 360 003 | 327 328 | 277 061 |
| Personal income tax | .. | 0 | 766 | 1 150 | 125 837 | 140 554 | 200 150 | 266 523 | 292 710 | 259 296 |
| 1120 On capital gains | .. | .. | .. | .. | .. | .. | .. | .. | .. | .. |
| 1200 Corporate | .. | 455 346 | 1 216 718 | 2 065 235 | 3 513 146 | 4 032 596 | 4 560 099 | 4 639 084 | 5 402 837 | 5 473 839 |
| 1210 On profits | .. | 455 346 | 1 216 718 | 2 065 235 | 3 513 146 | 4 032 596 | 4 560 099 | 4 639 084 | 5 402 837 | 5 473 839 |
| Income tax on small businesses | .. | 0 | 4 620 | 9 380 | 14 563 | 18 567 | 22 848 | 25 540 | 26 824 | 28 852 |
| Single tax | .. | 4 238 | 8 411 | 715 | 5 | 3 | 2 | 1 | 0 | 0 |
| Single tax on maquiladoras companies | .. | 0 | 1 401 | 3 310 | 10 892 | 12 087 | 20 194 | 27 070 | 31 201 | 35 229 |
| IRACIS | .. | 451 108 | 1 202 286 | 2 051 830 | 3 487 686 | 4 001 939 | 4 517 056 | 4 586 475 | 5 344 811 | 1 302 426 |
| Business income tax (IRE) | .. | 0 | 0 | 0 | 0 | 0 | 0 | 0 | 0 | 3 239 933 |
| Tax on dividends and income (IDU) | .. | 0 | 0 | 0 | 0 | 0 | 0 | 0 | 0 | 867 399 |
| 1220 On capital gains of corporates | .. | .. | .. | .. | .. | .. | .. | .. | .. | .. |
| 1300 Unallocable between 1100 and 1200 | 73 726 | 0 | 0 | 0 | 0 | 0 | 0 | 0 | 0 | 0 |
| Others | 73 726 | .. | .. | .. | .. | .. | .. | .. | .. | .. |
| **2000 Social security contributions** | **28 882** | **919 527** | **2 265 097** | **3 552 640** | **7 044 316** | **7 048 846** | **8 052 403** | **8 209 087** | **8 729 492** | **8 954 858** |
| 2100 Employees | .. | .. | .. | .. | .. | .. | .. | .. | .. | .. |
| 2110 On a payroll basis | .. | .. | .. | .. | .. | .. | .. | .. | .. | .. |
| 2120 On an income tax basis | .. | .. | .. | .. | .. | .. | .. | .. | .. | .. |
| 2200 Employers | .. | .. | .. | .. | .. | .. | .. | .. | .. | .. |
| 2210 On a payroll basis | .. | .. | .. | .. | .. | .. | .. | .. | .. | .. |
| 2220 On an income tax basis | .. | .. | .. | .. | .. | .. | .. | .. | .. | .. |
| 2300 Self-employed or non-employed | .. | .. | .. | .. | .. | .. | .. | .. | .. | .. |
| 2310 On a payroll basis | .. | .. | .. | .. | .. | .. | .. | .. | .. | .. |
| 2320 On an income tax basis | .. | .. | .. | .. | .. | .. | .. | .. | .. | .. |
| 2400 Unallocable between 2100, 2200 and 2300 | 28 882 | 919 527 | 2 265 097 | 3 552 640 | 7 044 316 | 7 048 846 | 8 052 403 | 8 209 087 | 8 729 492 | 8 954 858 |
| 2410 On a payroll basis | 28 882 | 919 527 | 2 265 097 | 3 552 640 | 7 044 316 | 7 048 846 | 8 052 403 | 8 209 087 | 8 729 492 | 8 954 858 |
| 2420 On an income tax basis | 0 | 0 | 0 | 0 | 0 | 0 | 0 | 0 | 0 | 0 |
| **3000 Taxes on payroll and workforce** | **0** | **0** | **0** | **0** | **0** | **0** | **0** | **0** | **0** | **0** |
| **4000 Taxes on property** | **17 162** | **71 777** | **276 985** | **276 119** | **435 473** | **571 590** | **565 323** | **415 570** | **443 521** | **401 222** |
| 4100 Recurrent taxes on immovable property | 17 162 | 0 | 196 504 | 258 423 | 405 806 | 540 423 | 529 986 | 389 962 | 417 177 | 375 800 |
| 4110 Households | 17 162 | .. | 196 504 | 258 423 | 405 806 | 540 423 | 529 986 | 389 962 | 417 177 | 375 800 |
| Real estate tax | 17 162 | .. | 190 924 | 249 697 | 390 772 | 514 404 | 501 873 | 359 235 | 378 712 | 342 625 |
| Tax on vacant lots | 0 | .. | 2 046 | 2 925 | 4 818 | 10 284 | 13 600 | 17 411 | 20 985 | 19 608 |
| Large estate and land tax | 0 | .. | 3 533 | 5 801 | 10 216 | 15 736 | 14 513 | 13 315 | 17 480 | 13 566 |
| 4120 Others | 0 | .. | 0 | 0 | 0 | 0 | 0 | 0 | 0 | 0 |
| 4200 Recurrent taxes on net wealth | 0 | 0 | 0 | 0 | 0 | 0 | 0 | 0 | 0 | 0 |
| 4210 Individual | .. | .. | .. | .. | .. | .. | .. | .. | .. | .. |
| 4220 Corporate | .. | .. | .. | .. | .. | .. | .. | .. | .. | .. |
| 4300 Estate, inheritance and gift taxes | 0 | 0 | 0 | 0 | 0 | 0 | 0 | 0 | 0 | 0 |
| 4310 Estate and inheritance taxes | .. | .. | .. | .. | .. | .. | .. | .. | .. | .. |
| 4320 Gift taxes | .. | .. | .. | .. | .. | .. | .. | .. | .. | .. |
| 4400 Taxes on financial and capital transactions | 0 | 71 777 | 80 466 | 15 955 | 29 601 | 29 897 | 33 872 | 24 583 | 24 912 | 24 857 |
| Real estate transfer tax | .. | 0 | 6 412 | 11 766 | 22 406 | 22 978 | 26 263 | 17 228 | 17 216 | 13 595 |
| Municipal Seal and Stamp Paper Tax | .. | 0 | 2 923 | 3 857 | 6 912 | 6 515 | 7 464 | 7 326 | 7 346 | 11 205 |
| Registration and stamp duties | .. | 71 777 | 71 130 | 332 | 282 | 403 | 144 | 30 | 350 | 57 |
| 4500 Non-recurrent taxes | 0 | 0 | 0 | 0 | 0 | 0 | 0 | 0 | 0 | 0 |
| 4510 On net wealth | .. | .. | .. | .. | .. | .. | .. | .. | .. | .. |
| 4520 Other non-recurrent taxes | .. | .. | .. | .. | .. | .. | .. | .. | .. | .. |
| 4600 Other recurrent taxes on property | 0 | 0 | 16 | 1 742 | 66 | 1 269 | 1 466 | 1 025 | 1 432 | 565 |
| **5000 Taxes on goods and services** | **438 444** | **2 080 878** | **5 813 827** | **9 462 461** | **14 279 329** | **15 225 947** | **16 813 348** | **17 901 774** | **17 610 929** | **16 929 091** |
| 5100 Taxes on production, sale, transfer, etc | 438 444 | 2 080 878 | 5 685 560 | 9 245 877 | 13 860 634 | 14 746 697 | 16 356 200 | 17 550 296 | 17 230 758 | 16 557 669 |
| 5110 General taxes | 0 | 1 150 496 | 3 496 977 | 5 991 694 | 9 768 800 | 10 482 238 | 11 221 710 | 11 851 395 | 11 794 402 | 11 787 033 |
| 5111 Value added taxes | 0 | 1 150 496 | 3 496 977 | 5 991 694 | 9 768 800 | 10 482 238 | 11 221 710 | 11 851 395 | 11 794 402 | 11 787 033 |
| 5112 Sales tax | .. | 0 | 0 | 0 | 0 | 0 | 0 | 0 | 0 | 0 |
| 5113 Other | .. | 0 | 0 | 0 | 0 | 0 | 0 | 0 | 0 | 0 |
| 5120 Taxes on specific goods and services | 438 444 | 930 382 | 2 188 583 | 3 254 183 | 4 091 834 | 4 264 459 | 5 134 490 | 5 698 901 | 5 436 356 | 4 770 635 |
| 5121 Excises | 300 219 | 456 561 | 1 335 412 | 1 710 531 | 2 404 222 | 2 589 108 | 2 890 013 | 3 156 091 | 2 992 813 | 2 773 235 |
| Fuels | 41 087 | 316 694 | 1 000 894 | 1 126 143 | 1 775 479 | 1 830 782 | 2 032 235 | 2 300 311 | 2 084 712 | 2 032 124 |
| Other excises | 259 132 | 136 194 | 309 463 | 537 887 | 616 342 | 745 189 | 843 123 | 841 900 | 886 475 | 724 578 |
| Animal health and quality service | 0 | 3 673 | 24 923 | 46 501 | 12 401 | 13 137 | 14 656 | 13 881 | 13 875 | 16 533 |
| Livestock trade | 0 | 0 | 132 | 0 | 0 | 0 | 0 | 0 | 7 751 | 0 |
| 5122 Profits of fiscal monopolies | 0 | 0 | 0 | 0 | 0 | 0 | 0 | 0 | 0 | 0 |
| 5123 Customs and import duties | 138 225 | 473 821 | 838 494 | 1 524 252 | 1 659 535 | 1 642 818 | 2 206 934 | 2 512 883 | 2 420 302 | 1 984 697 |
| 5124 Taxes on exports | 0 | 0 | 0 | 0 | 0 | 0 | 0 | 0 | 0 | 0 |
| 5125 Taxes on investment goods | 0 | 0 | 0 | 0 | 0 | 0 | 0 | 0 | 0 | 0 |

## Table 5.22. **Paraguay** *(cont.)*

Details of tax revenue / Ingresos tributarios detallados

*Million PYG*

| | 1990 | 2000 | 2007 | 2010 | 2015 | 2016 | 2017 | 2018 | 2019 | 2020 |
|---|---|---|---|---|---|---|---|---|---|---|
| 5126 Taxes on specific services | 0 | 0 | 14 677 | 19 401 | 28 076 | 32 533 | 37 542 | 29 927 | 23 241 | 12 704 |
| Advertising | .. | .. | 3 613 | 5 249 | 7 428 | 8 424 | 9 489 | 7 387 | 6 741 | 6 384 |
| Public transport | .. | .. | 4 173 | 4 363 | 4 297 | 4 316 | 4 080 | 4 196 | 3 420 | 1 255 |
| Gambling | .. | .. | 162 | 16 | 4 654 | 3 683 | 7 131 | 6 448 | 6 617 | 2 666 |
| Advertising and gambling | .. | .. | 5 361 | 8 884 | 9 357 | 12 715 | 14 821 | 9 796 | 4 447 | 1 317 |
| Other taxes on specific services | .. | .. | 1 368 | 888 | 2 341 | 3 395 | 2 021 | 2 099 | 2 017 | 1 082 |
| 5127 Other taxes on internat. trade and transactions | 0 | 0 | 0 | 0 | 0 | 0 | 0 | 0 | 0 | 0 |
| 5128 Other taxes | 0 | 0 | 0 | 0 | 0 | 0 | 0 | 0 | 0 | 0 |
| 5130 Unallocable between 5110 and 5120 | 0 | 0 | 0 | 0 | 0 | 0 | 0 | 0 | 0 | 0 |
| 5200 Taxes on use of goods and perform activities | 0 | 0 | 126 958 | 216 347 | 395 856 | 451 842 | 426 115 | 350 893 | 379 208 | 370 331 |
| 5210 Recurrent taxes | .. | .. | 107 077 | 183 622 | 329 518 | 386 360 | 365 303 | 315 178 | 329 087 | 334 724 |
| 5211 Paid by households: motor vehicles | .. | .. | 0 | 0 | 0 | 0 | 0 | 0 | 0 | 0 |
| 5212 Paid by others: motor vehicles | .. | .. | 28 343 | 52 365 | 94 393 | 106 200 | 109 084 | 106 872 | 109 402 | 103 274 |
| Motor vehicle licences | .. | .. | 28 343 | 52 365 | 94 393 | 106 200 | 109 084 | 106 872 | 109 402 | 103 274 |
| 5213 Paid in respect of other goods | .. | .. | 78 735 | 131 257 | 235 125 | 280 161 | 256 219 | 208 305 | 219 685 | 231 450 |
| Licencing fees | .. | .. | 75 323 | 126 965 | 229 686 | 274 468 | 250 528 | 203 605 | 214 555 | 225 717 |
| slaughter tax | .. | .. | 3 363 | 4 271 | 5 074 | 5 584 | 5 395 | 4 635 | 4 991 | 5 585 |
| Tax to the owners of animals | .. | .. | 48 | 21 | 365 | 109 | 296 | 65 | 140 | 148 |
| 5220 Non-recurrent taxes | .. | .. | 19 881 | 32 725 | 66 338 | 65 482 | 60 812 | 35 715 | 50 121 | 35 607 |
| Tax on construction | .. | .. | 16 168 | 31 696 | 65 403 | 64 284 | 60 092 | 34 999 | 49 375 | 34 930 |
| Luxury automobile tax | .. | .. | 2 750 | 91 | 54 | 152 | 7 | 0 | 0 | 0 |
| Trademarks registration | .. | .. | 962 | 938 | 881 | 1 045 | 713 | 716 | 746 | 677 |
| 5300 Unallocable between 5100 and 5200 | 0 | 0 | 1 309 | 237 | 22 838 | 27 409 | 31 034 | 585 | 962 | 1 092 |
| **6000 Other taxes** | **49 807** | **44 875** | **84 608** | **250 812** | **173 684** | **190 709** | **213 344** | **162 652** | **201 917** | **145 946** |
| 6100 Paid solely by business | 0 | 0 | 0 | 0 | 0 | 0 | 0 | 0 | 0 | 0 |
| 6200 Other | 49 807 | 44 875 | 84 608 | 250 812 | 173 684 | 190 709 | 213 344 | 162 652 | 201 917 | 145 946 |
| Taxes replaced | 0 | 0 | 0 | 0 | 0 | 0 | 0 | 0 | 0 | 0 |
| Other | 49 807 | 44 875 | 84 608 | 250 812 | 173 684 | 190 709 | 213 344 | 162 652 | 201 917 | 145 946 |

.. Not available

*Note:* Year ending 31st December.

The data are on a cash basis.

The figures for years before 2006 exclude local government tax revenues as the data are not available. This affects data in categories 4000, 5000 and 6000.

Heading 1200: Business income tax (IRE) and tax on dividends and income (IDU) have been included in this edition. They were introduced in 2019 for modernisation and simplification of the national tax system.

Heading 2000: Social security contributions before 1999 do not include social security contributions collected by decentralised institutions as the data are not available.

*Source:* Subsecretaría de Estado de Tributación, Ministerio de Hacienda del Paraguay (Tax Undersecretary, Ministry of Finance of Paraguay); Centro Interamericano de Administraciones Tributarias (Inter-American Centre of Tax Administrations).

StatLink https://doi.org/10.1787/888934309758

# Table 5.23. **Peru / Perú**

Details of tax revenue / Ingresos tributarios detallados

*Million PEN*

| | 1990 | 2000 | 2007 | 2010 | 2015 | 2016 | 2017 | 2018 | 2019 | 2020 |
|---|---|---|---|---|---|---|---|---|---|---|
| **Total tax revenue** | **637** | **26 771** | **59 187** | **74 803** | **106 183** | **106 042** | **107 028** | **121 844** | **127 989** | **109 416** |
| **1000 Taxes on income, profits and capital gains** | **37** | **5 078** | **24 139** | **27 317** | **37 772** | **40 360** | **39 846** | **43 979** | **46 753** | **40 124** |
| 1100 Of individuals | 3 | 2 117 | 4 645 | 6 518 | 11 137 | 11 760 | 13 008 | 13 598 | 14 744 | 13 182 |
| First category | .. | 167 | 217 | 160 | 443 | 504 | 532 | 580 | 624 | 503 |
| Second category | .. | 7 | 611 | 869 | 1 287 | 1 536 | 1 581 | 1 772 | 2 412 | 1 767 |
| Fourth category | .. | 234 | 408 | 521 | 783 | 871 | 894 | 960 | 1 023 | 1 002 |
| Fifth category | .. | 1 641 | 3 241 | 4 735 | 8 044 | 8 248 | 8 444 | 9 162 | 9 760 | 9 178 |
| Tax debt payments | .. | 68 | 168 | 233 | 581 | 601 | 1 558 | 1 125 | 926 | 733 |
| 1110 On income and profits | .. | .. | .. | .. | .. | .. | .. | .. | .. | .. |
| 1120 On capital gains | .. | .. | .. | .. | .. | .. | .. | .. | .. | .. |
| 1200 Corporate | 32 | 2 526 | 18 724 | 19 561 | 24 266 | 24 786 | 24 604 | 28 830 | 29 449 | 23 352 |
| 1210 On profits | 32 | 2 526 | 18 724 | 19 561 | 24 266 | 24 786 | 24 604 | 28 830 | 29 449 | 23 352 |
| Third category | .. | 2 023 | 13 258 | 14 652 | 16 817 | 16 496 | 15 499 | 17 268 | 17 679 | 13 804 |
| Income tax on mining | .. | 0 | 0 | 0 | 208 | 236 | 638 | 770 | 545 | 430 |
| Income tax special regime | .. | 47 | 60 | 118 | 310 | 335 | 323 | 344 | 354 | 271 |
| Other incomes corporate | .. | 18 | 95 | 148 | 167 | 215 | 233 | 251 | 257 | 220 |
| Tax debt payments | .. | 438 | 3 829 | 2 856 | 3 066 | 3 204 | 3 327 | 5 244 | 5 438 | 3 863 |
| Temporary tax on net assets | .. | 0 | 1 483 | 1 788 | 3 697 | 4 300 | 4 585 | 4 953 | 5 176 | 4 764 |
| 1220 On capital gains of corporates | .. | .. | .. | .. | .. | .. | .. | .. | .. | .. |
| 1300 Unallocable between 1100 and 1200 | 1 | 436 | 770 | 1 239 | 2 369 | 3 814 | 2 233 | 1 550 | 2 560 | 3 589 |
| Income tax on non-residents | 1 | 487 | 961 | 1 511 | 3 248 | 5 205 | 3 462 | 3 560 | 4 135 | 5 658 |
| Income tax refunds | 0 | -51 | -191 | -272 | -879 | -1 391 | -1 228 | -2 009 | -1 575 | -2 069 |
| **2000 Social security contributions** | **50** | **3 185** | **5 244** | **7 929** | **12 681** | **13 186** | **13 676** | **14 873** | **15 453** | **14 680** |
| 2100 Employees | .. | 566 | 1 005 | 2 468 | 3 508 | 3 646 | 3 796 | 4 216 | 4 202 | 3 910 |
| 2110 On a payroll basis | .. | 566 | 978 | 1 700 | 3 371 | 3 550 | 3 662 | 3 940 | 4 023 | 3 728 |
| 2120 On an income tax basis | .. | 0 | 26 | 767 | 137 | 97 | 134 | 275 | 179 | 182 |
| Solidarity contribution for pension plan | .. | .. | 26 | 767 | 137 | 97 | 134 | 275 | 179 | 182 |
| 2200 Employers | .. | 2 515 | 4 221 | 5 454 | 9 170 | 9 536 | 9 878 | 10 653 | 11 245 | 10 767 |
| 2210 On a payroll basis | .. | 2 432 | 4 039 | 5 216 | 8 926 | 9 282 | 9 591 | 10 299 | 10 883 | 10 344 |
| 2220 On an income tax basis | .. | 83 | 182 | 238 | 244 | 255 | 287 | 354 | 362 | 423 |
| 2300 Self-employed or non-employed | .. | 95 | 8 | 7 | 2 | 3 | 2 | 4 | 6 | 3 |
| 2310 On a payroll basis | .. | 0 | 0 | 0 | 0 | 0 | 0 | 0 | 0 | 0 |
| 2320 On an income tax basis | .. | 95 | 8 | 7 | 2 | 3 | 2 | 4 | 6 | 3 |
| 2400 Unallocable between 2100, 2200 and 2300 | 50 | 9 | 11 | 0 | 0 | 0 | 1 | 1 | 0 | 0 |
| 2410 On a payroll basis | 50 | 9 | 11 | 0 | 0 | 0 | 1 | 1 | .. | .. |
| 2420 On an income tax basis | 0 | 0 | 0 | 0 | 0 | 0 | 0 | 0 | .. | .. |
| **3000 Taxes on payroll and workforce** | **0** | **1 176** | **-40** | **57** | **92** | **91** | **91** | **99** | **99** | **96** |
| Extraordinary solidarity tax (IES) | .. | 1 151 | 9 | 3 | 5 | 1 | 0 | 1 | 0 | 1 |
| IES refunds | .. | -2 | -48 | -2 | -1 | 0 | -2 | 0 | -3 | 0 |
| National Housing Fund (FONAVI) | .. | 27 | 0 | 0 | 0 | 0 | 0 | 0 | 0 | 0 |
| Contributions to SENATI | .. | 0 | 0 | 56 | 88 | 90 | 93 | 98 | 102 | 96 |
| **4000 Taxes on property** | **87** | **323** | **1 931** | **2 231** | **2 429** | **2 637** | **2 573** | **2 680** | **3 063** | **2 418** |
| 4100 Recurrent taxes on immovable property | 0 | 298 | 554 | 727 | 1 463 | 1 629 | 1 718 | 1 748 | 2 026 | 1 749 |
| 4110 Households | .. | .. | .. | .. | .. | .. | .. | .. | .. | .. |
| 4120 Others | .. | .. | .. | .. | .. | .. | .. | .. | .. | .. |
| 4200 Recurrent taxes on net wealth | 49 | 0 | 0 | 0 | 0 | 0 | 0 | 0 | 0 | 0 |
| 4210 Individual | .. | .. | .. | .. | .. | .. | .. | .. | .. | .. |
| 4220 Corporate | .. | .. | .. | .. | .. | .. | .. | .. | .. | .. |
| 4300 Estate, inheritance and gift taxes | 0 | 0 | 0 | 0 | 0 | 0 | 0 | 0 | 0 | 0 |
| 4310 Estate and inheritance taxes | .. | .. | .. | .. | .. | .. | .. | .. | .. | .. |
| 4320 Gift taxes | .. | .. | .. | .. | .. | .. | .. | .. | .. | .. |
| 4400 Taxes on financial and capital transactions | 38 | 25 | 1 377 | 1 504 | 966 | 1 008 | 855 | 932 | 1 037 | 669 |
| Financial transactions tax | 0 | 0 | 1 031 | 944 | 161 | 168 | 175 | 200 | 224 | 207 |
| Real estate transfer tax | 0 | 25 | 347 | 560 | 805 | 840 | 680 | 732 | 813 | 463 |
| Tax Law Decree 519 | 38 | 0 | 0 | 0 | 0 | 0 | 0 | 0 | 0 | 0 |
| 4500 Non-recurrent taxes | 0 | 0 | 0 | 0 | 0 | 0 | 0 | 0 | 0 | 0 |
| 4510 On net wealth | .. | .. | .. | .. | .. | .. | .. | .. | .. | .. |
| 4520 Other non-recurrent taxes | .. | .. | .. | .. | .. | .. | .. | .. | .. | .. |
| 4600 Other recurrent taxes on property | 0 | 0 | 0 | 0 | 0 | 0 | 0 | 0 | 0 | 0 |
| **5000 Taxes on goods and services** | **454** | **16 263** | **27 142** | **36 353** | **51 102** | **48 247** | **50 061** | **58 551** | **60 366** | **51 219** |
| 5100 Taxes on production, sale, transfer, etc | 454 | 16 239 | 27 075 | 36 199 | 50 820 | 47 943 | 49 774 | 58 257 | 60 064 | 50 978 |
| 5110 General taxes | 109 | 9 646 | 20 151 | 29 094 | 42 612 | 39 462 | 41 036 | 49 038 | 49 197 | 42 377 |
| 5111 Value added taxes | 109 | 9 646 | 20 151 | 29 094 | 42 612 | 39 462 | 41 036 | 49 038 | 49 197 | 42 377 |
| VAT (internal) | 69 | 6 992 | 13 586 | 19 629 | 30 410 | 31 040 | 32 114 | 35 125 | 37 892 | 32 708 |
| VAT (imports) | 41 | 4 961 | 11 673 | 15 908 | 21 259 | 21 652 | 22 529 | 25 541 | 25 613 | 22 671 |
| VAT refunds | 0 | -2 307 | -5 107 | -6 442 | -9 056 | -13 231 | -13 606 | -11 628 | -14 307 | -13 003 |
| 5112 Sales tax | 0 | 0 | 0 | 0 | 0 | 0 | 0 | 0 | 0 | 0 |
| 5113 Other | 0 | 0 | 0 | 0 | 0 | 0 | 0 | 0 | 0 | 0 |
| 5120 Taxes on specific goods and services | 345 | 6 593 | 6 924 | 7 105 | 8 208 | 8 482 | 8 737 | 9 219 | 10 867 | 8 602 |

## Table 5.23. **Peru / Perú** *(cont.)*

Details of tax revenue / Ingresos tributarios detallados

*Million PEN*

| | 1990 | 2000 | 2007 | 2010 | 2015 | 2016 | 2017 | 2018 | 2019 | 2020 |
|---|---|---|---|---|---|---|---|---|---|---|
| 5121 Excises | 232 | 3 518 | 4 445 | 4 875 | 5 796 | 6 175 | 6 588 | 7 011 | 8 668 | 7 231 |
| Fuels | 151 | 2 145 | 2 419 | 2 410 | 2 211 | 2 423 | 2 604 | 2 565 | 3 212 | 2 950 |
| Gasoline sales tax | 3 | 97 | 174 | 210 | 332 | 312 | 363 | 437 | 456 | 316 |
| Other excises | 78 | 1 304 | 1 872 | 2 258 | 3 284 | 3 479 | 3 711 | 4 295 | 5 005 | 3 971 |
| Excise tax refunds | 0 | -28 | -20 | -4 | -31 | -39 | -91 | -286 | -4 | -5 |
| 5122 Profits of fiscal monopolies | 0 | 0 | 0 | 0 | 0 | 0 | 0 | 0 | 0 | 0 |
| 5123 Customs and import duties | 64 | 2 960 | 2 198 | 1 803 | 1 775 | 1 606 | 1 448 | 1 455 | 1 424 | 1 159 |
| 5124 Taxes on exports | 2 | 0 | 0 | 0 | 0 | 0 | 0 | 0 | 0 | 0 |
| 5125 Taxes on investment goods | 0 | 0 | 0 | 0 | 0 | 0 | 0 | 0 | 0 | 0 |
| 5126 Taxes on specific services | 0 | 115 | 281 | 427 | 637 | 701 | 702 | 754 | 774 | 212 |
| Casinos and slot machines | .. | 81 | 109 | 187 | 279 | 298 | 297 | 318 | 310 | 69 |
| Tourism tax | .. | 0 | 87 | 105 | 144 | 173 | 174 | 193 | 215 | 72 |
| Municipal taxes on services | .. | 34 | 85 | 135 | 214 | 230 | 230 | 243 | 250 | 70 |
| 5127 Other taxes on internat. trade and transactions | 48 | 0 | 0 | 0 | 0 | 0 | 0 | 0 | 0 | 0 |
| 5128 Other taxes | 0 | 0 | 0 | 0 | 0 | 0 | 0 | 0 | 0 | 0 |
| 5130 Unallocable between 5110 and 5120 | 0 | 0 | 0 | 0 | 0 | 0 | 0 | 0 | 0 | 0 |
| 5200 Taxes on use of goods and perform activities | 0 | 25 | 67 | 154 | 282 | 303 | 288 | 294 | 302 | 241 |
| 5210 Recurrent taxes | .. | 25 | 67 | 154 | 282 | 303 | 288 | 294 | 302 | 241 |
| 5211 Paid by households: motor vehicles | .. | .. | .. | .. | .. | .. | .. | .. | .. | .. |
| 5212 Paid by others: motor vehicles | .. | .. | .. | .. | .. | .. | .. | .. | .. | .. |
| 5213 Paid in respect of other goods | .. | .. | .. | .. | .. | .. | .. | .. | .. | .. |
| 5220 Non-recurrent taxes | .. | 0 | 0 | 0 | 0 | 0 | 0 | 0 | 0 | 0 |
| 5300 Unallocable between 5100 and 5200 | 0 | 0 | 0 | 0 | 0 | 0 | 0 | 0 | 0 | 0 |
| **6000 Other taxes** | **9** | **745** | **770** | **914** | **2 108** | **1 522** | **780** | **1 662** | **2 254** | **878** |
| 6100 Paid solely by business | 0 | 84 | 82 | 108 | 179 | 185 | 140 | 133 | 135 | 93 |
| Single simplified regime | .. | 84 | 82 | 108 | 179 | 185 | 140 | 133 | 135 | 93 |
| University Development Fund | .. | 0 | 0 | 0 | 0 | 0 | 0 | 0 | 0 | 0 |
| 6200 Other | 9 | 662 | 688 | 806 | 1 929 | 1 337 | 639 | 1 529 | 2 119 | 785 |
| Tax debt payments | 9 | 542 | 510 | 714 | 922 | 1 068 | 1 109 | 1 320 | 1 843 | 1 165 |
| Other taxes | 0 | 133 | 253 | 280 | 1 790 | 1 114 | 785 | 1 225 | 1 389 | 868 |
| Other tax refunds | 0 | -14 | -74 | -188 | -783 | -845 | -1 255 | -1 016 | -1 112 | -1 249 |

.. Not available

*Note:* Year ending 31st December.

The data are on a cash basis.

The figures for years up to 2000 exclude local government tax revenues as the data are not available.

Heading 2000: All contributions pertaining to pensions are only made by employees and contributions to healthcare are made by employers. The exceptions are special regimes which apply to self-employed and are levied on an income basis.

Heading 3000: Contributions to SENATI are included in heading 3000. The tax revenue is classified under the central government. In Peru this revenue is classified under a separate unit considered to be different to the central government.

Heading 5123: Import tax refunds are classified under 6200 because they cannot be distinguished from other tax refunds.

*Source:* Superintendencia Nacional de Aduanas y de Administración Tributaria (National Superintendence of Customs and Tax Administration - SUNAT); Banco de la Nación (Bank of the Nation); Ministerio de Economía y Finanzas (Ministry of Economy and Finance); Servicio Nacional de Adiestramiento en Trabajo Industrial (National Industrial Work Training Service).

StatLink https://doi.org/10.1787/888934309777

## Table 5.24. **Saint Lucia / Santa Lucía**

Details of tax revenue / Ingresos tributarios detallados

*Million XCD*

| | 1990 | 2000 | 2007 | 2010 | 2015 | 2016 | 2017 | 2018 | 2019 | 2020 |
|---|---|---|---|---|---|---|---|---|---|---|
| **Total tax revenue** | .. | **480** | **765** | **828** | **1 045** | **1 090** | **1 107** | **1 157** | **1 180** | **908** |
| **1000 Taxes on income, profits and capital gains** | .. | **137** | **196** | **224** | **242** | **259** | **247** | **269** | **258** | **213** |
| 1100 Of individuals | .. | 49 | 71 | 83 | 105 | 106 | 124 | 131 | 134 | 109 |
| 1110 On income and profits | .. | 49 | 71 | 83 | 105 | 106 | 124 | 131 | 134 | 109 |
| Personal income tax | .. | 49 | 71 | 83 | 105 | 106 | 104 | 113 | 116 | 95 |
| Arrears on personal income tax | .. | 0 | 0 | 0 | 0 | 0 | 21 | 18 | 18 | 14 |
| 1120 On capital gains | .. | .. | .. | .. | .. | .. | .. | .. | .. | .. |
| 1200 Corporate | .. | 63 | 92 | 95 | 78 | 99 | 102 | 115 | 111 | 90 |
| 1210 On profits | .. | 63 | 92 | 95 | 78 | 99 | 102 | 115 | 111 | 90 |
| Corporate income tax | .. | 63 | 92 | 95 | 78 | 99 | 89 | 92 | 93 | 75 |
| Arrears on corporate income tax | .. | 0 | 0 | 0 | 0 | 0 | 13 | 23 | 18 | 15 |
| 1220 On capital gains of corporates | .. | .. | .. | .. | .. | .. | .. | .. | .. | .. |
| 1300 Unallocable between 1100 and 1200 | .. | 26 | 33 | 46 | 58 | 53 | 21 | 23 | 13 | 14 |
| Withholdings | .. | 7 | 5 | 14 | 25 | 24 | 24 | 28 | 16 | 19 |
| Arrears | .. | 25 | 35 | 42 | 44 | 39 | 7 | 5 | 7 | 5 |
| Tax Refunds | .. | -6 | -8 | -10 | -10 | -10 | -10 | -10 | -9 | -10 |
| **2000 Social security contributions** | .. | **48** | **77** | **92** | **111** | **112** | **114** | **120** | **127** | **115** |
| 2100 Employees | .. | .. | .. | .. | .. | .. | .. | .. | .. | .. |
| 2110 On a payroll basis | .. | .. | .. | .. | .. | .. | .. | .. | .. | .. |
| 2120 On an income tax basis | .. | .. | .. | .. | .. | .. | .. | .. | .. | .. |
| 2200 Employers | .. | .. | .. | .. | .. | .. | .. | .. | .. | .. |
| 2210 On a payroll basis | .. | .. | .. | .. | .. | .. | .. | .. | .. | .. |
| 2220 On an income tax basis | .. | .. | .. | .. | .. | .. | .. | .. | .. | .. |
| 2300 Self-employed or non-employed | .. | .. | 0 | 1 | 1 | 1 | 1 | 1 | 1 | 1 |
| 2310 On a payroll basis | .. | .. | 0 | 1 | 1 | 1 | 1 | 1 | 1 | 1 |
| 2320 On an income tax basis | .. | .. | 0 | 0 | 0 | 0 | 0 | 0 | 0 | 0 |
| 2400 Unallocable between 2100, 2200 and 2300 | .. | 48 | 76 | 91 | 110 | 112 | 113 | 119 | 126 | 114 |
| 2410 On a payroll basis | .. | 48 | 76 | 91 | 110 | 112 | 113 | 119 | 126 | 114 |
| 2420 On an income tax basis | .. | 0 | 0 | 0 | 0 | 0 | 0 | 0 | 0 | 0 |
| **3000 Taxes on payroll and workforce** | .. | **0** | **0** | **0** | **0** | **0** | **0** | **0** | **0** | **0** |
| **4000 Taxes on property** | .. | **11** | **37** | **19** | **23** | **26** | **26** | **26** | **25** | **19** |
| 4100 Recurrent taxes on immovable property | .. | 2 | 5 | 3 | 11 | 12 | 12 | 10 | 8 | 6 |
| 4110 Households | .. | .. | .. | .. | .. | .. | .. | .. | .. | .. |
| 4120 Others | .. | .. | .. | .. | .. | .. | .. | .. | .. | .. |
| 4200 Recurrent taxes on net wealth | .. | 0 | 0 | 0 | 0 | 0 | 0 | 0 | 0 | 0 |
| 4210 Individual | .. | .. | .. | .. | .. | .. | .. | .. | .. | .. |
| 4220 Corporate | .. | .. | .. | .. | .. | .. | .. | .. | .. | .. |
| 4300 Estate, inheritance and gift taxes | .. | 0 | 0 | 0 | 0 | 0 | 0 | 0 | 0 | 0 |
| 4310 Estate and inheritance taxes | .. | .. | .. | .. | .. | .. | .. | .. | .. | .. |
| 4320 Gift taxes | .. | .. | .. | .. | .. | .. | .. | .. | .. | .. |
| 4400 Taxes on financial and capital transactions | .. | 9 | 32 | 16 | 12 | 14 | 14 | 17 | 18 | 13 |
| 4500 Non-reccurrent taxes | .. | 0 | 0 | 0 | 0 | 0 | 0 | 0 | 0 | 0 |
| 4510 On net wealth | .. | .. | .. | .. | .. | .. | .. | .. | .. | .. |
| 4520 Other non-recurrent taxes | .. | .. | .. | .. | .. | .. | .. | .. | .. | .. |
| 4600 Other recurrent taxes on property | .. | 0 | 0 | 0 | 0 | 0 | 0 | 0 | 0 | 0 |
| **5000 Taxes on goods and services** | .. | **284** | **456** | **493** | **670** | **694** | **720** | **742** | **770** | **561** |
| 5100 Taxes on production, sale, transfer, etc | .. | 277 | 430 | 467 | 642 | 663 | 694 | 715 | 742 | 551 |
| 5110 General taxes | .. | 101 | 122 | 119 | 347 | 335 | 318 | 329 | 339 | 241 |
| 5111 Value added taxes | .. | 0 | 0 | 0 | 346 | 335 | 318 | 329 | 339 | 241 |
| VAT (domestic) | .. | .. | .. | .. | 184 | 177 | 176 | 181 | 184 | .. |
| VAT (imports) | .. | .. | .. | .. | 163 | 159 | 142 | 148 | 156 | .. |
| 5112 Sales tax | .. | 101 | 122 | 119 | 0 | 0 | 0 | 0 | 0 | 0 |
| Consumption tax (domestic) | .. | 11 | 10 | 6 | 0 | .. | .. | .. | .. | 0 |
| Consumption tax (Imports) | .. | 90 | 112 | 114 | 0 | .. | .. | .. | .. | 0 |
| 5113 Other | .. | 0 | 0 | 0 | 0 | 0 | 0 | 0 | 0 | 0 |
| 5120 Taxes on specific goods and services | .. | 176 | 308 | 348 | 295 | 328 | 376 | 385 | 402 | 311 |
| 5121 Excises | .. | 34 | 49 | 85 | 92 | 112 | 128 | 134 | 140 | 125 |
| Excise tax (domestic) | .. | 28 | 3 | 14 | 4 | 4 | 5 | 5 | 5 | 4 |
| Excise tax (imports) | .. | 0 | 43 | 68 | 74 | 87 | 103 | 109 | 114 | 103 |
| Fuel Surcharge | .. | 3 | 4 | 4 | 15 | 21 | 21 | 20 | 21 | 19 |
| Surcharge on international calls | .. | 4 | 0 | 0 | 0 | 0 | 0 | 0 | 0 | 0 |
| 5122 Profits of fiscal monopolies | .. | 0 | 0 | 0 | 0 | 0 | 0 | 0 | 0 | 0 |
| 5123 Customs and import duties | .. | 108 | 194 | 187 | 179 | 189 | 202 | 206 | 205 | 161 |
| Import Duty | .. | 64 | 107 | 101 | 106 | 114 | 121 | 123 | 122 | 92 |
| Thruput Charge | .. | 1 | 3 | 6 | 3 | 4 | 5 | 4 | 4 | 4 |
| Service Charge (imports) and security charges | .. | 33 | 66 | 64 | 70 | 72 | 76 | 79 | 80 | 65 |
| Environmental Levy | .. | 9 | 18 | 16 | 0 | 0 | 0 | 0 | 0 | 0 |
| 5124 Taxes on exports | .. | 0 | 0 | 0 | 0 | 0 | 0 | 0 | 0 | 0 |
| 5125 Taxes on investment goods | .. | 0 | 0 | 0 | 0 | 0 | 0 | 0 | 0 | 0 |

## Table 5.24. **Saint Lucia / Santa Lucía** *(cont.)*

Details of tax revenue / Ingresos tributarios detallados

*Million XCD*

| | 1990 | 2000 | 2007 | 2010 | 2015 | 2016 | 2017 | 2018 | 2019 | 2020 |
|---|---|---|---|---|---|---|---|---|---|---|
| 5126 Taxes on specific services | .. | 34 | 65 | 76 | 24 | 26 | 46 | 45 | 57 | 24 |
| Hotel occupancy tax | .. | 23 | 34 | 34 | 1 | 0 | 0 | 0 | 1 | 0 |
| Insurance premium tax | .. | 4 | 7 | 7 | 8 | 8 | 9 | 9 | 10 | 10 |
| Cellular tax | .. | 0 | 12 | 18 | 0 | 0 | 0 | 0 | 0 | 0 |
| Passenger facility fee | .. | 0 | 3 | 5 | 4 | 3 | 4 | 3 | 3 | 1 |
| Travel tax | .. | 3 | 3 | 4 | 4 | 4 | 5 | 5 | 4 | 0 |
| Airport tax | .. | 5 | 6 | 9 | 7 | 11 | 29 | 28 | 39 | 13 |
| 5127 Other taxes on internat. trade and transactions | .. | 0 | 0 | 0 | 0 | 0 | 0 | 0 | 0 | 0 |
| 5128 Other taxes | .. | 0 | 0 | 0 | 0 | 0 | 0 | 0 | 0 | 0 |
| 5130 Unallocable between 5110 and 5120 | .. | 0 | 0 | 0 | 0 | 0 | 0 | 0 | 0 | 0 |
| 5200 Taxes on use of goods and to perform activities | .. | 7 | 25 | 26 | 29 | 31 | 26 | 28 | 28 | 9 |
| 5210 Recurrent taxes | .. | 7 | 25 | 26 | 29 | 31 | 26 | 28 | 28 | 9 |
| 5211 Paid by households: motor vehicles | .. | 0 | 0 | 0 | 0 | 0 | 0 | 0 | 0 | 0 |
| 5212 Paid by others: motor vehicles | .. | 0 | 0 | 0 | 0 | 0 | 0 | 0 | 0 | 0 |
| 5213 Paid in respect of other goods | .. | 7 | 25 | 26 | 29 | 31 | 26 | 28 | 28 | 9 |
| 5220 Non-recurrent taxes | .. | 0 | 0 | 0 | 0 | 0 | 0 | 0 | 0 | 0 |
| 5300 Unallocable between 5100 and 5200 | .. | 0 | 0 | 0 | 0 | 0 | 0 | 0 | 0 | 0 |
| **6000 Other taxes** | **..** | **0** | **0** | **0** | **0** | **0** | **0** | **0** | **0** | **0** |
| 6100 Paid solely by business | .. | .. | .. | .. | .. | .. | .. | .. | .. | .. |
| 6200 Other | .. | .. | .. | .. | .. | .. | .. | .. | .. | .. |

.. Not available

*Note:* Year ending 31st March. For example, the data for 2020 represent April 2020 to March 2021.

The data are on a cash basis.

The figures do not include local tax revenues because data are not available.

Heading 2000: A small amount of voluntary contributions have been identified and removed since 2003 in this edition. Social security contributions for the self-employed have been identified and placed under heading 2310 since 2003 in this edition. Social security contributions follow financial year from July to June, instead of April to March. For example, social security contributions in 2020 are between 1st July 2019 and 30th June 2020.

Heading 5123: Data for security charge are estimated for 2020.

Heading 5213: Data for 2020 include some of the licences and fees under taxes on use of goods and permissions in Estimates of Revenue and Expenditure 2021-2022 from the Department of Finance.

*Source:* The Central Statistical Office of Saint Lucia; Department of Finance of Saint Lucia; National Insurance Corporation of Saint Lucia.

StatLink https://doi.org/10.1787/888934309796

## Table 5.25. **Trinidad and Tobago / Trinidad y Tobago**

Details of tax revenue / Ingresos tributarios detallados

*Million TTD*

| | 1990 | 2000 | 2007 | 2010 | 2015 | 2016 | 2017 | 2018 | 2019 | 2020 |
|---|---|---|---|---|---|---|---|---|---|---|
| **Total tax revenue** | **4 923** | **10 953** | **37 099** | **39 720** | **46 559** | **33 984** | **31 164** | **36 813** | **38 417** | **31 258** |
| **1000 Taxes on income, profits and capital gains** | **2 595** | **6 224** | **26 853** | **27 213** | **29 628** | **17 057** | **16 133** | **19 413** | **22 391** | **15 332** |
| 1100 Of individuals | 669 | 2 325 | 3 426 | 4 674 | 7 752 | 7 458 | 6 570 | 6 842 | 7 215 | 6 209 |
| 1110 On income and profits | 669 | 2 325 | 3 426 | 4 674 | 7 752 | 7 458 | 6 570 | 6 842 | 7 215 | 6 209 |
| Health surcharge | 92 | 149 | 170 | 185 | 264 | 226 | 218 | 184 | 191 | 170 |
| Insurance surrender tax | 6 | 7 | 16 | 22 | 42 | 46 | 48 | 57 | 65 | 59 |
| Individuals (Ch. 75:01) | 571 | 2 169 | 3 239 | 4 467 | 7 445 | 7 187 | 6 303 | 6 601 | 6 960 | 5 980 |
| 1120 On capital gains | .. | .. | .. | .. | .. | .. | .. | .. | .. | .. |
| 1200 Corporate | 1 856 | 3 704 | 22 252 | 21 659 | 20 810 | 8 608 | 8 736 | 11 713 | 13 816 | 8 186 |
| 1210 On profits | 1 856 | 3 704 | 22 252 | 21 659 | 20 810 | 8 608 | 8 736 | 11 713 | 13 816 | 8 186 |
| Oil companies | 1 439 | 2 441 | 16 206 | 13 834 | 10 513 | 1 036 | 1 116 | 2 093 | 3 755 | 1 762 |
| Other companies | 383 | 1 041 | 4 797 | 6 630 | 9 481 | 7 003 | 6 919 | 8 858 | 8 694 | 5 641 |
| Business levy | 0 | 65 | 138 | 206 | 215 | 438 | 603 | 608 | 649 | 571 |
| National recovery impost | 34 | 0 | 0 | 0 | 0 | 0 | 0 | 0 | 0 | 0 |
| Unemployment Fund | 0 | 157 | 1 111 | 989 | 601 | 131 | 99 | 153 | 718 | 211 |
| 1220 On capital gains of corporates | .. | .. | .. | .. | .. | .. | .. | .. | .. | .. |
| 1300 Unallocable between 1100 and 1200 | 70 | 195 | 1 175 | 881 | 1 067 | 990 | 827 | 858 | 1 360 | 938 |
| **2000 Social security contributions** | **183** | **702** | **1 502** | **2 645** | **4 261** | **4 252** | **4 608** | **4 670** | **4 706** | **4 686** |
| 2100 Employees | .. | .. | .. | .. | .. | .. | .. | .. | .. | .. |
| 2110 On a payroll basis | .. | .. | .. | .. | .. | .. | .. | .. | .. | .. |
| 2120 On an income tax basis | .. | .. | .. | .. | .. | .. | .. | .. | .. | .. |
| 2200 Employers | .. | .. | .. | .. | .. | .. | .. | .. | .. | .. |
| 2210 On a payroll basis | .. | .. | .. | .. | .. | .. | .. | .. | .. | .. |
| 2220 On an income tax basis | .. | .. | .. | .. | .. | .. | .. | .. | .. | .. |
| 2300 Self-employed or non-employed | .. | .. | .. | .. | .. | .. | .. | .. | .. | .. |
| 2310 On a payroll basis | .. | .. | .. | .. | .. | .. | .. | .. | .. | .. |
| 2320 On an income tax basis | .. | .. | .. | .. | .. | .. | .. | .. | .. | .. |
| 2400 Unallocable between 2100, 2200 and 2300 | 183 | 702 | 1 502 | 2 645 | 4 261 | 4 252 | 4 608 | 4 670 | 4 706 | 4 686 |
| 2410 On a payroll basis | .. | .. | .. | .. | .. | .. | .. | .. | .. | .. |
| 2420 On an income tax basis | .. | .. | .. | .. | .. | .. | .. | .. | .. | .. |
| **3000 Taxes on payroll and workforce** | **0** | **0** | **0** | **0** | **0** | **0** | **0** | **0** | **0** | **0** |
| **4000 Taxes on property** | **90** | **175** | **385** | **194** | **406** | **332** | **322** | **362** | **405** | **260** |
| 4100 Recurrent taxes on immovable property | 39 | 64 | 84 | 22 | 3 | 3 | 3 | 4 | 50 | 2 |
| 4110 Households | .. | .. | .. | .. | .. | .. | .. | .. | .. | .. |
| 4120 Others | .. | .. | .. | .. | .. | .. | .. | .. | .. | .. |
| 4200 Recurrent taxes on net wealth | 0 | 0 | 0 | 0 | 0 | 0 | 0 | 0 | 0 | 0 |
| 4210 Individual | .. | .. | .. | .. | .. | .. | .. | .. | .. | .. |
| 4220 Corporate | .. | .. | .. | .. | .. | .. | .. | .. | .. | .. |
| 4300 Estate, inheritance and gift taxes | 1 | 0 | 0 | 0 | 0 | 0 | 0 | 0 | 0 | 0 |
| 4310 Estate and inheritance taxes | 1 | .. | .. | .. | .. | .. | .. | .. | .. | .. |
| 4320 Gift taxes | 0 | .. | .. | .. | .. | .. | .. | .. | .. | .. |
| 4400 Taxes on financial and capital transactions | 49 | 111 | 301 | 172 | 403 | 329 | 319 | 359 | 356 | 258 |
| Stamp duties | 49 | 111 | 301 | 172 | 403 | 329 | 319 | 359 | 356 | 258 |
| 4500 Non-recurrent taxes | 0 | 0 | 0 | 0 | 0 | 0 | 0 | 0 | 0 | 0 |
| 4510 On net wealth | .. | .. | .. | .. | .. | .. | .. | .. | .. | .. |
| 4520 Other non-recurrent taxes | .. | .. | .. | .. | .. | .. | .. | .. | .. | .. |
| 4600 Other recurrent taxes on property | 0 | 0 | 0 | 0 | 0 | 0 | 0 | 0 | 0 | 0 |
| **5000 Taxes on goods and services** | **2 055** | **3 852** | **8 358** | **9 667** | **12 264** | **12 344** | **10 101** | **12 368** | **10 915** | **10 980** |
| 5100 Taxes on production, sale, transfer, etc | 1 973 | 3 603 | 8 010 | 9 282 | 11 678 | 11 765 | 9 675 | 12 024 | 10 612 | 10 752 |
| 5110 General taxes | 980 | 1 890 | 5 105 | 6 358 | 7 569 | 7 617 | 5 876 | 8 087 | 6 836 | 7 417 |
| 5111 Value added taxes | 927 | 1 890 | 4 829 | 6 032 | 7 223 | 7 005 | 5 050 | 7 245 | 5 848 | 6 682 |
| 5112 Sales tax | 54 | 0 | 0 | 0 | 0 | 0 | 1 | 0 | 0 | 0 |
| 5113 Other | 0 | 0 | 276 | 325 | 346 | 612 | 825 | 842 | 988 | 734 |
| Green Fund | .. | .. | 276 | 325 | 346 | 612 | 803 | 813 | 957 | 689 |
| Tax on online purchases | .. | .. | 0 | 0 | 0 | 0 | 22 | 29 | 31 | 46 |
| 5120 Taxes on specific goods and services | 993 | 1 713 | 2 904 | 2 924 | 4 108 | 4 148 | 3 798 | 3 936 | 3 777 | 3 336 |
| 5121 Excises | 481 | 801 | 614 | 708 | 703 | 735 | 739 | 793 | 680 | 703 |
| Alcohol products | .. | .. | .. | 156 | 154 | 168 | 150 | 183 | 187 | 205 |
| Beer | .. | .. | .. | 202 | 189 | 181 | 202 | 202 | 173 | 197 |
| Petroleum products | .. | .. | .. | 105 | 88 | 132 | 102 | 98 | 23 | 6 |
| Cigarette products | .. | .. | .. | 243 | 243 | 226 | 253 | 269 | 262 | 274 |
| Malt beverages | .. | .. | .. | 2 | 29 | 28 | 33 | 41 | 35 | 21 |
| 5122 Profits of fiscal monopolies | 0 | 0 | 0 | 0 | 0 | 0 | 0 | 0 | 0 | 0 |
| 5123 Customs and import duties | 260 | 748 | 2 004 | 1 905 | 3 014 | 3 016 | 2 684 | 2 732 | 2 672 | 2 301 |
| 5124 Taxes on exports | 0 | 0 | 0 | 0 | 0 | 0 | 0 | 0 | 0 | 0 |
| 5125 Taxes on investment goods | 0 | 0 | 0 | 0 | 0 | 0 | 0 | 0 | 0 | 0 |

## Table 5.25. **Trinidad and Tobago / Trinidad y Tobago** *(cont.)*

Details of tax revenue / Ingresos tributarios detallados

*Million TTD*

| | 1990 | 2000 | 2007 | 2010 | 2015 | 2016 | 2017 | 2018 | 2019 | 2020 |
|---|---|---|---|---|---|---|---|---|---|---|
| 5126 Taxes on specific services | 49 | 163 | 284 | 311 | 391 | 397 | 375 | 411 | 425 | 331 |
| Insurance premium tax | 0 | 56 | 130 | 167 | 191 | 181 | 163 | 170 | 180 | 159 |
| Transaction tax on financial services | 0 | 23 | 42 | 53 | 75 | 87 | 93 | 97 | 103 | 92 |
| Hotel room tax | 0 | 23 | 48 | 46 | 64 | 54 | 52 | 52 | 55 | 34 |
| Betting and entertainment taxes | 4 | 17 | 0 | 12 | 0 | 0 | 0 | 0 | 0 | 0 |
| Other taxes on goods and services | 45 | 44 | 63 | 33 | 61 | 75 | 67 | 93 | 86 | 46 |
| 5127 Other taxes on internat. trade and transactions | 202 | 0 | 2 | 1 | 0 | 0 | 1 | 0 | 0 | 0 |
| 5128 Other taxes | 0 | 0 | 0 | 0 | 0 | 0 | 0 | 0 | 0 | 0 |
| 5130 Unallocable between 5110 and 5120 | 0 | 0 | 0 | 0 | 0 | 0 | 0 | 0 | 0 | 0 |
| 5200 Taxes on use of goods and perform activities | 81 | 249 | 348 | 386 | 586 | 580 | 426 | 344 | 303 | 228 |
| 5210 Recurrent taxes | 81 | 249 | 348 | 386 | 586 | 580 | 426 | 344 | 303 | 228 |
| Motor vehicle taxes and duties | 76 | 239 | 338 | 375 | 575 | 569 | 415 | 334 | 291 | 221 |
| 5211 Paid by households: motor vehicles | .. | .. | .. | .. | .. | .. | .. | .. | .. | .. |
| 5212 Paid by others: motor vehicles | .. | .. | .. | .. | .. | .. | .. | .. | .. | .. |
| 5213 Paid in respect of other goods | 5 | 10 | 10 | 10 | 11 | 11 | 11 | 11 | 12 | 7 |
| Liquor and miscellaneous business licence fees | 5 | 10 | 10 | 10 | 11 | 11 | 11 | 11 | 12 | 7 |
| 5220 Non-recurrent taxes | 0 | 0 | 0 | 0 | 0 | 0 | 0 | 0 | 0 | 0 |
| 5300 Unallocable between 5100 and 5200 | 0 | 0 | 0 | 0 | 0 | 0 | 0 | 0 | 0 | 0 |
| **6000 Other taxes** | **0** | **0** | **0** | **0** | **0** | **0** | **0** | **0** | **0** | **0** |
| 6100 Paid solely by business | .. | .. | .. | .. | .. | .. | .. | .. | .. | .. |
| 6200 Other | .. | .. | .. | .. | .. | .. | .. | .. | .. | .. |

.. Not available

*Note:* Fiscal year ending on 30th September. For example, the data for 2020 represent October 2019 to September 2020.

The data are on a cash basis.

The figures exclude local government tax revenues as the data are not available.

Heading 1100: Lottery winnings tax has been identified and classified under heading 1110 ("Income taxes on individuals") in this edition. It was previously classified under heading 5126. This tax was introduced in 2018 and is levied on all lottery prize money in excess of USD 1000, paid to a ticket holder. Income taxes on individuals include "Individuals (Ch. 75:01)" and lottery winnings tax.

Heading 2000: Social security contributions follow financial year from July to June, instead of October to September. For example, social security contributions in 2020 are between 1st July 2019 and 30th June 2020. The figures include total contribution income of National Insurance Board minus refunds. A small amount of voluntary contributions have been identified and removed from the figures since 2013.

Heading 5126: Other taxes on goods and services under heading 5126 include mainly club gaming tax which is charged on all gambling tables and other gambling devices from a licenced gambling operator.

*Source:* Ministry of Finance; The National Insurance Board.

StatLink https://doi.org/10.1787/888934309815

## Table 5.26. **Uruguay**

Details of tax revenue / Ingresos tributarios detallados

*Million UYU*

| | 1990 | 2000 | 2007 | 2010 | 2015 | 2016 | 2017 | 2018 | 2019 | 2020 |
|---|---|---|---|---|---|---|---|---|---|---|
| **Total tax revenue** | **2 399** | **64 183** | **141 132** | **212 907** | **398 274** | **441 875** | **494 901** | **534 519** | **573 642** | **600 015** |
| **1000 Taxes on income, profits and capital gains** | **114** | **8 698** | **20 540** | **42 583** | **84 141** | **101 738** | **125 295** | **140 527** | **149 920** | **159 783** |
| 1100 Of individuals | 0 | 3 597 | 8 362 | 19 148 | 45 451 | 51 679 | 68 948 | 78 571 | 85 847 | 91 819 |
| Personal income tax (IRP) | .. | 3 597 | 3 519 | 0 | 0 | 0 | 0 | 0 | 0 | 0 |
| 1110 On income and profits | .. | .. | 4 262 | 16 790 | 39 613 | 44 817 | 60 570 | 69 083 | 75 944 | 80 407 |
| IRPF second category | .. | .. | 4 262 | 14 643 | 34 881 | 39 883 | 54 327 | 61 077 | 67 254 | 70 295 |
| Social security assistance | .. | .. | 0 | 2 651 | 6 576 | 7 480 | 9 448 | 11 091 | 12 336 | 14 198 |
| Personal income tax refunds | .. | .. | 0 | -504 | -1 844 | -2 545 | -3 204 | -3 085 | -3 646 | -4 086 |
| 1120 On capital gains | .. | .. | 581 | 2 358 | 5 838 | 6 862 | 8 377 | 9 488 | 9 903 | 11 412 |
| IRPF first category | .. | .. | 581 | 2 358 | 5 838 | 6 862 | 8 377 | 9 488 | 9 903 | 11 412 |
| 1200 Corporate | 114 | 5 102 | 11 829 | 21 772 | 34 814 | 45 535 | 51 169 | 56 316 | 58 071 | 61 487 |
| 1210 On profits | 114 | 5 102 | 11 829 | 21 772 | 34 814 | 45 535 | 51 169 | 56 316 | 58 071 | 61 487 |
| Income tax for economic activities (IRAE) | 0 | 0 | 709 | 21 437 | 34 720 | 45 461 | 51 081 | 56 316 | 58 071 | 61 487 |
| Industry and commerce income tax (IRIC) | 97 | 5 096 | 11 055 | 333 | 94 | 73 | 88 | 0 | 0 | 0 |
| Agricultural income tax (IRA) | 10 | 3 | 65 | 2 | 0 | 1 | 0 | 0 | 0 | 0 |
| Tax on agricultural activities (IMAGRO) | 7 | 3 | 0 | 0 | 0 | 0 | 0 | 0 | 0 | 0 |
| 1220 On capital gains of corporates | .. | .. | .. | .. | .. | .. | .. | .. | .. | .. |
| 1300 Unallocable between 1100 and 1200 | 0 | 0 | 349 | 1 662 | 3 875 | 4 523 | 5 179 | 5 639 | 6 002 | 6 477 |
| Non-resident income tax (IRNR) | .. | .. | 349 | 1 662 | 3 875 | 4 523 | 5 179 | 5 639 | 6 002 | 6 477 |
| **2000 Social security contributions** | **717** | **17 679** | **28 485** | **49 742** | **109 282** | **119 101** | **131 545** | **139 561** | **151 589** | **150 185** |
| 2100 Employees | .. | .. | .. | .. | .. | .. | .. | .. | .. | .. |
| 2110 On a payroll basis | .. | .. | .. | .. | .. | .. | .. | .. | .. | .. |
| 2120 On an income tax basis | .. | .. | .. | .. | .. | .. | .. | .. | .. | .. |
| 2200 Employers | .. | .. | .. | .. | .. | .. | .. | .. | .. | .. |
| 2210 On a payroll basis | .. | .. | .. | .. | .. | .. | .. | .. | .. | .. |
| 2220 On an income tax basis | .. | .. | .. | .. | .. | .. | .. | .. | .. | .. |
| 2300 Self-employed or non-employed | .. | .. | .. | .. | .. | .. | .. | .. | .. | .. |
| 2310 On a payroll basis | .. | .. | .. | .. | .. | .. | .. | .. | .. | .. |
| 2320 On an income tax basis | .. | .. | .. | .. | .. | .. | .. | .. | .. | .. |
| 2400 Unallocable between 2100, 2200 and 2300 | 717 | 17 679 | 28 485 | 49 742 | 109 282 | 119 101 | 131 545 | 139 561 | 151 589 | 150 185 |
| 2410 On a payroll basis | 717 | 17 679 | 28 485 | 49 742 | 109 282 | 119 101 | 131 545 | 139 561 | 151 589 | 150 185 |
| 2420 On an income tax basis | 0 | 0 | 0 | 0 | 0 | 0 | 0 | 0 | 0 | 0 |
| **3000 Taxes on payroll and workforce** | **0** | **0** | **0** | **0** | **0** | **0** | **0** | **0** | **0** | **0** |
| **4000 Taxes on property** | **213** | **5 508** | **13 243** | **18 965** | **32 422** | **36 441** | **38 460** | **40 508** | **44 178** | **46 398** |
| 4100 Recurrent taxes on immovable property | 87 | 3 248 | 5 686 | 8 140 | 14 884 | 16 812 | 18 180 | 19 648 | 21 056 | 22 400 |
| Primary education tax | 0 | 378 | 691 | 1 064 | 2 386 | 2 474 | 2 781 | 2 961 | 3 271 | 3 474 |
| Farm property tax | 0 | 155 | 0 | 189 | 886 | 852 | 764 | 728 | 750 | 941 |
| Property tax surcharge | 0 | 0 | 0 | 0 | 503 | 511 | 543 | 476 | 471 | 610 |
| Primary education tax refunds | 0 | 0 | 0 | 0 | 0 | 0 | 0 | -3 | -2 | -1 |
| Other property taxes | 87 | 2 715 | 4 995 | 6 887 | 11 109 | 12 975 | 14 092 | 15 485 | 16 567 | 17 377 |
| 4110 Households | .. | .. | .. | .. | .. | .. | .. | .. | .. | .. |
| 4120 Others | .. | .. | .. | .. | .. | .. | .. | .. | .. | .. |
| 4200 Recurrent taxes on net wealth | 94 | 1 769 | 5 392 | 8 760 | 14 776 | 16 652 | 17 057 | 17 473 | 19 717 | 20 335 |
| 4210 Individual | 64 | 108 | 340 | 382 | 606 | 684 | 711 | 760 | 707 | 676 |
| 4220 Corporate | 30 | 1 661 | 5 052 | 8 378 | 14 170 | 15 968 | 16 346 | 16 713 | 19 010 | 19 659 |
| Corporate wealth tax | 28 | 1 507 | 4 805 | 8 165 | 14 167 | 15 967 | 16 345 | 16 713 | 19 010 | 19 659 |
| Tax on financial investment companies (ISAFI) | 1 | 154 | 247 | 213 | 3 | 1 | 1 | 1 | 0 | 1 |
| 4300 Estate, inheritance and gift taxes | 0 | 0 | 0 | 0 | 0 | 0 | 0 | 0 | 0 | 0 |
| 4310 Estate and inheritance taxes | .. | .. | .. | .. | .. | .. | .. | .. | .. | .. |
| 4320 Gift taxes | .. | .. | .. | .. | .. | .. | .. | .. | .. | .. |
| 4400 Taxes on financial and capital transactions | 31 | 476 | 1 831 | 1 740 | 2 241 | 2 439 | 2 662 | 2 819 | 2 841 | 3 078 |
| Property transfer tax (ITP) | 11 | 372 | 1 405 | 1 347 | 1 601 | 1 724 | 1 927 | 1 984 | 1 859 | 2 120 |
| Tax on transfer of rights over athletes | 0 | 0 | 50 | 3 | 0 | 0 | 0 | 0 | 0 | 0 |
| Auction tax | 20 | 104 | 376 | 390 | 639 | 714 | 735 | 835 | 982 | 958 |
| 4500 Non-recurrent taxes | 0 | 0 | 0 | 0 | 0 | 0 | 0 | 0 | 0 | 0 |
| 4510 On net wealth | .. | .. | .. | .. | .. | .. | .. | .. | .. | .. |
| 4520 Other non-recurrent taxes | .. | .. | .. | .. | .. | .. | .. | .. | .. | .. |
| 4600 Other recurrent taxes on property | 1 | 15 | 335 | 326 | 522 | 538 | 560 | 567 | 564 | 585 |
| Corporation control tax (ICOSA) | 1 | 15 | 236 | 325 | 522 | 538 | 560 | 567 | 564 | 585 |
| Financial system control tax (ICOSIFI) | 0 | 0 | 99 | 0 | 0 | 0 | 0 | 0 | 0 | 0 |
| **5000 Taxes on goods and services** | **1 358** | **32 139** | **77 673** | **100 282** | **170 279** | **182 082** | **196 669** | **210 711** | **224 394** | **240 075** |
| 5100 Taxes on production, sale, transfer, etc | 1 301 | 29 562 | 74 369 | 96 494 | 162 739 | 172 823 | 186 355 | 199 329 | 212 218 | 227 321 |
| 5110 General taxes | 660 | 18 009 | 50 943 | 69 951 | 114 627 | 123 262 | 129 663 | 137 400 | 145 846 | 157 644 |
| 5111 Value added taxes | 660 | 17 995 | 49 064 | 69 921 | 114 627 | 123 262 | 129 663 | 137 400 | 145 846 | 157 644 |
| 5112 Sales tax | 1 | 14 | 1 879 | 30 | 0 | 0 | 0 | 0 | 0 | 0 |
| Social security financing tax (COFIS) | 0 | 0 | 1 859 | 30 | .. | .. | .. | .. | .. | .. |
| Other sales taxes | 1 | 14 | 20 | 0 | .. | .. | .. | .. | .. | .. |
| 5113 Other | 0 | 0 | 0 | 0 | 0 | 0 | 0 | 0 | 0 | 0 |
| 5120 Taxes on specific goods and services | 641 | 11 553 | 23 426 | 26 543 | 48 111 | 49 561 | 56 692 | 61 928 | 66 372 | 69 678 |

## Table 5.26. **Uruguay** *(cont.)*

Details of tax revenue / Ingresos tributarios detallados

*Million UYU*

| | 1990 | 2000 | 2007 | 2010 | 2015 | 2016 | 2017 | 2018 | 2019 | 2020 |
|---|---|---|---|---|---|---|---|---|---|---|
| 5121 Excises | 393 | 7 896 | 13 409 | 17 300 | 31 197 | 32 528 | 37 779 | 39 214 | 42 183 | 44 212 |
| Fuels | 203 | 4 067 | 5 694 | 6 551 | 14 096 | 15 222 | 17 129 | 18 662 | 20 094 | 22 157 |
| Tobacco products | 80 | 1 741 | 3 085 | 4 236 | 5 778 | 6 144 | 6 995 | 7 518 | 7 703 | 7 944 |
| Motor vehicles | 20 | 656 | 1 333 | 2 289 | 4 017 | 3 960 | 4 313 | 3 789 | 3 799 | 4 626 |
| Non-alcoholic beverages | 19 | 464 | 804 | 1 172 | 2 131 | 2 330 | 2 547 | 2 687 | 2 754 | 2 879 |
| Agricultural products | 4 | 299 | 1 396 | 1 349 | 2 223 | 2 227 | 2 369 | 2 636 | 2 998 | 3 256 |
| Beer | 8 | 205 | 372 | 602 | 1 102 | 1 109 | 1 357 | 1 526 | 1 494 | 1 688 |
| Advances of import excises | 0 | 27 | -250 | -136 | 312 | -62 | 1 372 | 704 | 1 591 | -465 |
| Greases and lubricants | 5 | 119 | 306 | 390 | 525 | 559 | 623 | 652 | 677 | 815 |
| Alcoholic beverages | 22 | 212 | 415 | 562 | 789 | 774 | 766 | 617 | 677 | 714 |
| Other excises | 32 | 106 | 254 | 283 | 224 | 265 | 309 | 423 | 397 | 598 |
| 5122 Profits of fiscal monopolies | 0 | 0 | 0 | 0 | 0 | 0 | 0 | 0 | 0 | 0 |
| 5123 Customs and import duties | 214 | 1 967 | 7 077 | 8 478 | 15 440 | 15 384 | 17 198 | 20 878 | 22 124 | 23 099 |
| 5124 Taxes on exports | 1 | 32 | 274 | 325 | 582 | 658 | 664 | 770 | 858 | 908 |
| 5125 Taxes on investment goods | 0 | 0 | 0 | 0 | 0 | 0 | 0 | 0 | 0 | 0 |
| 5126 Taxes on specific services | 34 | 1 392 | 2 145 | 440 | 892 | 991 | 1 052 | 1 067 | 1 207 | 1 458 |
| Bank asset tax (IMABA) | 31 | 1 092 | 686 | 2 | 0 | 0 | 0 | 0 | 0 | 0 |
| Income tax for insurance companies | 3 | 76 | 336 | 366 | 763 | 845 | 902 | 916 | 1 004 | 1 270 |
| Other services taxes | 0 | 224 | 1 123 | 72 | 129 | 146 | 150 | 152 | 202 | 189 |
| 5127 Other taxes on internat. trade and transactions | 0 | 265 | 520 | 0 | 0 | 0 | 0 | 0 | 0 | 0 |
| 5128 Other taxes | 0 | 0 | 0 | 0 | 0 | 0 | 0 | 0 | 0 | 0 |
| 5130 Unallocable between 5110 and 5120 | 0 | 0 | 0 | 0 | 0 | 0 | 0 | 0 | 0 | 0 |
| 5200 Taxes on use of goods and perform activities | 57 | 2 576 | 3 303 | 3 788 | 7 540 | 9 259 | 10 313 | 11 382 | 12 176 | 12 754 |
| 5210 Recurrent taxes | 57 | 2 576 | 3 303 | 3 788 | 7 540 | 9 259 | 10 313 | 11 382 | 12 176 | 12 754 |
| 5211 Paid by households: motor vehicles | 0 | 0 | 0 | 0 | 0 | 0 | 0 | 0 | 0 | 0 |
| 5212 Paid by others: motor vehicles | 57 | 2 576 | 3 303 | 3 788 | 7 540 | 9 259 | 10 313 | 11 382 | 12 176 | 12 754 |
| 5213 Paid in respect of other goods | 0 | 0 | 0 | 0 | 0 | 0 | 0 | 0 | 0 | 0 |
| 5220 Non-recurrent taxes | 0 | 0 | 0 | 0 | 0 | 0 | 0 | 0 | 0 | 0 |
| 5300 Unallocable between 5100 and 5200 | 0 | 0 | 0 | 0 | 0 | 0 | 0 | 0 | 0 | 0 |
| **6000 Other taxes** | **-3** | **159** | **1 191** | **1 335** | **2 151** | **2 513** | **2 933** | **3 212** | **3 560** | **3 574** |
| 6100 Paid solely by business | -10 | -145 | 626 | 586 | 796 | 850 | 925 | 980 | 1 039 | 1 033 |
| Small business tax (minimum VAT) | 0 | 296 | 563 | 586 | 796 | 850 | 925 | 980 | 1 039 | 1 033 |
| Credit card tax | 0 | 0 | 63 | 0 | 0 | 0 | 0 | 0 | 0 | 0 |
| Other tax refunds | -10 | -440 | 0 | 0 | 0 | 0 | 0 | 0 | 0 | 0 |
| 6200 Other | 7 | 303 | 565 | 748 | 1 355 | 1 663 | 2 008 | 2 232 | 2 521 | 2 542 |

.. Not available

*Note:* Year ending 31st December.

The data are on a cash basis.

Figures for local tax revenues are estimated for 2020 as data are not available.

Heading 2000: Figures for 1990-98 are estimated by the General Tax Directorate (DGI). The figures have included income from Social Security Bank (BPS) published by the Ministry of Economy and Finance since 1999.

Heading 5112: The tax on the sale of goods by public auctions recorded under other sales taxes is classified in category 4000 in ECLAC data.

*Source:* Dirección General Impositiva (General Tax Directorate); Ministerio de Economía y Finanzas (Ministry of Economy and Finance).

StatLink https://doi.org/10.1787/888934309834

## Table 5.27. **Venezuela**

Details of tax revenue / Ingresos tributarios detallados

VES

| | 1990 | 2000 | 2007 | 2010 | 2015 | 2016 | 2017 | 2018 | 2019 | 2020 |
|---|---|---|---|---|---|---|---|---|---|---|
| **Total tax revenue** | **4 115** | **108 486** | **838 614** | **1 200 840** | .. | .. | .. | .. | .. | .. |
| **1000 Taxes on income, profits and capital gains** | **3 444** | **46 856** | **375 642** | **368 365** | **2 847 864** | .. | .. | .. | .. | .. |
| 1100 Of individuals | .. | .. | .. | .. | .. | .. | .. | .. | .. | .. |
| 1110 On income and profits | .. | .. | .. | .. | .. | .. | .. | .. | .. | .. |
| 1120 On capital gains | .. | .. | .. | .. | .. | .. | .. | .. | .. | .. |
| 1200 Corporate | 3 148 | 33 683 | 199 585 | 86 998 | 473 879 | .. | .. | .. | .. | .. |
| 1210 On profits | 3 148 | 33 683 | 199 585 | 86 998 | 473 879 | .. | .. | .. | .. | .. |
| Oil | 3 148 | 33 683 | 199 585 | 86 998 | 473 879 | .. | .. | .. | .. | .. |
| 1220 On capital gains of corporates | .. | .. | .. | .. | .. | .. | .. | .. | .. | .. |
| 1300 Unallocable between 1100 and 1200 | 297 | 13 173 | 176 057 | 281 367 | 2 373 986 | 7 331 699 | 31 378 510 | .. | .. | .. |
| **2000 Social security contributions** | **202** | **5 905** | **42 176** | **96 896** | .. | .. | .. | .. | .. | .. |
| 2100 Employees | .. | .. | .. | .. | .. | .. | .. | .. | .. | .. |
| 2110 On a payroll basis | .. | .. | .. | .. | .. | .. | .. | .. | .. | .. |
| 2120 On an income tax basis | .. | .. | .. | .. | .. | .. | .. | .. | .. | .. |
| 2200 Employers | .. | .. | .. | .. | .. | .. | .. | .. | .. | .. |
| 2210 On a payroll basis | .. | .. | .. | .. | .. | .. | .. | .. | .. | .. |
| 2220 On an income tax basis | .. | .. | .. | .. | .. | .. | .. | .. | .. | .. |
| 2300 Self-employed or non-employed | .. | .. | .. | .. | .. | .. | .. | .. | .. | .. |
| 2310 On a payroll basis | .. | .. | .. | .. | .. | .. | .. | .. | .. | .. |
| 2320 On an income tax basis | .. | .. | .. | .. | .. | .. | .. | .. | .. | .. |
| 2400 Unallocable between 2100, 2200 and 2300 | 202 | 5 905 | 42 176 | 96 896 | .. | .. | .. | .. | .. | .. |
| 2410 On a payroll basis | .. | .. | .. | .. | .. | .. | .. | .. | .. | .. |
| 2420 On an income tax basis | .. | .. | .. | .. | .. | .. | .. | .. | .. | .. |
| **3000 Taxes on payroll and workforce** | **0** | **0** | **0** | **0** | **0** | **0** | **0** | .. | .. | .. |
| **4000 Taxes on property** | **11** | **3 999** | **27 147** | **2 217** | **29 459** | **90 877** | **24 353 035** | .. | .. | .. |
| 4100 Recurrent taxes on immovable property | 0 | 0 | 0 | 0 | 0 | 0 | 0 | .. | .. | .. |
| 4110 Households | .. | .. | .. | .. | .. | .. | .. | .. | .. | .. |
| 4120 Others | .. | .. | .. | .. | .. | .. | .. | .. | .. | .. |
| 4200 Recurrent taxes on net wealth | 0 | 0 | 0 | 0 | 0 | 0 | 0 | .. | .. | .. |
| 4210 Individual | .. | .. | .. | .. | .. | .. | .. | .. | .. | .. |
| 4220 Corporate | .. | .. | .. | .. | .. | .. | .. | .. | .. | .. |
| 4300 Estate, inheritance and gift taxes | 11 | 191 | 1 050 | 2 217 | 29 459 | 90 877 | 361 298 | .. | .. | .. |
| 4310 Estate and inheritance taxes | 11 | 191 | 1 050 | 2 217 | 29 459 | 90 877 | 361 298 | .. | .. | .. |
| 4320 Gift taxes | 0 | 0 | 0 | 0 | 0 | 0 | 0 | .. | .. | .. |
| 4400 Taxes on financial and capital transactions | 0 | 3 808 | 26 097 | 0 | 0 | 0 | 23 991 737 | .. | .. | .. |
| Bank debits | .. | 2 918 | 26 097 | .. | .. | .. | 0 | .. | .. | .. |
| Registration of immovable property rights | .. | 890 | 0 | .. | .. | .. | 0 | .. | .. | .. |
| Tax on Large Financial Transactions (IGTF) | .. | 0 | 0 | .. | .. | .. | 23 991 737 | .. | .. | .. |
| 4500 Non-recurrent taxes | 0 | 0 | 0 | 0 | 0 | 0 | 0 | .. | .. | .. |
| 4510 On net wealth | .. | .. | .. | .. | .. | .. | .. | .. | .. | .. |
| 4520 Other non-recurrent taxes | .. | .. | .. | .. | .. | .. | .. | .. | .. | .. |
| 4600 Other recurrent taxes on property | 0 | 0 | 0 | 0 | 0 | 0 | 0 | .. | .. | .. |
| **5000 Taxes on goods and services** | **457** | **51 726** | **393 649** | **733 363** | **9 128 199** | **25 580 149** | **148 669 517** | .. | .. | .. |
| 5100 Taxes on production, sale, transfer, etc | 457 | 51 726 | 393 649 | 733 363 | 9 128 199 | 25 580 149 | 148 669 517 | .. | .. | .. |
| 5110 General taxes | 0 | 32 716 | 278 954 | 561 005 | 7 027 427 | 19 070 779 | 112 990 174 | .. | .. | .. |
| 5111 Value added taxes | 0 | 32 716 | 278 954 | 561 005 | 7 027 427 | 19 070 779 | 112 990 174 | .. | .. | .. |
| 5112 Sales tax | .. | 0 | 0 | 0 | 0 | 0 | 0 | .. | .. | .. |
| 5113 Other | .. | 0 | 0 | 0 | 0 | 0 | 0 | .. | .. | .. |
| 5120 Taxes on specific goods and services | 457 | 19 011 | 114 695 | 172 357 | 2 100 772 | 6 509 370 | 35 679 343 | .. | .. | .. |
| 5121 Excises | 157 | 7 742 | 29 778 | 88 722 | 1 165 755 | 4 399 252 | 29 679 186 | .. | .. | .. |
| Oil | 57 | 4 679 | 7 039 | 12 798 | 0 | 0 | 0 | .. | .. | .. |
| Alcoholic beverages | 58 | 852 | 9 081 | 21 915 | 444 982 | 1 568 778 | 14 113 397 | .. | .. | .. |
| Tobacco | 42 | 2 201 | 13 641 | 54 009 | 720 772 | 2 830 474 | 15 565 789 | .. | .. | .. |
| Matches | 0 | 9 | 17 | 0 | 0 | 0 | 0 | .. | .. | .. |
| 5122 Profits of fiscal monopolies | 0 | 0 | 0 | 0 | 0 | 0 | 0 | .. | .. | .. |
| 5123 Customs and import duties | 300 | 9 716 | 82 713 | 81 333 | 932 598 | 2 103 519 | 5 986 482 | .. | .. | .. |
| 5124 Taxes on exports | 0 | 0 | 0 | 0 | 0 | 0 | 0 | .. | .. | .. |
| 5125 Taxes on investment goods | 0 | 0 | 0 | 0 | 0 | 0 | 0 | .. | .. | .. |
| 5126 Taxes on specific services | 0 | 1 552 | 2 204 | 2 302 | 2 419 | 6 600 | 13 675 | .. | .. | .. |
| Telecommunications | 0 | 1 505 | 1 658 | 0 | 0 | 0 | 0 | .. | .. | .. |
| Casinos, bingo and slot machines | 0 | 47 | 546 | 2 302 | 2 419 | 6 600 | 13 675 | .. | .. | .. |
| 5127 Other taxes on internat. trade and transactions | 0 | 0 | 0 | 0 | 0 | 0 | 0 | .. | .. | .. |
| 5128 Other taxes | 0 | 0 | 0 | 0 | 0 | 0 | 0 | .. | .. | .. |
| 5130 Unallocable between 5110 and 5120 | 0 | 0 | 0 | 0 | 0 | 0 | 0 | .. | .. | .. |
| 5200 Taxes on use of goods and perform activities | 0 | 0 | 0 | 0 | 0 | 0 | 0 | .. | .. | .. |
| 5210 Recurrent taxes | .. | .. | .. | .. | .. | .. | .. | .. | .. | .. |
| 5211 Paid by households: motor vehicles | .. | .. | .. | .. | .. | .. | .. | .. | .. | .. |
| 5212 Paid by others: motor vehicles | .. | .. | .. | .. | .. | .. | .. | .. | .. | .. |
| 5213 Paid in respect of other goods | .. | .. | .. | .. | .. | .. | .. | .. | .. | .. |
| 5220 Non-recurrent taxes | .. | .. | .. | .. | .. | .. | .. | .. | .. | .. |

## Table 5.27. **Venezuela** *(cont.)*

Details of tax revenue / Ingresos tributarios detallados

*VES*

| | 1990 | 2000 | 2007 | 2010 | 2015 | 2016 | 2017 | 2018 | 2019 | 2020 |
|---|---|---|---|---|---|---|---|---|---|---|
| 5300 Unallocable between 5100 and 5200 | 0 | 0 | 0 | 0 | 0 | 0 | 0 | .. | .. | .. |
| **6000 Other taxes** | **0** | **0** | **0** | **0** | **158 333** | **263 062** | **1 225 170** | .. | .. | .. |
| 6100 Paid solely by business | .. | .. | .. | .. | 0 | 0 | 0 | .. | .. | .. |
| 6200 Other | .. | .. | .. | .. | 158 333 | 263 062 | 1 225 170 | .. | .. | .. |

.. Not available

*Note:* Year ending 31st December.

The data are on a cash basis.

Tax data have not been available since 2018.

The figures exclude state and local government tax revenues as the data are not available.

The figures between 2015 and 2017 should be interpreted with caution as they have been affected by the high rate of inflation over this period.

Total tax revenue data were not available between 2014 and 2017 due to missing data for social security contributions since 2014 and oil revenues since 2016 (classified in heading 1210 taxes on corporate profits).

*Source:* Servicio Nacional Integrado de Administración Aduanera (National Integrated Service of Customs); Ministerio de Finanzas (Ministry of Finance).

StatLink https://doi.org/10.1787/888934309853

*Chapter 6*

# Tax revenues by sub-sectors of general government

*Capítulo 6*

# Ingresos tributarios por sub-sectores de gobierno general

# Chapter 6 / Capítulo 6

## Tax revenues by sub-sectors of general government

Revenues of Latin American, Caribbean and OECD countries have been attributed to the different levels of government according to the revised guidelines set out in the final version of the 2008 System of National Accounts (SNA). Under this, revenues are generally attributed to the level of government that exercises the authority to impose the tax or has the final discretion to set and vary the tax rate.

## Ingresos tributarios por sub-sectores de gobierno general

Los ingresos de los países latinoamericanos, del Caribe y de los países de la OCDE se han atribuido a los diferentes niveles de gobierno de acuerdo con lo recogido en la versión final 2008 del Sistema de Cuentas Nacionales (SCN), según el cual, los ingresos se atribuyen por lo general al nivel de gobierno que ejerce la facultad de aplicar el impuesto o que puede a su discreción establecer y modificar la tasa del impuesto.

## Table 6.1. **Antigua and Barbuda, tax revenues by sub-sectors of government**

*Million XCD*

| | Federal government | | | | | State/Regional | | | | |
|---|---|---|---|---|---|---|---|---|---|---|
| | 1990 | 2000 | 2010 | 2015 | 2020 | 1990 | 2000 | 2010 | 2015 | 2020 |
| **1000 Taxes on income, profits and capital gains** | .. | **38** | **92** | **89** | **87** | .. | .. | .. | .. | .. |
| 1100 Of individuals | .. | 0 | 33 | 37 | 0 | .. | .. | .. | .. | .. |
| 1200 Corporate | .. | 37 | 59 | 52 | 87 | .. | .. | .. | .. | .. |
| 1300 Unallocable between 1100 and 1200 | .. | 0 | 0 | 0 | 0 | .. | .. | .. | .. | .. |
| **2000 Social security contributions** | .. | **0** | **0** | **0** | **0** | .. | .. | .. | .. | .. |
| 2100 Employees | .. | .. | .. | .. | .. | .. | .. | .. | .. | .. |
| 2200 Employers | .. | .. | .. | .. | .. | .. | .. | .. | .. | .. |
| 2300 Self-employed or non-employed | .. | .. | .. | .. | .. | .. | .. | .. | .. | .. |
| 2400 Unallocable between 2100, 2200 and 2300 | .. | .. | .. | .. | .. | .. | .. | .. | .. | .. |
| **3000 Taxes on payroll and workforce** | .. | **0** | **0** | **0** | **0** | .. | .. | .. | .. | .. |
| **4000 Taxes on property** | .. | **13** | **49** | **52** | **56** | .. | .. | .. | .. | .. |
| 4100 Recurrent taxes on immovable property | .. | 0 | 18 | 18 | 18 | .. | .. | .. | .. | .. |
| 4200 Recurrent taxes on net wealth | .. | 0 | 0 | 0 | 0 | .. | .. | .. | .. | .. |
| 4300 Estate, inheritance and gift taxes | .. | 0 | 0 | 0 | 0 | .. | .. | .. | .. | .. |
| 4400 Taxes on financial and capital transactions | .. | 13 | 32 | 34 | 38 | .. | .. | .. | .. | .. |
| 4500 Non-recurrent taxes | .. | 0 | 0 | 0 | 0 | .. | .. | .. | .. | .. |
| 4600 Other recurrent taxes on property | .. | 0 | 0 | 0 | 0 | .. | .. | .. | .. | .. |
| **5000 Taxes on goods and services** | .. | **217** | **435** | **481** | **467** | .. | .. | .. | .. | .. |
| 5100 Taxes on production, sale, transfer, etc | .. | 217 | 429 | 478 | 464 | .. | .. | .. | .. | .. |
| 5110 General taxes | .. | 0 | 179 | 307 | 273 | .. | .. | .. | .. | .. |
| 5120 Taxes on specific goods and services | .. | 217 | 250 | 171 | 191 | .. | .. | .. | .. | .. |
| 5130 Unallocable between 5110 and 5120 | .. | 0 | 0 | 0 | 0 | .. | .. | .. | .. | .. |
| 5200 Taxes on use of goods and perform activities | .. | 0 | 6 | 3 | 3 | .. | .. | .. | .. | .. |
| 5300 Unallocable between 5100 and 5200 | .. | 0 | 0 | 0 | 0 | .. | .. | .. | .. | .. |
| **6000 Other taxes** | .. | **0** | **0** | **0** | **0** | .. | .. | .. | .. | .. |
| 6100 Paid solely by business | .. | .. | .. | .. | .. | .. | .. | .. | .. | .. |
| 6200 Other | .. | .. | .. | .. | .. | .. | .. | .. | .. | .. |
| **Total tax revenue** | .. | **268** | **577** | **623** | **610** | .. | .. | .. | .. | .. |

*Million XCD*

| | Local government[1] | | | | | Social Security Funds[2] | | | | |
|---|---|---|---|---|---|---|---|---|---|---|
| | 1990 | 2000 | 2010 | 2015 | 2020 | 1990 | 2000 | 2010 | 2015 | 2020 |
| **1000 Taxes on income, profits and capital gains** | .. | .. | .. | .. | .. | .. | .. | **0** | **0** | **0** |
| 1100 Of individuals | .. | .. | .. | .. | .. | .. | .. | .. | .. | .. |
| 1200 Corporate | .. | .. | .. | .. | .. | .. | .. | .. | .. | .. |
| 1300 Unallocable between 1100 and 1200 | .. | .. | .. | .. | .. | .. | .. | .. | .. | .. |
| **2000 Social security contributions** | .. | .. | .. | .. | .. | .. | .. | **83** | **113** | **122** |
| 2100 Employees | .. | .. | .. | .. | .. | .. | .. | .. | .. | .. |
| 2200 Employers | .. | .. | .. | .. | .. | .. | .. | .. | .. | .. |
| 2300 Self-employed or non-employed | .. | .. | .. | .. | .. | .. | .. | .. | .. | .. |
| 2400 Unallocable between 2100, 2200 and 2300 | .. | .. | .. | .. | .. | .. | .. | 83 | 113 | 122 |
| **3000 Taxes on payroll and workforce** | .. | .. | .. | .. | .. | .. | .. | **0** | **0** | **0** |
| **4000 Taxes on property** | .. | .. | .. | .. | .. | .. | .. | **0** | **0** | **0** |
| 4100 Recurrent taxes on immovable property | .. | .. | .. | .. | .. | .. | .. | .. | .. | .. |
| 4200 Recurrent taxes on net wealth | .. | .. | .. | .. | .. | .. | .. | .. | .. | .. |
| 4300 Estate, inheritance and gift taxes | .. | .. | .. | .. | .. | .. | .. | .. | .. | .. |
| 4400 Taxes on financial and capital transactions | .. | .. | .. | .. | .. | .. | .. | .. | .. | .. |
| 4500 Non-recurrent taxes | .. | .. | .. | .. | .. | .. | .. | .. | .. | .. |
| 4600 Other recurrent taxes on property | .. | .. | .. | .. | .. | .. | .. | .. | .. | .. |
| **5000 Taxes on goods and services** | .. | .. | .. | .. | .. | .. | .. | **0** | **0** | **0** |
| 5100 Taxes on production, sale, transfer, etc | .. | .. | .. | .. | .. | .. | .. | .. | .. | .. |
| 5110 General taxes | .. | .. | .. | .. | .. | .. | .. | .. | .. | .. |
| 5120 Taxes on specific goods and services | .. | .. | .. | .. | .. | .. | .. | .. | .. | .. |
| 5130 Unallocable between 5110 and 5120 | .. | .. | .. | .. | .. | .. | .. | .. | .. | .. |
| 5200 Taxes on use of goods and perform activities | .. | .. | .. | .. | .. | .. | .. | .. | .. | .. |
| 5300 Unallocable between 5100 and 5200 | .. | .. | .. | .. | .. | .. | .. | .. | .. | .. |
| **6000 Other taxes** | .. | .. | .. | .. | .. | .. | .. | **0** | **0** | **0** |
| 6100 Paid solely by business | .. | .. | .. | .. | .. | .. | .. | .. | .. | .. |
| 6200 Other | .. | .. | .. | .. | .. | .. | .. | .. | .. | .. |
| **Total tax revenue** | .. | .. | .. | .. | .. | .. | .. | **83** | **113** | **122** |

.. Not available

1. Local government tax revenues are not available.
2. Figures for 2019 and 2020 are estimated.

StatLink https://doi.org/10.1787/888934309872

## Table 6.2. **Argentina, tax revenues by sub-sectors of government**

*Million ARS*

| | Federal government | | | | | State/Regional | | | | |
|---|---|---|---|---|---|---|---|---|---|---|
| | 1990 | 2000 | 2010 | 2015 | 2020 | 1990 | 2000 | 2010 | 2015 | 2020 |
| **1000 Taxes on income, profits and capital gains** | **542** | **11 303** | **78 427** | **384 536** | **1 470 348** | **0** | **0** | **0** | **0** | **0** |
| 1100 Of individuals | 141 | 3 937 | 23 980 | 188 218 | 634 425 | .. | .. | .. | .. | .. |
| 1200 Corporate | 357 | 6 575 | 50 664 | 185 725 | 756 440 | .. | .. | .. | .. | .. |
| 1300 Unallocable between 1100 and 1200 | 43 | 792 | 3 783 | 10 593 | 79 483 | .. | .. | .. | .. | .. |
| **2000 Social security contributions[1]** | **0** | **0** | **0** | **0** | **0** | **0** | **0** | **0** | **0** | **0** |
| 2100 Employees | .. | .. | .. | .. | .. | .. | .. | .. | .. | .. |
| 2200 Employers | .. | .. | .. | .. | .. | .. | .. | .. | .. | .. |
| 2300 Self-employed or non-employed | .. | .. | .. | .. | .. | .. | .. | .. | .. | .. |
| 2400 Unallocable between 2100, 2200 and 2300 | .. | .. | .. | .. | .. | .. | .. | .. | .. | .. |
| **3000 Taxes on payroll and workforce** | **0** | **0** | **0** | **0** | **0** | **0** | **0** | **0** | **0** | **0** |
| **4000 Taxes on property** | **616** | **1 254** | **32 674** | **117 274** | **667 346** | **549** | **2 614** | **10 864** | **48 908** | **211 797** |
| 4100 Recurrent taxes on immovable property | 0 | 0 | 0 | 0 | 0 | 419 | 1 809 | 5 035 | 21 738 | 113 243 |
| 4200 Recurrent taxes on net wealth | 246 | 1 084 | 5 248 | 18 538 | 209 929 | 0 | 0 | 0 | 0 | 0 |
| 4300 Estate, inheritance and gift taxes | 0 | 0 | 0 | 0 | 0 | 0 | 0 | 0 | 0 | 0 |
| 4400 Taxes on financial and capital transactions | 330 | 100 | 27 423 | 98 736 | 457 417 | 130 | 804 | 5 829 | 27 170 | 98 554 |
| 4500 Non-recurrent taxes | 40 | 70 | 3 | 0 | 0 | 0 | 0 | 0 | 0 | 0 |
| 4600 Other recurrent taxes on property | 0 | 0 | 0 | 0 | 0 | 0 | 0 | 0 | 0 | 0 |
| **5000 Taxes on goods and services** | **4 669** | **27 592** | **198 346** | **634 068** | **3 004 971** | **967** | **6 947** | **54 746** | **255 256** | **1 118 832** |
| 5100 Taxes on production, sale, transfer, etc | 4 671 | 28 174 | 201 402 | 642 899 | 3 037 153 | 791 | 6 114 | 51 148 | 238 221 | 1 046 083 |
| 5110 General taxes | 1 594 | 19 009 | 116 386 | 433 076 | 1 905 385 | 791 | 6 114 | 51 148 | 238 221 | 1 046 083 |
| 5120 Taxes on specific goods and services | 3 077 | 9 166 | 85 016 | 209 822 | 1 131 767 | 0 | 0 | 0 | 0 | 0 |
| 5130 Unallocable between 5110 and 5120 | 0 | 0 | 0 | 0 | 0 | 0 | 0 | 0 | 0 | 0 |
| 5200 Taxes on use of goods and perform activities[2] | .. | .. | .. | .. | .. | 177 | 833 | 3 598 | 17 035 | 72 748 |
| 5300 Unallocable between 5100 and 5200 | -3 | -583 | -3 056 | -8 831 | -32 182 | 0 | 0 | 0 | 0 | 0 |
| **6000 Other taxes** | **214** | **395** | **2 386** | **6 931** | **35 384** | **78** | **1 309** | **3 110** | **10 533** | **24 753** |
| 6100 Paid solely by business | 0 | 354 | 2 093 | 5 624 | 29 169 | 0 | 0 | 0 | 0 | 0 |
| 6200 Other[3] | 214 | 41 | 294 | 1 306 | 6 215 | 78 | 1 309 | 3 110 | 10 533 | 24 753 |
| **Total tax revenue** | **6 040** | **40 544** | **311 834** | **1 142 808** | **5 178 049** | **1 594** | **10 870** | **68 720** | **314 697** | **1 355 382** |

*Million ARS*

| | Local government[4] | | | | | Social Security Funds | | | | |
|---|---|---|---|---|---|---|---|---|---|---|
| | 1990 | 2000 | 2010 | 2015 | 2020 | 1990 | 2000 | 2010 | 2015 | 2020 |
| **1000 Taxes on income, profits and capital gains** | .. | .. | .. | .. | .. | **0** | **0** | **0** | **0** | **0** |
| 1100 Of individuals | .. | .. | .. | .. | .. | .. | .. | .. | .. | .. |
| 1200 Corporate | .. | .. | .. | .. | .. | .. | .. | .. | .. | .. |
| 1300 Unallocable between 1100 and 1200 | .. | .. | .. | .. | .. | .. | .. | .. | .. | .. |
| **2000 Social security contributions[1]** | .. | .. | .. | .. | .. | **2 583** | **9 670** | **102 460** | **415 410** | **1 548 052** |
| 2100 Employees | .. | .. | .. | .. | .. | .. | 2 486 | 37 990 | 163 590 | 626 400 |
| 2200 Employers | .. | .. | .. | .. | .. | .. | 6 069 | 54 713 | 235 610 | 864 329 |
| 2300 Self-employed or non-employed | .. | .. | .. | .. | .. | 98 | 1 115 | 9 757 | 16 210 | 57 323 |
| 2400 Unallocable between 2100, 2200 and 2300 | .. | .. | .. | .. | .. | 2 485 | 0 | 0 | 0 | 0 |
| **3000 Taxes on payroll and workforce** | .. | .. | .. | .. | .. | **0** | **0** | **0** | **0** | **0** |
| **4000 Taxes on property** | .. | .. | .. | .. | .. | **0** | **0** | **0** | **0** | **0** |
| 4100 Recurrent taxes on immovable property | .. | .. | .. | .. | .. | .. | .. | .. | .. | .. |
| 4200 Recurrent taxes on net wealth | .. | .. | .. | .. | .. | .. | .. | .. | .. | .. |
| 4300 Estate, inheritance and gift taxes | .. | .. | .. | .. | .. | .. | .. | .. | .. | .. |
| 4400 Taxes on financial and capital transactions | .. | .. | .. | .. | .. | .. | .. | .. | .. | .. |
| 4500 Non-recurrent taxes | .. | .. | .. | .. | .. | .. | .. | .. | .. | .. |
| 4600 Other recurrent taxes on property | .. | .. | .. | .. | .. | .. | .. | .. | .. | .. |
| **5000 Taxes on goods and services** | .. | .. | .. | .. | .. | **0** | **0** | **0** | **0** | **0** |
| 5100 Taxes on production, sale, transfer, etc | .. | .. | .. | .. | .. | .. | .. | .. | .. | .. |
| 5110 General taxes | .. | .. | .. | .. | .. | .. | .. | .. | .. | .. |
| 5120 Taxes on specific goods and services | .. | .. | .. | .. | .. | .. | .. | .. | .. | .. |
| 5130 Unallocable between 5110 and 5120 | .. | .. | .. | .. | .. | .. | .. | .. | .. | .. |
| 5200 Taxes on use of goods and perform activities[2] | .. | .. | .. | .. | .. | .. | .. | .. | .. | .. |
| 5300 Unallocable between 5100 and 5200 | .. | .. | .. | .. | .. | .. | .. | .. | .. | .. |
| **6000 Other taxes** | .. | .. | .. | .. | .. | **0** | **0** | **0** | **0** | **0** |
| 6100 Paid solely by business | .. | .. | .. | .. | .. | .. | .. | .. | .. | .. |
| 6200 Other[3] | .. | .. | .. | .. | .. | .. | .. | .. | .. | .. |
| **Total tax revenue** | .. | .. | .. | .. | .. | **2 583** | **9 670** | **102 460** | **415 410** | **1 548 052** |

.. Not available

1. The figures may be under-estimated as they exclude certain types of social security contributions for which data are not readily available.
2. In ECLAC data, tax on ownership of motor vehicles is classified in category 4000.
3. The tax debt payments in 2016 include revenue following the implementation of a new voluntary disclosure regime in July 2016 (Law 27260).
4. The figures exclude local government tax revenues as the data are not available.

StatLink https://doi.org/10.1787/888934309891

## Table 6.3. **Bahamas, tax revenues by sub-sectors of government**

*Million BSD*

| | Federal government | | | | | State/Regional | | | | |
|---|---|---|---|---|---|---|---|---|---|---|
| | 1990 | 2000 | 2010 | 2015 | 2020 | 1990 | 2000 | 2010 | 2015 | 2020 |
| **1000 Taxes on income, profits and capital gains** | **0** | **0** | **0** | **0** | **0** | .. | .. | .. | .. | .. |
| 1100 Of individuals | 0 | 0 | 0 | 0 | 0 | .. | .. | .. | .. | .. |
| 1200 Corporate | 0 | 0 | 0 | 0 | 0 | .. | .. | .. | .. | .. |
| 1300 Unallocable between 1100 and 1200 | 0 | 0 | 0 | 0 | 0 | .. | .. | .. | .. | .. |
| **2000 Social security contributions** | **0** | **0** | **0** | **0** | **0** | .. | .. | .. | .. | .. |
| 2100 Employees | .. | .. | .. | .. | .. | .. | .. | .. | .. | .. |
| 2200 Employers | .. | .. | .. | .. | .. | .. | .. | .. | .. | .. |
| 2300 Self-employed or non-employed | .. | .. | .. | .. | .. | .. | .. | .. | .. | .. |
| 2400 Unallocable between 2100, 2200 and 2300 | .. | .. | .. | .. | .. | .. | .. | .. | .. | .. |
| **3000 Taxes on payroll and workforce** | **0** | **0** | **0** | **0** | **0** | .. | .. | .. | .. | .. |
| **4000 Taxes on property** | **56** | **208** | **269** | **298** | **173** | .. | .. | .. | .. | .. |
| 4100 Recurrent taxes on immovable property | 19 | 32 | 92 | 107 | 99 | .. | .. | .. | .. | .. |
| 4200 Recurrent taxes on net wealth | 0 | 0 | 0 | 0 | 0 | .. | .. | .. | .. | .. |
| 4300 Estate, inheritance and gift taxes | 0 | 0 | 0 | 0 | 0 | .. | .. | .. | .. | .. |
| 4400 Taxes on financial and capital transactions | 37 | 176 | 177 | 191 | 74 | .. | .. | .. | .. | .. |
| 4500 Non-recurrent taxes | 0 | 0 | 0 | 0 | 0 | .. | .. | .. | .. | .. |
| 4600 Other recurrent taxes on property | 0 | 0 | 0 | 0 | 0 | .. | .. | .. | .. | .. |
| **5000 Taxes on goods and services** | **386** | **620** | **780** | **1 203** | **1 686** | .. | .. | .. | .. | .. |
| 5100 Taxes on production, sale, transfer, etc | 354 | 552 | 657 | 993 | 1 533 | .. | .. | .. | .. | .. |
| 5110 General taxes | 0 | 0 | 0 | 219 | 880 | .. | .. | .. | .. | .. |
| 5120 Taxes on specific goods and services | 354 | 552 | 657 | 775 | 654 | .. | .. | .. | .. | .. |
| 5130 Unallocable between 5110 and 5120 | 0 | 0 | 0 | 0 | 0 | .. | .. | .. | .. | .. |
| 5200 Taxes on use of goods and perform activities | 32 | 69 | 123 | 209 | 152 | .. | .. | .. | .. | .. |
| 5300 Unallocable between 5100 and 5200 | 0 | 0 | 0 | 0 | 0 | .. | .. | .. | .. | .. |
| **6000 Other taxes** | **-4** | **21** | **60** | **0** | **0** | .. | .. | .. | .. | .. |
| 6100 Paid solely by business | 0 | 0 | 0 | 0 | .. | .. | .. | .. | .. | .. |
| 6200 Other | -4 | 21 | 60 | 0 | .. | .. | .. | .. | .. | .. |
| **Total tax revenue** | **438** | **849** | **1 109** | **1 500** | **1 858** | .. | .. | .. | .. | .. |

*Million BSD*

| | Local government[1] | | | | | Social Security Funds[2] | | | | |
|---|---|---|---|---|---|---|---|---|---|---|
| | 1990 | 2000 | 2010 | 2015 | 2020 | 1990 | 2000 | 2010 | 2015 | 2020 |
| **1000 Taxes on income, profits and capital gains** | .. | .. | .. | .. | .. | **0** | **0** | **0** | **0** | **0** |
| 1100 Of individuals | .. | .. | .. | .. | .. | .. | .. | .. | .. | .. |
| 1200 Corporate | .. | .. | .. | .. | .. | .. | .. | .. | .. | .. |
| 1300 Unallocable between 1100 and 1200 | .. | .. | .. | .. | .. | .. | .. | .. | .. | .. |
| **2000 Social security contributions** | .. | .. | .. | .. | .. | **66** | **115** | **167** | **260** | **246** |
| 2100 Employees | .. | .. | .. | .. | .. | .. | .. | 60 | 98 | .. |
| 2200 Employers | .. | .. | .. | .. | .. | .. | .. | 104 | 157 | .. |
| 2300 Self-employed or non-employed | .. | .. | .. | .. | .. | .. | .. | 3 | 6 | .. |
| 2400 Unallocable between 2100, 2200 and 2300 | .. | .. | .. | .. | .. | 66 | 115 | 0 | -1 | 246 |
| **3000 Taxes on payroll and workforce** | .. | .. | .. | .. | .. | **0** | **0** | **0** | **0** | **0** |
| **4000 Taxes on property** | .. | .. | .. | .. | .. | **0** | **0** | **0** | **0** | **0** |
| 4100 Recurrent taxes on immovable property | .. | .. | .. | .. | .. | .. | .. | .. | .. | .. |
| 4200 Recurrent taxes on net wealth | .. | .. | .. | .. | .. | .. | .. | .. | .. | .. |
| 4300 Estate, inheritance and gift taxes | .. | .. | .. | .. | .. | .. | .. | .. | .. | .. |
| 4400 Taxes on financial and capital transactions | .. | .. | .. | .. | .. | .. | .. | .. | .. | .. |
| 4500 Non-recurrent taxes | .. | .. | .. | .. | .. | .. | .. | .. | .. | .. |
| 4600 Other recurrent taxes on property | .. | .. | .. | .. | .. | .. | .. | .. | .. | .. |
| **5000 Taxes on goods and services** | .. | .. | .. | .. | .. | **0** | **0** | **0** | **0** | **0** |
| 5100 Taxes on production, sale, transfer, etc | .. | .. | .. | .. | .. | .. | .. | .. | .. | .. |
| 5110 General taxes | .. | .. | .. | .. | .. | .. | .. | .. | .. | .. |
| 5120 Taxes on specific goods and services | .. | .. | .. | .. | .. | .. | .. | .. | .. | .. |
| 5130 Unallocable between 5110 and 5120 | .. | .. | .. | .. | .. | .. | .. | .. | .. | .. |
| 5200 Taxes on use of goods and perform activities | .. | .. | .. | .. | .. | .. | .. | .. | .. | .. |
| 5300 Unallocable between 5100 and 5200 | .. | .. | .. | .. | .. | .. | .. | .. | .. | .. |
| **6000 Other taxes** | .. | .. | .. | .. | .. | **0** | **0** | **0** | **0** | .. |
| 6100 Paid solely by business | .. | .. | .. | .. | .. | .. | .. | .. | .. | .. |
| 6200 Other | .. | .. | .. | .. | .. | .. | .. | .. | .. | .. |
| **Total tax revenue** | .. | .. | .. | .. | .. | **66** | **115** | **167** | **260** | **246** |

.. Not available

1. Local government tax revenues are not available.
2. The data for social security contributions are estimated for 2019 and 2020.

StatLink https://doi.org/10.1787/888934309910

## Table 6.4. **Barbados, tax revenues by sub-sectors of government**

*Million BBD*

| | Federal government | | | | | State/Regional | | | | |
|---|---|---|---|---|---|---|---|---|---|---|
| | 1990 | 2000 | 2010 | 2015 | 2020 | 1990 | 2000 | 2010 | 2015 | 2020 |
| **1000 Taxes on income, profits and capital gains** | **250** | **599** | **766** | **714** | **976** | .. | .. | .. | .. | .. |
| 1100 Of individuals | 140 | 293 | 395 | 433 | 308 | .. | .. | .. | .. | .. |
| 1200 Corporate | 95 | 269 | 294 | 215 | 613 | .. | .. | .. | .. | .. |
| 1300 Unallocable between 1100 and 1200 | 15 | 37 | 76 | 66 | 55 | .. | .. | .. | .. | .. |
| **2000 Social security contributions** | **0** | **0** | **0** | **0** | **0** | .. | .. | .. | .. | .. |
| 2100 Employees | .. | .. | .. | .. | .. | .. | .. | .. | .. | .. |
| 2200 Employers | .. | .. | .. | .. | .. | .. | .. | .. | .. | .. |
| 2300 Self-employed or non-employed | .. | .. | .. | .. | .. | .. | .. | .. | .. | .. |
| 2400 Unallocable between 2100, 2200 and 2300 | .. | .. | .. | .. | .. | .. | .. | .. | .. | .. |
| **3000 Taxes on payroll and workforce** | **0** | **0** | **0** | **0** | **0** | .. | .. | .. | .. | .. |
| **4000 Taxes on property** | **147** | **108** | **130** | **143** | **189** | .. | .. | .. | .. | .. |
| 4100 Recurrent taxes on immovable property | 46 | 95 | 118 | 133 | 182 | .. | .. | .. | .. | .. |
| 4200 Recurrent taxes on net wealth | 0 | 0 | 0 | 0 | 0 | .. | .. | .. | .. | .. |
| 4300 Estate, inheritance and gift taxes | 0 | 0 | 0 | 0 | 0 | .. | .. | .. | .. | .. |
| 4400 Taxes on financial and capital transactions | 101 | 13 | 12 | 10 | 8 | .. | .. | .. | .. | .. |
| 4500 Non-recurrent taxes | 0 | 0 | 0 | 0 | 0 | .. | .. | .. | .. | .. |
| 4600 Other recurrent taxes on property | 0 | 0 | 0 | 0 | 0 | .. | .. | .. | .. | .. |
| **5000 Taxes on goods and services** | **495** | **889** | **1 276** | **1 410** | **1 223** | .. | .. | .. | .. | .. |
| 5100 Taxes on production, sale, transfer, etc | 424 | 788 | 1 105 | 1 291 | 1 171 | .. | .. | .. | .. | .. |
| 5110 General taxes | 197 | 492 | 768 | 861 | 706 | .. | .. | .. | .. | .. |
| 5120 Taxes on specific goods and services | 227 | 296 | 337 | 430 | 465 | .. | .. | .. | .. | .. |
| 5130 Unallocable between 5110 and 5120 | 0 | 0 | 0 | 0 | 0 | .. | .. | .. | .. | .. |
| 5200 Taxes on use of goods and perform activities | 71 | 101 | 171 | 119 | 52 | .. | .. | .. | .. | .. |
| 5300 Unallocable between 5100 and 5200 | 0 | 0 | 0 | 0 | 0 | .. | .. | .. | .. | .. |
| **6000 Other taxes** | **0** | **0** | **0** | **0** | **0** | .. | .. | .. | .. | .. |
| 6100 Paid solely by business | .. | .. | .. | .. | .. | .. | .. | .. | .. | .. |
| 6200 Other | .. | .. | .. | .. | .. | .. | .. | .. | .. | .. |
| **Total tax revenue** | **892** | **1 596** | **2 171** | **2 266** | **2 388** | .. | .. | .. | .. | .. |

*Million BBD*

| | Local government[1] | | | | | Social Security Funds | | | | |
|---|---|---|---|---|---|---|---|---|---|---|
| | 1990 | 2000 | 2010 | 2015 | 2020 | 1990 | 2000 | 2010 | 2015 | 2020 |
| **1000 Taxes on income, profits and capital gains** | .. | .. | .. | .. | .. | **0** | **0** | **0** | **0** | **0** |
| 1100 Of individuals | .. | .. | .. | .. | .. | .. | .. | .. | .. | .. |
| 1200 Corporate | .. | .. | .. | .. | .. | .. | .. | .. | .. | .. |
| 1300 Unallocable between 1100 and 1200 | .. | .. | .. | .. | .. | .. | .. | .. | .. | .. |
| **2000 Social security contributions** | .. | .. | .. | .. | .. | **134** | **295** | **565** | **627** | **595** |
| 2100 Employees | .. | .. | .. | .. | .. | .. | .. | .. | .. | .. |
| 2200 Employers | .. | .. | .. | .. | .. | .. | .. | .. | .. | .. |
| 2300 Self-employed or non-employed | .. | .. | .. | .. | .. | .. | .. | .. | .. | .. |
| 2400 Unallocable between 2100, 2200 and 2300 | .. | .. | .. | .. | .. | 134 | 295 | 565 | 627 | 595 |
| **3000 Taxes on payroll and workforce** | .. | .. | .. | .. | .. | **0** | **0** | **0** | **0** | **0** |
| **4000 Taxes on property** | .. | .. | .. | .. | .. | **0** | **0** | **0** | **0** | **0** |
| 4100 Recurrent taxes on immovable property | .. | .. | .. | .. | .. | .. | .. | .. | .. | .. |
| 4200 Recurrent taxes on net wealth | .. | .. | .. | .. | .. | .. | .. | .. | .. | .. |
| 4300 Estate, inheritance and gift taxes | .. | .. | .. | .. | .. | .. | .. | .. | .. | .. |
| 4400 Taxes on financial and capital transactions | .. | .. | .. | .. | .. | .. | .. | .. | .. | .. |
| 4500 Non-recurrent taxes | .. | .. | .. | .. | .. | .. | .. | .. | .. | .. |
| 4600 Other recurrent taxes on property | .. | .. | .. | .. | .. | .. | .. | .. | .. | .. |
| **5000 Taxes on goods and services** | .. | .. | .. | .. | .. | **0** | **0** | **0** | **0** | **0** |
| 5100 Taxes on production, sale, transfer, etc | .. | .. | .. | .. | .. | .. | .. | .. | .. | .. |
| 5110 General taxes | .. | .. | .. | .. | .. | .. | .. | .. | .. | .. |
| 5120 Taxes on specific goods and services | .. | .. | .. | .. | .. | .. | .. | .. | .. | .. |
| 5130 Unallocable between 5110 and 5120 | .. | .. | .. | .. | .. | .. | .. | .. | .. | .. |
| 5200 Taxes on use of goods and perform activities | .. | .. | .. | .. | .. | .. | .. | .. | .. | .. |
| 5300 Unallocable between 5100 and 5200 | .. | .. | .. | .. | .. | .. | .. | .. | .. | .. |
| **6000 Other taxes** | .. | .. | .. | .. | .. | **0** | **0** | **0** | **0** | **0** |
| 6100 Paid solely by business | .. | .. | .. | .. | .. | .. | .. | .. | .. | .. |
| 6200 Other | .. | .. | .. | .. | .. | .. | .. | .. | .. | .. |
| **Total tax revenue** | .. | .. | .. | .. | .. | **134** | **295** | **565** | **627** | **595** |

.. Not available

1. Local government tax revenues are not available.

StatLink https://doi.org/10.1787/888934309929

## Table 6.5. **Belize, tax revenues by sub-sectors of government**

*Million BZD*

| | Federal government[1] | | | | | State/Regional | | | | |
|---|---|---|---|---|---|---|---|---|---|---|
| | 1990 | 2000 | 2010 | 2015 | 2020 | 1990 | 2000 | 2010 | 2015 | 2020 |
| **1000 Taxes on income, profits and capital gains** | **37** | **76** | **248** | **254** | **217** | .. | .. | .. | .. | .. |
| 1100 Of individuals | 21 | 19 | 52 | 82 | 87 | .. | .. | .. | .. | .. |
| 1200 Corporate | 12 | 51 | 189 | 159 | 121 | .. | .. | .. | .. | .. |
| 1300 Unallocable between 1100 and 1200 | 4 | 6 | 7 | 13 | 10 | .. | .. | .. | .. | .. |
| **2000 Social security contributions** | **0** | **0** | **0** | **0** | **0** | .. | .. | .. | .. | .. |
| 2100 Employees | .. | .. | .. | .. | .. | .. | .. | .. | .. | .. |
| 2200 Employers | .. | .. | .. | .. | .. | .. | .. | .. | .. | .. |
| 2300 Self-employed or non-employed | .. | .. | .. | .. | .. | .. | .. | .. | .. | .. |
| 2400 Unallocable between 2100, 2200 and 2300 | .. | .. | .. | .. | .. | .. | .. | .. | .. | .. |
| **3000 Taxes on payroll and workforce** | **0** | **0** | **0** | **0** | **0** | .. | .. | .. | .. | .. |
| **4000 Taxes on property** | **33** | **11** | **16** | **29** | **25** | .. | .. | .. | .. | .. |
| 4100 Recurrent taxes on immovable property | 0 | 0 | 0 | 0 | 0 | .. | .. | .. | .. | .. |
| 4200 Recurrent taxes on net wealth | 0 | 0 | 0 | 0 | 0 | .. | .. | .. | .. | .. |
| 4300 Estate, inheritance and gift taxes | 0 | 0 | 0 | 0 | 0 | .. | .. | .. | .. | .. |
| 4400 Taxes on financial and capital transactions | 33 | 11 | 16 | 29 | 25 | .. | .. | .. | .. | .. |
| 4500 Non-recurrent taxes | 0 | 0 | 0 | 0 | 0 | .. | .. | .. | .. | .. |
| 4600 Other recurrent taxes on property | 0 | 0 | 0 | 0 | 0 | .. | .. | .. | .. | .. |
| **5000 Taxes on goods and services** | **97** | **211** | **409** | **580** | **532** | .. | .. | .. | .. | .. |
| 5100 Taxes on production, sale, transfer, etc | 94 | 207 | 400 | 571 | 526 | .. | .. | .. | .. | .. |
| 5110 General taxes | 0 | 82 | 199 | 275 | 232 | .. | .. | .. | .. | .. |
| 5120 Taxes on specific goods and services | 94 | 125 | 200 | 296 | 294 | .. | .. | .. | .. | .. |
| 5130 Unallocable between 5110 and 5120 | 0 | 0 | 0 | 0 | 0 | .. | .. | .. | .. | .. |
| 5200 Taxes on use of goods and perform activities | 3 | 4 | 9 | 9 | 6 | .. | .. | .. | .. | .. |
| 5300 Unallocable between 5100 and 5200 | 0 | 0 | 0 | 0 | 0 | .. | .. | .. | .. | .. |
| **6000 Other taxes** | **0** | **0** | **0** | **0** | **0** | .. | .. | .. | .. | .. |
| 6100 Paid solely by business | .. | .. | .. | .. | .. | .. | .. | .. | .. | .. |
| 6200 Other | .. | .. | .. | .. | .. | .. | .. | .. | .. | .. |
| **Total tax revenue** | **167** | **298** | **673** | **864** | **774** | .. | .. | .. | .. | .. |

*Million BZD*

| | Local government[1] | | | | | Social Security Funds | | | | |
|---|---|---|---|---|---|---|---|---|---|---|
| | 1990 | 2000 | 2010 | 2015 | 2020 | 1990 | 2000 | 2010 | 2015 | 2020 |
| **1000 Taxes on income, profits and capital gains** | **0** | **0** | **0** | **0** | **0** | **0** | **0** | **0** | **0** | **0** |
| 1100 Of individuals | .. | .. | .. | .. | .. | .. | .. | .. | .. | .. |
| 1200 Corporate | .. | .. | .. | .. | .. | .. | .. | .. | .. | .. |
| 1300 Unallocable between 1100 and 1200 | .. | .. | .. | .. | .. | .. | .. | .. | .. | .. |
| **2000 Social security contributions** | **0** | **0** | **0** | **0** | **0** | **10** | **18** | **60** | **77** | **110** |
| 2100 Employees | .. | .. | .. | .. | .. | .. | .. | .. | .. | .. |
| 2200 Employers | .. | .. | .. | .. | .. | .. | .. | .. | .. | .. |
| 2300 Self-employed or non-employed | .. | .. | .. | .. | .. | .. | .. | .. | .. | .. |
| 2400 Unallocable between 2100, 2200 and 2300 | .. | .. | .. | .. | .. | 10 | 18 | 60 | 77 | 110 |
| **3000 Taxes on payroll and workforce** | **0** | **0** | **0** | **0** | **0** | **0** | **0** | **0** | **0** | **0** |
| **4000 Taxes on property** | **1** | **2** | **7** | **5** | **6** | **0** | **0** | **0** | **0** | **0** |
| 4100 Recurrent taxes on immovable property | 1 | 2 | 7 | 5 | 6 | .. | .. | .. | .. | .. |
| 4200 Recurrent taxes on net wealth | 0 | 0 | 0 | 0 | 0 | .. | .. | .. | .. | .. |
| 4300 Estate, inheritance and gift taxes | 0 | 0 | 0 | 0 | 0 | .. | .. | .. | .. | .. |
| 4400 Taxes on financial and capital transactions | 0 | 0 | 0 | 0 | 0 | .. | .. | .. | .. | .. |
| 4500 Non-recurrent taxes | 0 | 0 | 0 | 0 | 0 | .. | .. | .. | .. | .. |
| 4600 Other recurrent taxes on property | 0 | 0 | 0 | 0 | 0 | .. | .. | .. | .. | .. |
| **5000 Taxes on goods and services** | **0** | **0** | **0** | **0** | **0** | **0** | **0** | **0** | **0** | **0** |
| 5100 Taxes on production, sale, transfer, etc | .. | .. | .. | .. | .. | .. | .. | .. | .. | .. |
| 5110 General taxes | .. | .. | .. | .. | .. | .. | .. | .. | .. | .. |
| 5120 Taxes on specific goods and services | .. | .. | .. | .. | .. | .. | .. | .. | .. | .. |
| 5130 Unallocable between 5110 and 5120 | .. | .. | .. | .. | .. | .. | .. | .. | .. | .. |
| 5200 Taxes on use of goods and perform activities | .. | .. | .. | .. | .. | .. | .. | .. | .. | .. |
| 5300 Unallocable between 5100 and 5200 | .. | .. | .. | .. | .. | .. | .. | .. | .. | .. |
| **6000 Other taxes** | **0** | **0** | **0** | **0** | **0** | **0** | **0** | **0** | **0** | **0** |
| 6100 Paid solely by business | .. | .. | .. | .. | .. | .. | .. | .. | .. | .. |
| 6200 Other | .. | .. | .. | .. | .. | .. | .. | .. | .. | .. |
| **Total tax revenue** | **1** | **2** | **7** | **5** | **6** | **10** | **18** | **60** | **77** | **110** |

.. Not available

1. The data for 2020 are revised estimates as presented by the Approved Estimates of Revenue and Expenditure for Fiscal Year 2021/2022.

StatLink https://doi.org/10.1787/888934309948

# Table 6.6. **Bolivia, tax revenues by sub-sectors of government**

*Million BOB*

| | Federal government | | | | | State/Regional | | | | |
|---|---|---|---|---|---|---|---|---|---|---|
| | 1990 | 2000 | 2010 | 2015 | 2020 | 1990 | 2000 | 2010 | 2015 | 2020 |
| **1000 Taxes on income, profits and capital gains** | **68** | **1 209** | **6 294** | **12 809** | **7 402** | .. | .. | .. | .. | .. |
| 1100 Of individuals | 68 | 214 | 263 | 508 | 470 | .. | .. | .. | .. | .. |
| 1200 Corporate | 0 | 995 | 6 031 | 12 302 | 6 931 | .. | .. | .. | .. | .. |
| 1300 Unallocable between 1100 and 1200 | 0 | 0 | 0 | 0 | 0 | .. | .. | .. | .. | .. |
| **2000 Social security contributions** | **0** | **0** | **0** | **0** | **0** | .. | .. | .. | .. | .. |
| 2100 Employees | .. | .. | .. | .. | .. | .. | .. | .. | .. | .. |
| 2200 Employers | .. | .. | .. | .. | .. | .. | .. | .. | .. | .. |
| 2300 Self-employed or non-employed | .. | .. | .. | .. | .. | .. | .. | .. | .. | .. |
| 2400 Unallocable between 2100, 2200 and 2300 | .. | .. | .. | .. | .. | .. | .. | .. | .. | .. |
| **3000 Taxes on payroll and workforce** | **0** | **0** | **0** | **0** | **0** | .. | .. | .. | .. | .. |
| **4000 Taxes on property** | **1** | **3** | **367** | **424** | **421** | .. | .. | .. | .. | .. |
| 4100 Recurrent taxes on immovable property | 0 | 0 | 0 | 0 | 0 | .. | .. | .. | .. | .. |
| 4200 Recurrent taxes on net wealth | 0 | 0 | 0 | 0 | 0 | .. | .. | .. | .. | .. |
| 4300 Estate, inheritance and gift taxes | 1 | 3 | 20 | 36 | 0 | .. | .. | .. | .. | .. |
| 4400 Taxes on financial and capital transactions | 0 | 0 | 347 | 388 | 421 | .. | .. | .. | .. | .. |
| 4500 Non-recurrent taxes | 0 | 0 | 0 | 0 | 0 | .. | .. | .. | .. | .. |
| 4600 Other recurrent taxes on property | 0 | 0 | 0 | 0 | 0 | .. | .. | .. | .. | .. |
| **5000 Taxes on goods and services** | **907** | **6 656** | **17 791** | **34 759** | **25 866** | .. | .. | .. | .. | .. |
| 5100 Taxes on production, sale, transfer, etc | 907 | 6 656 | 17 791 | 34 759 | 25 866 | .. | .. | .. | .. | .. |
| 5110 General taxes | 584 | 3 953 | 12 541 | 25 247 | 19 124 | .. | .. | .. | .. | .. |
| 5120 Taxes on specific goods and services | 324 | 2 702 | 5 250 | 9 511 | 6 742 | .. | .. | .. | .. | .. |
| 5130 Unallocable between 5110 and 5120 | 0 | 0 | 0 | 0 | 0 | .. | .. | .. | .. | .. |
| 5200 Taxes on use of goods and perform activities | 0 | 0 | 0 | 0 | 0 | .. | .. | .. | .. | .. |
| 5300 Unallocable between 5100 and 5200 | 0 | 0 | 0 | 0 | 0 | .. | .. | .. | .. | .. |
| **6000 Other taxes** | **30** | **42** | **451** | **2 452** | **3 190** | .. | .. | .. | .. | .. |
| 6100 Paid solely by business | 4 | 6 | 12 | 25 | 25 | .. | .. | .. | .. | .. |
| 6200 Other | 26 | 36 | 439 | 2 427 | 3 165 | .. | .. | .. | .. | .. |
| **Total tax revenue** | **1 005** | **7 910** | **24 903** | **50 444** | **36 878** | .. | .. | .. | .. | .. |

*Million BOB*

| | Local government[1] | | | | | Social Security Funds[2] | | | | |
|---|---|---|---|---|---|---|---|---|---|---|
| | 1990 | 2000 | 2010 | 2015 | 2020 | 1990 | 2000 | 2010 | 2015 | 2020 |
| **1000 Taxes on income, profits and capital gains** | .. | **0** | **0** | **0** | **0** | .. | **0** | **0** | **0** | **0** |
| 1100 Of individuals | .. | .. | .. | .. | .. | .. | .. | .. | .. | .. |
| 1200 Corporate | .. | .. | .. | .. | .. | .. | .. | .. | .. | .. |
| 1300 Unallocable between 1100 and 1200 | .. | .. | .. | .. | .. | .. | .. | .. | .. | .. |
| **2000 Social security contributions** | .. | **0** | **0** | **0** | **0** | .. | **666** | **5 265** | **14 235** | **16 893** |
| 2100 Employees | .. | .. | .. | .. | .. | .. | .. | .. | .. | .. |
| 2200 Employers | .. | .. | .. | .. | .. | .. | .. | .. | .. | .. |
| 2300 Self-employed or non-employed | .. | .. | .. | .. | .. | .. | .. | .. | .. | .. |
| 2400 Unallocable between 2100, 2200 and 2300 | .. | .. | .. | .. | .. | .. | 666 | 5 265 | 14 235 | 16 893 |
| **3000 Taxes on payroll and workforce** | .. | **0** | **0** | **0** | **0** | .. | **0** | **0** | **0** | **0** |
| **4000 Taxes on property** | .. | **0** | **0** | **0** | **0** | .. | **0** | **0** | **0** | **0** |
| 4100 Recurrent taxes on immovable property | .. | .. | .. | .. | .. | .. | .. | .. | .. | .. |
| 4200 Recurrent taxes on net wealth | .. | .. | .. | .. | .. | .. | .. | .. | .. | .. |
| 4300 Estate, inheritance and gift taxes | .. | .. | .. | .. | .. | .. | .. | .. | .. | .. |
| 4400 Taxes on financial and capital transactions | .. | .. | .. | .. | .. | .. | .. | .. | .. | .. |
| 4500 Non-recurrent taxes | .. | .. | .. | .. | .. | .. | .. | .. | .. | .. |
| 4600 Other recurrent taxes on property | .. | .. | .. | .. | .. | .. | .. | .. | .. | .. |
| **5000 Taxes on goods and services** | .. | **0** | **0** | **0** | **0** | .. | **0** | **0** | **0** | **0** |
| 5100 Taxes on production, sale, transfer, etc | .. | .. | .. | .. | .. | .. | .. | .. | .. | .. |
| 5110 General taxes | .. | .. | .. | .. | .. | .. | .. | .. | .. | .. |
| 5120 Taxes on specific goods and services | .. | .. | .. | .. | .. | .. | .. | .. | .. | .. |
| 5130 Unallocable between 5110 and 5120 | .. | .. | .. | .. | .. | .. | .. | .. | .. | .. |
| 5200 Taxes on use of goods and perform activities | .. | .. | .. | .. | .. | .. | .. | .. | .. | .. |
| 5300 Unallocable between 5100 and 5200 | .. | .. | .. | .. | .. | .. | .. | .. | .. | .. |
| **6000 Other taxes** | .. | **575** | **1 381** | **2 585** | **2 715** | .. | **0** | **0** | **0** | **0** |
| 6100 Paid solely by business | .. | 0 | 0 | 0 | 0 | .. | .. | .. | .. | .. |
| 6200 Other | .. | 575 | 1 381 | 2 585 | 2 715 | .. | .. | .. | .. | .. |
| **Total tax revenue** | .. | **575** | **1 381** | **2 585** | **2 715** | .. | **666** | **5 265** | **14 235** | **16 893** |

.. Not available

1. The figures exclude local government tax revenues for the period 1990-1993 as the data are not available.
2. The data for social security contributions include contributions to Bolivia's pension system (since its nationalisation in 2010) and healthcare related funds.

StatLink https://doi.org/10.1787/888934309967

## Table 6.7. **Brazil, tax revenues by sub-sectors of government**

*Million BRL*

| | Federal government | | | | | State/Regional | | | | |
|---|---|---|---|---|---|---|---|---|---|---|
| | 1990 | 2000 | 2010 | 2015 | 2020 | 1990 | 2000 | 2010 | 2015 | 2020 |
| **1000 Taxes on income, profits and capital gains** | **1** | **68 667** | **258 738** | **400 993** | **525 627** | **0** | **0** | **0** | **0** | **0** |
| 1100 Of individuals | 0 | 3 406 | 87 828 | 148 739 | 224 582 | .. | .. | .. | .. | .. |
| 1200 Corporate | 0 | 25 430 | 128 255 | 164 057 | 200 032 | .. | .. | .. | .. | .. |
| 1300 Unallocable between 1100 and 1200 | 0 | 39 831 | 42 656 | 88 196 | 101 014 | .. | .. | .. | .. | .. |
| **2000 Social security contributions** | **0** | **0** | **0** | **0** | **0** | **0** | **0** | **0** | **0** | **0** |
| 2100 Employees | .. | .. | .. | .. | .. | .. | .. | .. | .. | .. |
| 2200 Employers | .. | .. | .. | .. | .. | .. | .. | .. | .. | .. |
| 2300 Self-employed or non-employed | .. | .. | .. | .. | .. | .. | .. | .. | .. | .. |
| 2400 Unallocable between 2100, 2200 and 2300 | .. | .. | .. | .. | .. | .. | .. | .. | .. | .. |
| **3000 Taxes on payroll and workforce** | **0** | **5 437** | **21 348** | **37 891** | **40 056** | **0** | **0** | **0** | **0** | **0** |
| **4000 Taxes on property** | **0** | **17 726** | **27 044** | **35 791** | **23 710** | **0** | **329** | **2 956** | **7 148** | **9 627** |
| 4100 Recurrent taxes on immovable property | 0 | 234 | 485 | 1 105 | 1 761 | 0 | 0 | 437 | 687 | 1 105 |
| 4200 Recurrent taxes on net wealth | 0 | 0 | 0 | 0 | 0 | 0 | 0 | 0 | 0 | 0 |
| 4300 Estate, inheritance and gift taxes | 0 | 0 | 0 | 0 | 0 | 0 | 329 | 2 518 | 6 461 | 8 521 |
| 4400 Taxes on financial and capital transactions | 0 | 17 492 | 26 559 | 34 686 | 21 949 | 0 | 0 | 0 | 0 | 0 |
| 4500 Non-recurrent taxes | 0 | 0 | 0 | 0 | 0 | 0 | 0 | 0 | 0 | 0 |
| 4600 Other recurrent taxes on property | 0 | 0 | 0 | 0 | 0 | 0 | 0 | 0 | 0 | 0 |
| **5000 Taxes on goods and services** | **1** | **75 502** | **256 256** | **357 270** | **389 590** | **1** | **87 573** | **290 423** | **434 286** | **572 760** |
| 5100 Taxes on production, sale, transfer, etc | 1 | 75 502 | 250 857 | 348 492 | 389 416 | 1 | 82 279 | 269 056 | 398 068 | 524 582 |
| 5110 General taxes[1] | 0 | 48 358 | 182 188 | 253 356 | 279 915 | 1 | 82 279 | 269 056 | 398 068 | 524 582 |
| 5120 Taxes on specific goods and services | 0 | 27 144 | 68 669 | 95 136 | 109 502 | 0 | 0 | 0 | 0 | 0 |
| 5130 Unallocable between 5110 and 5120 | 0 | 0 | 0 | 0 | 0 | 0 | 0 | 0 | 0 | 0 |
| 5200 Taxes on use of goods and perform activities | 0 | 0 | 5 399 | 8 778 | 173 | 0 | 5 294 | 21 367 | 36 219 | 48 178 |
| 5300 Unallocable between 5100 and 5200 | 0 | 0 | 0 | 0 | 0 | 0 | 0 | 0 | 0 | 0 |
| **6000 Other taxes** | **0** | **1 479** | **5 548** | **5 423** | **18 734** | **0** | **322** | **15 662** | **26 656** | **19 172** |
| 6100 Paid solely by business | 0 | 0 | 0 | 0 | 0 | 0 | 0 | 0 | 0 | 0 |
| 6200 Other | 0 | 1 479 | 5 548 | 5 423 | 18 734 | 0 | 322 | 15 662 | 26 656 | 19 172 |
| **Total tax revenue** | **1** | **168 811** | **568 934** | **837 368** | **997 718** | **1** | **88 224** | **309 040** | **468 091** | **601 559** |

*Million BRL*

| | Local government | | | | | Social Security Funds | | | | |
|---|---|---|---|---|---|---|---|---|---|---|
| | 1990 | 2000 | 2010 | 2015 | 2020 | 1990 | 2000 | 2010 | 2015 | 2020 |
| **1000 Taxes on income, profits and capital gains** | **0** | **0** | **0** | **0** | **0** | **0** | **0** | **0** | **0** | **0** |
| 1100 Of individuals | .. | .. | .. | .. | .. | .. | .. | .. | .. | .. |
| 1200 Corporate | .. | .. | .. | .. | .. | .. | .. | .. | .. | .. |
| 1300 Unallocable between 1100 and 1200 | .. | .. | .. | .. | .. | .. | .. | .. | .. | .. |
| **2000 Social security contributions** | **0** | **0** | **0** | **0** | **0** | **1** | **83 469** | **316 530** | **503 222** | **611 542** |
| 2100 Employees | .. | .. | .. | .. | .. | .. | .. | 75 509 | 114 653 | .. |
| 2200 Employers | .. | .. | .. | .. | .. | 0 | 18 709 | 240 280 | 369 094 | 127 503 |
| 2300 Self-employed or non-employed | .. | .. | .. | .. | .. | .. | .. | .. | .. | .. |
| 2400 Unallocable between 2100, 2200 and 2300 | .. | .. | .. | .. | .. | 1 | 64 760 | 741 | 19 474 | 484 039 |
| **3000 Taxes on payroll and workforce** | **0** | **0** | **0** | **0** | **0** | **0** | **0** | **0** | **0** | **0** |
| **4000 Taxes on property** | **0** | **5 469** | **23 285** | **41 426** | **58 253** | **0** | **0** | **0** | **0** | **0** |
| 4100 Recurrent taxes on immovable property | 0 | 4 519 | 17 444 | 31 521 | 44 964 | .. | .. | .. | .. | .. |
| 4200 Recurrent taxes on net wealth | 0 | 0 | 0 | 0 | 0 | .. | .. | .. | .. | .. |
| 4300 Estate, inheritance and gift taxes | 0 | 0 | 0 | 0 | 0 | .. | .. | .. | .. | .. |
| 4400 Taxes on financial and capital transactions | 0 | 950 | 5 840 | 9 904 | 13 290 | .. | .. | .. | .. | .. |
| 4500 Non-recurrent taxes | 0 | 0 | 0 | 0 | 0 | .. | .. | .. | .. | .. |
| 4600 Other recurrent taxes on property | 0 | 0 | 0 | 0 | 0 | .. | .. | .. | .. | .. |
| **5000 Taxes on goods and services** | **0** | **6 106** | **35 873** | **60 572** | **76 333** | **0** | **0** | **0** | **0** | **0** |
| 5100 Taxes on production, sale, transfer, etc | 0 | 6 106 | 35 873 | 60 572 | 76 333 | .. | .. | .. | .. | .. |
| 5110 General taxes[1] | 0 | 6 106 | 32 756 | 54 455 | 66 796 | .. | .. | .. | .. | .. |
| 5120 Taxes on specific goods and services | 0 | 0 | 3 117 | 6 118 | 9 537 | .. | .. | .. | .. | .. |
| 5130 Unallocable between 5110 and 5120 | 0 | 0 | 0 | 0 | 0 | .. | .. | .. | .. | .. |
| 5200 Taxes on use of goods and perform activities | 0 | 0 | 0 | 0 | 0 | .. | .. | .. | .. | .. |
| 5300 Unallocable between 5100 and 5200 | 0 | 0 | 0 | 0 | 0 | .. | .. | .. | .. | .. |
| **6000 Other taxes** | **0** | **377** | **5 456** | **8 509** | **8 533** | **0** | **0** | **0** | **0** | **0** |
| 6100 Paid solely by business | 0 | 0 | 0 | 0 | 0 | .. | .. | .. | .. | .. |
| 6200 Other | 0 | 377 | 5 456 | 8 509 | 8 533 | .. | .. | .. | .. | .. |
| **Total tax revenue** | **0** | **11 952** | **64 613** | **110 507** | **143 119** | **1** | **83 469** | **316 530** | **503 222** | **611 542** |

.. Not available

1. The PASEP (Program of Formation of the Patrimony of the Public Servants) contributions are added to the PIS (Social Integration Program) contributions in heading 5110 for the years prior to 2000.

StatLink https://doi.org/10.1787/888934309986

## Table 6.8. **Chile, tax revenues by sub-sectors of government**

*Million CLP*

| | Federal government | | | | | State/Regional | | | | |
|---|---|---|---|---|---|---|---|---|---|---|
| | 1990 | 2000 | 2010 | 2015 | 2020 | 1990 | 2000 | 2010 | 2015 | 2020 |
| **1000 Taxes on income, profits and capital gains** | **412 974** | **1 841 630** | **8 329 060** | **11 840 521** | **12 540 335** | **..** | **..** | **..** | **..** | **..** |
| 1100 Of individuals | 99 154 | 604 100 | 1 492 837 | 3 199 876 | 3 976 009 | .. | .. | .. | .. | .. |
| 1200 Corporate | 219 586 | 882 896 | 4 448 745 | 6 839 133 | 9 429 787 | .. | .. | .. | .. | .. |
| 1300 Unallocable between 1100 and 1200 | 94 233 | 354 634 | 2 387 478 | 1 801 512 | -865 461 | .. | .. | .. | .. | .. |
| **2000 Social security contributions** | **66 738** | **232 728** | **371 386** | **434 658** | **510 829** | **..** | **..** | **..** | **..** | **..** |
| 2100 Employees | 61 200 | 209 907 | 310 558 | 370 744 | 399 998 | .. | .. | .. | .. | .. |
| 2200 Employers | 5 538 | 22 821 | 60 828 | 63 914 | 110 830 | .. | .. | .. | .. | .. |
| 2300 Self-employed or non-employed | 0 | 0 | 0 | 0 | 0 | .. | .. | .. | .. | .. |
| 2400 Unallocable between 2100, 2200 and 2300 | 0 | 0 | 0 | 0 | 0 | .. | .. | .. | .. | .. |
| **3000 Taxes on payroll and workforce** | **0** | **0** | **0** | **0** | **0** | **..** | **..** | **..** | **..** | **..** |
| **4000 Taxes on property** | **59 682** | **255 371** | **245 044** | **379 603** | **534 971** | **..** | **..** | **..** | **..** | **..** |
| 4100 Recurrent taxes on immovable property | 10 331 | 3 578 | 8 805 | 15 249 | 25 367 | .. | .. | .. | .. | .. |
| 4200 Recurrent taxes on net wealth | 0 | 0 | 0 | 0 | 0 | .. | .. | .. | .. | .. |
| 4300 Estate, inheritance and gift taxes | 3 444 | 10 906 | 39 338 | 92 236 | 155 433 | .. | .. | .. | .. | .. |
| 4400 Taxes on financial and capital transactions | 45 907 | 240 886 | 196 901 | 272 118 | 354 171 | .. | .. | .. | .. | .. |
| 4500 Non-recurrent taxes | 0 | 0 | 0 | 0 | 0 | .. | .. | .. | .. | .. |
| 4600 Other recurrent taxes on property | 0 | 0 | 0 | 0 | 0 | .. | .. | .. | .. | .. |
| **5000 Taxes on goods and services** | **1 063 677** | **4 719 255** | **10 330 378** | **16 181 720** | **19 422 146** | **..** | **..** | **..** | **..** | **..** |
| 5100 Taxes on production, sale, transfer, etc | 1 060 304 | 4 684 525 | 10 294 165 | 16 129 953 | 19 209 620 | .. | .. | .. | .. | .. |
| 5110 General taxes | 664 421 | 3 306 350 | 8 399 926 | 13 273 958 | 15 963 032 | .. | .. | .. | .. | .. |
| 5120 Taxes on specific goods and services[1] | 395 883 | 1 378 175 | 1 894 239 | 2 855 995 | 3 246 588 | .. | .. | .. | .. | .. |
| 5130 Unallocable between 5110 and 5120 | 0 | 0 | 0 | 0 | 0 | .. | .. | .. | .. | .. |
| 5200 Taxes on use of goods and perform activities | 3 374 | 34 730 | 36 213 | 51 767 | 212 526 | .. | .. | .. | .. | .. |
| 5300 Unallocable between 5100 and 5200 | 0 | 0 | 0 | 0 | 0 | .. | .. | .. | .. | .. |
| **6000 Other taxes** | **-23 356** | **-112 195** | **-61 117** | **-579 308** | **-175 017** | **..** | **..** | **..** | **..** | **..** |
| 6100 Paid solely by business | 0 | 0 | 0 | 0 | 0 | .. | .. | .. | .. | .. |
| 6200 Other | -23 356 | -112 195 | -61 117 | -579 308 | -175 017 | .. | .. | .. | .. | .. |
| **Total tax revenue** | **1 579 715** | **6 936 788** | **19 214 751** | **28 257 194** | **32 833 263** | **..** | **..** | **..** | **..** | **..** |

*Million CLP*

| | Local government | | | | | Social Security Funds | | | | |
|---|---|---|---|---|---|---|---|---|---|---|
| | 1990 | 2000 | 2010 | 2015 | 2020 | 1990 | 2000 | 2010 | 2015 | 2020 |
| **1000 Taxes on income, profits and capital gains** | **0** | **0** | **0** | **0** | **0** | **0** | **0** | **0** | **0** | **0** |
| 1100 Of individuals | .. | .. | .. | .. | .. | .. | .. | .. | .. | .. |
| 1200 Corporate | .. | .. | .. | .. | .. | .. | .. | .. | .. | .. |
| 1300 Unallocable between 1100 and 1200 | .. | .. | .. | .. | .. | .. | .. | .. | .. | .. |
| **2000 Social security contributions** | **0** | **0** | **0** | **0** | **0** | **92 821** | **344 030** | **1 122 601** | **1 817 831** | **2 594 038** |
| 2100 Employees | .. | .. | .. | .. | .. | 92 821 | 344 030 | 1 122 601 | 1 817 831 | 2 594 038 |
| 2200 Employers | .. | .. | .. | .. | .. | 0 | 0 | 0 | 0 | 0 |
| 2300 Self-employed or non-employed | .. | .. | .. | .. | .. | 0 | 0 | 0 | 0 | 0 |
| 2400 Unallocable between 2100, 2200 and 2300 | .. | .. | .. | .. | .. | 0 | 0 | 0 | 0 | 0 |
| **3000 Taxes on payroll and workforce** | **0** | **0** | **0** | **0** | **0** | **0** | **0** | **0** | **0** | **0** |
| **4000 Taxes on property** | **49 637** | **298 666** | **653 563** | **1 041 671** | **1 476 033** | **0** | **0** | **0** | **0** | **0** |
| 4100 Recurrent taxes on immovable property | 49 637 | 298 666 | 653 563 | 1 041 671 | 1 476 033 | .. | .. | .. | .. | .. |
| 4200 Recurrent taxes on net wealth | 0 | 0 | 0 | 0 | 0 | .. | .. | .. | .. | .. |
| 4300 Estate, inheritance and gift taxes | 0 | 0 | 0 | 0 | 0 | .. | .. | .. | .. | .. |
| 4400 Taxes on financial and capital transactions | 0 | 0 | 0 | 0 | 0 | .. | .. | .. | .. | .. |
| 4500 Non-recurrent taxes | 0 | 0 | 0 | 0 | 0 | .. | .. | .. | .. | .. |
| 4600 Other recurrent taxes on property | 0 | 0 | 0 | 0 | 0 | .. | .. | .. | .. | .. |
| **5000 Taxes on goods and services** | **55 045** | **322 514** | **854 778** | **1 415 658** | **1 843 465** | **0** | **0** | **0** | **0** | **0** |
| 5100 Taxes on production, sale, transfer, etc | 13 705 | 105 302 | 238 739 | 385 532 | 399 440 | .. | .. | .. | .. | .. |
| 5110 General taxes | 0 | 0 | 0 | 0 | 0 | .. | .. | .. | .. | .. |
| 5120 Taxes on specific goods and services[1] | 13 705 | 105 302 | 238 739 | 385 532 | 399 440 | .. | .. | .. | .. | .. |
| 5130 Unallocable between 5110 and 5120 | 0 | 0 | 0 | 0 | 0 | .. | .. | .. | .. | .. |
| 5200 Taxes on use of goods and perform activities | 41 340 | 217 212 | 616 039 | 1 030 126 | 1 444 025 | .. | .. | .. | .. | .. |
| 5300 Unallocable between 5100 and 5200 | 0 | 0 | 0 | 0 | 0 | .. | .. | .. | .. | .. |
| **6000 Other taxes** | **0** | **0** | **0** | **0** | **0** | **0** | **0** | **0** | **0** | **0** |
| 6100 Paid solely by business | .. | .. | .. | .. | .. | .. | .. | .. | .. | .. |
| 6200 Other | .. | .. | .. | .. | .. | .. | .. | .. | .. | .. |
| **Total tax revenue** | **104 682** | **621 180** | **1 508 341** | **2 457 329** | **3 319 498** | **92 821** | **344 030** | **1 122 601** | **1 817 831** | **2 594 038** |

.. Not available

1. ECLAC classifies Oil Prices Stabilisation Fund (FEPP) revenues as non-tax revenues.

StatLink https://doi.org/10.1787/888934310005

## Table 6.9. **Colombia, tax revenues by sub-sectors of government**

*Million COP*

| | Federal government | | | | | State/Regional[1] | | | | |
|---|---|---|---|---|---|---|---|---|---|---|
| | 1990 | 2000 | 2010 | 2015 | 2020 | 1990 | 2000 | 2010 | 2015 | 2020 |
| **1000 Taxes on income, profits and capital gains** | **771 694** | **7 103 525** | **26 218 852** | **52 656 876** | **61 812 525** | **0** | **0** | **0** | **0** | **0** |
| 1100 Of individuals | 47 210 | 1 499 345 | 5 192 384 | 9 215 137 | 12 977 788 | .. | .. | .. | .. | .. |
| 1200 Corporate | 359 758 | 5 119 828 | 20 405 209 | 41 401 857 | 45 978 957 | .. | .. | .. | .. | .. |
| 1300 Unallocable between 1100 and 1200 | 364 726 | 484 352 | 621 258 | 2 039 882 | 2 855 780 | .. | .. | .. | .. | .. |
| **2000 Social security contributions** | **0** | **0** | **0** | **0** | **0** | **0** | **0** | **0** | **0** | **0** |
| 2100 Employees | .. | .. | .. | .. | .. | .. | .. | .. | .. | .. |
| 2200 Employers | .. | .. | .. | .. | .. | .. | .. | .. | .. | .. |
| 2300 Self-employed or non-employed | .. | .. | .. | .. | .. | .. | .. | .. | .. | .. |
| 2400 Unallocable between 2100, 2200 and 2300 | .. | .. | .. | .. | .. | .. | .. | .. | .. | .. |
| **3000 Taxes on payroll and workforce** | **0** | **1 286 803** | **4 022 503** | **2 797 308** | **3 670 490** | **0** | **0** | **0** | **0** | **0** |
| **4000 Taxes on property** | **0** | **1 036 584** | **5 196 303** | **12 094 140** | **9 057 760** | **0** | **0** | **0** | **0** | **0** |
| 4100 Recurrent taxes on immovable property | .. | 0 | 0 | 0 | 0 | .. | .. | .. | .. | .. |
| 4200 Recurrent taxes on net wealth | .. | 0 | 1 970 530 | 5 352 940 | 957 137 | .. | .. | .. | .. | .. |
| 4300 Estate, inheritance and gift taxes | .. | 0 | 0 | 0 | 0 | .. | .. | .. | .. | .. |
| 4400 Taxes on financial and capital transactions | .. | 1 036 584 | 3 225 773 | 6 741 200 | 7 476 295 | .. | .. | .. | .. | .. |
| 4500 Non-recurrent taxes | .. | 0 | 0 | 0 | 624 327 | .. | .. | .. | .. | .. |
| 4600 Other recurrent taxes on property | .. | 0 | 0 | 0 | 0 | .. | .. | .. | .. | .. |
| **5000 Taxes on goods and services** | **1 035 934** | **11 108 594** | **35 382 852** | **51 831 190** | **60 110 745** | **263 429** | **1 481 725** | **3 406 301** | **4 986 314** | **6 575 397** |
| 5100 Taxes on production, sale, transfer, etc | 1 035 934 | 11 108 594 | 35 382 852 | 51 831 190 | 60 110 745 | 263 429 | 1 349 930 | 3 032 733 | 4 456 650 | 5 548 940 |
| 5110 General taxes | 583 078 | 8 445 776 | 28 811 682 | 41 659 696 | 53 912 648 | 0 | 0 | 0 | 0 | 0 |
| 5120 Taxes on specific goods and services | 452 856 | 2 662 818 | 6 571 170 | 10 171 494 | 6 198 096 | 263 429 | 1 349 930 | 3 032 733 | 4 456 650 | 5 548 940 |
| 5130 Unallocable between 5110 and 5120 | 0 | 0 | 0 | 0 | 0 | 0 | 0 | 0 | 0 | 0 |
| 5200 Taxes on use of goods and perform activities | 0 | 0 | 0 | 0 | 0 | 0 | 131 795 | 373 568 | 529 665 | 1 026 457 |
| 5300 Unallocable between 5100 and 5200 | 0 | 0 | 0 | 0 | 0 | 0 | 0 | 0 | 0 | 0 |
| **6000 Other taxes** | **78 306** | **480 784** | **483 762** | **419 939** | **286 914** | **0** | **241 471** | **1 374 970** | **2 624 769** | **2 519 571** |
| 6100 Paid solely by business | 0 | 0 | 0 | 0 | 0 | .. | 0 | 0 | 0 | 0 |
| 6200 Other | 78 306 | 480 784 | 483 762 | 419 939 | 286 914 | .. | 241 471 | 1 374 970 | 2 624 769 | 2 519 571 |
| **Total tax revenue** | **1 885 934** | **21 016 290** | **71 304 272** | **119 799 453** | **134 938 434** | **263 429** | **1 723 196** | **4 781 271** | **7 611 084** | **9 094 967** |

*Million COP*

| | Local government[1] | | | | | Social Security Funds[2] | | | | |
|---|---|---|---|---|---|---|---|---|---|---|
| | 1990 | 2000 | 2010 | 2015 | 2020 | 1990 | 2000 | 2010 | 2015 | 2020 |
| **1000 Taxes on income, profits and capital gains** | **0** | **0** | **0** | **0** | **0** | **0** | **0** | **0** | **0** | **0** |
| 1100 Of individuals | .. | .. | .. | .. | .. | .. | .. | .. | .. | .. |
| 1200 Corporate | .. | .. | .. | .. | .. | .. | .. | .. | .. | .. |
| 1300 Unallocable between 1100 and 1200 | .. | .. | .. | .. | .. | .. | .. | .. | .. | .. |
| **2000 Social security contributions** | **0** | **0** | **0** | **0** | **0** | **203 596** | **4 989 000** | **11 478 085** | **13 585 138** | **18 615 408** |
| 2100 Employees | .. | .. | .. | .. | .. | .. | .. | .. | .. | .. |
| 2200 Employers | .. | .. | .. | .. | .. | .. | .. | .. | .. | .. |
| 2300 Self-employed or non-employed | .. | .. | .. | .. | .. | .. | .. | .. | .. | .. |
| 2400 Unallocable between 2100, 2200 and 2300 | .. | .. | .. | .. | .. | 203 596 | 4 989 000 | 11 478 085 | 13 585 138 | 18 615 408 |
| **3000 Taxes on payroll and workforce** | **0** | **0** | **0** | **0** | **0** | **0** | **0** | **0** | **0** | **0** |
| **4000 Taxes on property** | **56 160** | **991 070** | **3 338 935** | **6 061 965** | **9 109 598** | **0** | **0** | **0** | **0** | **0** |
| 4100 Recurrent taxes on immovable property | 56 160 | 991 070 | 3 338 935 | 6 061 965 | 9 109 598 | .. | .. | .. | .. | .. |
| 4200 Recurrent taxes on net wealth | 0 | 0 | 0 | 0 | 0 | .. | .. | .. | .. | .. |
| 4300 Estate, inheritance and gift taxes | 0 | 0 | 0 | 0 | 0 | .. | .. | .. | .. | .. |
| 4400 Taxes on financial and capital transactions | 0 | 0 | 0 | 0 | 0 | .. | .. | .. | .. | .. |
| 4500 Non-recurrent taxes | 0 | 0 | 0 | 0 | 0 | .. | .. | .. | .. | .. |
| 4600 Other recurrent taxes on property | 0 | 0 | 0 | 0 | 0 | .. | .. | .. | .. | .. |
| **5000 Taxes on goods and services** | **89 290** | **1 590 132** | **5 622 489** | **8 899 062** | **11 066 402** | **0** | **0** | **0** | **0** | **0** |
| 5100 Taxes on production, sale, transfer, etc | 89 290 | 1 590 132 | 5 622 489 | 8 400 241 | 10 300 667 | .. | .. | .. | .. | .. |
| 5110 General taxes | 89 290 | 1 140 090 | 4 522 121 | 7 025 204 | 8 954 004 | .. | .. | .. | .. | .. |
| 5120 Taxes on specific goods and services | 0 | 450 042 | 1 100 368 | 1 375 037 | 1 346 662 | .. | .. | .. | .. | .. |
| 5130 Unallocable between 5110 and 5120 | 0 | 0 | 0 | 0 | 0 | .. | .. | .. | .. | .. |
| 5200 Taxes on use of goods and perform activities | 0 | 0 | 0 | 498 821 | 765 735 | .. | .. | .. | .. | .. |
| 5300 Unallocable between 5100 and 5200 | 0 | 0 | 0 | 0 | 0 | .. | .. | .. | .. | .. |
| **6000 Other taxes** | **81 017** | **288 942** | **1 930 282** | **4 200 992** | **4 839 779** | **0** | **0** | **0** | **0** | **0** |
| 6100 Paid solely by business | 0 | 0 | 0 | 0 | 0 | .. | .. | .. | .. | .. |
| 6200 Other | 81 017 | 288 942 | 1 930 282 | 4 200 992 | 4 839 779 | .. | .. | .. | .. | .. |
| **Total tax revenue** | **226 467** | **2 870 144** | **10 891 707** | **19 162 019** | **25 015 779** | **203 596** | **4 989 000** | **11 478 085** | **13 585 138** | **18 615 408** |

.. Not available

1. The data correspond to the reported consolidated revenues of the territorial entities (departments and municipalities).
2. All of the health contributions pertaining to FOSYGA (Solidarity and Guarantee Fund) are classified as social security contributions from 2013. Prior to 2013, only the portion of the contributions used to finance the subsidised regime was included and the part to finance the contributory regime was classified in the social security sector as "other incomes".

StatLink https://doi.org/10.1787/888934310024

# Table 6.10. **Costa Rica, tax revenues by sub-sectors of government**

*Million CRC*

| | Federal government | | | | | State/Regional | | | | |
|---|---|---|---|---|---|---|---|---|---|---|
| | 1990 | 2000 | 2010 | 2015 | 2020 | 1990 | 2000 | 2010 | 2015 | 2020 |
| **1000 Taxes on income, profits and capital gains** | **11 820** | **128 805** | **748 093** | **1 247 308** | **1 651 249** | .. | .. | .. | .. | .. |
| 1100 Of individuals | .. | .. | 202 849 | 386 241 | 556 084 | .. | .. | .. | .. | .. |
| 1200 Corporate | .. | .. | 450 312 | 659 951 | 692 551 | .. | .. | .. | .. | .. |
| 1300 Unallocable between 1100 and 1200 | 11 820 | 128 805 | 94 932 | 201 116 | 402 613 | .. | .. | .. | .. | .. |
| **2000 Social security contributions[1]** | **1 345** | **18 677** | **61 193** | **63 458** | **79 428** | .. | .. | .. | .. | .. |
| 2100 Employees | .. | .. | .. | .. | .. | .. | .. | .. | .. | .. |
| 2200 Employers | 0 | 0 | 0 | 0 | 0 | .. | .. | .. | .. | .. |
| 2300 Self-employed or non-employed | .. | .. | .. | .. | .. | .. | .. | .. | .. | .. |
| 2400 Unallocable between 2100, 2200 and 2300 | 1 345 | 18 677 | 61 193 | 63 458 | 79 428 | .. | .. | .. | .. | .. |
| **3000 Taxes on payroll and workforce** | **0** | **0** | **0** | **0** | **0** | .. | .. | .. | .. | .. |
| **4000 Taxes on property** | **366** | **3 007** | **18 270** | **37 334** | **39 956** | .. | .. | .. | .. | .. |
| 4100 Recurrent taxes on immovable property | 0 | 0 | 3 527 | 4 076 | 4 655 | .. | .. | .. | .. | .. |
| 4200 Recurrent taxes on net wealth | 0 | 0 | 0 | 0 | 0 | .. | .. | .. | .. | .. |
| 4300 Estate, inheritance and gift taxes | 0 | 0 | 0 | 0 | 0 | .. | .. | .. | .. | .. |
| 4400 Taxes on financial and capital transactions | 366 | 3 007 | 14 743 | 33 258 | 35 300 | .. | .. | .. | .. | .. |
| 4500 Non-recurrent taxes | 0 | 0 | 0 | 0 | 0 | .. | .. | .. | .. | .. |
| 4600 Other recurrent taxes on property | 0 | 0 | 0 | 0 | 0 | .. | .. | .. | .. | .. |
| **5000 Taxes on goods and services** | **52 248** | **444 870** | **1 696 593** | **2 536 562** | **2 611 481** | .. | .. | .. | .. | .. |
| 5100 Taxes on production, sale, transfer, etc | 49 867 | 425 630 | 1 598 789 | 2 385 807 | 2 497 206 | .. | .. | .. | .. | .. |
| 5110 General taxes | 21 326 | 222 775 | 920 298 | 1 368 601 | 1 649 531 | .. | .. | .. | .. | .. |
| 5120 Taxes on specific goods and services[2] | 28 541 | 202 856 | 678 491 | 1 017 206 | 847 675 | .. | .. | .. | .. | .. |
| 5130 Unallocable between 5110 and 5120 | 0 | 0 | 0 | 0 | 0 | .. | .. | .. | .. | .. |
| 5200 Taxes on use of goods and perform activities | 2 380 | 19 240 | 97 804 | 150 755 | 114 275 | .. | .. | .. | .. | .. |
| 5300 Unallocable between 5100 and 5200 | 0 | 0 | 0 | 0 | 0 | .. | .. | .. | .. | .. |
| **6000 Other taxes[3]** | **9 251** | **23 956** | **92 452** | **162 200** | **166 912** | .. | .. | .. | .. | .. |
| 6100 Paid solely by business | 0 | 0 | 0 | 0 | 0 | .. | .. | .. | .. | .. |
| 6200 Other | 9 251 | 23 956 | 92 452 | 162 200 | 166 912 | .. | .. | .. | .. | .. |
| **Total tax revenue** | **75 030** | **619 314** | **2 616 600** | **4 046 862** | **4 549 026** | .. | .. | .. | .. | .. |

*Million CRC*

| | Local government | | | | | Social Security Funds | | | | |
|---|---|---|---|---|---|---|---|---|---|---|
| | 1990 | 2000 | 2010 | 2015 | 2020 | 1990 | 2000 | 2010 | 2015 | 2020 |
| **1000 Taxes on income, profits and capital gains** | **0** | **0** | **0** | **0** | **0** | **0** | **0** | **0** | **0** | **0** |
| 1100 Of individuals | .. | .. | .. | .. | .. | .. | .. | .. | .. | .. |
| 1200 Corporate | .. | .. | .. | .. | .. | .. | .. | .. | .. | .. |
| 1300 Unallocable between 1100 and 1200 | .. | .. | .. | .. | .. | .. | .. | .. | .. | .. |
| **2000 Social security contributions[1]** | **0** | **0** | **0** | **0** | **0** | **32 645** | **278 392** | **1 389 338** | **2 241 674** | **2 892 160** |
| 2100 Employees | .. | .. | .. | .. | .. | .. | .. | .. | .. | .. |
| 2200 Employers | .. | .. | .. | .. | .. | 3 447 | 37 313 | 207 206 | 318 652 | 387 840 |
| 2300 Self-employed or non-employed | .. | .. | .. | .. | .. | .. | .. | .. | .. | .. |
| 2400 Unallocable between 2100, 2200 and 2300 | .. | .. | .. | .. | .. | 29 198 | 241 079 | 1 182 132 | 1 923 022 | 2 504 321 |
| **3000 Taxes on payroll and workforce** | **0** | **0** | **0** | **0** | **0** | **7 575** | **61 796** | **260 664** | **423 616** | **537 654** |
| **4000 Taxes on property** | **1 200** | **5 390** | **45 436** | **85 927** | **122 994** | **0** | **0** | **0** | **0** | **0** |
| 4100 Recurrent taxes on immovable property | 1 200 | 5 390 | 45 436 | 85 927 | 122 970 | .. | .. | .. | .. | .. |
| 4200 Recurrent taxes on net wealth | 0 | 0 | 0 | 0 | 0 | .. | .. | .. | .. | .. |
| 4300 Estate, inheritance and gift taxes | 0 | 0 | 0 | 0 | 0 | .. | .. | .. | .. | .. |
| 4400 Taxes on financial and capital transactions | 0 | 0 | 0 | 0 | 0 | .. | .. | .. | .. | .. |
| 4500 Non-recurrent taxes | 0 | 0 | 0 | 0 | 24 | .. | .. | .. | .. | .. |
| 4600 Other recurrent taxes on property | 0 | 0 | 0 | 0 | 0 | .. | .. | .. | .. | .. |
| **5000 Taxes on goods and services** | **1 262** | **11 981** | **70 321** | **125 341** | **133 636** | **0** | **0** | **0** | **0** | **0** |
| 5100 Taxes on production, sale, transfer, etc | 0 | 83 | 1 513 | 3 093 | 3 304 | .. | .. | .. | .. | .. |
| 5110 General taxes | .. | 0 | 0 | 0 | 0 | .. | .. | .. | .. | .. |
| 5120 Taxes on specific goods and services[2] | .. | 83 | 1 513 | 3 093 | 3 304 | .. | .. | .. | .. | .. |
| 5130 Unallocable between 5110 and 5120 | .. | 0 | 0 | 0 | 0 | .. | .. | .. | .. | .. |
| 5200 Taxes on use of goods and perform activities | 1 262 | 11 898 | 68 808 | 122 248 | 130 332 | .. | .. | .. | .. | .. |
| 5300 Unallocable between 5100 and 5200 | 0 | 0 | 0 | 0 | 0 | .. | .. | .. | .. | .. |
| **6000 Other taxes[3]** | **0** | **1 242** | **8** | **155** | **58** | **0** | **0** | **0** | **0** | **0** |
| 6100 Paid solely by business | .. | 0 | 0 | 0 | 0 | .. | .. | .. | .. | .. |
| 6200 Other | .. | 1 242 | 8 | 155 | 58 | .. | .. | .. | .. | .. |
| **Total tax revenue** | **2 461** | **18 613** | **115 765** | **211 422** | **256 688** | **40 220** | **340 187** | **1 650 002** | **2 665 291** | **3 429 814** |

.. Not available

1. The data include social security contributions paid by the governments for their employees as well as the contributions for special regimes (teachers and magistrates). In ECLAC data, social security contributions also include INA (National Institute of Apprenticeship), IMAS (Joint Social Aid Institute) and FODESAF (Social Development and Family Allowances Fund).
2. In ECLAC data, the tax on ownership of vehicles, aircraft and boats is classified in category 4000.
3. The tax revenue of decentralised bodies is classified under the central government. In Costa Rica this revenue is classified under a separate unit (decentralised) considered to be different to the central government.

StatLink https://doi.org/10.1787/888934310043

## Table 6.11. **Cuba, tax revenues by sub-sectors of government**

*Million CUP*

| | Federal government[1] | | | | | State/Regional | | | | |
|---|---|---|---|---|---|---|---|---|---|---|
| | 1990 | 2000 | 2010 | 2015 | 2020 | 1990 | 2000 | 2010 | 2015 | 2020 |
| **1000 Taxes on income, profits and capital gains** | .. | .. | **1 857** | .. | .. | .. | .. | .. | .. | .. |
| 1100 Of individuals | .. | .. | 0 | .. | .. | .. | .. | .. | .. | .. |
| 1200 Corporate | .. | .. | 1 857 | .. | .. | .. | .. | .. | .. | .. |
| 1300 Unallocable between 1100 and 1200 | .. | .. | 0 | .. | .. | .. | .. | .. | .. | .. |
| **2000 Social security contributions** | .. | .. | **0** | .. | .. | .. | .. | .. | .. | .. |
| 2100 Employees | .. | .. | .. | .. | .. | .. | .. | .. | .. | .. |
| 2200 Employers | .. | .. | .. | .. | .. | .. | .. | .. | .. | .. |
| 2300 Self-employed or non-employed | .. | .. | .. | .. | .. | .. | .. | .. | .. | .. |
| 2400 Unallocable between 2100, 2200 and 2300 | .. | .. | .. | .. | .. | .. | .. | .. | .. | .. |
| **3000 Taxes on payroll and workforce** | .. | .. | **289** | .. | .. | .. | .. | .. | .. | .. |
| **4000 Taxes on property** | .. | .. | **0** | .. | .. | .. | .. | .. | .. | .. |
| 4100 Recurrent taxes on immovable property | .. | .. | .. | .. | .. | .. | .. | .. | .. | .. |
| 4200 Recurrent taxes on net wealth | .. | .. | .. | .. | .. | .. | .. | .. | .. | .. |
| 4300 Estate, inheritance and gift taxes | .. | .. | .. | .. | .. | .. | .. | .. | .. | .. |
| 4400 Taxes on financial and capital transactions | .. | .. | .. | .. | .. | .. | .. | .. | .. | .. |
| 4500 Non-recurrent taxes | .. | .. | .. | .. | .. | .. | .. | .. | .. | .. |
| 4600 Other recurrent taxes on property | .. | .. | .. | .. | .. | .. | .. | .. | .. | .. |
| **5000 Taxes on goods and services** | .. | .. | **5 757** | .. | .. | .. | .. | .. | .. | .. |
| 5100 Taxes on production, sale, transfer, etc | .. | .. | 5 757 | .. | .. | .. | .. | .. | .. | .. |
| 5110 General taxes | .. | .. | 4 924 | .. | .. | .. | .. | .. | .. | .. |
| 5120 Taxes on specific goods and services | .. | .. | 833 | .. | .. | .. | .. | .. | .. | .. |
| 5130 Unallocable between 5110 and 5120 | .. | .. | 0 | .. | .. | .. | .. | .. | .. | .. |
| 5200 Taxes on use of goods and perform activities | .. | .. | 0 | .. | .. | .. | .. | .. | .. | .. |
| 5300 Unallocable between 5100 and 5200 | .. | .. | 0 | .. | .. | .. | .. | .. | .. | .. |
| **6000 Other taxes** | .. | .. | **569** | .. | .. | .. | .. | .. | .. | .. |
| 6100 Paid solely by business | .. | .. | .. | .. | .. | .. | .. | .. | .. | .. |
| 6200 Other | .. | .. | .. | .. | .. | .. | .. | .. | .. | .. |
| **Total tax revenue** | .. | .. | **8 472** | .. | .. | .. | .. | .. | .. | .. |

*Million CUP*

| | Local government[2] | | | | | Social Security Funds | | | | |
|---|---|---|---|---|---|---|---|---|---|---|
| | 1990 | 2000 | 2010 | 2015 | 2020 | 1990 | 2000 | 2010 | 2015 | 2020 |
| **1000 Taxes on income, profits and capital gains** | .. | .. | **1 746** | .. | .. | **0** | **0** | **0** | **0** | **0** |
| 1100 Of individuals | .. | .. | 554 | .. | .. | .. | .. | .. | .. | .. |
| 1200 Corporate | .. | .. | 1 193 | .. | .. | .. | .. | .. | .. | .. |
| 1300 Unallocable between 1100 and 1200 | .. | .. | 0 | .. | .. | .. | .. | .. | .. | .. |
| **2000 Social security contributions** | .. | .. | **0** | .. | .. | **691** | **1 181** | **2 974** | **4 322** | **6 433** |
| 2100 Employees | .. | .. | .. | .. | .. | .. | .. | .. | .. | .. |
| 2200 Employers | .. | .. | .. | .. | .. | .. | .. | .. | .. | .. |
| 2300 Self-employed or non-employed | .. | .. | .. | .. | .. | .. | .. | .. | .. | .. |
| 2400 Unallocable between 2100, 2200 and 2300 | .. | .. | .. | .. | .. | 691 | 1 181 | 2 974 | 4 322 | 6 433 |
| **3000 Taxes on payroll and workforce** | .. | .. | **4 125** | .. | .. | **0** | **0** | **0** | **0** | **0** |
| **4000 Taxes on property** | .. | .. | **0** | .. | .. | **0** | **0** | **0** | **0** | **0** |
| 4100 Recurrent taxes on immovable property | .. | .. | .. | .. | .. | .. | .. | .. | .. | .. |
| 4200 Recurrent taxes on net wealth | .. | .. | .. | .. | .. | .. | .. | .. | .. | .. |
| 4300 Estate, inheritance and gift taxes | .. | .. | .. | .. | .. | .. | .. | .. | .. | .. |
| 4400 Taxes on financial and capital transactions | .. | .. | .. | .. | .. | .. | .. | .. | .. | .. |
| 4500 Non-recurrent taxes | .. | .. | .. | .. | .. | .. | .. | .. | .. | .. |
| 4600 Other recurrent taxes on property | .. | .. | .. | .. | .. | .. | .. | .. | .. | .. |
| **5000 Taxes on goods and services** | .. | .. | **6 526** | .. | .. | **0** | **0** | **0** | **0** | **0** |
| 5100 Taxes on production, sale, transfer, etc | .. | .. | 6 526 | .. | .. | .. | .. | .. | .. | .. |
| 5110 General taxes | .. | .. | 5 601 | .. | .. | .. | .. | .. | .. | .. |
| 5120 Taxes on specific goods and services | .. | .. | 925 | .. | .. | .. | .. | .. | .. | .. |
| 5130 Unallocable between 5110 and 5120 | .. | .. | 0 | .. | .. | .. | .. | .. | .. | .. |
| 5200 Taxes on use of goods and perform activities | .. | .. | 0 | .. | .. | .. | .. | .. | .. | .. |
| 5300 Unallocable between 5100 and 5200 | .. | .. | 0 | .. | .. | .. | .. | .. | .. | .. |
| **6000 Other taxes** | .. | .. | **106** | .. | .. | **0** | **0** | **0** | **0** | **0** |
| 6100 Paid solely by business | .. | .. | .. | .. | .. | .. | .. | .. | .. | .. |
| 6200 Other | .. | .. | .. | .. | .. | .. | .. | .. | .. | .. |
| **Total tax revenue** | .. | .. | **12 503** | .. | .. | **691** | **1 181** | **2 974** | **4 322** | **6 433** |

.. Not available

1. The figures include central government tax revenues between 2002 and 2012. Central tax revenues are not available for other years.
2. The figures include local government tax revenues between 2002 and 2012. Local tax revenues are not available for other years.

StatLink https://doi.org/10.1787/888934310062

## Table 6.12. **Dominican Republic, tax revenues by sub-sectors of government**

*Million DOP*

| | Federal government | | | | | State/Regional | | | | |
|---|---|---|---|---|---|---|---|---|---|---|
| | 1990 | 2000 | 2010 | 2015 | 2020 | 1990 | 2000 | 2010 | 2015 | 2020 |
| **1000 Taxes on income, profits and capital gains** | **1 650** | **10 708** | **53 492** | **119 580** | **188 486** | .. | .. | .. | .. | .. |
| 1100 Of individuals | .. | 4 088 | 17 088 | 35 549 | 58 747 | .. | .. | .. | .. | .. |
| 1200 Corporate | .. | 4 605 | 21 325 | 61 455 | 90 442 | .. | .. | .. | .. | .. |
| 1300 Unallocable between 1100 and 1200 | 1 670 | 2 015 | 15 080 | 22 576 | 39 297 | .. | .. | .. | .. | .. |
| **2000 Social security contributions** | **0** | **0** | **0** | **0** | **0** | .. | .. | .. | .. | .. |
| 2100 Employees | .. | .. | .. | .. | .. | .. | .. | .. | .. | .. |
| 2200 Employers | .. | .. | .. | .. | .. | .. | .. | .. | .. | .. |
| 2300 Self-employed or non-employed | .. | .. | .. | .. | .. | .. | .. | .. | .. | .. |
| 2400 Unallocable between 2100, 2200 and 2300 | .. | .. | .. | .. | .. | .. | .. | .. | .. | .. |
| **3000 Taxes on payroll and workforce[1]** | **0** | **0** | **1 385** | **2 366** | **3 141** | .. | .. | .. | .. | .. |
| **4000 Taxes on property** | **74** | **689** | **13 315** | **19 044** | **25 252** | .. | .. | .. | .. | .. |
| 4100 Recurrent taxes on immovable property | 9 | 115 | 555 | 1 755 | 2 857 | .. | .. | .. | .. | .. |
| 4200 Recurrent taxes on net wealth | 0 | 0 | 2 449 | 3 445 | 4 522 | .. | .. | .. | .. | .. |
| 4300 Estate, inheritance and gift taxes | 11 | 96 | 231 | 418 | 523 | .. | .. | .. | .. | .. |
| 4400 Taxes on financial and capital transactions | 40 | 377 | 8 658 | 12 067 | 15 634 | .. | .. | .. | .. | .. |
| 4500 Non-recurrent taxes | 3 | 32 | 488 | 591 | 779 | .. | .. | .. | .. | .. |
| 4600 Other recurrent taxes on property | 11 | 70 | 934 | 769 | 936 | .. | .. | .. | .. | .. |
| **5000 Taxes on goods and services** | **4 487** | **35 927** | **175 290** | **274 137** | **340 031** | .. | .. | .. | .. | .. |
| 5100 Taxes on production, sale, transfer, etc | 4 418 | 35 209 | 168 791 | 263 675 | 328 258 | .. | .. | .. | .. | .. |
| 5110 General taxes | 970 | 9 912 | 81 226 | 147 039 | 194 408 | .. | .. | .. | .. | .. |
| 5120 Taxes on specific goods and services | 3 449 | 25 297 | 87 566 | 116 636 | 133 851 | .. | .. | .. | .. | .. |
| 5130 Unallocable between 5110 and 5120 | 0 | 0 | 0 | 0 | 0 | .. | .. | .. | .. | .. |
| 5200 Taxes on use of goods and perform activities | 69 | 718 | 6 498 | 10 463 | 11 773 | .. | .. | .. | .. | .. |
| 5300 Unallocable between 5100 and 5200 | 0 | 0 | 0 | 0 | 0 | .. | .. | .. | .. | .. |
| **6000 Other taxes** | **159** | **495** | **0** | **1** | **1** | .. | .. | .. | .. | .. |
| 6100 Paid solely by business | 0 | 0 | .. | 0 | 0 | .. | .. | .. | .. | .. |
| 6200 Other | 159 | 495 | .. | 1 | 1 | .. | .. | .. | .. | .. |
| **Total tax revenue** | **6 371** | **47 820** | **243 482** | **415 128** | **556 911** | .. | .. | .. | .. | .. |

*Million DOP*

| | Local government[2] | | | | | Social Security Funds[3] | | | | |
|---|---|---|---|---|---|---|---|---|---|---|
| | 1990 | 2000 | 2010 | 2015 | 2020 | 1990 | 2000 | 2010 | 2015 | 2020 |
| **1000 Taxes on income, profits and capital gains** | .. | .. | .. | .. | .. | **0** | **0** | **0** | **0** | **0** |
| 1100 Of individuals | .. | .. | .. | .. | .. | .. | .. | .. | .. | .. |
| 1200 Corporate | .. | .. | .. | .. | .. | .. | .. | .. | .. | .. |
| 1300 Unallocable between 1100 and 1200 | .. | .. | .. | .. | .. | .. | .. | .. | .. | .. |
| **2000 Social security contributions** | .. | .. | .. | .. | .. | **53** | **490** | **1 845** | **1 483** | **2 661** |
| 2100 Employees | .. | .. | .. | .. | .. | .. | .. | 1 720 | 1 321 | .. |
| 2200 Employers | .. | .. | .. | .. | .. | .. | .. | 125 | 163 | .. |
| 2300 Self-employed or non-employed | .. | .. | .. | .. | .. | .. | .. | 0 | 0 | .. |
| 2400 Unallocable between 2100, 2200 and 2300 | .. | .. | .. | .. | .. | 53 | 490 | 0 | 0 | 2 661 |
| **3000 Taxes on payroll and workforce[1]** | .. | .. | .. | .. | .. | **0** | **0** | **0** | **0** | **0** |
| **4000 Taxes on property** | .. | .. | .. | .. | .. | **0** | **0** | **0** | **0** | **0** |
| 4100 Recurrent taxes on immovable property | .. | .. | .. | .. | .. | .. | .. | .. | .. | .. |
| 4200 Recurrent taxes on net wealth | .. | .. | .. | .. | .. | .. | .. | .. | .. | .. |
| 4300 Estate, inheritance and gift taxes | .. | .. | .. | .. | .. | .. | .. | .. | .. | .. |
| 4400 Taxes on financial and capital transactions | .. | .. | .. | .. | .. | .. | .. | .. | .. | .. |
| 4500 Non-recurrent taxes | .. | .. | .. | .. | .. | .. | .. | .. | .. | .. |
| 4600 Other recurrent taxes on property | .. | .. | .. | .. | .. | .. | .. | .. | .. | .. |
| **5000 Taxes on goods and services** | .. | .. | .. | .. | .. | **0** | **0** | **0** | **0** | **0** |
| 5100 Taxes on production, sale, transfer, etc | .. | .. | .. | .. | .. | .. | .. | .. | .. | .. |
| 5110 General taxes | .. | .. | .. | .. | .. | .. | .. | .. | .. | .. |
| 5120 Taxes on specific goods and services | .. | .. | .. | .. | .. | .. | .. | .. | .. | .. |
| 5130 Unallocable between 5110 and 5120 | .. | .. | .. | .. | .. | .. | .. | .. | .. | .. |
| 5200 Taxes on use of goods and perform activities | .. | .. | .. | .. | .. | .. | .. | .. | .. | .. |
| 5300 Unallocable between 5100 and 5200 | .. | .. | .. | .. | .. | .. | .. | .. | .. | .. |
| **6000 Other taxes** | .. | .. | .. | .. | .. | **0** | **0** | **0** | **0** | **0** |
| 6100 Paid solely by business | .. | .. | .. | .. | .. | .. | .. | .. | .. | .. |
| 6200 Other | .. | .. | .. | .. | .. | .. | .. | .. | .. | .. |
| **Total tax revenue** | .. | .. | .. | .. | .. | **53** | **490** | **1 845** | **1 483** | **2 661** |

.. Not available

1. This heading includes the mandatory non-pensions contributions to the Instituto de Formacion Tecnico Profesinal (INFOTEP). The tax revenue is classified under the central government. In Dominican Republic this revenue is classified under a separate unit (decentralised) considered to be different to the central government.
2. The figures exclude local government tax revenues as the data are not available.
3. The figures exclude social security contributions to general government managed by the private sector.

StatLink https://doi.org/10.1787/888934310081

## Table 6.13. **Ecuador, tax revenues by sub-sectors of government**

*Million USD*

| | Federal government | | | | | State/Regional | | | | |
|---|---|---|---|---|---|---|---|---|---|---|
| | 1990 | 2000 | 2010 | 2015 | 2020 | 1990 | 2000 | 2010 | 2015 | 2020 |
| **1000 Taxes on income, profits and capital gains** | **138** | **267** | **2 909** | **4 935** | **4 453** | **..** | **..** | **..** | **..** | **..** |
| 1100 Of individuals | .. | 10 | 80 | 192 | 155 | .. | .. | .. | .. | .. |
| 1200 Corporate | .. | 53 | 1 046 | 1 723 | 1 333 | .. | .. | .. | .. | .. |
| 1300 Unallocable between 1100 and 1200 | 138 | 204 | 1 783 | 3 020 | 2 965 | .. | .. | .. | .. | .. |
| **2000 Social security contributions** | **0** | **0** | **0** | **0** | **0** | **..** | **..** | **..** | **..** | **..** |
| 2100 Employees | .. | .. | .. | .. | .. | .. | .. | .. | .. | .. |
| 2200 Employers | .. | .. | .. | .. | .. | .. | .. | .. | .. | .. |
| 2300 Self-employed or non-employed | .. | .. | .. | .. | .. | .. | .. | .. | .. | .. |
| 2400 Unallocable between 2100, 2200 and 2300 | .. | .. | .. | .. | .. | .. | .. | .. | .. | .. |
| **3000 Taxes on payroll and workforce** | **0** | **0** | **0** | **0** | **0** | **..** | **..** | **..** | **..** | **..** |
| **4000 Taxes on property** | **0** | **0** | **43** | **88** | **56** | **..** | **..** | **..** | **..** | **..** |
| 4100 Recurrent taxes on immovable property | .. | .. | 3 | 9 | 0 | .. | .. | .. | .. | .. |
| 4200 Recurrent taxes on net wealth | .. | .. | 35 | 49 | 31 | .. | .. | .. | .. | .. |
| 4300 Estate, inheritance and gift taxes | .. | .. | 5 | 29 | 24 | .. | .. | .. | .. | .. |
| 4400 Taxes on financial and capital transactions | .. | .. | 0 | 0 | 0 | .. | .. | .. | .. | .. |
| 4500 Non-recurrent taxes | .. | .. | 0 | 0 | 0 | .. | .. | .. | .. | .. |
| 4600 Other recurrent taxes on property | .. | .. | 0 | 0 | 0 | .. | .. | .. | .. | .. |
| **5000 Taxes on goods and services** | **668** | **1 596** | **5 969** | **10 959** | **8 402** | **..** | **..** | **..** | **..** | **..** |
| 5100 Taxes on production, sale, transfer, etc | 665 | 1 574 | 5 814 | 10 623 | 8 203 | .. | .. | .. | .. | .. |
| 5110 General taxes | 302 | 923 | 3 759 | 6 468 | 5 398 | .. | .. | .. | .. | .. |
| 5120 Taxes on specific goods and services | 363 | 651 | 2 054 | 4 155 | 2 805 | .. | .. | .. | .. | .. |
| 5130 Unallocable between 5110 and 5120 | 0 | 0 | 0 | 0 | 0 | .. | .. | .. | .. | .. |
| 5200 Taxes on use of goods and perform activities | 3 | 22 | 156 | 336 | 200 | .. | .. | .. | .. | .. |
| 5300 Unallocable between 5100 and 5200 | 0 | 0 | 0 | 0 | 0 | .. | .. | .. | .. | .. |
| **6000 Other taxes** | **0** | **0** | **4** | **10** | **20** | **..** | **..** | **..** | **..** | **..** |
| 6100 Paid solely by business | .. | .. | 0 | 0 | 0 | .. | .. | .. | .. | .. |
| 6200 Other | .. | .. | 4 | 10 | 20 | .. | .. | .. | .. | .. |
| **Total tax revenue** | **806** | **1 863** | **8 925** | **15 992** | **12 931** | **..** | **..** | **..** | **..** | **..** |

*Million USD*

| | Local government[1] | | | | | Social Security Funds[2] | | | | |
|---|---|---|---|---|---|---|---|---|---|---|
| | 1990 | 2000 | 2010 | 2015 | 2020 | 1990 | 2000 | 2010 | 2015 | 2020 |
| **1000 Taxes on income, profits and capital gains** | **1** | **2** | **15** | **75** | **50** | **0** | **0** | **0** | **0** | **0** |
| 1100 Of individuals | .. | .. | 0 | 0 | 0 | .. | .. | .. | .. | .. |
| 1200 Corporate | .. | .. | .. | .. | .. | .. | .. | .. | .. | .. |
| 1300 Unallocable between 1100 and 1200 | 1 | 2 | 15 | 75 | 50 | .. | .. | .. | .. | .. |
| **2000 Social security contributions** | **0** | **0** | **0** | **0** | **0** | **243** | **228** | **2 541** | **5 062** | **5 443** |
| 2100 Employees | .. | .. | .. | .. | .. | .. | .. | .. | .. | .. |
| 2200 Employers | .. | .. | .. | .. | .. | .. | .. | .. | .. | .. |
| 2300 Self-employed or non-employed | .. | .. | .. | .. | .. | .. | .. | .. | .. | .. |
| 2400 Unallocable between 2100, 2200 and 2300 | .. | .. | .. | .. | .. | 243 | 228 | 2 541 | 5 062 | 5 443 |
| **3000 Taxes on payroll and workforce** | **0** | **0** | **0** | **0** | **0** | **0** | **0** | **0** | **0** | **0** |
| **4000 Taxes on property** | **16** | **17** | **116** | **216** | **278** | **0** | **0** | **0** | **0** | **0** |
| 4100 Recurrent taxes on immovable property | 13 | 8 | 66 | 125 | 172 | .. | .. | .. | .. | .. |
| 4200 Recurrent taxes on net wealth | 0 | 0 | 0 | 0 | 0 | .. | .. | .. | .. | .. |
| 4300 Estate, inheritance and gift taxes | 0 | 0 | 0 | 0 | 0 | .. | .. | .. | .. | .. |
| 4400 Taxes on financial and capital transactions | 0 | 0 | 0 | 0 | 0 | .. | .. | .. | .. | .. |
| 4500 Non-recurrent taxes | 0 | 0 | 0 | 0 | 0 | .. | .. | .. | .. | .. |
| 4600 Other recurrent taxes on property | 3 | 9 | 50 | 91 | 107 | .. | .. | .. | .. | .. |
| **5000 Taxes on goods and services** | **10** | **13** | **97** | **246** | **207** | **0** | **0** | **0** | **0** | **0** |
| 5100 Taxes on production, sale, transfer, etc | 6 | 6 | 49 | 89 | 65 | .. | .. | .. | .. | .. |
| 5110 General taxes | 4 | 5 | 41 | 79 | 61 | .. | .. | .. | .. | .. |
| 5120 Taxes on specific goods and services | 1 | 2 | 8 | 10 | 3 | .. | .. | .. | .. | .. |
| 5130 Unallocable between 5110 and 5120 | 0 | 0 | 0 | 0 | 0 | .. | .. | .. | .. | .. |
| 5200 Taxes on use of goods and perform activities | 5 | 7 | 48 | 157 | 142 | .. | .. | .. | .. | .. |
| 5300 Unallocable between 5100 and 5200 | 0 | 0 | 0 | 0 | 0 | .. | .. | .. | .. | .. |
| **6000 Other taxes** | **2** | **2** | **1** | **0** | **0** | **0** | **0** | **0** | **0** | **0** |
| 6100 Paid solely by business | 0 | 0 | 0 | 0 | 0 | .. | .. | .. | .. | .. |
| 6200 Other | 2 | 2 | 1 | 0 | 0 | .. | .. | .. | .. | .. |
| **Total tax revenue** | **29** | **34** | **228** | **537** | **535** | **243** | **228** | **2 541** | **5 062** | **5 443** |

.. Not available

1. Local tax revenues come from the Development Bank of Ecuador.
2. Social security contributions are collected from non-financial public sector operations published by the Central Bank of Ecuador.

StatLink https://doi.org/10.1787/888934310100

## Table 6.14. **El Salvador, tax revenues by sub-sectors of government**

*Million USD*

| | Federal government | | | | | State/Regional | | | | |
|---|---|---|---|---|---|---|---|---|---|---|
| | 1990 | 2000 | 2010 | 2015 | 2020 | 1990 | 2000 | 2010 | 2015 | 2020 |
| **1000 Taxes on income, profits and capital gains** | **95** | **429** | **996** | **1 545** | **1 954** | .. | .. | .. | .. | .. |
| 1100 Of individuals | .. | .. | 590 | 774 | 820 | .. | .. | .. | .. | .. |
| 1200 Corporate | .. | .. | 420 | 622 | 934 | .. | .. | .. | .. | .. |
| 1300 Unallocable between 1100 and 1200 | 95 | 429 | -14 | 148 | 201 | .. | .. | .. | .. | .. |
| **2000 Social security contributions** | **0** | **0** | **0** | **0** | **0** | .. | .. | .. | .. | .. |
| 2100 Employees | .. | .. | .. | .. | .. | .. | .. | .. | .. | .. |
| 2200 Employers | .. | .. | .. | .. | .. | .. | .. | .. | .. | .. |
| 2300 Self-employed or non-employed | .. | .. | .. | .. | .. | .. | .. | .. | .. | .. |
| 2400 Unallocable between 2100, 2200 and 2300 | .. | .. | .. | .. | .. | .. | .. | .. | .. | .. |
| **3000 Taxes on payroll and workforce[1]** | **0** | **0** | **21** | **30** | **36** | .. | .. | .. | .. | .. |
| **4000 Taxes on property** | **26** | **12** | **16** | **107** | **21** | .. | .. | .. | .. | .. |
| 4100 Recurrent taxes on immovable property | 0 | 0 | 0 | 0 | 0 | .. | .. | .. | .. | .. |
| 4200 Recurrent taxes on net wealth | 16 | 0 | 0 | 0 | 0 | .. | .. | .. | .. | .. |
| 4300 Estate, inheritance and gift taxes | 0 | 0 | 0 | 0 | 0 | .. | .. | .. | .. | .. |
| 4400 Taxes on financial and capital transactions | 10 | 12 | 16 | 107 | 21 | .. | .. | .. | .. | .. |
| 4500 Non-recurrent taxes | 0 | 0 | 0 | 0 | 0 | .. | .. | .. | .. | .. |
| 4600 Other recurrent taxes on property | 0 | 0 | 0 | 0 | 0 | .. | .. | .. | .. | .. |
| **5000 Taxes on goods and services** | **259** | **903** | **1 871** | **2 266** | **2 574** | .. | .. | .. | .. | .. |
| 5100 Taxes on production, sale, transfer, etc | 259 | 903 | 1 863 | 2 254 | 2 561 | .. | .. | .. | .. | .. |
| 5110 General taxes | 133 | 714 | 1 433 | 1 764 | 2 033 | .. | .. | .. | .. | .. |
| 5120 Taxes on specific goods and services | 127 | 189 | 431 | 490 | 528 | .. | .. | .. | .. | .. |
| 5130 Unallocable between 5110 and 5120 | 0 | 0 | 0 | 0 | 0 | .. | .. | .. | .. | .. |
| 5200 Taxes on use of goods and perform activities | 0 | 0 | 7 | 12 | 12 | .. | .. | .. | .. | .. |
| 5300 Unallocable between 5100 and 5200 | 0 | 0 | 0 | 0 | 0 | .. | .. | .. | .. | .. |
| **6000 Other taxes** | **58** | **0** | **0** | **0** | **0** | .. | .. | .. | .. | .. |
| 6100 Paid solely by business | 0 | 0 | .. | .. | .. | .. | .. | .. | .. | .. |
| 6200 Other | 58 | 0 | .. | .. | .. | .. | .. | .. | .. | .. |
| **Total tax revenue** | **438** | **1 344** | **2 903** | **3 947** | **4 585** | .. | .. | .. | .. | .. |

*Million USD*

| | Local government | | | | | Social Security Funds[2] | | | | |
|---|---|---|---|---|---|---|---|---|---|---|
| | 1990 | 2000 | 2010 | 2015 | 2020 | 1990 | 2000 | 2010 | 2015 | 2020 |
| **1000 Taxes on income, profits and capital gains** | .. | .. | **0** | **0** | **0** | **0** | **0** | **0** | **0** | **0** |
| 1100 Of individuals | .. | .. | .. | .. | .. | .. | .. | .. | .. | .. |
| 1200 Corporate | .. | .. | .. | .. | .. | .. | .. | .. | .. | .. |
| 1300 Unallocable between 1100 and 1200 | .. | .. | .. | .. | .. | .. | .. | .. | .. | .. |
| **2000 Social security contributions** | .. | .. | **0** | **0** | **0** | **104** | **325** | **470** | **608** | **700** |
| 2100 Employees | .. | .. | .. | .. | .. | .. | 75 | 165 | 214 | 246 |
| 2200 Employers | .. | .. | .. | .. | .. | .. | 176 | 306 | 393 | 454 |
| 2300 Self-employed or non-employed | .. | .. | .. | .. | .. | .. | 13 | 0 | 0 | 0 |
| 2400 Unallocable between 2100, 2200 and 2300 | .. | .. | .. | .. | .. | 104 | 62 | 0 | 0 | 0 |
| **3000 Taxes on payroll and workforce[1]** | .. | .. | **0** | **0** | **0** | **0** | **0** | **0** | **0** | **0** |
| **4000 Taxes on property** | .. | .. | **3** | **5** | **6** | **0** | **0** | **0** | **0** | **0** |
| 4100 Recurrent taxes on immovable property | .. | .. | 3 | 5 | 6 | .. | .. | .. | .. | .. |
| 4200 Recurrent taxes on net wealth | .. | .. | 0 | 0 | 0 | .. | .. | .. | .. | .. |
| 4300 Estate, inheritance and gift taxes | .. | .. | 0 | 0 | 0 | .. | .. | .. | .. | .. |
| 4400 Taxes on financial and capital transactions | .. | .. | 0 | 0 | 0 | .. | .. | .. | .. | .. |
| 4500 Non-recurrent taxes | .. | .. | 0 | 0 | 0 | .. | .. | .. | .. | .. |
| 4600 Other recurrent taxes on property | .. | .. | 0 | 0 | 0 | .. | .. | .. | .. | .. |
| **5000 Taxes on goods and services** | .. | .. | **7** | **12** | **10** | **0** | **0** | **0** | **0** | **0** |
| 5100 Taxes on production, sale, transfer, etc | .. | .. | 0 | 0 | 0 | .. | .. | .. | .. | .. |
| 5110 General taxes | .. | .. | .. | .. | .. | .. | .. | .. | .. | .. |
| 5120 Taxes on specific goods and services | .. | .. | .. | .. | .. | .. | .. | .. | .. | .. |
| 5130 Unallocable between 5110 and 5120 | .. | .. | .. | .. | .. | .. | .. | .. | .. | .. |
| 5200 Taxes on use of goods and perform activities | .. | .. | 7 | 12 | 10 | .. | .. | .. | .. | .. |
| 5300 Unallocable between 5100 and 5200 | .. | .. | 0 | 0 | 0 | .. | .. | .. | .. | .. |
| **6000 Other taxes** | .. | .. | **63** | **86** | **92** | **0** | **0** | **0** | **0** | **0** |
| 6100 Paid solely by business | .. | .. | 0 | 0 | 0 | .. | .. | .. | .. | .. |
| 6200 Other | .. | .. | 63 | 86 | 92 | .. | .. | .. | .. | .. |
| **Total tax revenue** | .. | .. | **74** | **104** | **108** | **104** | **325** | **470** | **608** | **700** |

.. Not available

1. Vocational training contributions to the Instituto Salvadoreño de Formación Profesional (INSAFORP) are included in heading 3000. The tax revenue is classified under the central government. In El Salvador this revenue is classified under a separate unit considered to be different to the central government.
2. Social security contributions are those paid to the Salvadoran Institute of Social Security (ISSS), National Public Employees Pension Institute (INPEP), Social Security Institute of the Armed Forces (IPSFA) and Salvadoran Institute of Teacher Welfare (ISBM). The figures exclude contributions to the privately managed regime and may include a small amount of voluntary contributions which is undistinguishable from the public social security contribution data.

StatLink https://doi.org/10.1787/888934310119

## Table 6.15. **Guatemala, tax revenues by sub-sectors of government**

*Million GTQ*

| | Federal government | | | | | State/Regional | | | | |
|---|---|---|---|---|---|---|---|---|---|---|
| | 1990 | 2000 | 2010 | 2015 | 2020 | 1990 | 2000 | 2010 | 2015 | 2020 |
| **1000 Taxes on income, profits and capital gains** | **507** | **3 293** | **7 745** | **13 628** | **16 751** | .. | .. | .. | .. | .. |
| 1100 Of individuals | 25 | 143 | 1 225 | 1 826 | 2 816 | .. | .. | .. | .. | .. |
| 1200 Corporate | 482 | 3 149 | 6 520 | 11 801 | 13 935 | .. | .. | .. | .. | .. |
| 1300 Unallocable between 1100 and 1200 | 0 | 0 | 0 | 0 | 0 | .. | .. | .. | .. | .. |
| **2000 Social security contributions** | **0** | **0** | **0** | **0** | **0** | .. | .. | .. | .. | .. |
| 2100 Employees | .. | .. | .. | .. | .. | .. | .. | .. | .. | .. |
| 2200 Employers | .. | .. | .. | .. | .. | .. | .. | .. | .. | .. |
| 2300 Self-employed or non-employed | .. | .. | .. | .. | .. | .. | .. | .. | .. | .. |
| 2400 Unallocable between 2100, 2200 and 2300 | .. | .. | .. | .. | .. | .. | .. | .. | .. | .. |
| **3000 Taxes on payroll and workforce[1]** | **0** | **0** | **447** | **736** | **859** | .. | .. | .. | .. | .. |
| **4000 Taxes on property** | **149** | **199** | **582** | **358** | **404** | .. | .. | .. | .. | .. |
| 4100 Recurrent taxes on immovable property | 0 | 6 | 1 | 1 | 1 | .. | .. | .. | .. | .. |
| 4200 Recurrent taxes on net wealth | 0 | 0 | 0 | 0 | 0 | .. | .. | .. | .. | .. |
| 4300 Estate, inheritance and gift taxes | 0 | 0 | 0 | 0 | 0 | .. | .. | .. | .. | .. |
| 4400 Taxes on financial and capital transactions | 149 | 194 | 581 | 357 | 403 | .. | .. | .. | .. | .. |
| 4500 Non-recurrent taxes | 0 | 0 | 0 | 0 | 0 | .. | .. | .. | .. | .. |
| 4600 Other recurrent taxes on property | 0 | 0 | 0 | 0 | 0 | .. | .. | .. | .. | .. |
| **5000 Taxes on goods and services** | **1 477** | **10 317** | **23 255** | **31 719** | **37 993** | .. | .. | .. | .. | .. |
| 5100 Taxes on production, sale, transfer, etc | 1 449 | 10 131 | 22 750 | 31 002 | 37 090 | .. | .. | .. | .. | .. |
| 5110 General taxes | 762 | 6 259 | 16 980 | 23 271 | 28 760 | .. | .. | .. | .. | .. |
| 5120 Taxes on specific goods and services | 687 | 3 872 | 5 770 | 7 730 | 8 330 | .. | .. | .. | .. | .. |
| 5130 Unallocable between 5110 and 5120 | 0 | 0 | 0 | 0 | 0 | .. | .. | .. | .. | .. |
| 5200 Taxes on use of goods and perform activities | 28 | 186 | 505 | 717 | 903 | .. | .. | .. | .. | .. |
| 5300 Unallocable between 5100 and 5200 | 0 | 0 | 0 | 0 | 0 | .. | .. | .. | .. | .. |
| **6000 Other taxes** | **0** | **7** | **2 575** | **3 907** | **5 070** | .. | .. | .. | .. | .. |
| 6100 Paid solely by business | .. | 0 | 0 | 0 | 0 | .. | .. | .. | .. | .. |
| 6200 Other | .. | 7 | 2 575 | 3 907 | 5 070 | .. | .. | .. | .. | .. |
| **Total tax revenue** | **2 133** | **13 815** | **34 605** | **50 347** | **61 077** | .. | .. | .. | .. | .. |

*Million GTQ*

| | Local government | | | | | Social Security Funds[2] | | | | |
|---|---|---|---|---|---|---|---|---|---|---|
| | 1990 | 2000 | 2010 | 2015 | 2020 | 1990 | 2000 | 2010 | 2015 | 2020 |
| **1000 Taxes on income, profits and capital gains** | .. | **0** | **0** | **0** | **0** | **0** | **0** | **0** | **0** | **0** |
| 1100 Of individuals | .. | .. | .. | .. | .. | .. | .. | .. | .. | .. |
| 1200 Corporate | .. | .. | .. | .. | .. | .. | .. | .. | .. | .. |
| 1300 Unallocable between 1100 and 1200 | .. | .. | .. | .. | .. | .. | .. | .. | .. | .. |
| **2000 Social security contributions** | .. | **0** | **0** | **0** | **0** | **436** | **2 569** | **6 312** | **9 778** | **12 742** |
| 2100 Employees | .. | .. | .. | .. | .. | .. | .. | .. | .. | .. |
| 2200 Employers | .. | .. | .. | .. | .. | .. | .. | .. | .. | .. |
| 2300 Self-employed or non-employed | .. | .. | .. | .. | .. | .. | .. | .. | .. | .. |
| 2400 Unallocable between 2100, 2200 and 2300 | .. | .. | .. | .. | .. | 436 | 2 569 | 6 312 | 9 778 | 12 742 |
| **3000 Taxes on payroll and workforce[1]** | .. | **0** | **0** | **0** | **0** | **0** | **0** | **0** | **0** | **0** |
| **4000 Taxes on property** | .. | **147** | **620** | **692** | **711** | **0** | **0** | **0** | **0** | **0** |
| 4100 Recurrent taxes on immovable property | .. | 147 | 620 | 692 | 711 | .. | .. | .. | .. | .. |
| 4200 Recurrent taxes on net wealth | .. | 0 | 0 | 0 | 0 | .. | .. | .. | .. | .. |
| 4300 Estate, inheritance and gift taxes | .. | 0 | 0 | 0 | 0 | .. | .. | .. | .. | .. |
| 4400 Taxes on financial and capital transactions | .. | 0 | 0 | 0 | 0 | .. | .. | .. | .. | .. |
| 4500 Non-recurrent taxes | .. | 0 | 0 | 0 | 0 | .. | .. | .. | .. | .. |
| 4600 Other recurrent taxes on property | .. | 0 | 0 | 0 | 0 | .. | .. | .. | .. | .. |
| **5000 Taxes on goods and services** | .. | **0** | **0** | **0** | **0** | **0** | **0** | **0** | **0** | **0** |
| 5100 Taxes on production, sale, transfer, etc | .. | .. | .. | .. | .. | .. | .. | .. | .. | .. |
| 5110 General taxes | .. | .. | .. | .. | .. | .. | .. | .. | .. | .. |
| 5120 Taxes on specific goods and services | .. | .. | .. | .. | .. | .. | .. | .. | .. | .. |
| 5130 Unallocable between 5110 and 5120 | .. | .. | .. | .. | .. | .. | .. | .. | .. | .. |
| 5200 Taxes on use of goods and perform activities | .. | .. | .. | .. | .. | .. | .. | .. | .. | .. |
| 5300 Unallocable between 5100 and 5200 | .. | .. | .. | .. | .. | .. | .. | .. | .. | .. |
| **6000 Other taxes** | .. | **0** | **0** | **0** | **0** | **0** | **0** | **0** | **0** | **0** |
| 6100 Paid solely by business | .. | .. | .. | .. | .. | .. | .. | .. | .. | .. |
| 6200 Other | .. | .. | .. | .. | .. | .. | .. | .. | .. | .. |
| **Total tax revenue** | .. | **147** | **620** | **692** | **711** | **436** | **2 569** | **6 312** | **9 778** | **12 742** |

.. Not available

1. Contributions to INTECAP and contributions to IRTRA are included in heading 3000. The tax revenues are classified under the central government. In Guatemala these revenues are classified under a separate unit considered to be different to the central government.
2. Corresponds to social security contributions to the Guatemalan Social Security Institute (IGSS) and payments by public employees to the government's pension fund.

StatLink https://doi.org/10.1787/888934310138

## Table 6.16. **Guyana, tax revenues by sub-sectors of government**

*Million GYD*

| | Federal government[1] | | | | | State/Regional | | | | |
|---|---|---|---|---|---|---|---|---|---|---|
| | 1990 | 2000 | 2010 | 2015 | 2020 | 1990 | 2000 | 2010 | 2015 | 2020 |
| **1000 Taxes on income, profits and capital gains** | **1 752** | **16 179** | **39 561** | **55 011** | **105 756** | .. | .. | .. | .. | .. |
| 1100 Of individuals | 333 | 7 734 | 17 816 | 23 300 | 39 711 | .. | .. | .. | .. | .. |
| 1200 Corporate | 1 375 | 8 266 | 21 427 | 31 200 | 64 992 | .. | .. | .. | .. | .. |
| 1300 Unallocable between 1100 and 1200 | 43 | 179 | 317 | 511 | 1 053 | .. | .. | .. | .. | .. |
| **2000 Social security contributions** | **0** | **0** | **0** | **0** | **0** | .. | .. | .. | .. | .. |
| 2100 Employees | .. | .. | .. | .. | .. | .. | .. | .. | .. | .. |
| 2200 Employers | .. | .. | .. | .. | .. | .. | .. | .. | .. | .. |
| 2300 Self-employed or non-employed | .. | .. | .. | .. | .. | .. | .. | .. | .. | .. |
| 2400 Unallocable between 2100, 2200 and 2300 | .. | .. | .. | .. | .. | .. | .. | .. | .. | .. |
| **3000 Taxes on payroll and workforce** | **0** | **0** | **0** | **0** | **0** | .. | .. | .. | .. | .. |
| **4000 Taxes on property** | **53** | **701** | **2 068** | **3 676** | **4 390** | .. | .. | .. | .. | .. |
| 4100 Recurrent taxes on immovable property | 40 | 681 | 1 562 | 3 201 | 3 847 | .. | .. | .. | .. | .. |
| 4200 Recurrent taxes on net wealth | 0 | 0 | 0 | 0 | 0 | .. | .. | .. | .. | .. |
| 4300 Estate, inheritance and gift taxes | 13 | 20 | 31 | 37 | 44 | .. | .. | .. | .. | .. |
| 4400 Taxes on financial and capital transactions | 0 | 0 | 476 | 438 | 499 | .. | .. | .. | .. | .. |
| 4500 Non-recurrent taxes | 0 | 0 | 0 | 0 | 0 | .. | .. | .. | .. | .. |
| 4600 Other recurrent taxes on property | 0 | 0 | 0 | 0 | 0 | .. | .. | .. | .. | .. |
| **5000 Taxes on goods and services** | **2 200** | **20 798** | **59 360** | **83 924** | **106 683** | .. | .. | .. | .. | .. |
| 5100 Taxes on production, sale, transfer, etc | 2 162 | 20 530 | 58 846 | 83 227 | 105 489 | .. | .. | .. | .. | .. |
| 5110 General taxes | 1 399 | 14 861 | 27 044 | 35 374 | 49 907 | .. | .. | .. | .. | .. |
| 5120 Taxes on specific goods and services | 763 | 5 669 | 31 802 | 47 853 | 55 582 | .. | .. | .. | .. | .. |
| 5130 Unallocable between 5110 and 5120 | 0 | 0 | 0 | 0 | 0 | .. | .. | .. | .. | .. |
| 5200 Taxes on use of goods and perform activities | 38 | 268 | 514 | 697 | 1 194 | .. | .. | .. | .. | .. |
| 5300 Unallocable between 5100 and 5200 | 0 | 0 | 0 | 0 | 0 | .. | .. | .. | .. | .. |
| **6000 Other taxes** | **1 037** | **204** | **757** | **599** | **1 897** | .. | .. | .. | .. | .. |
| 6100 Paid solely by business | 0 | 0 | 0 | 0 | 0 | .. | .. | .. | .. | .. |
| 6200 Other | 1 037 | 204 | 757 | 599 | 1 897 | .. | .. | .. | .. | .. |
| **Total tax revenue** | **5 041** | **37 882** | **101 746** | **143 210** | **218 726** | .. | .. | .. | .. | .. |

*Million GYD*

| | Local government[2] | | | | | Social Security Funds[3] | | | | |
|---|---|---|---|---|---|---|---|---|---|---|
| | 1990 | 2000 | 2010 | 2015 | 2020 | 1990 | 2000 | 2010 | 2015 | 2020 |
| **1000 Taxes on income, profits and capital gains** | .. | .. | **0** | **0** | **0** | **0** | **0** | **0** | **0** | **0** |
| 1100 Of individuals | .. | .. | .. | .. | .. | .. | .. | .. | .. | .. |
| 1200 Corporate | .. | .. | .. | .. | .. | .. | .. | .. | .. | .. |
| 1300 Unallocable between 1100 and 1200 | .. | .. | .. | .. | .. | .. | .. | .. | .. | .. |
| **2000 Social security contributions** | .. | .. | **0** | **0** | **0** | **191** | **4 868** | **10 047** | **16 644** | **24 706** |
| 2100 Employees | .. | .. | .. | .. | .. | .. | .. | .. | .. | .. |
| 2200 Employers | .. | .. | .. | .. | .. | .. | .. | .. | .. | .. |
| 2300 Self-employed or non-employed | .. | .. | .. | .. | .. | .. | .. | .. | .. | .. |
| 2400 Unallocable between 2100, 2200 and 2300 | .. | .. | .. | .. | .. | 191 | 4 868 | 10 047 | 16 644 | 24 706 |
| **3000 Taxes on payroll and workforce** | .. | .. | **0** | **0** | **0** | **0** | **0** | **0** | **0** | **0** |
| **4000 Taxes on property** | .. | .. | **0** | **0** | **0** | **0** | **0** | **0** | **0** | **0** |
| 4100 Recurrent taxes on immovable property | .. | .. | .. | .. | .. | .. | .. | .. | .. | .. |
| 4200 Recurrent taxes on net wealth | .. | .. | .. | .. | .. | .. | .. | .. | .. | .. |
| 4300 Estate, inheritance and gift taxes | .. | .. | .. | .. | .. | .. | .. | .. | .. | .. |
| 4400 Taxes on financial and capital transactions | .. | .. | .. | .. | .. | .. | .. | .. | .. | .. |
| 4500 Non-recurrent taxes | .. | .. | .. | .. | .. | .. | .. | .. | .. | .. |
| 4600 Other recurrent taxes on property | .. | .. | .. | .. | .. | .. | .. | .. | .. | .. |
| **5000 Taxes on goods and services** | .. | .. | **0** | **0** | **0** | **0** | **0** | **0** | **0** | **0** |
| 5100 Taxes on production, sale, transfer, etc | .. | .. | .. | .. | .. | .. | .. | .. | .. | .. |
| 5110 General taxes | .. | .. | .. | .. | .. | .. | .. | .. | .. | .. |
| 5120 Taxes on specific goods and services | .. | .. | .. | .. | .. | .. | .. | .. | .. | .. |
| 5130 Unallocable between 5110 and 5120 | .. | .. | .. | .. | .. | .. | .. | .. | .. | .. |
| 5200 Taxes on use of goods and perform activities | .. | .. | .. | .. | .. | .. | .. | .. | .. | .. |
| 5300 Unallocable between 5100 and 5200 | .. | .. | .. | .. | .. | .. | .. | .. | .. | .. |
| **6000 Other taxes** | .. | .. | **113** | **41** | **75** | **0** | **0** | **0** | **0** | **0** |
| 6100 Paid solely by business | .. | .. | 0 | 0 | 0 | .. | .. | .. | .. | .. |
| 6200 Other | .. | .. | 113 | 41 | 75 | .. | .. | .. | .. | .. |
| **Total tax revenue** | .. | .. | **113** | **41** | **75** | **191** | **4 868** | **10 047** | **16 644** | **24 706** |

.. Not available

1. Central government tax revenues are based on Budget Estimates by the Ministry of Finance.
2. Local government tax revenues include payments of local taxes by public corporations and come from Bank of Guyana.
3. Social security figures include contributions to National Insurance Scheme.

StatLink https://doi.org/10.1787/888934310157

# Table 6.17. **Honduras, tax revenues by sub-sectors of government**

*Million HNL*

| | Federal government | | | | | State/Regional | | | | |
|---|---|---|---|---|---|---|---|---|---|---|
| | 1990 | 2000 | 2010 | 2015 | 2020 | 1990 | 2000 | 2010 | 2015 | 2020 |
| **1000 Taxes on income, profits and capital gains** | **431** | **2 907** | **13 232** | **25 003** | **25 587** | .. | .. | .. | .. | .. |
| 1100 Of individuals | 157 | 992 | 4 528 | 8 147 | 11 214 | .. | .. | .. | .. | .. |
| 1200 Corporate | 274 | 1 916 | 8 705 | 16 856 | 14 373 | .. | .. | .. | .. | .. |
| 1300 Unallocable between 1100 and 1200 | 0 | 0 | 0 | 0 | 0 | .. | .. | .. | .. | .. |
| **2000 Social security contributions** | **0** | **0** | **0** | **0** | **0** | .. | .. | .. | .. | .. |
| 2100 Employees | .. | .. | .. | .. | .. | .. | .. | .. | .. | .. |
| 2200 Employers | .. | .. | .. | .. | .. | .. | .. | .. | .. | .. |
| 2300 Self-employed or non-employed | .. | .. | .. | .. | .. | .. | .. | .. | .. | .. |
| 2400 Unallocable between 2100, 2200 and 2300 | .. | .. | .. | .. | .. | .. | .. | .. | .. | .. |
| **3000 Taxes on payroll and workforce[1]** | **0** | **0** | **485** | **1 007** | **935** | .. | .. | .. | .. | .. |
| **4000 Taxes on property** | **16** | **266** | **994** | **2 635** | **2 954** | .. | .. | .. | .. | .. |
| 4100 Recurrent taxes on immovable property | 16 | 189 | 254 | 298 | 282 | .. | .. | .. | .. | .. |
| 4200 Recurrent taxes on net wealth | 0 | 78 | 359 | 334 | 328 | .. | .. | .. | .. | .. |
| 4300 Estate, inheritance and gift taxes | 0 | 0 | 0 | 0 | 0 | .. | .. | .. | .. | .. |
| 4400 Taxes on financial and capital transactions | 0 | 0 | 0 | 2 003 | 2 344 | .. | .. | .. | .. | .. |
| 4500 Non-recurrent taxes | 0 | 0 | 380 | 0 | 0 | .. | .. | .. | .. | .. |
| 4600 Other recurrent taxes on property | 0 | 0 | 0 | 0 | 0 | .. | .. | .. | .. | .. |
| **5000 Taxes on goods and services** | **1 401** | **12 436** | **28 937** | **50 027** | **55 520** | .. | .. | .. | .. | .. |
| 5100 Taxes on production, sale, transfer, etc | 1 401 | 12 436 | 28 937 | 50 027 | 55 520 | .. | .. | .. | .. | .. |
| 5110 General taxes | 344 | 5 146 | 16 050 | 32 273 | 35 815 | .. | .. | .. | .. | .. |
| 5120 Taxes on specific goods and services | 1 057 | 7 290 | 12 887 | 17 754 | 19 705 | .. | .. | .. | .. | .. |
| 5130 Unallocable between 5110 and 5120 | 0 | 0 | 0 | 0 | 0 | .. | .. | .. | .. | .. |
| 5200 Taxes on use of goods and perform activities | 0 | 0 | 0 | 0 | 0 | .. | .. | .. | .. | .. |
| 5300 Unallocable between 5100 and 5200 | 0 | 0 | 0 | 0 | 0 | .. | .. | .. | .. | .. |
| **6000 Other taxes** | **1** | **2** | **9** | **8** | **9** | .. | .. | .. | .. | .. |
| 6100 Paid solely by business | 0 | 0 | 0 | 0 | 0 | .. | .. | .. | .. | .. |
| 6200 Other | 1 | 2 | 9 | 8 | 9 | .. | .. | .. | .. | .. |
| **Total tax revenue** | **1 849** | **15 612** | **43 657** | **78 680** | **85 005** | .. | .. | .. | .. | .. |

*Million HNL*

| | Local government[2] | | | | | Social Security Funds | | | | |
|---|---|---|---|---|---|---|---|---|---|---|
| | 1990 | 2000 | 2010 | 2015 | 2020 | 1990 | 2000 | 2010 | 2015 | 2020 |
| **1000 Taxes on income, profits and capital gains** | **0** | **0** | **0** | **0** | **0** | **0** | **0** | **0** | **0** | **0** |
| 1100 Of individuals | .. | .. | .. | .. | .. | .. | .. | .. | .. | .. |
| 1200 Corporate | .. | .. | .. | .. | .. | .. | .. | .. | .. | .. |
| 1300 Unallocable between 1100 and 1200 | .. | .. | .. | .. | .. | .. | .. | .. | .. | .. |
| **2000 Social security contributions** | **0** | **0** | **0** | **0** | **0** | **179** | **1 727** | **8 671** | **13 524** | **23 138** |
| 2100 Employees | .. | .. | .. | .. | .. | .. | .. | .. | .. | .. |
| 2200 Employers | .. | .. | .. | .. | .. | .. | .. | .. | .. | .. |
| 2300 Self-employed or non-employed | .. | .. | .. | .. | .. | .. | .. | .. | .. | .. |
| 2400 Unallocable between 2100, 2200 and 2300 | .. | .. | .. | .. | .. | 179 | 1 727 | 8 671 | 13 524 | 23 138 |
| **3000 Taxes on payroll and workforce[1]** | **0** | **0** | **0** | **0** | **0** | **0** | **0** | **0** | **0** | **0** |
| **4000 Taxes on property** | **0** | **0** | **0** | **0** | **0** | **0** | **0** | **0** | **0** | **0** |
| 4100 Recurrent taxes on immovable property | .. | .. | .. | .. | .. | .. | .. | .. | .. | .. |
| 4200 Recurrent taxes on net wealth | .. | .. | .. | .. | .. | .. | .. | .. | .. | .. |
| 4300 Estate, inheritance and gift taxes | .. | .. | .. | .. | .. | .. | .. | .. | .. | .. |
| 4400 Taxes on financial and capital transactions | .. | .. | .. | .. | .. | .. | .. | .. | .. | .. |
| 4500 Non-recurrent taxes | .. | .. | .. | .. | .. | .. | .. | .. | .. | .. |
| 4600 Other recurrent taxes on property | .. | .. | .. | .. | .. | .. | .. | .. | .. | .. |
| **5000 Taxes on goods and services** | **0** | **0** | **0** | **0** | **0** | **0** | **0** | **0** | **0** | **0** |
| 5100 Taxes on production, sale, transfer, etc | .. | .. | .. | .. | .. | .. | .. | .. | .. | .. |
| 5110 General taxes | .. | .. | .. | .. | .. | .. | .. | .. | .. | .. |
| 5120 Taxes on specific goods and services | .. | .. | .. | .. | .. | .. | .. | .. | .. | .. |
| 5130 Unallocable between 5110 and 5120 | .. | .. | .. | .. | .. | .. | .. | .. | .. | .. |
| 5200 Taxes on use of goods and perform activities | .. | .. | .. | .. | .. | .. | .. | .. | .. | .. |
| 5300 Unallocable between 5100 and 5200 | .. | .. | .. | .. | .. | .. | .. | .. | .. | .. |
| **6000 Other taxes** | **90** | **960** | **2 216** | **2 495** | **4 306** | **0** | **0** | **0** | **0** | **0** |
| 6100 Paid solely by business | 0 | 0 | 0 | 0 | 0 | .. | .. | .. | .. | .. |
| 6200 Other | 90 | 960 | 2 216 | 2 495 | 4 306 | .. | .. | .. | .. | .. |
| **Total tax revenue** | **90** | **960** | **2 216** | **2 495** | **4 306** | **179** | **1 727** | **8 671** | **13 524** | **23 138** |

.. Not available

1. The employer contributions to National Institute of Vocational Training (INFOP) are included in heading 3000. The tax revenue is classified under the central government. In Honduras this revenue is classified under a separate unit considered to be different to the central government.
2. The figures may include non-tax revenues and central government transfers but it has not been possible to distinguish the different components of local government tax revenues.

StatLink https://doi.org/10.1787/888934310176

## Table 6.18. **Jamaica, tax revenues by sub-sectors of government**

*Million JMD*

| | Federal government[1] | | | | | State/Regional | | | | |
|---|---|---|---|---|---|---|---|---|---|---|
| | 1990 | 2000 | 2010 | 2015 | 2020 | 1990 | 2000 | 2010 | 2015 | 2020 |
| **1000 Taxes on income, profits and capital gains** | **3 639** | **35 457** | **105 917** | **129 233** | **155 632** | **..** | **..** | **..** | **..** | **..** |
| 1100 Of individuals | 1 687 | 17 441 | 54 798 | 74 538 | 72 692 | .. | .. | .. | .. | .. |
| 1200 Corporate | 1 280 | 7 627 | 33 091 | 40 198 | 61 823 | .. | .. | .. | .. | .. |
| 1300 Unallocable between 1100 and 1200 | 672 | 10 389 | 18 028 | 14 498 | 21 117 | .. | .. | .. | .. | .. |
| **2000 Social security contributions** | **0** | **0** | **0** | **0** | **0** | **..** | **..** | **..** | **..** | **..** |
| 2100 Employees | .. | .. | .. | .. | .. | .. | .. | .. | .. | .. |
| 2200 Employers | .. | .. | .. | .. | .. | .. | .. | .. | .. | .. |
| 2300 Self-employed or non-employed | .. | .. | .. | .. | .. | .. | .. | .. | .. | .. |
| 2400 Unallocable between 2100, 2200 and 2300 | .. | .. | .. | .. | .. | .. | .. | .. | .. | .. |
| **3000 Taxes on payroll and workforce** | **305** | **3 821** | **12 792** | **20 757** | **30 813** | **..** | **..** | **..** | **..** | **..** |
| **4000 Taxes on property** | **965** | **3 623** | **7 339** | **12 140** | **7 603** | **..** | **..** | **..** | **..** | **..** |
| 4100 Recurrent taxes on immovable property | 67 | 0 | 0 | 0 | 0 | .. | .. | .. | .. | .. |
| 4200 Recurrent taxes on net wealth | 0 | 0 | 0 | 0 | 0 | .. | .. | .. | .. | .. |
| 4300 Estate, inheritance and gift taxes | 0 | 0 | 0 | 0 | 0 | .. | .. | .. | .. | .. |
| 4400 Taxes on financial and capital transactions | 898 | 3 623 | 7 339 | 12 140 | 7 603 | .. | .. | .. | .. | .. |
| 4500 Non-recurrent taxes | 0 | 0 | 0 | 0 | 0 | .. | .. | .. | .. | .. |
| 4600 Other recurrent taxes on property | 0 | 0 | 0 | 0 | 0 | .. | .. | .. | .. | .. |
| **5000 Taxes on goods and services** | **2 824** | **43 907** | **149 544** | **240 795** | **315 268** | **..** | **..** | **..** | **..** | **..** |
| 5100 Taxes on production, sale, transfer, etc | 2 760 | 43 107 | 147 500 | 237 456 | 308 011 | .. | .. | .. | .. | .. |
| 5110 General taxes | 297 | 22 356 | 84 409 | 138 501 | 177 354 | .. | .. | .. | .. | .. |
| 5120 Taxes on specific goods and services | 2 463 | 20 752 | 63 091 | 98 955 | 130 658 | .. | .. | .. | .. | .. |
| 5130 Unallocable between 5110 and 5120 | 0 | 0 | 0 | 0 | 0 | .. | .. | .. | .. | .. |
| 5200 Taxes on use of goods and perform activities | 64 | 800 | 2 045 | 3 339 | 7 257 | .. | .. | .. | .. | .. |
| 5300 Unallocable between 5100 and 5200 | 0 | 0 | 0 | 0 | 0 | .. | .. | .. | .. | .. |
| **6000 Other taxes** | **16** | **266** | **748** | **994** | **1 824** | **..** | **..** | **..** | **..** | **..** |
| 6100 Paid solely by business | 0 | 0 | 0 | 0 | 0 | .. | .. | .. | .. | .. |
| 6200 Other | 16 | 266 | 748 | 994 | 1 824 | .. | .. | .. | .. | .. |
| **Total tax revenue** | **7 748** | **87 074** | **276 340** | **403 919** | **511 139** | **..** | **..** | **..** | **..** | **..** |

*Million JMD*

| | Local government[1] | | | | | Social Security Funds[1] | | | | |
|---|---|---|---|---|---|---|---|---|---|---|
| | 1990 | 2000 | 2010 | 2015 | 2020 | 1990 | 2000 | 2010 | 2015 | 2020 |
| **1000 Taxes on income, profits and capital gains** | **..** | **0** | **0** | **0** | **0** | **..** | **..** | **0** | **0** | **0** |
| 1100 Of individuals | .. | .. | .. | .. | .. | .. | .. | .. | .. | .. |
| 1200 Corporate | .. | .. | .. | .. | .. | .. | .. | .. | .. | .. |
| 1300 Unallocable between 1100 and 1200 | .. | .. | .. | .. | .. | .. | .. | .. | .. | .. |
| **2000 Social security contributions** | **..** | **0** | **0** | **0** | **0** | **..** | **..** | **8 199** | **16 449** | **24 994** |
| 2100 Employees | .. | .. | .. | .. | .. | .. | .. | .. | .. | .. |
| 2200 Employers | .. | .. | .. | .. | .. | .. | .. | .. | .. | .. |
| 2300 Self-employed or non-employed | .. | .. | .. | .. | .. | .. | .. | .. | .. | .. |
| 2400 Unallocable between 2100, 2200 and 2300 | .. | .. | .. | .. | .. | .. | .. | 8 199 | 16 449 | 24 994 |
| **3000 Taxes on payroll and workforce** | **..** | **0** | **0** | **0** | **0** | **..** | **..** | **0** | **0** | **0** |
| **4000 Taxes on property** | **..** | **639** | **2 600** | **7 271** | **7 996** | **..** | **..** | **0** | **0** | **0** |
| 4100 Recurrent taxes on immovable property | .. | 639 | 2 600 | 7 271 | 7 996 | .. | .. | .. | .. | .. |
| 4200 Recurrent taxes on net wealth | .. | 0 | 0 | 0 | 0 | .. | .. | .. | .. | .. |
| 4300 Estate, inheritance and gift taxes | .. | 0 | 0 | 0 | 0 | .. | .. | .. | .. | .. |
| 4400 Taxes on financial and capital transactions | .. | 0 | 0 | 0 | 0 | .. | .. | .. | .. | .. |
| 4500 Non-recurrent taxes | .. | 0 | 0 | 0 | 0 | .. | .. | .. | .. | .. |
| 4600 Other recurrent taxes on property | .. | 0 | 0 | 0 | 0 | .. | .. | .. | .. | .. |
| **5000 Taxes on goods and services** | **..** | **0** | **0** | **0** | **0** | **..** | **..** | **0** | **0** | **0** |
| 5100 Taxes on production, sale, transfer, etc | .. | .. | .. | .. | .. | .. | .. | .. | .. | .. |
| 5110 General taxes | .. | .. | .. | .. | .. | .. | .. | .. | .. | .. |
| 5120 Taxes on specific goods and services | .. | .. | .. | .. | .. | .. | .. | .. | .. | .. |
| 5130 Unallocable between 5110 and 5120 | .. | .. | .. | .. | .. | .. | .. | .. | .. | .. |
| 5200 Taxes on use of goods and perform activities | .. | .. | .. | .. | .. | .. | .. | .. | .. | .. |
| 5300 Unallocable between 5100 and 5200 | .. | .. | .. | .. | .. | .. | .. | .. | .. | .. |
| **6000 Other taxes** | **..** | **0** | **0** | **0** | **0** | **..** | **..** | **0** | **0** | **0** |
| 6100 Paid solely by business | .. | .. | .. | .. | .. | .. | .. | .. | .. | .. |
| 6200 Other | .. | .. | .. | .. | .. | .. | .. | .. | .. | .. |
| **Total tax revenue** | **..** | **639** | **2 600** | **7 271** | **7 996** | **..** | **..** | **8 199** | **16 449** | **24 994** |

.. Not available

1. The figures refer to fiscal year ending 31st March for 1990-2003 and then calendar year ending 31st December.

StatLink https://doi.org/10.1787/888934310195

## Table 6.19. **Mexico, tax revenues by sub-sectors of government**

*Million MXN*

| | Federal government | | | | | State/Regional | | | | |
|---|---|---|---|---|---|---|---|---|---|---|
| | 1990 | 2000 | 2010 | 2015 | 2020 | 1990 | 2000 | 2010 | 2015 | 2020 |
| **1000 Taxes on income, profits and capital gains[1]** | **34 668** | **276 548** | **683 604** | **1 230 555** | **1 768 639** | **3** | **0** | **0** | **0** | **0** |
| 1100 Of individuals | .. | .. | 313 473 | 609 384 | 872 598 | .. | .. | .. | .. | .. |
| 1200 Corporate | .. | .. | 246 745 | 592 443 | 832 120 | .. | .. | .. | .. | .. |
| 1300 Unallocable between 1100 and 1200 | 34 668 | 276 548 | 123 386 | 28 728 | 63 922 | 3 | .. | .. | .. | .. |
| **2000 Social security contributions** | **0** | **0** | **0** | **0** | **0** | **0** | **0** | **0** | **0** | **0** |
| 2100 Employees | .. | .. | .. | .. | .. | .. | .. | .. | .. | .. |
| 2200 Employers | .. | .. | .. | .. | .. | .. | .. | .. | .. | .. |
| 2300 Self-employed or non-employed | .. | .. | .. | .. | .. | .. | .. | .. | .. | .. |
| 2400 Unallocable between 2100, 2200 and 2300 | .. | .. | .. | .. | .. | .. | .. | .. | .. | .. |
| **3000 Taxes on payroll and workforce** | **818** | **0** | **0** | **0** | **0** | **972** | **11 215** | **36 818** | **70 221** | **105 456** |
| **4000 Taxes on property** | **3** | **0** | **0** | **0** | **0** | **894** | **7 018** | **13 137** | **22 481** | **26 447** |
| 4100 Recurrent taxes on immovable property | 0 | .. | .. | .. | .. | 482 | 5 238 | 8 522 | 14 245 | 17 631 |
| 4200 Recurrent taxes on net wealth | 0 | .. | .. | .. | .. | 0 | 0 | 0 | 0 | 0 |
| 4300 Estate, inheritance and gift taxes | 0 | .. | .. | .. | .. | 7 | 0 | 0 | 0 | 0 |
| 4400 Taxes on financial and capital transactions | 3 | .. | .. | .. | .. | 405 | 1 781 | 4 615 | 8 235 | 8 816 |
| 4500 Non-recurrent taxes | 0 | .. | .. | .. | .. | 0 | 0 | 0 | 0 | 0 |
| 4600 Other recurrent taxes on property | 0 | .. | .. | .. | .. | 0 | 0 | 0 | 0 | 0 |
| **5000 Taxes on goods and services** | **44 605** | **318 065** | **645 623** | **1 116 026** | **1 522 289** | **118** | **1 346** | **5 805** | **24 355** | **21 156** |
| 5100 Taxes on production, sale, transfer, etc | 44 029 | 309 283 | 627 187 | 1 115 525 | 1 521 797 | 45 | 910 | 2 470 | 4 357 | 5 253 |
| 5110 General taxes | 26 635 | 189 606 | 504 509 | 707 213 | 987 525 | 0 | 0 | 0 | 0 | 0 |
| 5120 Taxes on specific goods and services | 17 394 | 119 677 | 122 678 | 408 312 | 534 273 | 30 | 910 | 2 470 | 4 357 | 5 253 |
| 5130 Unallocable between 5110 and 5120 | 0 | 0 | 0 | 0 | 0 | 15 | 0 | 0 | 0 | 0 |
| 5200 Taxes on use of goods and perform activities | 576 | 8 782 | 18 436 | 501 | 491 | 73 | 436 | 3 335 | 19 998 | 15 902 |
| 5300 Unallocable between 5100 and 5200 | 0 | 0 | 0 | 0 | 0 | 0 | 0 | 0 | 0 | 0 |
| **6000 Other taxes** | **1 340** | **5 878** | **22 236** | **27 379** | **57 011** | **165** | **907** | **2 546** | **6 489** | **8 096** |
| 6100 Paid solely by business | 0 | 0 | 0 | 0 | 0 | 0 | 0 | 0 | 0 | 0 |
| 6200 Other | 1 340 | 5 878 | 22 236 | 27 379 | 57 011 | 165 | 907 | 2 546 | 6 489 | 8 096 |
| **Total tax revenue** | **81 434** | **600 491** | **1 351 463** | **2 373 960** | **3 347 939** | **2 152** | **20 485** | **58 307** | **123 545** | **161 155** |

*Million MXN*

| | Local government | | | | | Social Security Funds[2] | | | | |
|---|---|---|---|---|---|---|---|---|---|---|
| | 1990 | 2000 | 2010 | 2015 | 2020 | 1990 | 2000 | 2010 | 2015 | 2020 |
| **1000 Taxes on income, profits and capital gains[1]** | **2** | **0** | **0** | **0** | **0** | **0** | **0** | **0** | **0** | **0** |
| 1100 Of individuals | .. | .. | .. | .. | .. | .. | .. | .. | .. | .. |
| 1200 Corporate | .. | .. | .. | .. | .. | .. | .. | .. | .. | .. |
| 1300 Unallocable between 1100 and 1200 | 2 | .. | .. | .. | .. | .. | .. | .. | .. | .. |
| **2000 Social security contributions** | **0** | **0** | **0** | **0** | **0** | **17 165** | **138 223** | **277 459** | **409 249** | **576 019** |
| 2100 Employees | .. | .. | .. | .. | .. | .. | .. | .. | .. | .. |
| 2200 Employers | .. | .. | .. | .. | .. | .. | .. | .. | .. | .. |
| 2300 Self-employed or non-employed | .. | .. | .. | .. | .. | .. | .. | .. | .. | .. |
| 2400 Unallocable between 2100, 2200 and 2300 | .. | .. | .. | .. | .. | 17 165 | 138 223 | 277 459 | 409 249 | 576 019 |
| **3000 Taxes on payroll and workforce** | **7** | **2** | **93** | **1** | **0** | **0** | **0** | **0** | **0** | **0** |
| **4000 Taxes on property** | **1 017** | **6 946** | **25 818** | **35 193** | **40 014** | **0** | **0** | **0** | **0** | **0** |
| 4100 Recurrent taxes on immovable property | 554 | 4 710 | 17 202 | 23 715 | 26 275 | .. | .. | .. | .. | .. |
| 4200 Recurrent taxes on net wealth | 0 | 0 | 0 | 0 | 0 | .. | .. | .. | .. | .. |
| 4300 Estate, inheritance and gift taxes | 1 | 0 | 0 | 0 | 0 | .. | .. | .. | .. | .. |
| 4400 Taxes on financial and capital transactions | 462 | 2 236 | 8 616 | 11 477 | 13 739 | .. | .. | .. | .. | .. |
| 4500 Non-recurrent taxes | 0 | 0 | 0 | 0 | 0 | .. | .. | .. | .. | .. |
| 4600 Other recurrent taxes on property | 0 | 0 | 0 | 0 | 0 | .. | .. | .. | .. | .. |
| **5000 Taxes on goods and services** | **114** | **202** | **487** | **789** | **799** | **0** | **0** | **0** | **0** | **0** |
| 5100 Taxes on production, sale, transfer, etc | 97 | 133 | 466 | 728 | 665 | .. | .. | .. | .. | .. |
| 5110 General taxes | 0 | 0 | 0 | 0 | 0 | .. | .. | .. | .. | .. |
| 5120 Taxes on specific goods and services | 95 | 133 | 466 | 728 | 665 | .. | .. | .. | .. | .. |
| 5130 Unallocable between 5110 and 5120 | 2 | 0 | 0 | 0 | 0 | .. | .. | .. | .. | .. |
| 5200 Taxes on use of goods and perform activities | 17 | 69 | 21 | 61 | 134 | .. | .. | .. | .. | .. |
| 5300 Unallocable between 5100 and 5200 | 0 | 0 | 0 | 0 | 0 | .. | .. | .. | .. | .. |
| **6000 Other taxes** | **114** | **866** | **2 616** | **10 743** | **20 490** | **0** | **0** | **0** | **0** | **0** |
| 6100 Paid solely by business | 0 | 0 | 0 | 0 | 0 | .. | .. | .. | .. | .. |
| 6200 Other | 114 | 866 | 2 616 | 10 743 | 20 490 | .. | .. | .. | .. | .. |
| **Total tax revenue** | **1 254** | **8 016** | **29 014** | **46 726** | **61 302** | **17 165** | **138 223** | **277 459** | **409 249** | **576 019** |

.. Not available

1. In ECLAC data, income taxes are presented net of credit on salary figures.
2. In ECLAC data, social security contributions are presented net of transfers from the Federal government for the payment of IMSS (Mexican Social Security Institute) pensions.

StatLink https://doi.org/10.1787/888934310214

# Table 6.20. **Nicaragua, tax revenues by sub-sectors of government**

*Million NIO*

| | Federal government | | | | | State/Regional | | | | |
|---|---|---|---|---|---|---|---|---|---|---|
| | 1990 | 2000 | 2010 | 2015 | 2020 | 1990 | 2000 | 2010 | 2015 | 2020 |
| **1000 Taxes on income, profits and capital gains** | **..** | **1 144** | **8 351** | **21 313** | **32 460** | **..** | **..** | **..** | **..** | **..** |
| 1100 Of individuals | .. | 299 | 1 857 | 4 432 | 6 447 | .. | .. | .. | .. | .. |
| 1200 Corporate | .. | 845 | 6 494 | 16 881 | 26 013 | .. | .. | .. | .. | .. |
| 1300 Unallocable between 1100 and 1200 | .. | 0 | 0 | 0 | 0 | .. | .. | .. | .. | .. |
| **2000 Social security contributions** | **..** | **0** | **0** | **0** | **0** | **..** | **..** | **..** | **..** | **..** |
| 2100 Employees | .. | .. | .. | .. | .. | .. | .. | .. | .. | .. |
| 2200 Employers | .. | .. | .. | .. | .. | .. | .. | .. | .. | .. |
| 2300 Self-employed or non-employed | .. | .. | .. | .. | .. | .. | .. | .. | .. | .. |
| 2400 Unallocable between 2100, 2200 and 2300 | .. | .. | .. | .. | .. | .. | .. | .. | .. | .. |
| **3000 Taxes on payroll and workforce** | **..** | **0** | **0** | **0** | **0** | **..** | **..** | **..** | **..** | **..** |
| **4000 Taxes on property** | **..** | **11** | **20** | **90** | **55** | **..** | **..** | **..** | **..** | **..** |
| 4100 Recurrent taxes on immovable property | .. | 0 | 0 | 0 | 0 | .. | .. | .. | .. | .. |
| 4200 Recurrent taxes on net wealth | .. | 0 | 0 | 0 | 0 | .. | .. | .. | .. | .. |
| 4300 Estate, inheritance and gift taxes | .. | 0 | 0 | 0 | 0 | .. | .. | .. | .. | .. |
| 4400 Taxes on financial and capital transactions | .. | 11 | 20 | 90 | 55 | .. | .. | .. | .. | .. |
| 4500 Non-recurrent taxes | .. | 0 | 0 | 0 | 0 | .. | .. | .. | .. | .. |
| 4600 Other recurrent taxes on property | .. | 0 | 0 | 0 | 0 | .. | .. | .. | .. | .. |
| **5000 Taxes on goods and services** | **..** | **5 584** | **17 029** | **32 725** | **41 796** | **..** | **..** | **..** | **..** | **..** |
| 5100 Taxes on production, sale, transfer, etc | .. | 5 584 | 17 029 | 32 725 | 41 796 | .. | .. | .. | .. | .. |
| 5110 General taxes | .. | 2 931 | 10 353 | 20 714 | 25 293 | .. | .. | .. | .. | .. |
| 5120 Taxes on specific goods and services | .. | 2 653 | 6 676 | 12 011 | 16 503 | .. | .. | .. | .. | .. |
| 5130 Unallocable between 5110 and 5120 | .. | 0 | 0 | 0 | 0 | .. | .. | .. | .. | .. |
| 5200 Taxes on use of goods and perform activities | .. | 0 | 0 | 0 | 0 | .. | .. | .. | .. | .. |
| 5300 Unallocable between 5100 and 5200 | .. | 0 | 0 | 0 | 0 | .. | .. | .. | .. | .. |
| **6000 Other taxes** | **..** | **0** | **0** | **0** | **0** | **..** | **..** | **..** | **..** | **..** |
| 6100 Paid solely by business | .. | .. | .. | .. | .. | .. | .. | .. | .. | .. |
| 6200 Other | .. | .. | .. | .. | .. | .. | .. | .. | .. | .. |
| **Total tax revenue** | **..** | **6 739** | **25 400** | **54 128** | **74 311** | **..** | **..** | **..** | **..** | **..** |

*Million NIO*

| | Local government[1] | | | | | Social Security Funds | | | | |
|---|---|---|---|---|---|---|---|---|---|---|
| | 1990 | 2000 | 2010 | 2015 | 2020 | 1990 | 2000 | 2010 | 2015 | 2020 |
| **1000 Taxes on income, profits and capital gains** | **..** | **0** | **0** | **0** | **0** | **..** | **0** | **0** | **0** | **0** |
| 1100 Of individuals | .. | .. | .. | .. | .. | .. | .. | .. | .. | .. |
| 1200 Corporate | .. | .. | .. | .. | .. | .. | .. | .. | .. | .. |
| 1300 Unallocable between 1100 and 1200 | .. | .. | .. | .. | .. | .. | .. | .. | .. | .. |
| **2000 Social security contributions** | **..** | **0** | **0** | **0** | **0** | **..** | **1 678** | **8 090** | **18 194** | **29 014** |
| 2100 Employees | .. | .. | .. | .. | .. | .. | .. | .. | .. | .. |
| 2200 Employers | .. | .. | .. | .. | .. | .. | .. | .. | .. | .. |
| 2300 Self-employed or non-employed | .. | .. | .. | .. | .. | .. | .. | .. | .. | .. |
| 2400 Unallocable between 2100, 2200 and 2300 | .. | .. | .. | .. | .. | .. | 1 678 | 8 090 | 18 194 | 29 014 |
| **3000 Taxes on payroll and workforce** | **..** | **0** | **0** | **0** | **0** | **..** | **0** | **0** | **0** | **0** |
| **4000 Taxes on property** | **..** | **0** | **403** | **682** | **982** | **..** | **0** | **0** | **0** | **0** |
| 4100 Recurrent taxes on immovable property | .. | .. | 403 | 682 | 982 | .. | .. | .. | .. | .. |
| 4200 Recurrent taxes on net wealth | .. | .. | 0 | 0 | 0 | .. | .. | .. | .. | .. |
| 4300 Estate, inheritance and gift taxes | .. | .. | 0 | 0 | 0 | .. | .. | .. | .. | .. |
| 4400 Taxes on financial and capital transactions | .. | .. | 0 | 0 | 0 | .. | .. | .. | .. | .. |
| 4500 Non-recurrent taxes | .. | .. | 0 | 0 | 0 | .. | .. | .. | .. | .. |
| 4600 Other recurrent taxes on property | .. | .. | 0 | 0 | 0 | .. | .. | .. | .. | .. |
| **5000 Taxes on goods and services** | **..** | **0** | **1 922** | **3 874** | **4 763** | **..** | **0** | **0** | **0** | **0** |
| 5100 Taxes on production, sale, transfer, etc | .. | .. | 1 579 | 3 073 | 3 747 | .. | .. | .. | .. | .. |
| 5110 General taxes | .. | .. | 1 579 | 3 073 | 3 747 | .. | .. | .. | .. | .. |
| 5120 Taxes on specific goods and services | .. | .. | 0 | 0 | 0 | .. | .. | .. | .. | .. |
| 5130 Unallocable between 5110 and 5120 | .. | .. | 0 | 0 | 0 | .. | .. | .. | .. | .. |
| 5200 Taxes on use of goods and perform activities | .. | .. | 343 | 801 | 1 016 | .. | .. | .. | .. | .. |
| 5300 Unallocable between 5100 and 5200 | .. | .. | 0 | 0 | 0 | .. | .. | .. | .. | .. |
| **6000 Other taxes** | **..** | **0** | **347** | **690** | **915** | **..** | **0** | **0** | **0** | **0** |
| 6100 Paid solely by business | .. | .. | 0 | 0 | 0 | .. | .. | .. | .. | .. |
| 6200 Other | .. | .. | 347 | 690 | 915 | .. | .. | .. | .. | .. |
| **Total tax revenue** | **..** | **882** | **2 672** | **5 246** | **6 660** | **..** | **1 678** | **8 090** | **18 194** | **29 014** |

.. Not available

*Note:* Comparable statistics for 1990 cannot be shown due to the devaluation of the Nicaraguan cordoba.

1. Local tax revenue data in 2020 are estimated.

StatLink https://doi.org/10.1787/888934310233

## Table 6.21. **Panama, tax revenues by sub-sectors of government**

*Million PAB*

| | Federal government[3] | | | | | State/Regional | | | | |
|---|---|---|---|---|---|---|---|---|---|---|
| | 1990 | 2000 | 2010 | 2015 | 2020 | 1990 | 2000 | 2010 | 2015 | 2020 |
| **1000 Taxes on income, profits and capital gains** | **217** | **485** | **1 317** | **2 066** | **1 881** | .. | .. | .. | .. | .. |
| 1100 Of individuals | 140 | 295 | 440 | 799 | 965 | .. | .. | .. | .. | .. |
| 1200 Corporate | 66 | 159 | 603 | 851 | 596 | .. | .. | .. | .. | .. |
| 1300 Unallocable between 1100 and 1200 | 11 | 31 | 273 | 416 | 320 | .. | .. | .. | .. | .. |
| **2000 Social security contributions** | **0** | **0** | **0** | **0** | **0** | .. | .. | .. | .. | .. |
| 2100 Employees | .. | .. | .. | .. | .. | .. | .. | .. | .. | .. |
| 2200 Employers | .. | .. | .. | .. | .. | .. | .. | .. | .. | .. |
| 2300 Self-employed or non-employed | .. | .. | .. | .. | .. | .. | .. | .. | .. | .. |
| 2400 Unallocable between 2100, 2200 and 2300 | .. | .. | .. | .. | .. | .. | .. | .. | .. | .. |
| **3000 Taxes on payroll and workforce[1]** | **0** | **36** | **59** | **111** | **103** | .. | .. | .. | .. | .. |
| **4000 Taxes on property** | **32** | **43** | **138** | **199** | **126** | .. | .. | .. | .. | .. |
| 4100 Recurrent taxes on immovable property | 28 | 34 | 108 | 151 | 104 | .. | .. | .. | .. | .. |
| 4200 Recurrent taxes on net wealth | 0 | 0 | 0 | 0 | 0 | .. | .. | .. | .. | .. |
| 4300 Estate, inheritance and gift taxes | 0 | 0 | 0 | 0 | 0 | .. | .. | .. | .. | .. |
| 4400 Taxes on financial and capital transactions | 3 | 9 | 30 | 48 | 22 | .. | .. | .. | .. | .. |
| 4500 Non-recurrent taxes | 0 | 0 | 0 | 0 | 0 | .. | .. | .. | .. | .. |
| 4600 Other recurrent taxes on property | 0 | 0 | 0 | 0 | 0 | .. | .. | .. | .. | .. |
| **5000 Taxes on goods and services** | **349** | **565** | **1 547** | **2 496** | **1 765** | .. | .. | .. | .. | .. |
| 5100 Taxes on production, sale, transfer, etc | 332 | 546 | 1 473 | 2 376 | 1 657 | .. | .. | .. | .. | .. |
| 5110 General taxes | 80 | 69 | 766 | 1 357 | 963 | .. | .. | .. | .. | .. |
| 5120 Taxes on specific goods and services[2] | 251 | 477 | 707 | 1 019 | 695 | .. | .. | .. | .. | .. |
| 5130 Unallocable between 5110 and 5120 | 0 | 0 | 0 | 0 | 0 | .. | .. | .. | .. | .. |
| 5200 Taxes on use of goods and perform activities | 15 | 19 | 75 | 120 | 108 | .. | .. | .. | .. | .. |
| 5300 Unallocable between 5100 and 5200 | 2 | 0 | 0 | 0 | 0 | .. | .. | .. | .. | .. |
| **6000 Other taxes** | **26** | **27** | **41** | **37** | **20** | .. | .. | .. | .. | .. |
| 6100 Paid solely by business | 0 | 0 | 0 | 0 | 0 | .. | .. | .. | .. | .. |
| 6200 Other | 26 | 27 | 41 | 37 | 20 | .. | .. | .. | .. | .. |
| **Total tax revenue** | **624** | **1 157** | **3 102** | **4 910** | **3 894** | .. | .. | .. | .. | .. |

*Million PAB*

| | Local government | | | | | Social Security Funds[4] | | | | |
|---|---|---|---|---|---|---|---|---|---|---|
| | 1990 | 2000 | 2010 | 2015 | 2020 | 1990 | 2000 | 2010 | 2015 | 2020 |
| **1000 Taxes on income, profits and capital gains** | .. | **0** | **0** | **0** | **0** | **0** | **0** | **0** | **0** | **0** |
| 1100 Of individuals | .. | .. | .. | .. | .. | .. | .. | .. | .. | .. |
| 1200 Corporate | .. | .. | .. | .. | .. | .. | .. | .. | .. | .. |
| 1300 Unallocable between 1100 and 1200 | .. | .. | .. | .. | .. | .. | .. | .. | .. | .. |
| **2000 Social security contributions** | .. | **0** | **0** | **0** | **0** | **325** | **742** | **1 637** | **3 152** | **3 225** |
| 2100 Employees | .. | .. | .. | .. | .. | .. | .. | .. | .. | .. |
| 2200 Employers | .. | .. | .. | .. | .. | .. | .. | .. | .. | .. |
| 2300 Self-employed or non-employed | .. | .. | .. | .. | .. | .. | .. | .. | .. | .. |
| 2400 Unallocable between 2100, 2200 and 2300 | .. | .. | .. | .. | .. | 325 | 742 | 1 637 | 3 152 | 3 225 |
| **3000 Taxes on payroll and workforce[1]** | .. | **0** | **0** | **0** | **0** | **0** | **0** | **0** | **0** | **0** |
| **4000 Taxes on property** | .. | **0** | **0** | **0** | **0** | **0** | **0** | **0** | **0** | **0** |
| 4100 Recurrent taxes on immovable property | .. | 0 | .. | .. | .. | .. | .. | .. | .. | .. |
| 4200 Recurrent taxes on net wealth | .. | 0 | .. | .. | .. | .. | .. | .. | .. | .. |
| 4300 Estate, inheritance and gift taxes | .. | 0 | .. | .. | .. | .. | .. | .. | .. | .. |
| 4400 Taxes on financial and capital transactions | .. | 0 | .. | .. | .. | .. | .. | .. | .. | .. |
| 4500 Non-recurrent taxes | .. | 0 | .. | .. | .. | .. | .. | .. | .. | .. |
| 4600 Other recurrent taxes on property | .. | 0 | .. | .. | .. | .. | .. | .. | .. | .. |
| **5000 Taxes on goods and services** | .. | **43** | **76** | **131** | **119** | **0** | **0** | **0** | **0** | **0** |
| 5100 Taxes on production, sale, transfer, etc | .. | 0 | 0 | 0 | 0 | .. | .. | .. | .. | .. |
| 5110 General taxes | .. | 0 | .. | .. | .. | .. | .. | .. | .. | .. |
| 5120 Taxes on specific goods and services[2] | .. | 0 | .. | .. | .. | .. | .. | .. | .. | .. |
| 5130 Unallocable between 5110 and 5120 | .. | 0 | .. | .. | .. | .. | .. | .. | .. | .. |
| 5200 Taxes on use of goods and perform activities | .. | 43 | 76 | 131 | 119 | .. | .. | .. | .. | .. |
| 5300 Unallocable between 5100 and 5200 | .. | 0 | 0 | 0 | 0 | .. | .. | .. | .. | .. |
| **6000 Other taxes** | .. | **0** | **0** | **0** | **0** | **0** | **0** | **0** | **0** | **0** |
| 6100 Paid solely by business | .. | 0 | .. | .. | .. | .. | .. | .. | .. | .. |
| 6200 Other | .. | 0 | .. | .. | .. | .. | .. | .. | .. | .. |
| **Total tax revenue** | .. | **43** | **76** | **131** | **119** | **325** | **742** | **1 637** | **3 152** | **3 225** |

.. Not available

1. In CIAT and ECLAC data, the tax on banks, financial institutions and currency exchange is classified as a property tax (4000).
2. The figures exclude documentos fiscales as they are not considered as tax revenues according to the OECD classification, described in the interpretative guide.
3. In ECLAC data, education insurance is classified as "Other taxes" (6000).
4. Social security contributions include regular and special contributions and professional risks premium collected by the Caja de Seguro Social (CSS).

StatLink https://doi.org/10.1787/888934310252

## Table 6.22. **Paraguay, tax revenues by sub-sectors of government**

*Million PYG*

| | Federal government | | | | | State/Regional | | | | |
|---|---|---|---|---|---|---|---|---|---|---|
| | 1990 | 2000 | 2010 | 2015 | 2020 | 1990 | 2000 | 2010 | 2015 | 2020 |
| **1000 Taxes on income, profits and capital gains** | **73 726** | **470 388** | **2 096 498** | **3 922 384** | **6 010 196** | **..** | **..** | **..** | **..** | **..** |
| 1100 Of individuals | .. | 15 042 | 31 263 | 409 238 | 536 357 | .. | .. | .. | .. | .. |
| 1200 Corporate | .. | 455 346 | 2 065 235 | 3 513 146 | 5 473 839 | .. | .. | .. | .. | .. |
| 1300 Unallocable between 1100 and 1200 | 73 726 | 0 | 0 | 0 | 0 | .. | .. | .. | .. | .. |
| **2000 Social security contributions** | **0** | **0** | **0** | **0** | **0** | **..** | **..** | **..** | **..** | **..** |
| 2100 Employees | .. | .. | .. | .. | .. | .. | .. | .. | .. | .. |
| 2200 Employers | .. | .. | .. | .. | .. | .. | .. | .. | .. | .. |
| 2300 Self-employed or non-employed | .. | .. | .. | .. | .. | .. | .. | .. | .. | .. |
| 2400 Unallocable between 2100, 2200 and 2300 | .. | .. | .. | .. | .. | .. | .. | .. | .. | .. |
| **3000 Taxes on payroll and workforce** | **0** | **0** | **0** | **0** | **0** | **..** | **..** | **..** | **..** | **..** |
| **4000 Taxes on property** | **17 162** | **71 777** | **332** | **91** | **57** | **..** | **..** | **..** | **..** | **..** |
| 4100 Recurrent taxes on immovable property | 17 162 | 0 | 0 | 0 | 0 | .. | .. | .. | .. | .. |
| 4200 Recurrent taxes on net wealth | 0 | 0 | 0 | 0 | 0 | .. | .. | .. | .. | .. |
| 4300 Estate, inheritance and gift taxes | 0 | 0 | 0 | 0 | 0 | .. | .. | .. | .. | .. |
| 4400 Taxes on financial and capital transactions | 0 | 71 777 | 332 | 91 | 57 | .. | .. | .. | .. | .. |
| 4500 Non-recurrent taxes | 0 | 0 | 0 | 0 | 0 | .. | .. | .. | .. | .. |
| 4600 Other recurrent taxes on property | 0 | 0 | 0 | 0 | 0 | .. | .. | .. | .. | .. |
| **5000 Taxes on goods and services** | **438 444** | **2 080 878** | **9 226 584** | **13 837 266** | **16 547 634** | **..** | **..** | **..** | **..** | **..** |
| 5100 Taxes on production, sale, transfer, etc | 438 444 | 2 080 878 | 9 226 493 | 13 837 212 | 16 547 634 | .. | .. | .. | .. | .. |
| 5110 General taxes | 0 | 1 150 496 | 5 991 694 | 9 768 800 | 11 787 033 | .. | .. | .. | .. | .. |
| 5120 Taxes on specific goods and services | 438 444 | 930 382 | 3 234 799 | 4 068 411 | 4 760 600 | .. | .. | .. | .. | .. |
| 5130 Unallocable between 5110 and 5120 | 0 | 0 | 0 | 0 | 0 | .. | .. | .. | .. | .. |
| 5200 Taxes on use of goods and perform activities | 0 | 0 | 91 | 54 | 0 | .. | .. | .. | .. | .. |
| 5300 Unallocable between 5100 and 5200 | 0 | 0 | 0 | 0 | 0 | .. | .. | .. | .. | .. |
| **6000 Other taxes** | **49 807** | **44 875** | **109 001** | **128 632** | **97 800** | **..** | **..** | **..** | **..** | **..** |
| 6100 Paid solely by business | 0 | 0 | 0 | 0 | 0 | .. | .. | .. | .. | .. |
| 6200 Other | 49 807 | 44 875 | 109 001 | 128 632 | 97 800 | .. | .. | .. | .. | .. |
| **Total tax revenue** | **579 139** | **2 667 918** | **11 432 415** | **17 888 373** | **22 655 687** | **..** | **..** | **..** | **..** | **..** |

*Million PYG*

| | Local government[1] | | | | | Social Security Funds[2] | | | | |
|---|---|---|---|---|---|---|---|---|---|---|
| | 1990 | 2000 | 2010 | 2015 | 2020 | 1990 | 2000 | 2010 | 2015 | 2020 |
| **1000 Taxes on income, profits and capital gains** | **..** | **..** | **0** | **0** | **0** | **0** | **0** | **0** | **0** | **0** |
| 1100 Of individuals | .. | .. | .. | .. | .. | .. | .. | .. | .. | .. |
| 1200 Corporate | .. | .. | .. | .. | .. | .. | .. | .. | .. | .. |
| 1300 Unallocable between 1100 and 1200 | .. | .. | .. | .. | .. | .. | .. | .. | .. | .. |
| **2000 Social security contributions** | **..** | **..** | **0** | **0** | **0** | **28 882** | **919 527** | **3 552 640** | **7 044 316** | **8 954 858** |
| 2100 Employees | .. | .. | .. | .. | .. | .. | .. | .. | .. | .. |
| 2200 Employers | .. | .. | .. | .. | .. | .. | .. | .. | .. | .. |
| 2300 Self-employed or non-employed | .. | .. | .. | .. | .. | .. | .. | .. | .. | .. |
| 2400 Unallocable between 2100, 2200 and 2300 | .. | .. | .. | .. | .. | 28 882 | 919 527 | 3 552 640 | 7 044 316 | 8 954 858 |
| **3000 Taxes on payroll and workforce** | **..** | **..** | **0** | **0** | **0** | **0** | **0** | **0** | **0** | **0** |
| **4000 Taxes on property** | **..** | **..** | **275 787** | **435 382** | **401 165** | **0** | **0** | **0** | **0** | **0** |
| 4100 Recurrent taxes on immovable property | .. | .. | 258 423 | 405 806 | 375 800 | .. | .. | .. | .. | .. |
| 4200 Recurrent taxes on net wealth | .. | .. | 0 | 0 | 0 | .. | .. | .. | .. | .. |
| 4300 Estate, inheritance and gift taxes | .. | .. | 0 | 0 | 0 | .. | .. | .. | .. | .. |
| 4400 Taxes on financial and capital transactions | .. | .. | 15 623 | 29 510 | 24 800 | .. | .. | .. | .. | .. |
| 4500 Non-recurrent taxes | .. | .. | 0 | 0 | 0 | .. | .. | .. | .. | .. |
| 4600 Other recurrent taxes on property | .. | .. | 1 742 | 66 | 565 | .. | .. | .. | .. | .. |
| **5000 Taxes on goods and services** | **..** | **..** | **235 877** | **442 063** | **381 458** | **0** | **0** | **0** | **0** | **0** |
| 5100 Taxes on production, sale, transfer, etc | .. | .. | 19 384 | 23 423 | 10 035 | .. | .. | .. | .. | .. |
| 5110 General taxes | .. | .. | 0 | 0 | 0 | .. | .. | .. | .. | .. |
| 5120 Taxes on specific goods and services | .. | .. | 19 384 | 23 423 | 10 035 | .. | .. | .. | .. | .. |
| 5130 Unallocable between 5110 and 5120 | .. | .. | 0 | 0 | 0 | .. | .. | .. | .. | .. |
| 5200 Taxes on use of goods and perform activities | .. | .. | 216 256 | 395 802 | 370 331 | .. | .. | .. | .. | .. |
| 5300 Unallocable between 5100 and 5200 | .. | .. | 237 | 22 838 | 1 092 | .. | .. | .. | .. | .. |
| **6000 Other taxes** | **..** | **..** | **141 811** | **45 052** | **48 146** | **0** | **0** | **0** | **0** | **0** |
| 6100 Paid solely by business | .. | .. | 0 | 0 | 0 | .. | .. | .. | .. | .. |
| 6200 Other | .. | .. | 141 811 | 45 052 | 48 146 | .. | .. | .. | .. | .. |
| **Total tax revenue** | **..** | **..** | **653 476** | **922 496** | **830 769** | **28 882** | **919 527** | **3 552 640** | **7 044 316** | **8 954 858** |

.. Not available

1. The figures for years before 2006 exclude local government tax revenues as the data are not available.
2. Social security contributions before 1999 do not include contributions collected by decentralised institutions as the data are not available.

StatLink https://doi.org/10.1787/888934310271

## Table 6.23. **Peru, tax revenues by sub-sectors of government**

*Million PEN*

| | Federal government | | | | | State/Regional | | | | |
|---|---|---|---|---|---|---|---|---|---|---|
| | 1990 | 2000 | 2010 | 2015 | 2020 | 1990 | 2000 | 2010 | 2015 | 2020 |
| **1000 Taxes on income, profits and capital gains** | **37** | **5 078** | **27 317** | **37 772** | **40 124** | .. | .. | .. | .. | .. |
| 1100 Of individuals | 3 | 2 117 | 6 518 | 11 137 | 13 182 | .. | .. | .. | .. | .. |
| 1200 Corporate | 32 | 2 526 | 19 561 | 24 266 | 23 352 | .. | .. | .. | .. | .. |
| 1300 Unallocable between 1100 and 1200 | 1 | 436 | 1 239 | 2 369 | 3 589 | .. | .. | .. | .. | .. |
| **2000 Social security contributions** | **0** | **0** | **0** | **0** | **0** | .. | .. | .. | .. | .. |
| 2100 Employees | .. | .. | .. | .. | .. | .. | .. | .. | .. | .. |
| 2200 Employers | .. | .. | .. | .. | .. | .. | .. | .. | .. | .. |
| 2300 Self-employed or non-employed | .. | .. | .. | .. | .. | .. | .. | .. | .. | .. |
| 2400 Unallocable between 2100, 2200 and 2300 | .. | .. | .. | .. | .. | .. | .. | .. | .. | .. |
| **3000 Taxes on payroll and workforce[1]** | **0** | **1 176** | **57** | **92** | **96** | .. | .. | .. | .. | .. |
| **4000 Taxes on property** | **87** | **0** | **944** | **161** | **207** | .. | .. | .. | .. | .. |
| 4100 Recurrent taxes on immovable property | 0 | 0 | 0 | 0 | 0 | .. | .. | .. | .. | .. |
| 4200 Recurrent taxes on net wealth | 49 | 0 | 0 | 0 | 0 | .. | .. | .. | .. | .. |
| 4300 Estate, inheritance and gift taxes | 0 | 0 | 0 | 0 | 0 | .. | .. | .. | .. | .. |
| 4400 Taxes on financial and capital transactions | 38 | 0 | 944 | 161 | 207 | .. | .. | .. | .. | .. |
| 4500 Non-recurrent taxes | 0 | 0 | 0 | 0 | 0 | .. | .. | .. | .. | .. |
| 4600 Other recurrent taxes on property | 0 | 0 | 0 | 0 | 0 | .. | .. | .. | .. | .. |
| **5000 Taxes on goods and services** | **454** | **16 205** | **36 064** | **50 606** | **50 908** | .. | .. | .. | .. | .. |
| 5100 Taxes on production, sale, transfer, etc | 454 | 16 205 | 36 064 | 50 606 | 50 908 | .. | .. | .. | .. | .. |
| 5110 General taxes | 109 | 9 646 | 29 094 | 42 612 | 42 377 | .. | .. | .. | .. | .. |
| 5120 Taxes on specific goods and services | 345 | 6 558 | 6 970 | 7 994 | 8 532 | .. | .. | .. | .. | .. |
| 5130 Unallocable between 5110 and 5120 | 0 | 0 | 0 | 0 | 0 | .. | .. | .. | .. | .. |
| 5200 Taxes on use of goods and perform activities | 0 | 0 | 0 | 0 | 0 | .. | .. | .. | .. | .. |
| 5300 Unallocable between 5100 and 5200 | 0 | 0 | 0 | 0 | 0 | .. | .. | .. | .. | .. |
| **6000 Other taxes** | **9** | **697** | **888** | **2 088** | **832** | .. | .. | .. | .. | .. |
| 6100 Paid solely by business | 0 | 84 | 108 | 179 | 93 | .. | .. | .. | .. | .. |
| 6200 Other | 9 | 614 | 780 | 1 909 | 739 | .. | .. | .. | .. | .. |
| **Total tax revenue** | **587** | **23 156** | **65 270** | **90 719** | **92 167** | .. | .. | .. | .. | .. |

*Million PEN*

| | Local government[2] | | | | | Social Security Funds | | | | |
|---|---|---|---|---|---|---|---|---|---|---|
| | 1990 | 2000 | 2010 | 2015 | 2020 | 1990 | 2000 | 2010 | 2015 | 2020 |
| **1000 Taxes on income, profits and capital gains** | .. | **0** | **0** | **0** | **0** | **0** | **0** | **0** | **0** | **0** |
| 1100 Of individuals | .. | .. | .. | .. | .. | .. | .. | .. | .. | .. |
| 1200 Corporate | .. | .. | .. | .. | .. | .. | .. | .. | .. | .. |
| 1300 Unallocable between 1100 and 1200 | .. | .. | .. | .. | .. | .. | .. | .. | .. | .. |
| **2000 Social security contributions** | .. | **0** | **0** | **0** | **0** | **50** | **3 185** | **7 929** | **12 681** | **14 680** |
| 2100 Employees | .. | .. | .. | .. | .. | .. | 566 | 2 468 | 3 508 | 3 910 |
| 2200 Employers | .. | .. | .. | .. | .. | .. | 2 515 | 5 454 | 9 170 | 10 767 |
| 2300 Self-employed or non-employed | .. | .. | .. | .. | .. | .. | 95 | 7 | 2 | 3 |
| 2400 Unallocable between 2100, 2200 and 2300 | .. | .. | .. | .. | .. | 50 | 9 | 0 | 0 | 0 |
| **3000 Taxes on payroll and workforce[1]** | .. | **0** | **0** | **0** | **0** | **0** | **0** | **0** | **0** | **0** |
| **4000 Taxes on property** | .. | **323** | **1 287** | **2 268** | **2 212** | **0** | **0** | **0** | **0** | **0** |
| 4100 Recurrent taxes on immovable property | .. | 298 | 727 | 1 463 | 1 749 | .. | .. | .. | .. | .. |
| 4200 Recurrent taxes on net wealth | .. | 0 | 0 | 0 | 0 | .. | .. | .. | .. | .. |
| 4300 Estate, inheritance and gift taxes | .. | 0 | 0 | 0 | 0 | .. | .. | .. | .. | .. |
| 4400 Taxes on financial and capital transactions | .. | 25 | 560 | 805 | 463 | .. | .. | .. | .. | .. |
| 4500 Non-recurrent taxes | .. | 0 | 0 | 0 | 0 | .. | .. | .. | .. | .. |
| 4600 Other recurrent taxes on property | .. | 0 | 0 | 0 | 0 | .. | .. | .. | .. | .. |
| **5000 Taxes on goods and services** | .. | **59** | **290** | **496** | **311** | **0** | **0** | **0** | **0** | **0** |
| 5100 Taxes on production, sale, transfer, etc | .. | 34 | 135 | 214 | 70 | .. | .. | .. | .. | .. |
| 5110 General taxes | .. | 0 | 0 | 0 | 0 | .. | .. | .. | .. | .. |
| 5120 Taxes on specific goods and services | .. | 34 | 135 | 214 | 70 | .. | .. | .. | .. | .. |
| 5130 Unallocable between 5110 and 5120 | .. | 0 | 0 | 0 | 0 | .. | .. | .. | .. | .. |
| 5200 Taxes on use of goods and perform activities | .. | 25 | 154 | 282 | 241 | .. | .. | .. | .. | .. |
| 5300 Unallocable between 5100 and 5200 | .. | 0 | 0 | 0 | 0 | .. | .. | .. | .. | .. |
| **6000 Other taxes** | .. | **48** | **26** | **19** | **46** | **0** | **0** | **0** | **0** | **0** |
| 6100 Paid solely by business | .. | 0 | 0 | 0 | 0 | .. | .. | .. | .. | .. |
| 6200 Other | .. | 48 | 26 | 19 | 46 | .. | .. | .. | .. | .. |
| **Total tax revenue** | .. | **430** | **1 603** | **2 784** | **2 569** | **50** | **3 185** | **7 929** | **12 681** | **14 680** |

.. Not available

1. Contributions to SENATI are included in heading 3000. The tax revenue is classified under the central government. In Peru this revenue is classified under a separate unit considered to be different to the central government.
2. The figures for years up to 2000 exclude local government tax revenues as the data are not available.

StatLink https://doi.org/10.1787/888934310290

# Table 6.24. **Saint Lucia, tax revenues by sub-sectors of government**

*Million XCD*

| | Federal government | | | | | State/Regional | | | | |
|---|---|---|---|---|---|---|---|---|---|---|
| | 1990 | 2000 | 2010 | 2015 | 2020 | 1990 | 2000 | 2010 | 2015 | 2020 |
| **1000 Taxes on income, profits and capital gains** | .. | **137** | **224** | **242** | **213** | .. | .. | .. | .. | .. |
| 1100 Of individuals | .. | 49 | 83 | 105 | 109 | .. | .. | .. | .. | .. |
| 1200 Corporate | .. | 63 | 95 | 78 | 90 | .. | .. | .. | .. | .. |
| 1300 Unallocable between 1100 and 1200 | .. | 26 | 46 | 58 | 14 | .. | .. | .. | .. | .. |
| **2000 Social security contributions** | .. | **0** | **0** | **0** | **0** | .. | .. | .. | .. | .. |
| 2100 Employees | .. | .. | .. | .. | .. | .. | .. | .. | .. | .. |
| 2200 Employers | .. | .. | .. | .. | .. | .. | .. | .. | .. | .. |
| 2300 Self-employed or non-employed | .. | .. | .. | .. | .. | .. | .. | .. | .. | .. |
| 2400 Unallocable between 2100, 2200 and 2300 | .. | .. | .. | .. | .. | .. | .. | .. | .. | .. |
| **3000 Taxes on payroll and workforce** | .. | **0** | **0** | **0** | **0** | .. | .. | .. | .. | .. |
| **4000 Taxes on property** | .. | **11** | **19** | **23** | **19** | .. | .. | .. | .. | .. |
| 4100 Recurrent taxes on immovable property | .. | 2 | 3 | 11 | 6 | .. | .. | .. | .. | .. |
| 4200 Recurrent taxes on net wealth | .. | 0 | 0 | 0 | 0 | .. | .. | .. | .. | .. |
| 4300 Estate, inheritance and gift taxes | .. | 0 | 0 | 0 | 0 | .. | .. | .. | .. | .. |
| 4400 Taxes on financial and capital transactions | .. | 9 | 16 | 12 | 13 | .. | .. | .. | .. | .. |
| 4500 Non-recurrent taxes | .. | 0 | 0 | 0 | 0 | .. | .. | .. | .. | .. |
| 4600 Other recurrent taxes on property | .. | 0 | 0 | 0 | 0 | .. | .. | .. | .. | .. |
| **5000 Taxes on goods and services** | .. | **284** | **493** | **670** | **561** | .. | .. | .. | .. | .. |
| 5100 Taxes on production, sale, transfer, etc | .. | 277 | 467 | 642 | 551 | .. | .. | .. | .. | .. |
| 5110 General taxes | .. | 101 | 119 | 347 | 241 | .. | .. | .. | .. | .. |
| 5120 Taxes on specific goods and services | .. | 176 | 348 | 295 | 311 | .. | .. | .. | .. | .. |
| 5130 Unallocable between 5110 and 5120 | .. | 0 | 0 | 0 | 0 | .. | .. | .. | .. | .. |
| 5200 Taxes on use of goods and perform activities | .. | 7 | 26 | 29 | 9 | .. | .. | .. | .. | .. |
| 5300 Unallocable between 5100 and 5200 | .. | 0 | 0 | 0 | 0 | .. | .. | .. | .. | .. |
| **6000 Other taxes** | .. | **0** | **0** | **0** | **0** | .. | .. | .. | .. | .. |
| 6100 Paid solely by business | .. | .. | .. | .. | .. | .. | .. | .. | .. | .. |
| 6200 Other | .. | .. | .. | .. | .. | .. | .. | .. | .. | .. |
| **Total tax revenue** | .. | **432** | **737** | **935** | **793** | .. | .. | .. | .. | .. |

*Million XCD*

| | Local government[1] | | | | | Social Security Funds | | | | |
|---|---|---|---|---|---|---|---|---|---|---|
| | 1990 | 2000 | 2010 | 2015 | 2020 | 1990 | 2000 | 2010 | 2015 | 2020 |
| **1000 Taxes on income, profits and capital gains** | .. | .. | .. | .. | .. | .. | **0** | **0** | **0** | **0** |
| 1100 Of individuals | .. | .. | .. | .. | .. | .. | .. | .. | .. | .. |
| 1200 Corporate | .. | .. | .. | .. | .. | .. | .. | .. | .. | .. |
| 1300 Unallocable between 1100 and 1200 | .. | .. | .. | .. | .. | .. | .. | .. | .. | .. |
| **2000 Social security contributions** | .. | .. | .. | .. | .. | .. | **48** | **92** | **111** | **115** |
| 2100 Employees | .. | .. | .. | .. | .. | .. | .. | .. | .. | .. |
| 2200 Employers | .. | .. | .. | .. | .. | .. | .. | .. | .. | .. |
| 2300 Self-employed or non-employed | .. | .. | .. | .. | .. | .. | .. | 1 | 1 | 1 |
| 2400 Unallocable between 2100, 2200 and 2300 | .. | .. | .. | .. | .. | .. | 48 | 91 | 110 | 114 |
| **3000 Taxes on payroll and workforce** | .. | .. | .. | .. | .. | .. | **0** | **0** | **0** | **0** |
| **4000 Taxes on property** | .. | .. | .. | .. | .. | .. | **0** | **0** | **0** | **0** |
| 4100 Recurrent taxes on immovable property | .. | .. | .. | .. | .. | .. | .. | .. | .. | .. |
| 4200 Recurrent taxes on net wealth | .. | .. | .. | .. | .. | .. | .. | .. | .. | .. |
| 4300 Estate, inheritance and gift taxes | .. | .. | .. | .. | .. | .. | .. | .. | .. | .. |
| 4400 Taxes on financial and capital transactions | .. | .. | .. | .. | .. | .. | .. | .. | .. | .. |
| 4500 Non-recurrent taxes | .. | .. | .. | .. | .. | .. | .. | .. | .. | .. |
| 4600 Other recurrent taxes on property | .. | .. | .. | .. | .. | .. | .. | .. | .. | .. |
| **5000 Taxes on goods and services** | .. | .. | .. | .. | .. | .. | **0** | **0** | **0** | **0** |
| 5100 Taxes on production, sale, transfer, etc | .. | .. | .. | .. | .. | .. | .. | .. | .. | .. |
| 5110 General taxes | .. | .. | .. | .. | .. | .. | .. | .. | .. | .. |
| 5120 Taxes on specific goods and services | .. | .. | .. | .. | .. | .. | .. | .. | .. | .. |
| 5130 Unallocable between 5110 and 5120 | .. | .. | .. | .. | .. | .. | .. | .. | .. | .. |
| 5200 Taxes on use of goods and perform activities | .. | .. | .. | .. | .. | .. | .. | .. | .. | .. |
| 5300 Unallocable between 5100 and 5200 | .. | .. | .. | .. | .. | .. | .. | .. | .. | .. |
| **6000 Other taxes** | .. | .. | .. | .. | .. | .. | **0** | **0** | **0** | **0** |
| 6100 Paid solely by business | .. | .. | .. | .. | .. | .. | .. | .. | .. | .. |
| 6200 Other | .. | .. | .. | .. | .. | .. | .. | .. | .. | .. |
| **Total tax revenue** | .. | .. | .. | .. | .. | .. | **48** | **92** | **111** | **115** |

.. Not available

1. Local government tax revenues are not available.

StatLink https://doi.org/10.1787/888934310309

## Table 6.25. **Trinidad and Tobago, tax revenues by sub-sectors of government**

*Million TTD*

| | Federal government | | | | | State/Regional | | | | |
|---|---|---|---|---|---|---|---|---|---|---|
| | 1990 | 2000 | 2010 | 2015 | 2020 | 1990 | 2000 | 2010 | 2015 | 2020 |
| **1000 Taxes on income, profits and capital gains** | **2 595** | **6 224** | **27 213** | **29 628** | **15 332** | .. | .. | .. | .. | .. |
| 1100 Of individuals | 669 | 2 325 | 4 674 | 7 752 | 6 209 | .. | .. | .. | .. | .. |
| 1200 Corporate | 1 856 | 3 704 | 21 659 | 20 810 | 8 186 | .. | .. | .. | .. | .. |
| 1300 Unallocable between 1100 and 1200 | 70 | 195 | 881 | 1 067 | 938 | .. | .. | .. | .. | .. |
| **2000 Social security contributions** | **0** | **0** | **0** | **0** | **0** | .. | .. | .. | .. | .. |
| 2100 Employees | .. | .. | .. | .. | .. | .. | .. | .. | .. | .. |
| 2200 Employers | .. | .. | .. | .. | .. | .. | .. | .. | .. | .. |
| 2300 Self-employed or non-employed | .. | .. | .. | .. | .. | .. | .. | .. | .. | .. |
| 2400 Unallocable between 2100, 2200 and 2300 | .. | .. | .. | .. | .. | .. | .. | .. | .. | .. |
| **3000 Taxes on payroll and workforce** | **0** | **0** | **0** | **0** | **0** | .. | .. | .. | .. | .. |
| **4000 Taxes on property** | **90** | **175** | **194** | **406** | **260** | .. | .. | .. | .. | .. |
| 4100 Recurrent taxes on immovable property | 39 | 64 | 22 | 3 | 2 | .. | .. | .. | .. | .. |
| 4200 Recurrent taxes on net wealth | 0 | 0 | 0 | 0 | 0 | .. | .. | .. | .. | .. |
| 4300 Estate, inheritance and gift taxes | 1 | 0 | 0 | 0 | 0 | .. | .. | .. | .. | .. |
| 4400 Taxes on financial and capital transactions | 49 | 111 | 172 | 403 | 258 | .. | .. | .. | .. | .. |
| 4500 Non-recurrent taxes | 0 | 0 | 0 | 0 | 0 | .. | .. | .. | .. | .. |
| 4600 Other recurrent taxes on property | 0 | 0 | 0 | 0 | 0 | .. | .. | .. | .. | .. |
| **5000 Taxes on goods and services** | **2 055** | **3 852** | **9 667** | **12 264** | **10 980** | .. | .. | .. | .. | .. |
| 5100 Taxes on production, sale, transfer, etc | 1 973 | 3 603 | 9 282 | 11 678 | 10 752 | .. | .. | .. | .. | .. |
| 5110 General taxes | 980 | 1 890 | 6 358 | 7 569 | 7 417 | .. | .. | .. | .. | .. |
| 5120 Taxes on specific goods and services | 993 | 1 713 | 2 924 | 4 108 | 3 336 | .. | .. | .. | .. | .. |
| 5130 Unallocable between 5110 and 5120 | 0 | 0 | 0 | 0 | 0 | .. | .. | .. | .. | .. |
| 5200 Taxes on use of goods and perform activities | 81 | 249 | 386 | 586 | 228 | .. | .. | .. | .. | .. |
| 5300 Unallocable between 5100 and 5200 | 0 | 0 | 0 | 0 | 0 | .. | .. | .. | .. | .. |
| **6000 Other taxes** | **0** | **0** | **0** | **0** | **0** | .. | .. | .. | .. | .. |
| 6100 Paid solely by business | .. | .. | .. | .. | .. | .. | .. | .. | .. | .. |
| 6200 Other | .. | .. | .. | .. | .. | .. | .. | .. | .. | .. |
| **Total tax revenue** | **4 740** | **10 251** | **37 074** | **42 298** | **26 572** | .. | .. | .. | .. | .. |

*Million TTD*

| | Local government[1] | | | | | Social Security Funds[2] | | | | |
|---|---|---|---|---|---|---|---|---|---|---|
| | 1990 | 2000 | 2010 | 2015 | 2020 | 1990 | 2000 | 2010 | 2015 | 2020 |
| **1000 Taxes on income, profits and capital gains** | .. | .. | .. | .. | .. | **0** | **0** | **0** | **0** | **0** |
| 1100 Of individuals | .. | .. | .. | .. | .. | .. | .. | .. | .. | .. |
| 1200 Corporate | .. | .. | .. | .. | .. | .. | .. | .. | .. | .. |
| 1300 Unallocable between 1100 and 1200 | .. | .. | .. | .. | .. | .. | .. | .. | .. | .. |
| **2000 Social security contributions** | .. | .. | .. | .. | .. | **183** | **702** | **2 645** | **4 261** | **4 686** |
| 2100 Employees | .. | .. | .. | .. | .. | .. | .. | .. | .. | .. |
| 2200 Employers | .. | .. | .. | .. | .. | .. | .. | .. | .. | .. |
| 2300 Self-employed or non-employed | .. | .. | .. | .. | .. | .. | .. | .. | .. | .. |
| 2400 Unallocable between 2100, 2200 and 2300 | .. | .. | .. | .. | .. | 183 | 702 | 2 645 | 4 261 | 4 686 |
| **3000 Taxes on payroll and workforce** | .. | .. | .. | .. | .. | **0** | **0** | **0** | **0** | **0** |
| **4000 Taxes on property** | .. | .. | .. | .. | .. | **0** | **0** | **0** | **0** | **0** |
| 4100 Recurrent taxes on immovable property | .. | .. | .. | .. | .. | .. | .. | .. | .. | .. |
| 4200 Recurrent taxes on net wealth | .. | .. | .. | .. | .. | .. | .. | .. | .. | .. |
| 4300 Estate, inheritance and gift taxes | .. | .. | .. | .. | .. | .. | .. | .. | .. | .. |
| 4400 Taxes on financial and capital transactions | .. | .. | .. | .. | .. | .. | .. | .. | .. | .. |
| 4500 Non-recurrent taxes | .. | .. | .. | .. | .. | .. | .. | .. | .. | .. |
| 4600 Other recurrent taxes on property | .. | .. | .. | .. | .. | .. | .. | .. | .. | .. |
| **5000 Taxes on goods and services** | .. | .. | .. | .. | .. | **0** | **0** | **0** | **0** | **0** |
| 5100 Taxes on production, sale, transfer, etc | .. | .. | .. | .. | .. | .. | .. | .. | .. | .. |
| 5110 General taxes | .. | .. | .. | .. | .. | .. | .. | .. | .. | .. |
| 5120 Taxes on specific goods and services | .. | .. | .. | .. | .. | .. | .. | .. | .. | .. |
| 5130 Unallocable between 5110 and 5120 | .. | .. | .. | .. | .. | .. | .. | .. | .. | .. |
| 5200 Taxes on use of goods and perform activities | .. | .. | .. | .. | .. | .. | .. | .. | .. | .. |
| 5300 Unallocable between 5100 and 5200 | .. | .. | .. | .. | .. | .. | .. | .. | .. | .. |
| **6000 Other taxes** | .. | .. | .. | .. | .. | **0** | **0** | **0** | **0** | **0** |
| 6100 Paid solely by business | .. | .. | .. | .. | .. | .. | .. | .. | .. | .. |
| 6200 Other | .. | .. | .. | .. | .. | .. | .. | .. | .. | .. |
| **Total tax revenue** | .. | .. | .. | .. | .. | **183** | **702** | **2 645** | **4 261** | **4 686** |

.. Not available

1. Data are not available for local government tax revenues.
2. The figures follow financial year from July to June.

StatLink https://doi.org/10.1787/888934310328

## Table 6.26. **Uruguay, tax revenues by sub-sectors of government**

*Million UYU*

| | Federal government | | | | | State/Regional | | | | |
|---|---|---|---|---|---|---|---|---|---|---|
| | 1990 | 2000 | 2010 | 2015 | 2020 | 1990 | 2000 | 2010 | 2015 | 2020 |
| **1000 Taxes on income, profits and capital gains** | **114** | **8 698** | **42 583** | **84 141** | **159 783** | .. | .. | .. | .. | .. |
| 1100 Of individuals | 0 | 3 597 | 19 148 | 45 451 | 91 819 | .. | .. | .. | .. | .. |
| 1200 Corporate | 114 | 5 102 | 21 772 | 34 814 | 61 487 | .. | .. | .. | .. | .. |
| 1300 Unallocable between 1100 and 1200 | 0 | 0 | 1 662 | 3 875 | 6 477 | .. | .. | .. | .. | .. |
| **2000 Social security contributions** | **0** | **0** | **0** | **0** | **0** | .. | .. | .. | .. | .. |
| 2100 Employees | .. | .. | .. | .. | .. | .. | .. | .. | .. | .. |
| 2200 Employers | .. | .. | .. | .. | .. | .. | .. | .. | .. | .. |
| 2300 Self-employed or non-employed | .. | .. | .. | .. | .. | .. | .. | .. | .. | .. |
| 2400 Unallocable between 2100, 2200 and 2300 | .. | .. | .. | .. | .. | .. | .. | .. | .. | .. |
| **3000 Taxes on payroll and workforce** | **0** | **0** | **0** | **0** | **0** | .. | .. | .. | .. | .. |
| **4000 Taxes on property** | **105** | **2 690** | **11 688** | **20 673** | **28 063** | .. | .. | .. | .. | .. |
| 4100 Recurrent taxes on immovable property | 0 | 533 | 1 252 | 3 775 | 5 023 | .. | .. | .. | .. | .. |
| 4200 Recurrent taxes on net wealth | 94 | 1 769 | 8 760 | 14 776 | 20 335 | .. | .. | .. | .. | .. |
| 4300 Estate, inheritance and gift taxes | 0 | 0 | 0 | 0 | 0 | .. | .. | .. | .. | .. |
| 4400 Taxes on financial and capital transactions | 11 | 372 | 1 350 | 1 601 | 2 120 | .. | .. | .. | .. | .. |
| 4500 Non-recurrent taxes | 0 | 0 | 0 | 0 | 0 | .. | .. | .. | .. | .. |
| 4600 Other recurrent taxes on property | 1 | 15 | 326 | 522 | 585 | .. | .. | .. | .. | .. |
| **5000 Taxes on goods and services** | **1 301** | **29 556** | **96 432** | **162 611** | **227 132** | .. | .. | .. | .. | .. |
| 5100 Taxes on production, sale, transfer, etc | 1 301 | 29 556 | 96 432 | 162 611 | 227 132 | .. | .. | .. | .. | .. |
| 5110 General taxes[1] | 660 | 18 009 | 69 951 | 114 627 | 157 644 | .. | .. | .. | .. | .. |
| 5120 Taxes on specific goods and services | 641 | 11 546 | 26 480 | 47 983 | 69 489 | .. | .. | .. | .. | .. |
| 5130 Unallocable between 5110 and 5120 | 0 | 0 | 0 | 0 | 0 | .. | .. | .. | .. | .. |
| 5200 Taxes on use of goods and perform activities | 0 | 0 | 0 | 0 | 0 | .. | .. | .. | .. | .. |
| 5300 Unallocable between 5100 and 5200 | 0 | 0 | 0 | 0 | 0 | .. | .. | .. | .. | .. |
| **6000 Other taxes** | **-10** | **-145** | **586** | **796** | **1 033** | .. | .. | .. | .. | .. |
| 6100 Paid solely by business | -10 | -145 | 586 | 796 | 1 033 | .. | .. | .. | .. | .. |
| 6200 Other | 0 | 0 | 0 | 0 | 0 | .. | .. | .. | .. | .. |
| **Total tax revenue** | **1 510** | **40 799** | **151 289** | **268 221** | **416 011** | .. | .. | .. | .. | .. |

*Million UYU*

| | Local government[2] | | | | | Social Security Funds[3] | | | | |
|---|---|---|---|---|---|---|---|---|---|---|
| | 1990 | 2000 | 2010 | 2015 | 2020 | 1990 | 2000 | 2010 | 2015 | 2020 |
| **1000 Taxes on income, profits and capital gains** | **0** | **0** | **0** | **0** | **0** | **0** | **0** | **0** | **0** | **0** |
| 1100 Of individuals | .. | .. | .. | .. | .. | .. | .. | .. | .. | .. |
| 1200 Corporate | .. | .. | .. | .. | .. | .. | .. | .. | .. | .. |
| 1300 Unallocable between 1100 and 1200 | .. | .. | .. | .. | .. | .. | .. | .. | .. | .. |
| **2000 Social security contributions** | **0** | **0** | **0** | **0** | **0** | **717** | **17 679** | **49 742** | **109 282** | **150 185** |
| 2100 Employees | .. | .. | .. | .. | .. | .. | .. | .. | .. | .. |
| 2200 Employers | .. | .. | .. | .. | .. | .. | .. | .. | .. | .. |
| 2300 Self-employed or non-employed | .. | .. | .. | .. | .. | .. | .. | .. | .. | .. |
| 2400 Unallocable between 2100, 2200 and 2300 | .. | .. | .. | .. | .. | 717 | 17 679 | 49 742 | 109 282 | 150 185 |
| **3000 Taxes on payroll and workforce** | **0** | **0** | **0** | **0** | **0** | **0** | **0** | **0** | **0** | **0** |
| **4000 Taxes on property** | **107** | **2 819** | **7 277** | **11 749** | **18 335** | **0** | **0** | **0** | **0** | **0** |
| 4100 Recurrent taxes on immovable property | 87 | 2 715 | 6 887 | 11 109 | 17 377 | .. | .. | .. | .. | .. |
| 4200 Recurrent taxes on net wealth | 0 | 0 | 0 | 0 | 0 | .. | .. | .. | .. | .. |
| 4300 Estate, inheritance and gift taxes | 0 | 0 | 0 | 0 | 0 | .. | .. | .. | .. | .. |
| 4400 Taxes on financial and capital transactions | 20 | 104 | 390 | 639 | 958 | .. | .. | .. | .. | .. |
| 4500 Non-recurrent taxes | 0 | 0 | 0 | 0 | 0 | .. | .. | .. | .. | .. |
| 4600 Other recurrent taxes on property | 0 | 0 | 0 | 0 | 0 | .. | .. | .. | .. | .. |
| **5000 Taxes on goods and services** | **57** | **2 583** | **3 851** | **7 668** | **12 943** | **0** | **0** | **0** | **0** | **0** |
| 5100 Taxes on production, sale, transfer, etc | 0 | 7 | 63 | 128 | 189 | .. | .. | .. | .. | .. |
| 5110 General taxes[1] | 0 | 0 | 0 | 0 | 0 | .. | .. | .. | .. | .. |
| 5120 Taxes on specific goods and services | 0 | 7 | 63 | 128 | 189 | .. | .. | .. | .. | .. |
| 5130 Unallocable between 5110 and 5120 | 0 | 0 | 0 | 0 | 0 | .. | .. | .. | .. | .. |
| 5200 Taxes on use of goods and perform activities | 57 | 2 576 | 3 788 | 7 540 | 12 754 | .. | .. | .. | .. | .. |
| 5300 Unallocable between 5100 and 5200 | 0 | 0 | 0 | 0 | 0 | .. | .. | .. | .. | .. |
| **6000 Other taxes** | **7** | **303** | **748** | **1 355** | **2 542** | **0** | **0** | **0** | **0** | **0** |
| 6100 Paid solely by business | 0 | 0 | 0 | 0 | 0 | .. | .. | .. | .. | .. |
| 6200 Other | 7 | 303 | 748 | 1 355 | 2 542 | .. | .. | .. | .. | .. |
| **Total tax revenue** | **171** | **5 705** | **11 876** | **20 772** | **33 819** | **717** | **17 679** | **49 742** | **109 282** | **150 185** |

.. Not available

1. The tax on the sale of goods by public auctions under this heading is classified in category 4000 in ECLAC data.
2. Local tax revenue data in 2020 are estimated.
3. Figures for 1990-98 are estimated by the General Tax Directorate (DGI). Since 1999 the figures include income from Social Security Bank (BPS) published by the Ministry of Economy and Finance.

StatLink https://doi.org/10.1787/888934310347

## Table 6.27. **Venezuela, tax revenues by sub-sectors of government**

VES

| | Federal government[2] | | | | | State/Regional[3] | | | | |
|---|---|---|---|---|---|---|---|---|---|---|
| | 1990 | 2000 | 2010 | 2015 | 2020 | 1990 | 2000 | 2010 | 2015 | 2020 |
| **1000 Taxes on income, profits and capital gains** | **3 444** | **46 856** | **368 365** | **2 847 864** | .. | .. | .. | .. | .. | .. |
| 1100 Of individuals | .. | .. | .. | .. | .. | .. | .. | .. | .. | .. |
| 1200 Corporate[1] | 3 148 | 33 683 | 86 998 | 473 879 | .. | .. | .. | .. | .. | .. |
| 1300 Unallocable between 1100 and 1200 | 297 | 13 173 | 281 367 | 2 373 986 | .. | .. | .. | .. | .. | .. |
| **2000 Social security contributions** | **0** | **0** | **0** | .. | .. | .. | .. | .. | .. | .. |
| 2100 Employees | .. | .. | .. | .. | .. | .. | .. | .. | .. | .. |
| 2200 Employers | .. | .. | .. | .. | .. | .. | .. | .. | .. | .. |
| 2300 Self-employed or non-employed | .. | .. | .. | .. | .. | .. | .. | .. | .. | .. |
| 2400 Unallocable between 2100, 2200 and 2300 | .. | .. | .. | .. | .. | .. | .. | .. | .. | .. |
| **3000 Taxes on payroll and workforce** | **0** | **0** | **0** | **0** | .. | .. | .. | .. | .. | .. |
| **4000 Taxes on property** | **11** | **3 999** | **2 217** | **29 459** | .. | .. | .. | .. | .. | .. |
| 4100 Recurrent taxes on immovable property | 0 | 0 | 0 | 0 | .. | .. | .. | .. | .. | .. |
| 4200 Recurrent taxes on net wealth | 0 | 0 | 0 | 0 | .. | .. | .. | .. | .. | .. |
| 4300 Estate, inheritance and gift taxes | 11 | 191 | 2 217 | 29 459 | .. | .. | .. | .. | .. | .. |
| 4400 Taxes on financial and capital transactions | 0 | 3 808 | 0 | 0 | .. | .. | .. | .. | .. | .. |
| 4500 Non-recurrent taxes | 0 | 0 | 0 | 0 | .. | .. | .. | .. | .. | .. |
| 4600 Other recurrent taxes on property | 0 | 0 | 0 | 0 | .. | .. | .. | .. | .. | .. |
| **5000 Taxes on goods and services** | **457** | **51 726** | **733 363** | **9 128 199** | .. | .. | .. | .. | .. | .. |
| 5100 Taxes on production, sale, transfer, etc | 457 | 51 726 | 733 363 | 9 128 199 | .. | .. | .. | .. | .. | .. |
| 5110 General taxes | 0 | 32 716 | 561 005 | 7 027 427 | .. | .. | .. | .. | .. | .. |
| 5120 Taxes on specific goods and services | 457 | 19 011 | 172 357 | 2 100 772 | .. | .. | .. | .. | .. | .. |
| 5130 Unallocable between 5110 and 5120 | 0 | 0 | 0 | 0 | .. | .. | .. | .. | .. | .. |
| 5200 Taxes on use of goods and perform activities | 0 | 0 | 0 | 0 | .. | .. | .. | .. | .. | .. |
| 5300 Unallocable between 5100 and 5200 | 0 | 0 | 0 | 0 | .. | .. | .. | .. | .. | .. |
| **6000 Other taxes** | **0** | **0** | **0** | **158 333** | .. | .. | .. | .. | .. | .. |
| 6100 Paid solely by business | .. | .. | .. | 0 | .. | .. | .. | .. | .. | .. |
| 6200 Other | .. | .. | .. | 158 333 | .. | .. | .. | .. | .. | .. |
| **Total tax revenue** | **3 913** | **102 581** | **1 103 944** | **12 163 855** | .. | .. | .. | .. | .. | .. |

VES

| | Local government[3] | | | | | Social Security Funds[2,4] | | | | |
|---|---|---|---|---|---|---|---|---|---|---|
| | 1990 | 2000 | 2010 | 2015 | 2020 | 1990 | 2000 | 2010 | 2015 | 2020 |
| **1000 Taxes on income, profits and capital gains** | .. | .. | .. | .. | .. | **0** | **0** | **0** | .. | .. |
| 1100 Of individuals | .. | .. | .. | .. | .. | .. | .. | .. | .. | .. |
| 1200 Corporate[1] | .. | .. | .. | .. | .. | .. | .. | .. | .. | .. |
| 1300 Unallocable between 1100 and 1200 | .. | .. | .. | .. | .. | .. | .. | .. | .. | .. |
| **2000 Social security contributions** | .. | .. | .. | .. | .. | **202** | **5 905** | **96 896** | .. | .. |
| 2100 Employees | .. | .. | .. | .. | .. | .. | .. | .. | .. | .. |
| 2200 Employers | .. | .. | .. | .. | .. | .. | .. | .. | .. | .. |
| 2300 Self-employed or non-employed | .. | .. | .. | .. | .. | .. | .. | .. | .. | .. |
| 2400 Unallocable between 2100, 2200 and 2300 | .. | .. | .. | .. | .. | 202 | 5 905 | 96 896 | .. | .. |
| **3000 Taxes on payroll and workforce** | .. | .. | .. | .. | .. | **0** | **0** | **0** | .. | .. |
| **4000 Taxes on property** | .. | .. | .. | .. | .. | **0** | **0** | **0** | .. | .. |
| 4100 Recurrent taxes on immovable property | .. | .. | .. | .. | .. | .. | .. | .. | .. | .. |
| 4200 Recurrent taxes on net wealth | .. | .. | .. | .. | .. | .. | .. | .. | .. | .. |
| 4300 Estate, inheritance and gift taxes | .. | .. | .. | .. | .. | .. | .. | .. | .. | .. |
| 4400 Taxes on financial and capital transactions | .. | .. | .. | .. | .. | .. | .. | .. | .. | .. |
| 4500 Non-recurrent taxes | .. | .. | .. | .. | .. | .. | .. | .. | .. | .. |
| 4600 Other recurrent taxes on property | .. | .. | .. | .. | .. | .. | .. | .. | .. | .. |
| **5000 Taxes on goods and services** | .. | .. | .. | .. | .. | **0** | **0** | **0** | .. | .. |
| 5100 Taxes on production, sale, transfer, etc | .. | .. | .. | .. | .. | .. | .. | .. | .. | .. |
| 5110 General taxes | .. | .. | .. | .. | .. | .. | .. | .. | .. | .. |
| 5120 Taxes on specific goods and services | .. | .. | .. | .. | .. | .. | .. | .. | .. | .. |
| 5130 Unallocable between 5110 and 5120 | .. | .. | .. | .. | .. | .. | .. | .. | .. | .. |
| 5200 Taxes on use of goods and perform activities | .. | .. | .. | .. | .. | .. | .. | .. | .. | .. |
| 5300 Unallocable between 5100 and 5200 | .. | .. | .. | .. | .. | .. | .. | .. | .. | .. |
| **6000 Other taxes** | .. | .. | .. | .. | .. | **0** | **0** | **0** | .. | .. |
| 6100 Paid solely by business | .. | .. | .. | .. | .. | .. | .. | .. | .. | .. |
| 6200 Other | .. | .. | .. | .. | .. | .. | .. | .. | .. | .. |
| **Total tax revenue** | .. | .. | .. | .. | .. | **202** | **5 905** | **96 896** | .. | .. |

.. Not available

1. Data for revenues from taxes on oil profits (classified under heading 1200) have not been available since 2016.
2. Tax data have not been available since 2018. The figures between 2015 and 2017 should be interpreted with caution as they have been affected by the high rate of inflation over this period.
3. The figures exclude state and local government tax revenues as the data are not available.
4. Data on social security contributions have not been available since 2014.

StatLink https://doi.org/10.1787/888934310366

# ANNEX A

# The OECD classification of taxes and interpretative guide[1]

## Table of contents

## A.1 The OECD classification of taxes

1. **1000. Taxes on income, profits and capital gains**
   - 1100. Taxes on income, profits and capital gains of individuals
     - 1110. On income and profits
     - 1120. On capital gains
   - 1200. Corporate taxes on income, profits and capital gains
     - 1210. On income and profits
     - 1220. On capital gains
   - 1300. Unallocable as between 1100 and 1200
2. **2000. Social security contributions**
   - 2100. Employees
     - 2110. On a payroll basis
     - 2120. On an income tax basis
   - 2200. Employers
     - 2210. On a payroll basis
     - 2220. On an income tax basis
   - 2300. Self-employed or non-employed
     - 2310. On a payroll basis
     - 2320. On an income tax basis
   - 2400 Unallocable as between 2100, 2200 and 2300
     - 2410. On a payroll basis
     - 2420. On an income tax basis
3. **3000. Taxes on payroll and workforce**
4. **4000. Taxes on property**
   - 4100. Recurrent taxes on immovable property
     - 4110. Households
     - 4120. Other
   - 4200 Recurrent taxes on net wealth
     - 4210. Individual
     - 4220. Corporate
   - 4300. Estate, inheritance and gift taxes
     - 4310. Estate and inheritance taxes
     - 4320. Gift taxes
   - 4400. Taxes on financial and capital transactions
   - 4500. Other non-recurrent taxes on property
     - 4510. On net wealth
     - 4520. Other non-recurrent taxes
   - 4600. Other recurrent taxes on property

5. **5000. Taxes on goods and services**

5100. Taxes on production, sale, transfer, leasing and delivery of goods and rendering of services

5110. General taxes

5111. Value added taxes

5112. Sales taxes

5113. Turnover and other general taxes on goods and services

5120. Taxes on specific goods and services

5121. Excises

5122. Profits of fiscal monopolies

5123. Customs and import duties

5124. Taxes on exports

5125. Taxes on investment goods

5126. Taxes on specific services

5127. Other taxes on international trade and transactions

5128. Other taxes on specific goods and services

5130. Unallocable as between 5110 and 5120

5200. Taxes on use of goods, or on permission to use goods or perform activities

5210. Recurrent taxes

5211. Paid by households in respect of motor vehicles

5212. Paid by others in respect of motor vehicles

5213. Other recurrent taxes

5220. Non-recurrent taxes

5300. Unallocable as between 5100 and 5200

6. **6000. Other taxes**

6100. Paid solely by business

6200. Paid by other than business or unidentifiable

## A.2. Coverage

### General criteria

1. In the OECD classification, the term "taxes" is confined to compulsory unrequited payments to the general government or to a supranational authority. Taxes are unrequited in the sense that benefits provided by government to taxpayers are not normally in proportion to their payments.

2. The term "tax" does not include fines, penalties and compulsory loans paid to government. Borderline cases between tax and non-tax revenues in relation to certain fees and charges are discussed in §12–15.

3. General government consists of the central administration, agencies whose operations are under its effective control, state and local governments and their administrations, certain social security schemes and autonomous governmental entities, excluding public enterprises. This definition of government follows that of the 2008 *System of National Accounts* (SNA).[2] In that publication, the general government sector and its sub-sectors are defined in Chapter 4, paragraphs 4.117 to 4.165.

4. Extra-budgetary units are part of the general government system. These are general government entities with individual budgets that are not fully covered by the main or general budget. These entities operate under the authority or control of a central, state, or local government. Extra-budgetary entities may have their own revenue sources, which may be supplemented by grants (transfers) from the general budget or from other sources. Even though their budgets may be subject to approval by the legislature, similar to that of budgetary accounts, they have discretion over the volume and composition of their spending. Such entities may be established to carry out specific government functions, such as road construction, or the nonmarket production of health or education services. Budgetary arrangements vary widely across countries, and various terms are used to describe these entities, but they are often referred to as "extra-budgetary funds" or "decentralised agencies."

5. Compulsory, unrequited payments collected by national governments and paid to supranational authorities are also included as taxes under the definition in paragraph 1. Taxes that are collected by national governments and paid to a supranational authority are included as tax revenues at the level of the supranational authority in the SNA2008 (paragraphs 22.60-61, 22.88 and 22.99 refer) and the ESA2010 (paragraph 20.165 refers). In Revenue Statistics, these taxes include customs duties, contributions to the EU Single Resolution Fund, and any other taxes collected by EU member states on behalf of the European Union. They are included in the tax revenue amounts in the country tables (Chapter 5) of the country in which they are collected and are attributed to the supranational level of government (see §102).

6. In countries where the church forms part of general government, church taxes are included, provided they meet the criteria set out in §1 above. As the data refer to receipts of general government and to supranational authorities, levies paid to non-government bodies, welfare agencies or social insurance schemes outside general government, trade unions or trade associations, even where such levies are compulsory, are excluded. Compulsory payments to general government earmarked for such bodies are, however, included, provided that the government is not simply acting in an agency capacity.[3] Profits from fiscal monopolies are distinguished from those of other public enterprises and are treated as taxes because they reflect the exercise of the taxing power of the state by the use of monopoly

powers (see §66–68), as are profits received by the government from the purchase and sale of foreign exchange at different rates (see §76).

7. Taxes paid by governments (e.g., social security contributions and payroll taxes paid by governments in their capacity as an employer, consumption taxes on their purchases or taxes on their property) are not excluded from the data provided. However, where it is possible to identify the amounts of revenue involved,[4] they are shown in Table 5.40 of this Report.

8. The relationship between this classification and that of the System of National Accounts (SNA) is set out in Sections A.9 and A.11 below. Because of the differences between the two classifications, the data shown in national accounts are sometimes calculated or classified differently from the practice set out in this guide. These and other differences are mentioned where appropriate (e.g., in §31 below) but it is not possible to refer to all of them. There may also be some differences between this classification and that employed domestically by certain national administrations (e.g., see §13 below), so that OECD and national statistics data may not always be consistent: any such differences, however, are likely to be very slight in terms of amounts of revenues involved.

### *Social security contributions*

9. Compulsory social security contributions, as defined in §40, and paid to general government, are treated here as tax revenues. They may, however, differ from other taxes in that the receipt of social security benefits depends, in most countries, upon appropriate contributions having been made, although the size of the benefits is not necessarily related to the amount of the contributions. Better comparability between countries is obtained by treating social security contributions as taxes, but they are listed under a separate heading so that they can be distinguished in any analysis.

10. The strict dividing line between tax revenues (compulsory unrequited payments to general government or a supranational authority) and non-tax compulsory payments (NTCPs) (payments that are either requited or made to other institutions) is clearly defined. However, within the range of different compulsory payments to governments existing across countries, it is not always straightforward in practice to decide whether specific payments are either taxes or NTCPs. For example, compulsory pension savings that are controlled by general government and that accumulate on an individual account earning a market return or a rate that compensates for inflation would at first sight be categorised as NTCPs as opposed to taxes. However, even these payments might still be 'unrequited' and therefore classify as taxes instead of NTCPs (for example if these pension savings are not paid out when the taxpayer dies before reaching the pension age and the funds are then used to provide a minimum pension to all taxpayers that are insured). These issues result in the social security revenue figures reported for most countries being based on the premise that all types of compulsory payments to general government are judged to some extent to have a re-distributional element. It should be noted that this conclusion is based on a typically broad interpretation of the term 'unrequited' in the tax definition.

11. Social security contributions which are either voluntary or not payable to general government (see §1) are not treated as taxes, though in some countries, as indicated in the country footnotes, there are difficulties in completely eliminating voluntary contributions and certain compulsory payments to the private sector from the revenue figures. Imputed social security contributions are also not treated as taxes.

### *Fees, user charges and licence fees*

12. Apart from vehicle licence fees, which are universally regarded as taxes, it is not easy to distinguish between those fees and user charges which are to be treated as taxes and those which are not, since, whilst a fee or charge is levied in connection with a specific service or activity, the strength of the link between the fee and the service provided may vary considerably, as may the relation between the amount of the fee and the cost of providing the service. Where the recipient of a service pays a fee clearly related to the cost of providing the service, the levy may be regarded as requited and under the definition of §1 would not be considered as a tax. In the following cases, however, a levy could be considered as 'unrequited':

*a)* where the charge greatly exceeds the cost of providing the service;

*b)* where the payer of the levy is not the receiver of the benefit (e.g., a fee collected from slaughterhouses to finance a service which is provided to farmers);

*c)* where government is not providing a specific service in return for the levy which it receives even though a licence may be issued to the payer (e.g., where the government grants a hunting, fishing or shooting licence which is not accompanied by the right to use a specific area of government land);

*d)* where benefits are received only by those paying the levy but the benefits received by each individual are not necessarily in proportion to his payments (e.g., a milk marketing levy paid by dairy farmers and used to promote the consumption of milk).

13. In marginal cases, however, the application of the criteria set out in §1 can be particularly difficult. The solution adopted — given the desirability of international uniformity and the relatively small amounts of revenue usually involved — is to follow the predominant practice among tax administrations rather than to allow each country to adopt its own view as to whether such levies are regarded as taxes or as non-tax revenue.[5]

14. A list of the main fees and charges in question and their normal[6] treatment in this publication is as follows:

| | |
|---|---|
| Non-tax revenues: | court fees; driving licence fees; harbour fees; passport fees; radio and television licence fees where public authorities provide the service |
| Taxes within heading 5200 | permission to perform such activities as distributing films; hunting, fishing and shooting; providing entertainment or gambling facilities; selling alcohol or tobacco; permission to own dogs or to use or own motor vehicles or guns; severance taxes |

15. In practice, it may not always be possible to isolate tax receipts from non-tax revenue receipts when they are recorded together. If it is estimated that the bulk of the receipts derive from non-tax revenues, the whole amount involved is treated as a non-tax revenue; otherwise, such government receipts are included and classified according to the rules provided in §33 below.

### *Royalties*

16. The ownership of subsoil assets in the form of deposits of minerals or fossil fuels (coal, oil, or natural gas) depends upon the way in which property rights are defined by law and also on international agreements in the case of deposits below international waters. In

some cases, either the ground below which the mineral deposits are located, the deposits themselves or both may belong to a local or central government unit.

17. In such cases, these general government units may grant leases to other institutional units that permit them to extract these deposits over a specified period of time in return for a payment or series of payments. These payments are often described as 'royalties' but they are essentially rent that accrues to owners of natural resources in return for putting these assets at the disposal of other units for specified periods of time. The rent may take the form of periodic payments of fixed amounts, irrespective of the rate of extraction, or, more commonly, they may be a function of the quantity, volume, or value of the asset extracted. Enterprises engaged in exploration on government land may make payments to general government units in exchange for the right to undertake test drilling or otherwise investigate the existence and location of subsoil assets. Such payments are also recorded as rents even though no extraction may take place. These payments are therefore classified as non-tax revenues.

18. The same principles apply when other institutional units are granted leases that permit them to fell timber in natural forests on land owned by general government units. These payments are also classified as non-tax revenues.

19. These rents or royalties paid to general government should not be confused with taxes on income and profits, severance taxes, business licenses, or other taxes. If the payments are levied on the profits from the extraction activity, then they should be classified as taxes on incomes, profits and gains (1000). In addition, any severance payments that are imposed on the extraction of minerals and fossil fuels from reserves owned privately or by another government should be classified as taxes. Payments related to the gross value of production should be classified as other taxes on goods and services (5128). Payments for a license or permit to conduct extraction operations should be classified as taxes on use of goods and on permission to use goods or perform activities (5213).

### *Fines and penalties*

20. In principle, fines and penalties charged on overdue taxes or penalties imposed for the attempted evasion of taxes should not be recorded as tax revenues. However, it may not be possible to separate payments of fines or other penalties from the revenues from the taxes to which they relate. In this case, the fines and penalties relating to a particular tax are recorded together with the revenues from that tax and fines and penalties paid with revenue from unidentifiable taxes are classified as other taxes in Category 6000. Fines not relating to tax offences (e.g., for parking offences), or not identifiable as relating to tax offences, are also not treated as tax revenues.

## A.3. Basis of reporting

### *Accrual or cash reporting*

21. The data reported in the *Revenue Statistics* publications for recent years are predominantly recorded on an accrual basis for OECD countries, i.e. recorded at the time that the tax liability was created. Further information is provided in the footnotes to the country table in Chapter 5 of the Report.

22. However, data for earlier years and for non-OECD countries are still predominantly recorded on a cash basis, i.e. at the time at which the payment was received by government. Thus, for example, taxes withheld by employers in one year but paid to the government

in the following year and taxes due in one year but actually paid in the following year are both included in the receipts of the second year. Corrective transactions, such as refunds, repayments and drawbacks, are deducted from gross revenues of the period in which they are made.

23. Data on tax revenues are recorded without offsets for the administrative expenses connected with tax collection. Similarly, where the proceeds of tax are used to subsidise particular members of the community, the subsidy is not deducted from the yield of the tax, though the tax may be shown net of subsidies in the national records of some countries.

24. As regards fiscal monopolies (heading 5122), only the amount actually transferred to the government is included in government revenues. However, if any expenditures of fiscal monopolies are considered to be government expenditures (e.g., social expenditures undertaken by fiscal monopolies at the direction of the government) they are added back for the purpose of arriving at tax revenue figures (see §66 below).

### *The distinction between tax and expenditure provisions*[7]

25. Because this publication is concerned only with the revenue side of government operations, no account being taken of the expenditure side, a distinction has to be made between tax and expenditure provisions. Normally there is no difficulty in making this distinction as expenditures are made outside the tax system and the tax accounts and under legislation separate from the tax legislation. In borderline cases, cash flow is used to distinguish between tax provisions and expenditure provisions. Insofar as a provision affects the flow of tax payments from the taxpayer to the government, it is regarded as a tax provision and is taken into account in the data shown in this publication. A provision which does not affect this flow is seen as an expenditure provision and is disregarded in the data recorded in this publication.

26. Tax allowances, exemptions and deductions against the tax base clearly affect the amount of tax paid to the government and are therefore considered as tax provisions. At the other extreme, those subsidies which cannot be offset against tax liability and which are clearly not connected with the assessment process, do not reduce tax revenues as recorded in this publication. Tax credits are amounts deductible from tax payable (as distinct from deductions from the tax base). Two types of tax credits are distinguished, those (referred to here as wastable tax credits) which are limited to the amount of the tax liability and therefore cannot give rise to a payment by the authorities to the taxpayer, and those (referred to as non-wastable tax credits) which are not so limited, so that the excess of the credit over the tax liability can be paid to the taxpayer.[8] A wastable tax credit, like a tax allowance, clearly affects the amount of tax paid to the government, and is therefore considered as a tax provision. The practice followed for non-wastable tax credits[9] is to distinguish between the 'tax expenditure component',[10] which is that portion of the credit that is used to reduce or eliminate a taxpayer's liability, and the 'transfer component', which is the portion that exceeds the taxpayer's liability and is paid to that taxpayer. Reported tax revenues should be reduced by the amount of the tax expenditure component but not by the amount of the transfer component. In addition, the amounts of the tax expenditure and transfer components should be reported as memorandum items in the country tables. Countries that are unable to distinguish between the tax expenditure and transfer components should indicate whether or not the tax revenues have been reduced by the total of these components, and provide any available estimates of the amounts of the two components.

Further information is given in Chapter 1 of the Report, which illustrates the effect of alternative treatments of non-wastable tax credits on tax to GDP.

### Calendar and fiscal years

27. National authorities whose fiscal years do not correspond to the calendar year show data, where possible, on a calendar year basis to permit maximum comparability with the data of other countries. There remain a few countries where data refer to fiscal years. For these the GDP data used in the comparative tables also correspond to the fiscal years.

## A.4. General classification criteria

### The main classification criteria

28. The classification of receipts among the main headings (1000, 2000, 3000, 4000, 5000 and 6000) is generally governed by the base on which the tax is levied: 1000 income, profits and capital gains; 2000 and 3000 earnings, payroll or number of employees; 4000 property; 5000 goods and services; 6000 multiple bases, other bases or unidentifiable bases. Where a tax is calculated on more than one base, the receipts are, where possible, split among the various headings (see §33 and §84). The headings 4000 and 5000 cover not only taxes where the tax base is the property, goods or services themselves but also certain related taxes. Thus, taxes on the transfer of property are included in 4400[11] and taxes on the use of goods or on permission to perform activities in 5200. In headings 4000 and 5000 a distinction is made in certain sub-headings between recurrent and non-recurrent taxes: recurrent taxes are defined as those levied at regular intervals (usually annually) and non-recurrent taxes are levied once and for all (see also §48 to §51, §54, §55 and §81 for particular applications of this distinction).

29. Earmarking of a tax for specific purposes does not affect the classification of tax receipts. However, as explained in §40 on the classification of social security contributions, the conferment of an entitlement to social benefits is crucial to the definition of the 2000 main heading.

30. The way that a tax is levied or collected (e.g., by use of stamps) does not affect classification.

### Classification of taxpayers

31. In certain sub-headings, distinctions are made between different categories of taxpayers. These distinctions vary from tax to tax:

*a) Between individuals and corporations in relation to income and net wealth taxes*

The basic distinction is that corporation income taxes, as distinct from individual income taxes, are levied on the corporation as an entity, not on the individuals who own it, and without regard to the personal circumstances of these individuals. The same distinction applies to net wealth taxes on corporations and those on individuals. Taxes paid on the profits of partnerships and the income of institutions, such as life insurance or pension funds, are classified according to the same rule. They are classified as corporate taxes (1200) if they are charged on the partnership or institution as an entity without regard to the personal circumstances of the owners. Otherwise, they are treated as individual taxes (1100). Usually, there is different legislation for the corporation taxes and for the individual taxes.[12] The distinction made here between individuals and corporations does not follow the sector classification between households, enterprises, and so on of the System of National Accounts for income and outlay accounts. The SNA classification requires certain unincorporated businesses[13] to be excluded from the household sector and included with non-financial enterprises and financial institutions. The tax on the profits of these businesses, however, cannot always be separated from the tax on the other income of their owners, or can be separated only on an arbitrary basis. No attempt at this separation is made here and the whole of the individual income tax is shown together without regard to the nature of the income chargeable.

*b) Between households and others in relation to taxes on immovable property*

Here the distinction is that adopted by the SNA for the production and consumption expenditure accounts. The distinction is between households as consumers (i.e. excluding non-incorporated business) on the one hand and producers on the other hand. However, taxes on dwellings occupied by households, whether paid by owner-occupiers, tenants or landlords, are classified under households. This follows the common distinction made between taxes on domestic property versus taxes on business property. Some countries are not, however, in a position to make this distinction.

*c) Between households and others in relation to motor vehicle licences*

Here the distinction is between households as consumers on the one hand and producers on the other, as in the production and consumption expenditure accounts of the SNA.

*d) Between business and others in relation to the residual taxes (6000)*

The distinction is the same as in c) above between producers on the one hand and households as consumers on the other hand. Taxes which are included under the heading 6000 because they involve more than one tax base or because the tax base does not fall within any of the previous categories but which are identifiable as levyable only on producers and not on households are included under 'business'. The rest of the taxes which are included under the heading 6000 are shown as 'other' or non-identified.

### *Surcharges*

32. Receipts from surcharges in respect of particular taxes are usually classified with the receipts from the relevant tax whether or not the surcharge is temporary. If, however, the surcharge has a characteristic which would render it classifiable in a different heading of the OECD list, receipts from the surcharge are classified under that heading separately from the relevant tax.

### *Unidentifiable tax receipts and residual sub-headings*

33. A number of cases arise where taxes cannot be identified as belonging entirely to a heading or sub-heading of the OECD classification and the following practices are applied in such cases:

*a)* The heading is known, but it is not known how receipts should be allocated between sub-headings: receipts are classified in the appropriate residual sub-heading (1300, 2400, 4520, 4600, 5128, 5130, 5300 or 6200).

*b)* It is known that the bulk of receipts from a group of taxes (usually local taxes) is derived from taxes within a particular heading or sub-heading, but some of the taxes in the group whose amount cannot be precisely ascertained may be classifiable in other headings or sub-headings: receipts are shown in the heading or sub-heading under which most of the receipts fall.

c) Neither the heading nor sub-heading of a tax (usually local) can be identified: the tax is classified in 6200 unless it is known that it is a tax on business in which case it is classified in 6100.

## A.5. Commentaries on items of the list

### *1000 — Taxes on income, profits and capital gains*

34. This heading covers taxes levied on the net income or profits (i.e. gross income minus allowable tax reliefs) of individuals and enterprises. Also covered are taxes levied on the capital gains of individuals and enterprises, and gains from gambling.

35. Included in the heading are:

*a)* taxes levied predominantly on income or profits, though partially on other bases. Taxes on various bases which are not predominantly income or profits are classified according to the principles laid down in §33 and §84;

*b)* taxes on property, which are levied on a presumed or estimated income as part of an income tax (see also §48(a), (c) and (d));

*c)* compulsory payments to social security fund contributions that are levied on income but do not confer an entitlement to social benefits. When such contributions do confer an entitlement to social benefits, they are included in heading 2000 (see §40);

*d)* receipts from integrated scheduler income tax systems are classified as a whole in this heading, even though certain of the scheduler taxes may be based upon gross income and may not take into account the personal circumstances of the taxpayer.

36. The main subdivision of this heading is between levies on individuals (1100) and those on corporate enterprises (1200). Under each subdivision a distinction is made between taxes on income and profits (1110 and 1210), and taxes on capital gains (1120 and 1220). If certain receipts cannot be identified as appropriate to either 1100 or 1200, or if in practice this distinction cannot be made (e.g., because there are no reliable data on the recipients of payments from which withholding taxes are deducted) they are classified in 1300 as not-allocable.

### *Treatment of credits under imputation systems*

37. Under imputation systems of corporate income tax, a company's shareholders are wholly or partly relieved of their liability to income tax on dividends paid by the company out of income or profits liable to corporate income tax. In countries with such systems,[14] part of the tax on the company's profits is available to provide relief against the shareholders' own tax liability. The relief to the shareholder takes the form of a tax credit, the amount of which may be less than, equal to, or more than the shareholder's overall tax liability. If the tax credit exceeds this tax liability the excess may be payable to the shareholder. As this type of tax credit is an integral part of the imputation system of corporate income tax, any payment to the shareholders is treated as a repayment of tax and not as expenditure (compare the treatment of other tax credits described in §26).

38. As the tax credit under imputation systems (even when exceeding tax liability) is to be regarded as a tax provision, the question arises whether it should be deducted from individual income tax receipts (1110) or corporate income tax receipts (1210). In this Report, the full amount of corporate income tax paid is shown under 1210 and no imputed tax is included under 1110. Thus, the full amount of the credit reduces the amount of 1110 whether

the credit results in a reduction of personal income tax liability or whether an actual refund is made because the credit exceeds the income tax liability. (Where, however, such tax credits are deducted from corporation tax in respect of dividends paid to corporations the amounts are deducted from the receipts of 1210).

### *1120 and 1220 — Taxes on capital gains*

39. These sub-headings comprise taxes imposed on capital gains, 1120 covering those levied on the gains of individuals and 1220 those levied on the gains of corporate enterprises, where receipts from such taxes can be separately identified. In many countries, this is not the case and the receipts from such taxes are then classified with those from the income tax. Heading 1120 also includes taxes on gains from gambling.

### *2000 — Social security contributions*

40. Classified here are all compulsory payments to general government that confer an entitlement to receive a (contingent) future social benefit. Such payments are usually earmarked to finance social benefits and are often paid to institutions of general government that provide such benefits. However, such earmarking is not part of the definition of social security contributions and is not required for a tax to be classified here. However, conferment of an entitlement is required for a tax to be classified under this heading. So, levies on income or payroll that are earmarked for social security funds but do not confer an entitlement to benefit are excluded from this heading and shown under personal income taxes (1100) or taxes on payroll and workforce (3000). Taxes on other bases, such as goods and services, which are earmarked for social security benefits are not shown here but are classified according to their respective bases because they generally confer no entitlement to social security benefits.

41. Contributions for the following types of social security benefits would, *inter alia*, be included: unemployment insurance benefits and supplements, accident, injury and sickness benefits, old-age, disability and survivors' pensions, family allowances, reimbursements for medical and hospital expenses or provision of hospital or medical services. Contributions may be levied on both employees and employers.

42. Contributions may be based on earnings or payroll ('on a payroll basis') or on net income after deductions and exemptions for personal circumstances ('on an income tax basis'), and the revenues from the two bases should be separately identified if possible. However, where contributions to a general social security scheme are on a payroll basis, but the contributions of particular groups (such as the self-employed) cannot be assessed on this basis and net income is used as a proxy for gross earnings, the receipts may still be classified as being on a payroll basis. In principle, this heading excludes voluntary contributions paid to social security schemes. When separately identifiable these are shown in the memorandum item on the financing of social security benefits. In practice, however, they cannot always be separately identified from compulsory contributions, in which case they are included in this heading.

43. Contributions to social insurance schemes which are not institutions of general government and to other types of insurance schemes, provident funds, pension funds, friendly societies or other saving schemes are not considered as social security contributions. Provident funds are arrangements under which the contributions of each employee and of the corresponding employer on his/her behalf are kept in a separate account earning interest and withdrawable under specific circumstances. Pension funds are separately organised

schemes negotiated between employees and employers and carry provisions for different contributions and benefits, sometimes more directly tied to salary levels and length of service than under social security schemes. When contributions to these schemes are compulsory or quasi-compulsory (e.g., by virtue of agreement with professional and union organisations) they are shown in the memorandum item (refer to Table 5.39 of the Report).

44. Contributions by government employees and by governments in respect of their employees, to social security schemes classified within general government are included in this heading. Contributions to separate schemes for government employees, which can be regarded as replacing general social security schemes, are also regarded as taxes.[15] Where, however, a separate scheme is not seen as replacing a general scheme and has been negotiated between the government, in its role as an employer, and its employees, it is not regarded as social security and contributions to it are not regarded as taxes, even though the scheme may have been established by legislation.

45. This heading excludes 'imputed' contributions, which correspond to social benefits paid directly by employers to their employees or former employees or to their representatives (e.g., when employers are legally obliged to pay sickness benefits for a certain period).

46. Contributions are divided into those of employees (2100), employers (2200), and self-employed or non-employed (2300), and then further sub-divided according to the basis on which they are levied. Employees are defined for this purpose as all persons engaged in activities of business units, government bodies, private non-profit institutions, or other paid employment, except the proprietors and their unpaid family members in the case of unincorporated businesses. Members of the armed forces are included, irrespective of the duration and type of their service, if they contribute to social security schemes. The contributions of employers are defined as their payments on account of their employees to social security schemes. Where employees or employers are required to continue the payment of social security contributions when the employee becomes unemployed these contributions, data permitting, are shown in 2100 and 2200 respectively. Accordingly, the sub-heading 2300 is confined to contributions paid by the self-employed and by those outside of the labour force (e.g., disabled or retired individuals).

### *3000 — Taxes on payroll and workforce*

47. These consist of taxes payable by enterprises assessed either as a proportion of the wages or salaries paid or as a fixed amount per person employed. They do not include compulsory social security contributions paid by employers or any taxes paid by employees themselves out of their wages or salaries

### *4000 — Taxes on property*

48. This heading covers recurrent and non-recurrent taxes on the use, ownership or transfer of property. These include taxes on immovable property or net wealth, taxes on the change of ownership of property through inheritance or gift and taxes on financial and capital transactions. The following kinds of tax are excluded from this heading:

*a)* taxes on capital gains resulting from the sale of a property (1120 or 1220);

*b)* taxes on the use of goods or on permission to use goods or perform activities (5200); see §78;

*c)* taxes on immovable property levied on the basis of a presumed net income which take into account the personal circumstances of the taxpayer. They are classified as income taxes along with taxes on income and capital gains derived from property (1100);

*d)* taxes on the use of property for residence, where the tax is payable by either proprietor or tenant and the amount payable is a function of the user's personal circumstances (pay, dependants, and so on). They are classified as taxes on income (1100);

*e)* taxes on building in excess of permitted maximum density, taxes on the enlargement, construction or alteration of certain buildings beyond a permitted value and taxes on building construction. They are classified as taxes on permission to perform activities (5200);

*f)* taxes on the use of one's own property for special trading purposes like selling alcohol, tobacco, meat or for exploitation of land resources (e.g., United States severance taxes). They are classified as taxes on permission to perform activities (5200).

### 4100 — *Recurrent taxes on immovable property*

49. This sub-heading covers taxes levied regularly in respect of the use or ownership of immovable property.

- these taxes are levied on land and buildings;
- they can be in the form of a percentage of an assessed property value based on a national rental income, sales price, or capitalised yield; or in terms of other characteristics of real property, ( for example size or location ) from which a presumed rent or capital value can be derived.
- such taxes can be levied on proprietors, tenants, or both. They can also be paid by one level of government to another level of government in respect of property under the jurisdiction of the latter.
- debts are not taken into account in the assessment of these taxes, and they differ from taxes on net wealth in this respect.

50. Taxes on immovable property are further sub-divided into those paid by households (4110) and those paid by other entities (4120), according to the criteria set out in §31(*b*) above.

### 4200 — *Recurrent taxes on net wealth*

51. This sub-heading covers taxes levied regularly (in most cases annually) on net wealth, i.e. taxes on a wide range of movable and immovable property, net of debt. It is sub-divided into taxes paid by individuals (4210) and taxes paid by corporate enterprises (4220) according to the criteria set out in §31(*a*) above. If separate figures exist for receipts paid by institutions, the tax payments involved are added to those paid by corporations.

### 4300 — *Estate, inheritance and gift taxes*

52. This sub-heading is divided into taxes on estates and inheritances (4310) and taxes on gifts (4320).[16] Estate taxes are charged on the amount of the total estate whereas inheritance taxes are charged on the shares of the individual recipients; in addition the latter may take into account the relationship of the individual recipients to the deceased.

### *4400 — Taxes on financial and capital transactions*

53. This sub-heading comprises, *inter alia*, taxes on the issue, transfer, purchase and sale of non-financial and financial assets (including foreign exchange or securities), taxes on cheques and other forms of payment, and taxes levied on specific legal transactions such as validation of contracts and the sale of immovable property. The heading does not include:

- *a)* taxes on the use of goods or property or permission to perform certain activities (5200);
- *b)* fees paid to cover court charges, charges for birth, marriage or death certificates, which are normally regarded as non-tax revenues (see §12);
- *c)* taxes on capital gains (1000);
- *d)* recurrent taxes on immovable property (4100);
- *e)* recurrent taxes on net wealth (4200);
- *f)* once-and-for-all levies on property or wealth (4500);
- *g)* stamp taxes not related to financial and capital transactions
  - *i)* Stamp taxes on the sale of specific products, such as alcoholic beverages or tobacco (5121);
  - *ii)* Stamp taxes restricted by law to imported products (5123) or to exported products (5124); or
  - *iii)* Stamp taxes not falling exclusively on a single category of transaction (6000).

### *4500 — Other non-recurrent taxes on property*

54. This sub-heading covers once-and-for-all, as distinct from recurrent, levies on property. It is divided into taxes on net wealth (4510) and other non-recurrent taxes on property (4520). Heading 4510 would include taxes levied to meet emergency expenditures, or for redistribution purposes. Heading 4520 would cover taxes levied to take account of increases in land value due to permission given to develop or provision of additional local facilities by general government, any taxes on the revaluation of capital and once-and-for-all taxes on particular items of property.

### *4600 — Other recurrent taxes on property*

55. These rarely exist in OECD member countries, but the heading would include taxes on goods such as cattle, jewellery, windows, and other external signs of wealth.

### *5000 — Taxes on goods and services*

56. All taxes and duties levied on the production, extraction, sale, transfer, leasing or delivery of goods, and the rendering of services (5100), or in respect of the use of goods or permission to use goods or to perform activities (5200) are included here. The heading thus covers:

- *a)* multi-stage cumulative taxes;
- *b)* general sales taxes — whether levied at manufacture/production, wholesale or retail level;
- *c)* value-added taxes;
- *d)* excises;
- *e)* taxes levied on the import and export of goods;

*f)* taxes levied in respect of the use of goods and taxes on permission to use goods, or perform certain activities;

*g)* taxes on the extraction, processing or production of minerals and other products.

57. Borderline cases between this heading and heading 4000 (taxes on property) and 6100 (other taxes on business) are referred to in §48, §53 and §80. Residual sub-headings (5300) and (5130) cover tax receipts which cannot be allocated between 5100 and 5200 and between 5110 and 5120, respectively; see §33.

### 5100 — *Taxes on the production, sale, transfer, leasing and delivery of goods and rendering of services*

58. This sub-heading consists of all taxes, levied on transactions in goods and services on the basis of their intrinsic characteristics (e.g., value, weight of tobacco, strength of alcohol, and so on) as distinct from taxes imposed on the use of goods, or permission to use goods or perform activities, which fall under 5200.

### 5110 — *General taxes on goods and services*

59. This sub-heading includes all taxes, other than import and export duties (5123 and 5124), levied on the production, leasing, transfer, delivery or sales of a wide range of goods and/or the rendering of a wide range of services, irrespective of whether they are domestically produced or imported and irrespective of the stage of production or distribution at which they are levied. It thus covers value-added taxes, sales taxes and multi-stage cumulative taxes. Receipts from border adjustments in respect of such taxes when goods are imported are added to gross receipts for this category, and repayments of such taxes when goods are exported are deducted. These taxes are subdivided into 5111 value-added taxes, 5112 sales taxes, 5113 turnover and other general taxes on goods and services.

60. Borderline cases arise between this heading and taxes on specific goods (5120) when taxes are levied on a large number of goods, for example, the United Kingdom purchase tax (repealed in 1973) and the Japanese commodity tax (repealed in 1988). In conformity with national views, the former United Kingdom purchase tax is classified as a general tax (5112) and the former Japanese commodity tax as excises (5121).

### 5111 — *Value-added taxes*

61. All general consumption taxes charged on value-added are classified in this sub-heading, irrespective of the method of deduction and the stages at which the taxes are levied. In practice, all OECD countries with value-added taxes normally allow immediate deduction of taxes on purchases by all but the final consumer and impose tax at all stages. In some countries the heading may include certain taxes, such as those on financial and insurance activities, either because receipts from them cannot be identified separately from those from the value-added tax, or because they are regarded as an integral part of the value-added tax, even though similar taxes in other countries might be classified elsewhere (e.g., 5126 as taxes on services or 4400 as taxes on financial and capital transactions).

### 5112 — *Sales taxes*

62. All general taxes levied at one stage only, whether at manufacturing or production, wholesale or retail stage are classified here.

### 5113 — *Turnover and other general taxes on goods and services*

63. These are multi-stage cumulative taxes and taxes where elements of consumption taxes are combined with multistage taxes. These taxes are levied each time a transaction takes place without deduction for taxes paid on inputs. Multi-stage taxes can be combined with elements of value-added or sales taxes.

### 5120 — *Taxes on specific goods and services*

64. Excises, profits generated and transferred from fiscal monopolies, and customs and imports duties as well as taxes on exports, foreign exchange transactions, investment goods and betting stakes and special taxes on services, which do not form part of a general tax of 5110, are included in this category.

### 5121 — *Excises*

65. Excises are taxes levied as a product specific unit tax on a predefined limited range of goods. Excises are usually levied at differentiated rates on nonessential or luxury goods, alcoholic beverages, tobacco, and energy. Excises may be imposed at any stage of production or distribution and are usually assessed as a specific charge per unit based on characteristics by reference to the value, weight, strength, or quantity of the product. Included are special taxes on individual products such as sugar, sugar beets, matches, and chocolates; taxes levied at varying rates on a certain range of goods; and taxes levied on tobacco goods, alcoholic drinks, motor fuels, and hydrocarbon oils. If a tax collected principally on imported goods also applies, or would apply, under the same law to comparable domestically produced goods, then the revenue from this tax is classified as arising from excises rather than from import duties. This principle applies even if there is no comparable domestic production or no possibility of such production. Taxes on the use of utilities such as water, electricity, gas, and energy are regarded as excises rather than taxes on specific services (5126). Excises exclude those taxes that are levied as general taxes on goods and services (5110); profits of fiscal monopolies (5122); customs and other import duties (5123); or taxes on exports (5124).

### 5122 — *Profits of fiscal monopolies*

66. This sub-heading covers that part of the profits of fiscal monopolies which is transferred to general government or which is used to finance any expenditures considered to be government expenditures (see §24). Amounts are shown when they are transferred to general government or used to make expenditures considered to be government expenditures.

67. Fiscal monopolies reflect the exercise of the taxing power of government by the use of monopoly powers. Fiscal monopolies are non-financial public enterprises exercising a monopoly in most cases over the production or distribution of tobacco, alcoholic beverages, salt, matches, playing cards and petroleum or agricultural products (i.e. on the kind of products which are likely to be, alternatively or additionally, subject to the excises of 5121), to raise the government revenues which in other countries are gathered through taxes on dealings in such commodities by private business units. The government monopoly may be at the production stage or, as in the case of government-owned and controlled liquor stores, at the distribution stage.

68. Fiscal monopolies are distinguished from public utilities such as rail transport, electricity, post offices, and other communications, which may enjoy a monopoly or quasi-monopoly position but where the primary purpose is normally to provide basic services rather than to raise revenue for government. Transfers from such other public enterprises

to the government are considered as non-tax revenues. The traditional concept of fiscal monopoly is not generally extended to include state lotteries, the profits of which are usually accordingly regarded as non-tax revenues. However, they can be included as tax revenues if the prime reason for their operation is to raise revenues to finance government expenditure. Fiscal monopoly profits are distinguished from export and import monopoly profits (5127) transferred from marketing boards or other enterprises dealing with international trade.

### 5123 — *Customs and other import duties*

69. Taxes, stamp duties and surcharges restricted by law to imported products are included here. Also included are levies on imported agricultural products which are imposed in member countries of the European Union and amounts paid by certain of these countries under the Monetary Compensation Accounts (MCA) system.[17] Customs duties collected by European Union member states on behalf of the European Union are reported under this heading at the supranational level of government in the country tables (in Chapter 5 of the Report). Excluded here are taxes collected on imports as part of a general tax on goods and services, or an excise applicable to both imported and domestically produced goods.

### 5124 — *Taxes on exports*

70. In the 1970s, export duties were levied in Australia, Canada and Portugal as a regular measure and they have been used in Finland for counter-cyclical purposes. Some member countries of the European Union pay, as part of the MCA system, a levy on exports (see note 16 to §69). Where these amounts are identifiable, they are shown in this heading. This heading does not include repayments of general consumption taxes or excises or customs duties on exported goods, which should be deducted from the gross receipts under 5110, 5121 or 5123, as appropriate.

### 5125 — *Taxes on investment goods*

71. This sub-heading covers taxes on investment goods, such as machinery. These taxes may be imposed for a number of years or temporarily for counter-cyclical purposes. Taxes on industrial inputs which are also levied on consumers [e.g., the Swedish energy tax which is classified under (5121)] are not included here.

### 5126 — *Taxes on specific services*

72. All taxes assessed on the payment for specific services, such as taxes on insurance premiums, banking services, gambling and betting stakes (e.g., from horse races, football pools, lottery tickets), transport, entertainment, restaurant and advertising charges, fall into this category. Taxes on entry to casinos, races, other similar events or venues as well as stamp taxes on specific services are also classified under this heading. Taxes levied on the gross income of companies providing a specific service (e.g. transportation [including airport and other passenger taxes] insurance, banking, entertainment, restaurants, and advertising) are also classified under this heading.

73. Tax revenues from bank levies and payments to deposit insurance and financial stability schemes are also included here:

- Compulsory payments of stability fees, bank levies and deposit insurance should generally be treated as tax revenues where the payments are made to general government or supranational authorities and are allocated to the governments' consolidated or general funds so that the government is free to make immediate use of the money for the purposes that it chooses. This principle would apply regardless of whether the government is promising to make payments to guarantee the banks' customer deposits in some future contingency.

- If the compulsory payments are made to general government and placed in funds that are earmarked to be entirely channelled back to the sector of the economy that comprises the companies that are subject to the payment, they would still generally be treated as tax revenues on the grounds that the funds would be available for the government and would reduce its budget deficit, the fee is unrequited for an individual entity and the amounts raised could be unrelated to any eventual pay out to depositors or expenditure on wider support for the financial sector.
- Payments to made to the smaller long-standing schemes for insuring 'retail' deposits, where the payment levels are consistent with the costs of insurance should be classified as fee for service.
- Any payments which involve governments realising the assets of a failed institution or receiving a priority claim on its assets in liquidation in order to fund payments of compensation to customers for their lost deposits would be treated as a fee for a service as opposed to tax revenues.
- Compulsory payments that are made to funds operated outside the government sector and non-state institutions backed by the deposit takers and all payments to voluntary schemes should not be treated as tax revenues.
- Contributions made to the EU Single Resolution Fund are also included here and recorded under the supranational level of government in the country tables.

74. Excluded from this sub-heading are:

*a)* taxes on services forming part of a general tax on goods and services (5110);

*b)* taxes on electricity, gas and energy (5121 as excises);

*c)* taxes on individual gains from gambling (1120 as taxes on capital gains of individuals and non-corporate enterprises) and lump-sum taxes on the transfer of private lotteries or on the permission to set up lotteries (5200);[18]

*d)* taxes on cheques and on the issue, transfer or redemption of securities (4400 as taxes on financial and capital transactions);

*e)* general taxes on turnover (5113).

### *5127 — Other taxes on international trade and transactions*

75. This sub-heading covers revenue received by the government from the purchase and sale of foreign exchange at different rates. When the government exercises monopoly powers to extract a margin between the purchase and sales price of foreign exchange, other than to cover administrative costs, the revenue derived constitutes a compulsory levy exacted in indeterminate proportions from both purchaser and seller of foreign exchange. It is the common equivalent of an import duty and export duty levied in a single exchange rate system or of a tax on the sale or purchase of foreign exchange. Like the profits of fiscal monopolies and import or export monopolies transferred to government, it represents the exercise of monopoly powers for tax purposes and is included in tax revenues.

76. The sub-heading covers also the profits of export or import monopolies, which do not however exist in OECD countries, taxes on purchase or sale of foreign exchange, and any other taxes levied specifically on international trade or transactions.

### 5128 — *Other taxes on specific goods and services*

77. This item includes taxes on the extraction of minerals, fossil fuels and other exhaustible resources from deposits owned privately or by another government together with any other unallocable receipts from taxes on specific goods and services. Taxes on the extraction of exhaustible resources are usually a fixed amount per unit of quality or weight, but can be a percentage of value. The taxes are recorded when the resources are extracted. Payments from the extraction of exhaustible resources from deposits owned by the government unit receiving the payment are classified as rent.

### 5200 — *Taxes on use of goods or on permission to use goods or perform activities*

78. This sub-heading covers taxes which are levied in respect of the use of goods as distinct from taxes on the goods themselves. Unlike the latter taxes – reported under 5100 –, they are not assessed on the value of the goods but usually as fixed amounts. Taxes on permission to use goods or to perform activities are also included here, as are pollution taxes not based upon the value of particular goods. It is sometimes difficult to distinguish between compulsory user charges and licence fees which are regarded as taxes and those which are excluded as non-tax revenues. The criteria which are employed are noted in §12–13.

79. Although the sub-heading refers to the 'use' of goods, registration of ownership rather than use may be what generates liability to tax, so that the taxes of this heading may apply to the ownership of animals or goods rather than their use (e.g., race horses, dogs and motor vehicles) and may apply even to unusable goods (e.g., unusable motor vehicles or guns).

80. Borderline cases arise with:

*a)* taxes on the permission to perform business activities which are levied on a combined income, payroll or turnover base and, accordingly, are classified following the rules in §84;

*b)* taxes on the ownership or use of property of headings 4100, 4200 and 4600. The heading 4100 is confined to taxes on the ownership or tenancy of immovable property and – unlike the taxes of 5200 – they are related to the value of the property. The net wealth taxes and taxes on chattels of 4200 and 4600 respectively are confined to the ownership rather than the use of assets, apply to groups of assets rather than particular goods and again are related to the value of the assets,

### 5210 — *Recurrent taxes on use of goods and on permission to use goods or perform activities*

81. The principal characteristic of taxes classified here is that they are levied at regular intervals and that they are usually fixed amounts. The most important item in terms of revenue receipts is vehicle licence taxes. This sub-heading also covers taxes on permission to hunt, shoot, fish or to sell certain products and taxes on the ownership of dogs and on the performance of certain services, provided that they meet the criteria set out in §12–13. The sub-divisions of 5210 are:

- user taxes on motor vehicles paid by households (5211);
- taxes on motor vehicles paid by others (5212); and
- other recurrent taxes (5213). This sub-heading covers business and professional licences paid by enterprises in order to obtain a licence to carry on a particular kind of business or profession when the levies are on a recurring basis. Licences such as taxi and casino licences are included. Dog licences and recurrent general licences for hunting, shooting

and fishing where the right to carry out these activities is not granted as part of a normal commercial transaction are also included under this heading.

82. Excluded from sub-heading 5213 are:

*a)* licences where the right to carry out such activities is granted as part of a normal commercial transaction (e.g., the granting of the licence is accompanied by the right to use a specific area which is owned by government);

*b)* payments relating to the checks carried out by the government on the suitability and or safety of the business premises or equipment, or on the quality or standard of goods or services produced as a condition for granting such a licence. These payments are not unrequited and should be treated as payments for services rendered, unless the amounts charged for the licences are out of all proportion to the costs of the checks carried out by governments.

### *5220 — Non-recurrent taxes on use of goods and on permission to use goods or perform activities*

83. This section covers non-recurrent taxes levied on the use of goods or on permission to use goods or perform activities and taxes levied each time goods are used. It includes taxes levied on the emission or discharge into the environment of noxious gases, liquids or other harmful substances.

- Payments for tradable emission permits issued by governments under cap and trade schemes should be recorded here at the time the emissions occur. No revenue should be recorded for permits that governments issue free of charge. The accrual basis of recording means that there can be a timing difference between the cash being received by government for the permits and the time the emission occurs. In the national accounts, this timing gives rise to a financial liability for government during the period.
- Payments made for the collection and disposal of waste or noxious substances by public authorities should be excluded as they constitute a sale of services to enterprises.

84. Other taxes falling under heading 5200 that are not levied recurrently are also included here. Thus, once-and-for-all payments for permission to sell liquor or tobacco or to set up betting shops are included provided they meet the criteria set out in §12–13.

### *6000 — Other taxes*

85. Taxes levied on a base, or bases, other than those described under headings 1000, 3000, 4000 and 5000, or on bases of which cannot be considered to be related to any one of these headings, are included here. Where taxes are levied on a multiple base and it is possible to estimate the receipts related to each base the separate amounts are included under the appropriate headings. If separate amounts cannot be estimated and it is known that most of the receipts are derived from one base, the whole of the receipts are classified according to that base. Otherwise, they are classified here. Other revenues included here are presumptive taxes not included elsewhere in the classification system, taxes on individuals in the form of a poll tax or capitation tax, stamp taxes not related to financial and capital transactions nor falling exclusively on a single category of transaction, expenditure taxes where personal deductions or exemptions are applied and unidentifiable tax receipts. A subdivision is made between taxes levied wholly or predominantly on business (6100) and those levied on others (6200).

## A.6. Conciliation with National Accounts

86. This section of the tables provides a re-conciliation between the OECD calculation of total tax revenues and the total of all taxes and social contributions paid to general government as recorded in the country's National Accounts. Where the country is a member of the European Union (EU), the comparison is between the OECD calculation of total tax revenues and the sum of tax revenues and social contributions recorded in the combination of the general government and the institutions of the EU sectors of the National Accounts.

## A.7. Memorandum item on the financing of social security benefits

87. In view of the varying relationship between taxation and social security contributions and the cases referred to in §40 to §46, a memorandum item collects together all payments earmarked for social security-type benefits, other than voluntary payments to the private sector. Data are presented as follows (refer Table 5.39 of the Report):

*a)* Taxes of 2000 series.

*b)* Taxes earmarked for social security benefits.

*c)* Voluntary contributions to the government.

*d)* Compulsory contributions to the private sector.

Guidance on the breakdown of (a) to (d) above is provided in §40 to §46.

## A.8. Memorandum item on identifiable taxes paid by government

88. Identifiable taxes actually paid by government are presented in a memorandum item classified by the main headings of the OECD classification of taxes. In the vast majority of countries, only social security contributions and payroll taxes paid by government can be identified. These are, however, usually the most important taxes paid by governments (refer to Table 5.40 of the Report).

## A.9. Relation of OECD classification of taxes to national accounting systems

89. A system of national accounts (SNA) seeks to provide a coherent framework for recording and presenting the main flows relating respectively to production, consumption, accumulation and external transactions of a given economic area, usually a country or a major region within a country. Government revenues are an important part of the transactions recorded in SNA. The final version of the 2008 SNA was jointly published by five international organisations: the United Nations, the International Monetary Fund, the European Union, the Organisation for Economic Co-operation and Development, and the World Bank in August 2009. The *System* is a comprehensive, consistent and flexible set of macroeconomic accounts. It is designed for use in countries with market economies, whatever their stage of economic development, and also in countries in transition to market economies. The important parts of the SNA's conceptual framework and its definitions of the various sectors of the economy have been reflected in the OECD's classification of taxes.

90. There are, however, some differences between the OECD classification of taxes and SNA concepts that are listed below. They arise because the aim of the former is to provide the maximum disaggregation of statistical data on what are generally regarded as taxes by tax administrations.

*a)* OECD includes compulsory social security contributions paid to general government in total tax revenues. Imputed and voluntary contributions plus those paid to private funds are not treated as taxes (§9 and §11 above);

*b)* there are different points of view on whether or not some levies and fees are classified as taxes (§12 and §13 above);

*c)* OECD excludes imputed taxes or subsidies resulting from the operation of official multiple exchange rates or from the central bank paying a rate of interest on required reserves that is different from other market rates;

*d)* there are differences in the treatment of non-wastable tax credits

91. As noted in §1 and §2, headings 1000 to 6000 of the OECD list of taxes cover all unrequited payments to general government or to a supranational authority, other than compulsory loans and fines. Such unrequited payments including fines, but excluding compulsory loans can be obtained from adding together the following figures in the 2008 SNA

- value-added type taxes (D.211);
- taxes and duties on imports, excluding VAT (D.212);
- export taxes (D.213);
- taxes on products, excluding VAT, import and export taxes (D.214);
- other taxes on production (D.29);
- taxes on income (D.51);
- other current taxes (D.59);
- actual social contributions (D.611 and D613), excluding voluntary contributions and payments to employment-related schemes that are not social security schemes
- capital taxes (D.91).

## A.10. The OECD classification of taxes and the International Monetary Fund (GFS) system

92. The coverage and valuation of tax revenues in the GFS system and the 2008 SNA are very similar. Therefore, the differences between the OECD classification and that of the 2008 SNA (see §90 above) also apply to the GFS. In addition the International Monetary Fund subdivides the OECD 5000 heading into section IV (Domestic Taxes on Goods and Services) and section V (Taxes on International Trade and Transactions). This reflects the fact that while the latter usually yield insignificant amounts of revenue in OECD countries, this is not the case in many non-OECD countries.

## A.11. Comparison of the OECD classification of taxes with other international classifications

93. The table below describes an item by item comparison of the OECD classification of taxes and the classifications used in the following:

*a)* System of National Accounts (2008 SNA);

*b)* European System of Accounts (2010 ESA);

*c)* IMF Government Finance Statistics Manual (GFSM2014).

94. These comparisons represent those that would be expected to apply in the majority of cases. However in practice some flexibility should be used in their application. This is because in particular cases, countries can adopt varying approaches to the classification of revenues in National Accounts.

| OECD Classification | | | | | 2008 SNA | 2010 ESA | GFSM2014 |
|---|---|---|---|---|---|---|---|
| 1000 | Taxes on income, profits and capital gains | | | | | | |
| | 1100 Individuals | | | | | | |
| | 1110 | Income and profits | | | D51-8.61a | D51A | 1111 |
| | 1120 | Capital gains | | | D51-8.61c, d | D51C, D | 1111 |
| | 1200 Corporations | | | | | | |
| | 1210 | Income and profits | | | D51-8.61b | D51B | 1112 |
| | 1220 | Capital gains | | | D51-8.61c | D51C | 1112 |
| | 1300 Unallocable as between 1100 and 1200 | | | | | | 1113 |
| 2000 | Social security contributions | | | | | | |
| | 2100 Employees | | | | D613-8.85 | D613 | 1211 |
| | 2200 Employers | | | | D611-8.83 | D611 | 1212 |
| | 2300 Self-employed, non-employed | | | | D613-8.85 | D613 | 1213 |
| | 2400 Unallocable as between 2100, 2200 and 2300 | | | | | | 1214 |
| 3000 | Taxes on payroll and workforce | | | | D29-7.97a | D29C | 112 |
| 4000 | Taxes on property | | | | | | |
| | 4100 Recurrent taxes on immovable property | | | | | | |
| | 4110 | Households | | | D59-8.63a | D59A | 1131 |
| | 4120 | Other | | | D29-7.97b | D29A | 1131 |
| | 4200 Recurrent net wealth taxes | | | | | | |
| | 4210 | Individual | | | D59-8.63b | D59A | 1132 |
| | 4220 | Corporations | | | D59-8.63b | D59A | 1132 |
| | 4300 Estate, inheritance and gift taxes | | | | | | |
| | 4310 | Estate and inheritance taxes | | | D91-10.207b | D91A | 1133 |
| | 4320 | Gift taxes | | | D91-10.207b | D91A | 1133 |
| | 4400 Taxes on financial and capital transactions | | | | D59-7.96d; D29-7.97e | D214B, C | 114114; 1161 |
| | 4500 Other non-recurrent taxes on property | | | | D91-10.207a | D91B | 1135 |
| | 4600 Other recurrent taxes on property | | | | D59-8.63c | D59A | 1136 |
| 5000 | Taxes on goods and services | | | | | | |
| | 5100 Taxes on production, sale and transfer of goods and services | | | | | | |
| | 5110 | General taxes on goods and services | | | | | |
| | | | 5111 | Value-added taxes | D211-7.89 | D211; D29G | 11411 |
| | | | 5112 | Sales taxes | D2122-7.94a; D214-7.96a | D21224; D214I | 11412 |
| | | | 5113 | Other general taxes on goods and services | D214-7.96a | D214I | 11413 |
| | 5120 | Taxes on specific goods and services | | | | | |
| | | | 5121 | Excises | D2122-7.94b; D214-7.96b | D21223; D214A, B, D | 1142 |
| | | | 5122 | Profits of fiscal monopolies | D214-7.96e | D214J | 1143 |
| | | | 5123 | Customs and other import duties | D2121-7.93 | D2121; D21221, 2 | 1151 |
| | | | 5124 | On exports | D213-7.95a | D214K | 1152-4 |
| | | | 5125 | On investment goods | | | |
| | | | 5126 | On specific services | D2122-7.94c; D214-7.96c | D21225; D214E, F, G, H; D29F | 1144; 1156 |
| | | | 5127 | Other taxes on international trade and transactions | D2122-7.94d D29-7.95b D29-7.97g D59-8.64d | D21226; D29D; D59E | 1153; 1155-6 |
| | | | 5128 | Other taxes on specific goods and services | | | 1146 |
| | 5130 | Unallocable between 5110 and 5120 | | | | | |
| | 5200 Taxes on use of goods and on permission to use goods or perform activities | | | | | | |
| | 5210 | Recurrent taxes on use of goods and on permission to use goods or perform activities | | | | | |
| | | | 5211 | Motor vehicle taxes households | D59-8.64c | D59D | 11451 |
| | | | 5212 | Motor vehicles taxes others | D29-7.97d | D214D; D29B | 11451 |
| | | | 5213 | Other recurrent taxes on use of goods and on permission to use goods or perform activities | D29-7.97c, d, f D59-8.64c | D29B, E, F; D59D | 11452 |

| OECD Classification | | | 2008 SNA | 2010 ESA | GFSM2014 |
|---|---|---|---|---|---|
| | | 5220 Non-recurrent taxes on permission to use goods or perform activities | | | 11452 |
| | 5300 | Unallocable as between 5100 and 5200 | | | |
| 6000 | Other taxes | | | | |
| | 6100 | Payable solely by business | | | 1161 |
| | 6200 | Payable by other than business, or unidentifiable | D59-8.64a, b | D59B, C | 1162 |

## A.12. Attribution of tax revenues by sub-sectors of general government

95. The OECD classification requires a breakdown of tax revenues by sub-sectors of government. The definition of each sub-sector and the criteria to be used to attribute tax revenues between these sub-sectors are set out below. They follow the guidance of the 2008 SNA and GFSM 2014.

### *Sub-sectors of general government to be identified*

*a) Central government*

96. The central government sub-sector includes all governmental departments, offices, establishments and other bodies which are agencies or instruments of the central authority whose competence extends over the whole territory, with the exception of the administration of social security funds. Central government therefore has the authority to impose taxes on all resident and non-resident units engaged in economic activities within the country.

*b) State, provincial or regional government*

97. This sub-sector consists of intermediate units of government exercising a competence at a level below that of central government. It includes all such units operating independently of central government in a part of a country's territory encompassing a number of smaller localities, with the exception of the administration of social security funds. In unitary countries, regional governments may be considered to have a separate existence where they have substantial autonomy to raise a significant proportion of their revenues from sources within their control and their officers are independent of external administrative control in the actual operation of the unit's activities.

98. At present, federal countries comprise the majority of cases where revenues attributed to intermediate units of government are identified separately. Colombia and Spain are the only two unitary countries in this position. In the remaining unitary countries, regional revenues are included with those of local governments.

*c) Local government*

99. This sub-sector includes all other units of government exercising an independent competence in part of the territory of a country, with the exception of the administration of social security funds. It encompasses various urban and/or rural jurisdictions (e.g., local authorities, municipalities, cities, boroughs, districts).

*d) Social security funds*

100. Social security funds form a separate sub-sector of general government. The social security sub-sector is defined in the 2008 SNA by the following extracts from paragraphs 4.124 to 4.126 and 4.147:

"Social security schemes are social insurance schemes covering the community as a whole or large section of the community that are imposed and controlled by government units. The schemes cover a wide variety of programmes, providing benefits in cash or in kind for old age, invalidity or death, survivors, sickness and maternity, work injury, unemployment, family allowance, health care, etc. There is not necessarily a direct link between the amount of the contribution paid by an individual and the benefits he or she may receive." (Paragraph 4.124).

"When social security schemes are separately organised from the other activities of government units and hold their assets and liabilities separately from the latter and engage in financial transactions on their own account they qualify as institutional units that are described as social security funds." (Paragraph 4.125).

"The amounts raised, and paid out, in social security contributions and benefits may be deliberately varied in order to achieve objectives of government policy that have no direct connection with the concept of social security as a scheme to provide social benefits to members of the community. They may be raised or lowered in order to influence the level of aggregate demand in the economy, for example. Nevertheless, so long as they remain separately constituted funds, they must be treated as separate institutional units in the SNA. (Paragraph 4.126).

"The social security funds sub-sector (of general government) consists of the social security funds operating at all levels of government. Such funds are social insurance schemes covering the community as a whole or large section of the community that are imposed by government units." (Paragraph 4.147).

101. This definition of social security funds is followed in the OECD classification with the two following exceptions which are excluded

- Schemes imposed by government and operated by bodies outside the general government sector, as defined in §3 of this manual; and
- Schemes to which all contributions are voluntary.

### *Supranational Authorities*

102. This sub-sector covers the revenue-raising operations of supra-national authorities within a country. In practice, the only relevant supranational authority in the OECD area is that of the institutions of the European Union (EU). Tax revenues collected by member countries and paid to the EU are included in the *Revenue Statistics* at the supranational level of government. Income taxes and social security contributions collected by European Institutions and paid by European civil servants who are resident of EU member countries should not be included.

### *Criteria to be used for the attribution of tax revenues*

103. When a government collects taxes and pays them over in whole or in part to other governments, it is necessary to determine whether the revenues should be considered to be those of the collecting government which it distributes to others as grants, or those of the beneficiary governments which the collecting government receives and passes on only as their agent. The criteria to be used in the attribution of revenues are set out in §104 to §107 which replicate paragraphs 3.70 to 3.73 from the 2008 SNA.

104. In general, a tax is attributed to the government unit that

*a)* exercises the authority to impose the tax (either as a principal or through the delegated authority of the principal),

*b)* has final discretion to set and vary the rate of the tax

105. Where an amount is collected by one government for and on behalf of another government, and the latter government has the authority to impose the tax, and set and vary its rate, then the former is acting as an agent for the latter and the tax is reassigned. Any amount retained by the collecting government as a collection charge should be treated as a payment for a service. Any other amount retained by the collecting government, such as under a tax-sharing arrangement, should be treated as a current grant. If the collecting government was delegated the authority to set and vary the rate, then the amount collected should be treated as tax revenue of this government.

106. Where different governments jointly and equally set the rate of a tax and jointly and equally decide on the distribution of the proceeds, with no individual government having ultimate overriding authority, then the tax revenues are attributed to each government according to its respective share of the proceeds. If an arrangement allows one government unit to exercise ultimate overriding authority, then all of the tax revenue is attributed to that unit.

107. There may also be the circumstance where a tax is imposed under the constitutional or other authority of one government, but other governments individually set the tax rate in their jurisdictions. The proceeds of the tax generated in each respective government's jurisdiction are attributed as tax revenues of that government.

108. The levies paid by the member states of the EU take the form specific levies which include

*a)* custom duties and levies on agricultural goods (5123),

*b)* gross monetary compensation accounts (5123 if relating to imports and 5124 if relating to exports);

*c)* contributions to the Single Resolution Fund (5126); and

*d)* Steel, coal, sugar and milk levies (5128).

109. The custom duties collected by member states on behalf of the EU are recorded

- on a gross of collection fee basis;
- using figures adjusted so that duties are shown on a 'final destination' as opposed to a 'country of first entry' basis where such adjustments can be made. These adjustments concern in particular duties collected at important (sea) ports. Although the EU duties are collected by the authorities of the country of first entry, when possible these duties should be excluded from the revenue of the collecting country and be included in the revenue of the country of final destination

110. These are the specific EU levies that most clearly conform to the attribution criterion described in §102 above. Consequently, these amounts are footnoted as a memorandum item to the EU member state country tables (in Chapter 5) and are shown as supranational revenues against each of the tax headings identified in §108.

### Notes

1. References in this OECD Interpretative Guide to Sections or Parts of "this Report" refer to OECD (2021), Revenue Statistics 2021, OECD Publishing, Paris.
2. All references to SNA are to the 2008 edition.
3. See section A.12 of this guide for a discussion of the concept of agency capacity.

4. It is usually possible to identify amounts of social security contributions and payroll taxes, but not other taxes paid by government.
5. If, however, a levy which is considered as non-tax revenue by most countries is regarded as a tax — or raises substantial revenue — in one or more countries, the amounts collected are footnoted at the end of the relevant country tables, even though the amounts are not included in total tax revenues.
6. Names, however, can frequently be misleading. For example, though a passport fee would normally be considered a non-tax revenue, if a supplementary levy on passports (as is the case in Portugal) were imposed in order to raise substantial amounts of revenue relative to the cost of providing the passport, the levy would be regarded as a tax under 5200.
7. A more detailed explanation of this distinction can be found in the special feature, 'Current issues in reporting tax revenues', in the 2001 edition of the *Revenue Statistics*.
8. Sometimes the terms 'non-refundable' and 'refundable' are used, but it may be considered illogical to talk of 'refundable' when nothing has been paid.
9. A different treatment, however, is accorded to non-wastable tax credits under imputation systems of corporate income tax (§37–39).
10. This is not strictly a true tax expenditure in the formal sense. Such tax expenditures require identification of a benchmark tax system for each country or, preferably, a common international benchmark. In practice it has not been possible to reach agreement on a common international benchmark.
11. Unless based on the profit made on a sale, in which case they would be classified as capital gains taxes under 1120 or 1220.
12. In some countries the same legislation applies to both individual and corporate enterprises for particular taxes on income. However, the receipts from such taxes are usually allocable between individuals and enterprises and can therefore be shown in the appropriate sub-heading.
13. For example, "… sufficiently self-contained and independent that they behave in the same way as corporations… (including) keeping a complete set of accounts" (2008 SNA, section 4.44).
14. In Canada — a country also referred to as having an imputation system — the (wastable) tax credit for the shareholder is in respect of domestic corporation tax deemed to have been paid whether or not a corporation tax liability has arisen. As there is no integral connection between the corporation tax liability and the credit given against income tax under such systems, these credits for dividends are treated, along with other tax credits, on the lines described in §26.
15. This may also apply where a scheme for government employees existed prior to the introduction of a general social security scheme.
16. In the 2008 SNA these are regarded as capital transfers and not as taxes (see section A.8).
17. This is the system by which the European Union adjusts for differences between the exchange rates used to determine prices under the Common Market Agricultural Policy and actual exchange rates. Payments under the system may relate to imports or exports and where these amounts are separately identifiable they are shown under the appropriate heading (5123 or 5124). In this Report, these amounts are shown gross (i.e. without deducting any subsidies paid out under the MCA system).
18. Transfers of profits of State lotteries are regarded as non-tax revenues (see also §68).

# Anexo A

# *Guía de interpretación de la OCDE*[1]

## *Índice*

## A.1. Clasificación de impuestos de la OCDE

1. 1000 **Impuestos sobre la renta, las utilidades y las ganancias de capital**

    1100 Impuestos sobre la renta, utilidades y ganancias de capital de personas físicas

        1110 Renta y utilidades

        1120 Ganancias de capital

    1200 Impuesto sobre la renta, utilidades y ganancias de capital de sociedades.

        1210 Renta y utilidades

        1220 Ganancias de capital

    1300 No clasificables entre 1100 y 1200

2. 2000 **Contribuciones a la seguridad social**

    2100 Empleados

        2110 Sobre la base de la nómina

        2120 Sobre la base del impuesto sobre la renta

    2200 Empleadores

        2210 Sobre la base de la nómina

        2220 Sobre la base del impuesto sobre la renta

    2300 Trabajadores por cuenta propia o no empleados

        2310 Sobre la base de la nómina

        2320 Sobre la base del impuesto sobre la renta

    2400 No clasificables entre 2100, 2200 y 2300

        2410 Sobre la base de la nómina

        2420 Sobre la base del impuesto sobre la renta

3. 3000 **Impuestos sobre la nómina y la fuerza de trabajo**

4. 4000 **Impuestos sobre la propiedad**

    4100 Impuestos recurrentes sobre la propiedad inmueble

        4110 Hogares

        4120 Otros

    4200 Impuestos recurrentes sobre la riqueza neta

        4210 Personas físicas

        4220 Sociedades

    4300 Impuestos sobre sucesiones, herencias y donaciones

        4310 Impuestos sobre sucesiones y herencias

        4320 Impuestos sobre donaciones

    4400 Impuestos sobre transacciones financieras y de capital

    4500 Otros impuestos no recurrentes sobre la propiedad

        4510 Otros impuestos sobre la riqueza neta

        4520 Otros impuestos no recurrentes

    4600 Otros impuestos recurrentes sobre la propiedad

**5. 5000 Impuestos sobre los bienes y servicios**

5100 Impuestos sobre la producción, venta, transferencia , arrendamiento y entrega de bienes y prestación de servicios

5110 Impuestos generales

5111 Impuestos sobre el valor agregado

5112 Impuestos sobre las ventas

5113 Otros impuestos generales sobre ingresos brutos y sobre bienes y servicios

5120 Impuestos sobre bienes y servicios específicos

5121 Impuestos selectivos

5122 Utilidades de los monopolios fiscales

5123 Derechos de aduanas y otros derechos de importación

5124 Impuestos sobre las exportaciones

5125 Impuestos sobre los bienes de inversión

5126 Impuestos sobre servicios específicos

5127 Otros impuestos sobre el comercio y las transacciones internacionales

5128 Otros impuestos sobre bienes y servicios específicos

5130 No clasificables entre 5110 y 5120

5200 Impuestos sobre el uso de bienes y sobre el permiso para usar bienes y realizar actividades

5210 Impuestos recurrentes

5211 Pagados por los hogares sobre vehículos automotores.

5212 Pagados por otros sobre vehículos automotores

5213 Otros impuestos recurrentes

5220 Impuestos no recurrentes

5300 No clasificables entre 5100 y 5200

**6. 6000 Otros impuestos**

6100 Pagados únicamente por empresas

6200 Pagados por otros distintos de las empresas o no identificables

## A.2. Cobertura

### *Criterios generales*

1. En la clasificación de la OCDE, el término "impuestos" se circunscribe exclusivamente a los pagos sin contraprestación efectuados al gobierno general o una autoridad supranacional. Los impuestos carecen de contraprestación en el sentido en que, normalmente, las prestaciones proporcionadas por el gobierno a los contribuyentes no guardan relación directa con los pagos realizados por estos.

2. El término "impuestos" no incluye las multas, sanciones pecuniarias, ni préstamos obligatorios pagados al gobierno. La delimitación entre ingresos tributarios y no tributarios en relación con ciertas tasas y cargos se abordan en los § 12-15.

3. El gobierno general comprende la Administración central y los organismos que se hallan bajo su control efectivo, los gobiernos estatales y locales y sus respectivas administraciones, y ciertos regímenes de seguridad social y entidades gubernamentales autónomas, excluidas las empresas públicas. Esta definición del gobierno proviene del *Sistema de Cuentas Nacionales* (SCN) 2008;[2] en esa publicación, el sector del gobierno general y sus subsectores se hallan definidos en el capítulo 4, párrafos 4.117 a 4.165 de la versión en inglés.

4. Las unidades extrapresupuestarias son parte del sistema de gobierno general. Estas son entidades del gobierno general con presupuestos individuales que no están completamente cubiertos por el presupuesto principal o general. Estas entidades operan bajo la autoridad o el control de un gobierno central, estatal o local. Las entidades extrapresupuestarias pueden tener sus propias fuentes de ingresos, que pueden complementarse con subvenciones (transferencias) del presupuesto general o de otras fuentes. A pesar de que sus presupuestos pueden estar sujetos a la aprobación de la legislatura, similar a la de las cuentas presupuestarias, tienen discreción sobre el volumen y la composición de sus gastos. Dichas entidades pueden establecerse para llevar a cabo funciones gubernamentales específicas, como la construcción de carreteras o la producción de servicios de salud o educación pública. Los arreglos presupuestarios varían ampliamente entre países, y se utilizan diversos términos para describir estas entidades, pero a menudo se los denomina "fondos extrapresupuestarios" o "agencias descentralizadas".

5. Los pagos obligatorios y sin contraprestación recaudados por los gobiernos nacionales y abonados a las autoridades supranacionales se considerarán también como impuestos según la definición del párrafo 1. Los ingresos tributarios que recaudan los gobiernos nacionales y que se pagan a una autoridad supranacional se asignan como ingresos fiscales a la autoridad supranacional en el SCN 2008 (véanse los párrafos 22.60-61, 22.88 y 22.99) y en el SEC 2010 (véase el párrafo 20.165). En las estadísticas tributarias, estos ingresos tributarios incluyen los derechos de aduana, las contribuciones al Fondo de Resolución Única de la UE y cualquier otro impuesto recaudado por los Estados miembros de la UE en nombre de la Unión Europea. Se incluyen en los importes de los ingresos tributarios en los cuadros de países (capítulo 5) del país en el que se recaudan y se atribuyen a la autoridad supranacional (véase el §102).

6. En los países en los que la Iglesia forma parte del gobierno general y las autoridades supranacionales, se computan los impuestos eclesiásticos, siempre que reúnan los criterios establecidos en el § 1. Además, habida cuenta de que los datos hacen referencia a las entradas que recibe el gobierno general, quedan excluidos los gravámenes abonados a órganos no gubernamentales, organismos de bienestar o regímenes de seguro social externos al gobierno general, y sindicatos u organizaciones profesionales, aun cuando dichos gravámenes sean

obligatorios; sin embargo, los pagos obligatorios al gobierno general asignados a esos entes sí están incluidos aquí siempre que el gobierno no actúe como mero agente de estos[3]. Las utilidades de los monopolios fiscales se diferencian de las de otras empresas públicas, y se tratan como impuestos porque reflejan el ejercicio del poder tributario del Estado mediante el uso de prerrogativas monopolísticas (véanse los § 66 68), al igual que las utilidades percibidas por el gobierno por la compra y la venta de divisas a diferentes tipos de cambio (véase el § 76).

7. Los impuestos pagados por el gobierno (p. ej., contribuciones a la seguridad social e impuestos sobre la nómina pagados por el gobierno en su calidad de empleador, impuestos sobre el consumo en sus compras o impuestos sobre sus propiedades) no se han excluido de los datos presentados. Sin embargo, cuando ha sido posible identificar las cantidades de ingreso implicadas[4], se han mostrado en el Cuadro 5.39 de la publicación Estadísticas Tributarias en países de la OCDE.

8. La relación entre esta clasificación y la del Sistema de Cuentas Nacionales (SCN) se aclara en los apartados A.9 y A.11 infra.; dado que estas dos clasificaciones no coinciden en todos sus aspectos, en ocasiones, los datos presentados en las cuentas nacionales se calculan o clasifican de forma diferente a lo establecido en la presente guía y, aunque esas y otras diferencias se han mencionado en determinados casos (p. ej., en el § 31 infra.), no ha sido posible hacer referencia a todas ellas. Por otra parte, pueden darse asimismo ciertas disparidades entre la presente clasificación y la empleada internamente por algunas administraciones nacionales (véase el § 13), por lo que quizá las estadísticas de la OCDE y las nacionales no siempre concuerden; sin embargo, es más que probable que esas diferencias sean mínimas en lo que a la cuantía de ingresos se refiere.

### *Contribuciones a la seguridad social*

9. Las contribuciones obligatorias a la seguridad social, tal y como se definen en el § 40, abonadas al gobierno general, se tratan aquí como ingresos tributarios. No obstante, pueden diferir de otros impuestos por el hecho de que la recepción de prestaciones de la seguridad social depende, en numerosos países, de que se hayan aportado las debidas contribuciones, aunque la magnitud de dichas prestaciones no tiene por qué estar supeditada obligatoriamente al importe de las contribuciones. Al tratar las contribuciones sociales como impuestos, se obtiene un mayor grado de comparabilidad entre países, aunque se han consignado en una categoría separada para poder distinguirlas en cualquier análisis.

10. La estricta distinción entre los ingresos tributarios (pagos obligatorios sin contraprestaciones directas a los gobiernos generales o una autoridad supranacional) y los pagos obligatorios no tributarios (NTCPs por sus siglas en inglés) (pagos que con derechos a contraprestaciones o que se realizan a otras instituciones) está claramente definida. Sin embargo, dentro del rango de diferentes pagos obligatorios realizados a los gobiernos en todos los países, no siempre es sencillo en la práctica decidir si los pagos específicos son impuestos o NTCPs. Por ejemplo, los ahorros de pensión obligatorios que son controlados por el gobierno general y que se acumulan en una cuenta individual obteniendo una rentabilidad del mercado o una tasa que compensa la inflación se clasificarían a primera vista como NTCPs en lugar de impuestos. Sin embargo, incluso estos pagos podrían no dar origen a "reembolsos" y clasificarse como impuestos en lugar de NTCPs (por ejemplo, si estos ahorros no se pagan cuando el contribuyente muere antes de alcanzar la edad de jubilación y los fondos se utilizan para proporcionar una pensión mínima a todos los contribuyentes que están asegurados). Estos problemas hacen que las cifras de ingresos de la seguridad social reportadas para la mayoría de los países se basen en la premisa de que todos los tipos de pagos obligatorios a las administraciones públicas

se consideran en cierta medida como elementos de redistribución. Cabe señalar que esta conclusión se basa en una interpretación generalmente amplia del término "no correspondido" en la definición del impuesto.

11. Por el contrario, las contribuciones a la seguridad social voluntarias o no pagaderas al gobierno general (véase el § 1) no se tratan como impuestos, aunque en ciertos países, tal y como se indica debidamente en cada caso en las notas que figuran al pie de los cuadros, plantea dificultades el eliminar tanto las contribuciones voluntarias como algunos pagos obligatorios al sector privado de las cifras de recaudo tributario. Las contribuciones a la seguridad social imputadas tampoco son considerados impuestos.

### *Tasas, cargos a usuarios y licencias*

12. Aparte de las tasas por licencia de vehículos, universalmente consideradas como impuestos, no resulta fácil distinguir entre las tasas y cargos a usuarios que deben tratarse como impuestos y las que no, ya que, aunque toda tasa o cargo se impone en conexión con un servicio o una actividad específicos, la intensidad del vínculo entre el derecho cobrado y el servicio prestado puede variar considerablemente, al igual que puede hacerlo la relación entre la cuantía de la tasa y el costo que supone proporcionar el servicio en cuestión. En todo caso, cuando el beneficiario del servicio pague una tasa claramente relacionada con el costo que supone prestar un servicio, puede inferirse que el gravamen tiene contraprestación y, de acuerdo con la definición reseñada en el § 1, no se considerará como impuesto. En sentido contrario, puede estimarse que el gravamen "carece de contraprestación" cuando:

*a)* el cargo exceda con creces el costo que supone prestar el servicio;

*b)* el pagador o sujeto pasivo del gravamen no sea el beneficiario del servicio (p. ej., tasas recaudadas de los mataderos para financiar un servicio proporcionado a los titulares de explotaciones agropecuarias);

*c)* el gobierno no proporcione un servicio específico a cambio del pago del gravamen, aun y cuando se emita un permiso en beneficio del sujeto pasivo (p. ej., cuando el gobierno concede licencias de caza, pesca o tiro que no otorgan el derecho a usar una zona específica propiedad del gobierno);

*d)* los servicios beneficien únicamente a los pagadores del gravamen, pero las utilidades recibidas por cada persona no guarden necesariamente proporción con sus pagos (p. ej., el gravamen sobre la comercialización de la leche que recae en los criadores de ganado lechero y que se utiliza para fomentar el consumo de la leche).

13. Pese a las anteriores consideraciones, en ciertos casos excepcionales la aplicación de los criterios plasmados en el § 1 puede resultar particularmente compleja. La solución adoptada – dada la conveniencia de uniformidad internacional y las cantidades de ingreso relativamente bajas implicadas por lo general– ha consistido en seguir la práctica dominante en la mayoría de las administraciones, en lugar de permitir que cada país aplique su propia visión sobre si estos gravámenes deben considerarse como ingresos tributarios o no tributarios.[5]

14. Seguidamente, se ofrece una lista de las principales tasas y cargos en cuestión, y su tratamiento normal[6] en esta publicación:

| | |
|---|---|
| Ingresos no tributarios: | tasas procesales, permisos de conducir, tasas portuarias, tasas por expedición de pasaportes, licencias de radio y televisión cuando las autoridades públicas proporcionan el servicio de difusión |

| | |
|---|---|
| Impuestos de la partida 5200 | permiso para realizar actividades tales como distribución cinematográfica; caza, pesca o tiro; suministro de instalaciones para actividades recreativas o de ocio o juegos de azar; venta de bebidas alcohólicas o tabaco; posesión de animales domésticos o uso de vehículos automotores; derechos sobre la extracción |

15. En la práctica, puede que no siempre resulte posible aislar las entradas tributarias de las no tributarias cuando estas se registran conjuntamente. En ese caso, si se considera que la mayoría de las entradas proviene de ingresos no tributarios, se tratará el importe total como tal; de lo contrario, esas entradas del gobierno se incluirán y clasificarán según las normas recogidas en el § 33.

### *Regalías*

16. La propiedad de los activos del subsuelo en forma de depósitos de minerales o combustibles fósiles (carbón, petróleo o gas natural) depende de la forma en que los derechos de propiedad están definidos por la ley y también de los acuerdos internacionales en el caso de depósitos bajo aguas internacionales. En algunos casos, ya sea en el terreno por debajo del cual se encuentran los depósitos minerales, los depósitos en sí o ambos pueden pertenecer a una unidad del gobierno local o central.

17. En tales casos, estas unidades del gobierno general pueden otorgar arrendamientos a otras unidades institucionales que les permitan extraer estos depósitos durante un período de tiempo específico a cambio de un pago o una serie de pagos. Estos pagos a menudo se describen como "regalías", pero son esencialmente rentas que se acumulan a los propietarios de los recursos naturales a cambio de poner estos activos a disposición de otros agentes durante períodos de tiempo específicos. El alquiler puede tomar la forma de pagos periódicos de cantidades fijas, independientemente de la tasa de extracción, o, más comúnmente, pueden ser una función de la cantidad, el volumen o el valor del activo extraído. Las empresas dedicadas a la exploración en tierras del gobierno pueden hacer pagos a las unidades del gobierno general a cambio del derecho a realizar perforaciones de prueba o investigar de otro modo la existencia y ubicación de los activos del subsuelo. Dichos pagos también se registran como rentas aunque no se realice ninguna extracción. Por lo tanto, estos pagos se clasifican como ingresos no tributarios.

18. Los mismos principios se aplican cuando a otras unidades institucionales se les conceden arrendamientos que les permiten talar madera en bosques naturales en tierras que son propiedad de unidades del gobierno general. Estos pagos también se clasifican como ingresos no tributarios.

19. Estas rentas o regalías pagadas al gobierno general no deben confundirse con los impuestos sobre los ingresos y las ganancias, los impuestos sobre la extracción de recursos naturales, las licencias comerciales u otros impuestos. Si los pagos se aplican a las ganancias de la actividad de extracción, entonces deben clasificarse como impuestos sobre ingresos, utilidades y ganancias (1000). Además, cualquier pago que se imponga a la extracción de minerales y combustibles fósiles de las reservas de propiedad privada o de otro gobierno se debe clasificar como impuestos. Los pagos relacionados con el valor bruto de la producción deben clasificarse como otros impuestos sobre bienes y servicios (5128). Los pagos de una licencia o permiso para realizar operaciones de extracción se deben clasificar como impuestos sobre el uso de bienes y sobre el permiso para usar bienes o realizar actividades (5213).

### *Multas y sanciones pecuniarias*

20. En principio, las multas y sanciones pecuniarias impuestas por el pago tardío de los impuestos o por el intento de evasión de los impuestos no deben registrarse como ingresos tributarios. Sin embargo, en ocasiones no es posible distinguir y separar los pagos por multas y penalidades del recaudo del impuesto a los que estos están relacionados. En este caso, las multas y sanciones pecuniarias vinculadas a un determinado impuesto se registran con los ingresos de ese impuesto. Las multas y penalidades pagadas sobre el recaudo de impuestos no identificados se clasifican como otros impuestos en la partida 6000. Las multas que no están relacionadas con delitos tributarios (por ejemplo, las infracciones por estacionamiento indebido), o que no puedan ser identificadas como ofensas tributarias, no serán tratadas como ingresos tributarios.

## A.3. Principios de registro

### *Criterio de devengo o de caja*

21. Los datos recogidos en las publicaciones *Estadísticas tributarias* de los últimos años relativos a los países de la OCDE se han registrado predominantemente según el criterio de devengo, esto es, se han computado en el momento en que nace la obligación. Se ofrece más información al respecto en las notas que figuran al pie de los cuadros de países en el Capítulo 5 del informe.

22. Sin embargo, los datos relativos a años anteriores y a países que no pertenecen a la OCDE han seguido registrándose principalmente según el criterio de caja, es decir, en el momento en que el gobierno recibió el pago. Por lo tanto, por ejemplo, los impuestos descontados por los empleadores en un año pero pagados al gobierno al año siguiente y los impuestos debidos un año pero liquidados el año después constan ambos en las entradas del segundo año. Las transacciones correctoras, tales como devoluciones, reembolsos y reintegros, se deducen de los ingresos brutos del periodo en que se realizan.

23. Los datos sobre ingresos tributarios se registran sin deducción de los gastos administrativos propios de la recaudación impositiva. De igual modo, cuando los recursos generados por un impuesto se emplean para subvencionar a miembros particulares de la comunidad, el subsidio no se descuenta del producto impositivo, aunque puede que el impuesto aparezca sin los subsidios en los registros nacionales de algunos países.

24. En lo que a los monopolios fiscales se refiere (5122), únicamente se incluye en los ingresos del gobierno el importe realmente transferido a este. Sin embargo, si cualquier gasto de los monopolios fiscales se considera gasto del gobierno (p. ej., gastos sociales emprendidos por los monopolios fiscales en beneficio del gobierno), se añadirán posteriormente con el fin de llegar a cifras de ingreso tributario (véase el § 66 infra.).

### *Distinción entre disposiciones tributarias y disposiciones relativas al gasto*[7]

25. Dado que la presente publicación aborda únicamente la actividad del gobierno desde el punto de vista del ingreso, sin tener en cuenta los aspectos relacionados con el gasto, resulta preciso realizar una distinción entre las disposiciones que rigen estos dos elementos. Por lo general, no existe dificultad alguna en diferenciar ambos aspectos, ya que los gastos operan en un ámbito externo al sistema tributario y sus cuentas, y se rigen por una legislación separada de la impositiva. En los casos de difícil delimitación, se emplea el flujo de caja para distinguir entre disposiciones tributarias y disposiciones relativas al gasto. En la medida en que una disposición incida en el flujo de pagos tributarios del contribuyente al gobierno, se

entenderá que reviste un carácter tributario y se tendrá en cuenta en los datos recogidos en esta publicación. Cualquier disposición que no afecte a ese flujo se reputará como relativa al gasto y no se tendrá en consideración en la información plasmada en la publicación.

26. Las desgravaciones, exenciones y deducciones tributarias sobre la base imponible afectan claramente a la cantidad transferida al gobierno y, por ende, se consideran disposiciones de naturaleza tributaria. En el extremo opuesto, los subsidios o exoneraciones que no compensen la obligación tributaria y que estén claramente desvinculados del proceso de evaluación, no reducen los ingresos tributarios consignados en esta publicación. De particular interés en este ámbito resultan los créditos fiscales, que son cantidades deducibles del impuesto liquidable (lo que los diferencia de las deducciones sobre la base imponible). Cabe distinguir dos tipos de créditos fiscales: los créditos fiscales no exigibles (a veces denominados desaprovechables), limitados al importe de la obligación tributaria y que, por ende, no pueden generar un pago de las autoridades al contribuyente; y los créditos fiscales exigibles (o no desaprovechables), que no están sometidos a dicho límite, de forma que toda cantidad que exceda la obligación tributaria puede abonarse al contribuyente[8]. Al igual que las desgravaciones, un crédito fiscal no exigible afecta claramente a la cantidad transferida al gobierno y, por ende, se considerará como tributario. La práctica seguida para los créditos fiscales exigibles[9] consiste en distinguir entre "el componente de gasto tributario"[10] que es la porción del crédito empleada en reducir o eliminar la obligación del contribuyente" y el "componente de transferencia", constituido por la parte que excede la obligación del contribuyente y que se paga a este. Al registrar los ingresos tributarios deberá restarse la parte equivalente al componente de gasto tributario, pero no la correspondiente al componente de transferencia. Además, las cantidades de ambos componentes deberán figurar como partidas informativas en los cuadros de países. Los países que no puedan diferenciar entre estos dos componentes deberán indicar si se ha restado de los ingresos tributarios el total de ellos y presentar las evaluaciones disponibles del valor que ambos representan. Para mayor información, consúltese el Capítulo 1 de la publicación Revenue Statistics de la OCDE, que examina el efecto de los diversos tratamientos de los créditos fiscales exigibles en la relación impuestos sobre PIB.

### *Calendario y ejercicio fiscal*

27. Las autoridades nacionales cuyos ejercicios fiscales no coinciden con el año calendario deben presentar los datos, siempre que sea posible, sobre la base del año calendario, a fin de permitir el mayor grado posible de comparación con la información de otros países. Subsisten algunos países en los que los datos hacen referencia a los ejercicios fiscales; para ellos, los datos relativos al PIB utilizados en los cuadros comparativos corresponden igualmente a los ejercicios fiscales.

## A.4. Criterios generales de clasificación

### *Principales criterios de clasificación*

28. El desglose de las entradas fiscales en las diversas categorías (1000, 2000, 3000, 4000, 5000 y 6000) se rige en general por la base sobre la cual recae el impuesto: 1000, renta, utilidades y ganancias de capital; 2000 y 3000, remuneraciones, nómina o número de empleados (fuerza de trabajo); 4000, propiedad; 5000, bienes y servicios; 6000, bases múltiples, otras bases o bases no identificables. Cuando un impuesto se calcula sobre más de una base, las entradas que genera se distribuyen, en la medida de lo posible, entre las diversas categorías (véanse los § 33 y 84). Las categorías 4000 y 5000 no sólo cubren aquellos impuestos en los que la

base tributaria está constituida por la propiedad, los bienes o los servicios en sí mismos, sino también ciertos impuestos afines; y así, por ejemplo, los impuestos sobre transmisiones patrimoniales se incluyen en la partida 4400,[11] y los impuestos sobre el uso de bienes y sobre el permiso para realizar actividades, en la 5200. En las categorías 4000 y 5000, se distingue en ocasiones entre impuestos recurrentes y no recurrentes: son impuestos recurrentes los que se recaudan a intervalos regulares (por lo general, anualmente), y no recurrentes, los que se imponen una sola vez (véanse los § 48 §51, §54 §55 y §81 para profundizar en las aplicaciones particulares de esta distinción).

29. La asignación de un impuesto a fines específicos no afecta a la clasificación de las entradas fiscales que genera. Sin embargo, tal y como se explica en el § 40 en relación con la clasificación de las contribuciones a la seguridad social, el hecho de que estas confieran un derecho a recibir prestaciones sociales es decisivo para la definición de la categoría 2000.

30. La forma en que se establece o recauda un impuesto (p.ej., mediante el uso de timbres) no afecta a su clasificación.

### Clasificación de los contribuyentes

31. En ocasiones, se distingue entre diversas clases de contribuyentes. Esas distinciones dependen de cada impuesto.

*a)* Entre personas físicas y sociedades en relación con los impuestos sobre la renta y sobre la riqueza neta

La distinción básica aquí es que los impuestos sobre la renta de las sociedades (impuesto de sociedades), a diferencia de los impuestos sobre la renta de las personas físicas, gravan a la sociedad como entidad y no a sus propietarios, independientemente de las circunstancias personales de estos; la misma distinción se aplica a los impuestos sobre la riqueza neta de las sociedades y de las personas físicas. Los impuestos liquidados sobre las utilidades de las asociaciones y sobre la renta de las instituciones, tales como seguros de vida o fondos de pensiones, se clasifican siguiendo la misma regla, y así, se considerarán impuestos sobre las sociedades (1200) si se cargan a la asociación o institución como persona jurídica sin tener en cuenta las circunstancias personales de sus propietarios, o impuestos sobre las personas físicas en el caso contrario (1100). Por lo general, los impuestos aplicados a las sociedades y a las personas físicas se rigen por legislaciones diferentes.[12] La distinción realizada aquí entre personas físicas y sociedades no sigue la categorización por sectores entre hogares, empresas, etcétera, del Sistema de Cuentas Nacionales para las cuentas de ingresos y desembolsos. La clasificación del SCN requiere que ciertas empresas no constituidas en sociedad[13] se excluyan del sector de los hogares y vengan a sumarse a las empresas no financieras y las instituciones financieras. Sin embargo, el impuesto sobre las utilidades de esos negocios no siempre puede separarse del impuesto sobre la renta de sus propietarios o, como mucho, puede deslindarse sólo arbitrariamente. Por ello, no se ha intentado reproducir aquí esa separación, y la totalidad del impuesto sobre la renta de las personas físicas se ha recogido en un solo bloque, independientemente de la naturaleza del ingreso imponible.

*b) Entre hogares y otros en relación con los impuestos sobre la propiedad inmueble*

Esta distinción es la misma que la adoptada por el SCN para las cuentas de gasto del consumo final de los hogares y de producción. Se trata pues de diferenciar a los hogares como consumidores (esto es, excluidas las empresas no constituidas en sociedad), por una parte, y a los productores, por otra. Los impuestos sobre las viviendas ocupadas por los hogares, tanto a cargo de los propietarios-ocupantes como de los arrendatarios o de los arrendadores, se incluyen en los hogares, lo que coincide con la diferenciación que suele hacerse comúnmente entre los impuestos sobre la propiedad doméstica y los impuestos sobre la propiedad empresarial. No obstante, algunos países no se hallan en situación de operar esta distinción.

*c) Entre hogares y otros en relación con las licencias de vehículos automotores*

Se distingue aquí entre los hogares como consumidores, por una parte, y los productores, por otra, al igual que en las cuentas de gasto del consumo final de los hogares y de producción del SCN.

*d) Entre empresas y otros en relación con los impuestos residuales (6000)*

La distinción es la misma que en c), esta vez, entre los productores, por una parte, y los hogares como consumidores, por otra. Los impuestos recogidos en la categoría 6000 bien porque gravan más de una base tributaria, o bien porque su base no entra dentro del ámbito de ninguna de las categorías anteriores pero es identificable como imponible sobre los productores, y no sobre los hogares, se incluyen en 'empresas'. El resto de los impuestos de la categoría 6000 se imputan a 'otros' o no identificables.

### *Recargos*

32. Las entradas procedentes de recargos relacionados con impuestos particulares se clasifican por lo general en base al impuesto correspondiente, ya sea el recargo temporal o no. Pero si el recargo posee una característica que lo califica para ser clasificada en una categoría diferente de la lista de la OCDE, las entradas generadas por el recargo se recogen en dicha categoría, separadas de las del correspondiente impuesto.

### *Entradas tributarias no identificables y partidas residuales*

33. En un cierto número de casos, no logra determinarse que los impuestos pertenezcan enteramente a una categoría o partida de la clasificación de la OCDE y, en esos casos, se aplican las siguientes pautas:

*a)* Se conoce la categoría, pero no la forma de distribuir las entradas entre las diversas subdivisiones: las entradas se clasifican en la correspondiente partida o subpartida residual (1300, 2400, 4520, 4600, 5128, 5130, 5300 o 6200).

*b)* Se sabe que la mayor parte de las entradas procedentes de un grupo de impuestos (normalmente, impuestos locales) proviene de impuestos de una categoría o una partida particulares, pero algunos de los impuestos del grupo cuya cuantía no puede determinarse con exactitud pueden clasificarse en otras categorías o partidas: las entradas se consignan en la categoría o partida a la que pertenezca la mayoría de ellas.

*c)* No puede identificarse ni la categoría ni la partida correspondiente al impuesto (normalmente, local): el impuesto se incorpora a la partida 6200, a menos que se conozca que se trata de un impuesto sobre las empresas, en cuyo caso se incluye en la partida 6100.

## A.5. Comentarios sobre ítems de la lista

### *1000 – Impuestos sobre la renta, las utilidades y las ganancias de capital*

34. Esta categoría cubre los impuestos aplicados a la renta o a las utilidades netas (esto es, la renta bruta menos las deducciones permitidas) de las personas físicas y las sociedades, así como los impuestos a los que se someten las ganancias de capital de esos mismos sujetos pasivos, y las ganancias obtenidas en juegos de azar.

35. Se incluyen en esta categoría:

*a)* los impuestos que gravan predominantemente la renta o las utilidades, aunque recaigan parcialmente sobre otras bases; los impuestos aplicados a varias bases que no sean mayoritariamente la renta o las utilidades se clasifican de acuerdo con los principios establecidos en los § 33 y 84;

*b)* los impuestos sobre la propiedad aplicados a un ingreso presunto o estimado como parte de un impuesto sobre la renta (véase el § 48(a), (c) y (d));

*c)* los pagos obligatorios al fondo de contribuciones de la seguridad social impuestos sobre la renta que no confieran un derecho a prestaciones sociales; si esas contribuciones otorgan derecho a prestaciones sociales, se incluyen en la categoría 2000 (véase el § 40);

*d)* el producto de los sistemas integrados de impuestos sobre la renta de régimen cedular se clasifican como un todo en esta categoría, aunque algunos de los impuestos cedulares puedan basarse en la renta bruta y no tener en cuenta las circunstancias personales del contribuyente.

36. La principal división de esta categoría se efectúa entre los gravámenes a personas físicas (1100) y aquellos a sociedades (1200). A su vez, en cada partida, se separa entre impuestos sobre la renta y las utilidades (1110 y 1210) e impuestos sobre las ganancias de capital (1120 y 1220). Si algunas entradas no pueden atribuirse pertinentemente a la partida 1100 o a la 1200, o si no puede realizarse esta distinción en la práctica (p. ej., por falta de datos fiables sobre los receptores de los pagos de los que se deducen los impuestos con retención en la fuente), las entradas se incorporan a la partida 1300 como “no clasificables”.

### *Tratamiento de los créditos fiscales en los sistemas de imputación*

37. En los sistemas de imputación del impuesto de sociedades, los accionistas están exentos, total o parcialmente, de responder en concepto del impuesto sobre la renta por los dividendos abonados por la compañía a partir de la renta o de las utilidades sometidas al impuesto de sociedades. En los países con este sistema,[14] una parte del impuesto sobre las utilidades de la sociedad está disponible para exonerar a los accionistas de su propia obligación tributaria. La exoneración del accionista reviste la forma de un crédito fiscal, cuyo importe puede ser inferior, igual o superior al pasivo tributario total del accionista. Si el crédito fiscal excede al pasivo tributario, puede que ese exceso sea pagadero al accionista. Dado que este tipo de crédito fiscal es parte integrante del sistema de imputación del impuesto sobre la renta de las sociedades, cualquier pago a los accionistas se trata como devolución tributaria, y no como gasto (compárese con el tratamiento de otros créditos fiscales descrito en el § 26).

38. Puesto que en los sistemas de imputación el crédito fiscal (incluso cuando excede la obligación tributaria) debe considerarse como disposición tributaria, se plantea la cuestión de determinar si deberá deducirse de las entradas en concepto de impuesto sobre la renta de las personas físicas (1110) o de las entradas atribuibles al impuesto sobre la renta de las sociedades (1210). En este informe, la cantidad total pagada a título del impuesto sobre la renta de las sociedades se recoge en la subpartida 1210, y el impuesto no imputado en la subpartida 1110. Por lo tanto, la cuantía total del crédito se resta de esta última subpartida, tanto si el crédito da lugar a una reducción de la obligación tributaria por renta personal, como si se realiza un reembolso porque el crédito fiscal excede el pasivo tributario por este concepto. (No obstante, si los créditos fiscales se deducen del impuesto de sociedades por dividendos repartidos a otras sociedades, las correspondientes cantidades se descuentan de las entradas registradas en la subpartida 1210.)

### *1120 y 1220 – Impuestos sobre las ganancias de capital*

39. Como su nombre indica, estas subpartidas engloban los impuestos sobre las ganancias de capital, ya de las personas físicas (1120), ya de las sociedades (1220), siempre que las entradas procedentes de estos impuestos puedan identificarse por separado. Ese no es el caso en numerosos países, y las entradas de estos impuestos se clasifican junto con las del impuesto sobre la renta. La subpartida 1120 contiene asimismo los impuestos sobre las ganancias obtenidas en juegos de azar.

### *2000 – Contribuciones a la seguridad social*

40. Entran en esta categoría todos los pagos obligatorios a las administraciones públicas que confieran un derecho a recibir una prestación social futura (contingente). Esos pagos suelen estar asignados al financiamiento de prestaciones sociales y, a menudo, se pagan a las instituciones del gobierno general que proporcionan dichas prestaciones. Sin embargo, esa asignación no forma parte de la definición de las contribuciones a la seguridad social y no es necesaria para que un impuesto sea clasificado en esta categoría, pero, para que un impuesto se incluya aquí, sí será preciso que confiera un derecho. Y así, los gravámenes sobre la renta o la nómina asignados a los fondos de seguridad social pero que no confieran el derecho a recibir prestaciones sociales quedan excluidos de la presente categoría y se registran bien entre los impuestos sobre la renta de las personas físicas (1100), bien junto con los impuestos sobre la nómina y la fuerza de trabajo (3000). Los impuestos aplicados sobre otras bases, como los bienes y servicios, no se consignarán aquí aunque estén asignados a prestaciones de la seguridad social, sino que se catalogarán según sus respectivas bases, ya que por lo general no otorgarán derecho alguno a prestaciones sociales.

41. Entre otras, se incluirán aquí las contribuciones a los siguientes tipos de prestaciones de la seguridad social: prestaciones y suplementos por seguro de desempleo; prestaciones por accidente, lesión o enfermedad; pensiones por jubilación, invalidez y supervivencia; ayudas familiares; reembolsos de gastos médicos u hospitalarios o prestación de servicios médicos u hospitalarios. Las contribuciones pueden recaudarse tanto de los empleados como de los empleadores.

42. Las contribuciones pueden tener como base bien las remuneraciones o la nómina ('sobre la base de la nómina'), bien la renta neta tras deducciones y exenciones por circunstancias personales ('sobre la base del impuesto sobre la renta'), y el producto de ambas bases deberá identificarse separadamente en la medida de lo posible. Cuando las contribuciones al régimen general de la seguridad social se basen en la nómina, pero las de grupos particulares (tales como los trabajadores por cuenta propia) no puedan evaluarse en función de esta base y se emplee en ese caso la renta neta como una aproximación de las remuneraciones brutas, las entradas seguirán clasificándose sobre la base de la nómina. En principio, esta categoría excluye las contribuciones voluntarias aportadas a los regímenes de seguridad social, que, cuando sea posible identificarlas de forma separada, se recogerán en la partida informativa sobre el financiamiento de las prestaciones sociales; sin embargo, en la práctica, estas aportaciones no siempre pueden desvincularse de las contribuciones obligatorias, en cuyo caso se incluirán igualmente en esta categoría.

43. Las contribuciones a los regímenes de seguro social no vinculados a instituciones del gobierno general, así como las aportaciones a otros tipos de sistemas de seguro, tales como planes de previsión o planes de pensiones, mutualidades u otros planes de ahorro, no se consideran contribuciones a la seguridad social. Los planes de previsión son acuerdos por los que las contribuciones de cada empleado y la parte correspondiente del empleador en

nombre de aquél se conservan en una cuenta separada que genera interés, de la que pueden retirarse en circunstancias específicas. Por su parte, los planes de pensiones son regímenes organizados separadamente, negociados entre empleados y empleadores, que conllevan disposiciones sobre diversas contribuciones y prestaciones, a veces más directamente vinculadas a los niveles salariales y a la duración del servicio que en otros esquemas sociales. Cuando las contribuciones a esos regímenes son obligatorias o cuasiobligatorias (p. ej., en virtud de un acuerdo con sindicatos u organizaciones profesionales), se hacen constar en la partida informativa (véase el Cuadro 5.38 de este Reporte).

44. Las contribuciones de los empleados del gobierno y de este con respecto a sus empleados a los regímenes de seguridad social incluidos en el gobierno general se clasifican en esta categoría. También se consideran impuestos las contribuciones de los empleados del gobierno a regímenes diferentes que puedan reputarse sustitutivos de los regímenes generales de seguridad social.[15] Por el contrario, cuando un régimen diferente no pueda considerarse sustitutivo de uno general y haya sido negociado entre el gobierno, en su papel de empleador, y sus empleados, no se estimará como régimen de seguridad social y, por lo tanto, las contribuciones a él no se tendrán como impuestos, aunque el régimen haya sido instaurado por la legislación.

45. Esta categoría excluye las contribuciones 'imputadas', que corresponden a las prestaciones sociales pagadas directamente por los empleadores a sus empleados, antiguos empleados o personas a cargo de estos (p. ej., cuando los empleadores están legalmente obligados a correr con las prestaciones por enfermedad durante cierto tiempo).

46. Las contribuciones se dividen en tres partidas principales – empleados (2100), empleadores (2200) y trabajadores por cuenta propia o no empleados (2300) – y se subdividen posteriormente en función de la base que gravan. A efectos de la presente publicación, se entiende por empleados todas las personas contratadas en actividades de unidades empresariales, órganos gubernamentales, instituciones privadas sin ánimo de lucro u otro tipo de empleo remunerado, con excepción de los dueños de empresas no constituidas en sociedad y de los miembros no remunerados de sus familias. También se consideran empleados los miembros de las Fuerzas Armadas, independientemente de la duración y del tipo de su servicio, siempre que coticen a regímenes de la seguridad social. Por su parte, las contribuciones de los empleadores se definen como las aportaciones que estos realizan por cuenta de sus empleados a los sistemas de seguridad social. Si los empleados o los empleadores tienen la obligación de continuar cotizando a la seguridad social en el caso de desempleo de un empleado, esas contribuciones se muestran en las partidas 2100 y 2200, respectivamente, siempre que los datos lo permitan. En consecuencia, la partida 2300 queda reservada a las contribuciones abonadas por los trabajadores por cuenta propia y por quienes no se hallan incluidos en la población activa (p. ej., incapacitados o jubilados).

### *3000 – Impuestos sobre la nómina y la fuerza de trabajo*

47. Consiste en los impuestos pagados por las firmas o empresas, ya sea como una proporción de los salarios o la nómina, ya como una cantidad fija por persona empleada. No incluyen pagos a la seguridad social obligatorios pagados por empleadores u otros impuestos pagados por los empleados mismos de sus salarios o remuneraciones.

### *4000 – Impuestos sobre la propiedad*

48. Esta categoría engloba los impuestos, recurrentes y no recurrentes, sobre el uso, la titularidad o la transmisión de la propiedad, lo que incluye impuestos sobre la propiedad

inmueble y la riqueza neta, sobre el cambio de titularidad en la propiedad por herencia o donación, y sobre transacciones financieras y de capital. Quedan excluidas de esta categoría los siguientes tipos de impuestos:

*a)* los impuestos sobre las ganancias de capital procedentes de la venta de propiedad (1120 o 1220);

*b)* los impuestos sobre el uso de bienes y sobre el permiso para usar bienes o realizar actividades (5200): véase el § 78;

*c)* los impuestos sobre los bienes inmuebles gravados sobre la base de un ingreso neto presunto que tiene en cuenta las circunstancias personales del contribuyente: se clasifican como impuestos sobre la renta junto con los impuestos sobre la renta y sobre las ganancias de capital derivadas de la propiedad (1100);

*d)* los impuestos sobre el uso de la propiedad con fines residenciales, tanto si debe responder del impuesto el propietario como el arrendatario, siempre que la cantidad debida tenga en cuenta las circunstancias personales del usuario (ingresos, personas a cargo, etcétera): se integran en los impuestos sobre la renta (1100);

*e)* los impuestos sobre los edificios con una densidad máxima superior a la permitida; sobre la ampliación, construcción o modificación de ciertos edificios más allá de un valor umbral; y sobre la construcción de edificios: todos ellos se integran en los impuestos sobre el permiso para realizar actividades (5200);

*f)* los impuestos sobre el uso de la propiedad propia para fines comerciales especiales, tales como la venta de bebidas alcohólicas, tabaco o carne, o para la explotación de tierras (p. ej., impuestos sobre la extracción en Estados Unidos): se integran en los impuestos sobre el permiso para realizar actividades (5200).

### *4100 – Impuestos recurrentes sobre la propiedad inmueble*

49. Esta partida comprende los impuestos con que se grava de forma regular el uso o la titularidad de bienes inmuebles.

- Estos impuestos gravan las tierras y los edificios.
- Pueden consistir en un porcentaje del valor tasado de una propiedad, basado a su vez en un ingreso por alquiler hipotético, en el precio de venta, en un rendimiento capitalizado o en otras características de la propiedad inmueble (por ejemplo, el tamaño o la ubicación) de las que quepa inferir un alquiler o un valor de capital hipotéticos.
- Estos impuestos pueden aplicarse a los propietarios, a los arrendatarios o a ambos. También pueden pagarse de un nivel de gobierno a otro en relación con los bienes bajo jurisdicción de este último.
- Para la evaluación de estos impuestos, no se tienen en cuenta las deudas y, en ese sentido, difieren de los impuestos sobre la riqueza neta.

50. Los impuestos recurrentes sobre la propiedad inmueble se subdividen a su vez en los pagados por los hogares (4110) y los abonados por otros sujetos pasivos (4120), de acuerdo con los criterios establecidos en el § 31(b) supra.

### *4200 – Impuestos recurrentes sobre la riqueza neta*

51. Esta partida abarca los impuestos con que se grava periódicamente (por lo general, anualmente) la riqueza neta, esto es, los impuestos sobre un amplio abanico de bienes muebles e inmuebles, descontadas sus deudas. Esta partida se subdivide a su vez en los

impuestos pagados por las personas físicas (4210) y los abonados por las sociedades (4220), de acuerdo con los criterios establecidos en el § 31(a) supra. Si existen cifras separadas para las entradas correspondientes a pagos realizados por instituciones, se añaden a la subpartida de las sociedades.

### *4300 – Impuestos sobre sucesiones, herencias y donaciones*

52. Esta partida se divide entre impuestos sobre sucesiones o herencias (4310) e impuestos sobre donaciones (4320).[16] Los impuestos sobre sucesiones gravan el valor total de la sucesión o del caudal hereditario, mientras los impuestos sobre herencias se aplican a las cuotas recibidas por los causahabientes individualmente considerados o en función de la relación de estos con el difunto.

### *4400 – Impuestos sobre transacciones financieras y de capital*

53. Esta partida incluye, entre otros, los impuestos sobre la emisión, transmisión, compra y venta de activos no financieros y financieros (como divisas o valores), sobre los cheques y otras formas de pago y sobre transacciones legales específicas, tales como la validación de contratos o la venta de bienes inmuebles. La partida no incluye:

- *a)* los impuestos sobre el uso de bienes y sobre el permiso para realizar ciertas actividades (5200);
- *b)* las tasas abonadas en concepto de costos procesales o expedición de actas de nacimiento, matrimonio o defunción, que suelen considerarse como ingresos no tributarios (véase el § 12);
- *c)* los impuestos sobre ganancias de capital (1000);
- *d)* los impuestos recurrentes sobre la propiedad inmueble (4100);
- *e)* los impuestos recurrentes sobre la riqueza neta (4200);
- *f)* otros impuestos no recurrentes sobre la propiedad o la riqueza (4500);
- *g)* impuestos de timbre no relacionados con transacciones financieras y de capital
  - *i)* impuestos de timbre sobre la venta de productos específicos, tales como bebidas alcohólicas o tabaco (5121);
  - *ii)* impuestos de timbre restringidos por ley a productos importados (5123) o productos exportados (5124); o
  - *iii)* impuestos de timbre que no caen exclusivamente en una única categoría de transacción (6000).

### *4500 – Otros impuestos no recurrentes sobre la propiedad*[16]

54. Esta partida cubre los gravámenes sobre la propiedad que, a diferencia de los impuestos recurrentes, se recaudan una sola vez. Se divide en impuestos no recurrentes sobre la riqueza neta (4510) y otros impuestos no recurrentes sobre la propiedad (4520). La subpartida 4510 contiene los impuestos que se recaudan a fin de hacer frente a gastos excepcionales o de redistribuir la riqueza. Por su parte, la subpartida 4520 comprende los impuestos que gravan los incrementos de valor de la tierra, debido, por ejemplo, a permisos para su desarrollo concedidos por el gobierno general o a la provisión por parte de este de instalaciones locales adicionales; cualesquiera impuestos sobre la reevaluación del capital; y aquellos impuestos gravados una sola vez sobre determinados tipos de propiedad.

### 4600 – Otros impuestos recurrentes sobre la propiedad

55. Aunque este tipo de impuestos rara vez se dan en los países miembros de la OCDE, esta partida incluye los impuestos sobre bienes tales como ganado bovino, joyas, ventanas y otros signos externos de riqueza.

### 5000 – Impuestos sobre los bienes y servicios

56. Se incluyen en esta categoría todos los impuestos y derechos sobre la producción, extracción, venta, transmisión, arrendamiento y entrega de bienes, así como sobre la prestación de servicios (5100), y también los impuestos aplicados al uso de bienes y al permiso para usar bienes o realizar actividades (5200). Por lo tanto, esta categoría comprende:

- *a)* los impuestos acumulativos de etapas múltiples;
- *b)* los impuestos generales sobre las ventas aplicados, ya sea en la fabricación/producción, ya sea en la venta al por mayor o al por menor;
- *c)* los impuestos sobre el valor agregado;
- *d)* los impuestos selectivos;
- *e)* los impuestos sobre las importaciones y exportaciones de bienes;
- *f)* los impuestos sobre el uso de bienes y sobre el permiso para usar bienes o realizar ciertas actividades;
- *g)* los impuestos sobre la extracción, el procesamiento o la producción de minerales y otros productos.

57. Los casos de difícil delimitación entre esta categoría y la categoría 4000 (impuestos sobre la propiedad) o la partida 6100 (otros impuestos pagados únicamente por empresas) se tratan en los § 48, §53 y §80. La partida 5300 y la subpartida 5130, ambas residuales, incluyen, respectivamente, las entradas tributarias que no hayan podido clasificarse entre las partidas 5100 y 5200 o entre las subpartidas 5110 y 5120, respectivamente, véase §33.

### 5100 – Impuestos sobre la producción, venta, transmisión, arrendamiento y entrega de bienes, y la prestación de servicios

58. Esta partida comprende todos los impuestos aplicados a transacciones de bienes y servicios por las características intrínsecas de estos (p. ej., valor, peso del tabaco, graduación de las bebidas alcohólicas, etcétera) a diferencia de los impuestos determinados por el uso de bienes o por el permiso para usar bienes o realizar actividades, que entran dentro del ámbito de la partida 5200.

### 5110 – Impuestos generales

59. En esta subpartida, se incluyen todos los impuestos, aparte de los derechos de importación y exportación (5123 y 5124, respectivamente), que gravan la producción, el arrendamiento, la transmisión, la entrega o la venta de un amplio abanico de bienes o la prestación de una gran variedad de servicios, independientemente de que sean de producción nacional o importados, o de la etapa de producción o de distribución en la que recaigan. Por ende, comprende los impuestos sobre el valor agregado, los impuestos sobre las ventas y los impuestos acumulativos de etapas múltiples. A las entradas brutas generadas, se añaden las entradas por ajustes fronterizos en concepto de esos impuestos cuando se importan bienes, y se restan las devoluciones de dichos impuestos cuando se exportan bienes. Esta subpartida se divide a su vez en los epígrafes 5111, impuestos sobre el valor agregado; 5112,

impuestos sobre las ventas; y 5113, otros impuestos generales sobre los ingresos brutos y sobre bienes y servicios.

60. Suelen plantearse dificultades de delimitación entre esta subpartida y la dedicada a los impuestos sobre bienes y servicios específicos (5120) cuando los impuestos se aplican a un gran número de bienes, como, por ejemplo, en el caso del impuesto sobre las compras del Reino Unido (abolido en 1973) o el impuesto sobre mercancías de Japón (abolido en 1988). De acuerdo con las respectivas perspectivas nacionales, el antiguo impuesto sobre las compras británico se ha clasificado como impuesto general (5112), mientras el desaparecido impuesto sobre mercancías japonés se ha incluido entre los impuestos selectivos (5121).

### 5111 – *Impuestos sobre el valor agregado*

61. Todos los impuestos generales al consumo cargados sobre el valor agregado entran dentro de este epígrafe, independientemente del método de deducción y de las etapas en las que recaiga el impuesto. En la práctica, todos los países de la OCDE con este tipo de impuestos permiten que todos los intermediarios, excepto el consumidor final, se deduzcan inmediatamente los impuestos sobre las compras e imponen tributación en todas las etapas. Para algunos países, puede que se incluyan en este epígrafe otros impuestos, tales como los aplicados sobre actividades financieras y de seguros, o bien porque las entradas que generan no pueden identificarse separadamente de las procedentes del impuesto sobre el valor agregado, o bien porque se considera que forman parte de este último, aunque esos mismos impuestos puedan clasificarse diferentemente en terceros países (p. ej., como impuestos sobre servicios específicos (5126) o impuestos sobre transacciones financieras y de capital (4400).

### 5112 – *Impuestos sobre las ventas*

62. Se clasifican aquí todos los impuestos generales aplicados a una sola etapa, ya sea en la fabricación/producción, o en la venta al por mayor o al por menor.

### 5113 – *Otros impuestos generales sobre los ingresos brutos y sobre bienes y servicios*

63. Estos son impuestos acumulativos de etapas múltiples e impuestos en los que el impuesto al consumo se combina con otros impuestos multifásicos. Estos impuestos se aplican cada vez que se realiza una transacción sin deducción del valor de los impuestos pagados sobre los insumos. Los impuestos multifásicos pueden combinarse con elementos de los impuestos sobre el valor agregado o sobre las ventas.

### 5120 – *Impuestos sobre bienes y servicios específicos*

64. Se incluyen en esta subpartida los impuestos selectivos, las utilidades generadas y transferidas por los monopolios fiscales, y los derechos de aduana y otros derechos de importación, así como los impuestos sobre las exportaciones, las transacciones de divisas, los bienes de inversión y las apuestas, y los impuestos especiales sobre los servicios que no formen parte de uno de los impuestos generales de la subpartida 5110.

### 5121 – *Impuestos selectivos*

65. Los impuestos selectivos gravan la unidad de un producto específico de una gama predefinida y limitada de bienes. Los impuestos generalmente se aplican a tasas diferenciadas sobre bienes no esenciales o de lujo, bebidas alcohólicas, tabaco y la energía. Los selectivos pueden imponerse en cualquier etapa de la producción o distribución y generalmente se

aplican como un cargo específico por unidad en función de las características del bien con referencia al valor, peso, intensidad o cantidad del producto. Se incluyen impuestos especiales sobre productos como el azúcar, la remolacha azucarera, fósforos y chocolates; e impuestos que gravan a tasas variables una cierta gama de bienes; e impuestos aplicados a los productos de tabaco, bebidas alcohólicas, combustibles para motores e hidrocarburos. Si un impuesto recaudado principalmente sobre bienes importados también se aplica, o se aplicaría, bajo la misma ley a bienes comparables de producción nacional, entonces los ingresos de este impuesto se clasifican como impuestos selectivos más que de derechos de importación. Este principio se aplica incluso si no hay producción nacional comparable o no hay posibilidad de tal producción. Los impuestos sobre el uso de servicios como agua, electricidad, gas y energía se consideran como impuestos selectivos más que impuestos sobre servicios específicos (5126). Los selectivos no incluyen los gravámenes que se aplican como impuestos generales sobre bienes y servicios (5110); beneficios de los monopolios fiscales (5122); derechos de aduana y otros derechos de importación (5123); o impuestos a las exportaciones (5124).

### *5122 – Utilidades de los monopolios fiscales*

66. Este epígrafe comprende la parte de las utilidades de los monopolios fiscales transferida al gobierno general o usada para financiar gastos considerados como gastos del gobierno (véase el § 24). Las cantidades implicadas se registran cuando se transfieren al gobierno general o cuando se usan para gastos considerados como gastos del gobierno.

67. Los monopolios fiscales reflejan el ejercicio del poder tributario del gobierno mediante el uso de prerrogativas monopolísticas. Se trata de empresas públicas no financieras que ejercen un monopolio, en la mayoría de los casos sobre la producción o la distribución de tabaco, bebidas alcohólicas, sal, fósforos, cartas de juego, productos derivados del petróleo y productos agrícolas (es decir, sobre el tipo de productos susceptibles de estar sometidos, alternativa o adicionalmente, a los impuestos selectivos del epígrafe 5121), con el fin de recaudar ingresos para el gobierno que en otros países se obtienen gravando las operaciones que sobre dichos bienes efectúan las unidades empresariales privadas. El monopolio del gobierno puede intervenir en la etapa de producción o, en el caso de los establecimientos de licores propiedad del gobierno o bajo control de éste, en la etapa de distribución.

68. Cabe distinguir los monopolios fiscales de los servicios públicos, tales como el transporte ferroviario, la electricidad, los servicios de correos y otras comunicaciones, que pueden gozar también de una posición monopolística o cuasi-monopolística, pero cuyo fin primero suele ser la prestación de servicios básicos y no la obtención de ingresos para el gobierno; las transferencias de esas otras empresas públicas al gobierno se consideran ingresos no tributarios. Generalmente, el concepto tradicional de monopolio fiscal no abarca a las loterías estatales, cuyas utilidades usualmente se consideran, en consecuencia, ingresos no tributarios. No obstante, se pueden considerar como ingresos tributarios si su función principal es la de recaudar para financiar gasto gubernamental. Las utilidades de los monopolios fiscales se han separado de las de los monopolios de importación y exportación (5127) transferidas de juntas de comercialización u otras empresas dedicadas al comercio internacional.

### 5123 – *Derechos de aduana y otros derechos de importación*

69. Se incluyen aquí los impuestos, derechos de timbre y sobrecargas limitados por ley a los productos importados, así como los gravámenes sobre los productos agrícolas importados impuestos en los países miembros de la Unión Europea y las cantidades satisfechas por algunos de esos países a tenor del sistema de montantes compensatorios monetarios (MCM).[17] Los derechos de aduana recaudados por los Estados miembros de la Unión Europea en nombre de ésta ya se registran en este epígrafe a nivel de autoridad supranacional en los cuadros de países (Capítulo 4 de la publicación Revenue Statistics de la OCDE). Quedan excluidos aquí los impuestos recaudados de las importaciones como parte de un impuesto general sobre los bienes y servicios, así como los impuestos selectivos aplicables tanto a bienes importados como a bienes de producción nacional.

### 5124 – *Impuestos sobre las exportaciones*

70. En los años 1970, los derechos de exportación se aplicaban en Australia, Canadá y Portugal como una medida de carácter regular, y en Finlandia se han utilizado con fines contracíclicos. Algunos países miembros de la Unión Europea pagan un gravamen sobre las exportaciones, en el marco del sistema MCM (véase la nota a pie de página §16 en el § 69). Cuando las cantidades recaudadas son identificables, se integran en este epígrafe, que no incluye, sin embargo, las devoluciones de impuestos generales al consumo, de impuestos selectivos o de derechos de aduana sobre los bienes exportados, que se deducirán de las entradas brutas de 5110, 5121 o 5123, según corresponda.

### 5125 – *Impuestos sobre los bienes de inversión*

71. Este epígrafe cubre los impuestos sobre los bienes de inversión, tales como la maquinaria. Estos impuestos pueden cargarse por un cierto número de años o temporalmente con fines contracíclicos. No se incluyen aquí aquellos impuestos sobre los insumos industriales que recaen también en los consumidores (p. ej., el impuesto sobre la energía en Suecia, que se clasifica en 5121).

### 5126 – *Impuestos sobre servicios específicos*

72. Todos los impuestos sobre el pago por servicios específicos, tales como los impuestos sobre las primas de seguro, los servicios bancarios, los juegos de azar y las apuestas (p. ej., carreras de caballos, quinielas de fútbol, lotería), el transporte, las actividades recreativas o de ocio, los restaurantes y la publicidad, entran dentro de este epígrafe. También se clasifican en esta partida los impuestos sobre la entrada en casinos, carreras u otras manifestaciones o espacios similares, así como los impuestos de timbre sobre servicios específicos. También se clasifican aquí los impuestos sobre el ingreso bruto de las empresas que prestan un servicio específico (p. ej., transporte, como los impuestos de aeropuerto y otros impuestos de pasajeros; seguros; actividad bancaria; actividades recreativas o de ocio; restaurantes y publicidad).

73. Los ingresos tributarios procedentes de gravámenes bancarios y pagos a sistemas de seguro de depósitos y de estabilidad financiera se han incluido también en este epígrafe

- Los pagos obligatorios de tasas de estabilidad, gravámenes bancarios y primas de seguro de depósitos se tratarán por lo general como ingresos tributarios cuando se abonen al gobierno general o una autoridad supranacional y se asignen a los fondos consolidados o generales de este, de forma que el gobierno pueda utilizar libre e inmediatamente el dinero para los fines que elija. Este principio se aplicará independientemente de que el gobierno prometa revertir esos pagos para garantizar los depósitos de los clientes de los bancos en caso de necesidad futura.

- Si los pagos obligatorios se abonan al gobierno general y se destinan a fondos afectados exclusivamente a volver al sector de la economía que engloba a las sociedades sujetas a dichos pagos, éstos seguirán considerándose ingresos tributarios dado que los fondos estarán disponibles para el gobierno y podrán reducir su déficit presupuestario, que la tasa no conlleva contraprestación para una entidad individual y que las cantidades recaudadas no tienen relación con cualquier pago posterior a los depositantes o cualquier gasto realizado como medio de respaldo más amplio al sector financiero.
- Se clasificarán como tasa por servicio los pagos que deban aportarse a sistemas permanentes más reducidos para garantizar los depósitos de "particulares" cuando los niveles de pago concuerden con el coste del seguro.
- También se clasificarán como tasa por servicio, y no como ingreso tributario, los pagos que impliquen que el gobierno ejecute los activos de una institución en quiebra o tenga un derecho prioritario sobre la liquidación de activos de esta con objeto de financiar los pagos de compensación a los clientes por la pérdida de sus depósitos.

    *a)* Los pagos obligatorios a fondos gestionados fuera del sector público y a instituciones no estatales apoyadas por depositantes, así como todos los pagos a planes voluntarios, no deben tratarse como ingresos tributarios.

    *b)* También se incluyen aquí las contribuciones al Fondo de Resolución Única de la UE, que se atribuyen a la autoridad supranacional en los cuadros de los países.

74. Se excluyen de este epígrafe:

    *a)* los impuestos sobre servicios que formen parte de un impuesto general sobre los bienes y servicios (5110);

    *b)* los impuestos sobre la electricidad, el gas y la energía (5121, impuestos selectivos);

    *c)* los impuestos sobre las ganancias de las personas físicas en los juegos de azar (1120, impuestos sobre las ganancias de capital de las personas físicas o de las empresas no constituidas en sociedad) y los impuestos fijos sobre la transferencia de loterías privadas o sobre el permiso para crear loterías (5200);[18]

    *d)* los impuestos sobre los cheques y sobre la emisión, transmisión o compra y venta de valores (4400, impuestos sobre transacciones financieras y de capital);

    *e)* impuestos generales sobre los ingresos brutos (5113).

### *5127 – Otros impuestos sobre el comercio y las transacciones internacionales*

75. Este epígrafe abarca los ingresos percibidos por el gobierno por la compra y la venta de divisas a diferentes tipos de cambio. Cuando el gobierno ejerce poderes monopolísticos para obtener un margen entre los precios de compra y de venta de divisas superior al que sería necesario para cubrir los costos administrativos, el ingreso generado constituye un gravamen obligatorio impuesto en proporciones indeterminadas tanto sobre el comprador como sobre el vendedor de divisas. Es un equivalente común de los derechos de importación y exportación cargados en un sistema con tipo de cambio único o de un impuesto sobre la compraventa de divisas. Al igual que las utilidades de los monopolios fiscales o de los monopolios de importación y exportación transferidas al gobierno, representa el ejercicio de las prerrogativas monopolísticas con fines fiscales y, por lo tanto, se incluye en los ingresos tributarios.

76. El epígrafe engloba asimismo las utilidades de los monopolios de importación y exportación, que, sin embargo, son inexistentes en los países de la OCDE; los impuestos sobre la compraventa de divisas; y cualesquiera otros impuestos que recaigan sobre el comercio o las transacciones internacionales.

### 5128 – *Otros impuestos sobre bienes y servicios específicos*

77. Este epígrafe incluye los impuestos sobre la extracción de minerales, combustibles fósiles y otros recursos agotables de yacimientos de propiedad privada o de otro nivel de gobierno, así como cualesquiera otras entradas no clasificables procedentes de impuestos sobre bienes y servicios específicos. Los impuestos sobre la extracción de recursos agotables suelen traducirse en un importe fijo por cantidad o peso, pero también pueden adoptar un valor porcentual. Los impuestos se registran en el momento de extracción de los recursos. Los pagos por extracción de recursos agotables de yacimientos propiedad de la unidad de gobierno que recibe el pago se clasifican como alquiler.

### 5200 – *Impuestos sobre el uso de bienes y sobre el permiso para usar bienes o realizar actividades*

78. Esta partida incluye los impuestos aplicados al uso de bienes a diferencia de los impuestos sobre los propios bienes. Al contrario que los impuestos de este último tipo (registrados en la partida 5100), los impuestos considerados aquí no se basan en el valor de los bienes, sino que suelen revestir la forma de importes fijos. Los impuestos sobre el permiso para usar bienes o realizar actividades entran asimismo en esta partida, como, por ejemplo, los impuestos sobre la contaminación que no se basan en el valor de bienes particulares. En ocasiones, resulta complejo distinguir entre cargos obligatorios a los usuarios y tasas de licencia que se consideran como impuestos y aquellos que quedan excluidos por reputarse como ingresos no tributarios; los criterios de deslinde empleados se explican en los § 12 y §13.

79. Aunque el título de esta partida menciona el "uso" de bienes, es posible que sea el registro de la propiedad, y no el uso, lo que dé lugar a la obligación tributaria, y que los impuestos contenidos aquí se apliquen más al hecho de ser titular de ciertos animales o bienes (p. ej., caballos de carreras, perros y vehículos automotores) que al uso que se hace de ellos, o que recaigan incluso en bienes inutilizables (p. ej., vehículos automotores o armas inservibles).

80. Se plantean casos de difícil delimitación con respecto a:

*a)* los impuestos sobre el permiso para realizar actividades empresariales que parten de una base combinada de renta, nómina o volumen de ventas, que se clasifican de acuerdo con las normas del §84;

*b)* los impuestos sobre la propiedad o el uso de la propiedad de las partidas 4100, 4200 y 4600; la partida 4100 se dedica exclusivamente a los impuestos sobre la titularidad o la posesión de bienes inmuebles y, a diferencia de los impuestos de la partida 5200, recaen siempre sobre el valor de la propiedad; los impuestos sobre la riqueza neta (4200) y otros impuestos recurrentes sobre la propiedad (4600) se circunscriben al hecho de ser titular de propiedades, y no al uso de activos; se aplican a grupos de activos, y no a bienes particulares; y están en todo caso relacionados con el valor de los activos en cuestión.

### 5210 – Impuestos recurrentes sobre el uso de bienes y sobre el permiso para usar bienes o realizar actividades

81. La principal característica de los impuestos consignados aquí es que se recaudan a intervalos regulares y se cobran por lo general según una cantidad fija. En términos de ingresos, el elemento más importante está constituido por los impuestos por licencia de vehículos, aunque también integran esta subpartida los impuestos sobre los permisos de caza, pesca o tiro o sobre la venta de ciertos productos, así como los impuestos sobre la propiedad de animales domésticos y sobre la prestación de ciertos servicios siempre que estos reúnan los criterios establecidos en los § 12 y §13. Los epígrafes en que se divide la partida 5210 son:

- impuestos de uso sobre vehículos automotores pagados por los hogares (5211);
- impuestos sobre vehículos automotores abonados por otros (5212); y
- otros impuestos recurrentes (5213). Esta subpartida abarca las licencias comerciales y profesionales pagadas por las empresas para obtener una licencia para desarrollar un determinado tipo de negocio o profesión cuando los gravámenes se imponen de forma recurrente. Se incluyen licencias como las licencias de taxi o de casinos. También se incluyen las licencias de perros y las licencias generales periódicas de caza, pesca y tiro cuando el derecho a emprender esas actividades no se otorga como parte de una transacción comercial normal.

82. Se excluyen de la subpartida 5213:

*a)* las licencias cuando el derecho a emprender esas actividades se otorga como parte de una transacción comercial normal (p. ej., la concesión de la licencia va acompañada del derecho a usar una zona específica que es propiedad pública);

*b)* los pagos relativos a los controles efectuados por el gobierno para comprobar la idoneidad y/o la seguridad de los establecimientos o equipos comerciales o la calidad o normalización de los bienes o servicios producidos como condición para la concesión de dicha licencia. Dichos pagos no son unilaterales y deben tratarse como pagos por los servicios prestados, salvo que los importes cobrados por las licencias sean desproporcionados con relación a los gastos de los referidos controles efectuados por el gobierno.

### 5220 – Impuestos no recurrentes sobre el uso de bienes y sobre el permiso para usar bienes o realizar actividades

83. Se incluyen aquí los impuestos no recurrentes aplicados sobre el uso de bienes y sobre el permiso para utilizar bienes o realizar actividades, así como los impuestos aplicados cada vez que se utilizan los bienes.

- Entran en esta subpartida los impuestos sobre la emisión o liberación en el medio ambiente de gases y líquidos nocivos y otras sustancias peligrosas. Los pagos por permisos negociables de emisión expedidos por los gobiernos en el marco de programas de límites máximos y comercio de emisiones deberán registrarse aquí en la fecha en que se produzcan las emisiones. No se computarán ingresos por los permisos que los gobiernos expidan a título gratuito. El registro según el criterio de devengo implica que habrá una diferencia temporal entre el momento en que el gobierno reciba el pago por los permisos y el momento en que se produzca la emisión. En las cuentas nacionales, esta diferencia genera un pasivo para el gobierno durante ese periodo.

- Se excluirán los pagos efectuados por la recogida y eliminación de desechos o sustancias nocivas por parte de los poderes públicos, ya que constituyen una venta de servicios a las empresas.

84. También se incluyen aquí otros impuestos que entren dentro del ámbito de aplicación de la partida 5200 y que no se recauden recurrentemente. Por lo tanto, quedarán comprendidos los pagos únicos por permisos para la venta de alcohol o tabaco o para la creación de centros de apuestas, siempre que cumplan los criterios de los § 12 13.

#### *6000 – Otros impuestos*

85. Esta categoría recoge los impuestos que reposan en una o varias bases diferentes de las descritas en las categorías 1000, 3000, 4000 y 5000, o en bases que no puedan considerarse relacionadas a ninguna de estas categorías, se incluyen aquí. Los impuestos de base múltiple, y si es posible estimar las entradas relacionadas con cada base las cantidades desglosadas se repartirán en las correspondientes categorías de acuerdo a su base. Si no pueden calcularse los valores por separado y se sabe que la mayoría de las entradas proceden de una base determinada, el total de estas se atribuirán de acuerdo con dicha base. En caso contrario, las entradas se clasificarán aquí. Otros ingresos incluidos aquí son los impuestos presuntos no incluidos en el sistema de clasificación, los impuestos a las personas en forma de impuesto de capitación, impuestos de sellos no relacionados con las transacciones financieras y de capital que no pertenecen exclusivamente a una sola categoría de transacción, impuestos a los gastos donde se aplican deducciones o exenciones personales y recibos de impuestos no identificables. Esta categoría se subdivide entre los impuestos pagados completa o principalmente por las empresas (6100) y los abonados por otros sujetos pasivos (6200).

## A.6. Conciliación con las cuentas nacionales

86. Esta sección de los cuadros reconcilia el cálculo de la recaudación tributaria total realizado por la OCDE y el total de todos los impuestos y contribuciones sociales pagados al gobierno general tal y como figuran en el registro de las cuentas nacionales de cada país. Cuando el país es miembro de la Unión Europea (UE), la comparación se establece entre el cálculo de la recaudación tributaria total realizado por la OCDE y la suma de los ingresos tributarios y contribuciones sociales registrado en la combinación del gobierno general y de las instituciones de los sectores de la UE de las cuentas nacionales.

## A.7. Partida informativa sobre el financiamiento de las prestaciones sociales

87. A la vista de la variedad de relaciones entre la tributación y las contribuciones a la seguridad social y de los casos mencionados en los § 40 al §46, se ha previsto una partida informativa que recopile todos los pagos asignados a las prestaciones tipo de la seguridad social, aparte de los pagos voluntarios al sector privado. Los datos se presentan de la forma siguiente (véase el Cuadro 5.38 de este Reporte):

*a)* Impuestos de la categoría 2000.

*b)* Impuestos asignados a las prestaciones de la seguridad social.

*c)* Contribuciones voluntarias al gobierno.

*d)* Contribuciones obligatorias al sector privado.

Los § 40 al §46 ofrecen las debidas orientaciones para efectuar el desglose entre las rúbricas (a) a (d).

## A.8. Partida informativa sobre impuestos identificables pagados por el gobierno

88. Los impuestos identificables realmente pagados por el gobierno se presentan en una partida informativa, desglosados según las principales categorías de la clasificación de impuestos de la OCDE. En la vasta mayoría de los países, sólo pueden identificarse las contribuciones a la seguridad social y los impuestos sobre la nómina satisfechos por el gobierno, que, sin embargo, suelen ser los gravámenes más importantes liquidados por los gobiernos (véase el Cuadro 5.39 de este Reporte).

## A.9. Relación de la clasificación de impuestos de la OCDE con el Sistema de Cuentas Nacionales

89. El Sistema de Cuentas Nacionales (SCN) pretende proporcionar un marco coherente para registrar y presentar los principales flujos relacionados con la producción, el consumo, la acumulación y las transacciones con el exterior de una determinada zona económica, por lo general, un país o una región destacada de un país, y, en este sentido, los ingresos del gobierno constituyen una importante parte de las transacciones registradas en todo sistema de cuentas nacionales. En agosto de 2009, la versión final del SCN 2008 se publicó conjuntamente por cinco organizaciones internacionales: la Organización de las Naciones Unidas, el Fondo Monetario Internacional, la Unión Europea, la Organización para la Cooperación y el Desarrollo Económicos, y el Banco Mundial. La publicación está diseñada para ser empleada en países con economías de mercado, sea cual sea su estadio de desarrollo económico, así como en países en transición hacia economías de mercado. Las principales partes del marco conceptual y las definiciones de los diversos sectores económicos del SCN se han plasmado en la clasificación de impuestos de la OCDE.

90. Sin embargo, existen ciertas diferencias, reseñadas seguidamente, entre la clasificación de impuestos de la OCDE y los conceptos del SCN, debidas a que la finalidad de la clasificación de la OCDE consiste en lograr la máxima desagregación posible de los datos estadísticos en relación con lo que, por lo general, las Administraciones tributarias consideran como impuestos. Y así:

*a)* la OCDE incluye las contribuciones a la seguridad social obligatorias, pagadas al gobierno general en la recaudación tributaria total. No se consideran como impuestos las contribuciones imputadas y voluntarias, además de aquellas pagadas a fondos privados (véanse los §9 y §11 supra.);

*b)* los puntos de vista sobre la calificación de algunos gravámenes y tasas como impuestos son diferentes (§12 y §13 supra.);

*c)* la OCDE excluye los impuestos imputados o los subsidios procedentes de la aplicación de múltiples tipos de cambio oficiales, o del pago de una tasa diferente a otras del mercado sobre reservas requeridas que pueda hacer el banco central;

*d)* los créditos fiscales exigibles se tratan de forma diferente.

91. Tal y como se ha apuntado en los §1 y §2, las categorías 1000 a 6000 de la lista de impuestos de la OCDE cubren todos los pagos sin contraprestación al gobierno general o una autoridad supranacional, aparte de las multas y los préstamos obligatorios. Esos pagos sin contraprestación, incluidas las multas pero excluidos los préstamos obligatorios, pueden obtenerse añadiendo los siguientes valores del SCN 2008:

- impuestos sobre el valor agregado (D211);
- impuestos y derechos sobre las importaciones, IVA no incluido (D212);

- impuestos sobre las exportaciones (D213);
- impuestos sobre los productos, IVA e impuestos sobre las importaciones y exportaciones no incluidos (D214);
- otros impuestos sobre la producción (D29);
- impuestos sobre la renta (D51);
- otros impuestos corrientes (D59);
- las contribuciones efectivas a la seguridad social (D.611 y D1613), con exclusión de las contribuciones voluntarias y los pagos a planes de seguro social relacionados con el empleo que no sean planes de seguridad social;
- impuestos sobre el capital (D91).

## A.10. Relación de la clasificación de impuestos de la OCDE con el sistema de estadísticas de finanzas públicas del Fondo Monetario Internacional

92. La cobertura y la valoración de los ingresos tributarios en el sistema de estadísticas de finanzas públicas (EFP) y en el SCN 2008 son muy similares. Por lo tanto, a excepción del tratamiento dado a los créditos fiscales exigibles, las diferencias entre la clasificación de la OCDE y la del SCN 2008 (véase el § 90 supra.) son de aplicación igualmente al sistema de EFP. Además, el Fondo Monetario Internacional (FMI) escinde la categoría única 5000 de la OCDE en dos categorías distintas dedicadas a los impuestos nacionales sobre bienes y servicios (114) y a los impuestos sobre el comercio y las transacciones internacionales (115). Esto refleja el hecho de que, mientras estos últimos impuestos suelen generar insignificantes cantidades de ingresos en la zona de la OCDE, ese no es el caso en la mayoría de los países no pertenecientes a la Organización.

## A.11. Comparación de la clasificación de impuestos de la OCDE con otras clasificaciones internacionales

93. El cuadro siguiente recoge una comparación ítem por ítem entre la clasificación de impuestos de la OCDE y las clasificaciones empleadas en:

*a)* el Sistema de Cuentas Nacionales (SCN 2008);

*b)* el Sistema Europeo de Cuentas (SEC 2010);

*c)* el Manual de estadísticas de finanzas públicas del FMI (MEFP 2014).

94. Estas comparaciones representan equivalencias que podrán aplicarse en la mayoría de los casos. Con todo, deberán emplearse con cierta flexibilidad, ya que, en casos particulares, los países pueden adoptar enfoques diferentes para la clasificación de los ingresos en las cuentas nacionales.

| | Clasificación de la OCDE | SCN 2008 | SEC 2010 | MEFP 2014 |
|---|---|---|---|---|
| 1000 | Impuestos sobre los ingresos, utilidades y ganancias de capital | | | |
| 1100 | Personas | | | |
| 1110 | Ingresos y utilidades | D51-8.61a | D51A | 1111 |
| 1120 | Ganancias de capital | D51-8.61c, d | D51C, D | 1111 |
| 1200 | Corporaciones | | | |
| 1210 | Ingresos y ganancias | D51-8.61b | D51B | 1112 |
| 1220 | Ganancias de capital | D51-8.61c | D51C | 1112 |
| 1300 | No clasificables entre 1100 y 1200 | | | 1113 |
| 2000 | Contribuciones a la seguridad social | | | |
| 2100 | Empleados | D613-8.85 | D613 | 1211 |
| 2200 | Empleadores | D611-8.83 | D611 | 1212 |
| 2300 | Auto-empleados y no empleados | D613-8.85 | D613 | 1213 |
| 2400 | No asignables entre 2100, 2200 y 2300 | | | 1214 |
| 3000 | Impuestos sobre la nómina y fuerza de trabajo | D29-7.97a | D29C | 112 |
| 4000 | Impuestos sobre la propiedad | | | |
| 4100 | Impuestos recurrentes sobre la propiedad inmueble | | | |
| 4110 | Hogares | D59-8.63a | D59A | 1131 |
| 4120 | Otro | D29-7.97b | D29A | 1131 |
| 4200 | Impuestos recurrentes sobre la riqueza neta | | | |
| 4210 | Hogares | D59-8.63b | D59A | 1132 |
| 4220 | Corporaciones | D59-8.63b | D59A | 1132 |
| 4300 | Impuestos sobre sucesiones, herencias y donaciones | | | |
| 4310 | Impuestos sobre sucesiones y herencias | D91-10.207b | D91A | 1133 |
| 4320 | Impuestos sobre donaciones | D91-10.207b | D91A | 1133 |
| 4400 | Impuestos sobre transacciones financieras y de capital | D59-7.96d; D29-7.97e | D214B, C | 114114; 1161 |
| 4500 | Otros impuestos no recurrentes sobre la propiedad | D91-10.207a | D91B | 1135 |
| 4600 | Otros impuestos recurrentes sobre la propiedad | D59-8.63c | D59A | 1136 |
| 5000 | Impuestos sobre los bienes y servicios | | | |
| 5100 | Impuestos sobre la producción, venta y transmisión de bienes y prestación de servicios | | | |
| 5110 | Impuestos generales sobre bienes y servicios | | | |
| 5111 | Impuestos sobre el valor agregado | D211-7.89 | D211; D29G | 11411 |
| 5112 | Impuestos sobre las ventas | D2122-7.94a; D214-7.96a | D21224; D214I | 11412 |
| 5113 | Otros impuestos generales sobre los ingresos brutos y sobre bienes y servicios | D214-7.96a | D214I | 11413 |
| 5120 | Impuestos sobre bienes y servicios específicos | | | |
| 5121 | Impuestos selectivos | D2122-7.94b; D214-7.96b | D21223; D214A, B, D | 1142 |
| 5122 | Utilidades de los monopolios fiscales | D214-7.96e | D214J | 1143 |
| 5123 | Derechos de aduanas y otros derechos de importación | D2121-7.93 | D2121; D21221, 2 | 1151 |
| 5124 | Sobre las exportaciones | D213-7.95a | D214K | 1152-4 |
| 5125 | Sobre los bienes de inversión | | | |
| 5126 | Sobre servicios específicos | D2122-7.94c; D214-7.96c | D21225; D214E, F, G, H; D29F | 1144; 1156 |
| 5127 | Otros impuestos sobre el comercio y las transacciones internacionales | D2122-7.94d D29-7.95b D29-7.97g D59-8.64d | D21226; D29D; D59E | 1153; 1155-6 |
| 5128 | Otros impuestos sobre bienes y servicios específicos | | | 1146 |

| Clasificación de la OCDE | | | | SCN 2008 | SEC 2010 | MEFP 2014 |
|---|---|---|---|---|---|---|
| | | 5130 | No clasificables entre 5110 y 5120 | | | |
| | 5200 | Impuestos sobre el uso de bienes y sobre el permiso para usar bienes y realizar actividades | | | | |
| | | 5210 | Impuestos recurrentes | | | |
| | | | 5211 Sobre vehículos automotores: hogares | D59-8.64c | D59D | 11451 |
| | | | 5212 Sobre vehículos automotores: otros | D29-7.97d | D214D; D29B | 11451 |
| | | | 5213 Otros impuestos recurrentes en el uso de bienes y en el permiso para el uso de bienes y la realización de actividades | D29-7.97c, d, f D59-8.64c | D29B, E, F; D59D | 11452 |
| | | 5220 | Impuestos no recurrentes sobre el permiso para el uso de bienes o la realización de actividades | | | 11452 |
| | 5300 | No clasificables entre 5100 y 5200 | | | | |
| 6000 | Otros impuestos | | | | | |
| | 6100 | Pagados únicamente por empresas | | | | 1161 |
| | 6200 | Pagados por otros distintos de las empresas o no identificables | | D59-8.64a, b | D59B, C | 1162 |

## A.12. Atribución de ingresos tributarios por subsectores del gobierno general

95. La clasificación de la OCDE requiere un desglose de los ingresos tributarios por subsectores del gobierno general. Seguidamente, se establecen la definición de cada subsector y los criterios que deben emplearse para atribuir los ingresos tributarios entre ellos, que siguen las orientaciones del SCN 2008 y del MEFP 2014.

### *Identificación de los subsectores del gobierno general*

*a) Gobierno central*

96. El subsector del gobierno central incluye todos los departamentos, oficinas y establecimientos del gobierno, así como otros órganos que constituyen organismos o instrumentos de la autoridad central, cuya competencia se extiende a todo el territorio, con excepción de la administración de los fondos de seguridad social. En consecuencia, el gobierno central tiene la facultad de someter a tributación a todas las unidades residentes y no residentes que emprendan actividades económicas en el país.

*b) Gobierno estatal, provincial o regional*

97. Este subsector está compuesto por unidades intermedias del gobierno que ejercen su competencia a un nivel inferior al del gobierno central. Incluye a todas las unidades que operan independientemente del gobierno central en una parte del territorio de un país que engloba numerosas pequeñas localidades, con la excepción de la administración de los fondos de seguridad social. En los países unitarios, puede considerarse que los gobiernos regionales tienen una existencia separada, en la que cuentan con la suficiente autonomía como para recaudar sus ingresos de fuentes bajo su control, y sus funcionarios son independientes del control administrativo externo en el ejercicio de las actividades de la unidad.

98. En la actualidad, los países federales representan la mayoría de los casos en los que los ingresos atribuidos a unidades intermedias del gobierno se identifican de forma separada. España es el único país unitario en ese caso; en el resto de los países unitarios, los ingresos regionales se computan junto con los de los gobiernos locales.

*c) Gobierno local*

99. Este subsector incluye todas las demás unidades del gobierno que ejercen una competencia independiente en parte del territorio de un país, con excepción de la administración de los fondos de seguridad social. Engloba varios entes urbanos o rurales (p. ej., autoridades locales, municipios, ciudades, delegaciones, distritos).

*d) Fondos de seguridad social*

100. Los fondos de seguridad social forman un subsector separado del gobierno general. El SCN 2008 define el subsector de la seguridad social según lo expuesto en sus párrafos 4.124 a 4.126 y 4.147, citados seguidamente:

*"Los regímenes de seguridad social son sistemas de seguros sociales que cubren a la comunidad en su conjunto o a amplios sectores de la misma, y que son impuestos y controlados por unidades del gobierno. Los sistemas abarcan una gran variedad de programas, y ofrecen prestaciones en dinero o en especie por vejez, invalidez o muerte, supervivencia, enfermedad y maternidad, accidentes de trabajo, desempleo, ayudas familiares, asistencia sanitaria, etc. No existe necesariamente una relación directa entre la cuantía de la contribución pagada por un individuo y las prestaciones que este pueda recibir." (Párrafo 4.124)*

*"Cuando los sistemas de seguridad social se organizan por separado de las demás actividades de las unidades del gobierno, mantienen sus activos y pasivos separados de estas últimas, y realizan operaciones financieras por cuenta propia, se califican de unidades institucionales, que reciben el nombre de fondos de seguridad social." (Párrafo 4.125)*

*"Las cantidades recaudadas y pagadas por contribuciones y prestaciones de la seguridad social pueden modificarse deliberadamente con el fin de alcanzar determinados objetivos de la política del gobierno que no tengan relación directa con el concepto de la seguridad social como sistema destinado a ofrecer prestaciones sociales a los miembros de la comunidad. Pueden aumentarse o disminuirse, por ejemplo, con el fin de influir en el nivel de la demanda agregada de la economía. No obstante, mientras se mantengan como fondos constituidos por separado, han de ser tratados, en el SCN, como unidades institucionales diferentes." (Párrafo 4.126)*

*"El subsector de los fondos de seguridad social [del gobierno general] está conformado por los fondos de seguridad social que operan en todos los niveles del gobierno. Dichos fondos son sistemas de seguros sociales que cubren a la comunidad en su conjunto o a amplios sectores de la misma, y que son impuestos por unidades del gobierno." (Párrafo 4.147)*

101. La clasificación de la OCDE sigue esta definición de los fondos de seguridad social con las dos siguientes excepciones, por las se excluyen:

- los sistemas impuestos por el gobierno pero administrados por órganos externos al sector del gobierno general, tal y como se ha definido en el § 3 de este manual; y
- los sistemas en los que todas las contribuciones son voluntarias.

### *Autoridades supranacionales*

102. Este subsector engloba las operaciones de recaudación fiscal de autoridades supranacionales dentro de un país. En la práctica, la única autoridad supranacional que cabe tener en cuenta en la zona de la OCDE es la que conforman las instituciones de la Unión Europea (UE). Los ingresos tributarios recaudados por los países miembros y remitidos a la UE se incluyen en las estadísticas tributarias a nivel de autoridad supranacional. No se deben incluir los impuestos sobre la renta y las contribuciones a la seguridad social recaudados por las instituciones de la Unión Europea y pagados por funcionarios de la Unión Europea residentes en países miembros de la Unión Europea.

### *Criterios de atribución de los ingresos tributarios*

103. Cuando un gobierno recauda impuestos y los transfiere, en todo o en parte, a otros gobiernos, es necesario determinar si esos ingresos se imputarán al gobierno recaudador que los distribuye a otros en forma de donaciones, o si se atribuirán a los gobiernos beneficiarios para los que el gobierno recaudador actúa como mero agente, recibiendo el producto de los impuestos y transfiriéndolos posteriormente. Los criterios de atribución de los ingresos se establecen en los §104–§107 siguientes, y siguen lo dispuesto en los puntos 3.70 a 3.73 del SCN 2008.

104. Por regla general, un impuesto se atribuye a la unidad de gobierno que:

*a)* ejerce la facultad de aplicar el impuesto (como entidad principal o a través de la autoridad delegada por la entidad principal); y

*b)* puede a su discreción establecer y modificar la tasa del impuesto.

105. Cuando un gobierno recauda impuestos para y en nombre de otro, y este último tiene la facultad de aplicar el impuesto y establecer y modificar su tasa impositiva, entonces el gobierno recaudador actúa como agente de este, y el impuesto se reasigna. Cualquier cantidad retenida por el gobierno recaudador como cargo por la recaudación deberá tratarse como pago por un servicio. Cualquier otra cantidad retenida por el gobierno recaudador, por ejemplo, en el marco de un arreglo de coparticipación de impuestos, deberá tratarse como una donación corriente. Si se delegó al gobierno recaudador la autoridad para establecer y modificar la tasa impositiva entonces las cantidades recaudadas deberán tratarse como ingresos tributarios de este gobierno.

106. Cuando diferentes gobiernos establecen conjuntamente y por igual la tasa de un impuesto y el uso de los recursos, sin que ninguno de ellos tengan la autoridad final y exclusiva, entonces los ingresos tributarios se atribuyen a cada gobierno según la proporción de recursos que le corresponda; si el acuerdo permite a una unidad del gobierno ejercer el control final y exclusivo, entonces todos los ingresos tributarios se atribuirán a dicha unidad.

107. También puede ocurrir que un gobierno tenga la autoridad constitucional o de otra índole de aplicar un impuesto, pero que otros gobiernos establezcan individualmente la tasa de ese impuesto en sus jurisdicciones; los recursos generados por el impuesto en cuestión en la jurisdicción de cada gobierno se atribuirán como ingresos tributarios a los respectivos gobiernos.

108. Los gravámenes satisfechos por los Estados miembros de la Unión Europea (UE) revisten la forma de:

*a)* derechos de aduana y gravámenes sobre los bienes agrícolas (5123);

*b)* cuentas de compensación monetaria brutas (5123 en relación con las importaciones y 5124 en relación con las exportaciones);

*c)* contribuciones al Fondo de la Resolución Única (5126); y

*d)* gravámenes sobre el acero, el carbón, el azúcar y la leche (5128).

109. Los derechos de aduana recaudados por los Estados miembros de la UE en nombre de esta se registran de la siguiente forma:

- sobre la base de un coeficiente de recaudación bruta;
- ajustando los resultados, siempre que sea posible, de forma que esos derechos se muestren en relación con una base de "destino final", por oposición a la base de "país de primera entrada"; estos ajustes atañen particularmente a los derechos colectados en importantes

puertos (marítimos); aunque los derechos de la UE se perciben por las autoridades del país de primera entrada, siempre que sea posible cabrá excluir esos derechos del ingreso del país recaudador e incluirlos en el ingreso del país de destino final.

110. Son los gravámenes específicos de la UE los que cumplen más claramente con el criterio de asignación descrito en el §102 anterior. Por consiguiente, estas cantidades se indican en notas a pie de página en los cuadros por país de los Estados miembros de la UE (en el capítulo 5) y aparecen como ingresos supranacionales en cada uno de los epígrafes fiscales identificados en el §108.

## Notas

1. Las referencias a la publicación *Revenue Statistics* de la OCDE en esta Guía Interpretativa, aluden a OECD (2021), *Revenue Statistics 2021*, Publicaciones de la OCDE, París.
2. ·Todas las referencias al SCN deberán entenderse hechas a la edición de 2008.
3. Véase el apartado K de la presente guía para el análisis del concepto de agente.
4. Por lo general, es posible identificar la cuantía de las contribuciones a la seguridad social y de los impuestos sobre la nómina, pero no otros impuestos asumidos por el gobierno.
5. Sin embargo, si un gravamen considerado como ingreso no tributario en la mayoría de los países se califica de tributario –o permite recaudar sustanciales ingresos– en uno o más países, las entradas en concepto de dicho gravamen se indican en las notas que figuran al pie de los cuadros de países, pero no se incluyen en la recaudación tributaria total.
6. Obsérvese, no obstante, que los nombres pueden dar lugar a confusión. Por ejemplo, aunque una tasa sobre los pasaportes se trataría normalmente como ingreso no tributario, si se impone un gravamen suplementario sobre los pasaportes (como en el caso de Portugal) con el fin de conseguir un ingreso sustancialmente mayor que el costo que supone proporcionar el pasaporte, dicho gravamen deberá considerarse como un impuesto sobre el uso de bienes (5200).
7. Para una explicación más detallada de esta distinción, consúltese el estudio especial sobre cuestiones de actualidad en relación con el registro de los ingresos tributarios Current issues in reporting tax revenues, en la edición 2001 de Revenue Statistics.
8. En ocasiones, se emplean asimismo los términos "no reembolsable" y "reembolsable", pero puede parecer ilógico hablar de "reembolsable" cuando no se ha pagado nada.
9. Con la excepción del diferente tratamiento dado a los créditos fiscales exigibles en los sistemas de imputación del impuesto sobre sociedades (§§ 37 39)
10. No se trata aquí de verdaderos gastos tributarios en sentido formal, ya que tales gastos requieren que se identifique un sistema tributario de referencia para cada país o, mejor si cabe, una referencia internacional común y, en la práctica, no se ha logrado acuerdo sobre esta última.
11. A menos que se basen en la plusvalía obtenida con la venta, en cuyo caso se clasificarían como impuestos sobre las ganancias de capital, en las subpartidas 1120 o 1220.
12. Con todo, algunos países aplican la misma legislación a ambos en impuestos particulares sobre la renta, aunque las entradas procedentes de dichos impuestos suelen ser fácilmente atribuibles a uno u otro caso y pueden, por lo tanto, consignarse en la debida partida.
13. Por ejemplo, "[...] que son suficientemente autónomas e independientes y se comportan como si fueran sociedades [...] (incluido en el hecho de llevar) conjuntos completos de cuentas" (SCN 2008, 4.44).
14. En Canadá, país en el que se considera que rige un sistema de imputación, el crédito fiscal (no exigible) para el accionista nace en relación con el impuesto nacional sobre sociedades que se reputa haber pagado, tanto si ha surgido una obligación tributaria para la sociedad como si no. Habida cuenta de que no existe una conexión íntegra entre la obligación tributaria de la sociedad y el crédito concedido en relación con el impuesto sobre la renta en esos sistemas, los créditos por dividendos se tratan, junto con otros créditos fiscales, según lo descrito en el § 26.
15. Esto puede darse, por ejemplo, cuando ya existía un régimen para los empleados del gobierno previo a la introducción de un régimen general de seguridad social.
16. En el SCN 2008, se consideran transferencias de capital y no impuestos (véase la sección A.8.).

17. Mediante este sistema, la Unión Europea ajusta las diferencias entre los tipos de cambio empleados para determinar los precios de la política agrícola común (PAC) y los tipos de cambio reales. Los pagos realizados en este sistema pueden estar relacionados con importaciones o exportaciones y, cuando ha sido posible identificar por separado las respectivas cantidades, se han mostrado en el correspondiente epígrafe (5123 o 5124). En el presente informe, esas cantidades se han consignado en valores brutos (esto es, sin deducir ningún subsidio otorgado en el marco del sistema MCM).

18. Las transferencias de las utilidades de las loterías del Estado se consideran ingresos no tributarios (véase el § 68).

www.ingramcontent.com/pod-product-compliance
Ingram Content Group UK Ltd.
Pitfield, Milton Keynes, MK11 3LW, UK
UKHW051457290926
15471UKWH00008B/1250

9 789264 939141